Expanding Our Political Horizons

READINGS IN CANADIAN POLITICS AND GOVERNMENT

JAMES JOHN GUY
University College of Cape Breton

D0939128

HARCOURT BRACE CANADA

Harcourt Brace & Company, Canada

Toronto Montreal Fort Worth New York Orlando
Philadelphia San Diego London Sydney Tokyo

Canadian Cataloguing in Publication Data

Main entry under title:

Expanding our political horizons : readings in
    Canadian politics and government

Includes bibliographical references and index.
ISBN 0-7747-3515-5

1. Canada—Politics and government. I. Guy,
James John, 1943–   .

JL81.E87 1997   320.971   C96-930109-X

Director of Product Development: Heather McWhinney
Senior Acquisitions Editor: Daniel J. Brooks
Projects Manager: Liz Radojkovic
Developmental Editor: Megan Mueller
Director of Publishing Services: Jean Davies
Editorial Manager: Marcel Chiera
Supervising Editor: Semareh Al-Hillal
Production Manager: Sue-Ann Becker
Production Co-ordinator: Sheila Barry
Copy Editor: Darlene Zeleney
Cover and Interior Design: Sonya V. Thursby/Opus House
Typesetting and Assembly: MacTrix DTP
Printing and Binding: Webcom Limited

Cover Art: Brian Burnett, *Bridge to the Universe* (1987). Acrylic on canvas. 3.04 x 3.96 metres (10 x 13 feet). Irregular (five-sided). Photo courtesy of the artist. Reproduced by permission of the artist. Collection: Cineplex Canada.

This lively painting comprises a series of superimposed frames establishing the position of a Canadian city (Windsor, Ontario) in the centre of North America and in the middle of a tumultuous galaxy. In the main frame, the Ambassador Bridge joins Windsor to Detroit, Michigan. This is one of the busiest thoroughfares linking Canada to the United States, and beyond. The expansive, dynamic, and inclusive nature of the painting strikes a chord with the themes discussed in this reader.

This book was printed in Canada.

1 2 3 4 5   01 00 99 98 97

For my wife, Patti

The story of Canada is a compelling one. It is about the struggle of a multicultural and bilingual society to stay together and to find mutually beneficial ways of living together within one of the largest governing systems in the world. Current changes in Canada's political life foreshadow many transformations in the structures, issues, and processes that will make up Canadian government in the twenty-first century. In short, Canadian politics today are exciting, important, and controversial.

All introductory politics and government courses try to interest students in the controversial political issues that affect their lives. I believe that a reader can also stimulate that interest by exposing students to many different perspectives through short presentations, while providing a firm grounding in the basics of Canadian politics and government.

The purpose of this book, *Expanding Our Political Horizons: Readings in Canadian Politics and Government*, is not to convince students that a particular political position is "best," or to celebrate the virtues of any one ideology—indeed, there are traces of liberalism, conservatism, socialism, nationalism, and feminism throughout the book. Rather, its main task is to stimulate informed critical thinking about fundamental issues affecting all Canadians and to present those issues in a format that makes students want to learn about Canadian politics. An introductory reader succeeds if most of the students using it develop three things: an understanding of the major issues facing their country, an interest in learning more about Canadian government and politics, and the critical ability to evaluate media reports

about Canadian political issues. This reader's formula for success is to provide students with a manageable number of selections under a comprehensive range of topics, and to present readable, educative, and diverse perspectives on current Canadian political issues.

For obvious reasons, students tend not to read dull, lengthy, difficult articles; indeed, such materials do little to help them expand their knowledge. Each of the articles in *Expanding Our Political Horizons* is clearly written, well organized, and free of unnecessary jargon, having been selected with a view to helping students broaden their understanding of government and politics in Canada. The readings are concise and make their points quickly and succinctly. This allows for the inclusion of a greater number of selections, and thereby exposes students to a broader range of perspectives. And while each article can stand on its own as a coherent perspective on a particular topic, the presence of several, often conflicting, perspectives allows a more intense light to be shed on the topic and enriches the student's understanding, as well as his or her capacity for critical thought.

Instructors will be happy to know that the topics covered in this reader constitute the major areas of concern typically treated in introductory courses to Canadian politics and government. The book offers a collection of first-rate analyses by political scientists, sociologists, historians, journalists, and participants in Canada's political and governing system. All the readings raise issues of enduring concern and seek to place recent events in a broader historical and developmental context as we approach the twenty-first century.

The theme of governance—that is, all of the political skills, administrative methods, decision-making institutions, and public participation that we, as a society, bring to government—is particularly appropriate at this point in Canadian history. It brings to light the challenges involved in keeping Canada united in the face of many divisive forces. "Governance" also refers to the broader political arrangements through which we govern ourselves, and to the relationships between and among the various levels of government in Canada. The theme of governance draws our attention to questions of aboriginal government, the participation of women in government, and the place of Quebec in Canadian society. These issues constitute the enduring foundations of Canadian political life, and familiarity with them enables us to recognize and think critically about the difficult choices we face as citizens and voters.

The readings in this volume are gathered into ten broad parts that generally correspond to the major subdivisions in most introductory textbooks on Canadian politics and government and that can easily be adapted to whatever approach individual teachers prefer in organizing an introductory course. In addition to covering the core topics, I have included parts on municipal politics and government, the provinces, the media and political opinion, and the economy, in order to achieve a comprehensive view of all levels of politics and government in Canada.

Each part provides several readings on different aspects of the topic at hand. Where appropriate, careful attention has been paid to providing a historical and developmental perspective. All parts contain current analytical articles that draw on the best research or opinion in Canadian political science as well as on the insights of analysts who capture the human dimension of politics and government.

To make the articles as readable and accessible as possible, each part is introduced by a feature entitled "Close-Up," designed to animate student interest in the topic and to provide additional background and

depth to particular events, institutions, groups, ideas, and organizations mentioned in the articles that follow. Some of the Close-Ups treat current issues, some historical ones, but all are vivid and informative. The Close-Up is immediately followed by an introductory essay that suggests the major issues relating to governance and provides the historical, political, and social context for the topic. These part openers are more than just an introduction to the readings; they also teach students about the general topic area. They define basic concepts of political science and make reference to some of the essential functions of Canadian political institutions, as would a standard textbook. In fact, instructors may find that, with these comprehensive introductions, the reader serves well as a teaching tool in its own right.

Each part-opening section also contains a Glossary, to reinforce some of the important terms used in the readings. The concise definitions offered here will facilitate understanding for first-year students.

"Thinking It Over"—a set of thought-provoking questions at the end of each part-opening section—is a feature intended to generate reflection and discussion about the readings in each part and their relation to other readings in the book. The answers to these questions are found in the selections; where possible, the location of the relevant discussion in the reading (or readings) is cited. This feature can easily be adapted to serve as suggested essay topics or essay questions on course examinations. It is designed to do more than simply pose questions. Some of the questions and comments direct students to comparative reading; others seek to stimulate debate.

Those who use this reader will find that it provides an expanded vision of Canada as articulated by many of our most perceptive scholars and politicians. Their interpretations and prescriptions may not always provide final explanations, but the purpose here is not and cannot be to offer definitive solutions. Rather, it is to expose students to the complexity and challenge of such ideas. With this in mind, students will arrive at their own best judgements as to what the important issues and questions really are.

ACKNOWLEDGEMENTS

Many people contributed to the completion of this book. The pleasures of writing and compiling it have been increased by the many colleagues, students, and friends who offered helpful criticism and support along the way.

At the University College of Cape Breton I must thank a number of special colleagues for their generous encouragement of my book. Dr. Robert Morgan, director of research, helped enormously with travel support and other administrative assistance along the way. Our president, Dr. Jacke Scott, provided for these efforts with her usual cordial support. Margaret MacLeod was always there to put the manuscript in order and to answer my constant questions about "making computers go." A special thank you to Carol Ann Sheppard for helping compile the bibliography and for being so generous with her time. Four very helpful librarians, Mary Campbell, Cathy Chisholm, Catherine Steeves, and Laura Peverel, came through with the right information in my obsessive search for the right readings to include in each part of the reader. A special thanks to Catherine Steeves for helping me research a number of the Close-Ups presented in our part openers.

The Department of Politics, Government, and Public Administration at the University College of Cape Breton, which I have had the privilege of chairing, comprises some of the most talented political scientists in the country. They are Beryl Davis, Brian Howe, David Johnson, and Mohini Gupta, who together make up the team with which I am so proud to be associated. They make working hard worth it, and they deserve all the credit for making the writing of this book an easier enterprise.

I want to express my appreciation to those who contributed original articles to this reader. Special thanks go to Brian Howe, David Johnson, Beryl Davis, Federal Court Justice Allen Linden, Richard Jenkins, and Andrew Heard.

A number of anonymous reviewers, recruited by Harcourt Brace, made very useful recommendations to improve the contents of the reader. The book is a better learning instrument because of their valuable input. Their identities have since been made known to me; they are Peter Woolstencroft at the University of Waterloo, Patrick Malcolmson at St. Thomas University, and Nelson Wiseman at the University of Toronto. I thank them for their kind suggestions.

Of course, I wish to thank a number of the many talented people at Harcourt Brace Canada. This is really a wonderful company with which to publish one's efforts. I am grateful to all of them for their professional guidance, enthusiasm, and support for this project. Thanks to Dan Brooks, who planted the idea of this reader in my mind. He believed in the project when I was feeling doubtful, and he was right again.

In an undertaking of this magnitude, an author realizes early on that the success of a textbook is closely tied to the professional editors associated with the project. Fortunately for me, I was assigned Megan Mueller as developmental editor. Megan applied her affable self, her perceptive insights, and her many editorial skills to the manuscript. I'd especially like to thank Semareh Al-Hillal for supervising this project and for her helpfulness and infinite patience.

Finally, everyone at home makes it all worth while. I give my unqualified thanks, filled with love, to my wife, Patti, my daughter, Katha, and my son, Trevor, for their wonderful support.

A Note from the Publisher

Thank you for selecting *Expanding Our Political Horizons: Readings in Canadian Politics and Government*, by James John Guy. The author and publisher have devoted considerable time to the careful development of this book. We appreciate your recognition of this effort and accomplishment.

We want to hear what you think about *Expanding Our Political Horizons*. Please take a few minutes to fill in the stamped reader reply card at the back of the book. Your comments and suggestions will be valuable to us as we prepare new editions and other books.

CONTRIBUTORS

JANINE BRODIE
York University

KEITH BROWNSEY
Mount Royal College

SANDRA BURT
University of Waterloo

ROBERT M. CAMPBELL
Trent University

DAVID CHEAL
University of Winnipeg

BERYL DAVIS
University College of Cape Breton

G. BRUCE DOERN
Carleton University

CHRISTOPHER DUNN
Memorial University

RAND DYCK
Laurentian University

THE HONOURABLE EUGENE A. FORSEY
1904–1991

IAN GREENE
York University

MAGNUS GUNTHER
Trent University

JAMES J. GUY
University College of Cape Breton

ANDREW HEARD
Simon Fraser University

LAURENCE HEWICK
Wilfrid Laurier University

RONALD HIRSHHORN
Queen's University

R. BRIAN HOWE
University College of Cape Breton

MICHAEL HOWLETT
Simon Fraser University

RICHARD JENKINS
Queen's University

DAVID JOHNSON
University College of Cape Breton

RAIS A. KHAN
University of Winnipeg

GRAHAM KNIGHT
McMaster University

THE HONOURABLE JUSTICE ALLEN M. LINDEN
The Federal Court of Canada

MICHAEL MANDEL
Osgoode Law School, York University

MARCEL MASSÉ
President of the Queen's Privy Council of Canada
Minister of Intergovernmental Affairs and Minister
responsible for Public Service Renewal

PETER McCORMICK
University of Lethbridge

JAMES D. McNIVEN
Dalhousie University

ROLF MIRUS
University of Alberta

LESLIE PAL
Carleton University

RICHARD PHIDD
University of Guelph

A. PAUL PROSS
Dalhousie University

BRYNE PURCHASE
Queen's University

MARTIN ROBIN
Simon Fraser University

PETER H. RUSSELL
University of Toronto

ANDREW SANCTON
University of Western Ontario

CHRISTOPHER A. SARLO
Nipissing University

DAVID SIEGEL
Brock University

ROGER S. SMITH
University of Alberta

A. BRIAN TANGUAY
Wilfrid Laurier University

DAVID TARAS
University of Calgary

CHARLES TAYLOR
McGill University

PAUL THOMAS
University of Manitoba

SUSAN THORNE
Associate Editor, *The Businesskeeper*

C. RICHARD TINDAL
St. Lawrence College

SUSAN NOBES TINDAL
Barrister, Solicitor, and Notary Public,
Mill Street Law Offices

MANON TREMBLAY
Université d'Ottawa

MARY ELLEN TURPEL
University of Saskatchewan

S.M. WADDAMS
University of Toronto

JOSEPH WEARING
Trent University

PETER WEARING
Canadian Facts

ANTHONY WESTELL
Journalist and former Director,
School of Journalism, Carleton University

RANDALL WHITE
MacDonald White Associates

CONRAD WINN
Carleton University

LISA YOUNG
University of Toronto

CONTENTS

The Struggle to Govern Ourselves

CLOSE-UP: CANADA'S FIRST GOVERNMENTS

Canada will never be a wholly governable nation-state until it reconciles its relations with the many peoples of the First Nations. Aboriginal governments preceded all other political reality in Canada, providing fundamental services to their people from birth to death, governing them and regulating their activities over a wide range of functions within their respective societies.

Some aboriginal governments even provided for the union of their peoples using the principles of federalism, checks and balances, restrictions on the power of leaders, opportunities for political participation, and natural rights and fundamental equalities. Women and sometimes even children played major decision-making roles in many of these First Nations governments.

Most First Nations governments kept records of their internal and external transactions as well as of their judicial decisions. Chiefs were obligated to communicate with the people, sending messages to them and considering requests from them. The chiefs were expected to tolerate anger and criticism by the people and to reflect an endless patience and calm deliberation. Aboriginal leaders tended to view themselves as servants of the people rather than their masters. As such, they were not to accumulate more wealth than their people had. In fact, chiefs were almost always pressured to give away their material possessions. If leaders failed to follow rules such as these, they could be recalled or impeached.

By contemporary standards, most of these First Nations governments were of a democratic character, dispensing law, rights, and justice equally in their societies; keeping extensive records of their community and judicial decisions; requiring the accountability of their chiefs; and ruling with the consent of the governed. They made and honoured treaties with other aboriginal and foreign governments, practised diplomacy, and engaged in intergovernmental relations on a regular basis.

The First Nations comprised a great variety of political cultures living in vast territories. Some were nomadic or seminomadic hunters and gatherers. These First Nations included the Algonkin, Chippewa, Huron, Inuit, Iroquois, Mi'kmaq, and Naskapi. Some say the Iroquois invented federalism and governed themselves with a sense of distinction and justice. The Iroquois were a Confederacy of five nations: Seneca, Cayuga, Onondaga, Oneida, and Mohawk.

Contact between European settlers and aboriginal cultures elicited a variety of responses on both sides. Some aboriginal peoples tried to adapt to the invaders by trading with them and by accepting alliances as a means of gaining an advantage over rival aboriginal groups. Others resisted Euro-Canadian intrusions by harassing settlers, farmers, and herders.

One of the worst atrocities against aboriginal peoples anywhere in the Americas took place in Newfoundland. The Beothuks were gradually exterminated by fishermen and settlers, whose attacks on these peaceful and friendly people became a murdering sport. The European settlers called the Beothuks "nuisance Indians" because they competed in the Newfoundland fishery. Beothuk villages were pillaged for furs and other valuable possessions. The last of the Beothuks, a young woman named Shawandithit, died in St. John's in 1829.

Like the British and the French before them, Canadians viewed aboriginals as separate peoples with whom they could make treaties and whom they could treat differently under special rules of government. Underlying Canada's official policies toward aboriginal peoples was the intent that they would gradually disappear through **assimilation**. Although reservations separated aboriginal people from Canadian society, powerful pressures nonetheless existed to force compliance with Canadian cultural norms. Early Canadian governments were self-righteous and patronizing in their treatment of aboriginal societies. They believed they were culturally superior to the governments of the First Nations in ideology, technology, and social organization.

Not surprisingly, Canada's First Nations governments received little benefit from Confederation. The Constitution Act, 1867, stipulated that "Indians and lands reserved for the Indians" were under the exclusive jurisdiction of the federal government. With that power, and through eleven so-called numbered treaties between 1821 and 1921, Ottawa gained control over vast swaths of land in exchange for Native reserves. In assigning "Indians" to specific territory, the Canadian government promised protection from white encroachment, and thereby effectively made Indians dependent on non-Native governments at all levels, federal, provincial, and municipal. Without power or land, riven by disease and poverty, Canada's aboriginal people began to lose their ability to govern in traditional ways.

As more reserves were created, it became evident that the isolation the Native people sought was impossible. Canadian farmers, miners, ranchers, and herders came to occupy ever more remote aboriginal lands. Canadian settlers became more intent on assimilating Native people by trying to undermine their aboriginal organizations while making them accept white political and social values and integrating them into the wider Canadian society.

Efforts to assimilate the Indians were supposedly made for their own "good." In keeping with this ideology, in 1884, the federal government, on the advice of Christian missionaries, passed the Indian Act in order to ban the potlatch festival, making it illegal for aboriginals in British Columbia to hold traditional celebrations heralding the investiture of chiefs, honouring the dead, and celebrating high-ranking marriages. Whereas aboriginals viewed the potlatch as a unifying community gathering, the missionaries saw it as a "pagan way of life" that threatened the established order. By 1951, Parliament had lifted the ban, but the era of the great potlatch had long ended—and many aboriginal communities had disintegrated. The racist legacy of the Indian Act continues to this day, reflecting who we are as a people and the systems of government we build.

Today, in seemingly endless court battles across Canada, aboriginal groups are asserting their right to govern their lands and their peoples. They draw their authority to govern themselves from the distant past, from spiritual and human rights, from the long occupancy of the lands they claim, from the binding international treaties they signed, from colonial laws, and, more recently, from decisions of the Supreme Court of Canada on governing rights.

In the two most recent rounds of constitutional negotiations in this country, in 1987 and 1992, the idea of aboriginal governments exercising their traditional powers of governance over their land and people without intervention from Canada's federal and provincial governments was too radical a notion, too great an unknown, for many Canadians to accept as an enshrined provision of their constitution.

Most Canadians refer to the prospect of the First Nations' governing their own affairs as **aboriginal self-government**; for aboriginals, however, it is simply their rightful "government." Many First Nations even reject the term "self-government" as inaccurate and demeaning to their history and integrity. They point out that if there is "aboriginal self-government," there must also be "Canadian self-government."

Perhaps, one day, the legal position of aboriginal governments may be firmly established in the Canadian Constitution. Aboriginal groups will first have to overcome the tendency to splinter and create factions among the 600 000 people who constitute their many nations. If such divisive behaviour can be avoided, aboriginal leaders may be able to turn their energies more fully toward the needs of their lands and their peoples.

INTRODUCTION: RETHINKING WHO WE ARE

The readings in this opening section address the multidimensional question of who Canadians are and how they govern themselves. Each contributor helps us to see some of the complexities in these questions. From what they have written, we will learn that the struggle to govern ourselves has always had something to do with our Constitution, the effectiveness of our parliaments, our vast geography, how we treat and regard aboriginal peoples, the fact that the majority of Canadians — women — are underrepresented by our political institutions, how we relate to the Americans, and the overall sense we have of ourselves as a people.

As the second Quebec referendum on sovereignty approached in 1995, concern about Canada's national identity grew in all parts of the country. The referendum was yet another catalyst for national self-examination. In the end, it painfully revealed how divided Quebeckers were on the issue (50.6 percent said No, 49.4 percent said Yes). It also revealed the helplessness Canadians outside Quebec felt when it came to keeping Quebec within Canada: in the final moments of the campaign, thousands rallied to convey to the Québécois, with great emotion, an urgent and confused vision of a united Canada.

Canada's fate — whether of disintegration or of holding together in some form of renewed confederation — will be the example to avoid or to follow for other large multicultural federations such as Russia and Brazil, as well as for every nation-state that has to accommodate powerful internal forces of nationalism.

Now, at a time when we must reevaluate the roles and functions of our governments, Canadians are perplexed by the implications of altering the state forms that we have valued so highly for so long — social pluralism, **political equality**, the universality of public policy benefits, and the provision of a social safety net through government-funded programs, to name a few. Equally important to our national identity will be the outcome of the debate over the fate of social programs in an era of severe fiscal constraint.

Anthony Westell (Chapter 2) and Janine Brodie (Chapter 3) discuss how the current state of affairs will inevitably require us to reconfigure our governments, the institutions we have in place, the ways we make decisions, the way we elect our leaders, and the way we organize our provincial and federal governments to keep our country from unravelling.

Such considerations lead us to the question of how much our values will change in the future. What political values will we share in the coming century? What political beliefs are expendable in the face of necessary fiscal restraint? How will we judge ourselves and be judged as a civilized society? How will we treat others and expect others to treat us?

RETHINKING HOW WE GOVERN OURSELVES

Government in Canada is a complex network of organizations, programs, and policies reaching into every corner of Canadian life. At the close of the twentieth century, our governments wield tremendous influence over the fate of the Canadian economy. In all our capital cities, they are the largest employers. They provide Canadians with a host of so-called essential services. Governments control a massive bureaucracy that employs thousands, and regulate a wide range of social and economic activities that most Canadians consider vital to their prosperity.

In the early days of Confederation, people expected little from their governments. Most people were self-employed, and their lives centred on their own communities. Indeed, Canadians once lived out their lives without benefit of the majority of the government services we depend on today.

In recent years, the federal and provincial governments' serious debt and deficit levels have fuelled a debate over the size, scope, and power of government that dominates Canada's political agenda in the 1990s. Even though downsizing, retraction, and cutbacks began in the 1980s, they will likely remain the order of the day for the foreseeable future. Canadians must therefore reevaluate the philosophies of government that we have come to cherish and that are very much ingrained in our political psyche. This is what Marcel Massé, who has served as president of the Queen's Privy Council of Canada, minister of intergovernmental affairs, and minister responsible for public service renewal, argues in his paper, "Getting Government 'Right': The Challenges of Governing Canada" (Chapter 1).

Throughout our history, our parliamentary system of government, with a monarch as the formal head of state, has distinguished us from our hemispheric neighbours, particularly the United States and the countries of Latin America. Unlike our neighbours to the south, we rejected the political pathway of revolution and took on what we regarded as the stable, parliamentary, approach to constitutional monarchy and democracy. With this choice, we adopted a different political ideology from that of our neighbours — one emphasizing "peace, order and good government" rather than "life, liberty and the pursuit of happiness" — for very pragmatic reasons. Unlike Americans, who consistently distrusted government, Canadians entered into an early partnership with their governments to fight a hostile northern environment and, eventually, hostile economic cycles and social conditions. Today, that partnership is being challenged as Canadians reassess their capacity as a society to pay for the traditional structures and services their governments have historically provided for them.

Canada's was the first governing system in the world to combine parliamentary institutions with a federal structure of government. In fact, these institutions are not necessarily complementary and may even have compounded the difficulties inherent in how we govern ourselves. A **parliamentary system** of government combined with a **federal system** can be adversarial, expensive, and inefficient. As Anthony Westell points out in Chapter 2, such a governmental system may not be the most suitable to deliver on the expectations Canadians have of government.

FIRST CANADIANS RECLAIM THEIR LAND

In addition to all these issues, there is a new militancy among Canada's **indigenous people**. They want Canada to admit that they never gave up their right to govern their land and their people. In constitutional terms, they want Canada to concede that they never relinquished their original **sovereignty** — that Canadian sovereignty was imposed upon aboriginal people, who in fact had been treated as sovereign nations even by the arriving colonists. This means that the concept of "two founding nations" — English and French — must also be reevaluated, as it does a great disservice to those residents of Canada who were here long before either the French or the English.

National Chief of the Assembly of First Nations Ovide Mercredi sent a strong signal to the Canadian government in 1991 when he said: "*We* are the founding nations of Canada, and we will not allow the lie of two founding nations to continue." Not to conciliate ourselves with the governments of the First Nations on this question would be to allow our national identity to contain racist and **imperialist** overtones.

THE FUTURE OF QUEBEC

Sooner or later, all governments in Canada will have to come to grips with the scope of the governing authority of Quebec. The issue will not go away with simple defeat or passage of a referendum on whether Quebec should stay in Canada. Indeed, as

Westell points out, the possibility of Quebec's secession seems to be an inherent and unavoidable consequence of Canadian federalism. In view of this, it is worth remembering that conciliation, not confrontation, has historically been the Canadian way on issues that divide us and threaten to pull us apart.

The Aboriginal Referendum held in three Quebec communities in 1995 rejected sovereignty, perhaps not least because the question of the right of aboriginal governments to rule their own peoples within an independent Quebec remained unresolved. This is a fundamental moral and political question for all Canadians. In his speech following the Yes vote in the 1995 referendum, former premier of Quebec Jacques Parizeau made controversial statements regarding minority rights that raised grave concerns about the fate of minorities living in a separate and independent Quebec. The questions of self-determination and minority rights were drawn closer together in the light of such considerations. These complex matters are brilliantly analyzed by Cree aboriginal scholar Mary Ellen Turpel of the University of Saskatchewan in her article "Does the Road to Québec Sovereignty Run through Aboriginal Territory?" (Chapter 5).

A nationalist and sovereignist Quebec existing within the confines of Canada's egalitarian federal system creates a fundamental contradiction at the centre of Canadian politics — one that has ultimately led many government leaders in Quebec to consider a unilateral declaration of independence (UDI). The parameters of UDI and the goal of sovereignty are outlined by the National Executive Council of the Parti Québécois in *The PQ's Plan for Sovereignty*, translated by Robert Chodos and excerpted in Chapter 4 of this section. The document was a precursor of Quebec's Declaration of Sovereignty, issued after the PQ's return to power in 1994, which set down the basic values and objectives that a new Quebec nation-state would try to achieve.

A UDI would leave unsettled a number of major issues, including the aboriginal question and treaty obligations, the debt and monetary and fiscal

questions, borders, and the right of transit. Moreover, many regard a provincial government's breaking away from the Canadian federation as strictly illegal. For these people, separation would amount to a declaration by the Quebec government that the laws of Canada no longer apply within its claimed jurisdiction. Would Ottawa resort to the use of force to protect its vision of Canada? Would the federal government intervene to protect the constitutional rights of Canadians who happen to live in Quebec? Would the government of Quebec resort to force to protect its claimed jurisdiction?

There are those who believe Canadians have yet to witness a "defining moment" as a nation-state, comparable to the Glorious Revolution in Great Britain or to the American Revolution or the Civil War in the United States — a time or event that forges a clear national identity. As we conclude this century, however, the question of Quebec's and Canada's destiny is perhaps approaching a pivotal point. Reluctantly, Canadians may be on the verge of experiencing the very defining moment that they have long needed, but always avoided.

THINKING IT OVER

1. Why does Marcel Massé (Chapter 1) call on his colleagues to "get government right"? Outline the three goals of Massé's directive. What strategies does he identify? In your view, is what Massé postulates as the corrective for governments enough to "get government right"?

2. Anthony Westell (Chapter 2) takes a much broader view than does Massé — he wants to "reinvent Canada." Can Westell's strategies be related in any way to Massé's? Are Westell's recommendations for change realistic? Should Canada have more or less government in the twenty-first century?

3. What does Janine Brodie (Chapter 3) mean by "changing state forms"? How will the newer ways in which we conduct our governments affect the social net, that is, health care, welfare, and social services? Can you find any common

ground among the views expressed by Massé, Westell, and Brodie? What will happen to Canadians if they do not change their state forms in response to global pressures? Are we moving too quickly? Will changing the ways in which we govern ourselves affect how we think about ourselves?

4. How realistic is the manifesto of the Parti Québécois (Chapter 4)? Could Quebec's nationalism be reconciled with new approaches to government in Canada? How much sovereignty can one province exercise and still remain part of a federated Canada? Can Canada survive the separation of Quebec? Indeed, can Canada survive the constant threat of the separation of Quebec?

5. Can an independent Quebec demand the protection of international law and deny similar legal protections to the aboriginal peoples living within its boundaries? As Mary Ellen Turpel (Chapter 5) asks, "Does the road to Quebec sovereignty run through aboriginal territory?"

6. Two persistent and unresolved issues that are addressed in all the readings in this section have haunted Canadians in their struggle to govern themselves: (1) the inclusion of Quebec as a willing and full participant in the federal governing system, and (2) the recognition of aboriginal governments as sovereign and independent of the governments of Canada and the provinces. Do you think these matters can ever be resolved?

GLOSSARY

aboriginal self-government This term is interpreted and used very differently by non-aboriginal Canadians and aboriginal people. For non-aboriginals it usually means a right of governance to be granted to aboriginal peoples living in Canada, whereas most First Nations leaders consider self-government a natural right already possessed by the many peoples who lived in Canada long before Europeans settled here and established their parliamentary system of government.

assimilation The social and political process whereby a distinct racial, cultural, or ethnic group takes on the values of a more dominant group, which can itself be influenced and modified by the values of the entering group. Complete assimilation leads to intermarriage and the adoption of the customs, attitudes, and skills of the dominant group.

ceremonial head of state In Canada, this position is occupied by the Queen and in her absence by the governor general, who represents the traditional legality of the Canadian state.

federal system A system of government, such as exists in Canada, in which powers and jurisdictions are constitutionally divided and/or shared among the national government and the subnational governments (such as the provincial governments).

francophone French-speaking or French speaker; a person whose native or principal language is French. The term can also refer to French speakers who wish to protect and encourage the culture of Quebec and other places in Canada where French is the dominant language.

imperialist The term is used in reference to the empire-building strategies of monarchical governments, which result in a subordinate–superordinate relationship wherein one political community gains sovereignty over another. The term is also used in an evaluative sense, as a condemnation of the aggressive acts of certain states.

indigenous people The original inhabitants of a place; those living in a country before explorers from Europe or other places colonized their lands. In Canada, indigenous people are also referred to as aboriginals, Native people, or First Nations.

international law The vast body of laws, rules, regulations, and procedures that have been developed by the international community to regulate the behaviour of states in their interactions with one another.

Keynesian welfare state John Maynard Keynes (1883–1946), a British economist, advocated in *The General Theory of Employment, Interest and Money* (1936) deficit financing by governments so as to stimulate economic growth and address the problem of unemployment, and for the state to make substantial provision by law and administration for those in need — the sick, poor, elderly, disabled, and indigent.

minority rights The democratic rights accorded to groups that comprise fewer people than the majority in the national, provincial, or local population.

parliamentary system A system of government based on the fusion of powers of the executive and legislative branches, where, by custom and convention, the political executive are members of the legislature.

political equality With respect to voting, political equality usually means that each voter has one and only one ballot.

self-determination The internationally recognized doctrine that postulates the right of a group of people who consider themselves separate and distinct from others to determine for themselves the state in which they will live and the form of government that state will have.

sovereignty The status of a state whereby its authority and power to make decisions cannot be overturned or reversed by any other agency, body, or government.

state form The fundamental configuration of government — for example, the parliamentary legislative organization, the bureaucracy, the judiciary, and the division of powers in a federal system.

unilateral The term used when a state depends completely on its own resources for security and the advancement of its national interest and tends to act alone in the exercise of its policies in the international system.

ADDITIONAL READINGS

Bell, David. 1992. *The Roots of Disunity*. Toronto: Oxford University Press.

Chodos, Robert, Rae Murphy, and Eric Hamovitch. 1991. *The Unmaking of Canada*. Toronto: James Lorimer & Company.

Cook, Ramsay. 1995. *Canada, Quebec, and the Uses of Nationalism*. Toronto: McClelland & Stewart.

Dickason, Olive Patricia. 1992. *Canada's First Nations: A History of the Founding Peoples from Earliest Times*. Toronto: McClelland & Stewart.

Jutras, Hélène. 1995. *Quebec Is Killing Me*. Ottawa: The Golden Dog Press.

Lemco, Jonathan. 1994. *Turmoil in the Peaceful Kingdom: The Quebec Sovereignty Movement and Its Implications for Canada and the United States*. Toronto: University of Toronto Press.

McRoberts, Kenneth. 1990. *Quebec: Social Change and Political Crisis*. Toronto: McClelland & Stewart.

Smith, Allan. 1994. *Canada — An American Nation: Essays on Continentalism, Identity, and the Canadian Frame of Mind*. Montreal: McGill-Queen's University Press.

Taras, David, et al. 1993. *A Passion for Identity*. Scarborough, Ont.: Nelson Canada.

Taylor, Charles. 1992. *Multiculturalism and the Politics of Recognition: An Essay*. Princeton, NJ: Princeton University Press.

———. 1994. *Multiculturalism: Examining the Politics of Recognition*. Princeton, NJ: Princeton University Press.

Watts, Ronald, and Douglas Brown, eds. 1991. *Options for a New Canada*. Toronto: University of Toronto Press.

Wine, Jeri, and Janice Ristock. 1991. *Women and Social Change*. Toronto: James Lorimer & Company.

Young, Robert, ed. 1992. *Confederation in Crisis*. Toronto: James Lorimer & Company.

Getting Government "Right": The Challenges of Governing Canada

MARCEL MASSÉ

THE OBJECTIVES OF "GETTING GOVERNMENT RIGHT"

What are the goals of "getting government right"? The goals are intertwined. At the most basic level, the initiative has to do with helping to reaffirm public confidence in government generally, and in the federal government in particular. I say "helping to reaffirm" because public confidence depends on many factors, not all of which will be addressed through this initiative. For example, the question of ethical behaviour by politicians has a big impact on public attitudes. This has been a central theme of the new Government since the day it assumed office, but it is not a focus of my particular mandate.

Nonetheless, the area covered by my mandate relates closely to the theme of public confidence. The reality of the fiscal situation both federally and provincially reinforces the notion that the reach of governments in Canada extends well beyond their grasp. Over time, governments collectively have promised more than they could deliver ... and delivered more than they can afford. Too many citizens have fallen into the habit of turning to government to solve problems that should be addressed in other ways. Governments have neither the capacity nor the resources to cope with all the issues which people bring to their door. We have to find a new equilibrium where the role of government is more sensibly and reasonably aligned with its competence and its resources, both financial and human.

Another problem in this country is that we have had great difficulty finding working accommodations with the provinces. Too often, the history of federal-provincial relations has been one of acrimony, entrenched positions and grandstanding.

In my view, the responsibility for this is shared. Both federal and provincial governments have been guilty, from time to time, of obstinacy and narrow-mindedness. Can we get beyond this kind of relationship? I think the citizens of Canada are telling us we have to. They are tired of politicians who are more interested in scoring points than in solving problems, who are more concerned with protecting turf than with serving the public.

BUILDING A FRAMEWORK

To move the "getting government right" agenda ahead, we are developing a framework within which the process of discussion and negotiation with provinces can take place. This framework involves several components.

First, we must identify the essential functions of the federal government of the future, taking into account changing circumstances and priorities. This will involve defining criteria which help to specify those kinds of responsibilities which need to be

---

SOURCE: "Getting Government 'Right': The Challenge of Implementation," unpublished paper. Reprinted by permission of the author.

maintained at the federal level in order to protect the overall national interest and the integrity of the state.

Second, we will also want to look at what kind of process might best be employed to move federal-provincial discussions away from the kind of recrimination and bickering which has too often been seen in the past. We want, in the phrase popular today, to see if it is possible to "reinvent" the process of negotiation with the provinces so that it is more productive, so that there is less arguing over turf and more emphasis on solving problems in the interests of citizens.

Third, we need to develop a citizen-centred approach to federal-provincial relations. In doing this, it may prove possible to take a leaf from the book of those who write about quality management. Organizations which provide high-quality service are those which, among other things, take an "outside-in" perspective on their services. Instead of organizing themselves in the way which is most administratively or bureaucratically convenient, they start with the interests and concerns of their clients.

In the conventional approach to federal-provincial relations, too often, the basic preoccupation on both sides has not been, "how do we meet citizens' needs in the most efficient way?" but "how do we make sure that our jurisdiction's interests and prerogatives are protected?" This is hardly the way to encourage mutual accommodation. Nor is it a good way to restore taxpayers' confidence in our public institutions.

In these kinds of negotiations, there has been a tendency to lose sight of the interests of those members of the public whom both governments are elected to serve. This time, we must try to do better. Our guiding objective should not be simply "disentanglement," which suggests a reordering and sorting out of what exists now, but "service enhancement," which suggests collaborative, citizen-focussed initiatives in which the interests of taxpayers and service recipients take precedence over all others. Perhaps we will develop a pilot approach and test it in a few areas, then refine and improve it and apply it more generally. We will see.

A fourth part of this framework will involve establishing some timetables in collaboration with provinces. In addition, we will no doubt want to set some kind of financial objectives which will assist with the goal of deficit reduction and provide a context for more detailed negotiations.

A fifth part of this framework involves deciding how to break this initiative down into manageable components at the federal level. Our thinking is still evolving at this stage.

One approach might be to mount three different but linked initiatives. One initiative could involve those departments of government where the paramount federal interest is clear and where there is not the same need for close daily collaboration with provinces as there is elsewhere.

With the changes under way in our international environment, such as the end of the Cold War, the collapse of the Soviet Union, and the formation of trading blocs, there is clearly a need to rethink some of the basic premises upon which government has been based. We need to make sure that this kind of review takes place within the context I have just described.

Another initiative could involve those departments with considerable operational linkages with the provinces. These are the departments where there is the greatest danger of overlap or duplication with the federal government.

A final kind might involve those areas of government where major cross-functional policy reviews are either under way or planned. I refer to such fields as health care, income security, fiscal transfers and the like.

However we decide to subdivide the issues, we will need to clarify the federal-provincial interfaces and to provide a framework within which the negotiations would be conducted so as to ensure a coherent and a coordinated approach across the federal government.

THE RENEWAL OF GOVERNANCE

Why are governments changing? One important reason is the widespread economic recession and the debt load which many jurisdictions have accumulated. Canada is no exception to this; indeed we are, unfortunately, a leader. Today, no one can afford inefficient government. And even if government is run productively, countries are inquiring, how much government can we afford? Sometimes even well-administered programs cannot be paid for. Thus, the size and role of the public sector are coming in for close scrutiny.

Governments are also reviewing their roles and activities because, with the growing pressure of international business competition, it is becoming evident that government has a choice: it can be either part of the solution or part of the problem. That is, efficient service-oriented governments can open up the channels of commerce and help domestic businesses to compete. Governments which tie their citizens and businesses up in needless red tape stifle the country's ability to penetrate new markets or maintain position in established ones.

Another source of change is information technology. This technology is redefining jobs, organizations and relationships. It creates pressures in the public sector just as it does in the business world for institutions to adapt to the challenges which it presents, to harness its power and exploit its possibilities.

Yet another cause of reform is the increasing level of education among citizens in many countries. This in turn increases demands for governments to be accountable and efficient.

Pressures for change also arise from the poor reputation which many governments seem to have acquired over the years. The most important asset of government is the confidence of the citizens who elect it. Today, in Canada as elsewhere, there is too much evidence of an erosion of confidence in the public sector. Certainly those of us who were involved in last fall's election were made very aware of this by the voters. Governments are being called upon to adapt in various ways to remedy this serious problem.

In short, there are good reasons for governments to make major changes to the way they operate, and many are responding to this challenge. For example, concerns about finances and about service quality have been one of the motivating forces behind recent trends, in some jurisdictions, to restructure government operations. Thus, as some of you may be aware, both Britain and New Zealand have moved large sections of government out of traditional departmental structures into new types of executive agencies. These are just a couple of instances of interesting new approaches to the structures, systems and relationships of government which are being adopted all over the world.

THE OBJECTIVES OF RENEWAL

Today, the development of a response to the pressures for change requires action beyond the purview of the public service. While there is a need for administrative reform within the public service itself, a subject I will return to in a few pages, there is a need for action on a broader plane. To effect improvements in areas such as fiscal restraint, program redesign or relations with the private sector and citizens requires initiative and leadership from politicians.

So the objectives of renewal to which this government subscribes are quite broad in their scope. Here they are.

In my view, the overall aim must be to give citizens services they need, to deliver them efficiently and responsively, and to bring our financial books back into balance. I believe if we achieve this we will go a long way toward restoring confidence in our government institutions.

Within this framework there are a number of more specific goals which we must attain.

One of these is *to define more clearly where each level of government can make its best contribution and to coordinate the work of each more effectively.* In doing this, we must eradicate instances of duplication and inefficiency. We do not wish to reopen constitutional questions; rather we wish to use administrative arrangements to make practical decisions so that the level of government best suited to delivering a program or service does so, and that limited public resources are used as efficiently as possible.

While engaged in this process, we must work with the provinces, and other levels of government where appropriate, to present a seamless face to citizens interested in related services. That is, if several levels of government are involved in delivering services to related groups of clients, we have an obligation to make it easy for citizens to access clusters of related services, without having to trek from office to office.

All this may involve redesigning federal and provincial programs in quite basic ways. Obviously, our progress will depend a great deal on how the process of collaboration with our provincial colleagues evolves: we cannot advance far without their commitment and help.

A second, related goal is *to restructure federal programs so that they are as cost-effective as possible, targeted on the highest priority needs of our citizens and country, and responsive to clients.* The goal of easy access which I just mentioned applies here, to exclusively federal programs delivered by one or more departments, just as much as it does in the sphere of federal-provincial relations.

A third goal is *to renew and enhance the public service of Canada.* This involves preserving its best features, building on its strengths, reshaping its institutions, supporting the loyal people who work there, helping them to adapt to the demands of the future and assisting them through the difficult transitions that lie ahead.

How are we working to achieve these goals?

ELEMENTS OF THE STRATEGY

I sometimes perceive the work of reform to be like assembling a giant jigsaw puzzle, with many pieces, some larger, some smaller. Key pieces are as follows.

Major Policy Reviews

First, there are the major policy reviews flowing from the government's "red book," *Creating Opportunity.* Several of these are already under way and others are being developed.

These policy reviews are asking the big questions about the goals of groups of federal programs. They are not just about expenditure restraint, though obviously this is a key concern. They are intended to look at the purposes of these programs, the kinds of services

which they provide to Canadians and their performance. The reviews will also look at linkages with provincial programs and in some cases municipal ones.

What we expect is that through these reviews, a number of the objectives of renewal which I have just articulated will be achieved in particular areas of government policy, and that we will emerge with less duplication with other jurisdictions, with a more client-centred approach and with better integration of related programs. One of the great advantages of these reviews is that they are not centred on one particular program: they can examine several programs concurrently and this provides opportunities for rethinking that are less easy to realize when the focus is more limited.

The "Program Review"

We are also embarking on a process which was announced in the Budget, an examination of those federal government programs outside the purview of the major policy reviews. We are in the process right now of deciding how this review process will be carried out. This process will complement the policy reviews and provide a vehicle to advance the goals of renewal in other parts of the federal government.

Federal-Provincial Relations

Another part of the puzzle involves federal-provincial relations. As the Minister responsible for Intergovernmental Affairs I have a special interest in this sphere. We are working to review our relationships with the provinces on a number of fronts. We hope to be able to improve the efficiency of our overall system of government by streamlining the delivery of selected programs and services. We also hope to deal with the issue of overlap and duplication, both perceived and real, by clarifying responsibilities and perhaps shifting some activities between levels of government.

In working with the provinces, we should examine the possibilities which may be offered through the more effective use of technology, both to enhance the productivity of existing programs and to open up possibilities for more integrated delivery of related services to citizens. By entering into collaborative arrangements with other governments, and in some cases with the private sector as well, we hope to extend the notion of "one-stop shopping" to a wide range of services. Similar cooperative approaches in certain areas of regulation have the potential to lessen reporting requirements and delays faced by business and private citizens.

Openness

If we are to deliver services to citizens that they need and value, we need to run government in an open manner.

Open government is hardly a new theme. Governments are constantly wrestling with the problem of how to secure citizens' input to decisions, how to make representative government work better and how to enhance citizens' sense of confidence in government institutions. This is, in a sense, the basic challenge of democratic government.

No one has found a simple solution to this challenge, but it is one at which we have to continue to work. In the context of the renewal process I am describing today, we must strive to engage citizens openly and honestly in discussions about policy. We must keep abreast of new approaches to involving citizens, and if there are lessons to be learned from other jurisdictions, we must try to profit from them.

Our government has already taken some steps toward enhancing public involvement in key decisions through the consultations undertaken as a lead-up to the last Budget. Other consultative initiatives are being carried out in the context of the major policy reviews I mentioned above.

However, this is just a start. Finding ways to secure the effective engagement of citizens in the renewal process is a challenge which will be continuous as we move forward.

Financial Targets

One of the most important aspects of renewal is the financial component. The various initiatives which

I have just described have to recognize the fact that we are out of money. We are now financing the interest on our accumulated debt by borrowing, adding even more to the overall burden. This process cannot continue.

Thus an essential part of renewal — the outside frame within which the puzzle must fit, if you like — involves defining and implementing financial policies which gradually bring the government back into financial balance. We have made a start in this direction with the Budget tabled in February 1994. More work needs to be done to continue the process of restraint and define the borders of this frame, not only for the next three years, but beyond.

Renewal of the Public Service

From the viewpoint of those present today, another very important component of renewal has to do with the federal public service. We have a public service with a remarkable international reputation. We receive a steady stream of people from other countries interested in learning more about our Cabinet system, our line departments, our merit principle, our training courses. Though we are often critical of our institutions in this country, one has only to spend a few days abroad dealing with officials from other bureaucracies to realize that we have a real asset in the public service of Canada.

However, despite the reputation which the public service has acquired over the years, it cannot be immune from the winds of change which I have been describing. The irritation which Canadians exhibit with respect to their government institutions, the frustrations which they experience, challenge us to become more service-oriented, to realize economies, to become ever more results-oriented in our work.

To me, public service renewal comprises several facets. A key dimension involves the continued application of the ideas and principles associated with Public Service 2000. While I see no need to perpetuate the name of that program, my Parliamentary Secretary, John English, gave a speech on my behalf to a conference organized by the Institute of Public Administration of Canada, and that speech endorsed what I consider to be the core idea associated with PS 2000, namely: making organizations more client-centred.

This concept involves familiar themes: making organizations more open and consultative; greater accountability for results at all levels, particularly at the top; the importance of effective management of people; the value of continuous learning; the need to eradicate silly rules and red tape; greater delegation of authority; more scope for initiative and innovation; public reporting on performance; and the like. Progress has been made in a number of departments in the last few years on these fronts, but much more remains to be done. This process needs to continue and be given further momentum both at the centre of the public service and in a number of line departments.

The "people" side of the public service deserves special prominence. The major policy reviews which I mentioned previously will undoubtedly have implications for the organizations and people of the public service. Renewal involves the adaptation of institutions through a period of transition, in ways yet to be defined.

When organizations change, people are affected, sometimes radically. Adapting to meet the challenges of the balance of this century and to prepare for the next requires us to give increased attention to the people, to give more prominence to human resource management issues. We have to do our best to ensure that training gets the priority it deserves, that adequate support is provided to people who are adversely affected by change, that morale is bolstered and maintained in difficult times, that we communicate effectively with our people, that we involve them appropriately in planning and implementation, that we recruit and develop as many top quality young people as possible, and so on.

Our success in this regard will be judged not only by *what* we do, but also by *how* we do it.

In considering how our institutions might change, we will want to look at the possibilities offered by creating a clearer division between policy-making and executive functions in government. Several other jurisdictions — Britain, Holland,

Sweden, New Zealand, for example — have adopted this idea in various ways. One hears both good and not-so-good reports about the results.

COMMUNITIES AND CITIZENS

Through all this work on the administrative machinery of government, it will be my intention as much as possible to maintain a "citizens first" perspective. We must become more effective in government at learning to see ourselves from the perspective of the taxpayer and the people and organizations who feel the impact of our regulations or are clients for services. It is easy, in any big bureaucracy, to become mesmerized by internal concerns, to live inside the castle walls without taking much account of what is going on outside. Governments have to become better at making the "outside-in" orientation I mentioned previously part of their culture.

On the subject of citizens' perspective, I think it is important that we recognize what is going on in Canada as well as in other countries which are experiencing problems of retrenchment akin to ours. Responsibilities are being devolved from more senior to subordinate levels of government, sometimes without commensurate funding. That is, subordinate governments get the mandate but not the money to carry it out. In other cases, responsibilities are being dropped altogether. When you continually have to borrow to finance what you are doing, there comes a point where you have to stop borrowing; and at that point you can no longer afford to do all the things you were doing before. It's no more complicated than that.

This process is going to require Canadians to adopt a new perspective on their governments. We have to find ways of encouraging citizens and communities to reassume responsibility for solving some problems and issues which in the last few decades they have placed on the doorstep of government. We need to find out more about how communities and citizens are dealing with this challenge, and to do what we can, with limited resources, to encourage what in French we call "responsabilisation"— responsibility-taking.

At present, when something goes wrong, the immediate tendency of some community activists is to call out for "*them*," that is, government, to do something about "*our*" problem, whether the problem is date-rape, tree-planting, littered beaches or tainted blood. Obviously there are many areas where government has to accept responsibility for action. But if we are to solve our financial crisis in the country, and also if we are to restore respect in our government institutions, we have to recognize the limits of both government resources and government competence. We have to challenge both individual citizens and community organizations such as businesses and non-profits to ask, more frequently, what are *we* going to do about *our* problems?

When governments are called upon to do everything, there are two inevitable consequences. One is that government will fail and fall into disrepute. And the second is a loss of a sense of civic responsibility and initiative. If we are going to "get government right" in Canada, we must not neglect this part of the challenge.

CONCLUSION

The challenge of "getting government right" is very large. I do not deceive myself that the process will be quick. It will take a long time — certainly through the mandate of this government, and probably well beyond.

Although there will be controversy along the way, I hope that it will be possible, at least in some measure, for this to be seen as a non-partisan issue. The problems of government today are beyond ideology — this is clear from the fact that both so-called left wing and right wing governments are embarking on reform programs, both here in Canada and around the world.

We have in Canada a country envied and admired internationally. Thousands of people would — and indeed do — pay dearly for the privilege of moving themselves and their children here. One of the features of this country which they admire most is the quality of our government.

For the benefit of both our own children and those of less fortunate people who may immigrate here, we have a responsibility to maintain our public institutions, to refashion them in the light of changing circumstances, and to enhance their vitality. We must make them places where people find challenging and fulfilling work, no longer haunted by the spectre of layoffs and cutbacks. It will not be easy. However, with consistency of purpose and a firm commitment I hope we shall succeed.

What's to Be Done?

ANTHONY WESTELL

We have discovered the roots of Canada's problems in the crisis of social democracy, in the failure of our federalism and our parliamentary form of government. In sum, our problems are systemic — that is to say, they are inherent in our system and we cannot solve them merely by electing a new prime minister at the head of a new government. We have to change our system of governance, review and probably change the way in which governments operate, and reform our social and economic policies.

It's a daunting task and prompts the question of how to begin, or to put it another way, What's to be done? As some will recognize, the question is adapted from the title of a famous book by Lenin, who thought he knew the answers, but the purpose here is to learn from his mistakes. In that slim volume he denied that the socialist revolution would emerge naturally and inevitably from the workers exploited by capitalism, and argued that at least in Russia revolution would have to be led by an elite of professional revolutionaries. This "rock hard" elite, mostly intellectuals to whom Communist ideology was a revealed truth beyond debate, would be the vanguard of a mass party of workers. While Lenin's ideas on organization and leadership made possible the Communist seizure of power in Russia — and were later imposed on Communist parties around the world — they were also, arguably, the explanation of the Soviet Union's rapid descent

into tyranny. The idea of a broad-based and essentially democratic movement had been compromised, and the absolute power of the ruling elite led to absolute corruption.

The lesson is that radical change is likely to succeed only when it is generated and monitored by the democratic process and is seen to enjoy majority support. It is one thing therefore to make the case for radical change in the Canadian system, but it would be presumptuous and a profound mistake — a sort of Leninism — to dictate what the change should be. If solutions are to work they must emerge from democratic debate and decision. It is for Canadians to invent the New Populism — that is, decide how best to regain control of their politics, how to make government work for them so that they can lead change instead of being dragged behind it, and so become victors rather than victims in the new global economy.

In the past we left the definition and solution of problems to our own elites, the politicians we elected and their professional advisers, the bureaucrats, with the academics and journalists in supporting roles. Indeed, that's the process prescribed by our parliamentary form of government: we elect representatives to manage our affairs more or less as they think best, and review their record only every few years. That's how we got Confederation, and it's how we have since tried to correct

SOURCE: Excerpted from *Reinventing Canada* (Toronto: Dundurn Press, 1994), pp. 76–90. Reprinted by permission of the publisher.

its deficiencies. Our heads of governments have met at countless constitutional conferences, agreed reluctantly that there are problems and that something must be done, and proposed numerous solutions. They have even gone through the motions of consulting the people by appointing parliamentary committees and task forces to hold public hearings. And some of their suggestions have been passed into law by some of the parliamentary legislatures, usually over the objections of opposition parties. But the mass of Canadians were not deeply involved until all eleven governments agreed upon the Charlottetown formula for change and submitted it to the people in a referendum in 1992. Whereupon the people said no.

It would be wrong to assume that all those who voted no were rejecting the Charlottetown accord on its merits, or even objecting to the way in which it was reached by negotiation among the elites. Many were expressing their anger at governments in general and the Mulroney government in particular because of the failure to solve economic problems. Others objected mainly to what they interpreted as concessions to Quebec, which they believed would give it a status superior to that of other provinces. But the 1993 election showed that there was tremendous dissatisfaction with the political structure and method of government operation. A post-election study of the vote revealed that more than half of those who voted in 1988 and again in 1993 changed parties, an astonishing and unprecedented level of volatility. Nevertheless, the system produced a majority Liberal government which promised not change but a return to the good old days, and it excluded from power new parties proposing change.

CHANGING THE SYSTEM

Most Canadians will probably agree that in order to regain control of government we need to reduce it in size and complexity. We can do that in two ways. One is to change the structure of our federalism so that government is smaller and closer to the people. The second is to change the way in which government operates. Let's deal first with changing structures. It is now generally accepted that if we are to reform Confederation — change our defective system — there is no going back to the old ways of decision-making by elites — what political scientists call elite accommodation. The elites failed in the task of producing a Charlottetown settlement acceptable to a majority of Canadians.

On the other hand, it is unrealistic to think that a cohesive and comprehensive package of reforms to the system can arise naturally from ordinary people busy with their daily lives, not well informed on the basic constitutional issues, and not much interested in what they regard as abstract constitutional problems. We do not expect the voters at election time to invent a detailed program for government to follow. We offer — or purport to offer — several programs and ask the voters to choose. To reinvent Canada we must adopt a similar procedure. The Citizens' Forum therefore was only a start on a process that now urgently needs to be continued. As the commissioners said in their report: "On many specific dilemmas facing Canadian government and society, no one yet has detailed answers. Certainly we do not. Many of these demand expert advice and research, and far more time than the eight months we had... We were not charged with reinventing federalism or rewriting the constitution."

Yet reinventing federalism is what needs to be done. The first task is to define the problems more clearly, explain the costs and benefits of alternative systems, and put them to Canadians in a way that requires hard choices rather than general expressions of hopes, prejudices, and uninformed opinions. Defining issues and explaining possible solutions is a job for experts. Debating, perhaps improving, and choosing among solutions is a job for the people, and the essence of a New Populism. What's to be done here is to suggest the questions that need to be asked, the range of possible answers, and a process to make it all happen.

DO WE NEED TO CHANGE AT ALL?

A debate on fundamentals must be prepared so that we can think about what some will say is unthinkable — for starters, whether Canada is a viable national state in the changing world. When the Bloc Québécois became the official Opposition in the Commons last year, there were loud protests precisely because the party argued that Confederation had failed and should be dissolved. So let us first deal with the notion that merely to question the viability of Canada is treason, or at least a betrayal of the national legacy. Of course it is not. Dissent by lawful means is the life force of democracy, and it includes the right and sometimes the duty to challenge in Parliament or elsewhere even the fundamentals of the country. After all, Confederation itself grew out of the failure of an earlier model of Canada. If Confederation is failing, it is the highest form of patriotism to face that problem and find solutions.

In fact, although national states such as Canada may seem to us to be the natural and best order of things simply because they are familiar, in historical perspective they are forever changing. A few centuries ago there were hundreds of separate nations of aboriginals on the North American continent. Using superior technologies to defeat them, the Europeans absorbed the aboriginal nations into French, English, and Spanish colonies. Next, new technologies of transportation and communication in the last century — notably railways and telegraphs — tied these colonies into three national states, Canada, the United States, and Mexico, by centralizing political and commercial power and homogenizing cultures.

As yesterday's technologies created national states, today's are creating superstates. The North American Free Trade Agreement aims to create a continental economy, and the treaty undeniably creates a degree of continental government. Similarly, across the Atlantic the European Community, now known as the European Union, is gathering national states into a continental superstate.

So no matter how much we may be attached to present arrangements, change is inevitable. At one level continental consolidation is under way, but at another level there is a process of disintegration within national states — a return to the identities that existed before the states were formed, and a flow of power from national to regional governments. Here in Canada, Québécois and aboriginal peoples are seeking some degree of independence. In the West there is a strong sense of regional identity and alienation from the centre. TV journalist Eric Malling reported in his "W-5" program (CTV, 31 March 1994):

> Say the word "constitution," and most of us hear "Quebec." For decades now the leaders of that province have argued that Canada might work better with less federal government... Well, the argument always gets tied up in language and culture, and usually ends in name calling. But guess what? Listen today and you hear a lot of the same things from the other side of the country, in British Columbia. No one talks seriously about separatism, but B.C. is booming these days. It already has a separate economy, and maybe some different arrangements with the rest of the country could make it even better off, and a lot happier.

Interviewed by Malling, Rafe Mair, former provincial politician and now an influential broadcaster, suggested the choice for British Columbia in the future was probably going to be between a "renegotiated Canada" and a closer association with adjoining U.S. states — a concept which already has a name, Cascadia, and even a flag.

Even Ontario, which has been proud to think of itself as a heartland of Confederation, is now complaining about the amount of wealth that the federal government transfers from it to poorer provinces. The last several federal governments have accepted the need to surrender spending power to the provinces to allow them more autonomy. In the United States, the notion of a cultural melting pot is seen increasingly to be a myth, or at least a pot that works only for whites of European descent.

Afro-Americans and Hispanics in particular claim their own cultural identities, and indeed legal and illegal immigrants from Mexico are on the way to regaining control of the vast territories seized from Mexico by the United States in the last century. The devolution of power from Washington to the states has been called the second great revolution in American federalism. In Western Europe, the United Kingdom is becoming less united, as Scotland and Wales each seek some degree of autonomy. There are similar tendencies in other developed democracies.

The formation of superstates and a return to regionalism or ethnic identity are not contradictory but complementary. Both replace national states. As globalism saps the power of national governments to manage the economy within their borders, they lose a major reason for their existence. The binding power of national identity based on common economic interests and distinct national cultures declines. People begin to question the purpose of the national state in which they live — as they are now doing in Canada. But the alternative, continental or global identity, remains amorphous, so people return for a sense of belonging to ethnic and regional loyalties.

We tend to view the decay of the state in which we live as a disaster. For example, at the time of Confederation many people living in the Maritimes, Quebec, and Ontario were opposed to surrendering their colonial identities to create a Canadian state. But changing states and national identities is not necessarily a bad thing. In the global economy, breaking up a large federal state and returning to more regional identities may be economically advantageous. In his new book, *Global Paradox* (William Morrow and Co., New York, N.Y., 1994), trend-watcher John Naisbitt says, "The bigger the world economy, the more powerful its smallest players." And it is true that the fastest-growing economies have been such small states as Singapore, Hong Kong, and Taiwan. The explanation may be that in a rapidly shifting global economy the countries that do best are those that can respond fastest to external market changes. To respond fast requires

consensus on policy, which can be achieved only if there is a high degree of social cohesion. Small countries — and those, like Japan, with a unifying cultural identity — are cohesive. Big countries spanning many regional economies and including many ethnic minorities are not cohesive, because there are too many competing interests. Instead of making national policy and acting on it, we argue about who will win and who will lose. What's good for the West may not be good for Ontario, and vice versa; and our political processes allow protracted and frequently inconclusive negotiation.

In the era of national economies serving national markets, size was an advantage. Now it may be a disadvantage. This is an argument for reorganizing large countries like Canada; to refuse to contemplate such changes, even though such a stance may seem patriotic, is to put the country at risk. We are not talking here about abolishing national states as we know them. With so much history behind them they will not swiftly disappear and no doubt will continue to play a leading role in international affairs. But we should consider how we can best organize our states, and begin to think in different ways about nationality and citizenship. Indeed, we are already thinking continentally in our economic and cultural lives.

The first question therefore answers itself. Canada as we know it will not survive. Change is unavoidable, and the real question is whether we shall welcome and manage the process or wait for events beyond our control to force it upon us with results we may not like.

WHAT ARE OUR OPTIONS IN DESIGNING A NEW CANADA?

In reforming the system of government the first choice is the one they faced in 1867 and then dodged, between a unitary and a federal state. As we have seen, John A. Macdonald favoured a unitary system with one strong central government for all Canada, but the Maritimes and Quebec objected. The outcome was a compromise that was called a confederation but was actually a federation.

We need now, in changed circumstances, to review and perhaps change that compromise.

The obvious advantage of a unitary system would be that it would eliminate one whole level of government, the provinces, or at least reduce provinces to an administrative role. There would be national policies for all, an end to federal-provincial fights over jurisdiction and tax revenues, and in theory at least administration would be streamlined and costs reduced. But the objections would surely be stronger today than they were in 1867. The original objections were to a loss of local identity based on history and custom, but economic imperatives were driving in the other direction, toward the formation of large states. Today, as we have noted, the trend is to return from national to local roots.

It is also an undeniable fact that government has become a vast undertaking and is beyond the effective supervision of any one legislature. Even when power and responsibility are divided between two levels of government there are frequent complaints that the federal or provincial parliaments are not dealing with this or that issue, that there is insufficient time for debate on legislation, and that bureaucrats and the courts rather than MPs are allowed to make policy. Above all, there is the sense that a remote central government is insensitive to local concerns. If responsibility for all the activities of government were to be concentrated in one parliament in far-away Ottawa, all these problems would necessarily be worse.

An alternative to a unitary system would be a more genuinely federal system. This could take one of a number of forms. We might for example choose a congressional form with the federal power divided between a prime minister nationally elected to represent the national interest, a senate representing the provinces, and a house of commons representing the voters in their constituencies. Or we could look at the German model, in which the regional states are directly represented by delegates in one of the two chambers of the central parliament. The federal parliament makes policy but its laws are largely administered by the states.

Another option would be to form what we claim already to have, a confederation. (States forming a federation surrender most of their powers to a superior level of national government, which is what happened in 1867. In a confederation, the states assign to the national government only limited powers and retain a large measure of autonomy.) The result would be to reduce very sharply the powers, duties, and size of the central government. A true Canadian confederation might be formed by the ten provinces and two or three territories as we know them, but it would probably be more practicable to base it on four or five regions. Ontario, Quebec, the Atlantic region, and the West might be the regions. Or perhaps the Prairies and the Northwest Territories would make one region, with British Columbia and the Yukon forming another. It might also be practicable to create for the purposes of government an additional region to represent self-governing aboriginal communities.

The regions or provinces would be sovereign except to the extent that they assigned powers to a central government, presumably to Ottawa. The idea would be to limit central powers to those necessary to manage the union, thereby allowing to the provinces or regions the maximum freedom to run their own economic, social, and cultural affairs in accordance with custom and democratic decision. Two obvious questions arise. How would such a small central government be appointed, and what powers would it have? It might be appointed by a parliament directly elected across Canada, as we have today. But that would be to set up once again two parallel structures of government, one national and one provincial or regional, with all the possibilities for political competition and wasteful overlapping from which we now suffer. In such a confederation, the regional or provincial governments would be senior and would probably wish to assign to the independently elected centre only the minimum necessary jurisdiction. This might include trade and other relations with foreign countries; national defence; immigration; monetary policy and the currency; criminal law; the Supreme Court to resolve constitutional disputes and administer, among other matters, the Charter of Rights and Freedoms; and the raising of revenues required to finance just those activities.

An alternative to an elected national parliament might be a central administration run by delegates appointed by elected governments in the provinces or regions. In such a system the provinces or regions would collectively control the central administration and might therefore be willing to expand its mandate to include programs of social and economic development. Such a confederacy would be similar to the European Union, in which national states meet at the centre to agree on community policies which bind them all. True, there is a European parliament whose MPs are elected and are independent of national governments, but the real power seems to reside with the national governments meeting in council, and with the international commission they have created.

To use another analogy, it would be a form of sovereignty-association for all provinces or regions, not just Quebec. And why not? We should at least consider whether a Canadian union that would satisfy Quebec might also be good for other regions. A decentralized confederacy run by the provinces or regions might look attractive to most Canadians — when they got over the shock of the new. It would eliminate the unfairly elected and ineffective federal Parliament and slash the vast federal bureaucracy; a slimmer administration with limited powers and lower costs would take their place. Because the central authority would be weaker, the peoples of the provinces or regions, with their different economies and customs, would have more latitude to decide how to organize their affairs. With different economic, social, and cultural policies, the provinces or regions would compete with each other and learn from each other. Political debate and responsibility would be focused at one level of government, close to the voters, where social cohesion is likely to be stronger than at the federal level and consensus easier to find. Issues of concern to all the provinces or regions would still be dealt with at the centre, including broad economic issues such as the choice between free trade and protectionism.

Some of the national symbols would probably be discarded, leaving it to each province or region to decide whether it wished to be a monarchy or a republic, to have a parliamentary or a congressional form of government, to be officially unilingual, bilingual, or even trilingual — with no federal presence to overshadow local distinctions. We could expect provinces or regions to accelerate the process, which is already under way, of strengthening ties with neighbouring U.S. regions, thereby moving toward a North American confederation. National programs such as old age pensions and unemployment insurance, which are supposed to unite all Canadians with their federal government, might be replaced by provincial or regional schemes suited to local needs and finances. And there would probably also be less willingness by Canadians in the wealthy regions to pay subsidies to those in the poorer regions. But such measures have not in the past produced national unity, and they may in fact retard economic restructuring in depressed regions. Conversely, a union of more functional democracies and more efficient local economies might strengthen pride in and a commitment to a new Canadian confederation.

DIRECT OR REPRESENTATIVE DEMOCRACY?

Whatever federal or confederal structure we favour, there is a basic choice to be made between direct and representative democracy. In a direct democracy the people come together to make their own decisions about public policy. In small communities in the past, for example, they held town hall meetings, discussed the problems, and decided on the solution by majority vote. But this was obviously impracticable in large provinces and even less workable when a whole country was involved. The solution was a system in which people elected a representative to travel to the provincial or national capital, put their point of view, and vote on their behalf. The representatives were often prominent citizens who were better educated than those they represented, and better informed on national issues because in the capital they heard many points of view. The idea developed therefore that representatives had a higher duty than merely speaking and voting as their constituents directed. They were to speak and vote as they thought best in the provincial or national interest, and because that would be good for the province or nation it would ultimately be good for their constituents also. If the constituents did not agree with the judgments made by their representative, they could remove him or her at the next election.

The referendum on the Charlottetown accord was an example of direct democracy and attracted a high level of public interest and involvement. The elected representatives prepared the accord but then asked the people to discuss it at length and vote yes or no. The people voted no and thereby rejected the judgments of their representatives. We have to wonder, however, to what extent most Canadians want to participate directly in government on a regular basis — and whether they are prepared to do the work required to participate responsibly. Governments make decisions every day, and MPs and members of provincial legislatures spend a great part of their time studying issues on which they must eventually vote. With a living to earn and perhaps a family to raise, the average citizen does not have the time or the interest to be constantly involved in government decision-making, but she or he probably does want to be consulted more frequently and effectively than in the past. This will require a major change in our system, which has been almost entirely representative, with infrequent recourse to referendums for such fundamental issues as changing the constitution.

HOW SHOULD GOVERNMENTS BE ELECTED?

Whatever structure of government we choose — unitary, federal, or confederal — we should look carefully at the various systems for electing our governments. But surely we would not confirm our present arrangement. Many better models are available, and the choice will depend to some extent on

the form of government. The U.S. congressional system, for example, has obvious flaws but it does require agreement between the president, who is elected to represent the nation, the senators, who represent the people in their states of the union, and the congressmen, who represent the people in their districts, or constituencies. Decision-making is often messy and protracted, but it is far more open and participatory than the Canadian system. It is sensitive to a fault to local and regional concerns, and this explains why party discipline is weak.

The handling of the NAFTA issue provides a useful example of how the Canadian and U.S. systems differ in operation. In Canada NAFTA was driven through the Commons by a Conservative government at the end of its term over the objections of the opposition parties, some of the provinces, and the majority of the people speaking through opinion polls. In the United States, President Clinton had to negotiate with individual members of the Congress to secure support, and while he was criticized for "buying" votes by promising government aid for constituencies, the voters could see what was being traded in each deal. The outcome of the long struggle, in doubt until the end, was probably as good an expression of the national will as could be achieved.

In Europe most democracies have some form of proportional representation which ensures that the representation of parties in the legislature reflects more or less the wishes of the people as expressed in the vote. This often means that no single party has a majority, making a coalition of two or more parties necessary. Each party in the coalition may speak for an ideology, a region, or even a religious point of view, but they are forced to compromise to find the best common expression of the will of the nation. Again, decision-making may be protracted, and there may be frequent changes of government, but it would be hard to prove from the record that such governments are less successful than Canadian governments.

Indeed, the Task Force on Canadian Unity, in its 1979 report, declared that our electoral system was corroding national unity because "the simple fact is that our elections produce a distorted image of the country." It proposed to modify the imbalance in the Commons by adding sixty seats, to be awarded to the parties in proportion to the votes they received. No action was taken despite the fact that the Task Force was chaired by two pillars of the political establishment, Jean-Luc Pépin, a Liberal, who had held several federal cabinet portfolios, and John Robarts, former Conservative premier of Ontario. The report was signed by others hardly less distinguished, including academics, politicians, and a labour leader. The NDP leader at the time, Ed Broadbent, later suggested implementing the Pépin-Robarts proposal, and Prime Minister Trudeau indicated he would assent if the Conservatives agreed. Conservative leader Joe Clark dissented, and that was that. Considering that in 1993 they won 16 percent of the vote, but less than 1 percent of the seats in the Commons, the PCs may think that Clark made a mistake. Under the proposal, they would have won twelve seats. The Royal Commission on Electoral Reform and Party Financing, appointed in 1979, had a broad mandate but decided for some reason that it was not supposed to consider such a basic reform as proportional representation — without which nothing else much mattered.

The usual argument against proportional representation is that it would encourage minor parties and probably elect a House of Minorities — a legislature in which there would be no majority party to form a stable government. In other words, if Canadians were allowed to elect the representatives they really wanted, it would turn out that there was no consensus on who should govern or what should be done, and there would have to be real debate, compromise, and perhaps even trade-offs between competing interests to win majority agreement on a legislative program. What a shockingly democratic idea!

A less shocking way to improve the electoral system would be what is called the single transferable vote. Voters rank candidates in the order of their preference, for example, making the Liberal their first choice, the New Democrat their second, the Green candidate their third, and so on. All the

first preferences are counted first, but if none of the candidates has more than 50 percent of the total, second preferences are allocated. This continues until one of the candidates has more than half the votes and is declared elected with the closest possible approximation of a majority mandate.

Our present system is biased to elect governments with the support of less than half the voters. Once in power, in Ottawa or in a province, these governments rule more or less as they wish, ignoring other parties and the majority of voters who support them. Any electoral system that compelled parties to compromise and form coalition governments would be more representative, and would encourage more open debate and greater public participation in decision-making.

CHANGING THE WAY GOVERNMENTS OPERATE?

The second way in which we can reduce the size of governments and bring them under better control is to change the way they operate. We look now to government both to make policies and to implement them through an army of slow-moving civil servants — or too often through bureaucrats who are less than civil and far from servants, because they administer regulations we cannot understand. It doesn't have to be this way. We can restructure governments so that they function as policy-makers and regulators but farm out operations to business and to non-profit community organizations. An influential guide to how this can be done is *Reinventing Government: How the Entrepreneurial Spirit Is Transforming the Public Sector* (Addison-Wesley Publishing Company, Reading, Mass., 1992), by David Osborne and Ted Gaebler. They studied the way in which some government departments in the U.S. were changing their ways of doing business and wrote:

We last "reinvented" our governments during the early decades of the twentieth century, roughly from 1900 through 1940. We did so . . . to cope with the emergence of a new industrial economy which created vast new problems and vast new opportunities in American life. Today the world of government is once again in great flux. The emergence of a post-industrial, knowledge-based, global economy has undermined old realities throughout the world, creating wonderful opportunities and frightening problems. Governments large and small, American and foreign, federal, state, and local, have begun to respond.

Osborne and Gaebler set out ten principles that should guide government. Here we can only summarize or paraphrase their ideas. Governments should:

1. "Steer rather than row." That is to say, they should set policy, deliver funds, and evaluate performance rather than operate programs.
2. Empower communities by giving them ownership of public programs instead of treating them as clients to be serviced by the bureaucracy.
3. Introduce competition into delivery of public services, requiring existing government departments and private companies to bid on contracts.
4. Be driven by a mission clearly defined, and not by rules, regulations, and budgets so detailed that they control the organization.
5. Be results-oriented, which means funding the output of programs rather than the inputs. For example, instead of funding schools on the basis of how many students enrol, fund on how many students they graduate at what level.
6. Be customer- rather than bureaucracy-driven — meeting the needs of the public rather than of the civil servants.
7. Be enterprising and harness the power of the profit motive, looking at problems as an opportunity to find solutions that make money instead of just costing money.
8. Anticipate and prevent problems, instead of finding cures after the problem has emerged.
9. Decentralize management, with hierarchy of authority giving way to participation and team work.
10. Structure markets to achieve public ends. For example, instead of introducing a program to collect bottles for recycling, legislate a deposit on bottles so that it is profitable for others to collect and return them.

Governments in Canada, as in the United States, have already adopted some of these principles. For example, programs for native peoples are increasingly "owned" and administered by native community organizations. The Canadian International Development Agency discovered years ago that working through non-governmental organizations (NGOs) was often the best way to deliver aid to communities in developing countries. The federal government retained the power to regulate air traffic but got out of the business of operating an airline when it "privatized" Air Canada, selling it to private investors more likely than civil servants to keep a close eye on efficiency and profitability. In many cities garbage is collected by private contractors who bid against each other for the municipal contract. Instead of building and operating public housing, governments assist community co-operatives to do the job. While providing facilities for recreation and sports, governments increasingly offset the cost by charging a fee to those who use them. The goal is not to cut back on public services but to provide them in a more economical manner, so that cuts are less likely to be required by budgetary constraints.

But the advantage of this new style of government is not merely economy. When community organizations rather than bureaucrats take responsibility for managing programs introduced by governments to solve public problems, it is a form of participatory democracy. Much more could be done, because developed democracies seem to be producing growing numbers of non-governmental organizations of volunteer workers, which undertake all manner of projects. Many are charitable — for example, food banks. Some are educational — for example, those promoting literacy. Others are organized around causes such as preserving the environment or aiding development abroad. Think of an issue in social reform and community development, and there will be at least one NGO working on it. They mobilize concerned citizens, with energy, education, and/or skills, who are prepared to donate part of their leisure time to tackling social problems. Why not hand over schools to NGOs made up of parents, teachers, and pupils? Perhaps community NGOs would be better than civil servants at assessing need and administering public welfare, and so on.

The greatest opposition would probably come from public service unions. They exist to protect the jobs and working conditions of their civil servant members, and fiercely resist any attempt to downsize government or to transfer work from the bureaucracy to the more competitive private sector. While their primary motive is the welfare of their members, they often support parties which claim to be social democratic. The argument seems to be that to preserve big government is to preserve social democracy, but this is a fundamental error. Social democracy depends not on big government but on good government which enjoys public respect because it is efficient, economical, and responsive to public need. Policies which produce that sort of government are social democratic; resistance to such policies is reactionary.

The Challenge of Governing:
Women and Changing State Forms

JANINE BRODIE

Canada, like all Western democracies, is currently experiencing a significant shift in the form of the state and its governing practices. Daily, our newspapers are filled with dire warnings about how, among other things,

- Canada must adjust in order to trade competitively in the new international market;
- federal and provincial governments must cut back their activities and their spending in order to become more efficient and reduce constraints on private-sector investment;
- social programs must be reduced and transformed to help those displaced by the new economic realities to enter the work force and become self-sufficient.

All of these messages mark a distinct departure from the governing assumptions of the postwar period. Following the Second World War, all Western liberal democracies, including Canada, designed their own particular versions of what is commonly called "the **Keynesian welfare state**." Although the versions differed somewhat, this particular **state form** was universally founded on similar assumptions and governing instruments. The postwar years brought new shared understandings about state intervention in the economy, expansion of the social-welfare system and government commitment to full employment, and

changes to the very meaning of citizenship itself. The postwar Keynesian state asserted the primacy of the public good over the "invisible hand" of the market and generated expectations that the state was responsible for meeting the basic social needs of its citizens. Moreover, an assumption was commonly made that it was the responsibility of the state to cushion national economies against disruptive international conditions.

It is now widely recognized that the pillars of the Keynesian welfare state have not survived the combined forces of prolonged economic crisis, the so-called globalization of production, and neo-liberal governing practices. The broad consensus that formed the foundation of the postwar welfare state has given way to a very different set of assumptions about the role of governments and the rights of citizens. It is now widely believed that the only means left to correct the mounting problems of slow economic growth, rising government debts, and widespread unemployment is restructuring. In Canada, restructuring entails maximizing exports, reducing social spending, curtailing state economic regulation, and enabling the private sector to reorganize the national economy as part of a continental trading bloc.

These new tenets of governing are rapidly transforming Canadian politics and public-policy priorities. Yet, little attention has thus far been paid to the impact these policy changes have had and will

SOURCE: Excerpted from *Women and Canadian Public Policy* (Toronto: Harcourt Brace, 1996), pp. v–vi and 1–7. Reprinted by permission of the publisher.

have on the everyday lives of Canadian women. The essays in [*Women and Canadian Public Policy*] are a first step in attempting to address this issue. [That] volume took shape in the winter of 1994, when a number of my colleagues at York University and I met at weekly seminars to contemplate the consequences that restructuring would have for Canadian women. [The seminar series] combined the expertise of feminist academics from a wide spectrum of disciplines, including political science, law, social work, sociology, and women's studies. This cross-fertilization of ideas proved very rewarding during the seminar series.

From the outset, the participants in the series emphasized that restructuring is affecting every facet of women's lives and that any exploration of Canadian women and public policy should not be limited to only those areas traditionally viewed as "women's issues." We begin, therefore, from the perspective that all public-policy issues are, in effect, "women's issues." Although policy-makers may believe that their initiatives in a particular policy field are gender-neutral, the essays in [*Women and Canadian Public Policy*] argue that this is rarely the case: because the organization of Canadian society remains profoundly gendered, men and women usually have quite separate experiences of policy changes.

Since restructuring involves significant changes in social, economic, and political life, many kinds of issues could have been examined in [*Women and Canadian Public Policy*]. In a sense, the essays [in that volume] only "scratch the surface" of the countless and often contradictory effects that the current round of restructuring is having and will have on Canadian women. However, we believe that the issues examined here provide a strong foundation for further research in the areas of restructuring, public policy, and gender.

SHIFTING STATE FORMS

When I was driving through the Maritime provinces in summer 1994, I was struck by a series of images that I thought rather nicely illustrated the central theme that informs this chapter. Canada is currently experiencing a dramatic shift in state form. This shift involves changing the rules, expectations, and opportunities that Canadian women have lived with for most of the postwar period. Canada, as our politicians seem fond of telling us and as our newspapers remind us daily, is currently undergoing the painful exercise of restructuring. Among other things, this process has brought about continental economic integration and the collapse of the branch-plant manufacturing sector, a seemingly uncontrollable public debt, the erosion of the public sector and the welfare state, and the impetus to redesign the social safety net. Yet, while terms such as "restructuring," "globalization," and "competitiveness" have become a part of our everyday language, how this discourse informs Canadian public policy and the everyday lives of Canadian women is given little attention.

During my trip to the Maritime provinces, I was immediately struck, upon entering New Brunswick, by how much road construction was going on and, especially, by the number of women on the road crews. Of course, these women were not operating the heavy machinery; instead, they had the mind-numbing task of turning a sign — slow/stop, slow/stop, slow/stop — for hours on end. Nevertheless, my first impression was that this represented a marked improvement. It was not so long ago that only male college students got these relatively well-paying summer jobs, and female students were relegated to summer waitressing for minimum wage, a job that always offered few employment protections and often involved sexual harassment. As I approached the second construction site, however, I realized that my first impression had been dead wrong. These women were not college students; they were older, and responsibility, stress, and poverty showed in their faces. As one construction site passed into another, the scene was repeated again and again. In fact, during my stay in the province, I don't think I saw one man signalling traffic to slow or stop.

I do not know whether this recurring spectacle was coincidental, nor did I ask. But my mind immediately turned to what I had been reading about New Brunswick — the province that federal Human Resource Development Minister Lloyd Axworthy calls an "incubator of reform." He coined the phrase in praising the province for its initiatives in social-welfare reform, which, he said, "rather than using [social assistance] in a passive way for people to get some limited income security, ... gives them a launching pad into the job market" (*Globe and Mail*, November 17, 1993, p. A1). These initiatives, NB WORKS and the Self-Sufficiency Project, attempt to nudge single parents (read: women) from the welfare rolls onto the job market. More recently, the federal and Manitoba governments have launched a $26.2-million program to help that province's 4000 single parents who are currently on welfare find work (*Globe and Mail*, September 10, 1993, p. A4). In each case, single mothers are being targeted as "a problem" within the existing welfare system. Legislation and practice are rapidly transforming mothers previously seen as unemployable into burdens on the state — potential members of the labour force who are responsible for their own maintenance and that of their children.

The issue is not that the state should resist welfare-policy reforms that provide single mothers on welfare, or any other disadvantaged group, with good jobs, some dignity, and a means to financial security and independence. Rather, the issue is whether, in a period of so-called jobless recovery, such initiatives can reasonably be expected to succeed. New Brunswick's premier, Frank McKenna, suggests that the likelihood of jobs becoming available should not be a concern: "if you have the training, the jobs will take care of themselves" (*Globe and Mail*, January 15, 1993). However, critics of the new thinking about "active" social policy are less convinced (McFarland, 1993). My point is simply that the policy universe, the economy, and politics are undergoing a period of flux in which questions regarding the appropriate role for the state in the economy and the rights of citizenship are being recast, renegotiated, and reregulated.

French philosopher Michel Foucault once suggested that social scientists begin their analysis with a basic assumption — namely, not "that everything is evil but rather than everything is dangerous" (quoted in Fink-Eitel, 1992, p. 10). Foucault was not advocating a philosophy of extreme paranoia. Instead, he was pointing out that the way we think about social problems is profoundly political. Power and knowledge are intimately related; within each historical period, they construct systems of domination and oppression, exclusion and silence, and perceptions of self and other. The current period of restructuring in Canada, which is based on new ideas about the economy and the state, is no different. The process of restructuring is changing the issues and challenges Canadian women face in their ongoing struggle for equality. Our project in [*Women and Canadian Public Policy*] is not to lament the passing of the old order, although evidence suggests that the shift away from it has left Canadian women disproportionately disadvantaged. Instead, our goal is to point to how the rapidly changing political and policy universe is creating new dangers that Canadian women must recognize and challenge. Our point here is that it is contingent upon feminists to examine closely the policy shifts that affect women's everyday lives in order to identify the various webs of subordination and domination on which the emerging order rests.

THE NEW GOVERNING ORTHODOXY

Canada, like all Western democracies, is currently experiencing a significant shift in state form and governing practices. It is now widely acknowledged that the foundations of the Keynesian welfare state (KWS) have been undermined by the combined forces of prolonged recession, the so-called globalization of production, and neoliberal governing practices. The broad consensus that grounded the KWS and structured the pattern of federal politics for almost a half-century has gradually, but certainly, given way to a very different set of assumptions about the role of government and the rights of citizens. These new assumptions lead to new forms of domination, at the same time reshaping the familiar ones rooted in gender, race, and class.

The new governing orthodoxy—"the neoliberal consensus"—holds that changing international realities put roughly the same demands on all governments; namely, that they

♦ maximize exports,
♦ reduce social spending,
♦ curtail state economic regulation, and
♦ enable market forces to restructure national economies as parts of transnational or regional trading blocs (Friedman, 1991, p. 35).

On the basis of these principles, Canadian governments are increasingly rejecting their former roles as promoters of domestic welfare and protectors of the national economy against unstable international forces. In the process, they have largely abandoned as futile the postwar goals of full employment and an inclusive social safety net. As Lloyd Axworthy announced, in *Improving Social Security in Canada: A Discussion Paper,*

> today's social security system doesn't deliver enough of what Canadians need, and spends too much money in the wrong places.... This generation must use its ingenuity to rebuild our social programs for a new era, just as an earlier generation after the Second World War forged solutions to meet the social needs of the post-war period. ...the key to dealing with social insecurity can be summed up in a single phrase: helping people get and keep jobs. This means many things, from action to improve the business climate for entrepreneurs, to getting the government's finances in order. (Canada, 1994, pp. 9–10)

Governments are effectively acting as the midwives of globalization, transforming the state apparatus, development strategies, and regulations to respond to the "perceived exigencies" of a global economy (Cox, 1991, p. 337). In particular, assumptions and governing practices are being refashioned to achieve the illusive and abstract states of "flexibility" and "competitiveness."

This neoliberal world view was first championed by the Reagan administration in the United States, and by Margaret Thatcher's Conservatives in Great Britain in the early 1980s. It was put at the top of the Canadian political agenda by the long-awaited report of the Macdonald Commission (Royal Commission on the Economic Union and Development Prospects for Canada), released in 1985. The commission successfully advanced the position that free trade with the United States and a neoliberal economic agenda were the *only* viable economic-development strategies left to Canada. With respect to free trade, in particular, Canadians were told to close their eyes and take "a leap of faith" because the globalization train had already left the station. If Canadians did not "jump aboard," they would most surely be left behind and would forfeit their living standards. Consequently, in its report, the commission advised all Canadian governments, federal and provincial, to

♦ adopt a market-driven development strategy,
♦ facilitate adjustment by reducing regulations on industry, and
♦ create new opportunities for private-sector growth (Brodie, 1990, pp. 218–223).

The Macdonald Commission had been appointed in 1982 by the federal Liberal party, which, at the time, seemed incapable of reversing the worst economic downturn Canada had had since the 1930s. Postwar macro-economic policies appeared unable to cope with stagflation—an increase in both inflation and joblessness. However, the newly elected Conservative government, under the leadership of Brian Mulroney, was quick to embrace the commission's prescriptions for economic renewal. In fact, the outgoing Trudeau government could not have given the Conservative party a better gift. It quickly launched into free-trade talks with the United States, although only two years earlier all but one of the Conservative leadership candidates (John Crosbie), including

Brian Mulroney, had roundly rejected the idea as a threat to Canadian jobs and sovereignty. The Conservative party also began, tentatively at first, to carve away at the welfare state.

An uncompromising neoliberal world view came to dominate the Mulroney government's front benches after its re-election in 1988 and the implementation of the Canada–U.S. Free Trade Agreement in 1989. Throughout the late 1980s, the Mulroney government had used mounting federal deficits as a rationale for cutting back the welfare state. By the early 1990s, however, the Conservatives' attack was directly linked to making Canada more "competitive"—primarily by forfeiting economic terrain to the private sector (Abele, 1992, p. 1). In its 1992 Budget Speech, for example, the Conservative government announced that its primary legislative priority was to promote greater "reliance on the private sector and market forces." Ranked immediately below this were the related goals of deficit reduction, inflation control, free trade, and the development of a new consensus about the role of government. For the federal Conservatives, a restructured economy required a restructured government that would provide only those public services that were "affordable" and did not interfere with Canadian "competitiveness" (*Toronto Star*, November 8, 1992). Indeed, so committed was the ruling party to this new world view that it attempted to make it constitutional in the early stages of the ill-fated Charlottetown Accord negotiations (Brodie, 1992).

MORE OF THE SAME

Historians may very well judge the Mulroney regime to be one of the most radical and overtly ideological in Canadian history. It ultimately collided with the Canadian voters in 1993, when they gave a landslide victory to the federal Liberal party. The Liberals promised little else than to be more compassionate managers of the economic transition. Since the election, moreover, the new government has charted the same neoliberal course and has used similar governing instruments, primarily the budget, to erode Canada's social safety net. The Liberal government, for example, ratified the North American Free Trade Agreement (NAFTA) in January 1994, even though it had failed to secure the side agreements it had identified during the election campaign as prerequisites for Canada's signing NAFTA. The Liberals also gave deficit reduction priority over employment and infrastructure development and have continued to attack the social-welfare system and system of federal–provincial cost-sharing that had been built up piecemeal during the postwar years.

The new minister of finance, Paul Martin, Jr., wore workboots instead of Bay Street brogues when he delivered his first budget on February 22, 1994. Although this choice of footwear was meant to convey to the public that the Liberal party was about jobs, it did not signal that the new federal government was preparing to repair Canada's fraying social safety net. Instead, Martin told Parliament that, "for years, governments have been promising more than they can deliver, and delivering more than they can afford. That has to end. We are ending it" (*Toronto Star*, February 23, 1994, p. A1). In the process, the federal government has begun a total redesign of the social-welfare system, a strategy begun within the federal bureaucracy during the Mulroney regime. In other words, the postwar KWS is no more.

In sum, then, the past decade has seen discredited most of the familiar assumptions that grounded governing practices in the postwar years. Daily, we receive a barrage of messages about the imperatives of trade, the deficit, a "jobless" recovery, the survival of our health-care system, the necessity for redesigning our social programs... the list goes on. These policy changes represent more than a series of ad hoc responses to a weak national economy and the changing global order. Instead, these changes represent a paradigm shift in governing practices—a historic remodelling of state form that, in turn, enacts changes, some intended and some not, in cultural forms, political identities, and the very terrain of the political. Restructuring, in other words, "conveys the notion of a 'brake,' if not a break, in secular trends, and a shift toward a *significantly different order and configuration of social, economic and political life.* It thus evokes a sequential combination of falling apart and building up again, deconstruction and attempted reconstruction" (Soja, 1989, p. 159; emphasis added).

REFERENCES

Abele, Francis. 1992. "The Politics of Competition." In Francis Abele, ed., *How Ottawa Spends, 1992–93.* Ottawa: Carleton University Press.

Brodie, Janine. 1990. *The Political Economy of Canadian Regionalism.* Toronto: Harcourt Brace Jovanovich.

———. 1992. "The Constitutional Confidence Game: The Economic Proposals and the Politics of Restructuring." Unpublished paper presented to the Department of Political Science, Carleton University.

Canada. 1994. *Improving Social Security in Canada: A Discussion Paper.* Hull: Human Resources Development Canada.

Cox, Robert. 1991. "The Global Political Economy and Social Choice." In Daniel Drache and Meric Gertler, eds., *The New Era of Global Competition: State Policy and Market Power.* Montreal and Kingston: McGill-Queen's University Press.

Fink-Eitel, Hinrich. 1992. *Foucault: An Introduction.* Philadelphia: Pennbridge Books.

Friedman, Harriet. 1991. "New Wines, New Bottles: The Regulation of Capital on a World Scale." *Studies in Political Economy,* 36.

McFarland, Joan. 1993. *Combining Economic and Social Policy Through Work and Welfare: The Impact on Women.* Paper presented to the Economic Equity Workshop, Status of Women, Ottawa.

Soja, Edward. 1989. *Postmodern Geographies.* London: Verso.

Sovereignty:
A Clear and Coherent Plan

NATIONAL EXECUTIVE COUNCIL
OF THE PARTI QUÉBÉCOIS

The referendum of October 26, 1992, marked the end of a five-year journey through the constitutional maze. From the point of view of the movement to make Quebec a sovereign state, this period turned out to be a very productive one.

The sustained and sometimes dramatic growth in popular support for sovereignty was one clear expression of the period's fertility. Just as remarkable, however, was the extraordinary number of reflections, debates, reports, position papers, and technical clarifications through which all aspects of sovereignty were formulated more explicitly than ever before. New clarity has been achieved on issues as diverse as currency, territorial integrity, and **minority rights**.

It is significant that this process involved all of Quebec society, especially through the work of the Commission on the Political and Constitutional Future of Quebec (the Bélanger-Campeau Commission) in 1990–91. Since the commission did not operate in an exclusively sovereignist perspective, its deliberations provided an opportunity to compare sovereignty with the alternative proposal of renewed federalism, making this initiative an extremely fruitful one.

The Bélanger-Campeau Commission was one of two exceptional forums that provided an opportunity for people to express themselves in oral testimony and written briefs, for experts to discuss and clarify technical questions, and for elected representatives to draw conclusions and elements of consensus bearing on Quebec's political future. However, the report of the Bélanger-Campeau Commission, the studies carried out by its secretariat, and the draft report of the Quebec National Assembly committee that studied questions relating to Quebec's accession to sovereignty have received limited distribution. It is worth taking another look at the major conclusions of these forums to help clarify and define some of the fundamental elements involved in making Quebec a sovereign state.

THE DEFINITION OF SOVEREIGNTY

For the first time, a consensus has been reached on the definition of sovereignty. This definition is the one that the Quebec government used in 1979 in the white paper it issued to lay the basis for the 1980 referendum. It also forms part of the current program of the Parti Québécois. The Bélanger-Campeau Commission endorsed it as well. And finally, the Quebec National Assembly adopted this definition by including it in Bill 150, its 1991 legislation providing for a referendum on sovereignty by October 26, 1992, unless the federal government developed a proposal that could be put to the people instead.

SOURCE: "Sovereignty: A Clear and Coherent Plan," in *The PQ's Plan for Sovereignty*, trans. Robert Chodos (Toronto: James Lorimer & Company, 1994), pp. 41–60. Reprinted by permission of the publisher.

The sovereignty of Quebec means that

♦ all taxes imposed in Quebec are collected by the Quebec government or authorities dependent on it;
♦ all laws that apply to Quebec citizens on Quebec soil emanate from the Quebec National Assembly;
♦ all international treaties, conventions, and agreements are negotiated by representatives of the Quebec government and ratified by the Quebec National Assembly.

These three elements — taxes, legislation, and treaties — encompass all government activity internally and internationally. Given the way today's world is organized, no state can afford to become isolated or withdrawn. In acquiring complete freedom of action, Quebec will also assume responsibility for conducting its relations with other members of the international community. Of primary importance will be relations with Canada. Quebec should ensure that the Canadian economic space is maintained. It can also pool a portion of its powers in any sector where the interests of two or more countries are involved. Quebec will look for these paths to the future wherever it is in its interest to do so.

ACCESSION TO SOVEREIGNTY

The Parti Québécois defined the process of acceding to sovereignty at its conventions in November 1988 and January 1991. It specified the major steps it will take to achieve the sovereignty of Quebec in the event that it is called on to form a government. These are the steps:

♦ From now until the time that it forms the next government, the Parti Québécois will promote Quebec sovereignty by concretely demonstrating its advantages.
♦ Once elected, a Parti Québécois government will do the following, as paraphrased below:

a. submit to the National Assembly for adoption a solemn declaration stating Quebec's wish to accede to full sovereignty;
b. following discussions with the federal government, proceed to fulfil its responsibility and its mandate to establish the timetable and modalities for transferring powers and determine the rules for dividing Canada's assets and debts;
c. submit to the National Assembly for adoption legislation instituting a constitutional commission whose terms of reference would be to draw up a proposed constitution for a sovereign Quebec.
♦ As quickly as possible, the government will ask the population, through a referendum, to speak on the sovereignty of Quebec and the constitutional mechanisms that would make the exercise of that sovereignty possible. This referendum will be the act that will bring into being a sovereign Quebec.
♦ The Quebec government will also propose mutually advantageous forms of economic association to the federal government. These proposals will include the institution of joint bodies, established through treaties, to manage the economic relationship between Canada and Quebec.

It is our intention to ensure that accession to sovereignty takes place in as democratic a framework as possible. Here we will specify, as far as we can, the steps and conditions that will lead to a sovereign Quebec.

THE QUEBEC CONSTITUTION

The Constitution of Quebec will be the supreme law of the land. It will define the institutions through which the people of Quebec choose to govern themselves, and it will guarantee all the fundamental rights and freedoms of Quebec citizens. It is only by giving itself a constitution that Quebec can become sovereign.

To start with, the constitution needs to recognize the sovereignty of the people and establish the bodies that will exercise state power in its name. For an initial period at least, it would appear to be in Quebec's interest essentially to hold over its existing institutions and make only those modifications that are immediately required by the change in its political status.

This means that the existing system of executive and legislative authority would be maintained. The only change would be the replacement of the lieutenant-governor, whose responsibilities could be exercised by a **ceremonial head of state** elected by a majority of members of the National Assembly. The National Assembly itself could be maintained in its present form, as the new powers it would obtain would not require it to change the way it functions.

Changes to the judicial system would involve the establishment of a Supreme Court of Quebec and the incorporation into the Quebec judicial structure of a number of courts that now operate under federal legislation. Just as federal civil servants will be integrated into the Quebec civil service, places can be found for federally appointed judges within Quebec courts — on condition, of course, of their allegiance to the new constitution.

It will also be a function of the constitution to lay out Quebecers' rights and freedoms. To this end, the Quebec Charter of Rights and Freedoms will be entrenched in the constitution.

The constitution should include new and clear guarantees of the rights of the Anglophone minority. Quebec owes much to Quebecers of English culture, and it should act to ensure that the constitution expresses and guarantees their fundamental and acquired rights in the best possible fashion.

In the same way, the rights of aboriginal peoples will be preserved. The Constitution of Quebec should include the same guarantees of ancestral and treaty rights now offered by the Constitution of Canada. In addition, in the spirit of the National Assembly's 1985 decision to recognize aboriginal peoples as distinct nations, the constitution will provide explicit recognition of their right to autonomous governments and protection for agreements that would put this autonomy into practice in a context of respect for Quebec's territorial integrity.

The constitution also needs to include an amending formula. In addition to these provisions, temporary measures will be taken to allow for Quebec's transition from provincial status to the status of a sovereign state, especially with regard to the continuity of laws and institutions.

This transitional constitution will be prepared by the constitutional commission that a Parti Québécois government will establish after being elected. It could also be within the commission's terms of reference to study more thorough changes to Quebec's institutions. Should such changes be considered desirable, they could then be adopted after Quebec became sovereign.

QUEBEC CITIZENSHIP

Every state determines who its citizens are — to which people it will accord nationality or citizenship. Quebec citizenship will be automatically granted to all Canadian citizens domiciled in Quebec at the moment of Quebec's accession to sovereignty, and from that time on, to all children born to Quebec parents inside or outside Quebec territory. All Canadian citizens born in Quebec but domiciled elsewhere in Canada or outside Canada at the time of accession to sovereignty because of the position they occupy — students, missionaries, businesspeople, members of the armed forces, civil servants, et cetera — will also become Quebec citizens. To facilitate its nationals' relations with other countries, Quebec will issue a passport identifying its bearer as possessing Quebec nationality.

Landed immigrants will be able to obtain Quebec citizenship once the waiting period under Canadian legislation in force at the time of accession to sovereignty has elapsed. From then on, Quebec will exercise full powers over immigration. With respect to refugees, Quebec will sign the 1951 Convention relating to the Status of Refugees and its protocol and the 1966 International Convention on Civil and Political Rights and its protocol, which are the most important multilateral agreements in this regard.

Quebec intends to grant Quebec citizenship automatically, with no waiting period, to any

Canadian citizen who decides to become domiciled in Quebec. It will propose to the government of Canada that a reciprocal agreement be concluded in this regard so that any Quebec citizen who settles in Canada can immediately become a Canadian citizen. The two countries could also agree not to establish immigration quotas affecting each other's nationals so that the advantages of the free movement of people prevailing before Quebec's accession to sovereignty would be maintained.

It will, of course, be Canada's responsibility to take any decisions it considers appropriate with regard to Canadian citizenship. It could, for example, decide to maintain Canadian citizenship for any Canadian citizen residing in Quebec before Quebec's accession to sovereignty, or for any such person who requests it. Like current Canadian legislation, Quebec citizenship legislation will recognize the possibility of its nationals' holding dual citizenship.

TERRITORY

What will be the borders of a sovereign Quebec? The work of the National Assembly's committee on questions relating to sovereignty has made it possible to clarify questions surrounding the issue of territory.

First of all, before Quebec becomes sovereign, under the provisions of the Canadian constitution, its borders cannot be changed without its consent. After it becomes sovereign, the framework for questions of its territorial integrity will be international law.

Thus, when Quebec becomes sovereign, its borders will be the borders of the current province of Quebec. Some people have maintained that the lands transferred to Quebec under federal legislation in 1898 and 1912, which extended its territory to the shores of Hudson Bay, Hudson Strait, and Ungava Bay, could then be cut off from Quebec. The committee submitted this question to a panel of five international experts. Their answer was unequivocal: the lands transferred in 1898 and 1912 are an unrestricted and integral part of

Quebec territory. The experts based their opinion on legislation passed by the Canadian and Quebec governments to put the James Bay Agreement into effect in 1975. They also pointed out that the aboriginal peoples of these lands renounced their traditional rights under the terms of article 2.1 of the James Bay Agreement: "The James Bay Crees and Inuit of Quebec hereby cede, release, surrender and convey all their Native claims, rights, titles and interests, whatever they may be, in and to land in the Territory and in Quebec, and Quebec and Canada accept such surrender."

The same panel of experts concluded that in the case of a hypothetical claim aimed at dismembering Quebec's territory, the principle of judicial continuity would lead to the conclusion that the territorial integrity of Quebec, guaranteed both by Canadian constitutional law and by **international law**, should prevail. In short, unless Quebec explicitly authorizes a change in its borders, its territory at the time it becomes sovereign will coincide with the territory it currently holds as a province within the Canadian federation.

Quebec will also need to take measures to guarantee the security of its territory. In this spirit, it will maintain armed forces proportionate to its size and needs. It will also assume its responsibilities in collective security and defence through existing international organizations such as the North Atlantic Treaty Organization (NATO) and the North American Aerospace Defence Command (NORAD).

CONTINUITY OF LAW

When Quebec becomes sovereign, its state will be entrusted with all the powers and responsibilities that modern states assume. In addition to the powers and responsibilities it now exercises as a province, it will assume the powers now exercised by the federal government in Quebec through Ottawa's exclusive and shared responsibilities and the federal spending power. How will Quebec manage this transition?

To avoid a legal hiatus, the government will propose that the National Assembly maintain federal legislation—such as the Criminal Code or the Bankruptcy Act—in effect until it can amend or recast these laws. In this way, the continuity of judicial proceedings that involve federal jurisdiction and are under way at the time Quebec becomes sovereign can be ensured. Whatever courts have to render judgement in these cases can then do so according to the provisions of the federal legislation in effect at the time they were undertaken.

CONTINUITY OF SERVICE TO INDIVIDUALS AND CORPORATIONS

The Quebec government will prepare appropriate legislative, regulatory, and administrative measures to ensure continuity of the services the federal government provides to individuals and corporations. It will take special care to establish mechanisms to avoid any interruption in payment of old age pensions, child tax benefits, unemployment insurance claims, veterans' allowances, financial assistance to aboriginal peoples, et cetera. Since Quebec will recover all taxes, it will be able to ensure that these services are maintained. Indeed, it will be able to do so at lower cost through the elimination of duplication and overlap and through the rationalization of some expenses.

It is important here to recall and reiterate the Parti Québécois's firm commitment to provide a job in the Quebec civil service for any federal civil servant from Quebec. The integration of federal civil servants into the Quebec civil service will make available the human resources needed to maintain services and take charge of new responsibilities.

DIVIDING PUBLIC PROPERTY AND THE DEBT

Some commentators have long maintained that the question of division of public property and the federal debt when Quebec becomes sovereign involves major difficulties. The Bélanger-Campeau Commission and the National Assembly committee

on sovereignty have brought some very pertinent reasoning to bear on this question.

As a matter of principle, a sovereign Quebec would become the owner of federal property within its borders without being required to pay an indemnity. In principle as well, Quebec would not be formally bound by the debt accumulated by the Canadian federal government. However, recognizing that part of the debt was incurred for its benefit, Quebec intends to share it.

In this spirit, the Bélanger-Campeau Commission worked out a methodology for dividing federal property and the debt. This methodology leads to the conclusion that through the combined effect of the recovery of Quebec taxes paid to Ottawa, the transfer of federal services, the division of federal property and the debt, and the elimination of duplication and overlap, Quebec's finances would become significantly healthier.

While limiting its work to only two examples, the Bélanger-Campeau Commission gave some indication of the possible impact of eliminating duplication and overlap. It identified potential annual savings of $522 million relating only to transportation and communication costs and the expenditures of the federal Department of Revenue.

In addition, in the fall of 1990, the Quebec government launched department-by-department studies of the impact of recovering federal services. Despite the relevance of these studies, the government has so far refused to publish their content or conclusions.

INTERNATIONAL RELATIONS

Quebec will quickly have to become part of the dense and complex fabric of multilateral relations among governments. Its first initiative will be its application for admission to the United Nations. Along with this application, Quebec will also immediately apply for membership in the major UN specialized agencies: the United Nations Educational, Scientific and Cultural Organization (UNESCO), the World Health Organization (WHO), the International Labor Organization (ILO), and the

UN Food and Agriculture Organization (FAO), as well as in some major technical organizations such as the International Civil Aviation Organization (ICAO), whose headquarters are in Montreal. Quebec will also apply for membership in the General Agreement on Tariffs and Trade (GATT), the World Bank, the International Monetary Fund (IMF) and the Organization for Economic Co-operation and Development (OECD).

It goes without saying that Quebec attaches special importance to its participation in the Agence de Coopération Culturelle et Technique — the organization of **Francophone** countries — and Francophone summits. In these forums, Quebec's status would naturally change from that of "participating government" to that of full member. Quebec will also seek to belong to the Organization of American States, the Commonwealth, and the Conference on Security and Cooperation in Europe.

In bilateral relations, ties with Canada will clearly be given top priority. In addition to the close economic relations that they will continue to maintain, Quebec and Canada have numerous interests and concerns in common, in areas as diverse as the environment, territorial defence and security, and transportation and communications. The task will be to define a new relationship on the basis of the historic ties between the two political communities. Thus, attention should be devoted to developing a framework of active cooperation between Quebec and Canada's Francophone minorities and between Quebec's Anglophone minority and the Anglophone majority in Canada. Cooperation should also be encouraged, to the extent that they wish it, between the aboriginal nations of Quebec and Canada.

Next on the priority list come the United States and France, roughly equal in importance although they have very different relationships with Quebec. Quebec's relations with the United States will be characterized by growing integration in the commercial, financial, and industrial spheres. For a number of years now, Quebec's sales to the United States have been growing much more quickly than its sales to the rest of Canada — that is, they have been growing along a north–south rather than an east–west axis.

This process of integration, so characteristic of our era, will continue and broaden. The North American Free Trade Agreement has begun to incorporate Mexico into the North American sphere, and Chile, Colombia, and Venezuela have already indicated their desire to become part of NAFTA. It will be very natural for Quebec to take its place in the continental framework. There is nothing theoretical or abstract about this conclusion. Total Quebec–U.S. trade (exports and imports) is equal to half of total Mexico–U.S. trade, nine times total Chile–U.S. trade, and twice total Brazil–U.S. trade. It is close to the level of trade that the United States maintains with France or Italy.

In the economic sphere, Quebec's relations with France will not be as intense as its relations with the United States. However, what France and Quebec can offer each other as ports of entry into their respective continents should not be ignored. In the areas of cultural life, communications, education, and research, the community of Francophone countries offers immense possibilities.

ECONOMIC ASSOCIATION WITH CANADA

That having been said, we must turn to what is quite properly Quebecers' leading concern with regard to sovereignty: economic association with Canada.

The intensity of economic exchange between Quebec and Canada makes maintaining the Canadian economic space a major consideration when we look at Quebec's accession to sovereignty. A broad consensus in Quebec favours maintaining this space. Preserving it is in Canada's interest as well, irrespective of the political systems prevailing in Canada and Quebec. As a result, the Quebec government will propose concluding an economic association treaty or sectoral agreements that would maintain the Canadian economic space as it currently exists.

This does not exclude the possibility of improving the economic space through subsequent negotiations. However, to ensure a smooth transition, it would be more useful and easier to seek to preserve it as it is than to try to renegotiate all its elements. By maintaining their economic union, Canada and Quebec would be entering into one of the most advanced forms of economic integration between sovereign states anywhere in the world.

The interests of Quebec and Canada in maintaining the economic union dovetail completely. Quebec constitutes the rest of Canada's second-largest export market, behind the United States but far ahead of any other country in the world. According to Statistics Canada, Quebec bought merchandise worth more than $20 billion from the rest of Canada in 1988.

The Canadian economic space consists of a number of elements. First, it includes a monetary union, with the Canadian dollar as the common currency. Second, a customs union provides for free movement of goods between Quebec and Canada and a common trade policy towards other countries, making it unnecessary to set up customs posts between the partners. Finally, free movement — in varying degrees — of services, capital, and people round out the economic space and make it a form of common market.

Through the work of the Bélanger-Campeau Commission and the National Assembly committee on sovereignty, it has been established that Quebec could maintain a number of the components of the Canadian economic space **unilaterally**.

The arguments put forward by detractors of Quebec sovereignty have long drawn on the anticipated difficulties of creating a Quebec currency. However, it has been established that Quebec could technically continue to use the Canadian dollar as its currency without anyone being able to stop it. Against that point, it has frequently been argued that if Quebec followed this course, it could not demand participation in setting monetary policy through the Bank of Canada. It is worth pointing out that since the establishment of the Canadian dollar, Quebec has never participated in the conduct of monetary policy. In any event, maintaining a common currency would represent a significant guarantee of stability.

At least some freedom of movement is a characteristic of the Canadian economic space. However, it takes different forms depending on whether it applies to capital, goods, services, or people. Everyone recognizes that it would be completely futile if not impossible to try to restrict the free movement of capital. With regard to the free movement of goods and services, it is clearly in the mutual interest of Quebecers and Canadians to maintain the existing customs union and free trade area. Canada might want to limit this aspect of the economic space to a free trade area alone. This would not present insurmountable problems, as free movement would still be protected.

Nor does a sovereign Quebec's membership in GATT involve any special problems. Since it was founded in the late 1940s, GATT has brought about a remarkable lowering of the obstacles to international trade. The recently concluded Uruguay Round will further reduce the obstacles that remain. As a member of GATT, Quebec will enjoy significant guaranteed access to international markets, including Canada's.

Membership in GATT will permit Quebec to take advantage of the "most-favoured-nation" clause. Under this clause, a country is required to offer every one of its trading partners treatment equivalent to the best treatment it offers any other country.

Free movement of people is a significant aspect of economic association. It is especially important for inhabitants of border regions who live in one country and work in a neighbouring one on a daily basis. A situation of this sort currently exists between Canada and United States, and this aspect of the movement of people is managed through international agreements. It would be entirely possible to establish agreements of the same kind between Canada and Quebec.

The question of dual citizenship arises in the same context. Current Canadian legislation recognizes the right to hold more than one citizenship. A sovereign Quebec will follow the same policy. Many Quebecers will apply to the Canadian government to maintain their Canadian citizenship. It is hardly likely that the Canadian government would decide to amend its legislation to allow for dual citizenship with every country except Quebec.

Maintenance of a Canada–Quebec economic space raises the question of how that space should be managed. There are a variety of actions that governments can take in this regard. The governments concerned can simply establish rules by which they are expected to abide. Another course is to establish formal dispute settlement mechanisms. Or governments can pool a portion of their powers by setting up institutions responsible for exercising those powers.

As an example of how this would work, the establishment of three major joint institutions could be envisaged. First, a council composed of ministers or representatives designated and delegated by the two countries could exercise decision-making power in matters specified under the economic association treaty. Second, a secretariat could be responsible for applying the treaty according to the directives of the council. Finally, a tribunal could be in charge of settling disputes. A form of Quebec participation in the

Bank of Canada could also be provided for. The ministers or delegates who would sit on the council would remain responsible to their respective parliaments, ensuring democratic control of the treaty or treaties governing the activity of these bodies.

Joint commissions responsible for managing specialized aspects of the association treaty could also be envisaged. For instance, a commission could oversee the rules concerning the transfer of pensions or specific environmental or transportation issues involving the two countries. All these questions should be approached with an open mind and with the goal of ensuring that a treaty providing for maintenance of the Canadian economic space is applied in the best possible way.

It is in the interest of both Quebec and Canada to make sure that the transition takes place as smoothly as possible and that the mechanisms set up to manage their mutual relations are as effective as they can be. They both have everything to gain in remaining receptive to proposals from the other partner so that they can quickly reach mutually advantageous common ground.

Does the Road to Québec Sovereignty Run through Aboriginal Territory?

MARY ELLEN TURPEL

The problem here is a denial of the past, or a narrowness of vision that sees the arrival and then spread of immigrants as the very purpose of history.

Hugh Brody[1]

Québec's resources are permanent; we do not owe them to a political system, or to specific circumstances. They are a gift of nature, which has favoured us more than others in this respect by allowing us to play a more important economic role, thanks to our resources.

Government of Québec[2]

It is important to respect the aspirations of Québecois to **self-determination**, if they act in accordance with international law.

At the same time, it is difficult to address in a totally dispassionate way the spectre of "Québec secession." Every time I begin to write about the international legal and Canadian constitutional dimensions of Québec separation or accession to full sovereignty from the perspective of aboriginal peoples'[3] status, one area of my so-called professional and personal "expertise" as an aboriginal woman and law professor, I am confronted with my concern for the status and rights of those most marginalized in this discussion — the aboriginal peoples in Québec.

The claim by Québecois for full sovereignty, as it has been conceived by many secessionists,[4] appears to rest on the erasure of the political status of aboriginal peoples and the denial of their most fundamental rights to self-determination. These are two most critical points, seemingly resisted by the main political parties in Québec, and not taken seriously enough outside Québec by Canadian politicians, intellectuals or the academic community. I am cautious with terminology here because just writing the expression "Québec secession" poses a problem — it conjures up an image of a single territory and a homogeneous people setting up a new state. The point of this essay is to demonstrate that it is not this simple.

How can it be presumed that there can be an accession to sovereign status for Québec without considering the pivotal matter of the status and rights of the aboriginal peoples in this scenario? What does it mean to "consider" the status and rights of aboriginal peoples in a secessionist scenario? It is not a perfunctory matter, or an administrative decision considering how best to transfer a head of jurisdiction (Indians and lands reserved for the Indians)[5] from the federal authority to a newly independent Québec state. It is more complex than this, in both a legal and political sense.[6] The political success of the secessionist movement will ultimately be judged on its democratic process, its

SOURCE: "Does the Road to Québec Sovereignty Run through Aboriginal Territory?" in Daniel Drache and Roberto Perin, eds., *Negotiating with a Sovereign Québec* (Toronto: James Lorimer & Company, 1992), pp. 93–106. Reprinted by permission of the publisher.

respect for fundamental human rights and, in the end, its political legitimacy in the eyes of the international community. I believe that the relations with aboriginal peoples could prove to be the key to assessing that legitimacy and could well influence the international recognition and acceptance of any new Québec state.

Who are the aboriginal peoples in Québec? Most people know something about the Crees in northern Québec because of their current opposition to the Great Whale hydro-electric project in the James Bay territory, or perhaps because of the *James Bay Northern Québec Agreement.*[7] However, it is not only the Crees whose homeland is captured in some sense by the provincial boundaries of Québec. There are also Inuit, Naskapi, Mikmaq, Maliseet, Mohawk, Montagnais, Abenaki, Algonquin, Atikawekw and Huron whose homelands are at least partially within the geographical boundaries of the Province of Québec. I say "partially" because, using the Mikmaq as a case in point, the Mikmaq of Gaspé comprise one of the seven districts of the Mikmaq nation, Mikmakik, which extends into Nova Scotia, New Brunswick, Newfoundland and Prince Edward Island. A District Chief from this region sits on the Mikmaq Grand Council, the traditional governing body of the Mikmaq people situated in Cape Breton, Nova Scotia. The administrative boundary of the province of Québec for Mikmaqs in the Gaspé is an arbitrary boundary unrelated to their identity, both territorially and spiritually.

To note this is nothing new for aboriginal peoples, given that all provincial boundaries are somewhat arbitrary from an aboriginal historical perspective. These provincial boundaries, internal to Canada, do not demarcate aboriginal homelands. Indeed, even certain international boundaries suffer likewise from a similar arbitrariness. I will use the Mohawks at Akwesasne as another case in point. Their community extends over two provincial boundaries (Ontario and Québec) and an international boundary with New York State. Their sense of division is compounded by the existence of three boundaries which in no way correspond to their own territorial, spiritual or political identity as Mohawks or members of the Iroquois Confederacy. What about "Québec secession" for these First Nations? While some aboriginal peoples in Québec do speak French, their cultural and linguistic identities are first and foremost shaped by their own First Nations culture, history and language.[8]

While the Province of Québec is undoubtedly no worse than any other province in terms of its history of a strained relationship with aboriginal peoples (although I would argue this is not an appropriate threshold for assessment), the recent confrontation with Mohawks at Oka in 1991 and the ongoing battle with the Crees over further hydroelectric development in the James Bay territory seem to have particularly embittered relationships between aboriginal peoples and the provincial government. Not surprisingly, when a future is laid out by the secessionists which envisages a fully sovereign state, claiming to exercise complete jurisdiction over peoples and resources within the current provincial boundaries, aboriginal peoples express concern. Given the recent political history of Québec, the impact of the change in political status of the province on aboriginal peoples' historic relationship with the Crown presents a chilling potential for a complete breakdown in the political relationship between aboriginal peoples and Québec.

Open discussion, dialogue and consideration of aboriginal peoples' status and rights need to begin immediately in Québec, but they also require an *informed basis*, founded on principles of equality of peoples, mutual respect and self-determination. There are basic human rights principles at issue in this debate and the legitimacy of the sovereignist movement may well stand or fall on how these principles are reconciled. The sovereignist movement cannot continue as a virtual steamroller ignoring or denying aboriginal peoples' status and rights and still hope to be successful. Thus far, the secessionists have not presented a framework for dialogue which embraces basic principles of respect for aboriginal peoples and their status and rights. Instead, aboriginal peoples have been offered vague assurances that they will be treated well by a new Québec state. When aboriginal peoples have articulated their concerns and set out some basic principles upon which to begin a dialogue with Québécois, they have been unjustifiably attacked and diminished. It seems that, on the part of the Québec sovereignists, there is no genuine commitment to understanding the aboriginal perspective on full sovereignty for Québec.

SELF-DETERMINATION: THE COMPETING CLAIMS

The explosive political atmosphere encircling the debate over full sovereignty and aboriginal peoples was revealed when the National Chief of the Assembly of First Nations, Ovide Mercredi, appeared in 1992 before the Québec National Assembly's Committee to Examine Matters Relating to the Accession of Québec to Sovereignty.[9] The National Chief, appearing with Chiefs and Elders from a number of the First Nations in Québec, told the Committee:

> There can be no legitimate secession by any people in Québec if the right to self-determination of First Nations is denied, suppressed or ignored in order to achieve independence. Our rights do not take a back seat to yours... Only through openness, of the mind and of the heart, can questions of such vital importance to your people and ours be reconciled. The alternative, which we do not favour, is confrontation...

The response to this, and other submissions, both by the Québec media and some members of the Committee, was one of outrage. It was as if the sovereignists were wilfully blinded to the principles articulated by aboriginal peoples in support of their rights. This is particularly frustrating given that, at many levels, the principles that aboriginal peoples advance for the basis of a political relationship with Canada or a sovereign Québec are not very different from Québec's position (self-determination, territory, identity). At least in some cases, I believe the aboriginal position could prove stronger legally and

politically. Since the Lesage era in the 1960s, French Canadians have argued that they want to be masters of their own house (*maîtres chez nous*). Aboriginal peoples have asserted an equally powerful concept — self-determination or self-government.

Sovereignists seem to see threats only when aboriginal peoples articulate their own perspectives. The worrisome point in this fury over the National Chief's appearance before the Committee on Sovereignty is that he is a committed moderate. There were no threats of violence, only pleas for dialogue and for measures to prevent a confrontation over the competing positions. As Chief Mercredi stated: "I, as National Chief, welcome constructive dialogue between First Nations and Quebecers on constitutional issues. We should build partnerships in support of our respective rights and not construct hierarchies of your rights over ours." Nevertheless, there seems to be a powerful drive towards castigating aboriginal peoples for advocating aboriginal and treaty rights. For example, the National Chief was chastised by Claude Masson of *La Presse* for speaking "exaggerated, insulting and outrageous words" and said that the aboriginal leadership "must behave like reasonable and responsible human beings and not like warriors or criminals with a right of life and death over everybody else."[10] This utter misrepresentation of the basic principles advanced by the National Chief, a leader who has worked hard to build alliances and open dialogue with Québec, demonstrates how wide the gulf is growing between sovereignists and aboriginal peoples. The era of disciplining aboriginal peoples for being different is over. Political support for the aspirations of Québécois will not be won in Canada or around the world with this type of denigration.

There has been an obvious strategic decision in the Québec independence movement to view aboriginal issues as business for a later date — after the accession to full sovereignty. The executive of the Parti Québécois has recently adopted a resolution to this effect. There seems to be little priority placed on dealing with aboriginal peoples' status and rights before accession.[11] In response to aboriginal suggestions that the situation is critical in Québec, there is a "why only pick on us" sentiment in the secessionist movement's response to aboriginal peoples, which is ill informed. Aboriginal peoples have been vigorously advancing their right to self-determination, territory and cultural rights at all levels in Canada and internationally. The *Delgamuukw* action in British Columbia is a case in point. This case, which is now before the British Columbia Court of Appeal, is an assertion of Gitksan and Wet'suewet'en political and territorial sovereignty against the federal and provincial Crown.

The movement for adequate recognition of aboriginal and treaty rights is not confined to Québec. With or without the prospect of Québec's secession, the rights will be advanced in that province, too. But in light of the sovereignist agenda, it is seen as critical here because the movement for full sovereignty calls into question aboriginal peoples' status and rights in a most immediate and far-reaching way—there will be a decision made about the future of all peoples in Québec, in a referendum to be held by October 26, 1992. Issues relating to that referendum—self-determination, territory and identity—are brought directly to the fore by the sovereignist agenda which, once engaged through Bill 150, is a veritable juggernaut. Aboriginal peoples cannot be expected to ignore what is coming at them full force.

Moreover, these issues deserve more than just passing consideration in the context of [a theoretical discussion] of negotiating with a sovereign Québec. From a human rights perspective, could there legitimately be a fully sovereign Québec without according equal consideration to the aspirations and choices of aboriginal peoples? To simply begin the discussion by sketching the contours of negotiations with a sovereign Québec may be putting the cart before the horse. For aboriginal peoples, Québécois, and Canadians there is a great deal at stake. Either one legitimizes *a priori* the reduction of First Nations peoples to the status of ethnic minorities with no right of self-determination, or one recognizes that there would be several other potential sovereign entities with which a Québec state would have to negotiate.

Negotiating with a sovereign Québec could only mean, for aboriginal peoples, a political relationship based on negotiating international treaties between emerging independent peoples. Existing treaties involving Canada, aboriginal peoples and Québec, such as the *James Bay Northern Québec Agreement*, would not have continuing validity, and Québec would not be able to claim the benefits of such treaties. If full sovereignty is declared by Québec, this would amount to a unilateral breach of that agreement. The *James Bay Northern Québec Agreement* was not only explicitly negotiated and ratified in a federal context, but also contained perpetual federal and provincial obligations that cannot be altered without the aboriginal parties' consent. A unilateral declaration of independence would be a clear breach of that agreement and Québec could not claim the benefits of the agreement while not respecting its negotiated terms.

Aboriginal peoples are not simply a head of jurisdiction, as seems to have been presumed by many Québécois and others outside the province. The first peoples in Canada are political entities—"peoples" in the international legal sense. This means that as peoples (with distinct languages, cultures, territories, populations and governments), aboriginal peoples have full rights of self-determination. For the purposes of discussions over sovereignty, aboriginal peoples must be seen to enjoy the status of peoples with a right to self-determination. This position is supported by both Canadian and international law. The International Bill of Rights (an instrument which I presume a fully sovereign Québec would want to respect in order to gain entry into the international community) recognizes the right of *all* peoples to self-determination. By this it is meant that peoples should freely determine their political status and that this should not be determined for them by a state, or an external actor.

Aboriginal peoples are independent political entities with distinct languages, cultures, histories, territories, spiritualities and governments. As such, they can choose or determine their future relationship with Canada or a sovereign Québec. This should not be determined for them by other peoples or governments. At present, the position of many sovereignists does not embrace self-determination for aboriginal peoples. It presumes that aboriginal peoples are not peoples or are too insignificant and dispersed to be independent political actors.[12] As academics and intellectuals, we should not promote recognition for a fully sovereign Québec if it means that aboriginal peoples' competing rights of self-determination will be compromised.

We need to recognize that when the political discourse shifts to Québec's secession, it moves from the familiar realm of federalist considerations of distinct society and the recognition and protection of distinct identities to the less certain context of political and territorial sovereignty. With this shift, there is a different grid structuring the debate, one with far broader implications. Once basic concepts of control over territory and peoples are put so squarely on the agenda by people in Québec, the struggles in which aboriginal peoples are engaged across Canada come sharply into focus. The basic presumption which operates in the minds of many sovereignists is that they either have, or will automatically acquire, sovereignty *over* aboriginal peoples in Québec. Flowing from this sovereignty, some Québécois believe that the French-Canadian majority in Québec can decide what it wants to do with aboriginal peoples. But what is the source of their sovereignty over aboriginal peoples and territories? Is it the right of the French-Canadian nation in Québec to self-determination?

It would seem clear that the French-Canadian people are faced with the competing rights to self-determination of aboriginal peoples. Moreover, the right to self-determination is not a right of the province of Québec.[13] In international law, provinces do not enjoy a right of self-determination; peoples do. Consequently, other peoples who may have competing claims, especially to territory, cannot be ignored. Sovereignists in Québec have, in effect, constructed their claim on the basis of the province of Québec as the entity which will exercise the right of self-determination. However, this would unjustly efface the competing and legitimate rights of aboriginal peoples.

As this short discussion illustrates, the competing self-determination claims by French Canadians and aboriginal peoples need to be carefully examined before we can deal with referenda or territory in an equitable and mutually respectful manner. Indeed, these three issues — self-determination, referendum and territorial claims — are critically interwoven in the current Canadian context. No single issue can stand alone without the others being considered. An independent Québec state would not meet with international recognition if aboriginal peoples were not treated as peoples, with full enjoyment of human rights, including the right of self-determination. Self-determination for aboriginal peoples may well require that they be involved as full, equal and independent participants in the decision about the accession of Québec to full sovereignty. I emphasize "independent" because aboriginal peoples must be dealt with as "peoples," not "minorities" subject to the political will of the province. As distinct political entities, aboriginal peoples must participate in that process through their leadership and not be presumed to be "represented" by members of the Québec National Assembly or the federal parliament.

The federal government also has obligations to recognize aboriginal peoples' right to self-determination. If there are to be negotiations with Québec on secession, then aboriginal peoples cannot be treated as a head of jurisdiction along with monetary issues or other items. Aboriginal peoples must each decide their relationship with a new Québec state. As United States President Woodrow Wilson stated in 1917, "...no right exists anywhere to hand peoples about from sovereignty to sovereignty as if they were property."[14] Aboriginal peoples cannot be handed from one sovereign (the federal Crown) to another (an independent Québec state) as if they were property. Yet this seems to be the presumption operating in Bill 150, the Allaire report and the Bélanger-Campeau commission report, where aboriginal peoples are viewed as minorities, authority over which can be simply transferred to a sovereign Québec.

The persistence of this mindset of viewing aboriginal peoples as minorities or of an inferior status to French or English newcomers goes to the very problem Hugh Brody identifies in the quotation set out at the beginning of this chapter: there is a narrowness of vision here which sees the arrival and spread of immigrants (whether they be French, English or otherwise) as the very purpose of history, including Canadian history. It is this vision which selects immigrant political objectives as superior to and more compelling than those of aboriginal peoples. Aboriginal perspectives and political aspirations are treated as secondary within the immigrant vision. Yet the immigrant vision has been vigorously challenged. Even some voices in Québec have challenged it, although they seem to fall on deaf ears. For example, Professor Daniel Turp (Université de Montréal), a leading sovereignist academic frequently cited by the Parti Québécois, acknowledged, when he appeared before the Committee on Accession, that "in my opinion [aboriginal peoples] constitute peoples who are self-identified as peoples ... this would confer on them a right to self-determination at the same level as Québec ... the same rules apply to aboriginal peoples as to Québécois." [15] This aspect of his opinion has been largely ignored by sovereignists who instead emphasise the right of the French in Québec to self-determination.

We know that the Canadian constitution is premised on a privileged reading of history, or the immigrant vision of (only) two founding nations, and that it has marginalized or excluded aboriginal visions. Aboriginal peoples, Québécois and other Canadians should strive to establish a more honourable and collaborative process. This entails fundamental changes to existing political processes and constitutional structures. Moreover, in the context of secession, it requires a full airing of opinions on aboriginal peoples' status and rights.

TERRITORY

In 1992, David Cliche, the Parti Québécois "native policy" adviser and a member of the executive of the Parti Québécois, argued that, upon secession, Québec will naturally take the territory within the current provincial boundaries. This position was endorsed by the leader of the Parti Québécois, Jacques Parizeau. What it ignores is that aboriginal peoples have no say in the matter. The decisions over the control of aboriginal territories should be made by aboriginal peoples, not Québec or the federal government. Cliche opposes this view and suggests that the sovereignists would offer the aboriginal people the best deal they could ever get. But this promise misses the point, because self-determination for aboriginal peoples is not about the prospects of a good deal some time in the future. It is about peoples deciding freely their political and territorial status now and not being forced into political arrangements without that independent collective decision.

The gulf in our respective understandings of the situation is a broad one. I believe that from an international legal perspective, and in terms of the political legitimacy of the sovereignist movement, only aboriginal peoples can decide their future status. This cannot be usurped by the sovereignists, just as French Canadians want to decide their future without this being unilaterally usurped by the federal government.

Much of the sovereignist argument on territorial claims has rested on a doctrine of international law called *uti possidetis juris*, which is offered to support the claim that they will enter independence with the territory they had before. In this case, the secessionists say the territory they had before is Québec within the current provincial boundaries. They sometimes call this the principle of "territorial integrity." This doctrine is said to displace the ordinary principle of occupation as a basis for territorial sovereignty. The international law on whether *uti possidetis* is compelling is dubious at best, with the leading scholars in the field wondering whether the doctrine is even a norm of international law. [16] Even the International Court of Justice has cautioned that this doctrine is problematic, as it conflicts with a significant principle in international law — self-determination. [17] The sovereignist claim to take the territory within the current provincial boundaries is weak, internationally, especially given that much land in the province is subject to aboriginal claims which have yet to be resolved, and which are tied in to aboriginal self-determination. The secessionists will have to present other arguments that can satisfy international legal standards if they hope to be recognized as a legitimate state with the existing provincial boundaries as their territorial base.

Control over aboriginal peoples' territories has been essential for the prosperity of Québec. This certainly was the experience following the boundary extensions of 1898 and 1912. It is clear that the secessionist position is rooted in a realization that these territories are of continued significance. Issues of control over territory are fundamental to the secessionists because mass development projects like James Bay II (Great Whale) are part of their economic plan. Aboriginal peoples have legitimate concerns about the territorial consequences of full sovereignty. Would this mean that a new Québec state can unilaterally make development decisions? James Bay may be but a glimpse of what aboriginal peoples could face with Québec secession and full claims to jurisdiction over their territories. It has been an enormous struggle, albeit increasingly successful, for the Crees to gain support for their opposition to further James Bay hydro-electric development. As Grand Chief Coon-Come reflects:

> Bourassa's dream [of hydro-electric development] has become our nightmare. It has contaminated our fish with mercury. It has destroyed the spawning grounds. It has destroyed the nesting grounds of the waterfowl. It has displaced and dislocated our people and broken the fabric of our society. And we have decided, knowing the behaviour of the animals, that we will not be like the fox who, when he sees danger, crawls back to his hole. We have come out to stop the destruction of our land.[18]

In this quotation notice that the Grand Chief says "our" when he refers to the land and to the fish. This contradicts the view of the government of Québec (excerpted at the outset of this chapter) that the land and resources of the province are a gift

of nature to the people of Québec, in which regard they are more favoured than others.

The territorial claims of the secessionists to the current provincial boundaries are legally and politically insecure. The territory was not given to Québécois as a gift of nature. It was a gift of the federal government in 1898 and 1912—a gift made without the consent of the owners, aboriginal peoples. French Canadians will have to support their territorial claim to the lands within the existing provincial boundaries with something other than erroneous theories about gifts of nature or *uti possidetis*.[19] No one can presume these are theirs to take when the original occupants of the land, aboriginal peoples, assert their rights. Voting in a referendum in support of this position is not enough either, legally or politically.

REFERENDUM: THE WHO/WHOM

In 1902, Lenin posited the critical question in politics as "who/whom": who rules whom, who decides for whom? Bill 150 provides for a referendum sometime between October 12 and 26, 1992. The who/whom question is pivotal. Bill 150 states that if the results of the referendum are in favour of secession, they will "constitute a proposal" that Québec acquire the status of a sovereign state one year to the day from the holding of the referendum. What question will be put to voters, who will vote, and the weighing of the results are all unclear at this point. For aboriginal peoples in Québec, the ambiguity of the referendum is threatening because if a vote is registered in favour of sovereignty, it could legitimize the appropriation of aboriginal territories and the assumption of authority over them. They would be the "whom" ruled by the "who" in a simple majority referendum.

Is a simple 50-plus-1 majority enough in these circumstances? If it was, this could mean that aboriginal peoples' self-determination rights would be overridden, as aboriginal peoples may simply be outvoted by larger populations in non-aboriginal regions of Québec. This kind of a referendum could not be held up internationally as supporting accession to sovereignty because of its implications for aboriginal peoples. Referendums are numbers games and aboriginal peoples would be set up for exclusion unless double majorities or separate referendums are employed. Aboriginal peoples will have to insist on double majorities, or independent (traditional) means for expressing their views on accession to full sovereignty. They cannot be lumped into a general referendum if the result is to be accepted for any purposes as a legitimate mandate for statehood.

While concerns about the status and rights of aboriginal peoples are grave, it is nevertheless important to stress that this is a great opportunity for the sovereignists to lead the way on self-determination. There is a natural alliance which could be struck between aboriginal peoples and the secessionists whereby aboriginal self-determination could be respected as a priority. This requires an immediate dialogue with aboriginal peoples within a framework of respect for the equally compelling right of aboriginal peoples to self-determination. This dialogue cannot be informed by the "trust us, we'll give you a good deal later" attitude which seems so popular among sovereignists.

Such an alliance would be a historic event and could lead to interesting and innovative political arrangements with Canada and a new Québec state. However, the basic principles for such an alliance, such as aboriginal self-determination, must be discussed and openly embraced by the sovereignist movement. This requires a reconsideration of elements of its vision of a new Québec state. Particularly, the territorial integrity position would have to be revised to embrace at least the principle of shared and co-managed resources. Currently, there is no indication that this is happening and the responsibility is really on the sovereignist side to demonstrate a willingness to respect the right of aboriginal self-determination.

As the title of this essay would suggest, the road to full sovereignty for Québec runs through aboriginal territory. There is no detour, no other path. There is only one road, and it must be a course of justice and respect for aboriginal peoples. The secessionists will be well advised to look carefully at the map of this road now that they have chosen the path of statehood. Should Québécois fail to deal with aboriginal self-determination, their movement stands to lose a great deal of legitimacy and support both in Canada and the international community.

NOTES

1. H. Brody, *Maps and Dreams* (Vancouver: Douglas and McIntyre, 1988), p. xiii.
2. Government of Québec, *Quebec-Canada: A New Deal* (Éditeur Officiel, 1979), p. 89. This is the official Parti Québécois publication circulated prior to the referendum on sovereignty-association in 1980.
3. Although my preferred expression is *First Nations*, I use the phrase *aboriginal peoples* throughout this paper because I want it to be clear that I am referring to both the First Nations (sometimes called "Indians") and Inuit.
4. Here I am particularly mindful of the comments of the members of the Committee on the Accession of Québec to Full Sovereignty, established pursuant to Bill 150 (An Act Respecting the Process for Determining the Political and Constitutional Future of Québec).
5. Now section 91(24) of the Constitution Act, 1867.
6. Of course, law and politics are hardly distinct. Some of the detail of the legal argument, at least on the issue of territory, can be found in Kent McNeil, "Aboriginal Nations and Québec's Boundaries: Canada Couldn't Give What It Didn't Have," in [*Negotiating with a Sovereign Québec*, edited by Daniel Drache and Roberto Perin (Toronto: James Lorimer & Company, 1992)]. For a detailed and superb legal analysis of aboriginal peoples' concerns *vis-à-vis* full sovereignty for Québec, see Grand Council of the Crees of Québec, *Status and Rights of the James Bay Crees in the Context of Quebec's Secession from Canada*, Submission to the United Nations Commission on Human Rights, 48th Session, February 21, 1992.
7. This is a land claim agreement or modern treaty entered into in 1975 by Cree, Inuit and the federal and provincial governments.
8. As Zebeedee Nungak, spokesperson for the Inuit Tapirisat of Canada and the Inuit in northern

Québec, rather graphically illustrated at the federally sponsored constitutional constituency assembly, "Identity, Values and Rights," he identifies as an Inuk first, a Canadian second, and a Québécois third. (February 7, 1992, Royal York Hotel, Toronto.) I say "graphically" because he held up a map of Québec which divided the province into the north and south, arguing that (to paraphrase) "the distinct society of the south cannot override the distinct society of the north."

9. The National Chief of the Assembly of First Nations, Ovide Mercredi, appeared on February 11, 1992. A copy of his text is on file with the author.

10. From the translation, reprinted in *The Globe and Mail,* February 18, 1992, p. 19.

11. The sovereignists often refer to a March 20, 1985, National Assembly resolution as a starting point for engaging with aboriginal peoples on issues relating to full sovereignty. However, it is important to note that this resolution was unilaterally imposed on the First Nations in Québec. As a unilaterally imposed document, it is not a basis for a relationship which respects self-determination for aboriginal peoples.

The Crees suggest, in their brief to the United Nations, that "it is unacceptable for the National Assembly or government of Quebec to unilaterally impose policies on First Nations. The contents of an acceptable Resolution were in the process of being negotiated. Also, a prior commitment had been expressly made by the Premier of Quebec that he would not table any resolution on this matter in the National Assembly without aboriginal consent." Submission of the Grand Council of the Crees of Québec, p. 166.

12. The secessionist position has been articulated in detail by Professor J. Brossard in his text, *L'accession* *à la souveraineté et le cas du Québec* (Montréal: Les Presses de l'Université de Montréal, 1977). This text has been referred to by the Committee on the Accession of Québec to Sovereignty as an accurate statement of the rights of French Canadians to self-determination.

13. Brossard acknowledges that the basis of the claim to accession is the rights of French Canadians to self-determination. He goes further to suggest that in theory it is only the French-Canadian nation that could participate in the decision on full sovereignty, thus excluding the anglophones. *L'accession à la souveraineté,* pp. 183–85. He admits that politically such an alternative is impracticable.

14. This is quoted in the Submission of the Grand Council of the Crees of Québec to the United Nations Commission on Human Rights.

15. He appeared before the Committee on Accession on October 9, 1991.

16. See, for example, I. Brownlie, *Principles of International Law,* 4th ed. (Oxford: Clarendon Press, 1989), p. 135.

17. *Frontier Dispute (Burkina Faso/Mali),* 80 I.L.R. 440 at 554 (separate opinion of Judge Luchaire).

18. Quoted in H. Thurston, "Power in a Land of Remembrance," *Audubon* 52 (Nov.–Dec. 1991): 58–9.

19. As the National Chief of the Assembly of First Nations stated in his presentation to the Committee on Accession, "The Quebec government's proposed principle concerning the territorial integrity of Quebec is an affront to First Nations. It is obvious that territorial integrity serves to consolidate your legal position to the extreme prejudice of the First Nations."

Canada's Constitution and the Struggle to Govern

CLOSE-UP: URGENT CONSTITUTION MAKING

In the second half of this century Canadians have often felt pressured and rushed into their constitutional agreements. Although supported by some in Quebec, a formula put forward in 1964 to patriate and amend the Canadian Constitution (the Fulton-Favreau formula) was generally bitterly opposed and ultimately vetoed. Pressure mounted in all parts of the country to contain the Quiet Revolution of the 1960s in Quebec by initiating the complex process of achieving constitutional harmony, wherein Quebeckers could feel at home in Canada. By the late 1960s, Pierre Trudeau's accession to power had set the stage for confrontation with Quebec. In October 1970 the kidnapping of James Cross, a British trade commissioner, and the murder of Pierre Laporte, a Quebec provincial Cabinet minister, spread fears of insurrection.

Feeling that something had to be done to appease radical forces in Quebec, Canadian leaders embarked on what would prove to be a long and often tortuous path of constitutional discussion and debate that culminated in the failed Meech Lake and Charlottetown accords, in 1990 and 1992, respectively. Both agreements drew criticism that we were moving too quickly on fundamental constitutional questions and rushing into a very complex social contract. Deadlines had become the driving force for initiating, negotiating, and implementing constitutional change in Canada.

But this situation is not new in Canadian history. Debate about the motives and constraints of the Fathers of Confederation permeated the 1860s, and provided grist for the mill of future historians and political scientists. Contrary to popular belief, the Constitution Act of 1867 was not the result of calm and rational deliberation, nor were its provisions grounded in a vision that embraced the complexities of an emerging multinational federal nation-state. Notwithstanding the intelligent quality of the Confederation Debates, the conditions under which the Fathers of Confederation worked were pressing.

By 1865, most of Canada's economic, social, and political elites were convinced that unless some display of unity was made, the country would be in great danger of being absorbed by the United States. Indeed, the threat of annexation, felt especially in the West, gave the idea of confederation a substantial boost. The American Civil War had just ended, raising the fear that the victorious northern states, with a million idle soldiers, might now decide to attack the colonies in Canada to gain control over all of North America. Some Americans spoke openly of conquering British territory in retaliation for Britain's support of the South during the Civil War. And the British government pushed Canadians to form a strong federation, to pay for Canada's defence and to avoid the possible breakdown of stable government in the old Province of Canada.

John A. Macdonald, quick to capitalize on the apparent need to rush forward, went to London to seek help for Canada's defence, armed with a document that proposed to unite the colonies in a confederation. Macdonald came home not with a promise of military aid against the Americans, but with London's assurance that it would pressure the Maritime colonies into supporting Canadian Confederation. Many in the Maritimes were seeking their own union; now Britain would encourage union on a larger scale, eventually to spread from the Atlantic to the Pacific.

In 1866, the Fenian Brotherhood, a 150 000-strong secret society of Irish Americans dedicated to fomenting rebellion against British rule in Ireland, decided to "bust Confederation" in Canada by means of armed border attacks. "And we'll go and capture Canada, for we've nothing else to do" was their marching song. They sang it as they crossed the Niagara River to occupy Fort Erie, Ontario, and at Pigeon Hill, Quebec. Nothing, as it turned out, would do more to hasten the process of writing a constitution for Canada.

The Fenian raids convinced New Brunswick and Nova Scotia, alarmed by threats against Campobello Island in New Brunswick, that Confederation, undertaken immediately, was necessary to their survival. Thus, the final impetus to write a constitution sprang not from patriotism but from fear, frustration, and a sense of urgency. In view of the threatening possibilities of the time, John A. Macdonald believed that Canada's Constitution should be drawn up as quickly as possible, laying down only the minimum conditions for union. The Constitution, he argued, "should be a mere skeleton and framework that would not bind us down."

Macdonald took a firm plan to Lord Carnarvon, Britain's colonial secretary, who, on February 19, 1867, as a member of the House of Lords, hastily moved the second reading of the British North America bill. Just a week later the bill passed the House of Lords, and within a month it had passed the Commons. A new country, comprising four provinces, was born.

From 1867 until 1982, the Canadian Constitution was amended and expanded from time to time at Westminster, as an ordinary piece of legislation. Amendments were often the result of hastily arranged federal–provincial agreements on this side of the Atlantic.

Efforts to **patriate** the Constitution intensified after 1967, Canada's centennial year, during a decade of profound political changes in both Quebec and English-speaking Canada, particularly the western provinces. The momentum for constitutional rectitude came from pressures to make concessions to Quebec.

The first series of major federal–provincial constitutional conferences, known as the Victoria Round, took place between 1968 and 1971. Subsequent rounds were held between 1977 and 1979 (following the election of the *indépendantiste* Parti Québécois government in Quebec) and between 1980 and 1982 (following the 1980 Quebec **referendum** on sovereignty-association). The result, with Quebec's declining abstention, was the Constitution Act, 1982, a patriated constitution with an amending formula and an appended Charter of Rights and Freedoms.

Quebec's absence from the constitutional agreement has remained an open wound in the national body. It resulted in the Meech Lake, or "Quebec," Round of federal–provincial talks, from 1986 to 1990. In 1990, the Meech Lake Constitutional Accord died a resounding death. Meech Lake was never formally put to the test of national public opinion. Had it been so tested, the political discontents of western Canada would have come to light, reflecting another threat to national unity in this country. Two years later, the Charlottetown Accord produced a new proposal for national unity that was crafted by Ottawa, the provinces, and aboriginal leaders. It too ended in failure, leading to the election of another Parti Québécois government in 1994 and yet another Quebec referendum on separation, in 1995, with the promise of more to come, until a Yes victory was secured.

Although constitutional considerations were not supposed to be revisited until 1997, they surfaced again with some urgency as the 1995 Quebec referendum campaign drew to a close with the Yes forces appearing to have gained majority support. At the last moment, Prime Minister Jean Chrétien promised changes to accommodate Quebec, even if it meant re-opening constitutional negotiations. After the referendum, the federal government hastily decided to give constitutional vetoes to Quebec (and the other provinces) as a way of recognizing Quebec's distinct society. But the **veto** law has no real constitutional status, because Ottawa cannot unilaterally amend the amending formula. Nevertheless, the fear of Canada's unravelling had once again pushed the panic button on constitutional change.

INTRODUCTION: WHAT SHOULD A CONSTITUTION BE?

Ideally, a constitution should be accepted by the vast majority of people in a country. It should take on the aura of a secular bible, venerated more than it is criticized, amended less often than particular interest groups might want it to be, and universally regarded as the first law of the land. People should embrace it, consult it for guidance, cite it for support, and respectfully debate the meaning of its provisions. Many Canadians would say that their Constitution does not yet fit the ideal. Eugene Forsey presents the nuts and bolts of Canada's Constitution in his excellent booklet *How Canadians Govern Themselves*, excerpted here in Chapter 6.

Since Confederation, Canadians have struggled to perfect their first constitutional documents. Their pride in their Constitution has occasionally bordered on chauvinism. At the Charlottetown Conference of 1864, the attorney general of New Brunswick advocated union with Canada because its "constitution will keep constantly expanding with the needs of the people." In contrast to some of our contemporary political leaders, he bragged about the "superiority" of the Canadian Constitution over that of the "States of America," where change "seems always to require a bloody revolution."

Although Canada's Constitution has been responsive enough to survive through a century of rapid and often radical change, is it adequate to the task of ensuring the country's survival into the next century? Can a constitution lacking a universally accepted set of amending formulas, written by a small circle of men in a bygone era, continue to serve a technologically advanced, multicultural society?

Constitutional change, or **amendment**, must ultimately address questions of Quebec's place in Canada, the jurisdiction of aboriginal governments, the equality of interprovincial relationships in

English-speaking Canada, and the socio-political entities recognized and empowered by the Charter of Rights and Freedoms.

In the aftermath of the failed Meech Lake and Charlottetown accords, the only way to retain Canada's constitutional viability among all parties concerned may be to recognize the distinct status of Quebec and of the aboriginal peoples.

DIFFERENT WAYS OF SEEING OUR CONSTITUTION

It is an understatement to say that Canadians see the Constitution through a range of very different lenses. Will our Constitution demonstrate its adaptive virtues by granting Quebec the powers it needs to remain part of Canada's federation and by enabling aboriginal peoples to operate their own governing institutions over sovereign territory, while allowing the rest of the country the powers needed to retain a strong government? Distinct societies are here to stay in Canada. Can we design a constitution that includes all of these influences?

The next round of constitutional debates will be difficult, as Peter Russell points out in "The End of Mega Constitutional Politics in Canada?" (Chapter 9). The inclusion and reconciliation of a nationalist, sovereignist society among equal provinces may still be at the heart of the problem. The challenge will be to avoid the hypocrisy of recognizing Quebec as the sociological "nation" that it is, while stripping the concept of any real meaning in order not to offend Canadians elsewhere.

The latter approach will satisfy no one, certainly not Quebec, whose nationalists now consider the concept of distinct society passé. As Charles Taylor explains in "The Constitutional Problem" (Chapter 8), French nationalists feel their nationality is fragile and continually under siege by the assimilating pressure of the dominant English language in North

America. A majority of Quebeckers still appear to be looking for ways to stay in Canada, but they agree to do so only with the assurance of an arrangement conducive to their survival as a people.

Canadians, especially French Canadians outside Quebec, need something very different. Their sense of Canadian nationality is also fragile, particularly in view of the fact that NAFTA has effectively erased the economic border with the United States. NAFTA has unleashed powerful American influences on Canada's economy and on Canadian society in general. English-speaking Canadians do not have the clearly differentiated identity that a distinct language and culture gives Quebec within Canada, and so have always relied on a strong and active federal government to protect Canadian culture.

In contrast to Quebeckers and aboriginals, who relate to Canada through the groups that form their peoples, English-speaking Canadians usually identify with the country as a whole, albeit often from the perspective of their own province. Yet, rather than wanting to increase regional powers, most want a central government with adequate powers to maintain a sense of national unity and common citizenship.

But while Canadians manifest considerable agreement on the general principles of democracy that they adopted with Confederation, consensus is far from complete. Canadians seek a constitutional framework that will reflect and protect their differences rather than their similarities, and they differ substantially on the nature of that framework.

RECONCILING OUR DIVERGENT INTERESTS

The situation is complicated by continuing First Nations territorial demands and demands for greater sovereignty over governing jurisdictions within Canada. Although some aboriginal peoples do not have discrete land bases, more than 600 Indian bands do. When Nunavut takes on its new status by the end of the century, the Inuit will comprise the majority of residents in the territory and will have quasi-provincial status. Other land-claims

settlements (such as those of the Métis) will give varying degrees of jurisdictional powers over defined territories occupied by aboriginal peoples. Such settlements will create complex political and governmental borders.

In Quebec, for example, the Cree's claims to a defined territory will alter both provincial and federal **jurisdictions**. Citizens of sovereign aboriginal communities can simultaneously be members of Canadian society, sharing the responsibilities of government with provinces and the federal government, while enjoying their inalienable rights to self-determination. But jurisdictional complexities will also emerge in large Canadian urban centres with aboriginal populations; although they make no claims on land, these groups will also want to govern their own affairs in areas such as justice and education.

Canadians are heading for a triple-tiered constitutional federalism, in which different governing jurisdictions will have to co-exist and interact authoritatively and efficiently. Furthermore, even within the confines of a reconstituted Canadian federalism, Quebec will enjoy enhanced **international recognition**. France and other nation-states within the francophone international community have already initiated and reciprocated bilateral and multilateral arrangements with Quebec. The extent to which they would be prepared to aid an independent Quebec remains to be seen.

Another aspect of constitutional change has been evident in the development of a Canadian Charter of Rights and Freedoms. Stimulated by the culture of concern for human rights that took root in the post–World War II era and that was symbolized by the 1948 United Nations Universal Declaration of Human Rights, Canada moved slowly but deliberately toward a declaration of rights for all its inhabitants. Our first legislated Bill of Rights came into existence under John Diefenbaker; **entrenchment** of the Charter of Rights and Freedoms took place in 1982. In Chapter 7, Michael Mandel discusses some important aspects of the postwar movement by the judiciary in Canada to establish an explicit Bill of Rights. Both the Bill of Rights and the

Charter profoundly changed the relationship of all Canadian residents to the constitutional order. The Bill of Rights encountered provincial opposition, a weakness compounded by the inclusion in the Charter of a **notwithstanding clause** and the fact that the Bill was not an entrenched constitutional document. And despite opposition from eight provinces, the Charter received widespread popular support from various **grass-roots** groups, including women's organizations, ethnic groups, the disabled, and many other constituencies across the country.

To sum up, when the next constitutional package is put forward, its quality can be assessed by how well it balances the distinctive political culture of each province, aboriginal third-order governments, and conceptions of who we are, what rights we enjoy, and how we treat one another in the country we call Canada.

THINKING IT OVER

1. Based on what you read in the four articles in this section, do you think a constitution drafted in the 1860s can serve the governing needs of a political system in the 1990s? Taking into account the new amendment formulas in Canada's Constitution, would you describe it as a flexible or an inflexible document? Will our Constitution be able to adapt to changing times?
2. One common misconception of our Constitution is that it provides a blueprint for the workings of Canadian government. Would we be better served by our Constitution if we amended it to reflect the written and unwritten aspects of parliamentary government? How do you think Eugene Forsey (Chapter 6) would answer this question?
3. Investigate why a Bill of Rights was not included in the Constitution Act, 1867. Then, based on Michael Mandel's article (Chapter 7), explain why one was added in 1960. Is the Canadian Bill of Rights still operative today? Is it constitutional?
4. What does Charles Taylor (Chapter 8) mean by "the constitutional problem"? How does the problem as outlined by Taylor relate to our current federal system? Can we fix our constitutional problem by fixing federalism?
5. Why is Peter Russell (Chapter 9) so cynical about the possibility of negotiating a new constitutional framework for Canada? What would it take for all Canadians to agree on a constitution? Can a national consensus ever be reached? Without constitutional recognition of Quebec as a sovereign entity within Canada's federal system, will Canadians continue to experience constitutional crises?
6. Canadians are changing the ways in which they have traditionally governed themselves at all levels. Will they be able to continue to restructure and renew the basic organization of government (state forms) without eventually having to amend the Constitution?

GLOSSARY

amendment A change made to a constitution, a proposed bill, an act, a resolution, an administrative order, or some other written document.

entrenchment The inclusion of an item in a constitution so that change to that item requires formal constitutional amendment.

grass-roots A term used to describe organizations of ordinary people who react to and participate in the political system. The grass roots comprise the people whose support is critical to the success of political parties, interest groups, and governments.

international recognition An official act or combination of acts, such as the exchange of ambassadors, the signing of treaties, the conduct of trade, or meetings of heads of state or government leaders, whereby a government or state is accepted as a legitimate member of the international community.

judicial activism The philosophy that judicial decisions should affect the direction of public policy and even provoke social change.

judicial review The power of a court, in the course of adjudication and litigation, to declare certain laws and actions of government to be unconstitutional.

jurisdiction The right or prerogative of a state or government to act with authority, within certain boundaries of control, over people, property, subjects, and situations within a defined political or geographical area.

notwithstanding clause Section 33 of the Constitution Act, 1982, allows Parliament or provincial legislatures to pass legislation notwithstanding certain provisions in the Charter.

patriate To "bring home" a government, a constitution, or decision-making powers, under the direct control of a given country or region. With the patriation of the Canadian Constitution, full governing authority and responsibility was transferred from the British government to Canada.

referendum An electoral process in which a legislative, political, or constitutional question is referred to an electorate for acceptance or rejection.

unconstitutional That which is declared to be not in accord with the accepted meaning, words, principles, practices, and provisions of a constitution.

veto The power to reject legislation or a constitutional initiative or provision.

xenophobia A fear or hatred of foreigners.

ADDITIONAL READINGS

Beatty, David. 1995. *Constitutional Law in Theory and Practice.* Toronto: University of Toronto Press.

Cairns, Alan. 1992. *Charter versus Federalism: The Dilemmas of Constitutional Reform.* Montreal: McGill-Queen's University Press.

———. 1995. *Reconfigurations: Canadian Citizenship and Constitutional Change.* Toronto: McClelland & Stewart.

Conklin, William. 1993. *Images of a Constitution.* Toronto: University of Toronto Press.

Conway, John. 1992. *Debts to Pay: English Canada and Quebec from the Conquest to the Referendum.* Toronto: James Lorimer & Company.

Gagnon, Alain. 1993. *Quebec: State and Society.* 2nd ed. Scarborough, Ont.: Nelson Canada.

Heard, Andrew. 1991. *Canadian Constitutional Conventions.* Don Mills, Ont.: Oxford University Press.

Hutchinson, Allan. 1995 *Waiting for CORAF: A Critique of Law and Rights.* Toronto: University of Toronto Press.

Knopff, Rainer, and F.L. Morton. 1992. *Charter Politics.* Scarborough, Ont.: Nelson Canada.

Leacock, Stephen. 1995. *Social Criticism: The Unresolved Riddle of Social Justice and Other Essays.* Toronto: University of Toronto Press.

Milne, David. 1991. *The Canadian Constitution.* Toronto: James Lorimer & Company.

Reesor, Bayard. 1991. *The Canadian Constitution in Historical Perspective.* Scarborough, Ont.: Prentice-Hall Canada.

Russell, Peter. 1993. *Constitutional Odyssey: Can Canadians Become a Sovereign People?* Toronto: University of Toronto Press.

Webber, Jeremy. 1994. *Reimagining Canada: Language, Culture, Community, and the Canadian Constitution.* Montreal: McGill-Queen's University Press.

Yates, Richard, and Ruth Yates. 1993. *Canada's Legal Environment.* Scarborough, Ont.: Prentice-Hall Canada.

Our Constitution

EUGENE A. FORSEY

The *British North America (BNA) Act* was the instrument that brought the federation, the new nation, into existence. It was an act of the British Parliament. But, except for two small points, it is simply the statutory form of resolutions drawn up by delegates from what is now Canada. Not a single representative of the British government was present at the conferences that drew up those resolutions, or took the remotest part in them.

The two small points on which our Constitution is not entirely homemade are, first, the legal title of our country, "Dominion," and, second, the provisions for breaking a deadlock between the Senate and the House of Commons.

The Fathers of Confederation wanted to call the country "the Kingdom of Canada." The British government was afraid of offending the Americans so it insisted on the Fathers finding another title. They did, from Psalm 72: "He shall have dominion also from sea to sea, and from the river unto the ends of the earth." It seemed to fit the new nation like the paper on the wall. They explained to Queen Victoria that it was "intended to give dignity" to the Union, and "as a tribute to the monarchical principle, which they earnestly desire to uphold."

To meet a deadlock between the Senate and the House of Commons, the Fathers had made no provision. The British government insisted that they produce something. So they did: sections 26 to 28 of the Act, which have been used only once, in 1990.

That the federation resolutions were brought into effect by an act of the British Parliament was the Fathers' deliberate choice. They could have chosen to follow the American example, and done so without violent revolution.

Sir John A. Macdonald, in the Confederation debates, made that perfectly clear. He said: "If the people of British North America after full deliberation had stated that it was for their interest, for the advantage of British North America to sever the tie (with Britain) I am sure that Her Majesty and the Imperial Parliament would have sanctioned that severance." But: "Not a single suggestion was made, that it could . . . be for the interest of the colonies . . . that there should be a severance of our connection . . . There was a unanimous feeling of willingness to run all the hazards of war (with the United States) rather than lose the connection."

Hence, the only way to bring the federation into being was through a British act.

That act, the *British North America Act, 1867* (now renamed the *Constitution Act, 1867*) contained no provisions for its own amendment, except a limited power for the provinces to amend their own constitutions. All other amendments had to be made by a fresh act of the British Parliament.

At the end of the First World War, Canada signed the peace treaties as a distinct power, and became a founding member of the League of Nations and the International Labour Organization. In 1926, the

SOURCE: Excerpted from *How Canadians Govern Themselves*, 3rd ed. (Ottawa: Minister of Supply and Services Canada, 1991), pp. 8–18. Reproduced with permission of the Minister of Supply and Services Canada, 1996.

Imperial Conference recognized Canada, Australia, New Zealand, South Africa, the Irish Free State and Newfoundland as "autonomous communities, in no way subordinate to the United Kingdom in any aspect of their domestic or external affairs." Canada had come of age.

This gave rise to a feeling that we should be able to amend our Constitution ourselves, without even the most formal intervention by the British Parliament. True, that Parliament usually passed any amendment we asked for. But more and more Canadians felt this was not good enough. The whole process should take place here. The Constitution should be "patriated," brought home.

Attempts to bring this about began in 1927. Until 1981, they failed, not because of any British reluctance to make the change, but because the federal and provincial governments could not agree on a generally acceptable method of amendment. Finally, after more than half a century of federal-provincial conferences and negotiations, the Senate and the House of Commons, with the approval of nine provincial governments, passed the necessary joint address asking for the final British act. This placed the whole process of amendment in Canada, and removed the last vestige of the British Parliament's power over our country.

The *Constitution Act, 1867*, remains the basic element of our written Constitution. But the written Constitution, the strict law of the Constitution, even with the latest addition, the *Constitution Act, 1982*, is only part of our whole working Constitution, the set of arrangements by which we govern ourselves. It is the skeleton; it is not the whole body.

Responsible government, the national Cabinet, the Prime Minister, the bureaucracy, political parties, federal-provincial conferences: all these are basic features of our system of government. But the written Constitution does not contain one word about any of them (except for that phrase in the preamble to the Act of 1867 about "a Constitution similar in principle to that of the United Kingdom"). The flesh, the muscles, the sinews, and the nerves of our Constitution have been added by legislation (for example, federal and provincial

elections acts, the *Parliament of Canada Act*, the legislative assembly acts, the public services acts), by custom (the Prime Minister, the Cabinet, responsible government, political parties, federal-provincial conferences), by judgements of the courts (interpreting what the Act of 1867 and its amendments mean), by agreements between the national and provincial governments.

If the written Constitution is silent on all these things, which are the living reality of our Constitution, what does it say? If it leaves out so much, what does it put in?

Before we answer that question, we must understand that our written Constitution, unlike the American, is not a single document. In addition to other documents, it includes 25 primary documents outlined in the *Constitution Act, 1982*: 14 acts of the British Parliament, seven of the Canadian, and four British orders-in-council.

The core of the collection is still the Act of 1867. This, with the amendments added to it down to the end of 1981, did 12 things.

- First, it created the federation, the provinces, the territories, the national Parliament, the provincial legislatures and some provincial cabinets.
- Second, it gave the national Parliament power to create new provinces out of the territories, and also the power to change provincial boundaries with the consent of the provinces concerned.
- Third, it set out the power of Parliament and of the provincial legislatures.
- Fourth, it vested the formal executive power in the Queen, and created the Queen's Privy Council for Canada (the legal basis for the federal Cabinet).
- Fifth, it gave Parliament power to set up a Supreme Court of Canada (which it did, in 1875).
- Sixth, it guaranteed certain limited rights equally to the English and French languages in the federal Parliament and courts and in the legislatures and courts of Quebec and Manitoba.
- Seventh, it guaranteed separate schools for the Protestant and Roman Catholic minorities in

Quebec and Ontario. It also guaranteed separate schools in any other province where they existed by law in 1867, or were set up by any provincial law after 1867. There were special provisions for Manitoba (created in 1870), which proved ineffective; more limited guarantees for Alberta and Saskatchewan (created in 1905); and for Newfoundland (which came into Confederation in 1949), a guarantee of separate schools for a variety of Christian denominations.

- Eight, it guaranteed Quebec's distinctive civil law.
- Ninth, it gave Parliament power to assume the jurisdiction over property and civil rights, or any part of such jurisdiction, in other provinces, provided the provincial legislatures consented. This power has never been used.
- Tenth, it prohibited provincial tariffs.
- Eleventh, it gave the provincial legislatures the power to amend the provincial constitutions, except as regards the office of Lieutenant-Governor.
- Twelfth, it gave the national government (the Governor General-in-Council, that is, the federal Cabinet) certain controls over the provinces: appointment, instruction and dismissal of lieutenant-governors (two have been dismissed); disallowance of provincial acts within one year after their passing (112 have been disallowed — the last in 1943 — from every province except Prince Edward Island and Newfoundland); power of lieutenant-governors to send provincial bills to Ottawa, unassented to (in which case they do not go into effect unless the central executive assents within one year; of 70 such bills, the last in 1961, from every province but Newfoundland, only 14 have gone into effect).

These are the main things the written Constitution did as it stood at the end of 1981. They provided the legal framework within which we could, and did, adapt, adjust, manoeuvre, innovate, compromise, arrange, by what Prime Minister Sir Robert Borden called "the exercise of the commonplace quality of common sense."

The final British act of 1982, the *Canada Act*, as we have seen, provided for the termination of the British Parliament's power over Canada and for the "patriation" of our Constitution. Under the terms of the *Canada Act*, the *Constitution Act, 1982*, was proclaimed in Canada and "patriation" was achieved.

Under the *Constitution Act, 1982*, the *British North America Act* and its various amendments (1871, 1886, 1907, 1915, 1930, 1940, 1960, 1964, 1965, 1974, 1975) became the *Constitution Acts, 1867 to 1975*.

There is a widespread impression that the *Constitution Act, 1982*, gave us a "new Constitution." It did not. In fact, that Act itself says that "the Constitution of Canada includes" 14 acts of the Parliament of the United Kingdom, seven acts of the Parliament of Canada, and four United Kingdom orders-in-council (giving Canada the original Northwest Territories and the Arctic Islands, and admitting British Columbia and Prince Edward Island to Confederation). Fifteen of the acts got new names; two of these, the old *British North America Act, 1867* (now the *Constitution Act, 1867*) and the *Manitoba Act, 1870*, suffered a few minor deletions. The part of the United Kingdom Statute of Westminster that is included lost one section.

The rest, apart from changes of name, were untouched by "patriation." What we got was not a new Constitution but the old one with a very few small deletions and four immensely important additions; in an old English slang phrase, the old Constitution with knobs on.

What are the big changes it made in our Constitution? The *Constitution Act, 1982*, established four legal formulas or processes for amending the Constitution. Until 1982, there had never been any legal amending formula (except for a narrowly limited power given to the national Parliament in 1949, a power now superseded).

The first formula covers amendments dealing with the office of the Queen, the Governor General, the lieutenant-governors, the right of a province to at least as many seats in the House of Commons as it had in the Senate in 1982, the use of the English and French languages (except amendments applying only to a single province), the composition of the Supreme Court of Canada and amendments to the amending formulas themselves.

Amendments of these kinds must be passed by the Senate and the House of Commons (or by the Commons alone, if the Senate has not approved the proposal within 180 days after the Commons has done so), and by the legislature of every province. This gives every single province a veto.

The second formula covers amendments concerning the withdrawal of any rights, powers or privileges of provincial governments or legislatures; the proportionate representation of the provinces in the House of Commons; the powers of the Senate and the method of selecting senators; the number of senators for each province, and their residence qualifications; the constitutional position of the Supreme Court of Canada (except its composition, which comes under the first formula); the extension of existing provinces into the territories; the creation of new provinces; generally, the *Canadian Charter of Rights and Freedoms* (which is dealt with later).

Such amendments must be passed by the Senate and the House of Commons (or, again, the Commons alone if the Senate delays more than 180 days), and by the legislatures of two-thirds of the provinces with at least half the total population of all the provinces (that is, the total population of Canada excluding the territories). This means that any four provinces taken together (for example, the four Atlantic provinces, or the four Western) could veto any such amendments. So could Ontario and Quebec taken together. The seven provinces needed to pass any amendment would have to include either Quebec or Ontario.

Any province can, by resolution of its legislature, opt out of any amendment passed under this formula that takes away any of its powers, rights or privileges; and if the amendment it opts out of transfers power over education or other cultural matters to the national Parliament, Parliament must pay the province "reasonable compensation."

The third formula covers amendments dealing with matters that apply only to one province, or to several but not all provinces. Such amendments must be passed by the Senate and the House of Commons (or the Commons alone, if the Senate delays more than 180 days), and by the legislature or legislatures of the particular province or provinces concerned. Such amendments include any changes in provincial boundaries, or changes relating to the use of the English or French language in a particular province, or provinces.

The fourth formula covers changes in the executive government of Canada or in the Senate and House of Commons (other than those covered by the first two formulas). These amendments can be made by an ordinary act of the Parliament of Canada.

The second big change made by the *Constitution Act, 1982*, is that the first three amending formulas "entrench" certain parts of the written Constitution, that is, place them beyond the power of Parliament or any provincial legislature to touch.

For example, the monarchy cannot now be touched except with the unanimous consent of the provinces. Nor can the governor generalship, nor the lieutenant-governorships, nor the composition of the Supreme Court of Canada (nine justices, of whom three must be from Quebec; all of them appointed by the federal government and removable only by address of the Senate and the House of Commons), nor the right of a province to at least as many members of the Commons as it had senators in 1982, nor the amending formulas themselves. On all of these, any single province can impose a veto. Matters coming under the second formula can be changed only with the consent of seven provinces with at least half the population of the ten.

The guarantees for the English and French languages in New Brunswick, Quebec and Manitoba cannot be changed except with the consent both of the provincial legislatures concerned and the Senate and House of Commons (or the Commons alone, under the 180-day provision). The guarantees for denominational schools in Newfoundland cannot be changed except with the consent of the legislature of Newfoundland; nor can the Labrador boundary.

The amending process under the first three formulas can be initiated by the Senate, or the House of Commons, or a provincial legislature. The ordinary act of Parliament required by the fourth formula can, of course, be initiated by either House.

Third, the new *Constitution Act* sets out a Charter of Rights and Freedoms that neither Parliament nor any provincial legislature acting alone can change. Any such changes come under the second formula (or, where they apply only to one or more, but not all, provinces, the third formula).

The rights and freedoms guaranteed are:

1. Democratic rights (for example, the right of every citizen to vote for the House of Commons and the provincial legislative assembly, and the right to elections at least every five years, though in time of real or apprehended war, invasion or insurrection, the life of a federal or provincial house may be prolonged by a two-thirds vote of the Commons or legislative assembly).
2. Fundamental freedoms (conscience, thought, speech, peaceful assembly, association).
3. Mobility rights (to enter, remain in, or leave Canada, and to move into, and earn a living in, any province subject to certain limitations, notably to provide for "affirmative action" programs for the socially or economically disadvantaged).
4. Legal rights (a long list, including such things as the right to a fair, reasonably prompt, public trial by an impartial court).
5. Equality rights (no discrimination on grounds of race, national or ethnic origin, religion, sex, age or mental or physical disability; again, with provision for "affirmative action" programs).
6. Official language rights.
7. Minority language education rights.

All these rights are "subject to such reasonable limits as can be demonstrably justified in a free and democratic society." The courts will decide what these limits might be.

The equality rights came into force on April 17, 1985, three years after the time of patriation of our Constitution. (This gave time for revision of the multitude of federal, provincial and territorial laws which may have required amendment or repeal.)

The fundamental, legal and equality rights in the Charter are subject to a "notwithstanding" clause. This allows Parliament, or a provincial legislature, to pass a law violating any of these rights (except the equality right that prohibits discrimination based on sex) simply by inserting in such law a declaration that it shall operate notwithstanding the fact that it is contrary to this or that provision of the Charter. Any such law can last only five years, but it can be re-enacted for further periods of five years. Any such legislation must apply equally to men and women.

The official language rights make English and French the official languages of Canada for all the institutions of the government and Parliament of Canada and of the New Brunswick government and legislature. Everyone has the right to use either language in Parliament and the New Brunswick legislature. The acts of Parliament, and the New Brunswick legislature, and the records and journals of both bodies, must be in both languages. Either language may be used in any pleading or process in the federal and New Brunswick courts. Any member of the public has the right to communicate with the government and Parliament of Canada, and the government and legislature of New Brunswick, and to receive available services, in either language where there is "a sufficient demand" for the use of English or French or where the nature of the office makes it reasonable. The Charter confirms the existing constitutional guarantees for English and French in the legislatures and courts of Quebec and Manitoba.

The minority language education rights are twofold.

1. In every province, citizens of Canada with any child who has received or is receiving primary or secondary schooling in English or French have the right to have all their children receive

their schooling in the same language, in minority language educational facilities provided out of public funds, where the number of children "so warrants." Also, citizens who have received their own primary schooling in Canada in English or French, and reside in the province where that language is the language of the English or French linguistic minority, have the right to have their children get their primary and secondary schooling in the language concerned, where numbers warrant.

2. In every province except Quebec, citizens whose mother tongue is that of the English or French linguistic minority have the right to have their children get their primary and secondary schooling in the language concerned, where numbers so warrant. This right will be extended to Quebec only if the legislature or government of Quebec consents.

Anyone whose rights and freedoms under the Charter have been infringed or denied can apply to a court of competent jurisdiction "to obtain such remedy as the court considers appropriate and just." If the court decides that any evidence was obtained in a manner that infringed or denied rights and freedoms guaranteed under the Charter, it must exclude such evidence "if it is established that . . . the admission of it would bring the administration of justice into disrepute."

The Charter (except for the language provisions for New Brunswick, which can be amended by joint action of Parliament and the provincial legislature) can be amended only with the consent of seven provinces with at least half the total population of the ten.

The Charter is careful to say that the guarantees it gives to certain rights and freedoms are "not to be construed as denying the existence of any other rights or freedoms that exist in Canada." It declares also that nothing in it "abrogates or derogates from any rights or privileges guaranteed by or under the Constitution of Canada in respect of denominational, separate or dissentient schools." These are, and remain, entrenched.

Before the Charter was added, our written Constitution entrenched certain rights of the English and French languages, the Quebec civil law, certain rights to denominational schools and free trade among the provinces. Apart from these, Parliament and the provincial legislatures could pass any laws they saw fit, provided they did not jump the fence into each others' gardens. As long as Parliament did not try to legislate on subjects that belonged to provincial legislatures, and provincial legislatures did not try to legislate on subjects that belonged to Parliament, Parliament and the legislatures were "sovereign" within their respective fields. There were no legal limits on what they could do (though of course provincial laws could be disallowed by the federal Cabinet within one year). The only ground on which the courts could declare either a federal or a provincial law **unconstitutional** (that is, null and void) was that it intruded into the jurisdictional territory of the other order of government (or, of course, had violated one of the four entrenched rights).

The Charter has radically changed the situation. Parliament and the legislatures will, of course, still not be allowed to jump the fence into each others' gardens. But both federal and provincial laws can now be challenged, and thrown out by the courts, on the grounds that they violate the Charter. This is something with which the Americans, with their Bill of Rights entrenched in their Constitution, have been familiar for almost 200 years. For us, it is almost completely new, indeed revolutionary.

Plainly, this enormously widens the jurisdiction of the courts. Before the Charter, Parliament and the provincial legislatures, "within the limits of subject and area" prescribed by the *Constitution Act, 1867*, enjoyed "authority as plenary and as ample as the Imperial Parliament in the plenitude of its power possessed and could bestow." In other words, within those limits, they could do anything. They were sovereign.

The Charter ends that. It imposes new limits. Just how restrictive they will turn out to be depends on the courts.

Section 1 of the Charter itself provides some leeway for Parliament and the legislatures. It says that the rights the Charter guarantees are "subject only to such reasonable limits prescribed by law as can be demonstrably justified in a free and democratic society." The courts will decide the meaning of "reasonable" and "demonstrably justified" and "a free and democratic society." Their decisions may leave Parliament and the legislatures with most of the powers they had before the Charter came into effect, or they may narrowly restrict many of those powers. It may take some years to find out.

The Charter also contains a provision that Parliament, or a provincial legislature, can override some important parts of the Charter by inserting in an act that would otherwise violate those provisions, a plain declaration that the act shall operate "notwithstanding" the Charter. Such an act is limited to five years, but can be extended for renewed periods of five years. This could allow a partial restoration of the sovereignty of Parliament and the provincial legislatures.

The fourth big change made by the *Constitution Act, 1982,* gives the provinces wide powers over their natural resources. Each province will now be able to control the export, to any other part of Canada, of the primary production from its mines, oil wells, gas wells, forests and electric power plants, provided it does not discriminate against other parts of Canada in prices or supplies. But the national Parliament will still be able to legislate on these matters, and if provincial and federal laws conflict, the federal will prevail. The provinces will also be able to levy indirect taxes on their mines, oil wells, gas wells, forests and electric power plants, and primary production from these sources. But such taxes must be the same for products exported to other parts of Canada and products not so exported.

All these changes, especially the amending formulas and the Charter, are immensely important. But they leave the main structure of government, and almost the whole of the division of powers between the national Parliament and the provincial legislatures, just what they were before.

Incidentally, they leave the provincial legislatures their power to confiscate the property of any individual or corporation and give it to someone else, with not a penny of compensation to the original owner. In two cases, Ontario and Nova Scotia did just that, and the Ontario Court of Appeal ruled: "The prohibition 'Thou shalt not steal' has no legal force upon the sovereign body. And there would be no necessity for compensation to be given." The Charter does not change this. The only security against it is the federal power of disallowance (exercised in the Nova Scotia case) and the fact that today very few legislatures would dare to try it, save in most extraordinary circumstances: the members who voted for it would be too much afraid of being defeated in the next election.

The *Constitution Act, 1982,* makes other changes, and one of these looks very significant indeed, although how much it will really mean remains to be seen. The *BNA Act, 1867,* gave the national Parliament exclusive authority over "Indians, and lands reserved for the Indians," and the courts have ruled that "Indians" includes the Inuit. Until 1982, that was all the Constitution said about the Native peoples.

The Constitution now has three provisions on the subject.

First, it says that the Charter's guarantee of certain rights and freedoms "shall not be construed so as to abrogate or derogate from any aboriginal, treaty or other rights or freedoms that pertain to the aboriginal peoples of Canada," including rights or freedoms recognized by the Royal Proclamation of 1763, and any rights or freedoms acquired by way of land claims settlement.

Second, "The existing aboriginal and treaty rights of the aboriginal peoples of Canada are hereby recognized and affirmed," and the Aboriginal peoples are defined as including the Indian, Inuit and Métis peoples.

Third, in 1983, the amending formula was used for the first time to add to the Aboriginal and treaty rights of Canada's Native peoples, rights or freedoms that already existed by way of land claims agreements or that might be so acquired, and to guarantee all the rights equally to men and women. The amendment also provided that there would be no amendments to the constitutional provisions relating to Indians and Indian reserves, or the Aboriginal rights and freedoms guaranteed by the Charter of Rights and Freedoms, without discussions at a conference of First Ministers with representatives of the Native peoples. The amendment came into force on June 21, 1984.

The *Constitution Act, 1982*, also contains a section on equalization and regional disparities. This proclaims: (1) that the national government and Parliament and the provincial governments and legislatures "are committed to promoting equal opportunities for the well-being of Canadians, furthering economic development to reduce disparities in opportunities, and providing essential public services of reasonable quality to all Canadians"; and (2) that the government and Parliament of Canada "are committed to the principle of making equalization payments to ensure that provincial governments have sufficient revenues to provide reasonably comparable levels of public services at reasonably comparable levels of taxation."

The 1982 Act also provides that the guarantees for the English and French languages do not abrogate or derogate from any legal or customary right or privilege enjoyed by any other language, and that the Charter shall be interpreted "in a manner consistent with the preservation and enhancement of the multicultural heritage of Canada."

Finally, the Act provides for English and French versions of the whole written Constitution, from the Act of 1867 to the Act of 1982, and makes both versions equally authoritative.

The Canadian Bill of Rights Movement

MICHAEL MANDEL

Even before World War II, **judicial activism** in defence of the socio-economic status quo, mostly kept within jurisdictional confines, but with emerging broader ambitions along American lines, was an important feature of Canadian politics. These ambitions were given a great boost by the War itself. From the War came the Canadian movement for an explicit Bill of Rights to ground judicial activism more firmly (Tarnopolsky, 1975: 3ff). The timing and the way the issue was debated in Parliament would lead us to believe that the movement was inspired by Nazi atrocities, or Canada's own mistreatment of Canadians of Japanese origin during the War. But the heightened anti-racist sentiment provoked by all of this found expression in more traditional legal forms, such as the criminal prohibitions against discriminatory publications in Ontario's *Racial Discrimination Act* of 1944 and the more expansive rights in the *Saskatchewan Bill of Rights Act* of 1947. The latter Act was the prototype for modern provincial Human Rights Codes. It provided specific rights to live free from racial, religious, and other specified types of discrimination in employment, housing, and other services, and backed them up with fines and injunctions. However, though it bound the government as well as individuals, its main object was the private sector. It gave the courts no power to nullify laws and was specifically made subject to the law by a provision that it was not to be "construed as derogating from any right, freedom

or liberty to which any person or class of persons is entitled under the law" (section 18). On the other hand, the Bill of Rights movement we are concerned with had to do with giving powers to the judiciary *against* the law, and its appeal to those who carried the ball had more to do with fears that emerged during the War about big government's intrusions in the private sector than about racism.

Lawyers were central to the movement. They had become uneasy about the restrictive economic measures which had been undertaken by Cabinet during the War, which by-passed Parliament and which often cut off access to the courts. Their concerns were expressed in a series of post-war articles written by an early distinguished advocate of entrenchment, Justice C.H. O'Halloran of the Supreme Court of British Columbia (O'Halloran, 1947). O'Halloran sounded the alarm about the possibilities of Canada becoming a dictatorship on the Nazi-Communist style — he equated the two — because of the diminishing importance of Parliament and the courts in the regulatory state. O'Halloran deplored the shift in power from Parliament to Cabinet and the civil service. Worse still was the establishment of regulatory tribunals which were placed by legislation beyond the control of the courts: "they adjudicate without being judges, the tribunals act as Courts without being Courts and often there is no appeal from their decisions to the Courts" (O'Halloran, 1947, No. 3: 23).

SOURCE: *The Charter of Rights and the Legalization of Politics in Canada* (Toronto: Thompson Educational Publishing, 1994), pp. 12–19. Reprinted by permission of the publisher.

What seemed to make this especially menacing for O'Halloran was post-war immigration of a non-British type, which he called

the infiltration of European philosophies (and ways of thinking which owe their origin to those philosophies) to a degree that the peculiar and distinguishing features of the system of law and government which we have inherited may gradually become submerged in what seem to be indigenous habits of thought, of European extraction, which are finding roots particularly among the increasing percentage of the population which has not been invigorated traditionally by the well-tried and long proven principles of the common law. (O'Halloran, 1947, No. 3: 21)[1]

Mixed in with the **xenophobia** was a good measure of cold-warriorism. According to O'Halloran, prominent among these many dangerous foreign ideologies was "Marxian Communism," which, "in its practice which Marx did not live to see," requires that "man must make a complete abandonment of self to the will of the Marxian dictator; he must accept Communist collectivism as his God, and the Communist factory as his church" (O'Halloran, 1947, No. 3: 26). It was not long after this that O'Halloran, in his judicial capacity, would rule that adherence to Marxism was outside the protection of the notion of "freedom of opinion," as he upheld a British Columbia ban on Communists becoming lawyers.

The corollary of O'Halloran's arguments against European ideologies was his homage to the American model of government. The emergence of the United States after the War as the pre-eminent economic and military power in the world lent tremendous prestige to its institutions, including its Bill of Rights. At the end of his four-part article, O'Halloran quoted a Canadian newspaper editorial of 1943 which described the celebration of "Bill of Rights week" in the United States. "It is one of those observances for which the American people seem to have a unique partiality," read the editorial (O'Halloran, 1947, No. 3: 29). O'Halloran ended his piece with the following words:

No Canadian can rest content unless he is convinced that his citizenship as such guarantees to him constitutionally equally full rights as are enjoyed by his friends and neighbours in the United States of America. (O'Halloran, 1947, No. 3: 30)

So, a sense of loss of control over government by the legal profession, a fear of new Canadians and collectivist ideologies, and the powerful and prestigious American example were all elements in the argument of those lawyers anxious to make the judiciary more central to the Canadian constitutional order. To this was added the growing international human rights rhetoric of the Cold War and the ringing declarations of the United Nations Charter and other international human rights documents, as the two contending ideologies tried to outdo each other in their demonstrated commitment to respect for humanity.

O'Halloran's call for a Bill of Rights struck a chord with the legal profession (How, 1948; Scott, 1949), and the idea of an entrenched Bill of Rights on the American plan found very strong support among lawyer-Parliamentarians. Even if it had been inspired by less democratic concerns, in Parliament it was always linked to issues of human rights. The Charter, meant by the likes of O'Halloran to *control* immigrants, was made synonymous by Parliamentarians with *enfranchising* them. A CCF member introduced a motion for a Bill of Rights in 1945 (but dropped it immediately in view of the government's promise of a new law on citizenship), and from 1946 the Conservatives' rising star, John Diefenbaker, was committed to it. Diefenbaker made a speech in its favour on April 2, 1946, on the introduction of the new citizenship law (which abolished national-origin designations—"hyphenated citizenship"—for a common Canadian citizenship). The speech was full of praise for the United States, "our friends and kinsmen across the line" (*House of Commons Debates*, April 2, 1946: 510), whose cosmopolitan features were invoked frequently ("no one thinks of Mr. Roosevelt as a Dutch-American": *House of Commons Debates*,

April 2, 1946: 511–13). And he placed the Bill of Rights squarely within the ideological struggle of the Cold War:

> Today in this world two ideologies face one another. If ever there was a time when we should assert and practise what our citizenship means, it is now. (*House of Commons Debates*, April 2, 1946: 514)

The proposal appears to have been a popular one with the electorate. In 1947, Diefenbaker tabled a petition with more than half a million names.[2] A Parliamentary debate on the issue took place that year upon Canada's adherence to the Charter of the United Nations and the Universal Declaration of Human Rights, as the Liberal government set up a committee to study the question of Canada's obligations under these documents. In the debate, the Tories expressed strong support for an entrenched Bill of Rights, invoking big government, the proliferation of orders-in-council, the ascendancy of boards and tribunals over courts, and the alleged abuses in the investigation of the Gouzenko spy scandal. The CCF also supported such a measure, for their part invoking Nazi atrocities, the treatment by the Canadian government of Canadians of Japanese descent during the war, the treatment of Jehovah's Witnesses by the government of Québec, and the inequality of women. The Liberals were more diffident, referring to British traditions (a Bill of Rights represented the "Americanization of Canada": *House of Commons Debates*, May 19, 1947: 3215) and to the existence of Soviet tyranny even though the Soviets had a fine-sounding Bill of Rights. On the other hand, one Liberal member pointed in alarm to the rise of the welfare state in Britain and thought the American system provided better guarantees against a Canadian Parliament's introducing a "system of complete socialism or communism":

> A system of complete socialism or communism cannot be introduced in the United States without a change in the constitution of the United States, whereas in Great Britain a complete system of communism can be introduced by the will of the present parliament. (*House of Commons Debates*, May 19, 1947: 3204)

However, only the ultra-conservative Union Nationale representatives from Québec were firmly opposed in principle:

> In the province of Québec, no one has the right to commit crimes in the name of freedom and I hope our leaders will never forget that "the word freedom may sometimes lead men into slavery." Because it cherishes freedom, the province of Québec does not want to be fouled by troublemakers, anarchists or advocates of revolution. Neither does she want to become a ghetto for the communist-minded Jews from the lowest strata in European countries. (*House of Commons Debates*, May 19, 1947: 3228)

The major stumbling block in the view of most of those opposed to a Bill of Rights was the collateral fact that it would interfere with provincial jurisdiction. French-speaking Québec Liberals, including future premier of Québec Jean Lesage, argued that a Bill of Rights should not even be discussed until Canada had attained "full maturity" with its own constitution capable of domestic amendment to replace the already irksome arrangement whereby an application had to be made to the United Kingdom for all changes to Canada's constitution because it was technically a mere Act of the British Parliament (*House of Commons Debates*, May 16, 1947: 3173, 3212).

Amendment of the *BNA Act* proved to be the stumbling block three years later when a Special Senate Committee reported in favour of a constitutional Bill of Rights but recommended postponing it until there was complete provincial consent and Canada was capable of amending its own constitution. In the meantime, the Committee recommended Parliament enact a strictly federal Bill of Rights (Canada, 1950: 302–307). No agreement on constitutional amendment was forthcoming and the purely federal Bill of Rights had to await the election of a majority Conservative government under John Diefenbaker in 1958.

In the meantime, there was growing sentiment in the legal profession for an end run around the political impasse by the assertion of a broader federal constitutional jurisdiction in civil rights. Three decisions of the Supreme Court of Canada in the 1950s found it warming more and more to the idea of fashioning its own constitutional Bill of Rights, following the lead of the pre-war *Alberta Statutes* case. All three decisions had to do with Québec laws enacted by the Duplessis regime, another provincial government out of step with the rest of Canada. The cases split the Court on ethnic lines and never quite achieved a majority for the "implied Bill of Rights" idea. In *Saumur* (1953), a Québec regulation which was applied in such a way as to discriminate against Jehovah's Witnesses in the distribution of pamphlets was nullified, with four (English) judges invoking an invented federal jurisdiction on "freedom of religion." In *Birks & Sons* (1955), Québec Sunday closing legislation was unanimously held invalid, with three (English) judges invoking freedom of religion. In *Switzman* (1957), the Court finally did away with Québec's anti-communist "Padlock Law," under which houses could be padlocked if used for the "propagation of Communism or Bolshevism," a law by then a bit long in the tooth after twenty years of effective use in the harassment of the Québec left. Two (English) judges said only Parliament could interfere with fundamental political liberties and one of them (Justice Abbott) went so far as to postulate fundamental rights type limitations on *both* Parliament and the provincial legislatures.

At the same time as the Supreme Court of Canada was staking out its own constitutional claims, the United States Supreme Court was entering the most liberal-activist period of its history with the appointment of Earl Warren as Chief Justice (Galloway, 1982: 155–63). The immediate post-1937 deference of the Court was followed by a "resurgence of judicial activism." A "major milestone in the growth of modern judicial power" was

the desegregation case of *Brown v. School Board* (*Brown*, 1954) and this activist impulse was sustained into the 1960s when

> issue after issue was opened to judicial cognizance and decision. By the 1970s, it almost seemed as if it were difficult to find an issue in which some federal judge somewhere might not intervene to lay down the law. (Wolfe, 1986: 7)

The influence of U.S. institutions and culture on Canadian life is nothing new, of course. That aspect of the Free Trade debate has been a rather permanent feature of Canadian history. But the Second World War was a major turning point. It demonstrated to everyone the irrevocable decline of the United Kingdom and the ascendancy of the United States as the foremost capitalist power in the world. This had great significance for a former colony of the one situated on the northern border of the other. Common defence agreements between the U.S. and Canada were concluded during the war (McNaught, 1976: 282), and when the nuclear age and the Cold War dawned with Canada right smack between the U.S. and the USSR, agreements such as NORAD in 1957 were inevitably to subordinate Canadians to the U.S. world outlook. If that were not enough, the economic factors were overwhelming. In the mid-1920s the United States had replaced Britain as the major source of foreign capital in Canada. By the end of the 1950s, 70 per cent of Canadian imports came from the U.S., which also accounted for 75 per cent of direct foreign investment, 60 per cent of the Canadian exports, and the ownership and control of more than half of Canadian manufacturing and resource industries (McNaught, 1976: 294; Clement, 1975: 102–105).

> The impact of American "culture patterns" through advertising, magazines, films and television, together with what seemed an almost involuntary entanglement in the American alliance system, could be seen as irreversible signposts to the future. (McNaught, 1976: 295)

Canada was not alone in the West in being on the receiving end of U.S. cultural dominance, even if proximity, language, and other similarities made us particularly vulnerable. The division of the world into two great blocs, one dominated by the U.S., made itself felt in many ways. One of these was the proliferation of the institution of **judicial review** in the post-war constitutions of states in the American sphere of influence. The U.S. model had already attracted European followers in the period between the wars; after World War II it spread like wildfire. In the case of defeated Germany and Japan, judicial review was actually dictated by the occupation authorities, though there were at least some pre-war antecedents and much post-war enthusiasm in Germany (Ehrmann, 1976: 142). In most countries under the American sphere of influence, for example, Italy (1948), France (1958), and the European Economic Communities (1957), the institution of judicial review was clearly a question of American influence rather than pressure, even of the inherent attractiveness of the institution of judicial review in meeting the internal exigencies of societies increasingly modelled on or dominated by the American economy and way of life. These internal exigencies were variations on those faced by the Americans themselves in the 1780s: the many threats posed to powerful interests by representative institutions. A similar explanation can be given for the spread of judicial review in South America during the U.S. colonization of the nineteenth century pursuant to the Monroe Doctrine (Ehrmann, 1976: 145–46), and, indeed, for the more recent adoption of judicial review in the ex-Soviet bloc after the collapse of the Soviet economies in the 1980s (Schwartz, 1992). The Soviet regimes had firmly resisted judicial review and some defenders see this as proof of a quasi-synonymity between judicial review and "liberty," a thesis requiring massive historical amnesia, if only on the question of the American institution of slavery. However, some understanding of the historical "causes" of the legalization of politics is fundamental to a proper assessment of the phenomenon.

Given this world-wide popularity of judicial review under Bills of Rights in the 1950s, when the newly elected Progressive Conservative government of John Diefenbaker made good on its campaign promises and introduced a *Canadian Bill of Rights* in 1959 applicable only to the federal government, the main criticism levelled against it by Canada's leading legal intellectuals was that it did not go far enough.

Most interesting in retrospect is the opinion of Bora Laskin, then of the Faculty of Law of the University of Toronto, who would later, as Chief Justice of Canada, be so closely connected with the whole entrenchment project:

> . . . the proposed Bill is unfortunate in its limited application to the federal level of government . . . It would be better that no Bill be proposed so that the common law tradition be maintained through the unifying force and position of the Supreme Court of Canada. And better too, in such case, to allow that court to continue unaided in developing constitutional doctrine which has already pointed to legal limitations on legislative encroachments on civil liberties. (Laskin, 1959: 78)

Expressing the strong centralist inclinations that would characterize his judicial career, Laskin argued that the recent Supreme Court holdings gave the federal government the power to entrench a constitutional Bill of Rights applicable to the provinces in at least some respects, and he argued strenuously that it should have exercised it (Laskin, 1959: 130–33).

Thus, by 1950 there was strong, probably majority, support for the principle of judicial review among Canadian legal intellectuals. This support was overwhelming by 1959. And it was shared by the political community. The only real obstacles were the extraneous but delicate questions of provincial rights and an amending formula. However, some members of the practising bar (Council of the Canadian Bar Association, 1959) and the senior judiciary were not yet ready to overthrow tradition and climb on the bandwagon. The period from the enactment of the *Canadian Bill of Rights* in 1960 to 1967 saw the growing enthusiasm dampened as claims were consistently rejected. During this period, Canadian lawyers watched with envy as the United States Supreme Court went into high gear. Though some lower courts tried to emulate their U.S. colleagues, Canadian superior courts firmly resisted the blandishments of litigants and the occasional dissenting justice to use the Diefenbaker document to adopt a U.S.-style posture with respect to federal law. Notable decisions of this period, especially in light of the about-face courts have recently taken on the same issues in the 1980s, were *Robertson and Rosetanni* (1963—"freedom of religion" not applicable to Sunday closing laws) and *McCaud* (1964—"right to a fair hearing" not applicable to parole boards). Nor was this a good time for the "implied Bill of Rights" theory. In *Oil, Chemical and Atomic Workers Union* (1963), provincial legislation outlawing political contributions from union dues was upheld, by a margin of four judges to three, as within the province's exclusive jurisdiction over labour relations.

Not that questions of civil rights were ignored in this period. Anti-discrimination sentiment in Canada was strong after the War, nurtured by the War itself, post-war immigration, anti-colonialist movements around the world, the drama of the U.S. civil rights movement and so on. Provincial human rights laws forbidding discrimination in accommodation and employment proliferated in the 1950s. In the 1960s they were being consolidated and strengthened in provincial Human Rights Codes enforced by Human Rights Commissions (Williams, 1986: 104–11). But it is important to distinguish between Human Rights Codes on the one hand and the movement for a Bill of Rights on the other. Prohibitions against discrimination in Human Rights Codes are enforced either by traditional means, such as fines or injunctions, or by means which may even *replace* the judiciary with boards composed of non-lawyers. But the movement represented by the *Canadian Bill of Rights* was for a general judicial veto power over legislation, which, in its modern manifestation, *even includes human rights legislation*. Though they overlap in

some respects, the differences in form are fundamental. In the period we have been looking at, it was the new role for the judiciary that was encountering obstacles.

NOTES

1. The xenophobic argument was sufficiently widespread to be used even by the moderate left. Eugene Forsey, appearing for the Canadian Congress of Labour before the *Senate Special Committee on Human Rights* in 1950, used it as one of the CCL's arguments—though not their main one—for an entrenched Bill of Rights despite Britain's lack of one: "Second: Canada is a land of many peoples and many traditions. But it gives prejudice extra targets, and it means that the British tradition is only one among many, some of them much less tolerant or much less alert to the dangers of intolerance." (Canada, 1950: 79)

2. He repeated this feat in 1949 (Romanow et al., 1984: 222–23).

REFERENCES

Canada. 1950. *Proceedings of the Special Committee of the Senate of Canada on Human Rights and Fundamental Freedoms. Report of the Committee.* Ottawa: King's Printer.

Clement, Wallace. 1975. *The Canadian Corporate Elite: An Analysis of Economic Power.* Toronto: McClelland & Stewart.

Ehrmann, H.W. 1976. *Comparative Legal Cultures.* Englewood Cliffs, N.J.: Prentice-Hall.

Galloway, Russell. 1982. *The Rich and the Poor in Supreme Court History, 1790–1982.* Greenbrae, Calif.: Paradigm Press.

How, W.G. 1948. "The Case for a Canadian Bill of Rights," *Canadian Bar Review* 26: 759.

Laskin, Bora. 1959. "An Inquiry into the Diefenbaker Bill of Rights." *Canadian Bar Review* 37: 77.

McNaught, Kenneth. 1976. *The Pelican History of Canada.* Rev. ed. Harmondsworth: Penguin Books.

O'Halloran, C.H. 1947. Inherent Rights. *Obiter Dicta*, 22 (No. 1): 35; (No. 2): 24; (No. 3): 21.

Romanov, Roy, John Whyte, and Howard Leeson. 1984. *Canada . . . Notwithstanding: The Making of the Constitution, 1976–1982.* Toronto: Carswell/Methuen.

Schwartz, Charles. 1992. *Social Credit Theory and Legislation in Alberta*. M.A. Thesis, Department of Political Economy, University of Manitoba.

Scott, F.R. 1949. "Dominion Jurisdiction over Human Rights and Fundamental Freedoms." *Canadian Bar Review* 27: 497.

Tarnopolsky, Walter Surma. 1975. *The Canadian Bill of Rights*. 2nd rev. ed. Toronto: McClelland & Stewart.

Williams, Cynthia. 1986. "The Changing Nature of Citizens Rights." In Alan Cairns and Cynthia Williams, *Constitutionalism, Citizenship and Society*. Toronto: University of Toronto Press.

Wolfe, Christopher. 1986. *The Rise of Modern Judicial Review: From Constitutional Interpretation to Judge-Made Law*. New York: Basic Books.

CASES CITED

Birks & Sons (Montreal) Ltd. v. City of Montreal, [1955] S.C.R. 799.

Brown v. Board of Education, 347 U.S. 483 (1954).

Exp. McCaud, [1965] 1 C.C.C. 168.

Oil, Chemical and Atomic Workers International Union, Local 16-601 v. Imperial Oil Ltd., [1963] S.C.R. 584.

Re Alberta Statutes, [1938] S.C.R. 100.

Robertson and Rosetanni v. The Queen, [1963] 41 D.L.R. (2d) 485.

Saumur v. City of Quebec, [1953] 2 S.C.R. 299.

Switzman v. Elbing, [1957] S.C.R. 285.

The Constitutional Problem

CHARLES TAYLOR

Quebec's constitutional problem can be summed up simply as the need to reconcile the imperatives that flow from certain fundamental facts. I see four such facts.

a. Quebec is a distinct society, the political expression of a nation, and the majority of this nation lives within its borders.
b. Quebec is the principal home of this nation, but branches of it have settled elsewhere in North America and mainly in Canada.
c. Quebec must open itself economically, as must any society that seeks prosperity at the turn of this century.
d. The economic openness must not be bought at the cost of political domination from outside. Such a danger exists by virtue of the fact that we share the continent with a superpower. Quebec therefore has an interest in political association with the other regions of what is currently Canada, so as to maintain a certain balance in North American political relations, and to enjoy a certain influence internationally.

In Quebec, some conflict has often been felt between these demands, and, in response to this conflict, some have preferred a radical option. This is the sovereignist position, as it has generally been defended over the last 25 years. To safeguard the full autonomy of Quebec as a political entity and to maintain the degree of economic openness already achieved, breaking all ties with francophones outside Quebec and abandoning all the benefits of a wider political collaboration with the rest of Canada is proposed.

But this would involve sacrificing some important benefits, so it would be essential to ensure that the radical option was really compelling. Regarding francophones outside Quebec, it is not just a question of historical and cultural ties — these, of course, are important in their own right. It is also necessary to take into account that these communities represent the dissemination of French in North America. The stronger they are and the more recognition they gain for themselves in their respective provinces, the more they enlarge the French presence. And that is a great advantage for us in Quebec, who are at the heart of the francophone population in America. The pressure on us is reduced when we are surrounded by a demographic and political space that is not homogeneous and monolithic.

Political collaboration with the other regions can also contribute to this dissemination of French. The process of bilingualism in Canada, the growing number of English Canadians who are learning French, the sometimes extraordinary expansion of immersion schools, all this is an undeniable advantage for Quebec francophones. Anything that enhances the prestige of French, that increases the

SOURCE: "The Constitutional Problem," trans. Ruth Abbey, in William Dodge, ed., *Boundaries of Identity: A Quebec Reader* (Toronto: Lester Publishing, 1992), pp. 264–71. Reprinted by permission of the author.

number of people capable of communicating in French, diminishes the pressure that a minority language will always experience in North America.

These gains have been underestimated and insufficiently appreciated in Quebec thanks to the political context in which they were made. The Trudeau government is largely responsible for the growth of bilingualism. But this government linked the growth of bilingualism with a categorical refusal of any special status for Quebec. Bilingualism was defended in the name of a philosophy that relied on a rigorously symmetrical federalism. It was conceived as an individual right, of French and English speakers, and not as the recognition of a *community*, in this case francophone, forced to protect itself and to ensure its growth.

The political dynamic of the Trudeau-Lévesque era has made us forget this program that is both logical and profoundly in tune with our historical aspirations. For the last quarter of a century it has been dismissed as utopian. We have felt compelled to choose between an anti-communitarian philosophy that recognizes only individual rights and that was dominant in Ottawa, and an independence strategy that gained ground in Quebec. It seemed that Quebec could only find the political status it needed at the expense of the dissemination of French outside its boundaries.

But this choice is not inevitable. It is no longer necessary to remain obsessed by the political configuration of the last 25 years. That era is finished. With the process manifested in the Bélanger-Campeau commission, we are starting a new phase. It is no longer a question of fixing our objectives against the background of a passing era. We want to define them for a future that is still undetermined. We don't have to constrain them from the start.

Now, apart from this question of the spread of French, there are some other advantages from collaboration with the other regions of contemporary Canada that must be taken into account. Without claiming to offer an exhaustive list, I would like to mention three.

First, Canada distinguishes itself from the United States by its social programs, for example,

our old age pensions and our health insurance. Canadians and Quebecers hold these programs dear. But they are not guaranteed forever. In the context of North American free trade, there will always be a certain pressure on us to align our social spending and taxation levels with those of our powerful neighbours. The different provinces and regions of Canada have a common interest in resisting this pressure. There is a definite solidarity between them. To the extent that cooperation between the regions can support the maintenance of these programs, which was the argument made for equalization, cooperation is in the interests of everyone. Quebec should not become indifferent to the fate of the other regions in this regard.

Quebec is also different from the United States, and from the Anglo Saxon world in general, in its style of economic management. The state plays a much more active role. We need only mention the important role of the Caisse de Dépôt et Placement de Québec in our recent development. And, it must be noted that Canada has always offered a climate hospitable to this type of government intervention. For historical as much as geographical reasons, English Canada has always been more open to state initiatives than the United States.

Moreover, it is to be hoped that the other regions of Canada, and also a future federal government, will adopt some of the measures that have contributed to Quebec's economic success. One of them, the generation of capital from the citizens' savings, could enlarge the range of possibilities if practised on a wider scale. It could permit the financing of large-scale projects or enterprises. For example, one resource that is currently underdeveloped in Quebec and in Canada is government-sponsored scientific research. Here, too, the results could be much more significant if we were to unify our efforts.

Finally, there is a very important reason for not withdrawing from the Canadian space to that behind our borders. The Canadian space contains vast resources, some still unknown. Rather than being forced to retreat, we must aim to participate in the development of the north. The advantages of such participation in terms of those factors and resources that we currently know about cannot be emphasized enough. The future wealth and opportunities of this vast space are in part unforeseeable. We cannot let ourselves be excluded from the game.

With the death of the Meech Lake Accord, something very profound happened in Quebec. Everybody feels it, but it is not easy to define. For me, the most significant element is that the traditional ambiguity of Quebec federalists has been resolved. I don't mean that they are no longer federalists. But the age-old uncertainty over whether it was necessary to make certain changes to the 1867 constitution or to remake our structures from head to foot has gone. On June 23, 1990, the 1867 constitution died morally in Quebec. It is necessary to create anew.

Of course, it is quite possible that the old misunderstandings between Quebec and English Canada that destroyed the previous structures will survive them, that they will plague the new relationships that we want to establish. That's possible, but it's far from being inevitable. Some of these misunderstandings were tied up with the old constitution. The image of Canada as a "mosaic," the norm of equality of the provinces, the *idée fixe* that there was only a "Canadian" nation, all these elements were tied to the existing structures and to the way in which these structures were explained and experienced in the other regions. Canada created a certain expectation in the minds of a majority of English Canadians, an expectation regarding the provinces and other parts of the country, that Quebec couldn't violate. The advantage of creating anew is that new structures that break explicitly with the past can be proposed. It will no longer be a question of treason, but rather of building a new country.

Contrary to those who believe that English Canada, having refused Meech Lake, couldn't agree to bigger changes, there is a real possibility that deeper changes will be easier to accept, especially if they are proposed within the framework of a new constitution rather than as re-arrangements of the Canada of old.

It seems to me that the system that would best meet the four types of demands outlined at the outset would be a federal system that is more decentralized than the current one. The 1867 constitution is very supple in certain regards. The proof is that it was conceived as a very centralist system but has evolved over recent decades into a more and more decentralized one.

Quebec — and in the case of a symmetrical federation, the other members of the federation — would have to keep current provincial powers, plus a certain number of others, such as labour, taxation, communications, agriculture and fisheries (this is not a complete list). The federal power would control defence, external affairs and currency. There would be some areas of mixed jurisdiction as well, such as immigration, industrial policy (including scientific research) and environmental policy.

This distribution would put an end to certain useless duplications of effort that we currently have, but would not avoid all overlap. That would be impossible. The fact is that we don't live in isolation and even certain fully provincial powers can't be exercised without regard for what is being done outside. Take health insurance as an example. To maintain an open economy in Canada, we have to be concerned with mobility. Our health insurance system is our business, but we have an interest in extending it to others. The same applies to retirement pensions, labour policy and many other domains.

In some cases, coordination will occur through interprovincial agreements, but in others it would be better to imagine a shared or concurrent jurisdiction; shared power in the case of immigration, for example, because free movement of people within the federation requires legislation that is accepted by both levels; concurrent power in a domain like scientific research, because here our problem is not an excess of initiatives, but a lack of funds. As for ecology, some very obvious coordination problems exist. Regulation by inter-governmental agreements may be possible, as is currently the case between Canada and the U.S. for acid rain and purification of the Great Lakes. But the size and urgency of these problems, and the magnitude of the changes that must be made, favour a mixed jurisdiction. To some extent, even foreign affairs should be considered a mixed domain since Quebec has developed an international identity in some areas of jurisdiction, and any new federal structure would have to recognize diplomatic representations that are already being made under the current regime.

Another issue relating to the distribution of powers is the native question, the resolution of which will require the granting of some powers of self-rule to the aboriginal communities. A purely Québécois solution for the Indians and Inuit of Quebec, which would leave other regions free to legislate within their communities as they like, could be possible. But there are clearly some advantages to a common solution affecting all the native populations of the Canadian federation. One reason for this is that certain tribes cross provincial boundaries. But beyond such geographic considerations, two or more systems would always invite comparison, as well as demands and criticism that could render the new structures unstable and impair their functioning.

THE NEW FEDERAL STRUCTURES

A federation uniting whom? Who would be Quebec's partners? Unfortunately, it is impossible to specify at the moment. What's more, it is not for us to decide. English Canada itself, once it has understood and accepted that the country has to be remade from head to foot, will determine its identity and find its own articulations.

It is therefore necessary to examine several hypotheses, so as to measure their impact on the federal model just outlined. I rule out one possibility, a catastrophic scenario, according to which English Canada would disintegrate under the weight of its internal divisions as soon as it saw that the current structure would not hold. This is a possible, but not probable, scenario. But this is not the major reason for my ruling it out — it is rather that such an outcome would leave us without a negotiating partner.

I envisage three possibilities: (i) English Canada recovers its unity, either as a unitary state or a federation, and seeks to combine with Quebec in a federation of two; (ii) English Canada takes account of its own regional differences and restructures itself under three or four regional governments who would become Quebec's interlocutors; (iii) English Canada remains as it currently is, composed of nine provinces.

It is clear that the federal system wouldn't be the same under all three scenarios. Under (i), a perfectly symmetrical federalism can be envisaged, because it is obvious that a united English Canada would also push for a considerable decentralization of powers. Under (iii), by contrast, it is more than probable that the system would be asymmetrical. This means that only Quebec would exercise fully the powers that I attributed above to all the members of the federation, while the other provinces would opt for a centralization of several powers.

Hypothesis (ii) would probably represent a situation in-between. In this case the system would resemble a symmetrical federalism, but there would possibly be some minor differences in the powers that the different constituent members would want to exercise.

Quebec should decide the powers it wants to exercise, but not try to dictate those of the others. If the lists of powers differ, it would be necessary to build a system of asymmetrical federalism. English Canada could then evolve towards greater decentralization, or a centralization that is in accord with its own wishes and the needs of the time.

Is it as simple as this? Talk of asymmetrical federalism means a special status for Quebec. We all know how its very invocation provoked the resistance of English Canada, and how dangerous it still appears to some of our compatriots. The rejection of such a status was an important feature of the opposition to the Meech Lake Accord.

But we shouldn't automatically assume that asymmetry is impossible or unworkable. The fact is that Quebec enjoys a considerable special status *under the current regime*. We live every day with an asymmetrical federalism. Quebec is the only province that collects its own taxes, has its own pension plan, is active in immigration, and so on. This sums up what was at stake in the Meech clause recognizing Quebec as a distinct society. The resistance was not at the practical level. This was rather a principled resistance, a defence of the principle of equality of all provinces. It's as if we could tolerate considerable divergences from this principle in fact so long as provincial equality was safely protected in the texts. It's a resistance at the level of feeling. This is not insignificant, of course. But the obstacles it creates shouldn't be exaggerated. For one thing, the distinct society idea also has considerable support in English Canada. Furthermore, the resistance is linked, as mentioned before, to the expectations that the traditional idea of Canada has created in certain of our compatriots. It is a matter of convincing them that we are no longer playing the same game, that we are not proposing to repair the Canada of old. There is a new deal.

Beyond a certain threshold, a federalism that is too asymmetrical would create problems, so the best scenario for us would probably be an English Canada that formed itself into three or four large regions.

THE STATUS OF MINORITIES

While recognizing that French will dominate in Quebec and English elsewhere, Quebec and the rest of Canada should establish together a minority code that would prevent linguistic minorities from simply being crushed. This code would ensure that no matter which of the two traditional languages is in the minority, they will both enjoy special status and will not be treated as another immigrant language.

We have three major reasons for wanting to make such an agreement. First, by virtue of the imperatives mentioned earlier, our ties of solidarity and interest with francophones outside Quebec push us towards it. Secondly, a mean-spirited and repressive policy towards minorities by one side or the other will poison relations between the two societies, and good relations are important no matter

what political regime prevails. Thirdly, Quebec itself, through several of its leaders, including the Premier and the Leader of the Opposition, has recently declared that it considers the anglophone minority to be a traditional and integral part of Quebec society.

CONSEQUENCES OF NEW FEDERATION

With regard to our standard of living, I believe that a new federal arrangement of the type proposed here would be the most favourable. This is because it keeps the Canadian economic space intact and can better guarantee the integrity of this economic space over the years, and because a federation would be able to mobilize the resources of this vast country in the most efficient way.

As for the Québécois identity, there are two things that must be asked of a constitutional structure: first, that it recognizes fully and explicitly the specificity of Quebec; and second, that it gives Quebec the powers necessary to defend and promote this uniqueness. I believe that the proposed federal structure adequately meets these two demands.

CONCLUSION

There are some who want to convince English Canada of our seriousness, to induce them to negotiate, by taking extreme positions. It is said that the only way to make them negotiate seriously is to declare sovereignty first, and negotiate later.

It is necessary to find a way of alerting English Canada to the seriousness of the situation. However, we must avoid becoming embroiled in the maze of amendment procedures currently in place. The problem with these procedures is that they leave us with the status quo by default. They put the burden of proof on those who want change.

It may be necessary to propose to English Canada something like a rerun of the Charlottetown Conference of 1864 — negotiations whose defeat would not leave us with the status quo but would signify the end of the country. Of course, this ultimatum would have a shock-effect. But it is probably necessary, given the reluctance of English Canada to recognize the evolution of Quebec. On the other hand, a shock also risks damaging the interlocutor and leaving English Canada less inclined to talk.

It may be useful, therefore, to combine the ultimatum with an expression of openness, recognizing that Quebec is not alone in wanting to remake the country. Other regions have their own agendas, as we have ours, and we should declare ourselves ready to listen to their demands just as we expect them to listen to ours.

It is up to all of us in Quebec to decide what Quebec wants. But to achieve our goal, it is also necessary to take account of what the others want. Firmness doesn't mean closedness. At once determined and open, we can begin the political reconstruction of the north of this continent.

The End of Mega Constitutional Politics in Canada?

PETER H. RUSSELL

On 26 October 1992, the Canadian people, for the first time in their history as a political community, acted as Canada's ultimate constitutional authority — in effect, as a sovereign people. In the referendum conducted on that day, a majority of Canadians in a majority of provinces, said "No" to the Charlottetown Accord proposals for constitutional change.

Though the referendum was only consultative and not legally binding, nonetheless the governments that supported the Accord — and these include the federal government, all ten provincial governments and the two territorial governments, plus organizations representing the four groupings of aboriginal peoples (status and non-status Indians, Inuit, and Metis) — will not proceed with ratification of the Accord in their legislative assemblies. The politicians will respect the vox populi.

The referendum may have killed more than the Accord. It may very well be the last time this generation of Canadians attempt a grand resolution of constitutional issues in order to prevent a national unity crisis. If in the next few years Canada plunges once again into the constitutional maelstrom, it will be because it is confronted with an actual, not an apprehended, crisis of national unity.

MEGA CONSTITUTIONAL POLITICS

Virtually all constitutional democracies are constantly engaged in low level, piecemeal constitutional change, whether through formal constitutional amendments, informal political practice, or judicial interpretation. This is ordinary constitutional politics. Canada's constitutional politics fits this pattern through most of its first century after confederation in 1867.

When constitutional politics moves well beyond disputing the merits of specific constitutional proposals and addresses the very nature and principles of the political community on which the constitution is based, it is a horse of a very different color. At this "mega" level, "precisely because of the fundamental nature of the issues in dispute — their tendency to touch citizens' sense of identity and self-worth — mega constitutional politics is exceptionally emotional and intense."[1] The constitutional question tends to dwarf all other issues in public discussions and media coverage when a country's constitutional politics is at the mega level.

Mega constitutional politics is not peculiar to Canada. The United States knew this kind of politics last in the Civil War. Recently, much of

SOURCE: "The End of Mega Constitutional Politics in Canada?" *PS: Political Science & Politics* 26, 1 (March 1993): 33–37. Reprinted by permission of the author and the American Political Science Association.

eastern Europe passed through mega constitutional upheavals. South Africa is now fully engaged in constitutional politics at the mega level, and western Europe approaches such politics as it moves towards federation. Belgium has been involved in constitutional politics of the mega variety almost as much as Canada. But Canada must surely win the prize — and a booby prize it well may be — for the duration and intensity of its involvement in mega constitutional politics. We were at it, almost non-stop, from 1967 to 1992.

THE PREVIOUS ROUNDS

The 26 October referendum was the final act of what the media and the players referred to as the "Canada Round" of constitutional politics. The Canada Round was the fifth round of constitutional politics since the mid 1960s. Like each of the previous rounds, the Canada Round produced a package of constitutional proposals, the Charlottetown Accord, whose main purpose was to provide an alternative to Quebec sovereignty. Though the context and agenda of all five rounds varied considerably, the fundamental objectives of the constitutional architects were always essentially the same — to strengthen national unity and stave off the threat of Quebec separation.

The first round began in the 1960s when Quebec's "Quiet Revolution" unleashed a surge of ethnic nationalism that suddenly widened the constitutional agenda. Although in principle Canada had been an autonomous, self-governing Dominion since 1927, it had not been able to convert its constitution from a British statute to a constitution amendable in Canada. This was because its federal and provincial leaders, despite numerous conferences, could not agree on a formula for amending the constitution in Canada. Finally in the mid 1960s, just as agreement seemed in sight, Quebec raised the ante. Quebec would agree to patriation of the constitution only if the federation was restructured to recognize Quebec's special status as the homeland of one of Canada's founding peoples.

A political struggle over the constitution at the mega level was fully engaged when Quebec's demands were countered by Pierre Elliott Trudeau. Trudeau had become federal Justice Minister in 1967 and Prime Minister in 1968. Instead of making concessions to Quebec, Trudeau's strategy was to initiate constitutional proposals designed to build a stronger sense of Canadian nationhood. An intense series of federal-provincial meetings ensued. For three years they were the country's main political preoccupation. The inter-governmental negotiations were dominated by Trudeau's agenda with a constitutional bill of rights as its centerpiece. In June 1971, Trudeau seemed on the brink of success when the first ministers came to a tentative agreement on the Victoria Charter built around his proposals. But within days the Quebec premier, Robert Bourassa, responding to Quebec nationalist criticisms of the Charter, withdrew his support.

Although legally Trudeau could have gone ahead and asked Britain to patriate Canada's constitution on his terms, he did not at that time feel sufficiently strong nor impatient enough to impose a constitutional settlement on Quebec.

The first round demonstrated the risks of waging constitutional politics at the mega level in order to strengthen national unity. Trudeau's agenda of Canadian national-building reforms did not win the hearts and minds of a majority of his fellow Quebecois. But the Trudeauian constitutional vision with its emphasis on the equal rights of the Canadian citizen rather than the powers of provinces garnered a strong following outside of Quebec. Ever since this first round Trudeau has been English Canada's constitutional hero. But rather than unifying the country, Trudeau's success gave a sharper ideological edge to its constitutional politics. When constitutional politics are elite driven, as they usually are, they may deepen rather than narrow divisions within the populace.

In round two the agenda widened and a more complex set of cleavages opened up. In the early 1970s the Trudeau government's energy and language policies alienated opinion in western Canada. Western premiers became constitutional activists.

Provincial leaders from "outer Canada" began to press for a restructured Senate in which the smaller provinces could check the perceived central Canadian (Ontario/Quebec) dominance of national policy. During the same period, Canada's aboriginal peoples showed signs of entering the constitutional fray. Quebec's ethnic nationalism provided an influential demonstration effect, and the infatuation of elites with wholesale constitutional revision promised opportunities for decolonization unavailable to native peoples in other countries dominated by white-settler majorities.

But the mega constitutional struggle was not resumed until 1976, when Quebec elected a separatist government, led by René Lévesque. This event unleashed another flurry of feverish constitutional activity. Federal and provincial leaders, aided and abetted by the country's chattering classes, engaged in a season of "new constitutionalism." The assumption was that unless a new constitutional arrangement could be worked out satisfying Quebec's demands as well as other sources of constitutional discontent in the country, the Canadian federation would break up. Another tense series of federal-provincial negotiations produced no accord and ended with the electoral defeat of the Trudeau Government in 1979.

The third round began with the 1980 Quebec referendum, which produced a 60 percent majority against the Parti Québécois' option of a sovereign Quebec in an economic association with Canada. Trudeau's Liberals defeated a short-lived Conservative minority government in the 1980 general election, and Trudeau aimed to take advantage of the Quebec separatists' defeat and consolidate Canadian unity by driving through his own program of constitutional reform. At the center of that program was patriation of the constitution with a charter of rights and freedoms. Using Gaullist techniques, Trudeau bypassed the provincial premiers to build public support for his "People's Package," even threatening to hold a referendum. In television hearings in the federal parliament, the constitutional advocates were not provincial premiers pressing for more power for their governments but civil liberties and public interest groups pressing for the constitutional rights of citizens.

In the end the Supreme Court of Canada persuaded Trudeau to negotiate with the provincial premiers before asking the British Parliament to patriate Canada's Constitution. This he did, reluctantly accepting modifications in the federal proposals, the most notable of which was a stronger role for provinces in the amending process and a legislative override attached to the Charter of Rights. These concessions were enough to obtain the agreement of all the provinces except Quebec. Quebec's resistance deterred neither Trudeau nor the British Parliament. And so, in 1982, Canada at last took custody of its constitution in its own hands but on terms that were repudiated by one of its primary constituent elements.

For Trudeau and his supporters that should have been the end of Canada's constitutional struggle. But not all Canadians were willing to accept Trudeau's verdict that "The federation was set to last a thousand years."[2] To begin with, there were the aboriginal peoples. The 1982 constitutional amendments included a vague affirmation of "the existing rights" of aboriginal peoples. This did not provide the explicit recognition native peoples sought for their inherent right of self-government. Through four successive constitutional conferences, from 1983 to 1987, aboriginal leaders failed to obtain that recognition from the federal and provincial governments. Nonetheless, these conferences established the aboriginal peoples' status as key players in Canada's constitutional politics.

But again it was Quebec that brought this fourth round to the all-absorbing mega level. With Lévesque and Trudeau replaced by more conciliatory leaders, the scene was set for an attempt at reconciling Quebec to the changes made in 1982. Robert Bourassa, enjoying a second coming as Quebec premier, brought forward, as Quebec's price for accepting the 1982 changes, the most minimalist set of demands of any Quebec administration since the "Quiet Revolution." In Brian Mulroney, Bourassa found an eager constitutional partner.

For a year Mulroney and Bourassa quietly negotiated a deal with the other provincial premiers whereby they would all support Quebec's conditions by obtaining the same accretions of power for themselves. The one exception was the essentially symbolic constitutional recognition of Quebec's "distinct society." The deal was consummated at Meech Lake on 30 April 1987, and when it was announced to a surprised and ungrateful nation, mega constitutional politics began in earnest.

The first ministers who negotiated the Meech Lake Accord failed to appreciate how much the 1982 amendments had transformed Canada's constitutional culture. They did not comprehend how much the Charter of Rights had converted a governments' constitution to a citizens' constitution,[3] nor how difficult it would be to combine the traditional practice of federal-provincial negotiations with the new requirement of legislative ratification. They compounded their difficulties by putting together a package which, under the new amending rules, required unanimous approval of all ten provincial legislatures plus the federal parliament and then announcing to the legislatures that they could debate the Meech Lake Accord all they wished so long as they did not change a word of it. Perhaps most fatally, the first ministers failed to commit themselves to any timetable and allowed the ratification debate to drag on for the three full years permitted by the constitution.

When time ran out in the spring of 1990, although the Accord had been ratified in all but two provincial legislatures, polling data showed that it was strongly opposed by a majority of Canadians outside of Quebec.[4] And while it may have had majority support in Quebec, it was by then a clear second choice to Quebec sovereignty. Round four ended with the country more divided than ever.

THE CANADA ROUND

The fifth round of mega constitutional politics, which Canadians have just lived through, has been by far the most exhausting, partly because, constitutionally speaking, Canadians were all tuckered-out from the previous rounds. But add to that the fact that in this round there was far more public participation than in any of the previous rounds. Not only was there the two-month referendum campaign at the end, but over the two years leading up to the Charlottetown Accord the public, through all kinds of committees and commissions, was "consulted" as never before.

Though relatively participatory, this pre-referendum process was fundamentally flawed. Throughout the public consultation stage, and indeed until the very end of the multi-lateral negotiations that produced the Accord, there was very little interaction between Quebec and what came to be known as the "Rest of Canada." The Canada Round was very much a two-nations round.

Immediately following the death of the Meech Lake Accord, Premier Bourassa, smarting from the rejection of Quebec's "minimal demands," cranked up the constitutional machine. In collaboration with separatist leader Jacques Parizeau he established a Quebec "estates general," chaired by two Quebec businessmen, Michel Bélanger and Jean Campeau, to consider Quebec's future. At the same time he encouraged a party committee chaired by Jean Allaire to consult Liberals throughout the province on constitutional options. These Quebec discussions focused entirely on the question of what Quebec needs to fulfill its national destiny. Not surprisingly, both Belanger/Campeau and Allaire concluded with highly autonomist reports. In May 1991 Quebec's National Assembly committed itself to a referendum on "the sovereignty of Quebec" not later than October 1992 and in the meantime to have a committee look at the "best offer" that might be forthcoming from the Rest of Canada.

Public discussions on the constitution got under way in the Rest of Canada just as the Quebec process was reaching its culmination. And the only way the public outside of Quebec could be persuaded to participate was by firm undertakings that unlike Meech this would not be a Quebec Round but a Canada Round. Thus the agenda was opened up to include all matters of constitutional discontent in the land, especially those neglected by the Meech

Lake Accord—aboriginal self-government and Senate reform. This meant that participants in the massive round of public hearings that went on at the federal and provincial levels in the Rest of Canada were playing an entirely different constitutional game from Quebec's.

It was this Rest of Canada process that created the agenda for the Charlottetown Accord. Its public discussion phase culminated at the end of February 1992 with release of the Beaudoin/Dobbie Report by a federal parliamentary committee following five mini constituent assemblies.[5] Through the spring and summer the Beaudoin/Dobbie proposals were modified and honed into a package of constitutional proposals through closed-door negotiations among the federal, provincial, and territorial governments and organizations representing the aboriginal peoples. Bourassa chose not to join this negotiating process until August. By then he was faced with a fully negotiated package which, though it contained pretty well all of Meech, had little else for Quebec and a lot more for the Rest of Canada, including an elected Senate in which Quebec would have no more power than any other province. It was at this point that the idea of guaranteeing Quebec 25 percent of the seats in the House of Commons—regardless of its population—was pulled like a rabbit out of a hat. It was the only way Bourassa could be persuaded to accept provincial equality in the upper house.

Unlike all the other components of the Charlottetown Accord the 25 percent guarantee had not been before the country in the two years of public discussion leading up to the Accord. It was a deal-maker but a referendum-breaker. Guaranteeing Quebec a secure place in the institutions of the central government is, potentially, a more integrative way of recognizing Quebec's special status than giving a whole lot of extra powers to its provincial legislature. But this novel idea was one for which the public had not been prepared. In Quebec it was not enough to serve as a surrogate for more provincial autonomy; outside Quebec it was considered grossly unfair and was by far the Accord's most objectionable feature.

THE FUTURE OF CONSTITUTIONAL POLITICS

The foregoing review of the five rounds of mega constitutional politics Canada has experienced over the last twenty-five years should make it clear why neither the people nor the politicians are in a hurry to launch a sixth round. The recent referendum may have demonstrated that Canadians are deeply divided in their sense of identity and political justice but it has, nonetheless, left them united in their constitutional fatigue. There are no politicians of any consequence in post-referendum Canada with any stomach for resuming the effort to fashion a grand constitutional restructuring designed to strengthen national unity and stem the tide of Quebec separatism. There are still some well-meaning intellectuals and some constitutional junkies who would like to have another kick at that can. But they will find no support from political leaders or the general public.

The federal election scheduled for 1993 may well bring about a change of government in Ottawa. But this is unlikely to change the picture. The pro-sovereignty Bloc Québécois (BQ) will be the only political party contesting that election on a constitutional platform. While the BQ may very well win the largest block of Quebec seats, its aim is not to restructure the Canadian federation but to break it up.

The resumption of mega constitutional politics in Canada now depends entirely on politics within Quebec. In Quebec, the prevailing mood after the referendum is entirely different from what it was after Meech Lake. The defeat of Meech immediately gave currency in Quebec to the myth of rejection—compounding the 1982 myth of imposition. In the year following Meech, Quebec was moving "serenely" towards sovereignty. Now the mood is entirely different. The rejection of the Charlottetown Accord by majorities both in Quebec and outside Quebec obviously cannot be interpreted as English Canada's rejection of Quebec. Premier Bourassa, though he campaigned strenuously for the Accord and lost, appears to have gained political strength in the process. Far from jumping on the sovereignist bandwagon, he is cleansing his party of its autonomist wing. Nor is the Parti Québécois in any position right now to stoke the *sovereigntiste* fires. Throughout the campaign the PQ was emphatic that a vote against the Accord was not a vote for sovereignty.

The picture could change dramatically over the next two years. Bourassa must call an election by late 1994. In that election, the constitutional issue will be front and center. Mega constitutional politics will resume after the next Quebec election if two conditions are met: first, the winning party is committed to obtaining more constitutional autonomy for Quebec; and second, the winning party subsequently wins a referendum in favor of some form of Quebec sovereignty. Then Canada will be in a real crisis of national unity, not just an apprehended crisis.

In these circumstances constitutional politics would likely take on a much more confrontational style. The long, elaborate process of public consultations and intergovernmental negotiations aimed at working out an accommodation of differences would be replaced by an exchange of ultimatums, threats, and counterthreats. The confrontation would not be over the right of French-speaking Quebeckers to form their own sovereign nation but about their right to force ethnic minorities in Quebec, especially aboriginal peoples, to be part of a sovereign Quebec. Such circumstances would pose a tremendous challenge to Canada's civilized ways; violence could supplant tedium as the central feature of our constitutional politics.

There is a good chance that Canada will avoid such an ugly turn of events. Premier Bourassa (or, if his health fails, his successor) may well duplicate René Lévesque's ironic feat of losing a referendum but winning the subsequent election. And he may be able to pull this off without having to promise Quebeckers some sort of restructuring of the federation as an alternative to independence. Only about one-third of Quebeckers support the complete, unqualified separation of Quebec from Canada. The constitutional status quo in a straight-up contest could prevail over pure independence.

The danger is that both sides may fudge their options so that Quebec will elect a government committed to a constitutional restructuring of the federation that the Rest of Canada has not the slightest interest in negotiating.

For Canada to forsake mega constitutional politics for a while does not mean that it will or should forsake any kind of constitutional reform. A great benefit of the country's exhaustion from dealing with big packages of constitutional reform would be to learn how to do ordinary, one-reform-at-a-time, constitutional politics.

The top priority, needing immediate attention, is the position of Canada's aboriginal peoples. In socio-economic terms, it is the native component of the population (roughly 4 percent) which suffers the greatest deprivation of substantive equality. And the continuing imposition of non-aboriginal rule over the aboriginal peoples constitutes Canada's most serious constitutional injustice. Canada's prolonged engagement with mega constitutional politics opened up an opportunity for aboriginal peoples to force a fundamental reconsideration of their colonized status. Aboriginal leaders have taken advantage of that opportunity to raise the constitutional expectations of their own people and to win majority support within the non-aboriginal community for the basic principle of aboriginal self-government within Canada.

On a regional basis, constitutional action on the aboriginal front is already under way. In November 1992, less than a month after the national referendum, another referendum in the Eastern Arctic, where 85 percent of the population are Inuit, voted in favor of a land claims settlement under which the region will be separated from the Northwest Territories and organized as the largely self-governing territory of Nunavut. In Yukon, after nearly twenty years of negotiations, agreement in principle has been reached on a land claim settlement giving that territory's native peoples a very large measure of self-government. Settlements of this kind are also under negotiation south of the sixtieth parallel in a number of provinces. Thanks to a 1983 constitutional amendment, provisions for aboriginal self-government obtained through these modern treaties are constitutionally secured.

For much of the aboriginal leadership, achieving self-government on a piecemeal, regional basis will not suffice. There will continue to be considerable pressure for another attempt at an across-the-board settlement of aboriginal issues. This pressure will be resisted by Canadian politicians. They will sense the inescapable linkage of the aboriginal question when it is dealt with on a national basis with all the other constitutional discontents. The aboriginal peoples themselves may have cause to question the wisdom of negotiating an omnibus constitutional settlement. Their Canada Round experience demonstrated both their own heterogeneity and the difficulty of reconciling the first ministers' negotiating style with the traditional relationship of aboriginal leaders to their communities.

Aside from the aboriginal issue, the other major elements of the Charlottetown Accord may be left alone for quite some time. There will be pressure from western Canada to do something about the Senate. But again, because it is virtually impossible to disentangle Senate reform from the Quebec issue, that pressure—which does not have a deep popular base—will not produce constitutional action.

There is some scope for micro constitutional reform through section 43 of the amending formula. Under this section, amendments concerning one or more provinces but not all provinces can be made with the agreement of the legislatures of the provinces affected and the federal parliament. Already New Brunswick's premier, Frank McKenna, has initiated a section 43 amendment that would make New Brunswick officially bilingual.

But if Canadians have any sense, they will, for quite some time, eschew formal constitutional change as the primary means of dealing with structural or institutional problems. There are a myriad of ways in which the Canadian federation can be made to work more efficiently and responsively without risking the heavy politics of formal constitutional amendment. Political will, not constitutional change, is all that is required to remove virtually all barriers to internal free trade. Similarly, a federal Prime Minister enlightened and bold enough to depart from the tradition of strict party discipline in the House of Commons and of political patronage in the selection of judges and senators could do much to enhance the credibility of the federation's central institutions. But don't hold your breath. It will be no more easy for politicians to break from these practices than for the intelligentsia to abandon its predilection for constitutional solutions to every national problem.

However, if Canadians are fortunate enough to kick their constitutional habit for a decent interval, the October referendum will have had more positive long-term results than its majority "No" might portend. Although that "No" means there was no popular consensus on a new set of constitutional arrangements, it may translate into a fairly long-term grumpy acquiescence in the constitutional status quo. That may be all it is reasonable to expect by way of agreement among the sovereign people of this multi-national state called Canada.

NOTES

1. Peter H. Russell, *Constitutional Odyssey: Can Canadians Become a Sovereign People?* (Toronto: University of Toronto Press, 1992), 75.
2. Andrew Cohen, *A Deal Undone: The Making and Breaking of the Meech Lake Accord* (Vancouver: Douglas and McIntyre, 1990), 165.
3. Alan C. Cairns, *Disruptions: Constitutional Struggles from the Charter to Meech Lake* (Toronto: McClelland and Stewart, 1991).
4. Cohen, *A Deal Undone*.
5. House of Commons, *Report of the Special Joint Committee on a Renewed Canada* (Ottawa, 28 Feb. 1992).

Parliament and Government

CLOSE-UP: THE BLOC IN THE CENTRE BLOCK — IRONY OR HYPOCRISY?

Parliamentary democracy can sometimes be ironic. Parliament provides a democratic forum for all Canadians, even those who might organize to separate from the rest of Canada. Parliament may be host to Canada's adversaries by virtue of its invitation to represent all interests that are democratically elected to the House of Commons and appointed to the Senate.

Many Canadians wondered during the 1993 federal election, as the Bloc Québécois swept Quebec, clinching 54 seats, how these sovereignist members could sit in the Canadian House of Commons as the official Opposition. What an electoral coup! How could the Bloc, which ran and elected its candidates in only one province, represent all Canadians? How could the BQ's leader, Lucien Bouchard, officially represent both official language communities while sitting in Canada's Parliament as a francophone sovereignist? Raised to the status of a living martyr after his brush with death in late 1994, Bouchard returned to Quebec to lead a referendum that could have dissolved the country.

What an irony! This was the first official Opposition with an agenda to separate from Canada. A populist republican francophone party whose manifesto status that its MPs "will have no other fidelity except towards Quebec" now found itself in the position of having to represent Canada's loyalty to the Queen of Canada, to Commonwealth ties, and to the imperial traditions of the parliamentary democracy of Westminster. That loyalty involves the guardianship of the majesty of the Canadian state in all of its institutions, its Royal prerogatives, traditions, and customs. The Bloc would now represent Canadian issues as if it were faithful to the traditional symbols of national unity.

A loose amalgam of separatists from across Quebec's political spectrum, led by a former Tory, the Bloc hardly fit the image of a traditional Opposition. Indeed, the irony of the Bloc's assuming the role of Her Majesty's Loyal Opposition garnered international attention as well as the skepticism and ire of the other parties in the House of Commons and the general public in Canada.

On the surface, the Bloc's behaviour in the House has been consistent with the traditional role of the official Opposition. Before the 1995 referendum, its daily attacks on the government seemed almost conventional. It spent most of its energy preparing for the theatre of the parliamentary **question period**. Day after day, the fiery former Conservative minister and pugnacious school board director from Roberval, Lucien Bouchard, would stand up to the challenge of government. Bouchard's bellicose exchanges with the government and other opposition parties provided the drama to punctuate otherwise drab news reports.

Almost every afternoon in Parliament, Bouchard and his House leader, Michel Gauthier, would rise to paint Ottawa as a relentless centralizing force that habitually crushed Quebec's demands. Quebec was shown to be at odds with the forces of federalism at virtually every turn of public policy: Ottawa's plan to reform the **social safety net** was a federal ploy to ignore Quebec's traditional demands for more autonomy in the delivery of services; Ottawa's youth employment program was an example of the costly overlap of jurisdictions; Ottawa's revision of the drug patent law was a threat to put the interests of Toronto drug companies over those of Montreal firms.

Fourth floor, Centre Block, House of Commons, is where the Bloc under Bouchard planned its daily attacks. By seven in the morning, the offices of Bouchard, Gauthier, and party Whip Gilles Duceppe were already busy. Staff and MPs pored over clippings and transcripts, looking for issues to raise in the House. By mid-morning, a list of potential issues was being prepared and staff researchers were getting to work on beefing up the questions. But the Canadian electorate was also aware that the Bloc and the PQ kept in close contact on the issues that inflame passions in Quebec.

Can it be said that the Bloc was a typical official Opposition under Bouchard's leadership? After all, the Canadian parliamentary system rests on the fundamental and essential confrontation between the government and the opposition. But the role of the opposition is only vaguely defined. Parliament's procedural bible, *Beauchesne's Rules and Forms of the House of Commons of Canada*, sixth edition, defines "official Opposition" thus: "The political party which has the right to be called the Official Opposition is the largest minority group which is prepared, in the event of the resignation of the government, to assume office."

By this definition, despite having the second-largest number of elected officials, the Bloc does not qualify as an official Opposition because it is not politically or ideologically prepared to assume office in the event of the resignation of the government. The governor general would never call on the BQ to form a government, even though the alternative, the Reform party, is itself almost as regional as the BQ, holding only two seats east of Saskatchewan. No other federalist party would ever consider supporting a sovereignist-separatist party from Quebec to replace the government.

Throughout 1993–95, the Bloc was careful to bring some all-Canadian issues, such as the peacekeepers' role in Bosnia and the American takeover of Canadian publishing firms, before Parliament. But it was the party's tough talk on Quebec that lent such an unprecedented character to the House. Even when the Bloc mounted a coherent social-democratic critique of government policy, its sovereignty goal rendered its views as an official Opposition illegitimate to most Canadians.

INTRODUCTION: DISTINGUISHING PARLIAMENT FROM GOVERNMENT

In Chapter 10 of this section, James J. Guy discusses the distinction between Parliament and government in our political system. In general, people tend to confuse Parliament and government, as they do the narrow and broad meanings of the term *government* itself. When the media report that "The government has just passed a bill into law," they are confusing the government, or the governing party, with Parliament as a whole. What they really mean

is that the government of the day, which sits in Parliament and has the mandate to govern for a limited period of time, has introduced a bill that its members have supported. When we refer to our "system of government," we are referring to a set of philosophies and to parliamentary institutions that comprise an executive and a legislative component. As a composite institution embracing these two components, Parliament provides the ongoing framework for making Canadian law.

From the government's perspective, Parliament is also a powerful tool for achieving the public agenda. By contrast, the **opposition** perceives Parliament as unreliable in protecting the interests of the majority of the electorate. Under Canada's electoral system of winning seats by pluralities, the popular vote is usually not reflected proportionally, and the majority of voters may consequently be inadequately represented in the most powerful legislative assembly in the country. One device that allows parliamentarians to make public their support for alternatives to government policies, and hence to indicate their representation of divergent views among their constituents, is the Private Member's Bill.

PRIVATE MEMBER'S BILL

A Private Member's Bill is a bill, introduced by an MP, that does not have government support. But as Susan Thorne points out in Chapter 13, with the development of a cohesive party structure and the increased burden of government work, private members' time in the House has gradually been reduced to only about five hours per week. Today, private members' bills do not often appear on the parliamentary agenda because they are pieces of legislation brought forward not by the government through its ministers, but rather through the initiative of an individual MP (in some cases, in support of an opposition party strategy).

It is also important to point out that the effectiveness of private members' bills is limited because they cannot involve financial expenditure. At present, the private member's bill serves largely to put a feather in the cap of an MP seeking to please his or her constituents. But current pressures to reform Parliament call upon MPs to play a far more independent legislative role — sometimes to vote against their party line — because national political parties no longer adequately reflect the regional demands of their constituents, which have taken on a greater urgency to be represented in the 1990s.

REPRESENTATION

Ours is a representative democracy, in which the elected members of the House of Commons and appointees to the Senate are expected to serve as our legislative representatives in Ottawa. One approach to the representation of constituents is to promote and support the opinions they are known to hold. The Reform party adopts this view of representation, almost obsessively requiring its leadership to reflect as regularly as possible the demands of both party members and constituents. Another way to represent constituents is by the old-fashioned Burkean rule, which holds that a representative is elected to decide, according to his or her own judgement and conscience, what is to be articulated on behalf of constituents.

The first approach would hold that, if women's issues are to be represented properly, then adequate numbers of women must be elected to Parliament to get the job done. From this perspective, a perfectly representative Parliament would have characteristics similar to those of the general Canadian population in terms of race, gender, ethnicity, occupation, religion, age, and other variables. In this regard, Parliament is and has always been highly "underrepresentative," and often simply "unrepresentative."

Women as a majority and other groups as minorities are significantly underrepresented. The circumstances determining women's presence in our parliamentary institutions are complex, involving issues such as who we choose to represent us and by what means, the fairness of our electoral system, points of access to political power for underrepresented groups, systemic discrimination against certain groups, and the urgent need for parliamentary reform. Lisa Young's contribution to this section, "Women in the House of Commons" (Chapter 14), touches on all of these factors, and offers many persuasive insights on the fundamental issue of female representation in our institutions of official politics.

PARLIAMENTARY REFORMS

Recently, pressures have been exerted to reform the institutions of Parliament. Not long after the election of the Liberals in 1993, the House of Commons implemented rule reforms that would give backbenchers more influence over government legislation. Prior to the reforms, the dominance of the Cabinet in the lawmaking process prevented backbenchers on both the government side and the opposition side from effective participation in the various stages of a bill before Parliament. The old rules limited debate, encouraged hardline partisan bickering in the standing committees, and gave opposition members little opportunity to make amendments to proposed legislation. A Cabinet minister can now send a bill to its relevant committee before the second-reading stage in the House of Commons. Committees can now deliberate without so many of the old pressures for strict party discipline, and can inject changes to the content of a bill to satisfy a broader range of perspectives. In addition, a minister can now approach a Commons committee to draft legislation and introduce it to the full membership of the House of Commons.

For some, reform is essentially a technical exercise aimed at refining and simplifying legislative operations. For others, reform needs to be directed at the institutions themselves — at the Senate, in particular. In Chapter 12, Randall White outlines three separate proposals for reforming the Senate. Proponents of Senate reform have always focussed on making the institution more useful, but not so powerful as to paralyze Parliament.

Magnus Gunther and Conrad Winn tell us, in Chapter 11, that the parliamentary reform debate in Canada goes beyond the specific issues raised above, and revolves in particular around concerns about regional fairness. Many Canadians — particularly in the West — think the federal government is controlled by central Canada. By reforming key institutions, they hope to make the federal system more democratic and more responsive to the needs of Canada's distinctive regions.

In Canada's system of government there are two basic ways in which regional interests can be addressed, and both have been considered for reform. One is by altering the division of constitutional powers between federal and provincial governments in order to achieve better and more efficient delivery of government services, and the other is by making federal institutions more reflective of regional diversity — for example, by making the Senate an elected body with specific regional representation.

The public's final verdict on parliamentary performance is always delivered at the polls. Our era is hard on legislatures and legislators: we expect Parliament to adapt readily to rapid socio-economic changes and to maintain its integrity and provide stability and continuity at the same time. Pressures for reform come from within the institution as well. The Reform party's mandate, for example, calls for revolutionary changes in the way Parliament operates.

Complicating the situation are other factors, from **partisan** wrangling to the frustration that the opposition and the public experience when it appears that the legislative process is over even before a bill has been given first reading in the House of Commons. For Parliament to survive, it will have to relieve these pressures by adjusting its procedures.

THINKING IT OVER

1. Based on the discussion in Chapter 10, explain in what way Parliament is a "system" of government. Are Canadians being served well by their parliaments as lawmaking bodies? Should we consider adopting a more efficient system, as suggested by Magnus Gunther and Conrad Winn (Chapter 11)? What are the advantages of separating the head of state and the head of government in the Canadian system?

2. Gunther and Winn (Chapter 11) point to the relationship between the executive and the legislative branches as a possible focus for reform. But what is it about Parliament that we want to reform? Why don't we leave Parliament as it is, and reform only the way in which we elect and appoint people to the House of Commons and the Senate?

3. Can we talk about reforming Parliament without doing something about the Senate? Summarize the three proposals in the article

by Randall White (Chapter 12). Which one makes most sense to you? Why?

4. A bill becomes law only after it has passed through a maze of complex procedures. Review the process and think about ways in which it could be reformed. Explain what a Private Member's Bill is, and summarize the success stories described by Susan Thorne in Chapter 13.

5. Do individual members of Parliament satisfy the representation needs of most of their constituents? In what ways can it be argued that Parliament is under- or unrepresentative? What improvements or reforms, if any, might be suggested to make Parliament a more representative body? Debate the statement that MPs are better off than the public they represent.

6. What does Lisa Young (Chapter 14) mean by the "mandate of difference"? What are some of the reasons Young identifies as contributing to the underrepresentation of women?

GLOSSARY

cross-party co-operation Co-operation among members of Parliament across party lines, a practice that tests the limits of party discipline and caucus solidarity.

head of government In the parliamentary system, the leader of the majority party in the legislature or a person able to form a coalition that will sustain the confidence of the legislature.

head of state The ceremonial executive who formally represents a nation-state, for example, a governor general, a monarch, or a president.

incumbency The state of holding an office or position. The term "incumbent" is often used in reference to a person who has previously won an election, is in office, and is running for the same position once more, against a first-time challenger.

mandate of difference The expectation among women and women's groups that women in legislatures will work within the system to open the political process to other women, serve as points of access for women's groups, introduce "private" issues

into the public agenda, and bring the multiplicity of women's perspectives into political debate.

opposition Members of Parliament who do not belong to the government party or who are not part of a governing coalition of parties.

partisanship A psychological attachment to a political party and its leadership that is often learned from family and peers and that usually grows stronger with age. The positive affect toward a political party tends to be reflected in attitudes and opinions, often in the face of adversity and pressure to change position on certain issues.

party discipline Refers to the ways in which members of a political party must accept the dictates of the party leadership and the provisions of the party platform, voting strategies, and parliamentary procedures.

question period The one-hour period held most days when Parliament is in session during which ministers have to answer questions put by the opposition as well as by members of the government party.

representation in content Substantive representation of the interests of a particular group, such as women, in elected parliamentary bodies.

representation in form The proportional numerical representation of a particular group or class of people, such as aboriginals, the unemployed, or women, in elected parliamentary bodies.

system of government The configuration of economic, political, judicial, and legislative decision-making institutions that a nation-state adopts in order to govern itself. In Western nation-states the two most frequently adopted systems are the presidential/congressional and the parliamentary. Some states are absolute monarchies. Many states combine aspects of the presidential and the parliamentary models of government.

ADDITIONAL READINGS

Atkinson, Michael. 1993. *Governing Canada: Institutions and Public Policy*. Toronto: Harcourt Brace.

Cassidy, Frank, ed. 1991. *Aboriginal Self-Determination*. Lantzville, BC: Oolichan Books.

Dawson, R. MacGregor. 1990. *The Government of Canada*. Revised by Norman Ward. Toronto: University of Toronto Press.

Eagles, Munroe, et al. 1991. *The Almanac of Canadian Politics*. Peterborough, Ont.: Broadview Press.

Fleming, Robert. 1992. *Canadian Legislatures, 1992*. Agincourt, Ont.: Global Press.

Gunther, Magnus, and Conrad Winn, eds. 1991. *House of Commons Reform*. Ottawa: Parliamentary Internship Program.

Lijphart, Arend. 1992. *Parliamentary versus Presidential Government*. London: Oxford University Press.

Normandin, P.G., ed. 1990. *The Canadian Parliamentary Guide, 1990*. Toronto: Info Globe.

Seidle, Leslie, ed. 1993. *Rethinking Government: Reform or Reinvention?* Ottawa: Renouf Publishing.

Sproule-Jones, Mark. 1993. *Governments at Work*. Toronto: University of Toronto Press.

White, Randall. 1990. *Voice of Region: The Long Journey to Senate Reform in Canada*. Toronto: Dundurn Press.

The Parliamentary System of Government

JAMES J. GUY

By the 1860s, the Canadian colonies had gained extensive parliamentary experience with their own legislative assemblies. And they liked what they had. At the time of Confederation, the parliamentary system of government had been operating in eastern and central Canada since the 1840s. Each province in Canada had a legislature, with a lieutenant-governor representing the Queen, and every province except Ontario had an appointed Upper House, called a legislative council or Senate, and an elected Lower House, called a legislative assembly (Assemblée nationale in Quebec).

By creating a federal Parliament, the Fathers of Confederation continued a **system of government** with which they were familiar, a system that had worked well in England for more than 700 years and in the years immediately preceding the federation of Canada.

Parliament essentially plays two different roles. One is to make laws — the general rules that govern Canadian society — to deal with all the major issues confronting Canada — the economy, the budget deficit and national debt, the tax structure, protection of the environment, and any other problem that has national importance. The other role is to act as a local representative, articulating the viewpoints of various interests in Canadian society and securing tangible benefits for each riding. These two roles often clash and, when they do, the latter seems to suffer the most consequences. Strong **party discipline** sometimes keeps each elected member of Parliament at odds with local interests. The powerful position of the Cabinet often discounts the ability of MPs to represent their constituents in Parliament.

Canadians, including those who are elected and appointed to serve as parliamentarians, expect Parliament not only to discuss openly the problems of the country but also to advance solutions. Most of the controversy over how well or how badly Parliament performs focusses on its lawmaking function. Members of Parliament, like citizens on the outside, are worried about the ability of Parliament to govern. Many of them are frustrated about the growing difficulty Parliament has in dealing with tough national issues, particularly economic issues, such as controlling the deficit and national debt, and moral issues, such as abortion. Just how does party discipline affect the ability of Parliament to govern?

Parliament is an institution that has called forth extreme assessments. Some heap it with criticism; others regard its performance in making public policy quite remarkable.

Some careful observers are dismayed that Parliament cannot govern effectively. Other equally thoughtful observers believe the critics exaggerate the weaknesses of Parliament and overlook its strengths.

SOURCE: Excerpted from *How We Are Governed: The Basics of Canadian Politics and Government* (Toronto: Harcourt Brace, 1995), pp. 131–32 and 40–43. Reprinted by permission of the publisher.

THE PARLIAMENTARY SYSTEM OF GOVERNMENT

Many of the basic features of British constitutional and institutional practice were adopted by Canadians as instruments for governing a large, complex society. The British North America Act, an act of the British Parliament, not only made Confederation a reality but established British parliamentary procedures, customs, and institutions in Canada. The act created a governing system in which British parliamentary institutions would function in both the national and the provincial governments. This "Westminster model" became a prototype of Canada's political system, modified to suit the political and governmental conditions created by Canada's vast size.

The ability to govern Canada is based on the assumptions that Parliament is legally supreme in the lawmaking process, that it possesses the sovereign right to govern, and that only its members are constitutionally empowered to represent the interests and viewpoints of the people of Canada. In the words of John H. Redekop (1983, 147), "no statutes can be enacted or amended, no taxes legally imposed and no funds legally appropriated unless formally approved by Parliament." Structured and legitimized by a constitution, Parliament is a governing body that consists of the Queen and her Canadian representative, the governor general, an elected House of Commons, and an appointed Senate.

In order to elect members of the House of Commons, Canada is divided into geo-political areas called "constituencies" or "ridings" (at present, there are 295 constituencies nation-wide). In each constituency, political parties choose a person to run in the election, or an individual may decide to run without party affiliation as an independent. On election day, the candidate who receives the largest number of votes is declared elected and is entitled to a seat in the House of Commons; he or she usually represents the platform of a political party as well as the many interests of constituents. The political party whose members win the most seats will, under normal circumstances, form the government. The leader of that party will be the prime minister.

While the Queen and her representative constitute the **head of state**, the prime minister is the **head of government** (see Figure 10.1). The prime minister and the Cabinet, whose members he or she chooses, are known collectively as "the government." The Cabinet has differentiated itself from Parliament, placing itself in the dominant position to control the lawmaking process, to oversee legislative proceedings, and to plan the general order of business and political agenda the country will consider. Government bills are rarely defeated in Parliament because the governing party almost always musters a majority of its legislative supporters in favour of its legislation.

Parliament itself is not the lawmaking body that many have come to believe; rather, it approves, amends, and rejects government proposals for laws. But Parliament mostly ratifies decisions made by the government, as they are presented by the appropriate minister and supported by a majority of members.

Although its involvement in the preparation of legislation is minimal, Parliament attempts to perform two important functions. The first function is to legitimize the actions of government, but only after rigorous deliberation. Parliament meets to scrutinize, debate, and compromise so as to make laws for all — laws that ideally are in the public interest. Most Canadians accept and obey government decisions because they think laws are made properly and rightfully in the parliamentary forum. Parliament remains the official meeting place in which the government of the day must explain, defend, and justify its policies.

The second function of Parliament is to act as a forum of representation for ordinary citizens. Here the institution may not meet the governing expectations of the public because, like the Cabinet, which is dominated by white Anglo-Saxon males, usually with business and professional connections, Parliament is a model of elite rule and is vastly unrepresentative of the people for whom it is supposed to speak. Usually about 90 percent of MPs are drawn from high-status occupations, compared with only 20 percent of all Canadians (Guppy, Freeman, and Buchan 1987).

Figure 10.1
Fusion of Powers

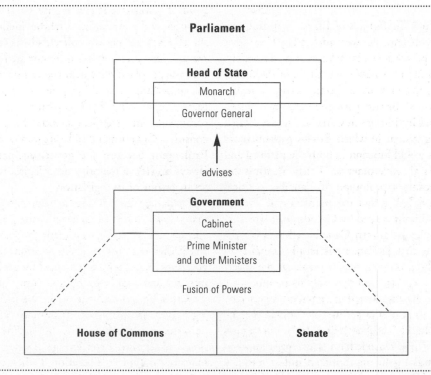

Very few women are elected to the House of Commons, and these few are almost all from highly educated and upper-income groups (see Figure 10.2). The character of Parliament as an exclusive club of upper-class white professionals and business persons affects the governability of Canada. Fundamental to the ability to govern is the ideal that Parliament will reflect the sociological composition of the people.

But can aboriginals and people of other ethnic and racial origins be properly represented by white, middle-aged males? Imagine what a more perfectly representative Parliament would look like: It would be 52 percent female, and would include more members of different ethnic and racial backgrounds; the average age would be 38 instead of 50; only about 1 percent, rather than nearly half, would be lawyers and the other 99 percent would be such people as plumbers, steelworkers, schoolteachers, professors, single mothers, and people who qualify for welfare. The representatives, the debates, and the rules processed through Parliament would have a very different character, being far more reflective of the needs of the general population.

The degree to which the membership of Parliament reflects the general population is called "descriptive representation." Taken to the extreme, descriptive representation is unlikely to occur in Canadian society. But it is certainly important for women, in particular, and people from various ethnic and racial backgrounds to feel they have authentic representation in the federal Parliament, in their provincial legislative assemblies, and on municipal councils. For many Canadians, legislatures are microcosms of society and provide visible

Figure 10.2

Distribution of Members of Parliament by Gender, 1980–1993

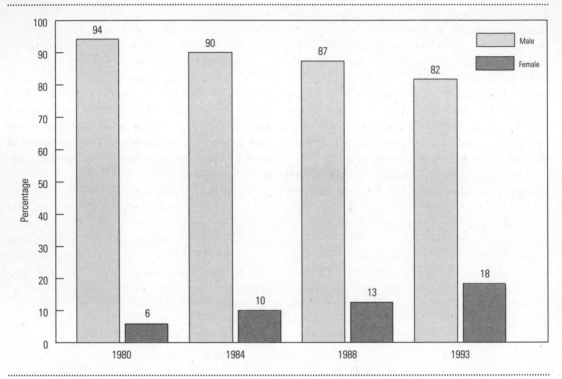

SOURCE: William Mishler and Harold Clarke, "Participation in Canada," in Michael Whittington and Glen Williams, eds., *Canadian Politics in the 1990s* (Toronto: Nelson Canada, 1990), p. 174. Reproduced by permission of the publisher.

evidence of whether governments are accessible to all citizens, regardless of gender, race, or national origin.

FEDERALISM AND GOVERNABILITY

One of the most contentious aspects of how we are governed in Canada is the federal–provincial relationship and how it steers the governing system in one direction or another. Canada's federalism has evolved as a system of government in which two levels, national and provincial, have governing authority over the same territory and the people who live and work there.

Frank R. Scott (1977, 35) noted that Canada's was the first governing system to combine parliamentary institutions with a federal structure of government. In this combination, governing institutions may not necessarily be complementary or may simply compound the difficulties we face in governing ourselves. A parliamentary system in combination with a federal system of government is adversarial; it can place political opponents in a combative and conflictive legislative relationship and make cooperation between levels of government difficult.

Canadians chose federalism because it permits a diversity of governmental organizations, political cultures, and public policies within a single nation-state. The practical problem for the framers of

Canada's federal system was to balance the need for a strong central government with the desire of the four original provinces to retain their decision-making autonomy in regional and local matters. Actually, the constitution makers of the 1860s foresaw a federation in which the central government could eventually exercise control over everything the provinces did (Milne, 1990). Strong centralizing powers were delegated specifically to, or reserved for, the federal government; other powers and jurisdictions were assigned to the provinces; and some were left for both levels to share.

The character of Canadian federalism has changed a great deal since 1867. Over the years, the provisions of federalism as outlined in the British North America Act, designating which aspects of governability were the jurisdiction of the provinces and which were that of the national government, have remained essentially the same, but the content of Canadian federalism has changed significantly.

Today, Canadian provinces retain remarkable governing vitality. In the course of Canada's federal history, they have become more powerful as subnational units, capable of successfully challenging federal jurisdiction in the courts, and skilful at organizing among themselves to strengthen provincial bargaining powers against Ottawa. Most of the provinces believe that, in many areas, they can govern more effectively and efficiently than can the federal government, especially in protecting and nurturing the health, safety, welfare, and morals of their people.

The constitutional division of powers between the federal government and the provinces has had an impact on the ability to govern. On the whole, federalism has constrained the federal government and continues to limit Canada's governability. Even in the 1990s, the debate continues over which level of government is best able to govern. Although Canada's federal system appears to be highly centralized, the federal government cannot govern Canada alone. It needs the co-operation of the provinces and their municipal governments.

The term "intergovernmental relations" is often used in Canada to refer to the complex web of interrelationships among governments — the federal government, the ten provincial governments, the two territorial governments, and the thousands of local governments — as they interact far more frequently than ever before.

Since the mid-1980s, one priority of the federal government has been to shift political power and economic responsibility to the provinces. As part of Ottawa's plan to reduce government spending, federal transfer payments and cost-sharing programs have been cut. Provincial and municipal officials have been compelled to look more to their own resources or to find new ones within their jurisdictions.

REFERENCES

Guppy, N., S. Freeman, and S. Buchan. 1987. "Representing Canadians: Changes in the Economic Backgrounds of Federal Politicians, 1965–1984." *Canadian Review of Sociology and Anthropology* 24: 417–30.

Milne, David. 1990. "Canada's Constitutional Odyssey." In Michael Whittington and Glen Williams, eds., *Canadian Politics in the 1990s*, 3rd ed. (pp. 313–35). Toronto: Nelson Canada.

Redekop, J.H. 1983. *Approaches to Canadian Politics*. 3rd ed. Scarborough, Ont.: Prentice-Hall Canada.

Scott, Frank R. 1977. *Essays on the Constitution: Aspects of Canadian Law and Politics*. Toronto: University of Toronto Press.

Parliamentary Reform: An Overview

MAGNUS GUNTHER
CONRAD WINN

The Canadian Parliament is neither greatly admired nor greatly understood, but this misfortune is not a recent phenomenon. Stephen Leacock's description of Parliament as "a place where men come together merely to hear the latest legislation and indulge in cheers, sighs, groans, votes and other experiences of vitality" is only marginally less despairing than the comment of the recent Speaker, the Honorable John Bosley, "If I had an impression when I [first] got here, it was that the institution was moribund and useless . . ." [1]

It is only fair to add that Mr. Bosley did in fact change his mind after sitting in the House for a few years:

I am no longer persuaded of [the useless and moribund nature of Parliament], having spent three years here . . . the institution has a lot more going for it . . . than it is generally given credit for in the public . . . the more one gets to know this institution, the more one realizes how effective it can be. [2]

Bosley's concern about Parliament's inadequacy, shared by many other members as well as a large segment of the Canadian public, has a long-standing pedigree. In his *Modern Democracies*, published in 1921, Lord Bryce raised the general question of whether there had been a decline in the power of legislatures, particularly in the late nineteenth and early twentieth centuries. Bryce did not provide an unequivocal answer to his own question except in the case of Australia and Canada, which had experienced no decline, he felt, since standards had never been high enough for the possibility of decline in the first place. [3]

Even in the case of Canada, there has nonetheless existed a myth of a golden age of legislative authority when individual legislators were not only able to hold executives accountable but were also able to initiate public policy in a significant way. The ability to dismiss an executive has traditionally been considered the legislature's most important power, as Walter Bagehot maintained in his well-known *The English Constitution*. [4]

Thomas Hockin's overview of Canada's legislative history shows that there was indeed such a golden age. Between 1848 and 1864, the "Assemblies were able to exercise their preeminence over the executive" in all the provinces and especially in the province of Canada. [5] For example, between 1855 and 1864, the Lower House of the Province of Canada brought about nine significant changes in government. But this "flexible" parliamentarism was an aberration, since executives could generally dominate the Lower House before 1848 and certainly after 1878, when the rise of mass parties led to the creation of the "structured" parliamentarism which prevails today.

The legislative Garden of Eden prior to 1878 was hardly the utopian equivalent of its biblical

SOURCE: "Parliamentary Reform: A Background Note and Introduction," in *House of Commons Reform* (Ottawa: Parliamentaryship Program, 1991), pp. 1–8. Reprinted by permission of the authors.

antecedent. The heightened power of parliamentarians made government itself almost impossible, providing Canada with a close approximation of the immobilism and unacceptably weak government characteristic of the Third and Fourth Republics in France. Canada's golden age was an age of crisis and instability, providing an illustration of how heightened parliamentary sovereignty can be a very mixed blessing. Professor Franks' book, *The Parliament of Canada*, is persuasive in its compelling argument that legislative reform should be judged by the criterion of whether it works rather than by any consideration of theoretical elegance.[6] An accurate assessment of whether or not any given reform would be successful requires both a realistic assessment of how the system currently works as well as of the expected benefits of change. Certain kinds of reform are impossible to achieve within the framework of our current parliamentary and constitutional system. There are trade-offs between executive authority and legislative participation which require open and honest acknowledgement. Perhaps it is time to think the unthinkable and ask whether the reforms that many of us are seeking would indeed require another kind of legislative system, for example, a congressional system along the American model. Before Canadians pine for another system, however, they need to understand better their own. In the Canadian House of Commons, government and opposition are intrinsically adversaries, unlike the situation in the U.S. Congress. Because of this intrinsic adversarial character, reform will tend to either strengthen the hand of government or strengthen the hand of the opposition. It is difficult to conceive of the possibility of strengthening the position of individual members without also in some respect weakening the hand of the executive.

The institutional framework within which politicians do their work sets powerful limits on the possible effects of evolutionary reforms as opposed to revolutionary change in the essential character of the system. For example, the existence of winner-take-all presidential elections in the United States goes a long way to explain the failure of third parties in American national politics. The costs of losing

are too great to justify persistent or recurrent third party candidacies. In the Canadian case, the executive's fundamental dependence on a legislative majority sets a real limit on the executive's ability and willingness to permit legislative autonomy and participation.

The Canadian dilemma of trade-offs between executive authority and legislative participation is illustrated by the way in which key reforms were brought about under the Liberal government in 1968, the first significant reform to parliamentary procedures in decades. In order to make more effective use of parliamentary time, the Trudeau government proposed and the opposition consented to changes which would see more work done (and legislative time saved) by referring most non-financial bills to committee after second reading and then having these bills reported back to the House before Third Reading. The power of opposition and of backbenchers in general seemed, in theory, to benefit from this change. But the government was only prepared to accept the change provided that there was also a procedure introduced (Standing Order C75) which would allow the government to pry bills out of committees, if stuck there, and prevent filibusters at the Report Stage. A battle royal ensued, ending only when the government resorted to closure to get C75 on the Standing Order book, thus recreating a kind of pipeline debate crisis.

The fact that the Canadian executive depends on a legislative majority while the American executive does not require legislative sanction for its own persistence means that committees in Canada can never have the autonomous law-making power of their American counterparts. Because the executive's legislative stakes are so much higher in Canada than in the United States our MPs will continue to want to vote with their parties rather than vote "freely" as do American Congressmen. Party discipline will not erode easily.

While the magnitude of the executive's legislative stakes remains much higher in Canada and while Members of Parliament will retain their partisan loyalty, their sense of frustration will not abate easily. Comments made in 1984 to the McGrath committee [a Commons legislative reform committee] by MP Keith Penner illustrate the frustrations and complex dilemmas caused by our legislative system:

> The executive suffocates and dominates to an alarming degree; and I want to know if this committee can do anything at all to redress or correct this frightening imbalance.
>
> I want to tell you, ... that the only times I have really felt good around here as a private member, as a backbencher, were during the minority of 1972 to 1974. I remember on numerous occasions having to call home and say I could not make it for dinner because the minister was having us in his office for coffee and sandwiches to discuss a policy issue. I can remember a backbencher shaking his finger under the nose of the finance minister and saying, "If you bring that in, do not count on me." And I loved it. It was fantastic. Parliament lived. I did not care when in the middle of a meal, with guests at home, the phone rang and the Whip said, "Get down here for a vote," because if I was on side, I did not care at all ... there were other times, in the last Parliament, when big Choo-Choo Charlie said to get down here for a vote or the government might fall, and I felt like saying that seems to me like a goddamned good reason to stay home.
>
> The other time when I felt good around here is when the government did not know where to go and it turned to the parliamentarians and said, "Can you come up with anything at all? Anything will do."
>
> We formed the special committee on Indian Policy, for example. It is only one example; I happened to be involved in it but the government did not have any ideas at all; they just drew a blank and told us to go to it, and there were no holds barred; that was great fun. We formed a committee without partisanship, as legislators, and we tried to find answers.[7]

Successful reform requires not only a realistic assessment of how the legislative system functions prior to reform and an empathetic appreciation of how members view their role, but also a careful consideration of *what one wants from reform*. For example, reforms to the parliamentary process could be explored in terms of their potential impact on the participation of women, income distribution, or the likelihood of an active human rights–oriented foreign policy for Canada. In practice, most discussions of reform focus on the distribution of powers and responsibilities among the principal institutions of our political system, without regard for policy consequences. A persistent theme is concern about an all-too-powerful executive. Such a concern ought logically to prompt interest in mechanisms available to Parliament for controlling and limiting government. Where the concern of reformers is the excessive power of bureaucracy, then the focus of the institutional change might be the role of Parliament in limiting "closed door" bargaining sessions among groups of public servants, both federal and provincial, representing or negotiating with different interest groupings. If on the other hand the object is to heighten ministerial control of the bureaucracy, then reform should focus on ways to bring the bureaucracy to heel.[8] Alternatively, the focus of reform might be to enhance the efficiency and effectiveness of the executive — for example, changes of the kind sought by the Trudeau government in 1968 for the purpose of enhancing the executive's ability to speed up legislation.

Finally, one's concern might be to augment the autonomy of the individual Member of Parliament at the expense of the party rather than the executive. If the purpose of reform is to improve the quality and quantity of information on government operations available to Members of Parliament irrespective of where they sit in the chamber, the focus of reform might well be the semi-autonomous agencies or agents of Parliament which do provide such information.

The purpose of reform is almost always an end result rather than a never-ending process. Yet the reality of reform is often a process which, if not quite never-ending, is nonetheless not fully satisfactory. Various factors can prompt or stimulate the process of reform; for example, new governments, motivated by their continuing "opposition mentality," are often the source of reform.

Five clear criteria by which institutional change can be assessed are as follows:

1. Does the reform make the House more efficient?
2. Does it make the opposition more effective?
3. Does it make the House more representative?
4. Does it promote more efficiency among the individual MPs?
5. Does it give Parliament more control of the executive?

With respect to the Lefebvre/McGrath reforms, the answer is a definite "yes" to all these questions, though on some matters the answer is more muted or uncertain.

NOTES

1. Canadian Study of Parliament Group, *Seminar on the Future of the House of Commons and Parliament and Accountability* (1982), p. 3. Leacock is quoted by P.G. Thomas, "Theories of Parliament and Parliamentary Reform," *Journal of Canadian Studies* (Summer 1979), p. 57.

2. Canadian Study of Parliament Group, *Seminar on the Future of the House of Commons*, p. 3.

3. G. Lowenberg, "The Role of Parliaments in Modern Political Systems," in G. Lowenberg, ed., *Modern Parliaments* (Chicago: Adine Athertine, 1971), p. 1.

4. W. Bagehot, *The English Constitution* (London: Oxford University Press, 1961), p. 140.

5. T.A. Hockin, "Flexible and Structured Parliamentarism: From 1848 to Contemporary Party Government," *Journal of Canadian Studies* 14 (Summer 1979), p. 8.

6. C.E.S. Franks, *The Parliament of Canada* (Toronto: University of Toronto Press, 1987).

7. Keith Penner, M.P., in Canadian Study of Parliament Group, *Seminar on the Future of the House of Commons*, p. 6.

8. C. Campbell and H.D. Clarke, "Conspectus, Some Thoughts on Parliamentary Reform," in H.D. Clarke et al., *Parliament: Policy and Representation* (Toronto: Methuen, 1980), pp. 307–11.

Three Proposals for a Reformed Senate

RANDALL WHITE

What follows summarizes three of the most prominent official proposals for an elected Canadian Senate advanced in the 1980s — one from the legislative branch of the federal government and two from provincial governments (one in Western and one in Atlantic Canada).

PROPOSAL I The first proposal was put forward by a joint committee of the federal Senate and House of Commons in Ottawa in 1984. What follows reproduces an abridged version of the chapter of the committee's report that outlines its specific recommendations. Everything that appears is taken directly from the report, but subsidiary parts of the original text have been omitted, to achieve a degree of brevity broadly comparable to the other proposals.

PROPOSAL II What follows reproduces the specific recommendations of the 1985 "Triple E" proposal developed by a committee of the Alberta Legislative Assembly and published in *Strengthening Canada*. Everything that appears is taken directly from the original document, with no omissions. For the sake of clarity one endnote has been added, taken from background material in the original document.

PROPOSAL III What follows reproduces a proposal tabled by the Government of Newfoundland and Labrador at the November 1989 First Ministers'

Conference in Ottawa. Unlike the other proposals, it is cast in the form of a potential constitutional amendment. Again, everything that appears is taken directly from the original document, the only omissions being material dealing with matters other than Senate reform. Two endnotes have been added, taken from background material in the original document.

The proposals have been reproduced with the kind permission of responsible authorities in Ottawa, Edmonton, and St. John's.

PROPOSAL I

EXCERPTS FROM *REPORT OF THE SPECIAL JOINT COMMITTEE OF THE SENATE AND OF THE HOUSE OF COMMONS ON SENATE REFORM.*
Ottawa, January 1984. Chapter 6. An Elected Senate: The Committee's Proposal.

Having concluded that an elected Senate would best meet our objectives for reform, the Committee faced a wide range of choices on questions such as the method of election, the distribution of seats among the provinces, and the powers of the Senate. The choices ranged from a Senate with powers equal to those of the House of Commons and with

SOURCE: *Voice of Region: The Long Journey to Senate Reform in Canada* (Toronto: Dundurn Press, 1990), pp. 278–89. Reprinted by permission of the publisher.

an equal number of seats for each province, to an advisory rather than a legislative body, with a distribution of seats proportionate to the population of each province.

We tried to strike a balance between these extremes. . . .

The Electoral System

The Committee had to choose between a majority system and proportional representation. . . .

Proportional representation is the system used to elect the Australian Senate and most western European legislatures. Essentially it gives each political party a number of parliamentary seats corresponding roughly to the percentage of votes cast for it. . . .

Opponents of proportional representation argue that if the system were used for Senate elections . . . it would facilitate the emergence of purely regional parties. . . .

We have been impressed by this argument and have concluded that Senate reform should not stray from its true objectives. . . .

. . . the Committee found the present single-member plurality system simple and satisfactory. Voters are familiar with the system, having used it for generations to elect representatives to all levels of government. . . .

We should not conclude these comments . . . without noting that we were urged by a number of witnesses to take a first-hand look at how proportional representation works in practice for Australian Senate elections. . . . We do recognize . . . that a comprehensive review of alternative electoral systems for the Canadian Senate should ideally include an on-the-spot examination of the system used in Australia.

Constituency Boundaries

. . . voters in each senatorial constituency would elect only one representative, as is the case in House of Commons elections. . . . Although population should be one criterion in determining the boundaries of Senate electoral districts, greater importance should be attached to geographic, community, linguistic and cultural factors than is the case for House of Commons constituencies. . . . At present Quebec is divided into 24 senatorial districts, the boundaries of which were delineated in 1856. They no longer have much relation to contemporary realities and should be abolished. . . .

The Senatorial Term and the Timing of Elections

We recognized that in choosing single-member constituencies we had to ensure that the role of elected senators would be quite clearly different from that of members of the House of Commons. Our proposal to restrict senators to a single term of office does this. . . .

It was difficult to decide how long the single term should be. . . . We . . . decided to recommend a nine-year term, with one-third of the senators being elected every three years. . . .

These triennial elections should be held separately from Commons elections and on fixed dates — for example, on the second Monday of March in every third year. A number of witnesses recommended that Commons and Senate elections be held simultaneously, with half the Senate being elected at each Commons election . . . we had . . . objections . . . the power to dissolve Parliament would give the government a certain measure of control over the Senate. We believe that senators would have more independence, and more authority as regional representatives, if their elections were separate. . . .

Legal Provisions Governing Senate Elections

Legal provisions will be needed governing such matters as who is eligible to vote or to stand as a candidate for election. These provisions should be set out in a new statute designed specifically to govern all aspects of Senate elections, including election expenses. . . .

The Distribution of Seats Between the Provinces and Territories

At present, Senate seats are divided according to the principle of four equal geographic regions — Ontario, Quebec, the Western provinces and the Atlantic provinces. The principle of equality is not followed strictly, because the four Atlantic provinces have a total of 30 seats in the Senate, compared with 24 for each of the other regions. . . .

A number of witnesses argued strongly that each province should have equal representation in the Senate. . . .

. . . In Canada the application of the equality principle would enable the five least populous provinces — that is, those accounting for 13.4% of the Canadian population — to have a majority in the Senate if they had the support of the territorial representatives, whatever their number. . . . Moreover, if this system were adopted, the only province with a francophone majority would see its relative weight in the Senate, which stood at 33 per cent of the seats in 1867 and today stands at 23 per cent, plummet to less than 10 per cent.

We therefore concluded that, while providing for substantial over-representation of the less populous provinces and territories, we should propose a distribution that reflects the Canadian reality more accurately than simple numerical equality can do. . . .

. . . most members of the Committee favoured the following distribution: Ontario and Quebec would retain the same number of seats that they have now (24), and the other provinces would be given 12 seats each, with the exception of Prince Edward Island, which would be given 6. Yukon and the Northwest Territories would both have increased representation. This formula would produce a Senate with 144 members. . . .

The Senate's Powers

Almost all the witnesses who spoke in favour of an elected Senate recommended that the Senate not be able to overturn a government. We agree fully.

In a parliamentary system, a government cannot serve two masters, whose wills might on occasion be diametrically opposed.

A number of witnesses maintained that an elected Senate ought to have the same legislative powers as the House of Commons or, more accurately, that it should continue to have the powers assigned to it by the *Constitution Act, 1867*. . . . If there were persistent disagreement between the two chambers, the disputed bill might be left in abeyance, or a joint committee composed of members from each house could try to agree on a mutually satisfactory redrafting. Some people proposed that if the disagreement persisted, a joint session of the two chambers could be held to resolve it by a majority vote; and if that failed, both houses could be dissolved and an election called.

. . . if the Senate enjoyed an absolute veto, the parliamentary process would become considerably more unwieldy than if it had just a suspensive veto. The government would have to be responsible to both houses. Double dissolution could mean a proliferation of elections, and the threat of dissolution could become an instrument of government control over senators. But the principal factor in our decision not to accord the Senate an absolute veto was the possibility, if not the probability, of our parliamentary institutions continually becoming deadlocked. . . .

We therefore decided that it was wiser and more in keeping with the character of parliamentary government to give the Senate the power to delay but not altogether prevent the adoption of measures voted by the House of Commons. The Senate would therefore have a suspensive veto of a maximum of 120 sitting days, divided into two equal periods of 60 days. Supply bills would not be subject to any delay. . . .

The Double Majority

To ensure additional protection for the French language and culture, we accept the argument of a number of witnesses that legislation of linguistic significance should be approved by a double major-ity in the Senate. Two methods for calculating such a majority were proposed to the Committee. One called for a majority of both francophone and anglophone senators. The other called for a major-ity of all senators that would have to include a majority of the francophone senators. . . .

Such a voting procedure would achieve its purpose only if the Senate veto on these matters were absolute . . .

We propose that, at the time of swearing in, sen-ators would be asked to declare whether they con-sider themselves francophone for purposes of the double majority.

Ratification of Appointments

We believe that order in council appointments to federal agencies whose decisions have important regional implications should be subject to Senate ratification within a period of perhaps 30 sitting days. If the Senate did not reject an appointment within that period, it would be deemed to have rat-ified it.

Internal Organization of the Senate

Under section 34 of the *Constitution Act, 1867*, the Speaker of the Senate is appointed and removed by the Governor General, on the recommendation of the Prime Minister. . . . We feel that the independence of the Senate would be increased if it would elect its own Speaker after each triennial election. . . .

. . . we believe that the government and opposi-tion supporters in the Senate should elect their own officers.

We considered the question of whether senators should be eligible for membership in the Cabinet. . . . The majority of Committee members . . . believes that if ministers are drawn from the Senate, cabinet solidarity would prevail over their responsibility as regional representatives. . . . We conclude therefore that senators should not be

eligible for cabinet office or for a position as par-liamentary secretary. . . .

Witnesses have suggested that regional caucuses should be created, grouping senators from a given region regardless of their party affiliation, in order to emphasize their role as regional representatives. Such a practice would accord with the spirit and general intent of our report. . . .

PROPOSAL II

REPORT OF THE ALBERTA SELECT SPECIAL COMMITTEE ON SENATE REFORM.
Edmonton, March 1985. Recommendations.

THE PURPOSE OF THE CANADIAN SENATE

IT IS RECOMMENDED THAT

The Senate of Canada should maintain as its primary purpose the objective established by the Fathers of Confederation, namely to represent the regions in the federal decision-making process.

In addition,
a) the Senate should continue to act as a body of "sober second thought";
b) another original purpose of the Senate, that is, to represent property owners, should be abandoned immediately;
c) the Senate should not be a forum for inter-governmental negotiations.

METHOD OF SELECTION

1. Current Membership

IT IS RECOMMENDED THAT

a) The tenure of current Senators should be termi-nated through an equitable severance process.
b) The termination of tenure should be accom-plished as quickly as possible to facilitate an imme-diate move to the new system.

2. Method of Selection and Basis of Representation of New Senators

IT IS RECOMMENDED THAT

a) The Senate should consist of 64 Senators, six representing each province and two representing each territory;

b) Senators should be elected on a first-past-the-post basis, a system now in use in federal and provincial elections;

c) Senators should represent constituencies whose boundaries are identical to provincial boundaries;

d) Senators should be elected for the life of two provincial legislatures;

e) In each province, three Senators should be elected during each provincial election, with each voter being able to vote for three candidates;

f) The qualifications for candidates to the Senate should be the same as those for Members of Parliament;

g) Upon winning an election, Senators should be required to resign from any provincial or civic elected office they hold.

POWERS OF THE SENATE

IT IS RECOMMENDED THAT

a) The Senate should have the power to initiate any legislation except a money or taxation bill;

b) Notwithstanding (a), the Senate should have the power to initiate supply resolutions relating to the Senate's own operational budget;

c) The Senate should have the power to amend any bill, after which the House of Commons would consider the amendment;

d) The Senate should have the power to veto any bill except a supply bill;

e) The Senate should retain the existing 180 day suspensive veto over constitutional issues;

f) The House of Commons should have the power to override a Senate veto on money or taxation bills by a simple majority;

g) The Senate should vote on a money or taxation bill within 90 days and on other bills within 180 days after it is sent to the House of Commons;

h) The House of Commons should be able to override any amendment (veto) passed by the Senate on a bill other than a money or taxation bill, by a vote that is greater in percentage terms than the Senate's vote to amend;

i) Non-military treaties should be subject to ratification by the Senate;

j) All changes affecting the French and English languages in Canada should be subject to a "Double Majority" veto, that is, a majority of all Senators combined with a majority of French-speaking Senators or English-speaking Senators, depending on the issue.[1]

SENATE ORGANIZATION

IT IS RECOMMENDED THAT

a) The traditional opposition and government roles in the current Senate be abolished, including the positions of Government Leader and Opposition Leader;

b) Senators should be physically seated in provincial designations, regardless of any party affiliations;

c) Each provincial delegation should select from its membership a chairman; chairmen should sit at the pleasure of the provincial delegation;

d) A Speaker should be elected by a majority of the Senate at a specified time every four years, and the Senate may, at any time, initiate an election for Speaker by a two-thirds vote;

e) The ten provincial chairmen, headed by the Speaker of the Senate, should constitute a "Senate Executive Council";

f) The Senate Executive Council should determine the order of business of the Senate, appointment of committee chairmen and membership of committees;

g) The characterization of legislation, that is, the determination of whether a bill is or is not a money or taxation bill, should be carried out by joint agreement of the Speakers of the House of Commons and the Senate, in accordance with the British definition of a supply bill;

h) Senate Executive Council members should receive remuneration and staff assistance in addition to that received by other Senators;

i) Senators should not be eligible for appointments to Cabinet.

OTHER RECOMMENDATIONS

IT IS RECOMMENDED THAT

a) The requirement that First Ministers' Conferences meet on a regular basis should be entrenched in the Constitution;

b) First Ministers should have the power to ratify Supreme Court appointments by a majority vote;

c) The use of emergency powers by the federal government should require ratification by a majority vote of First Ministers except in war time;

d) Federal powers of reservation and disallowance are antiquated and unnecessary and therefore should be abolished.

PROPOSAL III

CONSTITUTIONAL AMENDMENTS ON SENATE REFORM PROPOSED BY THE GOVERNMENT OF NEWFOUNDLAND AND LABRADOR.
First Ministers' Conference, Ottawa, November 1989.

The *Constitution Act, 1867* is amended . . . by adding thereto immediately after section 1 thereof, the following section:

2. (1) In order to uphold the fundamental characteristic of Canada and preserve the distinct society of Quebec . . . the Senate of Canada shall, solely for the purposes set out in paragraph (2), be divided into linguistic divisions in which all senators from every province in which English is the provincial official language shall constitute the English Division and all provinces in which French is the provincial official language shall constitute the French Division and each province where, by constitutional provision, English and French are provincial official languages shall constitute a separate Division.

(2) Every constitutional amendment affecting linguistic or cultural rights or the civil law system including the proportion of civil law judges on the Supreme Court of Canada shall be submitted to a separate vote in each linguistic division of the Senate and no such constitutional amendment shall be deemed to have been approved by the Senate unless it shall have been approved by the majority of the whole Senate and the majority in each division of the Senate. . . .

Sections 21 to 36 inclusive and Sections 51A and 53 of the *Constitution Act, 1867* are repealed and the following substituted therefore:

The Senate

21. The Upper House, styled the Senate, constituted by Section 17 of this Act, shall be composed of members called Senators who shall be drawn from throughout Canada in accordance with the provisions of sections 22 and 23.

22. (1) Each of the Provinces of Canada is at all times entitled to be represented in the Senate by 6 Senators.

(2) Any province which may be created pursuant to the provisions of the Constitution, after this section comes into force, shall on and after its creation be entitled to be represented in the Senate by 6 Senators.

23. (1) Senators shall be chosen by the people of Canada through popular election in accordance with the provisions of this section.

(2) Except as otherwise provided in sub-section 5, Senators shall be elected for a term of 6 years and Senators shall be eligible for re-election.

(3) Senate elections shall be held throughout Canada on the last Monday of October every three years.

(4) The first election, hereinafter referred to as "the initial election," will be held on the last Monday of October not less than one year nor more than two years after this provision comes into force.

(5) One half of the Senators elected from each Province at the initial election shall be elected for a term of 3 years and the balance of the Senators elected at the initial election shall be elected for a term of 6 years.

(6) The Parliament of Canada may make laws in relation to the method of election, the creation of senatorial districts, and procedures for the election of Senators, including laws in relation to the financing of elections, the funding of election campaigns, and the nomination of candidates.

24. Any person is eligible to be elected as a Senator for a Province if that person:

(a) Is a Canadian citizen;

(b) Is of the full age of 18 years as at the date of the election;

(c) Has been ordinarily resident within that province for an aggregate period of at least five years during the ten years immediately preceding the election and is resident within that province at the date of the election; and

(d) Is not a member of the House of Commons or a Legislative Assembly at the date of the election.

25. A Senator shall not be eligible to be a Minister.

26. If a vacancy occurs in the Senate through the death or resignation of a Senator at any time before the final year of the term, then such a vacancy shall be filled by a by-election to be held within 90 days. The Senator to be elected to fill the vacancy shall be elected for the balance of the term of the Senator who vacated the seat.

27. The Senate is empowered to establish its own procedures for the election of the Speaker of the Senate and the conduct of its business.[2]

28. (1) Bills proposed to Parliament, other than bills for appropriating money solely for the ordinary annual essential services of the government or for imposing any tax or impost, may originate in the Senate equally as in the House of Commons.

(2) A Bill shall not be taken to impose taxation, by reason only of its containing provisions for the imposition or appropriation of fines or other pecuniary penalties, or for the demand or payment of appropriation of fees for licences or services.

29. (1) A Bill certified by the Speaker of the House of Commons as being a Bill to appropriate money solely for the ordinary annual essential services of the government shall not be required to be passed by the Senate, if the Senate has not within 45 sitting days either passed the Bill as presented or amended it in a manner agreeable to the House of Commons.

(2) A Bill which appropriates revenue or money for the ordinary annual essential services of the government shall deal only with such appropriation.

30. Neither a defeat of a government-sponsored Bill, motion, or resolution in the Senate nor a specific confidence motion in the Senate shall constitute a vote of non-confidence in the government so as to require the government's resignation.

31. (1) A joint standing committee known as the Reconciliation Committee which shall be composed of ten Senators and ten members of the House of Commons is hereby established for the purpose of this section.

(2) The Senate and the House of Commons shall elect from among its members persons to be appointed to the Reconciliation Committee established pursuant to this section.

(3) Where any Bill that has been passed by one House and presented to the second House

(a) has been refused passage by the second House;

(b) has not been finally dealt with by the second House and not less than 45 sitting days have elapsed since the Bill was presented to the second House; or

(c) has been duly amended by the second House and the first House has duly advised the second House that it does not concur in all or some of the amendments made by the second House, the Bill in the form in which it was presented to the second House but with such amendments made by the second House as may be concurred in by the first House in the case of a Bill to which clause (c) applies, may be referred by the Speaker of either House to the Reconciliation Committee for the purpose of seeking to reconcile the differences and seek a mutually acceptable compromise.

32.   (1) No appointment of a person to be a chairman, president, chief executive officer or director of any of the Crown Corporations, Boards or Commissions subject to the application of the federal Financial Administration Act shall have effect until such time as the appointment of that person has been affirmed by the Senate.

(2) If no decision is taken by the Senate within 60 sitting days of a nomination being referred to it, then the appointment shall be deemed to have been affirmed by the Senate.

Section 47 of the *Constitution Act, 1982* is repealed.[3]

NOTES

1. Candidates to the Senate would declare themselves French- or English-speaking at the time of being nominated and would be judged in that way by the electorate.
2. This section would permit, for example, the establishment of a non-partisan Senate executive council made up of the chairpersons of the 10 provincial delegations, as proposed by the Alberta Task Force on Senate Reform.
3. This repeals a section of the current constitutional amending formula which allows the Senate to be bypassed on certain constitutional amendments. Its repeal is essential in order to ensure an effective vote by the linguistic divisions. Otherwise such votes could be overridden by the House of Commons after six months.

Private Member's Bill:
Success Stories in Canada's Parliament

SUSAN THORNE

Many texts about Canadian government mention Private Members' Bills only in passing or with a footnote, and many people who are not close to Parliament may be unfamiliar with this type of legislation. Even when a Bill is publicized in the press, as with Lynn McDonald's recent Non-Smokers' Act, readers may not realize that it represents something fairly unusual. Unusual because it is a piece of legislation put forward not by the government through its ministers, but rather through the initiative of an individual M.P.

Private Members' Bills may sometimes be associated with the Opposition but, in fact, members of all three political parties make use of this option in roughly equal measure. Another distinctive feature of these Bills is that Free Voting, without pressure from party Whips to take a certain stand, is practiced to a large extent — M.P.s of very different political stripes may be found on the same side of an issue.

Private Members' Bills used to suffer exceptionally high mortality rates: for example, of the hundreds submitted for first reading between 1944 and 1974, only 14 were enacted. But with Royal Assent for Bill C-255: the Public Pensions Reporting Act, on March 26, 1986, a new trend appears to have begun. C-255 could be seen as the harbinger of change, for it is the first of seven Private Members' Bills to pass successfully through both the House and the Senate during the 33rd Parliament. New procedural rules in 1986 made it easier for this type of legislation, and events suggest we will see it used increasingly by more M.P.s.

THE EARLY DAYS

In the early days of Confederation, most of the business of Parliament was initiated by private members. But with the development of a cohesive party structure and a greater burden of government work, private members' time was demarcated and gradually reduced to a maximum of four hours per week by 1955. A financial limitation also stated that Private Members' Bills could not involve the expenditure of public funds. Debate and voting had to be accomplished within a one-hour period, so that ninety percent of these Bills were "talked out" when speeches exhausted the allotted time.

Since there was little expectation that they would become law, Private Members' Bills were used largely for their publicity value, to draw attention to an issue or to goad the government to action. One of the great practitioners of this strategy was NDP Member Stanley Knowles, who introduced numerous Bills of his own over his long political career. He revived the use of the Private Member's Bill after the war with his 1946 Act to amend the existing legislation concerning striking railway workers, which eventually brought about an equivalent amendment on the part of the government.

SOURCE: "Private Member's Bill: Success Stories in Canada's Parliament," *The New Federation* (February/March 1990): 21–23. Reprinted by permission of New Federation House.

Many Private Members' Bills deal with moral or contentious issues which governments wish to avoid. Capital punishment, the rights of the unborn, and making Canada a nuclear-free zone were each the subject of at least one Bill in the eighties. Human rights, the subject of Pat Carney's 1980 Act to Prohibit Discrimination on the Grounds of Sexual Orientation, and freedom of information, the subject of Bill C-254, which sought access to certain records concerning Defence, are other frequent concerns.

Members of the Opposition and back-benchers of the majority party have found in these Bills one of the few available means of self-expression. A case in point is that of Jean Chrétien, who drew attention to himself with a Bill changing the name of TransCanada Airlines to Air Canada twenty-five years ago. A number of such Bills focus on matters of symbolic importance: holiday observances, like the one for a John A. Macdonald Day, the flag, or proposals for a new national anthem. The Beaver Bill, introduced in 1974 by the late Sean O'Sullivan using the Private Members' route, led to the official designation of the beaver as Canada's "sovereign symbol."

In 1986, reforms based on the recommendations of the McGrath Committee significantly changed the outlook for Private Members' Bills. Under the new rules, up to twenty Bills at a time are selected by random draw for debate, and a special committee can designate some as "votable," meaning that they will be brought to a vote after a maximum of five hours' deliberation. The traditional relaxing of party discipline for private members' business has been continued in the practice of calling Members' names for voting according to seating rows, rather than by party.

Some recent cases demonstrate the different possibilities for using the new procedure.

C-204: BANNING CIGARETTE ADVERTISING

The first bill to successfully pass through all the necessary steps under the new rules was a well-publicized one, Bill C-204: the Non-Smokers' Health Act. Its sponsor, New Democrat Lynn McDonald from the Toronto riding of Broadview-Greenwood, had put forward a similar but short-lived Bill before the new procedure was in place, and asserts that C-204 "wouldn't have had a hope without the McGrath Report."

McDonald's two-pronged Bill provided for the banning of all tobacco advertising, and guaranteed smoke-free zones in areas under federal jurisdiction, including trains and planes. The government seemed unresponsive. In one exchange with Ms. McDonald in the House, Health Minister Jake Epp voiced the opinion that banning cigarette ads would stop very few smokers.

However, the issue had captured public attention and the support of anti-smoking groups such as the Canadian Cancer Society. Within a year, Epp had made an apparent about-face with a Bill of his own, C-51: the Tobacco Products Control Act, containing less restrictive measures about print advertising and smoking in civil service work places.

With two similar Bills under discussion, both pressure groups and Members of the House were at times confused as to which to support. Certainly timing was important for the Epp legislation if it was to be passed before C-204, and McDonald is convinced the government tried to kill her Bill in Committee and at the Third Reading stage.

Former Speaker of the House John Bosley recalls that the question of party discipline vs independence was very much on Members' minds as the Final Reading for Bill C-204 approached in May 1988. "To my knowledge, there was a lot of conversation about how to vote; people were asking whether they should be free to vote according to their consciences." Conservative members in particular wondered how the government would look if this Bill passed when there was a Minister's Bill on the same subject.

One M.P. at the time maintains that the net effect of efforts to keep Tory members in line was to alienate some votes. The outcome was uncertain to the end, when a tally of 74 ayes and 57 nays vindicated McDonald's efforts. "Mine was the test case, the first controversial one," she says. "If it's something significant, you've got to build all-party support to succeed."

C-255: DISCLOSURE OF INFORMATION

Bill C-255, which received Royal Assent in March 1986, had its beginnings several years before, during the Clark government. In 1979, W. Paul McCrossen, Tory M.P. for York-Scarborough, was investigating the possible redesign of the public pension system for Sinclair Stevens when he realized there were no available figures on the total cost of public employees' pensions. It appeared that the total amount could be as high as ten billion dollars, enough to seriously affect the accuracy of government budgeting. In fact, John Crosbie's ill-fated December 1981 budget acknowledged in a footnote that funding of the pension plan was not included.

Two days after the submission of Crosbie's budget, the government was defeated and McCrossen was not re-elected. When he was returned to Parliament in the 1984 election, after several months as a lobbyist in Washington, D.C., he found that Liberal and NDP Members had also become interested in the issue. A Bill to require disclosure of pension information seemed assured of general support. Fortuitously, an Auditor-General's report was expressing concern about the topic at about the time C-255 was being drafted.

But, with the old procedural rules still in effect, controversy or long-winded opponents could "talk out" the Bill's time on the floor, so careful preparation was necessary. "The trick was to get it through in that one hour," McCrossen explains. For the Bill's First Reading, Finance Minister Michael Wilson agreed that only his Parliamentary Secretary and McCrossen would speak to the Bill. On its Final Reading, there was such a conspiracy of silence by all three parties that amendments were introduced and moved with no discussion: speeches were kept down to a total of twenty minutes and the Bill was ready for Senate deliberation on February 11, 1986.

"I was applying in Canada a process that I'd become accustomed to in the U.S., where all Bills are effectively Private Members' Bills," says McCrossen. In this situation, a Private Member's Bill was appropriate because the issue involved the employees of a number of ministries — from the R.C.M.P. to the M.P.s themselves — and was thus beyond the scope of any individual Minister's mandate.

McCrossen feels that C-255 had the benefit of widespread goodwill in the House, heightened by awareness of the McGrath Committee recommendations, soon to be implemented.

C-205: SAVING THE RAILWAY STATIONS

Another good illustration of multi-party collaboration was Gordon Taylor's Bill C-205: the Heritage Railway Stations Protection Act, which found supporters in all parts of the House.

Heritage Canada, alarmed at the 1982 demolition of West Toronto Station by CP Rail, had been lobbying to save Canada's historic railway stations, many of them important community landmarks, and most of them woefully unprotected by any legislation. Liberal M.P. Jesse Flis had introduced Bill C-253 in June 1984, but John Turner's election call not only stopped his Bill, but also cost Flis his seat.

Alberta Tory Gordon Taylor, M.P. for Bow River, took up the cause and presented his own Bill C-211, identical in content to its forerunner. This Bill was sidetracked by a committee referral and failed to be heard before the end of the session.

Undaunted, Taylor introduced a further incarnation of the same text, and it received First Reading on October 6 1986. At the time, he says, he felt he had unusually strong support from members of every party. Saskatchewan NDP Member Les Benjamin tried to facilitate the Bill's quick passage by moving that it be put through all three readings at once. Benjamin spoke eloquently of Regina's historic Union Station and declared: "I will beg, grovel, snivel . . . to save the stations."

Such measures seemed unnecessary. Bill C-205 moved smoothly through the House, receiving a unanimous vote on its final reading. Such approval seemed to ensure quick approval in the Senate.

But the pro-heritage forces had not reckoned on the powerful influence of Senator Ian Sinclair, past CEO of Canadian Pacific, and the man responsible for the destruction of West Toronto Station. Sinclair was solidly opposed to the Bill and was effective in having it sent off to committee not once but twice, a rare procedure for the Senate.

At this point, Heritage Canada mounted a newspaper campaign, urging readers to telephone party leaders in the Senate. As the telephones rang repeatedly with calls from all over the country, the extent of support for Bill C-205 became obvious.

On September 22, 1988, the Bill returned for its Third and Final Reading. Talk of an election was in the air, lending a sense of urgency to the proceedings. A last-minute motion was made to delay the Bill in order to check the correspondence of the French and English texts, but was withdrawn. When the vote was finally called, there was only one dissenter: Senator Ian Sinclair.

The success of this Bill was a dramatic conclusion to Taylor's political career: he retired with the dissolution of Parliament three months later.

C-292: FAIR BANKING PRACTICES

Paul McCrossen's experience with Bill C-292 suggests that Private Members' Bills can be an effective tool in pressuring the private sector as well as government.

Early in 1988, the Finance Committee, of which McCrossen was a member, was pressuring the Canadian Bankers' Association for changes in certain practices, such as charges to depositors for NSF cheques. The banks were unable to agree and the situation was at a stalemate.

The usual procedure at this point would have been for the Committee to produce a report for government consideration and response. But the demise of the current Parliament was anticipated,

so McCrossen took the singular step of drafting a Private Members' Bill which would implement the Committee's recommendations. Bill C-292: the Bank Act Bill (Amendment Regarding Fair Banking Practices) was tabled on June 6. Luck seemed to be on its side when it was picked the following week in the random draw for debate in the House. Then it was designated a votable Bill, ensuring more discussion time and an eventual vote.

Seeing that there was a strong possibility of the Bill's success, the banks re-opened talks with the Committee. A deal was struck: when all the banks had implemented the Committee's recommendations, C-292 would be withdrawn.

One by one the banks agreed, until only the Toronto-Dominion demurred; being singled out, it too backed down, in August. C-292 had accomplished its objective.

But McCrossen found himself with a peculiar problem. "You couldn't withdraw a Bill without unanimous consent of the House," he recounts. "There seemed to be no way of stopping the juggernaut." The Bill was listed for debate in its turn, and there was no procedure to defer this. McCrossen arranged to be out of town on the first occasion when the Bill's Third Reading was scheduled and it dropped to the bottom of the order of precedence. When it came up again for debate, McCrossen was ready to request unanimous consent for the Bill's withdrawal. By pre-arrangement, M.P. Bob Horner then asked that his own Bill C-264, concerning literature for illicit drug use, be given higher priority for debate — in effect, replacing McCrossen's Bill. The move enabled C-264, in danger of expiring before the end of the session, to clear both the House and the Senate within two weeks.

"While I didn't get a second Bill in my name, I count it as a Bill," McCrossen sums up regarding C-292.

As these accounts show, Private Members' Bills have the potential to be used in various ways. They also provide an opportunity for co-operation across party lines on an issue of merit. John Bosley sees in this an opportunity for "a restoration of the spirit of collegiality in the House. Through that, it becomes a place where one can iron out things beyond partisan interests."

Others would describe the recent developments as an imperfect revolution. The Non-Smokers' Health Act, given Royal Assent last June, has not yet been proclaimed. Lynn McDonald angrily dismisses the rationale for this delay — the need to draft further regulations for implementing the Act — as unlikely, given the full Parliamentary endorsement of C-204.

While the present government has brought in reforms which enhance the Private Member's role, it appears unprepared to accept the full consequences.

Women in the House of Commons: The Mandate of Difference

LISA YOUNG

Although women remain a minority in the Canadian House of Commons, their numbers are increasing steadily. By 1994, a woman (Kim Campbell) had become Canada's first female prime minister, although only for a few months. A woman had led a major opposition party (the NDP) and a woman had become deputy prime minister. Up from only 5 percent in 1980, women make up 18 percent of the membership of the House of Commons. Women's increasing presence in national politics raises the question of what implications, if any, the election of women will have on the political process and public policy in Canada.

There is no consensus among people who study women in politics about the extent to which the election of women will affect Canadian politics. Many studies of barriers to the election of women have implicitly assumed that the election of women will make governments more responsible to the needs and interests of women. This assumption is supported by research on women in American and Scandinavian legislatures (Mueller, 1987; Welch, 1985; Sinkkonen and Haavio-Mannila, 1981; Skjeie, 1988).

Other observers, however, posit an *inverse* relationship between women's numerical representation in electoral politics and political responsiveness to the women's movement. Mainstream political parties, they argue, can avoid and have avoided hard

programmatic commitments to the women's movement by recruiting highly visible and like-minded women. The recruitment of these women cannot translate into changes in public policy because parties, particularly those pursuing policy agendas inspired by neo-conservatism, are unwilling to address the structural sources of women's oppression (Gotell and Brodie, 1991).

This chapter will examine the factors that have contributed to the steadily increasing number of women elected to the Canadian House of Commons since 1972. It will also discuss the "mandate of difference" that the Canadian women's movement has created for the women elected to the Commons.

ELECTION OF WOMEN TO THE CANADIAN HOUSE OF COMMONS

In 1921, Agnes Macphail became the first woman elected to the Canadian House of Commons. Her election set a precedent, but did not presage a rapid increase in the number of women elected to the House. Between 1921 and 1972, the presence of women in the House of Commons ranged from zero after the 1949 election to five after the 1962 election. Of the eighteen women elected during this period, six were the widows of former members of Parliament and one was the wife of a former MP.

SOURCE: Adapted from "Fulfilling the Mandate of Difference: Women in the Canadian House of Commons," in Jane Arscott and Linda Trimble, *In the Presence of Women: Representation in Canadian Governments* (Toronto: Harcourt Brace, 1997), pp. 84–91. Used by permission of the publisher.

Barriers to Women

With women currently constituting about 18 percent of the membership of the House of Commons, Canadian women remain significantly underrepresented in numerical terms. Moreover, although one Aboriginal woman and several women from visible minority groups have been elected, the women in the House are not representative of the cultural diversity of Canadian women.

One reason for the persistent underrepresentation of women is the poor fit between the heavy demands of political careers and the family responsibilities women have traditionally assumed. This is all the more significant a barrier in Canada, as MPs may have to travel long distances between their constituencies and Ottawa on a regular basis. Because women were, at least until recently, less likely to have the professional status and networks that men considering political careers enjoyed, they faced particular challenges in terms of finding money to contest nominations and mount campaigns. Finally, rigid gender roles and perceptions that politics is a male

Table 14.1

Women as Proportion of Candidates and MPs by Party, 1980–1993

Year	Party	As Candidates		As MPs	
		No.	% of total	No.	% of total
1980	Lib	23	8	12	8
	PC	14	5	2	2
	NDP	32	11	2	6
	Total	69	8	16	5
1984	Lib	45	16	5	13
	PC	23	8	19	9
	NDP	64	23	4	13
	Total	132	16	28	10
1988	Lib	51	17	13	16
	PC	37	13	21	12
	NDP	84	29	5	12
	Total	172	19	39	13
1993	Lib	64	22	36	20
	PC	67	23	1	50
	NDP	113	38	1	11
	BQ	10	13	8	15
	Ref	23	11	7	14
	Total	277	24	53	18

SOURCE: 1980–88: Lisa Young, "Legislative Turnover and the Election of Women to the Canadian House of Commons," in Kathy Megyery, ed., *Women in Canadian Politics: Toward Equity in Representation* (Toronto: Dundurn Press, 1991), Table 3.1; 1993: Elections Canada, news release, September 28, 1993, and *Official Voting Results: Synopsis: 35th General Election* (Ottawa: Chief Electoral Officer of Canada, 1994).

preserve have made it difficult for women to consider a political career.

There are also aspects of the Canadian electoral system that pose barriers to the election of women. The persistence of these barriers is demonstrated both by the low proportion of MPs who are women and by the difference between the percentage of candidates who are women and the percentage of MPs who are women (see Table 14.1). Although the difference has narrowed over time, women candidates are still somewhat less likely to be elected than their male counterparts. This suggests that women continue to be more likely than men to be nominated in "unwinnable" ridings. It has proven difficult for parties to break this pattern. The combination of Canada's single member plurality electoral system and the extremely decentralized candidate selection process Canadian parties employ makes it very difficult for parties to adopt any kind of workable affirmative action program for women

or other underrepresented groups (Erickson, 1993; Young, 1994).

Increasing Numbers of Women Elected

Despite these barriers, the number of women elected to the House has increased steadily, if slowly, since 1972. Canadian women are better represented in numerical terms in the Canadian House than in the national legislature of any other industrialized country using a single member electoral system except New Zealand (see Table 14.2). When Canada is contrasted with the United States or Britain, it becomes clear that aspects of the Canadian political system have contributed to the steady increase in the number of women elected.

In comparative terms, the rate of turnover in the Canadian House of Commons is high, reflecting the small number of "safe" seats in Canadian elections and the tendency of many MPs to retire after

Table 14.2

Women as a Proportion of National Legislators, Selected Countries

Country (Year of Election)	Electoral System [a]	% of Total Seats Held by Women
Sweden (1994)	PR	41.0
Norway (1993)	PR	39.4
Iceland (1991)	PR	23.8
New Zealand (1993)	SMP	21.2
Australia House of Representatives (1993)	SMM	21.1
Germany (1990)	Mixed	20.5
Canada (1993)	SMP	18.3
Ireland (1992)	PR (STV)	12.1
U.S. House of Representatives (1994)	SMP	10.3
U.K. (1992)	SMP	9.2
Italy (1992)	PR	8.1
U.S. Senate (1994)	SMP	6.0

[a] *PR stands for a proportional representation system, and PR (STV) stands for a PR system using a single transferable vote instead of a list. SMP stands for a single member plurality, or first past the post, system, and SMM stands for a single member majority system. See Young, 1994.*

SOURCE: Lisa Young, *Electoral Systems and Representative Legislatures: Consideration of Alternative Electoral Systems* (Ottawa: Canadian Advisory Council on the Status of Women, 1994), p. 5; *New York Times*, September 27, 1994, p. A24; National Democratic Women's Network *Bulletin*, December 1994.

only one or two terms (Blake, 1991). Because the composition of the House of Commons changes significantly after almost every election, **incumbency** does not create as much of a barrier to the entry of new groups into the Canadian House as it would if the rate of turnover were lower (Young, 1991; Erickson, 1993).

Although access to adequate financial resources remains a problem for women considering a political career, Canadian electoral finance laws help to level the playing field. The *Election Expenses Act* of 1974 introduced limits on the amount that candidates and parties could spend in elections, created a generous tax deduction for contributions to candidates and parties, and provided for partial reimbursement of elections expenses to registered parties and candidates winning more than 15 percent of the vote. By preventing the excessive spending that characterizes American campaigns, broadening the contributor base, and reducing the personal financial risks assumed by candidates, these rules have made the financial barriers facing potential candidates less daunting than they would be in a system that was less extensively regulated.

In addition to these structural characteristics, several other factors encouraging the election of women came into play in the 1970s and 1980s. First, the position of women in Canadian society evolved significantly during this period. Women became more likely to gain a university education, pursue a career outside the home, and enter a profession. This gave some women — most of them middle-class and white — access to the personal and financial resources necessary to mount a competitive campaign.

Second, the Canadian women's movement has exerted pressure on the parties to nominate more women. In 1970, the Royal Commission on the Status of Women identified the absence of women from public life as a significant obstacle to the achievement of equality for Canadian women and called on political parties to nominate more women and to integrate women into the mainstream of party activity. This call was echoed by the newly formed National Action Committee on the Status

of Women (NAC) and by women in the media. Since the early 1970s, women have formed several organizations with the purpose of increasing the number of women elected. These groups include Women for Political Action (1971–79), the Feminist Party of Canada (1979–81), the Committee for '94 (1984–present), and Canadian Women for Political Representation (1986–88). There are also numerous groups working at the provincial level (Maillé, 1990). In addition, NAC, the Canadian Advisory Council on the Status of Women (CACSW), the Fédération des Femmes de Québec (FFQ), and other women's organizations and advisory councils have issued calls for the election of more women and have proposed reforms to the electoral system to reduce barriers to the entry of women.

The net effect of these efforts has been to increase public awareness of the underrepresentation of women, and to place pressure on the parties to remedy the situation. Groups like the Committee for '94 have also fostered the creation of informal networks of women involved in partisan politics, which have in turn facilitated the diffusion of ideas and information regarding techniques for electing women.

The final factor contributing to the growing number of women elected to the House of Commons is the effort of women within the parties. In recent years, the women's organizations within the three parties came to focus their attention on the election of women. Prior to the 1993 election, the NDP women's organization successfully advocated an affirmative action program (with the goal of gender parity) that required that constituency associations conduct a mandatory candidate search to look for female, visible minority, aboriginal, and disabled candidates before the nomination was held.

The PC and Liberal women's organizations have focussed on recruitment and training of potential candidates. The National PC Women's Federation established a "talent bank" as a means of recruiting female candidates for the 1993 election, and provided assistance to potential candidates through a mentoring program, help finding an official agent, and training in fundraising techniques (National PC Women's Federation, 1989).

REPRESENTATION OF WOMEN

The "Mandate of Difference"

The efforts of the women's movement and women in the parties to elect more women represents a strategic decision to seek power within the confines of the existing political system. Chantal Maillé (1990, p. 26) has suggested that the groups engaged in this "electoral project"

> simultaneously reached the conclusion that political power is the nerve centre of social change. They realized the necessity of appropriating this power and finding ways to overcome the series of obstacles identified as being responsible for the political under-representation of women.

The choice of pursuing the legislative route does not preclude the women's movement's pursuit of other avenues of political change, including use of the courts, traditional lobbying techniques, media campaigns, grassroots mobilization, and "unconventional" social protest. It does, however, represent an acceptance of the institutions of formal politics and a commitment to seeking change through the existing political system (Vickers, 1992). Although there is no unanimous support of this project in the Canadian women's movement, and although many activists believe it naïve to think that women working in established parties will further the interests of women, a significant segment of the movement remains committed to increasing the number of women in the Canadian House of Commons.

This electoral project goes beyond a call for employment equity in the "hiring" of politicians. Rather, it calls for the election of women *as women*. Embedded within the project is the assumption that the election of women will lead to substantive changes in the nature of political institutions and the content of public policy. Because of this assumed linkage between **representation in form**, or numerical representation, and **representation in content**, or substance (Brodie, 1991, p. 47), there is an expectation that women, once elected, will act

in the interests of women. This involves working within the political system to open the political process to other women, serving as points of access for women's groups, introducing "private" issues onto the public agenda, and bringing the multiplicity of women's perspectives into political debate. In this sense, the electoral project has created a "mandate of difference" for female politicians (Skjeie, 1991, p. 234). This mandate forms the basis on which feminist organizations and academics evaluate the performance of female politicians. It also presents a significant challenge to the representational practices that have traditionally governed parliamentary behaviour in Canada.

Representation in the Canadian House of Commons

The two most significant forces governing the behaviour of Canadian members of Parliament are partisanship and region. Parliamentary parties structure the organization of the House and influence virtually every aspect of a member's political life. Although this can be attributed in large part to the strict party discipline of the Canadian Parliament, it is also a consequence of most members' personal commitments to their party, the significant role that party affiliation plays in electoral politics, and the structuring of MPs' Ottawa lives along party lines.

As one might expect in a country characterized by inter-regional tensions and distinct provincial or regional political cultures, region follows party as a representational imperative for MPs. The significance of region is demonstrated by the formation in the Liberal and PC parties of formalized regional caucuses that bring together MPs and Senators from each region or province on a regular basis when the House is in session.

While acknowledging the salience of region as a representational imperative for MPs, most studies of legislative behaviour in Canada have denied that gender may constitute a similar imperative. Writing in 1974, Jackson and Atkinson (p. 139) argued that there is no demonstrated link between identity and policy preferences. More recent accounts of the Canadian

Parliament have ignored the issue, focussing instead on the role of MPs' *wives* (Franks, 1987, p. 89).

Although it might have been possible to dismiss the potential importance of gender for legislative behaviour in 1974, it is more difficult to do so today. During the period from 1972 to 1993, the feminist electoral project helped to open the three parliamentary parties to women and created a mandate of difference for these women. While its source is different from that of the regional representational imperative, the feminist mandate of difference creates similar expectations for female MPs. Just as many members of Parliament must represent regional concerns within the constraints of partisanship, female MPs in Canada often find themselves representing gender concerns within the constraints of both partisanship and regionalism.

It is difficult to determine the extent to which women MPs act as representatives of women in their parliamentary work. Much of this work goes on behind closed doors in Cabinet and party caucus meetings. One very visible form that this representation takes is **cross-party cooperation** among female legislators. For some feminist observers, cross-party cooperation on certain issues is seen as a manifestation of the limited alliances that are the "minimum expression of unitedness" among female legislators, a demonstration that feminism can transcend partisanship (Jonasdottir, 1988, p. 55). Cross-party cooperation is also seen as a temporary strategy women can use to compensate for their limited numbers in most elected bodies. Moreover, cooperation across party lines is a good indicator of some measure of gendered consciousness in a parliamentary system governed by tight party discipline, precisely because it flies in the face of the most significant behavioural norm within the institution: party solidarity.

REFERENCES

Blake, Donald E. 1991. "Party Competition and Electoral Volatility: Canada in Comparative Perspective." In Herman Bakvis, ed., *Representation, Integration and Political Parties in Canada*. Toronto: Dundurn.

Brodie, Janine. 1991. "Women and the Electoral Process in Canada." In Kathy Megyery, ed., *Women in Canadian Politics: Toward Equity in Representation*. Toronto: Dundurn Press.

Erickson, Lynda. 1993. "Making Her Way In: Women, Parties and Candidacies in Canada." In Joni Lovenduski and Pippa Norris, eds., *Gender and Party Politics*. London: Sage.

Franks, C.E.S. 1987. *The Parliament of Canada*. Toronto: University of Toronto Press.

Gotell, Lise, and Janine Brodie. 1991. "Women and Parties: More Than an Issue of Numbers." In Hugh Thorburn, ed., *Party Politics in Canada*, 6th ed. Toronto: Prentice-Hall.

Jackson, Robert, and Michael Atkinson. 1974. *The Canadian Legislative System*. Toronto: Macmillan.

Jonasdottir, Anna. 1988. "On the Concept of Interest, Women's Interests and the Limitations of Interest Theory." In Jones and Jonasdottir, eds., *The Political Interests of Gender: Developing Theory and Research with a Feminist Face*. London: Sage.

Kohn, Walter. 1984. "Women in the Canadian House of Commons." *American Review of Canadian Studies* 14.

Maillé, Chantal. 1990. *Primed for Power: Women in Canadian Politics*. Ottawa: Canadian Advisory Council on the Status of Women.

Mueller, Carol McClurg. 1987. "Collective Consciousness, Identity Transformation and the Rise of Women in Public Office in the United States." In Mary Fainsod Katzenstein and Carol McClurg Mueller, eds., *The Women's Movements of the United States and Western Europe*. Philadelphia: Temple University Press.

National P.C. Women's Federation. 1989. *Initiatives: Re-Election Driven–Revenue Driven—A Strategic Plan Towards 2000*. Ottawa: P.C. Women's Bureau.

Sinkkonen, Sirkka, and Elina Haavio-Mannila. 1981. "The Impact of the Women's Movement and Legislative Activity of Women MPs on Social Development." In Margherita Rendel, ed., *Power and Political Systems*. London: Croom Helm.

Skjeie, Hege. 1988. *The Feminization of Power: Norway's Political Experiment (1986–)*. Oslo: Institute for Social Research.

Vickers, Jill. 1992. "The Intellectual Origins of the Women's Movements in Canada." In Constance Backhouse and David H. Flaherty, eds., *Challenging Times: The Women's Movement in Canada and the United States.* Montreal: McGill-Queen's University Press.

Welch, Susan. 1985. "Are Women More Liberal Than Men in the U.S. Congress?" *Legislative Studies Quarterly* 10: 125–34.

Young, Lisa. 1994. *Electoral Systems and Representative Legislatures: Consideration of Alternative Electoral Systems.* Ottawa: Canadian Advisory Council on the Status of Women.

———. 1991. "Legislative Turnover and the Election of Women to the Canadian House of Commons." In Kathy Megyery, ed., *Women in Canadian Politics: Toward Equity in Representation.* Toronto: Dundurn Press.

Bureaucracy, Public Policy, and Administration

CLOSE-UP: CAN BUREAUCRACIES GO BAD?

Sometimes a government agency can lose sight of its legal mandate and break the very laws it is expected to implement. When this happens in government, administrative and political lines get blurred and an agency's functions begin to reflect what political scientists sometimes call a *bureaupathology*. When a bureaucracy violates the public policies of the very government it works for, something offensive happens to the fundamental principles of public administration.

Such was the case with the RCMP security service, now called the Canadian Security Intelligence Service (CSIS). From the late 1960s, behind its cloak of secrecy, Canada's security agency engaged in numerous illegal and unethical acts. Some of these included surreptitiously opening mail; entering homes and offices without search warrants; stealing the 100 000-name membership list of the Parti Québécois; creating files on 800 000 people of no particular security risk, often only because of their political affiliations or beliefs; burglarizing the offices of the Agence de Presse Libre du Québec; compiling information about gay communities; burning a barn used for separatist meetings in southern Quebec; keeping files containing embarrassing information on politicians; stealing dynamite; committing abduction; maintaining a spy in the federal Liberal party; even blacklisting Pierre Trudeau and paying someone to spy in the Quebec Liberal party.

Under the CSIS Act the domestic spy agency can investigate anyone who presents a threat to what the agency defines as "national security." The agency cannot make arrests or lay charges on its own, however, so it spends its time gathering information on perceived threats to security.

After the widespread negative publicity given to the above-mentioned acts of the RCMP, particularly during the 1970s, many Canadians believed that the bureaucratic "pathology" infecting Canada's security operations had been brought sufficiently under control. But royal commission hearings continued to generate public distrust of Canadian security operations, even among those who had traditionally respected the powerful symbolism of righteousness connected with the RCMP since the nineteenth century.

What was particularly unacceptable for Canadians was that a national security service would spy on law-abiding civilian groups, individuals, and organizations. Had the Crown spinned out of control on matters of security? Could the rights of Canadians and aliens living in Canada be violated simply to satisfy the desires of administrators working in the field of national security?

To complicate the situation, many Canadians were beginning to wonder why their country needed *two* security agencies. CSIS is Canada's domestice-security service; its foreign-policy counterpart is the Communications Security Establishment (CSE), which eavesdrops on foreign electronic communications and is responsible for the government's communications security. With the end of the Cold War, the role of CSIS and the CSE changed; both agencies are now operating in an environment of shifting international priorities and a new global balance of power. Both have refocussed their sights on counterterrorism and industrial sabotage.

Part of the solution appeared to be in the reorganization of the security function. In 1984, CSIS was separated from the Mounties, and a civilian watchdog committee was formed to keep an eye on its behaviour and to make sure it stayed on the straight and narrow.

Informed observers know that surveillance activity can easily get out of control. Some operations lend themselves to a degree of supervision; for example, the CSIS Act requires a judge's approval before electronic surveillance can proceed. But using "moles" or actually planting spies — an area of activity known in the trade as "human resources" — can be much more controversial and can push or even overstep the limits of administering government policy.

Informants, for example, can be unpredictable, difficult to control, and outrageously manipulative, to the point of breaking the law. The potential for bureaupathology is great, because the informant is actually selling information to the government. In such circumstances the potential for illegal and unethical activities is high. Given that dishonesty is fundamental to the profession of spying, governments involved in the activity can easily be compromised.

At the same time, government bureaucracies can become obsessed with self-preservation and the enhancement of their own status in the name of national security. By such defensive positioning they will inevitably become isolated, insulated, and secretive in relation to the society they are supposed to serve.

INTRODUCTION: PUBLIC ADMINISTRATION AS GOVERNING

Academics contribute theoretical knowledge to the practice of public administration. They believe that their distance from the everyday workings of public organizations and their applications of the rigours of social science research to the collection of data on public decision making lend a much-needed objectivity to the perspective they provide on the operations of government bureaucracies. But the thousands of civil servants who work at the various levels of Canadian government also believe they know something about the daily administration of public organizations. Many of them have extensive backgrounds in the academic study of public administration. They believe they possess the tools needed to implement **public policy**.

THE PUBLIC SERVICE AND PUBLIC ADMINISTRATION

In Chapter 15, David Johnson outlines ten aspects of public administration that make it "a crucially important element of Canadian government and society." He helps us understand public administration as both a field of knowledge and a set of professional procedures to deliver government services.

In Canada, the public service is clearly a major participant in the public-policy-making environment. That environment, comprising the country's political economy and social make-up, is quite complex, given free-trade agreements, a federal system of government, and ever-increasing pressures from interest groups, political parties, and the media. In Chapter 17, "The Canadian Political Economy and Core Institutions," Bruce Doern and Richard Phidd give us a good basic framework for analyzing the ideas, institutions, and structures connected with public-policy formulation in Canada.

At the highest levels of government, bureaucrats can initiate public policy without the public's awareness of their input and certainly without the public's electoral consent. Bureaucrats often help politicians and Cabinet ministers set the agenda on policy matters and advise them on the best ways to follow those agendas. Perhaps the most serious criticism of bureaucrats is that, without having been elected to their posts, they make independent choices that affect public policy and in the process play an uninvited political role in the governing system.

THE SCOPE OF PUBLIC POLICY

We often use the terms *public policy* and *decision making*, or *policy making*, interchangeably. Consider this example: When the Cabinet decides to reduce **transfer payments** to the provinces, Canada's *policy* on federalism becomes fiscally conservative. The Cabinet may announce that its *decision* to reduce transfers to the provinces was taken in pursuance of the government's *policy* to eliminate the deficit and reduce the federal debt.

According to this usage, a policy is something greater than a decision, but each decision gives some clue as to the general tendency of the public policy. Nor is a policy usually as abstract as a broad political principle or philosophy: as Brian Howe points out in Chapter 16, it is more concrete. It is what gives shape and consistency to the individual decisions of members of Parliament. When we speak of the "government's economic policy," we may not be referring to any one policy in particular, but to the general direction in which all individual policies seem to point. Howe expands our understanding of public policy in this regard by exploring how it is defined in the political science literature and by walking us through the various institutions and processes involved in the creation of public policies.

Indeed, the political science literature contains many definitions and views of public policy. In the eyes of policy analysts (and the policy-makers themselves), some are more apt than others. To help us analyze both the concept of and the processes involved in creating public policy, Leslie Pal, in Chapter 18, offers ten helpful tips for "good" policy analysis. His contribution provides a concise framework that students can apply at all levels of policy analysis.

THINKING IT OVER

1. Define public administration. What are the controls on public administrators? Why must they be so closely watched? Do government bureaucracies form their own political constituencies? On the basis of the readings in this section, outline how bureaucrats protect their interests in the public system.
2. It is generally agreed that a sharp distinction can no longer be drawn between politics and government administration in Canada. Discuss the items on David Johnson's "Top Ten List" (Chapter 15) that make the connection between politics and public administration.
3. Discuss whether the expert knowledge (expertise) of the professional career bureaucrat is needed for the formulation of sound public policy, as postulated in Chapter 15. Does the special knowledge of bureaucrats necessarily coincide with the national interest or even with regional community interests? Or do public administrators serve their own interests by cultivating professional expertise?
4. How does Brian Howe (Chapter 16) define public policy? What governing instruments are used in Canada to achieve policy goals? Who makes public policy, administrators or elected officials?
5. Bruce Doern and Richard Phidd (Chapter 17) outline the environment in which Canadian public policy is formulated. What four developments do they identify as major influences in that environment? What are the "core political institutions" that decisively influence the development of public policy in Canada? Why do the authors believe that these institutions cannot be observed in isolation?
6. Leslie Pal (Chapter 18) offers ten tips for understanding how to produce good public policy analysis. What are they? Does he give us good advice?

GLOSSARY

accountability The requirement that those who govern be responsible to those whom they govern; various laws, procedures, and administrative and political processes are in place to ensure that such responsibility is realized.

analysis The mental process by which an object of inquiry is separated into its constituent parts and the relationships among those parts are determined; it involves measuring and explaining the available information, and forecasting certain events based on it.

Cabinet committee system A form of governmental organization in which a Cabinet is broken down into smaller, functional sub-units, or committees, composed of ministers possessing related portfolios. The committees have a mandate to develop policies in their combined field of (special or general) interest.

error of law The breach of a fundamental rule of administrative law in a quasi-judicial administrative decision that stands as a ground for judicial review of that decision by a superior court. That court has the power to quash the decision and impose its own result or send the whole matter back to the original decision-maker for reconsideration.

ethical liberalism The stream of liberal thought that favours participatory democracy and positive state action in areas such as social welfare, regulation of the economy, and protection of basic human rights.

expertise The condition of possessing specialized, comprehensive knowledge of a particular discipline or field of study and action. Bureaucratic expertise is routinely gained through formal university education in the social sciences and law, as well as through practical experience in public administration.

governing instruments The instruments used by the Crown in its pursuit of a public policy objective. Governing instruments range from government advertising encouraging public adherence to policy, to the imposition of regulations with legal sanctions.

line departments Government departments in which lines of authority are hierarchical, that is, in which department officials are directly responsible and accountable to ministers.

meritocracy A system of personnel management in which decisions about employees are based on merit (education, experience, skills, talents, and aptitude). A meritocracy is the opposite of a patronage system. A public sector based on a meritocracy is likely to have a talented and professional work force — hence the public interest in the promotion of meritocracy over patronage.

patronage The practice of appointing political supporters to public office or to desirable positions on public boards, committees, and commissions.

personnel management system The government system concerned with establishing and developing the public sector work force. The federal personnel management system addresses such matters as the nature of hiring, promotion, demotion, and firing, as well as official bilingualism, pay equity and employment equity, professional training and upgrading, and collective bargaining and labour relations.

pluralism A social and political theory that accepts as a central feature of the policy-making process the influence of many different groups, none of which dominates the process.

plurality A measure of electoral success where there are more than two contenders. In such cases, it is possible that no single contender will win a majority of the vote (50% + 1); victory will then go to the contender who has won the most votes short of a majority, that is, the largest single percentage of the vote. For example: if contender A has 40 percent of the vote, contender B has 30 percent, and contender C has 30 percent, contender A wins with a plurality of 40 percent.

public personnel policy The rules and practices that pertain to the personnel of government departments and public agencies and that are geared to increasing the production, efficiency, and expertise of the civil service.

public policy A course of action or inaction consciously chosen by a government in response to social or political issues.

public sector The sector of the economy in which the employer is one of the three levels of government. The public sector includes not only government departments but also Crown corporations, regulatory agencies, and public schools. The line between the public and private sectors becomes blurred when one considers such institutions as hospitals and universities, which are included in what is known as the "broader public sector."

quasi-judicial The term used in reference to organizations that have an adjudicative function as well as an executive-administrative function. Regulatory agencies are the primary example: They not only develop regulatory policy but are also called upon to resolve legal disputes arising under such policy.

statism A theoretical perspective that assumes that elected officials and administrators enjoy substantial autonomy from outside pressure in setting public policy, and that policy consequently reflects their own beliefs and interests to a large degree. In contrast to those who favour a more restricted role for the state in policy-making and more public participation in the process, statists believe that the public should yield to the authority and power of the state.

transfer payments The federal public policy, supported by federal taxing powers, that consigns large sums of money to the provinces, either conditionally, in support of health, education, welfare, and resource development, or unconditionally, as formula-based equalization transfers.

ADDITIONAL READINGS

Abele, Frances. 1991. *How Ottawa Spends, 1991–92: The Politics of Fragmentation.* Ottawa: Carleton University Press.

Albo, Gregory, David Langille, and Leo Panitch, eds. 1993. *A Different Kind of State? Popular Power and Democratic Administration.* Don Mills, Ont.: Oxford University Press.

Canada. 1990. *Beneath the Veneer: Report of the Task Force on Barriers to Women in the Public Service,* Vol.1. Ottawa: Supply and Services Canada.

———. 1990. *Public Service 2000: The Renewal of the Public Service of Canada.* Ottawa: Supply and Services Canada.

Coleman, William, and Grace Skogstad. 1990. *Policy Communities and Public Policy in Canada.* Mississauga, Ont.: Copp Clark Pitman.

Doern, Bruce, and Richard Phidd. 1992. *Canadian Public Policy.* Scarborough, Ont.: Nelson Canada.

Gagnon, Yvan. 1995. *The Theory and Practice of Public Policy-Making in Canada.* Lewiston, NY: The Edwin Mellen Press.

Guy, James J. 1995. *How We Are Governed: An Introduction to Canadian Politics and Government.* Toronto: Harcourt Brace.

Johnson, A.W. 1994. *What Is Public Management?* Ottawa: Canadian Centre for Management Development.

Kernaghan, Kenneth, and John Langford. 1990. *The Responsible Public Servant.* Toronto: Institute of Public Administration of Canada.

Pross, A. Paul. 1992. *Group Politics and Public Policy.* Don Mills, Ont.: Oxford University Press.

Public Administration's "Top Ten List"

DAVID JOHNSON

There is a paradox at the heart of public administration. The exercise of state power within society touches all of us in so many ways — from the provision of public works such as water and sewage services, through to education and university funding policy, through to the socio-economic implications of free trade policy. And yet, despite the palpable importance which the state has in our lives, so many people are ill-informed about the theory and practice of public administration. In an effort to promote knowledge respecting public administration, the following pages will denote ten aspects of public administration which make it a crucially important element of Canadian government and society.

(1) PUBLIC ADMINISTRATION AND POLITICAL POWER

While there are many ways in which one can define power, its central idea is the ability to attain set ends. Once particular goals have been established, the successful realization of these objectives is the proof of power. Of course there are many characteristics of power: the ability to command obedience by law or authority; the capacity to influence others; the ability to marshal material resources; the capacity to command respect, trust, or fear. Not only is the concept of power broad but the uses of power are open-ended. Power can be used for good or ill; it can be used to promote individual and collective human well-being, or to advance the selfish and manipulative interests of particular individuals or groups. The concept of power itself, though, is neutral; it refers only to a capability. It is the ends to which it is used, and the means to attain ends, that become the substance of moral debate.

The political aspect of power focuses attention on power relations affecting individuals, groups, and the state. Political power is used not only to shape government institutions but to organize the working of the economy and the nature of social policy. Public administration, then, cannot be divorced from the practice of democratic politics. Within this society many individuals and groups are interested in the manner in which Canadians should be governed, and the types of social and economic policies that are best suited to promoting the interests of the country. As opinions differ with respect to these issues, political parties form, advocating differing approaches to issues of leadership while seeking mandates to govern through the winning of democratic elections.[1]

(2) PUBLIC ADMINISTRATION AND PUBLIC POLICY

It is axiomatic that public administration is related to public policy, given that political parties seek governmental power so as to gain the ability to enact and implement their vision of how the society should be governed. Indeed, the practice of public

SOURCE: "Public Administration's 'Top Ten List,'" July 1995, unpublished paper. Reprinted by permission of the author.

administration is nothing but the development, implementation, and evaluation of various public policies. The fields of public policy that interest governments are many, but among the major ones are foreign and defence policy; macro-economic policy; industrial and trade policy; social-welfare policy; justice policy; education policy; environmental policy; and multiculturalism policy.

The range of policies of interest to one government may not necessarily be the same for another government. One government may give priority to economic policy while downplaying social-welfare policy; another may seek to give equal weight to these while enhancing attention devoted to multicultural policy. Another government may totally disagree with the concept of multiculturalism, seeking its abolition as a policy field for government involvement. The range of policy fields and the weight accorded to each by any government will be influenced by a number of factors, including the temporal mood of the public on the popularity of certain policy fields; the strength of interest group support for particular fields; the economic importance of various fields to the general welfare of the country; and, not to be underestimated, the ideological orientation of the party in power.[2]

(3) PUBLIC ADMINISTRATION AND INSTITUTIONS

While the development of public policy is crucially important to public administration, so too is the implementation of such policy. And the means of implementation are found in the variety of institutions which comprise the **public sector**. Within Canada the public sector is composed of four types of institutions playing significant roles in the policy-making and implementation process.

Government Departments

The most commonly observed governmental institution is the government department. These are organizations of variable bureaucratic size and political-administrative importance, which have responsibility for managing the development and application of policy with respect to a particular field of policy. Some departments can be extremely large institutions, with tens of thousands of employees nation-wide, engaged in the implementation of hundreds of departmental programs, such as the Department of Agriculture. Others can be quite small, with a limited number of staff, primarily located in Ottawa, providing specialized services to the government, such as the Department of Justice. In all cases a department has as its formal head a minister—an elected member of the governing party—who, by virtue of this appointment, is entitled to sit in cabinet and engage in executive leadership for the country. Apart from these general cabinet duties the minister is expected to be responsible for the actions of his or her department. As will be seen, this is an awesome and difficult duty.

Central Agencies

Within the federal government, moreover, a number of central agencies exist to support policy-making within departments and to provide the prime minister and cabinet with sources of policy advice independent of particular departments and their vested interests. The major central agencies in Ottawa are five: the Prime Minister's Office, the Privy Council Office, the Treasury Board Secretariat, the Federal–Provincial Relations Office, and the Department of Finance. All of these bodies are so intricately involved in the policy process that one cannot understand policy-making and related policy evaluation without understanding their role. Departments and central agencies exist in a complex relationship: at times the relationship is convivial, with the bodies being mutually supportive; at other times the relationship can be antagonistic, as organizations clash over the manner in which policies are to be made, implemented, and evaluated.

Regulatory Agencies

Beyond departments and central agencies exist two other types of institutions: regulatory agencies and crown corporations. These are bodies designed to be relatively independent of the government of the day so as to allow them to undertake either **quasi-judicial** or commercial activities free from potential partisan interference. Regulatory agencies are bodies designed to regulate particular policy fields thus promoting social and economic ends deemed by the government to be important — such as economic stability, occupational health and safety, environmental protection, and the promotion of human rights. In each case regulatory agencies administer and implement particular legal rights as well as resolve legal disputes pertaining to these rights. As such, regulatory agencies possess not only an executive function but a judicial one. Hence the term "quasi-judicial" and the concern for their independence. Leading agencies in this country, at the federal level, are the Canadian Human Rights Commission, the Canadian Radio-television and Telecommunications Commission, the Canadian Immigration and Refugee Board, and the Canadian Parole Board. The importance of these agencies is to be observed simply by the public concern and controversy which surrounds every one of these bodies and by the debate in this country over the issue of deregulation.

Crown Corporations

Crown corporations, in turn, are public sector entities charged with responsibility to engage in commercial activities, either as a monopoly, as with Via Rail and provincial hydro-electric utilities, or in competition with private sector firms, as is the case with the CBC, Petro-Canada, or CN. Crown corporations have been created by differing governments for a variety of reasons. In certain cases their objective is to promote Canadian nationalism in particular industries, as with the CBC and the NFB in the fields of broadcasting and culture, or to promote Canadian economic interests in sectors dominated by foreign corporations, as with the role of Petro-Canada in the petroleum industry.

At other times crown corporations have been created to support and maintain industries which the private sector finds unworthy of support but which the government is committed to preserving, as with the establishment of the Cape Breton Development Corporation and the Cape Breton coal fields. In yet other cases, crown corporations are established to promote the development of new industries, as with De Havilland and Canadair and the aircraft industry, or to ensure that certain common and necessary services are provided to all Canadians, as is the case with Canada Post and the CBC. Crown corporations can also be established to provide state control over the sale of a particular product deemed by the government to be special and in need of careful management — as with the function of liquor control commissions in most provinces.

And as with regulatory agencies, the role of crown corporations is enveloped in controversy and debate. Many persons with a conservative predisposition seek their privatization while others with social-democratic values seek their maintenance and even expansion. Within the liberal centre opinion is divided, with many seeking the middle ground of crown corporation commercialization, meaning that political interest with respect to crown corporations will continue to be a characteristic feature of Canadian politics and public administration.[3]

(4) PUBLIC ADMINISTRATION AND THE PUBLIC SERVICE

A review of the institutions through which public policy is derived in this country highlights the importance of the public sector bureaucracy. Throughout the departments, central agencies, regulatory agencies, and crown corporations existing within the country, hundreds of thousands of public servants are involved in the processes of making public policies, of implementing and managing public policies, of evaluating the degree to which policies and related programs are being successfully or poorly administered, as well as of advising their responsible ministers, and the cabinet as a whole, of the ways and means through which policy and program delivery could be improved.

As can be observed, the scope of government action through public administration is enormous. In order to facilitate the efficient and effective implementation of these responsibilities, successive governments have created a public service comprising numerous persons with a range of professional skills to enable the governing institutions to fulfil their obligations. Because of the growth of government over this century, we have witnessed the development of a professional bureaucracy with the knowledge, skills, and expertise to engage in the policy-making and administrative actions required of public sector institutions.

Within the management ranks of the public service, moreover, there is a class of persons who have, as their career orientation and function, the management of public policy and administrative actions. Senior public service managers thus specialize in the application of political and administrative power within this society. In a society in which knowledge is correlated with power, public service managers possess both. This becomes problematic with respect to the relationship between bureaucracy and democracy. The bureaucracy possesses power within this society, but is this bureaucratic power subject to adequate democratic control?[4]

(5) PUBLIC ADMINISTRATION AND DEMOCRACY

The issue here is related to the tension between the professional bureaucracy and the elected ministers who are the formal leaders of the bureaucracy. The term "formal" is used to highlight the important "informal" relationships found here. One theory of democratic responsible government holds that the exercise of bureaucratic power is consistent with democracy provided that the institutions of the public service are ultimately subject to the authority and control of ministers who are themselves elected members of parliament. Their ability to be named ministers of the crown, in turn, is contingent on their party winning a majority, or at least a **plurality**, of seats at the most recent general election.

This is the formal understanding of responsible government. Problems arise, however, with respect to the actual power relationship between ministers and their senior public service officials. Simply put, do ministers have the time and the expertise to effectively govern the institutions for which they are responsible? Note that ministers possess a number of responsibilities beyond their ministerial duties. They remain MPs with legislative and constituency duties, and they are party members with party and caucus responsibilities. Beyond this limitation is the other factor that ministers are seldom, if ever, experts in the policy field over which they are given responsibility. Ministers are usually appointed to act as concerned generalists, overseeing the work of their departments; the experts in matters of policy development and administration, of course, are the permanent staff within the department.

Such **expertise**, coupled with the related conditions of longevity in the public service and their ability to devote all of their professional time and energy to their departmental duties, results in the senior executive members of departments possessing significant informal power within the institutions of government. Officials such as deputy ministers, assistant deputy ministers, regulatory agency and crown corporation heads, and senior managerial staff can all become major actors in the development, management, and evaluation of policies and programs simply because they are the ones with the greatest expertise respecting such matters. Ministers ostensibly "in charge" may find themselves reliant and dependent upon the "advice" of their senior staff. Under such conditions the real power relations are then reversed; effective authority over policy and administration thus lies in the hands of departmental staff, not the ministers.

It is precisely the fear of this occurrence that has resulted in a number of organizational initiatives being taken over the past three decades both to limit the influence of senior departmental officials and to enhance the executive capabilities of ministers. Central agencies themselves were designed to assist ministers by providing them with sources of policy and administrative advice separate from their own departments and related institutions. Similarly, the creation of the **cabinet committee system** was designed to enable ministers with related policy fields to come together on a formal basis to exchange information and advice respecting their policy fields.

Such innovations were to promote democratic control over the bureaucracy. But have they? This is a point of great debate. Clearly, ministers now possess a far greater range of institutional entities from which to gather advice. They are thus much less dependent upon their senior departmental advisers than was the case prior to the late 1960s. But, cabinet committees do represent another institutional burden on the precious time of ministers, and central agencies are generally but another set of institutions staffed by public servants. Have ministers simply exchanged one set of bureaucratic advisers for another?[5]

(6) PUBLIC ADMINISTRATION AND LAW

Given that public administration revolves around public policy it is axiomatic that law is integral to public administration, for laws are but the legal expressions of public policies. Much of what departments and regulatory agencies do revolves around the implementation of law. The Department of the Environment is very interested in the application of environmental protection legislation; similarly, the Immigration and Refugee Board is designed specifically to apply legislation respecting immigration and refugee determination, and to resolve legal disputes arising under such legislation. In turn, the courts become closely involved in the general process of public administration because they are called upon to pass judgement on the quality of the legal decision-making of such departments and agencies.

In general terms, two types of law are most important to public administration: constitutional law and administrative law. Constitutional law issues arise when a party (an individual, group, corporation, or other government) alleges that a particular law or part of a law is unconstitutional, thereby being null and void. There are two primary grounds for unconstitutionality of a law: that it violates the federal–provincial division of powers found in the *Constitution Act, 1867*, or that it violates one or more of the provisions found in the *Charter of Rights and Freedoms*.

In contrast to these broad matters, administrative law is much more precise. This field of law is concerned with the manner in which government departments and regulatory agencies actually exercise the legal powers which have been granted to them. Most departments and all regulatory agencies are specifically designed to apply law to particular policy fields. The legislation which they apply will denote not only their legal powers but the rights and obligations of individuals, groups, and corporations within the field. With workers' compensation policy, for example, workers' compensation boards possess legal power to apply the terms of workers' compensation acts involving the raising of revenues from employers and the disbursement of funds to injured workers. Within the acts, the rights of workers to make claims are outlined as are the rights of employers to contest such claims. The boards are then mandated with authority to resolve such disputes.

And, in the process of such dispute resolution, all departments and regulatory agencies are obligated to abide by certain fundamental rules of administrative law which will be enforced by the courts. These rules consist of the legal concepts of natural justice, bias, jurisdiction, and **error of law**. The rules of natural justice involve the procedural duties which must be followed by all adjudicators in rendering a decision, such as providing notice, allowing a right to counsel, and providing written reasons for a judgement. The rules of bias stipulate that an adjudicator must have no real or apparent conflict of interest with the case to be resolved. The rules of jurisdiction mandate that a decision-maker can only take into account and render a decision on matters that have been formally placed within its ambit of power. A liquor licence agency, for example, cannot issue or revoke drivers' licences.

And finally, the concept of error of law simply provides that should an agency make such an error in its decision-making, that error becomes a ground for judicial review of the impugned decision. This, in turn, will involve a superior court's reviewing the matter and assessing whether such a breach of administrative law occurred; if it did, the court would have the power to quash the decision of the administrative body and to order the matter to be reheard, this time in accordance with the law.[6]

(7) PUBLIC ADMINISTRATION AND MANAGEMENT

As those public servants involved in public administration are called upon to engage in policy-making and implementation, their work necessarily involves them in organizing and directing the means through which policy and program ends can be attained. The means of public administration move far beyond the institutions of government, extending to include the material and human resources required to engage in public administration. Two important issues confronting senior officials in government thus revolve around the manner in which to undertake financial and **public personnel policy**.

Financial management involves decision-making respecting the ways and means by which to organize and control the flow of financial resources — money — through an organization. Financial management thus involves issues of budget-making and resource allocation, as well as auditing and evaluation of monies spent. How can organizational budgets best be prepared? Who should have key responsibility for their preparation? And what organizational values should be given priority through the budget? Such seemingly bland questions belie great issues which go to the heart of bureaucratic politics within government organizations. Many officials support traditional, informal, and incremental budget systems which are easy to implement and which keep authority in their hands. Conversely, many officials in central agencies support newer forms of "rational" budgeting which call for detailed planning, priority setting, and cost–benefit analyses of existing and proposed policies and programs.

As control of money often results in overall political-administrative control, the resolution of such conflict is far from being of mere academic interest. The politics of the budgetary process is at the heart of much of routine life in government bureaucracies. In fact the Canadian federal government has adopted and discarded a host of budgetary approaches over the past two decades in an effort to develop an ideal model of budget-making. Interestingly, no one approach satisfies all actors in the process, and now with governments expressing great concerns over deficit and debt reduction and the "downsizing" of programs, the debate over budget-making rages on.

But there is more to management than budget-making. Governments need good people to staff the institutions of government, and the ways and means of organizing staff open up a host of questions and approaches. Should governments engage in **patronage** hiring? Should government distinguish between rank and file staffing and the making of appointments of senior executives to lead regulatory agencies and crown corporations? For example, why should a Liberal government not be allowed to appoint a Liberal, with years of executive experience, to head an agency, thereby replacing a Conservative appointee, if the government does not have confidence in the policy direction taken by the old Conservative appointee? Would such a change in personnel represent an example of illegitimate patronage, or just smart management?

If governments, however, are to eliminate patronage with respect to the decision-making on hiring, promotion, discipline, and removal that applies to the majority of ordinary public servants who are not senior executives, how should the personnel system be crafted? As observed in this country most governments have moved to a system of **meritocracy** with respect to the management of their personnel systems. Entry, advancement, and punishment, if need be, are to be based on merit — as evidenced through education, examinations, experience, performance evaluation, and professional upgrading.

But should other matters be allowed to enter the **personnel management system**? Should bilingualism be promoted as an attribute of merit? Should the federal public service be fully representative of francophones, meaning that roughly 25 percent of positions should be held by francophones? If so, should other social groups receive similar treatment? Should the public service be required to accurately represent women, visible minorities, natives, and the handicapped? For example, should half of all public service positions be held by women? Such questions, of course, lead into an analysis of the merits and demerits of personnel representationalism within organizations and the philosophy and politics of affirmative action and employment equity. Not only is this issue divisive among the general public but it is particularly hot within governments, as it is within the public service that policies of affirmative action and employment equity have been most vigorously implemented. Such personnel management approaches have many advocates, who see them as a means of ending invidious discrimination, but they also have many critics proclaiming that such policies merely perpetuate discrimination by promoting one form of sexism or racism or favouritism over another.

Suffice it to say that this issue is now at the heart of analysis respecting the manner in which public sector personnel management should be organized. Indeed, the issues here have sidelined another traditional personnel issue — that being the legitimacy of public sector collective bargaining and whether or not public servants should be given the right to strike. While sidelined, this issue has not ceased to exist; while many public servants chafe under wage restraint programmes, many others in the general public would prefer to witness public sector wages and benefits and collective bargaining rights diminished even further.[7]

(8) PUBLIC ADMINISTRATION AND EVALUATION

Policy-making and implementation, financial management and personnel administration, public sector decision-making of every sort calls for the making of choices respecting the application of power to particular issues and concerns. The quality of such decision-making becomes all important. Governments need to know if their actions, or non-actions, in particular policy fields are having desired effects. Governments need to assess the economy and efficiency of their actions so as to determine if valuable human and material resources are being well used, or whether such resources can be employed more effectively. In everything government does, policy and program evaluation is necessary.

A number of dynamics deserve to be mentioned with respect to policy and program evaluation. First, public administration is different from private sector administration in that the discipline of "the bottom line" is absent. The effectiveness of governmental action is usually not to be measured on a balance sheet; governments are not necessarily designed to earn a profit. Therefore, bringing private sector techniques to the issue of public service evaluation is usually of little assistance.

Second, the goals of government policies and programs are often articulated in broad, general terms, subject to a range of interpretations. The basic goal of the federal Department of Justice, for example, is to oversee the justice system in this country, to provide legal advice to all government departments, to maintain the federal courts, and to oversee the development and application of the *Criminal Code*. How is one to evaluate whether this mandate has been properly fulfilled at any point in time? Has the judiciary been well served by the appointments made by the Department? Does the *Criminal Code* reflect well the concerns of ordinary Canadians? Is the system of justice in Canada healthy or not? If not, how should it be reformed?

Third, the evaluation of government policies and programs is difficult because such matters can often have multiple objectives, often at cross purposes, with implementation extending across years. Has the policy of free trade, for example, benefited or harmed Canada? A profound question with no easy answers. Free trade policy with the United States and Mexico is designed to open North American markets to Canadian goods and services, enhancing the ability of Canadian businesses to prosper, thereby ultimately benefiting all Canadians. But how does one evaluate the tradeoffs in such a policy? And over what time? Many harmful effects of free trade can be observed now with job losses in particular industries, but supporters of the trade deal argue that its beneficial effects may not be witnessed for ten, fifteen, or twenty years. How is evaluation to be undertaken within these circumstances?[8]

(9) PUBLIC ADMINISTRATION AND ETHICS

As the work of ministers and public servants is important to the well-being of the country, it is not surprising that citizens as well as governments show an interest in witnessing the holders of governmental power exercising their duties in accordance with the highest standards of ethical behaviour. Sadly, much popular media reportage on the working of public administration involves cases in which standards of ethical behaviour have been breached. While all Canadian governments aspire to the highest standards of such behaviour, given that governments are composed of human beings, with all their weaknesses, governments have moved to establish strong codes of ethics to enforce within their public sectors.

Ethics involves the study, implementation, and enforcement of codes of behaviour designed to promote "proper" governmental behaviour and to proscribe and punish "improper" behaviour. Traditionally, the regulation of governmental ethics was left to the informal interactions of ministers and public servants. It was argued that these officials knew best how to exercise their powers within the social system of the bureaucracy and that the social conventions of government and a professional public service would lead to the enforcement of ethical behaviour.

The 1970s witnessed the inauguration of more formal methods of promoting governmental ethics. Now the federal government and most provincial governments have an array of ethics codes applicable to both ministers and public servants. In general, such codes stipulate that public office is not to be used for private gain. Ministers are forbidden, for example, from using their governmental powers to provide government contracts to companies owned by direct family members. Likewise, public servants are forbidden from using their official powers and knowledge to promote commercial ventures of their relatives or to profit from the sale of information in their possession. Ministers and public servants are also admonished to avoid the reality and even the appearance of a conflict of interest. Such conflicts arise when the decision-maker has, or is seen to have, a personal interest in the outcome of a particular matter, thereby rendering the decision-maker less than impartial.

While all such rules may be cumbersome they are designed to promote integrity in government by, it is hoped, demonstrating to Canadians that government decision-making is undertaken on account of the merits and justice of the particular issue, not on account of the material self-interest of particular officials.[9]

(10) PUBLIC ADMINISTRATION AND ACCOUNTABILITY

As public administration is centred on the organization and use of power so also is public administration rooted in the concept of **accountability**. A fundamental principle of democratic government holds that those who exercise governmental power must be accountable — answerable and responsive — to the people for the manner in which they have undertaken their duties. There are three broad approaches to accountability in this political system: the political, the legal, and the social.[10]

The first stresses the importance of parliamentary institutions and practices. Governments are held accountable to the people through the process of parliamentary scrutiny and debate, the pressure of question period, and ultimately through the working of party politics and the discipline of elections. Governments which lose the trust of a substantial proportion of the Canadian public cannot expect to retain power for extended periods of time.

Elections allow the people to judge governments, and those deemed by a majority or plurality to be unresponsive to their needs will be held accountable for this failing, and will be suitably punished.

The second approach to accountability revolves around the law and its application to governments. As already observed, governments not only make law but must abide by law. Laws not only delineate the rights and duties of individuals, groups, and corporations, but also establish the proper forms through which governmental power can be exercised. And when disputes arise respecting the legitimacy of governmental action, individuals, groups, corporations, and, indeed, other governments can hold a governmental decision-maker accountable for its actions before the courts. Independent and impartial courts thus have a major role to play in determining, shaping, and directing the scope of legal powers held by governments, and in ensuring that government action is always consistent with law and proper procedure. The processes of constitutional and administrative law, seemingly boring to the uninitiated, in reality are bulwarks of democratic accountability.

The third approach, related to the previous two, is that of social responsiveness, stressing the importance of group politics to the linkage of government to the public. As governments interact with the public, interest groups come to perform a major role in this relationship. Groups exist to provide information, advice, and opinion to governments; to support government initiatives when such initiatives are deemed by a group to be in the best interests of group members; and to criticize government policy and programs when this course of action is deemed necessary.

The development of policy and administration, in fact, is very much based on the government's building networks of support among groups, and on the inevitable mediating and balancing of competing group interests in such a manner as to establish a set of policies and programs which most people consider reasonable and responsive to the needs not only of affected groups but of the general public as well. Governments that can demonstrate general responsiveness to most group needs are those that can claim that their policies are generally accountable to the needs of the people. And this in turn is integral to any government's establishing a record upon which to gain re-election.

Accountability thus possesses a number of aspects but with one underlying current: the establishment of a relationship through which governments demonstrate their responsiveness to the public, and through which political parties, courts, interest groups, and individual citizens pass judgement on the quality of such responsiveness.

NOTES

1. Rand Dyck, *Canadian Politics: Critical Approaches* (Scarborough: Nelson Canada, 1993), ch. 1.
2. Stephen Brooks, *Public Policy in Canada: An Introduction*, 2nd ed. (Toronto: McClelland and Stewart, 1993), chs. 1–2.
3. Kenneth Kernaghan and David Siegel, *Public Administration in Canada: A Text*, 2nd ed. (Scarborough: Nelson Canada, 1991), chs. 8–10.
4. Reginald Whitaker, "Politicians and Bureaucrats in the Policy Process," in M.S. Whittington and G. Williams, eds., *Canadian Politics in the 1990s*, 4th ed. (Scarborough: Nelson Canada, 1995), ch. 21.
5. Richard J. Van Loon and Michael S. Whittington, *The Canadian Political System*, 4th ed. (Toronto: McGraw-Hill Ryerson Ltd., 1987), chs. 15, 17.
6. David P. Jones and Anne S. de Villars, *Principles of Administrative Law*, 2nd ed. (Toronto: Carswell, 1994), chs. 1–2.
7. Kernaghan and Siegel, *Public Administration in Canada*, chs. 23–27.
8. Stephen Brooks, "Bureaucracy," in James P. Bickerton and Alain-G. Gagnon, eds., *Canadian Politics*, 2nd ed. (Peterborough: Broadview Press, 1994), ch. 16.
9. Kernaghan and Siegel, *Public Administration in Canada*, ch. 14.
10. David Johnson, "Regulation, Accountability and Democracy: A Study of Select Ontario Regulatory Agencies" (doctoral dissertation, University of Toronto, 1990).

What Is Public Policy?

R. BRIAN HOWE

What is public policy? Where do we find it? How do we explain it? What are its limits? My purpose here is to respond to these questions in reference to political science literature on public policy in Canada. The first three questions will be dealt with by highlighting and clarifying what we find in the literature. The last question will be answered with an argument. I will argue that the current limits on public policy in Canada do not go far enough. On the basis of the constitution, policy at present is limited by federalism, which provides a jurisdictional check on what a particular level of government can do, and by the Charter of Rights and Freedoms, which provides a judicial check on what any government can do in the area of basic rights and freedoms. Policy must now conform to the federal division of powers and to respect for the largely political and legal rights in the Charter. My point will be that policy needs to be further limited by a constitutional Social Charter which requires respect for important social rights such as health care and education.

WHAT IS PUBLIC POLICY?

A handy introductory definition of public policy is provided by American political scientist Thomas Dye. Public policy, says Dye, is "whatever governments choose to do or not to do."[1] Central here is the element of choice by governmental or state authorities. Policy is a consciously designed course

of action—or inaction—by leading officials of the state, for example, cabinet ministers, senior bureaucrats, senior judges. Action or inaction which is unthinking would not qualify. For example, lack of state action in regulating the economy or in controlling discrimination would not qualify as public policy if no thought went into the inaction. Such inaction would qualify only if a determination was made to leave the economy alone, in the belief that market forces are more effective than state regulation, or to leave discrimination unregulated, in the belief that the problem is best dealt with privately rather than through law. Accordingly, deliberate choice by state officials is a key ingredient of public policy. Policy may be divided into domestic and foreign policy, and within domestic policy, into the fields of economic and social policy and policy on culture, justice, and the environment.

Policy is a set course of action or inaction that is usually broader than specific decisions or laws but narrower than general philosophical principles or aims.[2] Although many decisions or laws may be revealing of policy, they are not necessarily the same as policy. They usually pertain to particular matters, not to a general course of action or inaction, For example, the decision to increase the specific level of immigration for a given year is not necessarily indicative of a policy of open and large-scale immigration. Similarly, a law to prohibit discrimination by landlords in large apartment buildings is not necessarily indicative of public policy against discrimination.

SOURCE: "What Is Public Policy?" unpublished paper. Reprinted by permission of the author.

But neither is policy to be equated with broad political principles or general philosophical aims of a political nature. For example, the broad abstract principle of freedom of expression is an important general aim in Canadian society, but it is not the same thing as public policy. Policy exists at a more concrete level. While recognizing the importance of free expression, policies in Canada also control freedom of expression in areas such as pornography and the spread of hate. Policy thus is more narrow than philosophical goals but wider than particular decisions and laws.

Finally, policy involves not only the choice of goals to be achieved, but also the choice of means or instruments (commonly called **governing instruments**) in realizing goals. Doern and Phidd provide a useful typology of governing instruments based on the relative degree of coercion used in regulating society.[3] They refer to five types. First, there is self-regulation, involving no coercion. Here, state authorities choose not to intervene in society, allowing individuals and groups to regulate themselves. Medical associations, for example, may be allowed (as they still are) to regulate the professional conduct of their own members. Similarly, families may be allowed (as they have been in the past) to deal with problems of domestic conflict or violence themselves, the police being instructed not to get involved. The second instrument is exhortation, where state involvement is slight. Here, state officials intervene only through encouraging certain kinds of private behaviour. For reasons of cost or possible public opposition, the emphasis is on persuasion rather than on legal sanctions. Slogans are commonly used, such as "Be nice — clean your ice" or "Be healthy through Participaction."

The next three instruments involve increasing degrees of coercion. Expenditure is a third instrument where authorities of the state choose to intervene by public spending to realize some policy goal that is deemed important. This ranges from direct payments to individuals (e.g., pensions) and transfer payments (e.g., equalization grants) to subsidies, grants, loans, tax deductions, and tax credits. While costly, this instrument is selected because the state is seen to bear heavy responsibility for achieving the goal (e.g., health care) or because political pressure is so great (e.g., business pressure for subsidies). Regulation is a third instrument where authorities institute a code of formal rules to control private behaviour, backed up by legal sanctions. These rules usually are administered by special regulatory agencies, such as the Canadian Transportation Commission, or by regular **line departments** to remedy failures of market forces or to realize goals that cannot be realized through market forces. While this instrument involves more coercion, it is attractive because it is relatively inexpensive. For example, whereas social expenditure consumes over 50 percent of the federal budget, federal regulatory programs consume less than 5 percent. Finally, public ownership is an instrument where state intervention and coercion are at a maximum. Here, state authorities exert control not simply by means of spending or regulating but by the direct provision of goods and services to the public. This is carried out by public enterprises. It is done for purposes such as nation-building, providing economic or financial infrastructure, or carrying out risky ventures in the public interest that private enterprises are unwilling to do.

WHERE DO WE FIND IT?

If we were detectives, where would we find public policy? A logical first place to look would be in the law, particularly in legislation or statutory law. From the preamble and contents of a piece of legislation, we might find or infer underlying policy that guides the particulars of the legislation. For example, if we were interested in public policy on young offenders, we would be wise to consult the *Young Offender's Act* (1984) and its recent amendments. If were interested in environmental policy, we would consult the *Canadian Environmental Protection Act* (1988). If after examining the legislation we remained confused on the intent and goal of the underlying policy, we might refer to legislative debate preceding the enactment of the legislation, in particular to second reading stage, where the principles of the legislation are extensively discussed.

But legislation is not the only place we find public policy. Given the widespread delegation of powers to bureaucratic bodies responsible for legislation, we can find the setting of policy in the regulations, guidelines, or discretionary practices of senior officials. For example, in the field of worker's compensation, we find key policy set by senior officials in provincial workers' compensation boards. It is here where "accident" is defined and where levels of compensation are determined. Similarly, given the powers of judges to interpret legislation and the constitution, we can find policy in leading court rulings. For example, in defining the term "discrimination," judges have set policy through defining it broadly to include unintentional systemic exclusion as well as prejudice-based discrimination. Such an interpretation can set policy in a new direction. Finally, we can find policy in ministerial statements that are not put into legislation. A leading example was Canada's policy of official multiculturalism. Prime Minister Trudeau simply declared such a policy in 1971 in a speech to the House of Commons, but the policy was not given legislative effect. This did not occur until much later—with the 1988 *Multiculturalism Act*.

Do we find public policy simply on the basis of what state officials say it is in legislation or ministerial statements? Or do we also seek it on the basis of what is actually done or not done? Indeed, we might be missing a great deal if we rely solely on stated intentions. For example, in federal legislation on environmental protection, we find official commitment to the goals of environmentalism. But when we consult the budget of Environment Canada, the department mainly responsible for carrying out the policy, we find a relatively small budget of less than 1 percent of overall federal spending (during the early 1990s). In our role as detectives of public policy, this may help alert us to the possibility that environmental policy is more symbolic than substantial. At the very least, the example illustrates the importance of locating policy not simply on the basis of words expressed in legislation. As Thomas Dye's definition suggests, we must also look at the action or inaction of government.

HOW DO WE EXPLAIN IT?

How do we account for the origins and development of public policies in Canada? How would we explain, for example, the establishment of policy on income security after the Second World War, policies dealing with matters such as pensions, unemployment insurance, and social assistance?

Rather than trying to reinvent the wheel, it is wise to begin with existing theories. Theories can be conveniently divided into two types—society-centred and state-centred explanations.[4] In society-centred explanations, policy is seen largely to be the result of forces or pressures emanating from society. It is a situation in which the state and its officials are ultimately responding to the balance of societal forces. State officials may have a degree of autonomy in setting particular policies, but, overall, policy bears the stamp of pressures from society rather than the inclinations of authorities of the state.

There are different versions of the society-centred model. One of the leading ones is **pluralism**.[5] This theory assumes that policy is primarily the product of interest group politics. While state elites are influenced in some degree by electoral pressures or broad public opinion, these pressures have a limited bearing on public policy. Elections generally are about leaders rather than policies. And public opinion is rarely skewed enough in one direction to be a decisive factor in setting policy.

Most important, according to pluralist theory, are pressures from organized interests, especially interest groups (or pressure groups). The logic is this: Individuals with particular interests to promote (material or ideological) band together as interest groups. These groups compete with each other for influence, apply pressure on policy-makers, and affect policy. Income security policy, for example, can be seen to reflect the pressures and demands of organized labour and social advocacy groups. Policy is largely the product of group pressures, but no one group dominates the process. Rather, pluralism exists. Power is dispersed among a variety of competing groups—business, labour, professional, and so on. Although business interests may have an edge, or perhaps even a privileged position in the policy process (the position of neo-pluralism), no one group completely monopolizes power. One group may win out over a particular issue, but another group will typically win out over another. In the case of establishing income security, it so happened that organized labour and allied social advocacy groups won out.

A rival society-centred theory is neo-Marxism.[6] This theory assumes that policy is primarily the product of economic forces and class politics. Contrary to pluralism, the state is seen here not simply to respond to some interests at one time and to other interests at another. Rather, state policy is heavily biased in favour of the dominant business or capitalist class. This does not mean, of course, that state officials always side with particular businesses and business groups. Officials periodically make policy against particular business interests. For example, Trudeau's National Energy Programme (NEP) was against the interests of multinational oil companies.

But public policy in the overall sense, according to neo-Marxism, is biased in favour of the greater interests of the business class. Such policy is geared to the accumulation of capital but it is also geared, through social policy, to the legitimation of the existing order. Income security policy, for example, would receive the approval of business—especially big business, which can afford to be more generous—because it helps to legitimize a social system and economic order which benefits business. If it did not perform this function, it is doubtful the policy would have been developed.

Why does business have a monopoly on policy? One reason is that state elites tend to come from middle-upper- to upper-class backgrounds with business connections. Another is that business interest groups tend to have superior resources for applying political pressure. But the key reason is the logic of the capitalist economy. The political and electoral success of governmental authorities depends on the economic success of the business class in providing jobs and economic growth. Business interests need not always apply political pressure for favourable

policy. They may find such policy already in place for them.

In state-centred theory (**statism**), the perspective is much different. Policy here is seen to reflect the preferences and inclinations of state officials, enjoying substantial autonomy and setting policy as they see fit, apart from the pressures of interest groups or classes. Pressures from society are not unimportant but they tend to play a secondary role, often serving to justify what state officials want to do anyway.

At centre stage are relatively independent politicians, bureaucrats, and judges imposing their particular stamp on policy. They have the ability to do this for many reasons. They have substantial legal and financial resources at their disposal. Public opinion is often volatile or soft or contradictory with respect to public policy. Interest groups are often competitive, allowing state officials room to play one side off against the other and thus to steer an independent policy path. Politicians have the capacity for autonomous policy-making on the basis of democratic legitimacy and often because of public apathy; bureaucrats have it on the basis of technical expertise, control over information in the policy process, and their relative permanence in the government structure; and judges have it on the basis of their legitimate authority to interpret the law.

What motivates state officials to set policy as they do? According to public choice theory, the primary consideration is rational self-interest.[7] While this applies to politicians and special interest groups, it applies particularly to senior bureaucratic officials, who play a central role in the policy process. Just as self-interest guides economic behaviour, it also guides the policy behaviour of bureaucratic elites. They are motivated to expand their budgets, enlarge their programmes and policy responsibilities, and increase their personal status and salary level. Of particular concern to them is the maximization of their budget, given that their programmes and personal success depend to a large extent on how large a slice they get in the budget. Thus they use their resources—technical expertise, control over information—to initiate policies favourable to their budgetary situation. They use policy demands from advocacy groups in a self-serving way to justify policies that they themselves want, recommending these to the relevant politicians. Policy on income security, then, would reflect the budgetary desires of state officials responsible for health care, pensions, and social assistance. The large postwar growth in programmes here would reflect bureaucratic rational self-interest.

But for many, such a view is overly cynical. According to Ronald Manzer, the motivation has less to do with self-interest than with the underlying beliefs and values of leading public officials.[8] State elites are motivated to a large extent, says Manzer, by Canada's "public philosophy." At the core of this philosophy is liberalism. Liberalism, however, is not monolithic: it is divided into two rival strands, a conservative economic version of liberalism and a reformist ethical strand. The economic version influences policy-makers along the lines of a conservative, market-centred, and individual-responsibility-centred policy approach. The ethical reformist version spurs policy in the direction of government regulation of the economy and social programmes to remedy disadvantage and to respond to human needs. According to Manzer, the relative absence of income security before the Second World War was due in large part to the strength of economic liberalism in the public philosophy. The development of such a policy after the war reflected the growing presence of **ethical liberalism**. Finally, recent initiatives to downsize income security reflect a rejuvenation of economic liberalism. Thus, for Manzer, public policy is less a product of rational self-interest or interest groups pressures or the power of business than of underlying currents in the public philosophy.

WHAT ARE ITS LIMITS?

To return to Dye's definition, public policy is "whatever governments choose to do or not to do." But the word "whatever" is misleading. State officials cannot simply choose "whatever" in setting policy. They are constrained within certain limits.

There are boundaries around their ability to launch policy. Economic and technical limitations come to mind immediately. But there are also important political and constitutional boundaries. I will review the nature of these boundaries and suggest the need for a further extension of the boundaries.

One boundary is federalism. Under the constitution, there is a division of policy-making powers. The federal government is given responsibility for certain spheres of policy, provincial governments for other spheres. But as is well known, there is considerable overlap of policy responsibilities. For example, jurisdiction is concurrent in the areas of immigration and agriculture. Both levels of government legislate in matters of the environment, trade and commerce, and transportation. And both levels spend monies in the fields of health care, post-secondary education, and social assistance. There are few areas of public policy where both levels of government are not involved. But there are some. The federal government exercises exclusive responsibility in foreign and defence policy, monetary policy, criminal law policy, veteran affairs, and Indian affairs. The provinces have exclusive responsibility in elementary and secondary education and in municipal affairs. Thus, due to the boundaries established under federalism, there are jurisdictional limits to what policy-makers can do.

Another boundary is the constitutional provision of basic rights, especially those contained in the Charter of Rights. Policy-makers cannot set policy which violates or restricts fundamental rights and freedoms except under certain conditions. One condition is the demonstration of "reasonable limits" on rights and freedoms in the Charter. Another condition is the attachment by government of an override or notwithstanding clause in legislation that violates certain of the rights in the Charter. But apart from these conditions, policy is reined in by the limitation that it cannot override individual or collective rights in the Charter and that it must be in harmony with stated objectives in the Charter such as multiculturalism. This does not mean a clear-cut division between policy, on the one hand, and rights, on the other. Judges, in interpreting the

Charter, are in effect helping set the design and contours of public policy. They determine what counts as admissible legislation and what does not. They define the meaning of rights and freedoms and of reasonable limits. Nevertheless, an important boundary exists around policy set by government officials. Such action is subject to the limits of constitutional policy set by the courts under the authority of the Charter of Rights.

If public policy is limited by the Charter of Rights, which gives constitutional protection to political and legal rights, should not policy also be limited by a Social Charter of Rights, which would give similar protection to social and economic rights? I argue that it should. Social and economic rights (e.g., health care, pensions, education) may be no more important than political and legal rights (e.g., voting, free speech, legal counsel) but neither are they less important. Both sets of rights are basic and interdependent. The effective exercise of one requires as a condition the effective exercise of the other. The right to free speech is not fully effective without adequate health care, just as the right to education is not fully effective without freedom of expression.

Such interdependence has been recognized in Europe, leading to the adoption of the European Social Charter in 1961. Why not also in Canada? The logic is compelling. Just as the Charter of Rights is necessary to guard against policies which violate political rights, a Social Charter is necessary to check against policies which ignore or infringe social rights. Risks abound. Competitive economic pressures or mean-spiritedness may encourage government policy-makers to abandon or seriously weaken Canadian social programmes. A Social Charter, enforced by the courts or by a special Social Charter Commission, can help insulate Canadians against such a possibility. This, then, is another limit on public policy that is well worth exploring.

NOTES

1. Thomas Dye, *Understanding Public Policy* (Englewood Cliffs, N.J.: Prentice-Hall, 1978), p. 3.
2. For discussion, see Marsha Chandler and William Chandler, *Public Policy and Provincial Politics* (Toronto: McGraw-Hill Ryerson, 1979), pp. 2–3.
3. G. Bruce Doern and Richard Phidd, *Canadian Public Policy* (Scarborough: Nelson Canada, 1992), ch. 7.
4. See Robert Alford and Roger Friedland, *Powers of Theory* (Cambridge: Cambridge University Press, 1986), and Stephen Brooks, *Public Policy in Canada: An Introduction* (Toronto: McClelland & Stewart, 1993), ch. 2.
5. For a sophisticated version of pluralism, see A. Paul Pross, *Group Politics and Public Policy* (Toronto: Oxford University Press, 1986).
6. For example, Leo Panitch, "Elites, Classes, and Power in Canada," in M. Whittington and G. Williams, eds., *Canadian Politics in the 1990s* (Scarborough: Nelson Canada, 1995).
7. Michael Trebilcock, *The Choice of Governing Instrument* (Ottawa: Supply and Services, 1982).
8. Ronald Manzer, *Public Policies and Political Development in Canada* (Toronto: University of Toronto Press, 1985).

The Canadian Political Economy and Core Institutions

G. BRUCE DOERN
RICHARD PHIDD

Canadian public policy is made in the context of an evolving and changing political economy as well as social composition. It also occurs within an explicit set of liberal democratic political institutions that have been adapted and changed to meet new challenges. This article profiles the key features of the Canadian political economy and then takes stock of the main political institutions within which public policy formulation occurs. Our purpose here is not to offer a detailed account of the larger non-policy features of the main political institutions. Rather, we concentrate on highlighting features that are of relevance to public policy formulation.

The essential map of this terrain is different in the 1990s from that which might have been drawn in previous decades. Four developments make it different in degree as well as in kind: the rapid globalization of the economy; the launching of the Canada–U.S. Free Trade Agreement; the failure of the Meech Lake Accord; and the continuing experience with the policy consequences of the Canadian Charter of Rights and Freedoms. Each of these will be commented on briefly below.[1]

Canada's political origins demonstrate an explicit rejection of the American Revolution and an acceptance of the "peace, order, and good government" offered by British traditions and institutions, reflected especially in parliamentary government. At a basic constitutional level this also led to the adoption of a system of responsible cabinet-parliamentary government as opposed to the American system, which constructed an elaborate array of "checks and balances" between the three branches of government: the executive, the legislature, and the judiciary.[2] Canadian political leaders rejected the excesses of the American belief in individual liberty and distrust of government and authority. Even in the 1981 debate that led to an entrenched Charter of Rights, the Canadian system balanced its adherence to basic rights by providing for the right of legislative bodies to override these rights for a limited period of time. While Canada evolved into a liberal democratic state, it did so with a strong adherence to collectivist norms, whether of the Tory organic community-oriented variety or of a later social democratic kind.

The magnetic pull of the American giant has always been important — economically, politically, and culturally. The earliest definition of Canada's national and industrial policies after Confederation was an act of political will to counter American expansionism. It involved the deliberate creation of an east–west continental axis, physically and politically, to counter the efficiency of the north–south continental axis. In the last decades of the twentieth century the American influence, aided by mass communication, has exerted an even larger cultural pressure, which Canadians have simultaneously welcomed and resisted.

SOURCE: Excerpted from *Canadian Public Policy: Ideas, Structure, Process* (Toronto: Nelson, 1992), pp. 18–31. Reprinted by permission of the publisher.

The strong collectivist traditions in Canada are also a reflection of the central role of the relationships between French Canadians and English Canadians. In particular, the deeply rooted desire by French Canadians since "the Conquest" to preserve and enhance their collective cultural, religious, and linguistic independence, and even nationhood, is a central fact of Canadian political life.[3] The constant need to seek a new, delicate accommodation between French and English Canada affects many policy fields in ways that are not always obvious. Consequently, not only are policies on language and education so affected, but also policies tied to broader social issues (family allowances, for example), industrial location, and foreign policy.

Tensions in French–English relations have coincided as well with the growth and changing ethnic composition of Canada's population, and an increased focus on the rights and status of its native peoples. As a nation of immigrants, where immigration and settlement policy was once the centrepiece of economic development policy, the emergence of German, Italian, Ukrainian, and Polish Canadians, to name only a few of the ethnic groups, challenged the very definition of Canada, especially as viewed in western Canada, where a large proportion of these peoples were located and whose work and sacrifice opened the western frontier. Similar changes have occurred in large urban centres, where the immigration of visible minorities has transformed urban cultures and economies.

The enormous continental size and geographical composition of Canada, especially when contrasted with the thin ribbon of humanity that hugs the 49th parallel, imposes a spatial and physical reality to Canadian political life and public policy that even modern communications and the mass media cannot fully alter. Canada's most innovative contribution to social science, the work of Innis and others, was founded on an appreciation of this fundamental reality.[4] It focused on the importance of communication relationships between the centre and the periphery. As well, Innis showed the importance to Canadian economic development of basic staple resources, from furs and fish to grain and mineral resources. He also pointed out the limits and dependence created by reliance on a staples approach to economic development. In practical day-to-day public policy terms, the spatial and geographical realities cannot be underestimated. They affect the importance of staple resources as a central element of economic and industrial policy and of Canada's economic wealth and dependence; the importance of transportation and communication policy as a vehicle of national integration (with the infrastructure usually supplied by the state); the changing definition and response to demands for sensitive regional policy; the emotional and normative attachment, especially in western Canada but also in Atlantic Canada, to the question of resource ownership and the management of non-renewable resources; and the perception by Canada's trading partners, especially the United States, of Canada as a stable supplier of basic resources.

Canada's economy is essentially a capitalist one and thus is rooted in a belief in the value and efficiency of the market and in the individual freedom and defence of property rights that capitalism helps sustain. The right to own property was a particularly important value to the immigrant settlers. Though linked to the values of liberalism and individualism, there has always existed in Canada an ambivalence about the idea of efficiency inherent in capitalism. The numerous rough edges of Canadian capitalism have always been moderated by an inclination to use the state. Statism was reflected not only in the frequent use of public enterprise or crown corporations, but even earlier, in the extensive public subsidization and financing of major transportation networks.[5]

It must also be stressed that Canada's economy, like that of any continental country, is a regionally varied one. This reality arises from the physical and geographical attributes noted above. The geographic dispersal of natural resources such as fish, forests, grain, and minerals, the existence of different energy dependencies in each region, the proximity of different regions to population concentrations and therefore markets, and the widely varying modes and costs of transportation generate a need for regional policies and responses. They also result in distinctly different and often contradictory views about the soundness and appropriateness of national economic policy. These economic features are not ones that can be simplistically attributed to capitalism. They are influenced by capitalism, but they also predate and affect what capitalists and government entrepreneurs can do in the marketplace and in the exercise of political power.

Capitalism, however, does produce relations of dependence and economic subordination between those who own capital and those who supply their labour.[6] It also increasingly produces other "classes," such as government workers whose class orientations are at best vague and subject to other regional, ethnic, and individual cross pressures. The presence of capitalism raises fundamental questions about the role of class politics in the policy process. Several recent studies in Canada make it evident that the class aspects of Canadian politics cannot be viewed at the simplistic level of capitalists and workers in perpetual conflict, with the state operating as the agent of the owners of capital. It is increasingly acknowledged that the state has considerable autonomy. Nor can it be argued, on the basis of voting data and the failure of left-wing political parties such as the NDP to gain power at the national level, that class politics is irrelevant in electoral and party politics and hence in public policy. The truth lies somewhere in between.

The presence of capitalism and the ideas and beliefs associated with it and in opposition to it raises the age-old debate about efficiency versus equality. Because capitalism helps generate political parties of the left or socialist variety, it brings into organized political life a concern for the redistribution of income and power between rich and poor, between capital and labour, and among interests and regions.

A final but critical dual feature of Canadian capitalism and the Canadian economy is the considerable dependence on foreign trade and the extensive foreign ownership of the Canadian industrial and resource sectors, especially by American business interests.[7] About 25 to 30 percent of the income of Canadians is dependent upon foreign trade, much of it with the United States. These percentages are even higher in certain regions and subregions of Canada. The trade and foreign ownership imperatives affect and constrain Canada's conduct of policy both in foreign policy terms vis-à-vis the United States, and in domestic policy in fields such as energy, industrial, and regional policy. The presence of large blocks of concentrated foreign capital also affects the internal deliberations of major business interest groups, which must take positions that accommodate both indigenous capital and foreign-owned capital. Thus, foreign ownership and trade dependence are political and policy issues, not just because of the implied possible control by foreign enterprises operating through active support of their own foreign government, but also because they are a strong influence in the domestic counsels of Canadian federal and provincial governments and within major Canadian economic interest groups. These imperatives are reinforced by close relations among Canadian and American unions and by conflicts within the Canadian labour movement.[8]

THE CORE POLITICAL INSTITUTIONS

In the 1990s the core political institutions of Canadian politics include the Canada–U.S. Free Trade Agreement; federalism; the Charter of Rights and Freedoms; cabinet-parliamentary government; interest groups; the electoral system and political parties; and the mass media. The institutions interact with one another. One cannot understand their role in policy formulation by viewing each of them in isolation. Federalism and cabinet-parliamentary government interact with each other, partly through electoral competition and political party alliances and personalities. The media interact with all of the institutions because they are both an essential part of democratic life and a necessary forum for modern political communication and leadership. Interest groups seek to influence all the major institutions since they play a crucial intermediary role between the citizen and the state.

The Canada–U.S. Free Trade Agreement

The free trade agreement (FTA) between Canada and the United States was passed in 1988 and took effect in 1989.[9] Instituted by the Mulroney government, but with the support of seven provinces, the FTA creates by 1999 a tariff-free border as well as improving market access in areas such as services, agriculture, and resource trade. The most important aspects of the FTA for public policy purposes are threefold. First, it entrenches, in chapters 18 and 19 of the agreement, two mechanisms that together significantly institutionalize the overall Canada–U.S. decision-making relationship. Chapter 18 sets up an overall trade dispute resolution commission and also requires new forms of formal advance consultation on pending policy initiatives in many policy fields. Chapter 19 has a specific dispute panel to review procedurally decisions regarding the application of trade remedies such as countervail duties against alleged subsidy activities that confer advantage on either country's exporters.

These and other provisions ensure that the FTA now stands as a new quasi-constitutional pillar in the Canadian institutional pantheon. It is effectively a North American economic constitution that partly constrains the state from acting in ways to which it had become historically accustomed. Moreover, because of the political divisiveness that accompanied its debate and introduction, the FTA also has become a potent symbol for the ongoing debate between those interests that favour a strong role for the state and those that place greater faith in markets and capitalism.

Federalism

Federalism is based on a belief in the need to balance national integration and unity with regional and cultural differences. It incorporates ideas of centralization and decentralization. It imposes a dominant reality on the Canadian policy process, namely the need to practise some form of cooperative federalism regardless of the short-term rhetoric of day-to-day politics.

Federalism is first an article of belief, not just a document containing the deathless prose of the British North America Act or the more inspiring ideals of the Constitution Act, 1982, and the Charter of Rights and Freedoms.[10] It legitimizes the existence of separate, but interdependent, realms of political power. In particular, sections 91, 92, and 95 of the Constitution Act, 1867 (formerly the BNA Act) enumerate federal and provincial legislative powers and thus, in part, constrain what each level of government can do. Federalism sanctifies the right of constituent governments to pursue different policy priorities at different times. It also makes possible public policy experimentation and "learning" where one province or the federal government adopts an approach tried elsewhere and adapts it to its own situation. But policy and program interdependence between the two levels of government is also an evident feature of federalism. Public policy is profoundly affected by joint statutory agreements on taxation, equalization payments, and major social programs such as medicare, education, welfare, and employment training. Interdependence is a reality in environmental regulation, agricultural policy, labour relations, and in the industrial, resource, and energy policy fields, to mention only a few.

The growing dominance since the 1960s of "executive federalism," where policy is made in a series of "behind-the-scenes" multilateral bargains struck among ministers and senior officials, has led to concern about the process itself, about the policies it produces, and about the demoralizing inaction or mere tinkering it often produces. Indeed, in the immediate wake of the 1990 Meech Lake failure, many feared for the very existence of Canada as a viable political entity.

The Meech Lake Accord was an initiative of Prime Minister Brian Mulroney to bring Quebec back into the constitutional fold after Quebec's isolation from the 1982 Trudeau initiative that resulted in the patriation of the Canadian constitution from Britain and the entrenchment of a Charter of Rights and Freedoms. Had it been approved, the Meech Lake Accord would have done three main things of political and policy importance. First, it would have given some recognition to the existence of Quebec as a distinct society within Canada. Second, it would have recognized the right of the federal government to use its spending powers in areas of provincial jurisdiction, provided such use was approved by an appropriate number of provinces. Third, provinces would have the right to opt out of such joint initiatives with appropriate fiscal compensation, provided that their alternative programs were compatible with national objectives.

The Meech Lake Accord failed narrowly to win approval, in part because of outright disagreement over its substance, in part because of the "take it or leave it" process adopted, and in part because of its failure to address issues such as the rights of native peoples. In any event, its failure created a severe constitutional crisis and propelled angry demands by Quebeckers for independence or for an even more decentralized form of federalism than the Meech Lake formula had contained.[11] English Canadians were also increasingly less tolerant of the essential nature of their national political institutions. Western Canadians, in particular, had coupled their opposition to the accord with calls for an even more far-reaching establishment of a "triple E" Senate, "elected, equal, and effective," that would enhance regional representation in federal decision-making.

The Charter of Rights and Freedoms

The Charter of Rights and Freedoms became a central part of the Canadian constitution in 1982.[12] It sets out to protect several basic freedoms (of conscience and religion, association, and peaceful assembly) as well as basic legal rights (such as the right to be secure against unreasonable search and seizure, and the right to life, liberty, and security of person). The Charter also protects certain equality rights, including equal protection and equal benefit of the law without discrimination based on race, national or ethnic origin, colour, religion, sex, age, or mental or physical disability. These freedoms and rights can only be subject to such reasonable limits by law as can be demonstrably justified in a free and democratic society.

The intent of the Trudeau government in pressing for the Charter was that such protections would establish freedoms for all Canadians against the powers of both levels of government and would accordingly become a unifying symbol and reality of Canadians. Since 1982 hundreds of Charter cases have proceeded through the courts to test the exact meaning of these protections. Our interest in the Charter is primarily with its possible effects on the content and processes of policy formulation. While few consistent patterns of effect can be discerned, there is little doubt that public policy-making has been influenced in several ways.

First, the role of the courts in supervising the executive and administrative arms of government has undoubtedly increased. This will over time bring different styles of policy reasoning since the judicial mind will bring to bear different factors than the administrative or political mind. Second, the equality provisions, in particular, have influenced the content of some social policy in areas such as maternity benefits and other eligibility provisions. Third, as policy is developed, proposals are being assessed within the executive even more carefully to ensure that they do not offend the Charter and that they do not involve the government in litigation.

A further effect of the Charter is on the policy strategies of interest groups. Groups have to consider more carefully whether to lobby in their accustomed ways or occasionally take issues to court either in fact or as a threat. The government too may use the Charter or its fear of threatened litigation as a way of leveraging excessive demands by interest groups seeking discriminatory action in their favour. All of these effects in combination cannot help but alter the actual policy agenda, throwing up surprises and unexpected strategies and court decisions that send the government's planned agenda into some disarray.

Cabinet-Parliamentary Government

Cabinet-parliamentary government exists at both the federal and provincial levels of Canadian government. It is a system of government that has significant implications for the relations between the executive, the legislature, and the judiciary. The executive, comprising the Crown, the prime minister, the Cabinet, and the bureaucracy, has the main powers of initiation in matters of policy, finance, and legislation. Parliament and provincial legislatures represent public opinion, legislate, oppose, and criticize, but legally, and by convention, they do not initiate policy per se.

In recent years there has been a strong tendency to attribute a declining, low, or even nonexistent policy role to Parliament or the legislature itself.[13] Nonetheless, it is patently evident that the *existence* of an assembly, democratically elected by voters in geographically based constituencies and charged with holding the majority party (expressed in votes in the assembly) accountable, has important implications for policy formulation. Under a parliamentary system, governed by rigid rules of confidence and party discipline, the government majority party has the main power to initiate policy, especially through taxation and spending. This fact, coupled with the growing complexity and technical nature of public policy, has contributed further to the view that Parliament has virtually no policy role — only the power to oppose, criticize, and scrutinize. The policy role of Parliament is held to be that of a mere "refinery" or, somewhat more grandly, the ultimate source of legitimacy through its exercise of legislative procedures in the passage of bills. While it is difficult to argue that Parliament has much power — almost by definition this is so — the refinery concept and other similar labels nonetheless seriously underplay the role of Parliament, particularly the role it plays when governments have to "anticipate" the opposition political parties' views and strategies expressed and forged in the House of Commons. Moreover, in the Mulroney period, reforms gave some increased leverage to parliamentary committees.

There is, of course, little dispute that the executive branch of cabinet-parliamentary government is the fulcrum of policy-making. This applies to the role of the prime minister and other cabinet ministers, but also to the role of the senior bureaucracy

and the central agency apparatus that supports the Cabinet.[14] Policy is influenced by the central personal preferences and beliefs of the prime minster and of other ministers; by the inevitable and unavoidable need to delegate tasks to over forty ministers and hundreds of agencies; by the need to rank or balance ideas and to allocate resources of time, money, personnel, and political energy; by the size and representative composition of the Cabinet; by the advice, expertise, and longevity in office of senior officials; and by the presence, or lack, of resources, information, and knowledge.

Interest Groups

As a country with a strong belief in the right of persons to associate freely in groups, it is axiomatic that interest groups are important elements of Canadian politics and hence of public policy formulation.[15] While interest groups serve many important purposes for their members, our concern here is with their role in influencing policy development, by advocating change or marshalling political action to prevent changes unfavourable to them, by providing information to and withholding it from government, and by acting as a source of support for government. Interest groups are active in lobbying ministers and senior officials of the key departments and agencies that concern them.

Political Parties

The role of the electoral and party system in the development and formulation of public policy presents some puzzling paradoxes for the student of public policy, especially regarding the contrasting perspectives supplied by economists and political scientists. The latter have tended to downplay the formal policy role of parties by asserting that political parties are primarily agents for the recruitment of political leaders and the aggregation and mobilization of interests and voters for electoral purposes.[16] The two major Canadian parties, the Liberals and the Progressive Conservatives, are often viewed as cadre parties lacking even the British party traditions of the serious party "mandate" or platform and with only periodic policy meetings whose resolutions are not binding on the party leaders. The New Democratic Party, it is acknowledged, is more of a mass-based party and takes policy more seriously, but only, it is said by some, because it has no serious chance of gaining national office.

However, parties as electoral vehicles are the key link between voters and officer-holders. Both the governing and opposition parties cater to the views and perceptions of the *marginal* swing voter, especially in the swing constituency (electoral seats that were won or lost by a small plurality of votes). Political leaders, including central party advisers, often through the use of extensive public opinion polls, are particularly sensitive to the potential marginal vote changes in the fifty or so swing constituencies that make or break an election. Political parties help define what is to be viewed as "political" and how certain conceptions of politics, and therefore policies, can be successfully screened out of policy debates, out of the list of national priorities, and out of the very definition of the national interest.

The Mass Media

As with the other main institutions, the issue of the role of the mass media is important and complex.[17] Television and mass communications influence politics and public policy in several ways. An ability to communicate through the media is a prime factor in the selection and evaluation of leaders. It is said that a prime minister's dominance over policy and over the setting of the agenda is enhanced by an ability to command the media's attention. It is also evident that the media's short attention span makes it all the more difficult for government to hold any set of policy priorities constant for any extended period of time. Policies and decisions are often strategically timed either to minimize unfavourable coverage or to maximize coverage. The alleged bias of the media is held to be the major reason why governments and interest groups alike feel the need to spend increasing millions on policy advocacy advertising and on the marketing of their policies

and leaders. Some assert glibly that question period in the House of Commons could not function without *The Globe and Mail.*

Judgments about the political rise and fall of ministers and their strengths and weaknesses are formed partly by a tight network of gossip and information exchanged among journalists, ministers, ministerial aids, and senior bureaucrats. The media's role is held by many policy practitioners to be a central reason why, in public policymaking, *perception* may be more important than reality.

CONCLUSIONS

Canadian public policy is made within the larger national political economy and in the context of an important set of core institutions. These institutions now include the Canada–U.S. Free Trade Agreement and the Charter of Rights and Freedoms, as well as the more familiar institutions surveyed above. In the wake of the post–Meech Lake search for constitutional renewal, and in light of the rapid globalization of the economy, Canada's institutional setting for policy-making has never been subject to more challenges.

NOTES

1. See Thomas J. Courchene, "Global Competitiveness and the Canadian Federation," paper prepared for Conference on Global Competition and Canadian Federalism, University of Toronto, September 15, 1990; Richard Simeon, "Thinking About Constitutional Futures: A Framework," paper prepared for C.D. Howe Institute Conference, November 17, 1990; and G. Bruce Doern and Bryne Purchase, eds., *Canada at Risk: Canadian Public Policy in the 1990s* (Toronto: C.D. Howe Institute, 1990).
2. T.A. Hockin, *Government in Canada* (Toronto: McGraw-Hill Ryerson, 1976), and R.M. Dawson, *The Government of Canada*, revised by N. Ward (Toronto: University of Toronto Press, 1970). See also Reg Whitaker, "Images of the State in Canada," in Leo Panitch, ed., *The Canadian State* (Toronto: University of Toronto Press, 1977), ch. 2.

3. See Léon Dion, *Quebec: the Unfinished Revolution* (Montreal: McGill-Queen's University Press, 1976); Hubert Guindon, "The Modernization of Quebec and the Legitimacy of the Canadian State," *Canadian Review of Sociology and Anthropology* 15, no. 2 (1978), 227–45; Ramsay Cook, *Canada and the French Canadian Question* (Toronto: Macmillan, 1976); and Denis Monière, *Ideologies in Quebec* (Toronto: University of Toronto Press, 1981).

4. See Donald Creighton, *Harold Adams Innis: Portrait of a Scholar* (Toronto: University of Toronto Press, 1978), and Harold Innis, *Essays in Canadian Economic History* (Toronto: University of Toronto Press, 1956).

5. See Herschel Hardin, *A Nation Unaware: The Canadian Economic Culture* (Vancouver: J.J. Douglas, 1974); W.L. Morton, *The Canadian Identity*, 2nd ed. (Toronto: University of Toronto Press, 1972); and H.G. Aitken, "Defensive Expansionism: The State and Economic Growth in Canada," in W.T. Easterbrook and M.H. Watkins, eds., *Approaches to Canadian Economic History* (Toronto: McClelland and Stewart, 1967).

6. See Panitch, *The Canadian State*, and John Porter, *The Vertical Mosaic* (Toronto: University of Toronto Press, 1965), ch. 12.

7. See Robert Bothwell, Ian Drummond, and John English, *Canada Since 1945: Power, Politics and Provincialism* (Toronto: University of Toronto Press, 1981), ch. 5; and J. Fayerweather, *Foreign Investment in Canada* (Toronto: Oxford University Press, 1973).

8. See Gad Horowitz, *Canadian Labour in Politics* (Toronto: University of Toronto Press, 1968); John Anderson and Morley Gunderson, eds., *Union Management Relations in Canada* (Toronto: Addison-Wesley, 1982); and G. Swimmer and M. Thompson, eds., *Public Sector Industrial Relations in Canada* (Montreal: Institute for Research on Public Policy, 1983).

9. See G. Bruce Doern and Brian W. Tomlin, *Faith and Fear: The Free Trade Story* (Toronto: Stoddart, 1991).

10. See D.V. Smiley, *Canada in Question*, 3rd ed. (Toronto: McGraw-Hill Ryerson, 1980), ch. 1, and Garth Stevenson, *Unfulfilled Union* (Toronto: Macmillan, 1979).

11. See Simeon, "Thinking About Constitutional Futures."

12. See Peter H. Russell, "The Political Purposes of the Canadian Charter of Rights and Freedoms," *Canadian Bar Review* 61 (1983), 30–54; F.L. Morton and Leslie Pal, "The Impact of the Charter of Rights on Public Administration," *Canadian Public Administration* 28, no. 2 (1985), 221–43; and Michael Mandel, *The Charter of Rights and the Legalization of Politics in Canada* (Toronto: Thompson, 1991).

13. See Van Loon and Whittington, *The Canadian Political System*, ch. 19; Robert J. Jackson and M. Atkinson, *The Canadian Legislative System*, 2nd ed. (Toronto: Macmillan, 1980); and T. d'Aquino, G. Bruce Doern, and C. Blair, *Parliamentary Government in Canada: A Critical Assessment and Suggestions for Change* (Ottawa: Intercounsel Ltd., 1979).

14. G. Bruce Doern and Peter Aucoin, eds., *Public Policy in Canada* (Toronto: Macmillan, 1979), and T. Hockin, ed., *Apex of Power*, 2nd ed. (Toronto: Prentice-Hall, 1980).

15. A. Paul Pross, *Pressure Group Behaviour in Canadian Politics* (Toronto: McGraw-Hill Ryerson, 1975), and A. Paul Pross, *Group Politics and Public Policy* (Toronto: University of Toronto Press, 1986).

16. See, for example, H. Thorburn, ed., *Party Politics in Canada*, 4th ed. (Toronto: Prentice-Hall, 1979). For a broader view see M.J. Brodie and Jane Jenson, *Crisis, Challenge and Change: Party and Class in Canada* (Toronto: Methuen, 1980), and Conrad Winn and J. McMenemy, *Political Parties in Canada* (Toronto: McGraw-Hill Ryerson, 1976).

17. See Edwin R. Black, *Politics and the News* (Toronto: Butterworths, 1982); Douglas Hartle, *Public Policy, Decision Making and Regulation* (Montreal: Institute for Research on Public Policy, 1979).

Ten Tips for Good Policy Analysis

LESLIE PAL

Policy analysis is a practical activity, one in which good, bad, and mediocre results are both evident and recognizable. The following tips assume that good policy **analysis** is defined by its ability to clarify a problem and perhaps show plausible ways of dealing with it. It is fashionable to say that such criteria are purely relative and depend entirely on one's values and assumptions, but there is some ineffable quality to good work that does distinguish it from bad work in the long run. Good work has the rhythm and architecture of quality. These tips will not guarantee good work, but ignoring them is almost certain to lead to shoddy analysis.

1. DIVE DEEP Good analysis is almost always distinguished by a solid historical grasp of the issues and the problem. In some cases, historical depth may amount to no more than a few years; in others, it may require the analyst to retrieve decades of development and evolution. Background like this may never find its way into a report, and so it is tempting to skimp on it. The pressure of time also forces many analysts to do "quick and dirty" work. Avoid this, if possible.

2. KNOW THE LAW This maxim may lead the analyst through small mountains of legislative and judicial material, but it is the only way to crystallize the practical expression of policy. Analysis that confines itself to the rhetorical statements of intention that adorn policies inevitably will be misled.

3. COUNT THE STAKES Every public policy is set against a political context of winners and losers, values and interest. Ignoring these is fatal, but a sensitive accounting is extremely difficult. Weighing those interests and judging their salience is also necessary. Finally, the analyst cannot simply reduce values to interests. In many cases, arguments of ethics or principles are merely smokescreens for self-interest, but in others, there are real values at stake which are unconnected to any obvious short-term interest. Good analysis tries to be sensitive to these distinctions even if they cannot always be clearly made.

4. LOOK AT THE BIG PICTURE Practical policy analysis is usually undertaken at a specific level— for example, should these subsidies be revised or this program changed? It is tempting to keep one's analytical nose down in the dirt without looking up at the bigger picture, the long-term trends. This occasional glance to the wider context is essential if analysis is to be imaginative, bold, and fresh. In telecommunications policy the wider context might be the information revolution, in economic policy the emergence of the "symbols" economy, and in foreign policy the decline of the USSR. Looking at wider contexts sometimes induces a shift in the

SOURCE: Excerpted from *Public Policy Analysis: An Introduction* (Toronto: Nelson, 1992), pp. 276–80. Reprinted by permission of the publisher.

analyst's perspective, reassembling the elements of a problem or issue in novel ways.

5. BE CAUTIOUSLY SCEPTICAL OF EXPERTS People usually become experts by concentrating on one thing for a long time. True experts do not merely know a field, they help shape and define it. Moreover, they may derive their livelihood from the field they study. As a consequence, they sometimes develop prejudices, perspectives, beliefs, and convictions that blind them to new possibilities or different approaches. Good analysts use experts for help on detail and background, but are careful to solicit countervailing advice. If experts are to be consulted, always use more than one, preferably those known to have differing viewpoints.

6. BE CAUTIOUSLY RESPECTFUL OF COMMON SENSE The great conceit of modern science, social and natural, is its disdain for ordinary common sense. Common sense, after all, tells us that the sun revolves around the earth, while science — the disciplined pursuit and application of knowledge — tells us the truth, that the earth revolves around the sun. Policy analysis shares this conceit when it labels community preferences or common sense as "simplistic." People are never as stupid as they sometimes appear, and refined science can frequently paint itself into illogical corners. The current state of the world is a rather sorry advertisement for the benefits of policy research and scientific statecraft. Of course, this overestimates the influence of science on the political process, but it remains true that the explosion of expert policy advice over the last two decades has not coincided with many triumphs in social problem-solving. This is not the counsel of despair, just humility. Ordinary citizens can think too.

7. IF POSSIBLE, HAVE A BIAS TOWARD SMALL SOLUTIONS This is a variation of another, older maxim: "If it's not broken, don't fix it." "Improvement" for improvement's sake wastes time, money, and energy; so too can over-ambitious, grandiose attacks on policy problems. In other

words, "if it's broken, fix what's broken and leave the rest." Small solutions are difficult to define, and this may seem like the road to conservative policy-making. A few policy areas, like the environment, seem amenable only to "big" solutions. However, the use of small increments to deal with problems is possible in most policy areas. A small solution may be defined as one which has narrow scope (i.e., its target is focussed), and which relies on less coercive governing instruments. "Small solutions" may also be regarded as limited experiments that allow policy-makers to see whether their proposals work. A bias towards small solutions can thus become a willingness to try new ideas and experiment with old forms.

8. CHOOSE POLICY TARGETS THAT YOU HAVE A REASONABLE CHANCE OF CONTROLLING Aaron Wildavsky has noted that governments do some things better and more effectively than others. The global object of public policy is to change or maintain certain behaviours, but there is some wisdom in choosing means that can be reasonably well controlled and monitored. Anti-smoking messages are diffuse and inexact means to reduce the health risks of cigarettes; ordering manufacturers to reduce tar content or otherwise alter ingredients is more effective and direct. It may be difficult to improve levels of health or education, but governments can assure access to facilities like hospitals and schools. It is a tricky business to increase tolerance, but relatively easy to police open discrimination. The point is not to abandon the more grandiose goals, but simply to reformulate them in terms more amenable to realistic policy intervention.

9. DESPITE THE ABOVE, REMEMBER THAT PEOPLE HAVE DIFFERENT PREFERENCES — TRY TO STRUCTURE CHOICE INTO POLICY It is often in the interests of government to remove or reduce the range of choices when providing services. This enhances bureaucratic control and may reduce costs. It also sometimes reflects a latent distrust of ordinary citizens: without the benefit of expertise

or special training, how can they be expected to make the right decisions? Modern government sometimes seems close to being a tyranny of experts, where the only role for citizens is to pay the bills. Teachers want to control education, doctors the health-care system, and social workers the social services. Obviously there is a legitimate place for experts in these fields, but while bureaus must run efficiently, policies that involve providing services to people should try to allow clients the maximum feasible autonomy. Individuals have different needs and interests, and no bureaucracy, however competent, can hope to second guess all of them. Publicly run day-care centres, for example, may provide high standards of care as defined by experts, but not as defined by parents. Moreover, they may not be as convenient in location, price, or schedule as the friend next door. In cases like these, subsidies or vouchers are better than a monopoly service. Canada's publicly funded health-care system allows people to choose their own doctor; post-secondary students may apply to any of the country's universities. These are examples of policies that accommodate choice and allow beneficiaries to tailor program delivery to their own needs.

10. BE BALANCED IN CONSIDERING INTERESTS, BUT ERR ON THE SIDE OF WIDELY SPREAD OR DIFFUSE INTERESTS OVER CONCENTRATED, ORGANIZED INTERESTS Public policy is ultimately the expression of a community's sense of justice. It can no more be devoid of ethics than can any other part of the political process. While analysts must be fair-minded and balanced in their assessment of competing claims and interests, they must also face the unpleasant but universal fact that politics is about power: getting it, keeping it, and using it. Social and political systems tend to reflect the interests of the powerful, and are more receptive to them. But all wealth and power is justified not for its own sake but for its social benefit. Corporations are given tax breaks not so that they can make more money, but so that they employ people and do economically useful things. Concentrations of wealth are accepted because they are presumed to have been fairly gained and because they provide benefits to society at large. Labour unions and the organized professions are granted privileges to promote the general welfare, not merely to enhance their members' incomes.

Policy analysts must take the full measure of these claims, weigh them carefully, and determine whether they are genuine or self-serving. Given that privilege is almost always an advocate of its own cause, the analyst should have a small but healthy bias against this. Does economic regulation really serve a public purpose, or does it sometimes increase costs for consumers and protect vested interests from competition? Do tax breaks and shelters for investors really provide "trickle down" benefits for the unemployed? Analysts are often forced to ask questions like these, with only their judgment or instinct to guide them. In these moments, a bias favouring the less powerful is one useful, but not infallible, rule of thumb.

Ten tips will not an analyst make. One could apply them all, and still be wrong. What matters is a desire for excellence, complemented by conscience, fairness, and skill. All this makes the policy analyst seem part saint, part judge, and part scientist. While the world could use a few more saints, it needs skilful analysts too.

Law, the Courts, and Governing Ourselves

CLOSE-UP: POLICE, ORDER, AND GOOD GOVERNMENT

The phrase, "Peace, Order and good Government" in the Constitution Act, 1867, led the politicians of the day to create a national police force to administer and enforce the new laws of the country. Once established, a Canadian police force would be expected to play a major role in maintaining peace and order in the challenging and vast northern frontier. From the beginning, the police were identified not only with social order, but with good government as well.

The struggle to govern Canada always involved law enforcement by various government agencies. Indeed, our frontier mentality saw the need to fill the wilderness with rules, regulations, and enforcement officers as soon as possible. But the achievement of this goal, and the spread of law enforcement in the Canadian frontier, took time. In actuality, a lawless frontier lingered in Canada well into the twentieth century.

In the 1870s, a horse could be bought for a gallon of whisky — as could a person's life, usually an "Indian's." Fuelled by alcohol and racism, brutality and murder were commonplace in the Canadian frontier, especially at the whisky forts and in the lawless territories.

Clearly, the image of Canadians in the original Northwest Territories (present-day Alberta and Saskatchewan) as a lawful people is misleading, as is the traditional historical view of all Canadians as law-abiding and non-violent. Places called Slideout, Robbers' Roost, Whisky Gap, and Fort Whoop-Up were just a few of the sites in Canada that saw a great deal of violence, alcoholism, and abuse of Native people. Indeed, violence spurred by racism was a common event. These facts should not be overlooked as realities of Canadian history. Nor should we think that similar problems do not exist in our cities and towns in the 1990s.

AMERICAN INFLUENCE

In exchange for a rifle, traders from the United States could get a pile of valuable animal skins as high as the gun was long. But mostly, they came to Canada to peddle whisky. A buffalo skin would buy a quantity of a concoction made with alcohol, tobacco juice, water, and vitriol, and spiced with peppers and Jamaica ginger.

Many of the Americans who crossed the border in the latter half of the nineteenth century behaved in Canada just as they did at home: They were as lawless as the coyotes they liked to kill for sport. Also for sport, they would attack the people whom they commonly referred to as "Indians," burning their teepees, abusing their animals, raping the women, and murdering the children.

Canadian press reports referred to these individuals as "American scum" and demanded government action. After a time, Prime Minister John A. Macdonald took action by establishing the North-West Mounted Police, in August 1873. The

NWMP would send a signal to the Americans that Canada was not the United States and that civilian law was present and enforceable in the northern frontier. Macdonald had another motive as well. He wanted a police force in order to deal with the armed French Métis under the leadership of Louis Riel.

Macdonald's police recruits numbered about 300, and were accompanied by clerks, tradesmen, telegraphers, bartenders, lumberjacks, and some soldiers from Ontario, Quebec, New Brunswick, and Nova Scotia. They assembled in October 1873 at Collingwood, about 110 km north of Toronto, and travelled 800 km by steamer to Port Arthur (now Thunder Bay). Then, battling blizzards, they trudged 720 km to Lower Fort Garry, about 30 km north of Winnipeg, where many were sworn as North-West Mounted Police.

Gradually the whisky trade was wiped out: Americans and Canadians alike learned to fear and admire Queen Victoria's policemen. Tribal conflicts waned as mutual respect grew between the Mounties and the many aboriginal peoples. In about seven years, between 1893 and 1900, a measure of police order had come to the Canadian West, displacing the **anarchy** and lawlessness of the recent past. But some say it was not until the 1880s that a more durable "peace, order and good government" was established in the West.

Thus, in the earliest years after Confederation the police came to be regarded as the legitimate "governors" whose presence represented law and justice. Eventually in the public mind the police ceased to represent the totality of government and became just one agency of government that enforced the rules and regulations of government.

INTRODUCTION: LAW AND THE GOVERNING OF CANADA

To the political scientist, the concept of "the law" in Canada includes the processes, principles, standards, and rules that govern relationships among governments and that help to resolve conflicts between and among Canadians. "What Is Law?", the contribution by S.M. Waddams (Chapter 19),

gives us the nuts and bolts of this concept, taking us from its most fundamental applications to the role of judges in interpreting and administering legal challenges to public policy.

It is impossible to conceive of Canada functioning without the benefit of law, without carefully formulated legal principles, standards, and rules that keep us from unravelling as a society of law-abiding people. No reasonable person in Canada believes that complex social problems can be dealt with in the absence of statutes, courts, parliaments, Cabinet **orders-in-council**, public servants, police, and judges.

Canadians are very law-conscious. Increasingly, we are prone to litigation not just on material matters but on important questions of rights. When we encounter a social problem, we are likely to say, "There ought to be a law!" On reflection, however, we might conclude that we should be spared the extension of regulatory legal authority into all areas of our lives. Yet on all substantive issues, such as abortion, gun control, and the right to die by choice under special circumstances, Canadians expect their legislators to produce public policy.

Although the words **rule of law** were not mentioned in the Constitution Act, 1867, the idea is one of the most important legacies of the Fathers of Confederation. The rule of law means that the rulers, like those they rule, are answerable to the law, and that they are prohibited from interfering with the independent rulings of the courts. Just as there are laws that address the behaviour of ordinary citizens, so there are laws that focus on the behaviour of public officials. Thus, despite many signs to the contrary, especially in times of deep social and economic change, Canadians hold the rule of law in high esteem, as evidenced by our traditional respect for reason and for duly constituted authority.

COMMON LAW AND CIVIL LAW

Public law in Canada, including Quebec, is based largely on English **common law**, wherein judges dispense law based on custom and the precedents contained in the cumulative body of their decisions, dating back to the thirteenth century. When a case is before the courts, the lawyers and the judge try to find precedents — that is, decisions in earlier cases that involved principles similar to those in the case at hand. Most law governing the actions of Canadians is "statutory law," law enacted by Parliament or by provincial legislatures, but often embodying the original principles of English common law.

Public law in Canada's common-law system is that area of the law affecting the rights of the individual in relation to the state, or the Crown. It includes constitutional law, criminal law, administrative law, and international law. Public law is concerned with the most salient issues of public policy, although even a minor issue before the courts concerning the power of the state over the individual would be considered a matter of public law.

By contrast, **private law** deals with the relationships between or among private individuals or companies. Private law as practised in Quebec is governed by the **civil law**, at the heart of which is a set of unified codes, or authoritative written statements of the law. (Note that the term *civil law* has a second, broader, meaning: It also refers to private law in general *as opposed to* criminal law, which deals with offences against the state, in the common-law system.) Present law in Quebec is an adaptation of the original Code Napoléon, which served as a model for the contemporary Civil Code of Quebec. Under civil law, the latitude of the judge is considerably more restricted than under common law. In matters such as contracts, mortgages, and the law of property, judges are less able to assume a legislative role.

The Quebec legal system is described as a "mixed" or "hybrid" system, reflecting a bicultural legal heritage of the common-law and civil-law traditions. The Civil Code of Quebec is, like the use of the French language and other francophone cultural traits, a clear illustration of the distinctiveness of Quebec society in the legal, cultural, and linguistic landscape of Canada and North America.

THE ROLE OF THE COURTS

Canadian courts play a major role in governing this country. We must think of our courts as active governing institutions and not as passive bodies that react to the process of government from without. Our courts are confronted with issues of great importance, and their decisions help shape our rights and freedoms, as well as the quality of life that we enjoy.

Canada's court system is intergovernmental and hierarchical. Federalism determines the structure and harmony of the Canadian judiciary. In Chapter 20, "The Courts," Peter McCormick and Ian Greene give us an in-depth view of the Canadian judicial structure, outlining the role of our judges in that system and discussing the differences in the job of judicial interpretation in Canada's common-law system and in the civil-law tradition in Quebec. They describe the organization of the separate federal and provincial courts as a hierarchy of decision-making authority with the goal of producing a unified system of justice.

The Supreme Court of Canada, discussed in Chapter 21 by James Guy, stands at the pinnacle of the Canadian judiciary, but is only one part of Canada's decentralized system of justice, a system that encompasses a network of federal, provincial, and territorial courts. Most cases never reach the Supreme Court; those that do usually reach the Court through **original jurisdiction, appellate jurisdiction**, or, in the majority of cases, the granting of "**special leave of the court**."

The Supreme Court of Canada is a court of general jurisdiction. All types and categories of law — constitutional, statutory and common law, civil and criminal, federal and provincial — are cognizable by the Court. The Supreme Court of Canada combines the general power and responsibility of the House of Lords in the English system with a constitutional power and authority largely comparable to that of the United States Supreme Court.

In 1971, the Exchequer Court of Canada, created in 1875, was renamed the Federal Court of Canada and divided into trial and appellate divisions. Sometimes called the "unknown court," the Federal Court of Canada is located in Ottawa, but, when justified by demand or convenience, both its divisions will sit in other parts of the country.

Justice Allen Linden's authoritative and comprehensive description of this court is presented in Chapter 22.

Ours is a judicial system in which judges and their courts are constrained by the actions and preferences of many other political and governmental actors, including, to some extent, ordinary Canadian citizens. The degree to which people observe, understand, and criticize the actions of their courts is, of course, a key deteminant of the quality of the judicial branch of government in Canada's parliamentary democracy.

One criticism is this: Non-white minorities account for an increasing percentage of the Canadian population. The ethnic and racial complexion of many of our governing institutions is changing to reflect this fact. The judicial system, however, seems to be lagging behind. Can justice be meted out impartially in a judicial system composed largely of white Anglo-Saxon males?

THINKING IT OVER

1. S.M. Waddams (Chapter 19) tells us why defining law is not such an easy task. Why is it that law defies definition except in terms of culture? How is Canadian law influenced by the presence of so many distinctive cultures? What are some of the reasons why law is not easily equated with principles of universal justice?

2. What do Peter McCormick and Ian Greene (Chapter 20)) tell us about the role of our courts? Distinguish the common-law and the civil-law traditions in Canada. Do Canadian courts make or interpret law? Explain.

3. James Guy's article (Chapter 21) describes the Supreme Court of Canada. Design a better Supreme Court. Discuss the age and other characteristics of justices, the number of justices, the number of cases tried, and the overall workload in your ideal court. Does the profile of Madame Justice Claire L'Heureux-Dubé affect the assumptions you might have had about the Supreme Court? In what way?

4. Since the entrenchment of the Charter of Rights and Freedoms, judges have become more involved in the interpretation of the Canadian Constitution. Through judicial review, judges play a major role in the formation of law in the areas of civil and human rights. In view of this, should Canadians consider a formal recruitment system subject to legislative review prior to the appointment of their judges?

5. Why, according to Justice Allen Linden (Chapter 22), is the Federal Court of Canada called the "unknown court"? Briefly outline the evolution of the Court. What kinds of cases does the Federal Court hear?

6. The recent accumulation of judicial powers has caused some analysts to wonder whether judges are not assuming a policy-making role in our political process. Some critics of judicial power believe that the Supreme Court and the Federal Court are like superlegislatures. Based on the readings presented here, do you think Canadians should be concerned that our federal courts are using recently acquired powers of judicial review and statutory interpretation to expand their own role in defining Canadian public policy?

GLOSSARY

administrative law In Canada, this is the law of public administration as it relates to the organization, the duties, and the quasi-judicial and judicial powers of the executive branch of government.

anarchy The absence of government, authority, and leadership. The philosophy of anarchism holds that people are basically good, but that their institutions, especially governments and the state, have corrupted them. People are naturally social; they would get along better without the artificial structures of authority that stifle their communal instincts at every turn.

appellate jurisdiction A superior court's power to review the decision of a lower court.

assize Originally, the term meant a jury of men who sat together (*assideo*) and decided on the conviction or acquittal of an accused person. Today the term refers to the trial of a civil action before a travelling judge.

civil law The civil law deals mainly with private persons, corporations, civil status, marriages, property ownership, co-ownership, gifts, wills, trusts, contracts, loans, rentals, and pledges.

clerks Recent graduates of law school are hired as law clerks to serve a judge or a number of judges for a period of time. The judges employ their clerks in a variety of ways: to do research, summarize petitions, and write and critique drafts of legal opinions.

codification The collection of all of the relevant principles of law into a single statute or a body of statutes.

common law An Anglo-American body of rules based on judicial decisions as well as legislation, using the principles of precedent, equity, *stare decisis* (let the decision stand), *res judicata* (a matter already judicially settled), *ex aequo et bono* (out of equity and fairness), the interpretations of judges, and the supremacy of a constitution. Unlike civil law, the common law is flexible and adaptive, permitting a gradual and steady accommodation of change.

contract law The branch of private law that deals with drafting, interpreting, and enforcing contracts between persons.

court of first instance A court of primary jurisdiction — that is, the court in which an action is first brought to trial.

judicial independence The separate and impartial operation of the judiciary from the political and governing system that it serves.

judicial system All the personnel, such as judges and judicial administrators, and all the formal governmental organizations, such as courts, judicial, and other legal councils, that are empowered to make official juristic decisions.

natural justice The fundamental principles of justice that do not depend on convention but flow from natural reason as to the validity of their assertion, such as the injustice of sexual assault, murder, theft, or vandalism, and the injustice or unfairness of bureaucratic conduct. That no one should be a judge in his or her own cause and that all sides of a case should be heard and no one condemned unheard are examples of natural justice at it applies in criminal and administrative law.

order-in-council An order with immediate legal effect for Canadians made by the governor general or by a lieutenant-governor of a province, by and with the advice of the political executive, or the Privy Council.

original jurisdiction The authority, power, and capacity of a court to hear a case in the first instance, try it, and pass judgement on the law and facts.

private law All law pertaining to the relationships between or among private individuals or companies (as distinct from public law).

public law The area of the law affecting the rights of the individual in relation to the state, or the Crown.

registry of the court The administrative office of a court, staffed by appropriate officers, clerks, and other employees, where notices, memoranda, articles, and decisions are filed, registered, and stored.

relief The assistance or support, pecuniary or otherwise, ordered by a court to address damages suffered by a complainant.

resolution of disputes All the legal instruments (such as mediation, arbitration, and adjudication) available in the judicial, social, and political system to bring conflictive matters between individuals and groups to a peaceful settlement.

rule of law A fundamental principle of democratic government that proclaims the supremacy of the law as applied by an independent judiciary, establishing limits for public officials in exercising their power to govern. Under this principle all individuals are equal before the law.

special leave of the court Permission granted by a Supreme or Superior Court to hear a case.

tenure The right to hold a position or office as long as desired, without the possibility of arbitrary dismissal after the fulfilment of a probationary period or after meeting certain qualifications.

tort law The law that addresses any wrongful act, neglect, or default that results in loss or damage.

writs A formal order or command of a court that directs an individual, a corporation, or an official to do or refrain from doing something in particular;

for example, a writ of possession entitles the holder to recover the possession of land by commanding the sheriff to enter the land and return possession of it to the person(s) entitled under a judgement.

ADDITIONAL READINGS

Beatty, David. 1995. *Constitutional Law in Theory and Practice*. Toronto: University of Toronto Press.

Bogart, W.A. 1994. *Courts and Country: The Limits of Litigation and the Social and Political Life of Canada*. Don Mills, Ont.: Oxford University Press.

Carrigan, D. Owen. 1991. *Crime and Punishment in Canada*. Markham, Ont.: McClelland & Stewart.

Heard, Andrew. 1991. *Canadian Constitutional Conventions: The Marriage of Law and Politics*. Toronto: Oxford University Press.

Kaplan, William, and Donald McRae, eds. 1993. *Law, Policy, and International Justice: Essays in Honour of Maxwell Cohen*. Montreal, McGill-Queen's University Press.

Loo, Tina, and Lorna McLean. 1994. *Historical Perspectives on Law and Society in Canada*. Mississauga, Ont.: Copp Clark Longman.

Mandel, Michael. 1994. *The Charter of Rights and the Legalization of Politics in Canada*. Toronto: Wall and Thompson.

Manfredi, Christopher P. 1993. *Judicial Power and the Charter*. Toronto: McClelland & Stewart.

McCormick, Peter, and Ian Greene. 1990. *Judges and Judging: Inside the Canadian Judicial System*. Toronto: James Lorimer & Company.

Morton, F.L., ed. 1993. *Law, Politics and the Judicial Process in Canada*. Calgary: University of Calgary Press.

Russell, Peter. 1987. *The Judiciary in Canada: The Third Branch of Government*. Toronto: McGraw-Hill Ryerson.

Saywell, John, and George Vegh. 1991. *Making the Law: The Courts and the Constitution*. Mississauga, Ont.: Copp Clark Pitman.

What Is Law?

S.M. WADDAMS

INTRODUCTION

A question like "What is Law?" is not to be answered in a few words, or even in a few books. Indeed, those responding to the question, even lawyers, will always differ from each other in their answers, because the concept of law is so basic to our ideas of society that it has no clear meaning outside the writer's own social and political philosophy. No doubt Canadian law is one thing to a capitalist, and quite another to a Marxist. Furthermore, pre-revolutionary law in a Marxist state is one thing; post-revolutionary law is something quite different.

Aristotle said that the human person is a political animal. He did not, of course, have in mind the party politics of the twentieth century. He meant that human beings naturally live in a community (the polis or city-state being the particular kind of community he had in mind).[1] This view remains generally accepted. Despite the emphasis we place on the person as an individual, it can hardly be doubted that it is part of her nature to live in a community. As a recent commentator said, the human being is not purely a social animal, nor a solitary animal, he is a social and a solitary animal at the same time.[2] No complete description of humanity could possibly avoid reference to the community as well as to the individual.

A universal feature of human society has been conflict. Individuals have individual interests. On occasion, they conflict with each other. If a society is to survive it must develop a system of resolving conflicts between individuals, and conflicts between individuals on the one hand and the community on the other. The law is the system of resolving those conflicts.

SOCIAL SCIENCE OR HUMANITY?

Thus, the law in any society is the society's attempt to resolve the most basic of human tensions, that between the needs of the person as an individual and her needs as a member of a community. The law is the knife-edge on which the delicate balance is maintained between the individual on the one hand and the society on the other.

Law is, therefore, at the same time, a social science and a humanity. Indeed, it is fundamental to both, and constitutes the bridge between them. Until recently the study of law in most Canadian universities has been rather isolated both from the Social Sciences and the Humanities. In most universities the Faculty of Law is independent of the Faculty of Arts and Science. The Humanities and Social Sciences research libraries rarely include collections of law books. In the last few years, however, much greater interest has been shown in the law faculties, and in other divisions of the universities, in exploring the relationship between law and other academic disciplines.

SOURCE: *Introduction to the Study of Law* (Toronto: Carswell, 1987), pp. 1–10. Reprinted by permission of Carswell — a division of Thomson Canada Limited.

ACADEMIC STUDY OR PRACTICAL TRAINING?

Part of the reason for the isolation of the law in the university undoubtedly lies in the pragmatic nature of legal study. One can talk at considerable length about the reconciliation of the individual and the community, but the study of law brings the lawyer down very suddenly from the purity of theoretical speculation to the sordid reality of practical needs. Can the police compel a suspected bank robber to undergo surgery against his will in order to discover whether a foreign body lodged in his shoulder is a bullet? Well, on the one hand, the interests of the community require us to facilitate police investigations, and it would be very useful for the police to discover whether the object is a bullet. The safety of society requires an effective police and reasonable regularity in punishment of the guilty. But then, on the other hand, there is the sanctity of the human person, which every free society must respect. We cannot allow the police to cut people up to look at their insides even if it would make their job easier. Yes, but can we do it (the police will ask)? The police surgeon is free at four this afternoon. Can I stop them (the prisoner will ask you)? And how? And quickly? These are the questions that will be asked of lawyers and judges, and they demand answers. Mr. Justice Hugessen of the Quebec Court of Queen's Bench had to give one on July 7, 1972.[3]

Sometimes people are heard to advocate the study of law as a "liberal art," thereby implying that inquiry into what the law actually is can be eliminated and that the existing law schools should reform themselves or take their crass pragmatism elsewhere. The study of law, however, can never divorce itself from a living working system. A theoretical study of police powers without attention to what the police can actually do in a particular society is not a study of law. The bridge between the theoretical and the practical is of the essence. This is not to suggest that there is no place outside the law schools for the study of law. It will be suggested below what approach such study should take.

RULES OR PROCESS?

Many think of the law as a set of rules, and, in part, it is. The law does regulate conduct. However, the study of law is not the learning of rules. Perhaps the biggest surprise to a beginning law student is to discover the uncertainty of legal answers even to basic questions. I should rather say, especially to basic questions, for the more basic the question the greater the uncertainty. Definite answers can often be given to trivial questions: Is income tax payable on an employee's bonus? Is it an offence to sell securities without a licence? It is the fundamental questions that prove elusive: Is a man guilty of crime when compelled by necessity to do the forbidden act? Can damages be awarded for loss caused by a breach of contract, even though the loss could not reasonably have been anticipated? These questions raise fundamental issues about the nature and purpose of criminal law and punishment and of **contract law** and damages. They are not to be easily answered. It is questions of the latter type that mainly concern university law students. It has often been pointed out that the problems studied in law school do not reflect the experience of most lawyers in practice. The law schools make no apology for this. It would be absurd to suggest that a legal education should mirror the experience of practising lawyers. Most lawyers spend their time in executing routine transactions, and avoiding like the plague any problem of complexity or theoretical interest. A busy lawyer does not have time for such luxuries. But a law school goes out of its way to pick out the unusual and interesting case — the case that is on the edge of a legal principle — the case that causes conflict between two different principles.

A very well known case in criminal law is *The Queen v. Dudley and Stephens*.[4] The facts were dramatic. Three men and a boy were cast adrift on the open sea a thousand miles from land. Threatened with starvation, two of them killed and ate the boy. The existence of the report makes it unnecessary to add that they survived to face trial. Plainly the case raises many complex issues, legal and ethical, and is well worth some time in any curriculum. However, it can safely be predicted that not one in a million law graduates will run across a similar case in practice. The law schools do not apologize for emphasizing unusual cases; they go out of their way to look for them. *Dudley and Stephens* is one of the few cases on the defence of necessity in criminal law; and what other cases there are show that the law is in a state of great uncertainty. Even in more mundane areas, the law is full of uncertainty, and quite rapid change. Until recently most Canadian lawyers thought that a party complaining of breach of contract was not entitled to damages for mental distress, disappointment, anger, or frustration. In 1972, a court held a holiday tour operator liable for such damages to a customer whose holiday failed to match the expectations engendered by the defendant's glossy brochures.[5] What is the law after that case? Does the principle extend to the seller of a defective motor home, or to an employer who wrongly dismisses an employee, or to a solicitor who fails to provide proper legal services? No one can say until the courts decide. There are tenable arguments for and against extending the principle of liability to each of the classes of persons mentioned. As each decision is reported, the law changes, and it is still quite uncertain. It is much closer to the truth to regard the law as a continuing process of attempting to solve the problems of a changing society, than as a set of rules.

It has been said that everyone is presumed to know the law, but this is a fiction to support the rule that ignorance of the criminal law is no excuse. Plainly everyone does not know the law. Indeed, another rule, that a misrepresentation of law is of no legal consequence, has been justified on the basis that the law is so uncertain that any statement of law is equivalent only to an expression of an opinion! An eighteenth-century judge pointed out that "it would be very hard upon the profession, if the law was so certain, that every body knew it,"[6] and another judge is reputed to have said that everyone is presumed to know the law except Her Majesty's judges, who have a Court of Appeal set over them to correct their errors.

THE IDEA OF JUSTICE

Everyone knows that the law is not the same thing as justice. Generally, indeed, when the two words are mentioned in the same sentence, it is by way of contrast. It is rare that a resolution of a dispute leaves both parties equally happy, and it would be Utopian to expect that a working system should satisfy the losing party all the time. The best that can be expected is that the losing party will admit that she has had a fair hearing according to fair procedures and that the result has been determined by principles that she will recognize as the appropriate sort of principles to apply in such a case.

It is a well-known aphorism that hard cases make bad law — that is, sympathy for a party in a particular case may lead the court to distort a legal principle in order to secure a successful result for that party. There is a perpetual tension in the law between stability, certainty, and predictability on the one hand, and equity, fairness, and justice in the individual case on the other. An advocate of the former set of values spoke disparagingly of that "vague jurisprudence which is sometimes attractively styled justice as between man and man," which he then proceeded to dismiss as "well-meaning sloppiness of thought."[7] A later judge said that he would not be drawn by some abstract idea of justice to ignore his first duty, which was to administer the law.[8] Yet, despite heavy emphasis, particularly in the nineteenth and early twentieth centuries, on stable and predictable rules, a study of the actual decisions of judges shows that they will attempt to evade rules that seem to produce unfair results.

Justice is an elusive word. It commonly means "that point of view on a particular issue that I hold myself," as in "justice for the workers" or "let us fight for justice." Sometimes it is deliberately meaningless, as when the clergy pray for peace with justice in southern Africa, or a just settlement to the transit strike. The lawyer's concept of justice is much closer to the concept of rationality. If disputes are determined by fair procedures before an impartial tribunal honestly trying to give rational and consistent reasons for its results, we will not satisfy every litigant all the time, but we will come as close as humanly possible to administering justice. Professor John Willis, a distinguished Canadian law teacher, said that the law is a part of Western society's dream of a life governed by reason.

It is commonly thought that any dispute has a "right" or "just" result, and if only sufficient effort and goodwill is spent, that result can be found. But even a brief introduction to legal problems shows the weakness of this view. Consider the case of sale by a non-owner to a good-faith buyer. B steals A's watch and sells it to C, who pays value for it in good faith. Everyone can agree that justice requires B to repay. But what if B is not available, as is common in such cases, having disappeared, or is found without assets? It is not at all obvious what result "justice" requires in solving the dispute between A and C. A will assert: "This is my watch; give it back. If you were so foolish or unfortunate as to pay money to a rogue for something that he had no right to sell, so much the worse for you." C will say: "I have paid good money for this watch. I bought it in good faith, and if you had not left it lying around to be stolen, the problem would never have arisen. Further, you probably have insurance against loss by theft (or you should have). I am not insured against loss by law suit of my purchase." There is something in all of these points. No obvious solution leaps to the eye. In resolving a dispute of this sort, the court must have an eye not only to justice between the parties to the particular dispute, but to the long-term effects that the decision may have. Suppose the law is established in favour of C, the good-faith buyer. Might this encourage theft? It would mean that thieves could pass a good title to buyers — admittedly, only to good-faith buyers, but bad faith is always hard to prove, and the buyer might be a little less inclined to be suspicious of a good bargain if he knew that the law would generally give him a good title. Further, is it wise to recognize theft as an effective way of transferring title? Is there not a value in "stability of ownership"? On the other hand, if the law is established in A's favour, might it make owners careless in looking after their goods? Will it affect freedom of commerce if no buyer can be sure that

she is getting good title? Is there a value in "stability of transactions"? No obvious answer appears and, indeed, there can be no final resolution to the tension between stability of ownership and stability of transactions. Both are values that the law must recognize and protect. The difficult and interesting cases are those that bring the two principles into sharp conflict, and compel a choice. It is the attempt to make that choice rationally and consistently that we can reasonably call the administration of justice.

THE RULE OF LAW

The rule of law is another elusive phrase that is apt to be used in support of many different arguments. In one sense it describes an ordered society as opposed to one in which the person with the gun always gets his own way. It conjures up the vision of stability and tranquillity that the framers of Canadian confederation had in mind when they spoke of the "Peace, Order, and good Government of Canada."[9] A similar view underlies the mottos: "Freedom under the law" and "Equal Justice under law."

The rule of law suggests independence of the judiciary from the executive branch of government. It was established in the seventeenth century by Chief Justice Coke that even the King could not interfere with the ordinary processes of justice.[10] In the United States the Watergate crisis in 1974 reaffirmed the principle in holding that the President was bound to obey the court. In Canada in 1945, a government agency asserted the power under wartime emergency regulations to prevent the carrying out of an order of the court. Wilson J.'s response was in the following very fine language:

> If I have been unable to find an exact precedent for my decision in this matter, it is not, I hope, through lack of diligence but because the action attempted by the administrator is unprecedented. This is, so far as I know, the first instance in the annals of British jurisprudence in which an official has essayed to invalidate the order of a Court of Justice. It is, I think, somewhat alarming to

find an official of a minor administrative bureau attempting to assert a power which was, so long ago as the reign of James I, denied to the King himself. I refer, of course, to the glorious and courageous refusal of Coke and his brother Judges of the Court of King's Bench to obey the King's writ *de non procedendo rege inconsulto* [not to proceed without consulting the King] commanding them to stop or delay proceedings in their Court. . . . The whole value of the legal system— the integrity of the rule of law—is at once destroyed if it becomes possible for officials by arbitrary decisions made, not in the public court rooms but in the private offices of officialdom, without hearing the parties, without taking evidence, free of all obedience to settled legal principles, and subject to no appeal, effectively to overrule the Courts and deprive a Canadian citizen of a right he has established by the immemorial method of a trial at law.[11]

In the modern parliamentary system where the government often controls the majority of the Legislature, we are sometimes apt to confuse the government with Parliament itself. But it still remains an essential principle of our constitution that the government cannot itself make law, and has only those powers given to it by law. It is certainly not less important now than formerly for the courts to assert their ancient power of ensuring that officials of government at all levels do respect and obey the law.

The rule of law is also used to describe an ideal of rationality in the ordering of society, as opposed to the arbitrary making of decisions. It is often said that we should be governed by laws, not by the whims of persons. The concept is closely linked with the idea of justice described in the last section. We will be governed not necessarily by decisions that we would like, but by decisions made by impartial persons applying settled, consistent, and rationally defensible general principles.

The two meanings of the phrase sometimes conflict quite starkly. When a government is threatened by civil insurrection it may well announce that it proposes to restore the rule of law. Quite often it

will do so by suspending the ordinary democratic processes and infringing the ordinary civil liberties of its citizens, that is, by suspending the rule of law in the second sense. Of course, the government will generally claim that in such circumstances the democratic processes and civil liberties are suspended only temporarily in order to enable their long-term survival. Sometimes, but not always, history bears out that claim.

Another aspect of the rule of law is the avoidance of retroactive decision-making. Particularly in criminal law it is thought to be of importance that conduct lawful when engaged in should not retroactively be made punishable. This is called the principle of legality, often expressed in the Latin phrase *"nulla poena sine lege"*—no punishment without a law. A civil judicial decision that departs sharply from prior law is by its nature retroactive in its effect on the parties to a dispute, and this is one reason for judicial caution in law-making. In interpreting statutes the judges, for similar reasons, always lean in favour of finding that statutes are not retroactive in effect, that they do not make punishable conduct that was lawful at the time and do not take away vested rights without compensation.

The rule of law has been attacked by some on political grounds; it has been suggested that the concept is a myth that conceals the reality of class power. Of this kind of claim, the historian E.P. Thompson has written, on the basis of a study of eighteenth-century English criminal law:

> I am insisting . . . upon the obvious point, which some modern theorists have overlooked, that there is a difference between arbitrary power and the rule of law. We ought to expose the shams and inequities which may be concealed beneath this law. But the rule of law itself, the imposing of effective inhibitions upon power and the defence of the citizen from power's all-intrusive claims, seems to me to be an unqualified human good. . . . I am told that, just beyond the horizon, new forms of working-class power are about to arise which, being founded upon egalitarian productive relations, will require no inhibition and

can dispense with the negative restrictions of bourgeois legalism. A historian is unqualified to pronounce on such Utopian projections. All that he knows is that he can bring in support of them no historical evidence whatsoever. His advice might be: watch this new power for a century or two before you cut your hedges down.[12]

NOTES

1. Aristotle, *Politics*, i, 2, 9. 1253a (Newman ed.).
2. J. Bronowski, *The Ascent of Man* (1973), p. 411. "Justice is a universal of all cultures. It is a tightrope that man walks between his desire to fulfil his wishes, and his acknowledgement of social responsibility. No animal is faced with this dilemma: an animal is either social or solitary. Man alone aspires to be both, a social solitary."
3. *Re Laporte and The Queen* (1972), 8 C.C.C. (2d) 343 (Que. Q.B.).
4. (1884), 14 Q.B.D. 273.
5. *Jarvis v. Swans Tours Ltd.*, [1973] 1 Q.B. 233 (C.A.).
6. *Jones v. Randall* (1774), 1 Cowp. 37 at 40.
7. *Holt v. Markham*, [1923] 1 K.B. 504 at 513 (C.A.) *per* Scrutton L.J.
8. *Scruttons Ltd. v. Midland Silicones Ltd.*, [1962] A.C. 446 at 467–8 (H.L.) *per* Viscount Simonds.
9. Constitution Act, 1867 (U.K.), c. 3, s. 91.
10. See *Colt v. Coventry & Lichfield* (1617), 1 Roll Rep. 451.
11. *Re Bachand and Dupuis*, [1946] 2 D.L.R. 641 at 654–5 (B.C.S.C.). Reproduced with the permission of Canada Law Book Inc.
12. E.P. Thompson, *Whigs and Hunters* (Penguin, 1977) p. 266.

CHAPTER

20

The Courts

PETER McCORMICK

IAN GREENE

The **judicial system** in Canada operates under a number of basic concepts, and if we understand those concepts we can also more easily understand the judicial decision-making process.

THE PURPOSE OF COURTS

Throughout history most governments have established institutions for resolving disputes. These institutions are almost always called courts because in earlier days disputes were settled by the monarch from his throne in his courtroom.

There are three practical reasons why governments would want to establish courts. First, the orderly **resolution of disputes** between citizens, besides being a desirable alternative to combat, is a prerequisite for all other state activities in complex societies. Second, the more that citizens can rely on the even-handed enforcement of the contracts they make with each other, the more they can specialize in commercial activities and trust the trade relationships they enter into. Third, the fair resolution of disputes between the government and the citizen enhances the government's authority and legitimacy.

Courts, then, are government-sponsored dispute-resolution centres in which officials called judges have been given the power to decide controversies. The process by which disputes are settled in courts is known as "adjudication." Courts are successful to

the extent that (most) citizens consider the judges to be fair whether they win or lose, and therefore voluntarily comply with judicial decisions. Fairness implies that judges be impartial, meaning that they are not biased in advance for or against any of the parties in a dispute. One way of promoting impartiality is by providing judges with "independence," which means that they are not beholden to any of the parties in the disputes that come before them, including (and especially) the government.

Judicial independence is an essential feature of adjudication. But how can judges be independent from the government when the courts are considered to be one of the three branches of government, alongside the legislature and the executive? Moreover, judges are appointed and paid by the executive branch of government and have their offices and support staff provided by the executive branch. The Supreme Court of Canada wrestled with these issues in the *Valente* decision of 1985.

THE VALENTE CASE [31] AND JUDICIAL INDEPENDENCE

While driving his car at high speed along a street in Burlington, Ontario, in 1981, Walter Valente struck and killed three girls on their bicycles, as Paul T. Heron recounts in his commentary on the case. Valente was charged with dangerous driving,

SOURCE: *Judges and Judging: Inside the Canadian Judicial System* (Toronto: James Lorimer & Company, 1990), pp. 3–20 and 22–27. Reprinted by permission of the publisher.

Figure 20.1

Canadian Court Structure, 1990

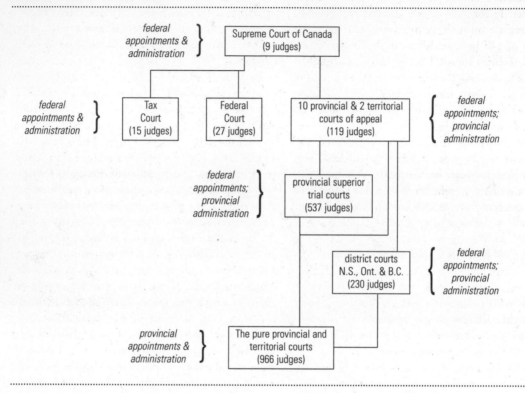

* By 1990 all provinces had merged their county and district courts with their superior courts.

a Canadian Criminal Code offence that carries a potential jail sentence.

Shortly after the Charter of Rights came into effect in 1982 the case came to the Provincial Court in Ontario, the lowest court in the judicial hierarchy. If we think of Canadian courts as a four-tiered hierarchy, the "capital 'P'" Provincial Courts are on the bottom, and above them are the "small 'p'" provincial superior trial courts, the provincial superior appeal courts, and finally the Supreme Court of Canada.

Valente instructed his lawyer, Noel Bates, to keep him out of jail, and Bates turned to the Charter of Rights, which declares that any person charged with an offence has the right to a hearing before an "independent and impartial tribunal." Bates was aware that Provincial Court judges do not have the same constitutional guarantees of independence as judges who are higher on the judicial ladder.

Our constitution declares that provincial superior court judges — judges on the second and third tier — can be removed from office only if the Senate and House of Commons jointly pass a resolution to this effect; the public nature of this procedure makes it difficult to remove judges and thereby protects them from retaliation for making decisions that displease individual cabinet ministers. The constitution also requires that the salaries of the provincial superior court judges be established publicly through a law of Parliament, thus preventing the Minister of Justice from arbitrarily reducing the salaries of judges who decide contrary to the government's wishes.

There are no such written constitutional guarantees of the independence of Provincial Court judges, so Bates argued that Provincial Court judges are not independent. He held that because the Provincial Court judge charged with hearing Valente's case was not independent, the judge had no authority to decide the case.

The Provincial Court judge considered the argument to have merit (some Provincial Court judges have for years been irritated that the superior courts have a higher constitutional status, and have unsuccessfully pressed the provincial government to take appropriate action), so he disqualified himself and referred the independence question to the Ontario Court of Appeal. Valente lost in the Court of Appeal; he appealed to the Supreme Court of Canada and lost again.

The Supreme Court held that judges are independent if three conditions are met. First, judges must have "security of **tenure**," meaning that they cannot be fired because the government disagrees with their decisions. Because Provincial Court judges in Ontario (and most other provinces) can be removed only after a judicial inquiry has determined that the judge should be dismissed, this condition was satisfied. Second, judges must have "financial security," a legislated right to a salary, so that the cabinet cannot secretly manipulate judges by raising or lowering their salaries or by threatening to do so. Third, judges must have "institutional independence," or the ability to control administrative actions in the courts that could affect judicial decision-making. The Supreme Court felt that the Ontario law that outlines the terms and conditions of the employment of Provincial Court judges met these three conditions, and that constitutional safeguards, while advantageous, were not strictly necessary.

The "security of tenure" condition means that judges in Canada are given permanent appointments that continue until the mandatory retirement age, which is 75 for superior court judges and 65

or 70 for most Provincial Court judges. (In New Brunswick, there is no compulsory retirement age for Provincial Court judges.) Under extraordinary circumstances a judge can be dismissed, but not by a cabinet minister or legislature acting alone. A judicial inquiry must take place to investigate the allegations of wrongdoing, and the inquiry must recommend dismissal. A judge cannot be removed for making an error in law, but only for behaviour inappropriate for a judge, such as taking a bribe or not fulfilling court-related duties. The reason why a judge cannot be removed for an error in law is that vengeful litigants with plenty of money to litigate, disappointed with a judicial decision, might harass a judge by pressing for his or her removal. If such situations could occur, a judge might be inclined to decide in favour of well-known "trouble-makers."

We asked the judges we interviewed in Ontario and Alberta to tell us what judicial independence implied to them. Although all the judges told us that it meant that no one — especially cabinet ministers — could interfere in the decision-making process, some judges thought that the principle had additional overtones. A third of the judges thought that judicial independence meant that the judiciary should control the flow of cases through the courts, and a few (13 per cent) thought that judges should have *complete* control over all aspects of court administration. Half the judges thought that judicial independence implied that even the chief judge could not give orders to the junior judges regarding case-flow management decisions. This lack of consensus about some of the implications of judicial independence has ramifications for the judges' perceptions of their role.

ADJUDICATION

Adjudication is a process by which the two parties in a dispute (the litigants) put their case before a neutral third party (the judge) for resolution. The judge makes a decision based on an objective set of standards (the law), and this decision can be enforced by the coercive powers of the state.

Usually, one party to the dispute wins and the other loses; decisions that result in compromises or simply "split the difference" are rare. The judge must reach his decision by first determining the facts of the case and then applying the law to those facts.

(To be sure, these are the types of cases that form the core of the court's adjudicative function; not all actual cases look like this. For example, some court cases are *ex parte* — they go uncontested or by default — meaning that the second disputant is invisible. As well, the court is often called upon simply to ratify a decision reached elsewhere, as in many modern divorce cases, and the "dispute" is largely a fiction. The core of the court's role, however, is a dispute involving the legal rights or obligations of two or more parties.)

Disputes that go to court are either *public* or *private*. Public law disputes are those in which the government is a party. These include criminal law, administrative law, and constitutional law cases. Private law disputes are conflicts between two private (or corporate) persons. These include real estate transactions, contracts, family law, and suits for negligence.

Adjudication is, of course, just one of many methods of dispute resolution. In *negotiation* the two disputing parties attempt to resolve their dispute without the aid of a neutral third party; they do not necessarily look to external objective standards and there is usually no enforcement mechanism obliging the parties to reach an agreement or to abide by it. In *mediation* the parties turn for help to a neutral mediator, who simply assists the two parties to negotiate but cannot impose a settlement. In *arbitration*, the neutral third party — an arbitrator — may impose a binding settlement but is not usually bound by the same strict set of objective standards — the whole body of law — as a judge.

Courts use the adjudicative method because of the need for predictability. Mediation and arbitration produce more varied outcomes, which certain parties can perceive, rightly or wrongly, as an indication of favouritism. At the same time, adjudication is not ideally suited to all disputes. Disputes involving parties who want a quicker and less

formal procedure, and disputes in which the state has no compelling interest, probably do not belong in court.

In private law cases, adjudication is ideally the dispute resolution method of last resort, to be used only when negotiation, mediation, or arbitration are impossible or fail. The adjudicative service is provided by the state so that a method of last resort will be available — so that private disputes can be settled without the disruption of public order.

In public law cases involving disputes between the state and private citizens, countries adhering to the principle of the rule of law submit such disputes to adjudication to promote the perception that the government is fair. The rule of law means that government officials may act only as authorized by legitimate laws — which usually means laws enacted by elected legislatures — and that the law must be applied equally to everyone. When the state uses adjudication to resolve disputes between, for example, the law enforcement authorities and the persons they accuse of crimes, it intends to ensure adherence to the rule of law.

Two great legal systems have developed in the world: the common law system and the civil law system.

THE COMMON LAW SYSTEM

The common law system is based on the judicial system of England and Wales, and its origins can be traced to the time of King Henry II in the twelfth century. Henry II inherited a justice system based primarily on local, traditional courts, so that the rules of commerce and the criminal law varied from one locality to another. Such a system not only discouraged inter-regional trade in England but also promoted disunity. The king and his advisory council created legislation to standardize some of the criminal and commercial laws across England, and the council itself heard disputes arising out of these laws.

Before long, the council experienced a "caseload crisis" not unlike backlog problems in many of today's courts. Travelling justices were appointed to relieve the pressure on the council and to provide a more convenient dispute-resolution service for the king's subjects. As caseload pressures continued, central courts separate from the king's council were created. The travelling judges together with the judges of the central courts had jurisdiction to settle certain disputes even in the absence of decrees from the king's council. Records were kept of their decisions, and judges began to refer to these records of old cases when deciding new cases. As much as possible, the precedents set by the old cases were followed in the new cases according to the principle of *stare decisis* ("let decided matters stand"). This judge-made law became known as the "common law," because it was judge-made law that the judges applied to all social classes across England and Wales.

According to the rules of *stare decisis* as they have developed over the centuries, every court must follow the precedents established by a higher court in the same court system, and the precedents of the highest court "trump" those of any lower courts. In the absence of conflicting precedents established by a higher court, a court usually follows its own precedents. The precedents of higher or equal status courts in another common law jurisdiction are influential, but not binding. For example, U.S. Bill of Rights precedents are often cited in Canadian Charter of Rights cases, but they are only sometimes followed. Precedents must be followed only when the facts in the current case and the precedent case are substantially the same. If a judge considers the facts in a current case to be significantly different, the judge may "distinguish" the precedent, and thus depart from it.

All courts in Canada must follow precedents established by the Supreme Court. The Supreme Court itself almost always follows its own precedents. In the mid-1970s the Court announced that it might occasionally overrule its own precedents (or those established by the Judicial Committee of the Privy Council in London, England, which was Canada's highest court of appeal until 1949) if it considered those precedents to be clearly wrong or inappropriate. Since that time, according to Peter Hogg (1992), the Supreme Court has overruled fewer than ten

precedents. Such overruling will not occur frequently because it would destroy the predictability of the adjudicative system. However, because judges can "distinguish" appropriate precedents, *stare decisis* is not quite as rigid as it might first appear.

One of the most difficult issues for judges is to decide when to follow *stare decisis* and when to "distinguish" a precedent case (that is, leave it aside as not relevant). Our survey of Alberta judges' views on this difficult question indicates that the majority of judges at all levels think that *stare decisis* should be followed in an almost mechanical fashion, although some judges strongly believe that rigid adherence to tradition falsely assumes that all wisdom is in the past.

In addition to *stare decisis*, a second essential characteristic of the common law world is the adversary system. According to the adversarial approach, it is the responsibility of the litigants to present the judge or judges with all the facts and theory needed to make a decision. Judges have neither the responsibility nor the opportunity to carry out an independent investigation of the facts. Although they do sometimes research legal theory and precedents on their own, they are not usually provided with all the resources necessary for this work because they are expected to rely primarily on the information presented by counsel for the litigants.

Only in recent years have Supreme Court of Canada judges and provincial appeal court judges been assigned law clerks to assist them with their legal research. Trial court judges rarely have such assistance. Thus, if judicial decisions seem to take into account only a narrow range of possible fact situations or legal interpretations, this is often because the lawyers presenting the case have narrowed the considerations in advance.

A third characteristic of the common law system is that judges do not receive specialized training in judging, but are appointed from among the ranks of lawyers. This tradition dates from thirteenth-century England. In the preceding century the quality of the king's judges had begun to deteriorate, perhaps because the kings were too busy with crusades and disputes with nobles to give the courts the attention they needed. The judges and court officials were poorly paid, and even though all the judges were clergymen, many resorted to accepting bribes. As a result, the end of the twelfth century saw a public outcry about corruption in the judicial system. In response, Edward I appointed a royal commission to investigate in 1289, thus setting a precedent to be followed by governments for centuries thereafter when confronted with public dissatisfaction with the administration of justice.

The commission found that about half of the judges in the common law courts were corrupt, and the king fired them. He was forced by circumstances to look outside the clergy for replacement judges. For about a century some businessmen had specialized in advising litigants about how to proceed in the increasingly complex judicial system. Edward appointed some of these "lawyers" to fill the vacancies in the judiciary. His solution to the crisis soon became a tradition. By early in the fourteenth century, lawyers had completely displaced clerics as judges in all but one of the royal courts. These lawyer-judges have ever since continued to wear robes in the clerical tradition.

THE CIVIL LAW SYSTEM

The common law world includes most Commonwealth countries and the United States; the rest of the world has adopted the civil law system, which developed in continental Europe beginning at the end of the eighteenth century. University scholars had become fascinated with Roman law, and they urged governments to adopt uniform codes of law based on the old Roman codes. For example, Napoleon I supervised the **codification** of French private and criminal law into a set of unified codes. The codes are organized in a logical sequence, from general principles to specific rules of law.

Judges in civil law countries usually receive specialized training as judges; it is not assumed that the training and experience of a lawyer by themselves are appropriate for judicial duties.

Another important difference between the common and civil law systems is that civilian judges place less emphasis on precedent than common law judges. According to the civil law approach, whenever the code is unclear, judges look for guidance to the general principles in the code, the reports of the "codificateurs" (the framers of the code), and finally scholarly writings—all before researching precedent judicial decisions. A third difference between the two systems is that civilian judges may often conduct their own investigations of the facts of a case; this is known as the "inquisitorial" approach. They need not rely entirely on evidence presented by counsel for the opposing sides.

Canada's legal system incorporates elements of both the common law and civil law approaches, although common definitely overshadows civil law. After conquering Quebec in 1759, the British authorities attempted to obtain the support of Quebeckers by allowing the colony to maintain its civil legal system in the private law field. Today, Quebec's legal system adheres to the civil law approach for private law matters, although the inquisitorial style of adjudication is not nearly as evident as in most other civil law countries; precedent plays a larger role because of the influence of common law. In public law matters, Quebec is a common law jurisdiction, like all the other provinces and the federal government. The Supreme Court of Canada, which is required by law to have three judges from Quebec, acts as a civil law court when it hears private law appeals from Quebec and as a common law court the rest of the time; understandably, Quebec scholars and judges have some reservations about the viability of this dual role.

IMPARTIALITY

In common or civil law countries that adhere to the liberal political ideology—liberalism stresses the maximization of individual freedom, the limitation of governmental powers through laws enacted by representative legislatures, and equality in the application of the law—judges are expected to be as impartial as possible. Impartiality implies that judges must hear a case with an open mind, without being biased in advance toward any of the litigants.

Absolute impartiality is a human impossibility, but the more that judges can demonstrate impartiality, the more respected and credible will be the adjudicative process.

A number of practices and principles have developed to promote judicial impartiality. The most important is the principle of judicial independence, as elaborated by the Supreme Court in the *Valente* case. Other methods of promoting impartiality are the presumption that judges will disqualify themselves if a litigant is a family member or associate, the prohibition against judges holding a second job, and the expectation that judges will, upon appointment, sever their association with groups that are likely to litigate or that advocate particular courses in public policy (such as political parties or anti-abortion groups).

THE CANADIAN COURT STRUCTURE

As the caseloads of courts grow in response to new laws, changing values, and population increases, governments tend to create new and more specialized courts, the result being a complex hodgepodge. Canada is no exception to this trend, but in addition Canada's court system has had to respond to another factor: federalism.

Some federal countries have established two separate hierarchies of courts — one to hear cases arising out of federal laws and the other primarily to hear cases arising out of state or provincial laws. The United States provides an example of this "dual" court system. In 1867 the Fathers of Confederation rejected the dual court model in favour of what Peter Russell (1987) calls an "integrated" court structure. The goal of the integrated approach is to allow for most cases arising out of both federal and provincial laws to be heard in the same court system, a system in which both the federal and provincial governments have some responsibilities.

At the very top of the system, however, the provinces currently have no responsibility, reflecting the desire of some of the Fathers of Confederation for federal dominance of the Canadian political system. The 1867 constitution granted the federal Parliament the power to establish a Supreme Court of Canada — which it did in 1875 — to appoint all its judges and to determine its jurisdiction. The Supreme Court has the constitutional and statutory authority to hear appeals involving cases arising out of both federal and provincial laws.

A significant number of Supreme Court cases involve constitutional interpretation: they settle disputes about the extent of federal and provincial powers and about the extent to which the powers of both Parliament and the provincial legislatures are limited by the Charter of Rights. It seems curious that this important court, which acts as a referee between the two orders of government, is staffed by appointees selected only by the federal order. The Meech Lake Accord set out to reduce this anomaly by giving the provincial premiers the right to nominate candidates for the Supreme Court, with the final selection to be made by the prime minister. Even with the failure of the Accord, it is possible that the provincial governments may gain the ability to be consulted over Supreme Court appointments through more informal channels.

As of April 1, 1990, the eight ordinary judges on the Supreme Court of Canada, who are known as "puisne" (pronounced pyoo'-ney, meaning "junior") judges, earned $166,800 per year. The chief justice earned $13,400 over and above the base salary.

The architects of the Canadian constitution decided to adopt a more fully integrated approach, based on courts for which both federal and provincial governments have responsibilities, immediately below the level of the Supreme Court. They did this for several reasons, although the possible inconvenience of a dual court system to the public was only a minor consideration — if it was considered at all. More importantly, the commitment of most of the anglophone Fathers of Confederation to a strong central government resulted in the idea that the federal government should have the power to appoint provincial superior court judges; this federal power made the idea of separate federal courts seem less attractive. As well, the provincial superior court judges of the time opposed the establishment of a rival system of courts. Perhaps the most important consideration was the fact that if the federal government was empowered to make appointments to the prestigious provincial superior courts, the new government would have at its disposal wonderful patronage opportunities that would encourage ambitious lawyers to work for the federal political parties. The result was section 96 of the British North America Act (renamed in 1982 to become the Constitution Act, 1867), which gave the federal cabinet the power to appoint provincial superior court judges, as well as provincial county and district court judges. Consequently, these federally appointed provincial judges became known as "section 96 judges."

The superior courts have trial and appeal divisions. The trial divisions are known by such names as Queen's Bench, Supreme Court, or High Court. The appeal divisions are usually known as The Court of Appeal of the province. The trial divisions have jurisdiction over serious and moderately serious Canadian Criminal Code cases and over private law cases involving sums of money exceeding the monetary limits of the small claims courts, and these courts preside over jury trials.

Canada's system of courts is modelled on the court system of England and Wales. Many superior court judges in England and Wales were travelling justices who held "**assizes**," or hearings, in the major county centres at least twice a year. If litigants did not want to wait for an assize, they could travel to London where the superior courts sat more frequently. Before Confederation the colonial governments had established superior courts on the English model, with travelling justices holding assizes in county towns twice a year. In the early years, because of the difficulties of travel to provincial capitals, local merchants demanded that judges be appointed permanently to sit in major centres outside the capitals. In response, in Upper Canada in 1794 Lieutenant-Governor Simcoe established a number of "district" courts in the major centres. The judges in these courts had an "inferior" status, but were empowered to hear many of the kinds of cases that superior court judges would otherwise

hear. Litigants could often choose between having a case settled before a district court judge, or waiting for a superior court judge's assize. The other common law colonies followed suit, with the result that eventually all the provinces except Quebec had district courts (sometimes known as county courts).

There may have been a marked difference between the abilities of district court judges and superior court judges in the past, so that it was worth maintaining the separate existence of the two courts to give litigants in outlying areas the chance to choose between a quick hearing before the district court judge, or waiting for the superior court assize where the services of a "better" judge would be available. With the development of higher standards in legal education, however, the pool of available talent for the county and district courts increased, so that the rationale for maintaining the county or district courts and the superior courts as separate entities diminished.

For example, our Ontario interviews indicated that three-fifths of the trial lawyers, crown attorneys, and court administrators did not consider the superior court trial judges to be superior in ability; outside of Toronto, this proportion jumped to three-quarters. Spurred on by this change in perception as well as by the desire for greater efficiency in the court system, since 1975 all provinces with county or district courts have merged their county and district courts with their superior courts.

There are about 800 provincial superior, county, and district court judges in Canada. The puisne superior court judges earn $140,400 per year, while puisne county and district court judges earn $135,400. The chief and associate chief judges earn $13,400 more than the puisne judges.

Section 101 of the Constitution Act, 1867, gave Parliament the right to establish not only a "general court of appeal" (Supreme Court) but also other federal courts "for the better Administration of the Laws of Canada." (Such federal courts, however, cannot hear federal Criminal Code cases; these cases must be heard in courts established by the provinces.) Pursuant to section 101, Parliament established the Exchequer Court in 1875 to hear cases involving federal taxes, patents, and copyrights; until 1887, the six judges of the Supreme Court of Canada also served as Exchequer Court judges. In 1971 Parliament abolished the Exchequer Court and replaced it with the Federal Court. The jurisdiction was expanded to include federal administrative law cases. The Federal Court has two divisions, one for trials and one for appeals. In 1983 Parliament created a third section 101 court—the Tax Court of Canada—to hear certain cases arising under federal taxation laws. The Federal Court now has 27 judges, and the Tax Court has 15.

Ottawa is responsible for providing the administrative support services for the Supreme Court of Canada, the Federal Court, and the Tax Court, as well as for appointing and paying all the judges of these courts. Federal Court and Tax Court judges earn $140,400 per year. The chief justices and associate chief justices of these courts earn $13,300 more than the puisne judges.

All of the other courts in Canada, including the provincial superior, county, and district courts, are established by provincial legislatures, and their administrative support is provided by the provincial governments. These provincial courts, which among them employ nearly 1800 judges, conduct all trials for cases arising out of either federal or provincial laws (except for the relatively few trials conducted by the Federal Court or the Tax Court).

The provincial legislatures have created two basic types of courts: "superior" courts and "inferior" courts. The superior courts have jurisdiction over the most serious criminal cases, including jury trials, civil or private law cases except for small claims cases (which are cases involving a set maximum that varies from $500 to $15,000, depending on the province or territory), and appeals from the inferior courts.

All the provinces have at one time had an inferior court known as the "Provincial Court." Unlike the provincial county, district, and superior courts, the provincial governments have the constitutional power to appoint all the judges to these "capital-P" provincial courts; therefore, following the lead of Peter Russell (1987) we will refer to them as "pure provincial" courts. (It should be kept in mind that

there are four kinds of courts established by the provinces. From "lowest" to "highest," these are the "Provincial," "county and district," "superior trial," and "superior appeal" courts. The fact that most provincial legislatures have chosen to name the lowest of these courts "*the* Provincial Court" often creates confusion.) The Ontario and Quebec legislatures have recently renamed their pure provincial courts the "Ontario Court of Justice Provincial Division" and "Court of Quebec," respectively. Before the late 1960s, Provincial Court judges were known as "magistrates" or "police magistrates."

The pure provincial courts are by far the busiest courts in the country, with over 90 per cent of all the cases heard in Canadian courts. Even though these courts have provincially appointed judges, our constitution gives the federal Parliament the right to assign them the responsibility for conducting trials under the federal Criminal Code. Therefore, a large portion of the caseload of the pure provincial courts is composed of minor to moderately serious violations of the federal Criminal Code. As well, the pure provincial courts hear cases under the Young Offenders Act, provincial offences such as highway traffic violations, and some family law cases such as adoption, child neglect, child and spousal abuse, and enforcement of maintenance orders. The pure provincial courts also hear small claims cases involving civil suits up to a maximum of between $500 and $15,000, depending on the province. (In New Brunswick, Prince Edward Island, and parts of Ontario, the provincial government has chosen to appoint persons already sitting as federally appointed judges to hear small claims cases. These judges, therefore, have both federal and provincial appointments.) There are nearly a thousand pure Provincial Court judges in Canada, and they earn between $70,000 and $105,000 per year, depending on the province they preside in.

In addition to the Provincial Court judges, most provinces have created positions for lower-status adjudicators who are usually called "justices of the peace," or JPs. These officials often double as court clerks, and few of them have legal education.

(Moreover, according to one of our studies, less than 30 per cent of the head court administrators in local courts, most of whom were also JPs, had any university or college training.) The JPs hear cases involving minor provincial or municipal offences, such as parking offences, but are occasionally given jurisdiction over some relatively serious cases.

Although JPs do perform adjudicative functions, we have not included them in our count of Canadian judges. This is partly because their status will remain unclear until the Supreme Court of Canada makes an authoritative decision on the matter [of standards of independence for JPs], and partly because JPs do not have the educational background or experience associated with being a "judge" in the common law world. (In Quebec, there are more than 150 "municipal court judges" who hear cases arising under municipal by-laws and minor traffic offences, but in Montreal, Laval, and Quebec City they have a more extensive jurisdiction, according to Russell. We have also excluded these officials from our count of judges.)

According to law, federally appointed judges must be selected from among lawyers who have been qualified to practise law by a provincial or territorial law society for at least ten years. Before the 1960s, the provincial legislatures did not require their magistrates to be lawyers. Since the transformation of magistrates' courts into the Provincial Courts, legislation in all the provinces except Alberta and Newfoundland has required that Provincial Court judges be selected from the bar. Even in Alberta and Newfoundland, however, as Russell has observed, very few non-lawyers are appointed.

Reform-minded political scientists such as Peter Russell and Carl Baar and judges such as Thomas G. Zuber have criticized the provincial court systems for being too hierarchical, too difficult for the average citizen to understand, and too fragmented to allow efficient operation. The Ontario Liberal Party's attorney general Ian Scott was the only provincial attorney general in this century who attempted a major restructuring of the provincial court system. In 1989, following the recommendations of the 1987 Zuber Commission Report, Scott announced some significant reforms. The first phase of the reform, now under way, creates an Ontario Court of Justice including all judges other than those in the Court of Appeal. This court has two divisions: General and Provincial. The General Division includes all superior court judges (except those on the Court of Appeal), all District Court judges, and the small claims court judges. The Provincial Division is formed from the criminal and family divisions of the old Provincial Court.

Besides the change in name, this reform has two major aspects to it which may influence court reform in the other provinces. First, to promote greater efficiency the administrative services for all the courts have been merged and reorganized on a regional basis rather than a "level of court" basis. Second, Scott hoped eventually to merge the General and Provincial Divisions into one trial court. The federal government will have to cooperate to bring about this unified court, because the Provincial Division judges will need federal appointments to attain the same status and jurisdiction as the superior court judges in the General Division. If federal cooperation is attained, Ontario will be left with just two courts: a unified Ontario Court of Justice, which will handle all civil and criminal trials, and a Court of Appeal.

Since Confederation, Ontario has tended to lead the other provinces in reform of the legal-judicial system. For example, in 1968 the province established the Provincial Court out of the former local magistrate's courts. Within 15 years all the other provinces had followed suit in what Peter Russell referred to as "a remarkable demonstration of Ontario's influence on provincial public administration" (1987, p. 126). If the reforms of the Ontario court system that Scott initiated are successful, this example may lead to similar changes in the other provinces.

CHIEF JUDGES AND JUSTICES

Each level of court has a judicial head known as a "Chief Judge" (the title used in the Provincial and district courts) or "Chief Justice" (the title used in the superior courts). Many of the courts have associate chief justices or judges to assist their respective chiefs with their administrative duties. The chiefs are selected by the prime minister (in consultation with the minister of justice) for federal appointments, and by the appropriate provincial attorney general for provincial appointments. The chief is either selected from among sitting judges (which is the usual practice) or appointed from outside the court.

The duties of the chiefs and associate chiefs vary with the nature of the court. In all the Provincial Courts, the chief judges assign judges to particular judicial districts and devise plans for assigning judges temporarily from less busy courthouses to more busy courthouses to assist with case processing. As well, the chief judge may want to influence how specific judges are assigned to cases when a court centre has more than one judge.

For example, in some multi-judge courthouses, cases are grouped together in certain courtrooms according to type (such as highway traffic offences, minor criminal offences, major criminal offences, offences involving women), and judges rotate monthly among the various courtrooms. This system can promote the practice of "judge-shopping" or "judge-avoidance," whereby lawyers invent excuses to delay until the judge they want turns up in the courtroom, or until the judge they want to avoid is absent. A third of the Ontario judges we questioned thought that this practice of judge-shopping and judge-avoidance contributed to unnecessary delays in the system. Another system of managing case-flow is to assign a case to a particular judge who will eventually hear the case regardless of delays.

In the district and superior trial courts, the chief judges and justices design the system for assigning cases to judges. The chief justices of superior courts set the travel schedules for the judges' circuits. In the courts of appeal (including the Federal Court of Appeal and the Supreme Court of Canada), the chief justices decide on the make-up of the appeal panels, and they preside over the "conferences" — discussions after hearings — of the panels which they have assigned themselves to.

In the provincial court system, there is a mixture of circuit points (courts presided over by a single non-resident judge for a set number of days per month), and local court centres in the larger towns and cities with a number of resident judges. Each multi-judge court at the Provincial or district level in each local court centre has a "senior judge." The senior judge is appointed by the Chief Judge, and is often the longest-serving judge in the local centre. The senior judge handles the administrative duties at the local centre on behalf of the chief judge.

Most jurisdictions in Canada have created positions for judges who have either reached the mandatory retirement age or chosen early retirement but wish to continue judging on a part-time basis. These semi-retired judges are known as "supernumerary" judges, and account for about 6 per cent of Canada's judges.

DIGNITY AND DECORUM

Courts are potentially violent places. A 10:00 a.m. visitor to almost any of the Provincial Courts in Canada's larger cities will see the courtrooms for ordinary criminal cases filled with dozens of people waiting for trial. The "docket," or list of cases scheduled for that day, is posted beside the courtroom door, and it may list 50 to 100 cases, including some dealing with breaking-and-entering, assault, and perhaps robbery. The people in the courtroom include accused persons, victims of crime, witnesses, and friends and family of these people. Accused persons and victims eye each other in close proximity. Witnesses are angry because their cases may already have been adjourned several times and each adjournment has made the witness miss a day of work. Security is often provided by an aging official whose primary job is to give directions to people entering the courthouse.

We questioned the judges about how they could keep order in an atmosphere like this. This response from an Ontario Provincial Court judge was typical:

> When I first became a judge, I thought that the whole idea of wearing robes was ridiculous. During the summer, the chief judge isn't so particular about having the judges wear robes because

the courtrooms are so hot. So I decided to go to court one day without my robes. It was the worst day I've ever had. First of all, no one knew who the judge was. People were arguing and bickering in the courtroom, and I thought some fights would break out. The next day I came in my robe, and I had no problem keeping order.

Robes, then — worn by judges in the common law world since the early times when judges were clerics — are not worn just for tradition's sake, but because of the strong sense of authority vested in them, an authority that has a pacifying effect. They also serve another function, as illustrated by an Ontario Supreme Court judge's comment:

> When my orderly comes to help me put on my robe in the morning, it changes me. It makes me realize that I am about to enter the courtroom and perform a very important function. I must listen to all the evidence impartially, and then make some decisions that may have a tremendous impact on people's lives. I have to leave my own prejudices and preferences behind for awhile and I have to take that role seriously. I don't think I could concentrate as well on that role without my robe. I think that the robe also reminds the people in the courtroom — lawyers, witnesses, and litigants — that they also have an important and serious job in the courtroom.

Several judges also told us that in addition to the way they dressed, the way they were *addressed* helped them to concentrate on the judicial role. Provincial and district court judges are addressed as "Your Honour," and superior court judges are addressed as "My Lord" or "My Lady." (This is because in the English system, superior court judges usually *were* lords.) The judges often made a point of telling us that they did not take these forms of address seriously outside the courtroom, but that nevertheless they thought they served a function.

When all else fails to keep order in the courtroom, judges can cite a disorderly person for "contempt of court," which was originally a common

law offence with a maximum sentence of life imprisonment. In some Canadian jurisdictions, statutes regulate the judges' ability to cite for contempt, but the maximum penalties are still severe. Before the Charter, even those criticizing judges outside the courtroom could be charged with contempt. The idea behind this power was that if citizens lose respect for judges, the consequences in terms of potential social disorder are serious; therefore the criticism of judges — even if accurate — cannot be tolerated.

It is perhaps a tribute to the atmosphere in courts created by the formal trappings and the judicial robe that judges rarely need to resort to citing for contempt to keep order. On the other hand, the concern — some might even say preoccupation — of some judges with their own dignity and decorous proceedings can, of course, have a down-side as well: many citizens (and not only those burdened with guilty consciences) can be totally intimidated and demoralized by the ordeal of appearing in court, even as a witness.

Half of the court personnel whom we interviewed in Ontario (judges, trial lawyers, crown attorneys, and court administrators) said that judges tended to develop a "swelled ego" because of their role in the courtroom. They often referred to this tendency as "judgeitis." Like any persons in positions of authority, including the police, medical doctors, and professors, it is sometimes difficult *not* to develop an unrealistically inflated self-view.

JUDICIAL DISCIPLINE

Persons who feel that a judge has engaged in behaviour inappropriate for a judge may complain to one of the judicial councils: to a provincial judicial council for Provincial Court judges, or to the Canadian Judicial Council for federally appointed judges. Provincial judicial councils vary from province to province but usually consist of senior judges, or a combination of judges, lawyers, and lay persons.

The Canadian Judicial Council is composed of all federally appointed chief justices and judges, and associate chief justices and judges of the provincial superior, district, and county courts, and of the Supreme Court of Canada, the Federal Court, and the Tax Court, a group consisting of 39 judges in 1990. In the 1987–88 fiscal year, the Canadian Judicial Council received 47 complaints, according to its Annual Report. In 1989–90 the number of complaints jumped to 83, almost double. None of the complaints from the public produced enough evidence to warrant a judicial inquiry.

Judicial councils represent an uneasy balance between "keeping the judges in line" and "protecting the judges" from groundless complaints; the fact that other judges play so large a role in the process may beg the question of which of these two functions is more important.

Procedures have developed in all liberal countries to promote fairness in the adjudicative process. In the common law jurisdictions these procedures are known as the "rules of natural justice." They include many of the legal rights now enshrined in sections 7 to 14 of the Charter of Rights, such as the presumption of innocence, the right to an impartial and independent judge, and the right to counsel. Another of these principles is that litigants have the right to appeal a trial judge's decision at least once.

APPEAL COURTS

Courts that are specifically established as appeal courts hear cases in panels of three judges or more.

This is because appeal courts frequently have to decide difficult questions about the meaning of the law, about which reasonable judges could differ. It is considered that several heads are more likely to make better decisions than one.

Provincial appeal courts usually sit in panels of three judges, although the court itself is usually composed of many more judges than this — for example, six in New Brunswick, and twenty-four in Quebec (including supernumerary judges). For more complex cases, a panel of five or even more can be struck, although by the late 1980s this was becoming increasingly unusual. In 1987, there was only a single reported decision of a provincial court of appeal using a seven-judge panel, and in 1989 the three prairie provinces handled their entire caseload without a single panel larger than three judges. Although the chief justice determines membership in the panels and assignment of cases to panels, he or she usually takes into consideration the preferences of the regular appeal court judges, and spontaneous last-minute substitutes or rotations are not uncommon.

REFERENCES

Hogg, Peter. 1992. *Constitutional Law of Canada*, 3rd ed. Toronto: Carswell.

Russell, Peter. 1987. *The Judiciary in Canada: The Third Branch of Government.* Toronto: McGraw-Hill Ryerson.

The Supreme Court of Canada

JAMES J. GUY

The Constitution Act, 1867, made no mention of a Supreme Court of Canada. The Fathers of Confederation granted statutory authority to Parliament, which, after having bills to establish a final court withdrawn in 1869 and 1870, succeeded in passing the Supreme Court Act, 1875. The fact that this federal statute gave existence, jurisdiction, and composition to the Supreme Court generated concern over the years among constitutional, legal, and political experts that the highest courts in the country could be removed by ordinary legislation. Accordingly, in 1982, the Supreme Court of Canada was entrenched in the Constitution by Sections 41(d) and 42(1)(d) of the Constitution Act, 1982. And, the Meech Lake Accord (Constitution Amendment, 1987) would have legitimized the current composition of the court as consisting of a *chief justice* and eight *puisne* (junior-rank) judges, with at least three justices from Québec to ensure that some justices have a background in the distinctive civil-law tradition of that province. In addition, the appointment process would have been entrenched, for the first time giving provinces a constitutional voice in the selection of Supreme Court justices by filling vacancies from provincial lists of nominees.

The early Supreme Court had only six justices and its first sittings were held in the Railway Committee Room of the House of Commons: thereafter the court sat in the old Supreme Court Building at the foot of Parliament Hill until 1946, when it took possession of its present building. But until 1949, the Judicial Committee of the Privy Council in England was the highest court of final appeal for Canadian civil cases, as it was for criminal cases until 1931. In 1949, the Supreme Court assumed that role. It sits only in Ottawa. Since 1949, the composition of the court's bench has followed the pattern of appointing three justices from Ontario, three from Québec, two from the western provinces, and one from the Atlantic region. This pattern had only one temporary deviation between 1979 and 1982, when there were two from Ontario and three from the West. All nine judges are appointed until age 75 by the governor-general-in-council.

Candidates must have at least ten years' experience in law practice. Normally, Supreme Court judges are selected from provincial courts of appeal; for example, Beverley McLachlin was appointed in March 1989 from the B.C. Supreme Court. But from time to time, practising lawyers are elevated directly to the high court, as exemplified by the appointment of John Sopinka in 1988, who replaced Justice Willard Estey as one of Ontario's representatives on the bench. Judges are removable from the Supreme Court by the governor-general-in-council (on the advice of the Cabinet), which removal is accompanied by a joint address to the Senate and the House of Commons.

The chief justice presides over and directs the work of the court as its principal administrator. For

SOURCE: *People, Politics and Government* (Scarborough, ON: Prentice-Hall, 1995), pp. 312–18. Reprinted by permission of the publisher.

this, the chief justice receives an annual salary of approximately $185,000. This position is one of great judicial influence rather than one of power. The chief justice has only one vote as do the other judges in deciding cases. The other eight puisne justices, whose annual salaries are about $160,000, unavoidably bring their own personal values and political philosophies to the bench. These men and women, ranging in age from their 50s to mid-70s, have usually left more lucrative careers in law and teaching to accept prestigious judicial appointments — initially to the supreme courts of their home provinces.

The Supreme Court, notorious for its lengthy deliberations, has the capacity to hear only about 100 cases of the several hundred filed each year. As one justice told an interviewer: "We're like an oversold airline; we have an airplane with 100 seats and 1000 passengers trying to get in." There are two classes of people who have the automatic right to appeal: those whose acquittal of a crime was reversed by a provincial appellate court on an appeal from the Crown and those whose conviction was upheld by an appellate court with one of the judges dissenting on a question of law. An appeal is accompanied by a lawyer's written arguments, called *factums*, which, together with the appeal books containing all of the trial transcripts and judgements from lower courts, frequently reach several thousand pages. One case involving Québec's Bill 101, which legislated French as the only official language in that province, contained 55 volumes of complex legal arguments.

In response to a 1987 report on the Supreme Court by the Canadian Bar Association, the court instituted reforms to streamline its operations for faster, more efficient, service. The court now limits most submissions to 40 pages and permits lawyers to beam their arguments to the Supreme Court's television screens via satellite (video-conferencing). The Supreme Court has adopted the latest technologies to deal with its ever-increasing workload. Several years ago, all of the court's record-keeping was computerized so that every document filed with the court can be tracked electronically. The court uses satellite-TV links for many of its routine hearings that are conducted to determine whether a full appeal will be heard. Such "applications for leave to appeal" do not require lawyers to come all the way to Ottawa for a 15-minute session with the judges. Most appeals are turned down. For example, in 1992, the Supreme Court refused to hear an appeal by a New Brunswick motorist who wanted a traffic ticket quashed because he was not given a choice of getting it in English or French.

In recent times, the Supreme Court has not hesitated to pass judgement on basic political and moral questions. For example, it ruled that TV cameras can be barred from federal and provincial legislatures because the assemblies of Canada have "inherent privileges" that are a cut above constitutional rights to a free media. It ruled that those found not guilty of a crime by reason of insanity cannot be automatically committed to a mental institution, and that evidence obtained illegally by the police was admissible in court. It has also ruled that police cannot recruit informers to try to get a confession from an accused person. It upheld the decision that mandatory retirement is a legitimate infringement of the Charter of Rights, because work benefits society as well as the majority of employees, and it concluded that the results of a polygraph (lie-detector) test have no place in the legal system.

Indeed, over the past two decades, Supreme Court judges have made important rulings on the guarantees of equality and individual freedom in Canadian society. And, since the Charter of Rights and Freedoms became law in 1982, the Supreme Court has decided over a hundred cases involving its provisions. Thus the court ruled that if police obtain authorization to bug private premises they also have the right to enter these premises secretly to plant the bug. In its ruling, the Supreme Court decided that even though Parliament does not say police can trespass, it undoubtedly meant to do so. Dismissing an appeal from Alberta's attorney general, a unanimous Supreme Court struck down the federal Lord's Day Act because it compelled all residents to observe the Christian Sabbath, thereby violating the right of individuals to determine their

Box 21.1   Profile of a Supreme Court Justice: Madame Justice Claire L'Heureux-Dubé

Before they are appointed to the Supreme Court of Canada, justices have earned solid reputations in the legal profession. Such is the case of Madame Justice Claire L'Heureux-Dubé, who is the second woman to be appointed to Canada's highest court. After putting herself through law school and graduating cum laude from the Faculty of Law at Laval University, she was called to the Québec Bar and practised law in her native Québec City from 1952 to 1973, where she quickly earned a distinguished record as counsel and justice. In February, 1973, she was appointed to the Supreme Court of Québec, and in 1979 to the Québec Court of Appeal, where she served as justice until her appointment to the Supreme Court of Canada in April, 1987.

Within a span of forty years, Justice L'Heureux-Dubé enhanced her professional experience as Lecturer in Family Law in the Cours de formation professionelle du Barreau du Québec; was a counsellor of the Québec Bar, and delegate in its General Council; was a five-year member of the Conseil consultatif de l'administration de la justice de la Province du Québec; spent three years in a judicial inquiry into certain matters relating to the Department of Manpower and Immigration in Montreal; accepted a three-year term as vice-president of the Canadian Consumers Council; spent four years as president of the Family Law Committee and of the Family Court Committee of the Québec Civil Code Revision Office; and devoted a year as vice-president of the Vanier Institute of the Family and chairman of the Editorial Board of the Canadian Bar Review.

Since the early 1980s, Justice L'Heureux-Dubé has been granted six honorary doctor of law degrees. She has published numerous professional articles in Canada and the United States. She has served as president of the International Commission of Jurists, and in 1992 took on the position of vice- president in order to continue her role there. In the same year, she was made a member of the International Academia of Comparative Law.

Throughout her busy legal career in Québec City, Madame Justice Claire L'Heureux-Dubé learned to work long hours, including nights and weekends, on matters of judicial importance. Likewise, on the High Court she begins most thought-filled weekdays in the same way — she gets up at six, often goes swimming at a downtown Ottawa hotel, eats breakfast, and reads the newspaper. By 8:00 a.m. she passes through the bronze doors in the entrance hall of the Supreme Court building, rides the elevator to the second floor, and enters the churchy atmosphere of her small book-lined chamber. There, she begins to read and answer correspondence, which might include memorandums to and from members of the court on current opinions circulated. She receives invitations of all kinds: requests to speak at lunches, dinners, and conferences. She is frequently asked to participate at seminars, conventions, and annual meetings, all of which consume precious time in preparing speeches and fulfilling the protocol of a Supreme Court justice. All of these engagements must be organized around the schedule of the Supreme Court, which holds three sessions during the year and sits about sixteen or seventeen weeks, from the end of September to the end of June.

Most of her office time is spent reading and writing. When she became a superior appellate court judge, she earned the reputation of being a good writer, an adventurous thinker, and a tireless reader. When Justice L'Heureux-Dubé arrives at her office, the factums for a case the court will hear are waiting on her desk. She must read these carefully because they contain the lawyers' presentations of the facts on which the legal contest is based, as well as their refutations of the means of the adverse party. She must interpret these in conference with her colleagues. Thus, the job demands a cautious professional approach, tactfulness, diplomacy, and most of all, patience. Law **clerks** are assigned various tasks. Sometimes she will direct them in the research to be done, while in other circumstances she will request specific answers, and when the research is completed, the law clerks and the justice will have discussions about it. Often the clerks are recent law-school graduates, recruited from all provinces, who share the invaluable experience of working closely with federal judges.

The court usually convenes for a session from 10:30 a.m. to 12:30 p.m., which is followed by a one-and-a-half hour lunch at the Court House. The afternoon session begins at 2:00 p.m. and continues to 4:30 p.m., when it is followed by a half-hour Conference of the Court to discuss the cases of the day. The justices enter

(continued)

the court through a door directly behind a long elevated bench, wearing black silk gowns with white-collared vests. At the formal opening and closing of each session, they usually wear their bright scarlet robes trimmed with Canadian white mink, which they also wear at the opening of each new session of Parliament. The most junior justices sit on the far flanks and the others range closer to the chief justice, who occupies the centre position. A *quorum* consists of five members, but the full court of nine sits for most of the cases, unless illness prevents the attendance of all the justices.

One day a month (motion day) is devoted to motion hearings. Motion days start at 9:30 a.m., the Court convenes at 10:30 a.m. and sits until about 4:30 p.m., and there is a one-and-a-half-hour break for lunch. Court motions are requests by parties to have their cases heard by the Supreme Court. The Court receives twenty to thirty motions a day. Justice L'Heureux-Dubé, like her colleagues, must consider the merits of a request before giving an opinion. Each motion requires a judge to spend valuable time reading and doing research. Some motions are accepted, others are rejected. Those that are accepted have their day in the high court.

Unless by *special leave of the court*, the only people who may argue before it, apart from the litigants themselves, are lawyers from any Canadian province or territory. When the arguments are being presented to the court, any justice may ask questions of the lawyers retained. Sometimes a decision will be rendered at the conclusion of the arguments, but usually decisions are reserved for further deliberation or to enable judges to write their reasons. Decisions are made by the majority and need not be unanimous; dissenting reasons are frequently given. On adjourning, the justices file out the back door of the court to the conference room directly across the corridor. At this time, Justice L'Heureux-Dubé sits by a circular oak table and begins the ritual of discussing the case she has just heard. Each judge speaks to the points and issues raised in the case. The proceedings in this room are more confidential than federal cabinet meetings.

The decisions of the Court are published in the *Supreme Court Reports* and lodged in the *Registry*, managed by the *registrar*, who holds the status of deputy minister responsible for the administration of the Supreme Court. Justice Claire L'Heureux-Dubé and her colleagues perform an essential governmental task — the peaceful settlement of legal disputes at the highest judicial level.

religious preferences. In a 5:0 decision, the court ruled that the provision banning the use of languages other than French on public signs (Bill 101) was invalid because it violated the Québec Charter of Rights. And in 1993, by a narrow margin of 5:4, the Supreme Court upheld the prohibition on assisted suicide in the Sue Rodriguez case, basing their decision on the interest of the Crown in protecting life.

No other branch of government is more removed from public scrutiny. The public's only real influence on the high court comes indirectly from the power to elect governments which appoint the justices to the Supreme Court. Appointments to the Supreme Court have never been an election issue in Canada. These summit judicial appointments receive little public scrutiny. Almost the only thing to appear in the newspapers is the name of the appointee, a few sentences about the person, and all sorts of quotes from professors and lawyers affirming "this person has the best legal mind in Canada." Senior lawyers are reluctant to criticize such appointments because they may wish to maintain goodwill among the judicial community in case they have to appear before the Supreme Court.

In Parliament, the tradition is to praise. In general there is no wish among parliamentarians to cast Canada's top court into disrepute by questioning the appointment of a specific member. In addition, the Canadian legal establishment is very much opposed to public hearings or some sort of ratification by a parliamentary body as in the United States, where the Senate hears evidence and testimony on the competence and appropriateness of presidential nominees and ratifies or does not ratify the appointment. To some, the idea of introducing ratification hearings smacks of the Americanization of Canada's political and judicial cultures — an Americanization already seen in the more activist role of the court itself since the entrenchment of the Charter of Rights and Freedoms.[1]

Appointments follow strict protocol. The government decides from which region the appointee should come. As already noted, *by law*, three judges must come from Québec; but by tradition, the remaining positions are filled according to the pattern of three from Ontario, two from the West, and one from Atlantic Canada, which some feel represents an unfair distribution of high-court appointments. Ottawa asks the legal community to point out top candidates. Some applicants make the first contact, either by mentioning their interest to their province's chief justice or by writing directly to the federal justice minister or prime minister. Most Supreme Court members are appointed from appellate courts.

Professionally, the current justices of the Supreme Court of Canada have the collective reputation for intensity on the bench. They often work eighty-hour weeks, including weekends, and, at an average age of 65, make up one of the youngest benches in the history of the court. But as private citizens, they do what most people do: raise their families, participate in sports such as swimming, tennis, and fishing, and go through the daily routines of managing their personal affairs.

An unwritten rule of the court is that justices should lead restrained social lives, and close their lifestyles to public scrutiny so that their judicial impartiality is preserved for cases pending their decision. Other restrictions affect judges' lives as well. They may not hold any other remunerative positions with the federal or provincial governments, nor can they engage in business. They must live in the National Capital Region or within forty kilometres thereof. For reasons such as these, a judge's life is a complex one.

Ideally, the court should have a mix of talents, ages, ethnicity, and backgrounds — men and women, academics, practising lawyers, judges with trial- and appeal-court experience. The bench should also possess other important qualities essential to the operation of the most powerful court in Canada. This means appointing judges who are honest, unbiased, neither racist nor sexist, industrious, empathetic, intelligent, and knowledgeable of the law.[2] It is up to Canadians to demand that their judicial branch of government reflect the norms and values in their society. And it is up to Canadians to ask whether their best interests are served in a Supreme Court to which appointments are left to the backroom machinations of the prime minister.

As a result of these general attitudes and conduct, Canada's judicial institutions are perceived to be beyond the scope of political influence. A recent judgement of the Federal Court removed the disqualification of judges from voting in federal and provincial elections. Change is rarely sudden in the Supreme Court. Governments may come and go, and with them their national policies, but the judges, whatever their political leanings, seem to prize continuity and predictability.

NOTES

1. A. Wayne Mackay, "Judicial Free Speech and Accountability: Should Judges Be Seen But Not Heard?", *National Journal of Constitutional Law* (Vol. 3, No. 2, Oct., 1993), 159–242.
2. P. McCormick and I. Greene, *Judges and Judging: Inside the Judicial System* (Toronto: Lorimer, 1990), Ch. 4.

The Unknown Court:
The Federal Court of Canada

THE HONOURABLE JUSTICE
ALLEN M. LINDEN

I am a member of an Unknown Court. Even though the Federal Court of Canada is more than twenty years old, it is still a mysterious, enigmatic Court to most Canadians, including many lawyers. It is, nevertheless, an important Court which hears matters of importance to all Canadians. I would like to tell you something of its history, the story of its creation, and describe briefly its workings and the people who populate it. Perhaps, as a result, it will be a little less "unknown" to you.

ORIGIN

In 1970, the fledgling Trudeau Government was trying to build a Just Society in Canada. One of its initiatives along these lines was a Bill with the appellation "C-192." In March of that year, then Minister of Justice John N. Turner rose in the House of Commons to speak in support of that legislative initiative, asking the members to allow the Bill to be read a second time and then to send it to the Standing Committee on Justice and Legal Affairs. The arguments he made in support of this Bill, and the Court it was to create, are still appropriate and instructive today. To understand the Court as it is today it is helpful to look back at the hopes and aspirations of its creators.

On March 2, 1970, this new governmental initiative was announced (perhaps one could even say

trumpeted) by the Department of Justice, as "launching the first major reorganization and reform of the structure of the Exchequer Court of Canada since 1887."[1] Of course, any history of the present Federal Court of Canada must begin with the former Exchequer Court.[2] This forerunner to our Court was created in 1875, the same year as the foundation of the Supreme Court, and both were established under section 101 of the *Constitution Act 1867*, for the better administration of the laws of Canada. As its name makes clear, the Exchequer Court's jurisdiction was originally to hear matters pertaining to federal revenue law. This jurisdiction was augmented in 1887 so that it would have exclusive jurisdiction in cases where the Crown was being sued, and concurrent jurisdiction with Provincial Courts when the Crown brought the suit. Over the years, other, more specialized areas of law were added to the Exchequer Judges' workload, among them admiralty law, as well as patents, trademarks and copyright. The Exchequer Court also had supervisory jurisdiction over federal administrative bodies, although this jurisdiction was shared with the Supreme Court of Canada and the Provincial Superior Courts.

There were substantial and compelling reasons for the creation of the Federal Court of Canada to replace the Exchequer Court. No one could have foreseen the growth that occurred in the nearly 100

SOURCE: "The Unknown Court: The Federal Court of Canada," unpublished paper. Reprinted by permission of the author.

years after the creation of the Exchequer Court in the number and influence of federal boards, commissions and tribunals. Such rapid development was not, however, matched with equivalent reformation of the judicial system charged with administrative review. Rather than having a single, national Court with jurisdiction over this quickly-expanding legal area, judicial review and supervision of this multitude of federal institutions were dealt with by a variety of Courts. Understandably, this resulted in uneven jurisprudence, creating difficulties for the board and tribunals, counsel, and those citizens who depended on the smooth functioning of the federal administrative system. The solution, as Mr. Turner stated in the House of Commons on March 25, 1970, was that "superintending jurisdiction should be vested in a single Court that enjoyed the same nation wide jurisdiction as the federal boards, commissions and tribunals themselves."[3]

A further advantage of a Federal Court was that, as a national institution, it could deal with national legal problems. Any **relief** given, or orders issued, would be effective across Canada. This was seen as especially advantageous in legal areas such as admiralty or intellectual property which, by their very nature, are inter-provincial or international. The Federal Court would be a national Court, finding national solutions to national problems.

The creation of this Court to ensure uniformity in the review of administrative bodies also gave Parliament the opportunity to modernize the remedies available in these cases. Before 1971, the superintending Courts found their remedial jurisdiction in the common law or in legislation which dated from before Confederation. These remedies were largely limited to the traditional prerogative writs. Creating a new Court furnished us with an opportunity to ensure that the administrative bodies operated within their proper procedures, according to the law and **natural justice**, without unduly hampering their independent decision-making ability. The Federal Court was to be permitted to supervise the Canadian administrative system in a manner sensitive to its particular structure and objectives. The old system of **writs** and relief in the nature of the writs

was left to the Trial Division which, under section 18, was to have review jurisdiction over federal boards, commissions or other tribunals making decisions on an administrative basis. The review jurisdiction of the Federal Court of Appeal, which was vested with the power of judicial review over federal boards, commissions or other tribunals making decisions on a judicial or quasi-judicial basis, reflected the new national approach to administrative review. As Mr. Justice Jackett stated: "Unlike the jurisdiction conferred by section 18 on the Trial Division, which is a jurisdiction in respect of pre-existing well-known remedies, the jurisdiction conferred by section 28 on the Court of Appeal would seem to be defined in the statute itself."[4] Section 28 was a new simplification of administrative procedure with "no cross-reference to pre-existing remedies."[5] It simply permitted the Federal Court of Appeal to set aside the decision of a tribunal for certain errors of jurisdiction, of law, and of fact.

I have just alluded to the Trial Division and the Federal Court of Appeal. Before the passage of the *Federal Court Act*,[6] the Supreme Court of Canada was the Court of Appeal from the Exchequer Court, which was a Court of original jurisdiction. There was no intermediate Appeal Court. As a result, the Supreme Court found itself overloaded with these appeals from a **Court of first instance**. The Federal Court, with its own Appeal Division, was designed to handle appeals from the Court of first instance, which would allow only the most important cases to proceed to the Supreme Court. This filtering process was put in place to ensure that the Supreme Court could be left to deal with matters of national import, such as constitutional questions and resolving interprovincial legal conflicts. Further, even matters proceeding directly to the Federal Court of Appeal would require leave to appeal to the Supreme Court.

Another advantage of the new Court was an improvement in accessibility. Under the old system, parties wishing to appeal from the Exchequer Court had to travel to Ottawa to make their arguments. With the advent of the Federal Court, this changed. Both the Appeal and the Trial Divisions were made into itinerant Courts, which would be more convenient for the parties involved in litigation. It was hoped that a travelling Court would "bring justice to the people, decentralize the operation of the present Court, make the Court more accessible, quicker and less expensive."[7] From the beginning the Federal Court was designed to put justice and the availability of justice first. It was meant to be a "people's Court."

The Federal Court of Canada was premised upon a far-reaching vision of the just interaction between the individual and his or her government. As Mr. Turner stated: "I believe that this is a further step toward balancing the rights between the citizen and the state, providing some sort of recourse against bigness, remoteness, alienation, distance from the decision making power. I believe it will give the average citizen the power to enforce his rights against the government and against the structures that the government sets up."[8] If the rapid growth of administrative bodies was to be a central part of the Canada emerging in the early 1970s, then a new Court was also to emerge which would provide citizens with fair and efficient legal protection.

The creation of the Federal Court must also be looked at from the standpoint of the political context of the time. The new Court was part of the "Just Society" program, which also included important statutory amendments (particularly in the criminal law) and the creation of the Law Reform Commission of Canada. At least one commentator has ventured the opinion that the Federal Court was an attempt by the federal government to increase its stature in the provinces, especially given the de-centralizing "centrifugal implications" of the growth of administrative bodies.[9] Whatever its intentions, Parliament's structuring of the Court to ensure accessibility and a presence in every region could not help but make this new "Federal" Court a part of the national landscape, from sea to sea.

PROCESS OF CREATION

Any discussion of the development of the Federal Court must include the part played by the then Chief Justice of the Exchequer Court of Canada, Wilbur Jackett. As the head of the Court that was to become the Federal Court, he had an interest in ensuring that the new institution was an effective and fair means of dispensing justice to Canadians. His booklet entitled *The Federal Court of Canada: A Manual of Practice* is still required reading for anyone interested in the Court, despite Chief Justice Jackett's own disclaimer that it is a "potboiler."[10] Along with Chief Justice Jackett, one must also mention the work of Mr. D.S. Maxwell, who was then the Deputy Minister of Justice. His helpful assistance is evident in the statements he made before the Standing Committee on Justice and Legal Affairs. These two individuals, along with Mr. Turner, were the key actors in the creation of the Federal Court of Canada.

But this new Court which was to have such an important impact upon administrative law was not created overnight. And neither should the acclaim or blame for the Court's various strengths and shortcomings fall solely on the shoulders of a few individuals. The Bill was the subject of intense scrutiny by a great many people within the legal community. Roughly 1,200 lawyers asked for copies of the Bill, one-third of whom made suggestions regarding various portions of the Bill which they felt needed attention. As Mr. Turner explained to the House of Commons:

> This bill received first reading on March 2. It received a very thorough review by the Standing Committee on Justice and Legal Affairs. It received the scrutiny of a good many top legal counsel throughout the country. As a matter of fact, I sent a mimeographed letter to all 14,000 members of the Canadian Bar Association thanks to its distribution system. The Canadian Bar Association designated a committee to review the bill.... I had the opportunity to appear on a panel discussion which was televised and videotaped and will be shown to all provincial subsections of the Canadian Bar Association.
>
> What I am saying is that the bill has received a good deal of public scrutiny from the legal

profession, from those organizations accustomed to appearing before federal boards and tribunals and from private citizens generally who are interested in the administration of justice.[11]

PUBLIC RESPONSE

When the Bill to create the Federal Court was unveiled, editorial writers at Canada's major newspapers welcomed the Court reform with enthusiasm. The Montreal *Gazette* described the new Court as "a giant step towards putting the citizen and the government on a more equal footing." The changes proposed were "long overdue" and were "an attempt to overhaul some of the more obvious and discriminatory weaknesses of the administration of justice."[12] The *Toronto Star* pointed out that the itinerant nature of the Court "would provide aggrieved parties with a much speedier and more convenient way of getting a hearing." The limit placed on the Court's review jurisdiction was called "a sound decision."[13] According to the *Globe and Mail* "the very least that can be said about the [Federal Court] bill is that it is a highly commendable effort to meet problems in a difficult and complex area."[14] And the Ottawa *Journal* pointed out that "the bill has no sex-appeal and it will probably not arouse much public interest. But few bills passed by this Parliament will be more in the public interest."[15]

The *Federal Court Act* was not without its critics. The consultation process produced some thoughtful criticism of Bill C-192. Numerous individuals from the academic community and the practising bar pointed out what they believed to be shortcomings with the Bill as it was drafted. Nowhere is this process more evident than in the minutes of the Standing Committee on Justice and Legal Affairs. Certain problems which did surface after the Federal Court Act was proclaimed were accurately forecast during Committee hearings. In his statements before the Committee, Professor G.V. Nichols pointed out that the wording of the Bill was "unnecessarily" complex, pointing specifically to sections 18 and 28. Professor Nichols was not the only person to make reference to problems which could arise out of these

sections, and he was neither alone nor entirely incorrect in stating that they would be "a prolific breeder of unproductive litigation" as to which division of the Court had jurisdiction.[16]

Other witnesses before the Committee pointed out potential difficulties posed by the Bill. The dangers of conflicting decisions and expensive extra litigation were alluded to by Professor G.D. Watson when he spoke regarding the necessity for litigants to sue the government in the Federal Court, and private parties involved in the same action in the Provincial Courts. Labour groups presented a brief expressing their concern that allowing the Appeal Division to review tribunal decisions on the basis that they are based on an "erroneous finding of fact that it made in a perverse or capricious manner or without due regard to the material before it"[17] would be to allow the Court too much influence over administrative bodies, particularly the labour boards.

It would be wrong to suggest, however, that there was always unanimity in the comment on the Bill. Indeed, sometimes the criticisms were directly contradictory. For example, while one expert pointed out that "the overall effect of sections 18 [and] 28 . . . may well be to restrict the traditional role of the courts . . .,"[18] another, shortly after the passage of the *Act*, stated that section 28 "arguably leaves little or nothing sacred from the scrutiny of the courts . . ."[19] Clearly, prognostication, rather like legislative drafting, is more of an art than a science.

Out of the consultative process came a number of amendments to the Bill, which fine-tuned its wording, allowing for the better functioning of the Court. But, for the most part, the structure and intent of the bill remained much the same as before. It should not be surprising, therefore, to find that the tenor and focus of the academic response to the new *Act* was much the same as that before the Bill became law. The academic community pointed out what were felt to be numerous problems with the *Act*: the maintenance of the old prerogative writs, keeping the need to distinguish between quasi-judicial and administrative functions, splitting the review jurisdiction between the two divisions of the

Court, the broadening (or narrowing, depending on one's perspective) of the Court's review jurisdiction, and the creation of new constitutional difficulties regarding the Court's jurisdiction.[20]

One should note, in defence of the Court, that a certain number of jurisdictional and other problems were to be expected in a Court of this nature. As has been pointed out, "this preoccupation [with the Federal Court's jurisdiction] is compelled because the jurisdiction of the Court is exceptional and statutory. It is to be contrasted with the jurisdiction of the provincial superior courts."[21] The very fact that the jurisdiction of the Court had to be statutorily defined meant that there would be issues surrounding its interpretation. This reality, combined with the special task the Court was created to undertake, and the special demands of the Canadian Constitution, could only result in much ink being spilled over the issue. It must be recalled that the legal academic's job is, in part, to probe legislation, to attempt to discover any weaknesses, and to press for improvements.

Some commentators were willing to adopt a wait-and-see attitude:

> The Federal Court, therefore, appears to provide a flexible but virtually all-inclusive recourse from federal administrative decisions or at least it purports to do so. . . . How the Federal Court is able to deal with its continuing problems remains to be seen.[22]

The private bar also had an ongoing interest in the Federal Court. This can be seen in the continuing debate about the Court which has been carried on by the Canadian Bar Association. Members of the C.B.A. were involved in the original consultative process for Bill C-192. After the bill became law, the C.B.A. persevered in its examination of the Court, its structure and its workings. In 1977, a C.B.A. Special Committee released its recommendations regarding the Court.[23]

The Special Committee was reconstituted in 1989 to study the controversial British Columbia proposal to abolish the Federal Court and give its jurisdiction to the Provincial Courts. This new Committee also studied the proposed Federal Court reforms of the current government, contained in Bill C-38. The Special Committee issued a Report on the B.C. proposal during the summer of 1990.[24] While it continued to back the C.B.A.'s position that **tort** and contract matters involving the federal crown be given to the provinces, it was not in favour of abolishing the Court, given the constitutional difficulties involved in such an action. Nevertheless, the B.C. proposal was put to the C.B.A. as a resolution at its Mid-Winter meeting in Regina in 1991, where it was "overwhelmingly" defeated. (A 42–42 tie vote was broken by the Chair.)

FURTHER DEVELOPMENTS

Over the years the Court has continued to enjoy an ever-strengthening position within the Canadian legal community. The success of the court can be measured in such basic ways as the number of judges which hear its cases. In 1971 there were twelve Judges, eight in Trial Division and four on the Appeal Bench. In four years, this number had grown to sixteen. Ten years later, in 1985, the original number of Judges had more than doubled, with fourteen Judges forming the Trial Division, and eleven in the Appeal Court.[25] Today the Federal Court of Appeal boasts of fourteen members while the Trial Division has swelled to include twenty-one Judges. The increase in the workload and influence of the Court is reflected in these numbers.

The main offices of the Federal Court of Canada are in Ottawa. The members of the Appeal Division are located in the Supreme Court Building, where there are also two courtrooms used by the Appeal and Trial Divisions. Members of the Trial Division have their offices in the Royal Bank Building on Sparks Street, and they make use of various locations to hear cases. A new building to house all members of the Federal Court is scheduled for construction next to the Supreme Court Building.

While the Court, like all large institutions, still has its critics, it is now being recognized and applauded for the work which it does. I can do worse than quote Professor J.M. Evans: "Having survived that most dangerous life-phase — adolescence — the Court is now better equipped to come into its own as a specialist public law Court, second in importance only to the Supreme Court of Canada."[26]

The Court survived this adolescent phase by continuing to fulfil its ambitious mandate: the provision of administrative legal justice in an efficient and fair manner in all areas of Canada. And according to recent comment on the Court, this has been remarkably successful:

> Certainly the court has struggled manfully to make itself accessible. It has established registry offices in sixteen locations across Canada. It hears cases in major cities in every province and in the northern territories. Despite the requirement that all of the court's judges reside in Ottawa, only 14 per cent of the matters heard by the court since 1978 have been heard in the national capital. This is just 2 per cent higher than the proportion of cases heard in Vancouver. Two-thirds of the cases since 1978 have been heard in Montreal and Toronto. The Federal Court judges have indeed become frequent flyers![27]

The accessible nature of the Court has certainly always been one of its strong points. While the principal **registry of the Court** is in Ottawa, a party can conduct business with it at any of the regional offices. The Federal Court achieves accessibility to citizens by travelling across Canada. The Court has offices in most major cities, from St. John's to Vancouver to Yellowknife. In some of these places, the Court has its own facilities while in others it makes use of existing courtrooms for its hearings. Members of the Appeal Division travel in panels of three, and are outside of Ottawa roughly every other week, while Trial Division Judges travel on their own and may be away from Ottawa for extended periods of time due to the demands of conducting trials. Accessibility is also facilitated by the Court's operating in both official languages across the country, as befits the Court's national character. It

would be safe to say that, in doing its job, this Court "goes that extra mile."

One might expect that a Court with such far-flung responsibilities, and such a diverse, and yet strictly circumscribed, jurisdiction would be extremely difficult to administer. But the Court has been extremely lucky in the people who have been responsible for its operation. Take, for example, the three former Chief Justices of the Court: the Honourable Wilbur R. Jackett, who, as I already mentioned, was instrumental in the creation of the Federal Court and its smooth transition from the Exchequer Court; the Honourable Arthur Thurlow, who saw the Court through much of its later growth and development; and the Honourable Frank Iacobucci, now a member of the Supreme Court of Canada. Our current Chief Justice, the Honourable Julius Isaac, must also be applauded for his role in seeing the Court through recent changes brought about by the amendment of the *Federal Court Act*. These people, along with the approximately two hundred others who are responsible for the operation of this Court, are what led the Canadian Bar Association to conclude that "overall, it is clear that from the time the court was established, it has been noted for the efficiency and dispatch with which it has performed its functions."[28] Professor Russell, a person not known for his effusive use of superlatives, recently wrote that the Federal Court is the "best administered Court in this country."

In 1983, the Federal Court undertook a pilot law clerks' program. This pilot program was so successful that a full-time law clerk program was established the following year. The program has continued to grow, and this year there are thirty-two clerks working at the Court — eleven with the Appeal Division and twenty-one with the Trial Court. This prestigious program attracts law students from every province, who share the invaluable experience of working closely with the Judges for one year. Clerks have gone on to further graduate study not only in Canada but in Britain, France and elsewhere. They have put their skills to work in private law firms and in government departments, particularly the federal Justice Department.

Former clerks now teach law in Ottawa, at McGill University in Montreal and other places. Clerking is both challenging and rewarding—and it has been rumoured that the Court and the Judges have benefited from this program as well.

The Court, as it has grown, has worked diligently to avoid the pitfalls alluded to by earlier commentators. One of the academic critics of the Court now points to the Appeal Division's record of decisions as illustrating that it has skilfully balanced the competing interests in ensuring that tribunals have followed the rules of natural justice.[29] Critics also worried that paragraph 28(1)(c), which allows review of tribunals based on "erroneous findings of fact... made in a perverse or capricious manner," would allow the Court free rein to interfere with administrative functioning. These fears have proved to be largely unfounded. "On the contrary, the Federal Court of Appeal appears to have drawn a 'tight net' around 28(1)(c) as a ground of review, so that in effect it amounts to no more than the traditional requirement that there be some evidence to support the decision under review.[30]

With amendments to legislation, principally the *Federal Court Act*, which came into force early in 1992, some of the early problems with the Court have been ironed out. Two changes are of particular significance. First, section 17 of the *Federal Court Act* has been amended to provide for concurrent jurisdiction with the Superior Courts of the provinces in all cases where relief is claimed against the Crown. This amendment was intended to do away with multiple proceedings that arose in suits against the Crown where third party claims based on common law or a provincial statute had to be brought in the Superior Courts of the provinces. Second, sections 18 and 28 of the *Federal Court Act* were amended to cut off the seemingly endless litigation over jurisdiction between the Trial Division and the Federal Court of Appeal in applications for judicial review. Under the new amendments, judicial review will proceed in the Trial Division unless the application is for review of a decision or order of one of fourteen bodies named specifically in section 28.

THE JUDGES [31]

A Court's strength lies in the learning, the background and the experience of its Judges. In this respect, the Federal Court is a particularly formidable institution. An overview of its Judges, past and present, reveals that they have a range and depth of experience from which the Court continues to benefit every day. Particularly outstanding is the history of governmental service by the members of the bench. At least six of our Judges have performed their public responsibilities by being members of the House of Commons. Other Judges have been members of provincial legislatures in Nova Scotia, Quebec and Saskatchewan. Many Judges are former federal cabinet ministers, and the portfolios they held were impressive as well as varied: Minister of Justice and Attorney General of Canada, Minister of State for National Revenue, Minister of Employment and Immigration, Secretary of State for External Affairs, Minister of Public Works and Minister of Veterans Affairs. One of our Judges is also a former provincial Attorney General, and another was the first Speaker of the House of Commons to be re-elected to that position after a change in government. These same individuals also served on some of the most important standing committees on Parliament Hill. Federal Court Judges have chaired the Standing Committee on Justice and Legal Affairs, the Committee on External Affairs, the Joint Committee on the Constitution of Canada and the Committee on Finance, Trade and Economic Affairs.

Two Judges of the Federal Court have been appointed to the Supreme Court of Canada. Three of our Judges, prior to their appointment to the Court, have had the honour of heading the Law Reform Commission of Canada. Two other Judges have been provincial ombudsmen (in Quebec and Nova Scotia). And this is by no means the extent of governmental experience on the Court. Judge's of the Federal Court have held the position of Deputy Minister of Justice, Deputy Attorney General and Deputy Solicitor General. Numerous Judges have held senior positions in the public service, especially in the Department of Justice, but also as Chair of the National Parole Board and as Director of Investigation and Research on Competition Policy. One Judge was a Director of the Bank of Canada and another served as both constitutional adviser to the Republic of the Seychelles and as an adviser to the government of Hong Kong on Human Rights. One of our Judges was part of the Canadian delegation to NATO and was President of the Commonwealth Parliamentary Association.

They have also distinguished themselves in academia. Our Judges are a remarkably learned crowd, having pursued their studies at prestigious and far-flung institutions. Members of the Court, past and present, have degrees from Harvard, from the Faculté de droit et des sciences économiques de Paris, from Oxford (including a Rhodes Scholar) and Cambridge, and from leading universities such as the University of California and Columbia University. Federal Court Judges have been deans of law schools at Dalhousie, Laval, New Brunswick, Toronto and Windsor Universities and Osgoode Hall. Over the years, many Judges have been professors of law in law schools all across Canada.

Federal Court Justices have also had experience outside of the academic world which contributes to the strength of the Court. Numerous Judges have, of course, worked as members of the practising bar from Bay and Wall Streets to small-town Canada. Others have been Crown prosecutors. On a less legalistic note, we have a former director of the Saskatchewan Rough Riders football team, as well as a past president of the Calgary Stampeders, and, not to forget another national passion, an ex-governor of Hockey Canada. Now, sadly, they are all just "bench-warmers."

Numerous Judges of the Court have also been members of the Canadian armed forces, and some have seen active duty. Several Judges worked for the Judge Advocate of the Canadian armed forces, and some participated in the war crimes trials after World War II. Federal Court Judges have also been involved in the arts. They have, naturally enough, been prolific authors, turning out law books on a wide variety of topics, from torts to the Constitution. But they have also written for a wider audience: we have a former newspaper columnist on the Court, for example. As an aside, this same Judge also showed his commitment to the arts by acting as a Director for Les Grands Ballets canadiens.

Federal Court Judges have, not surprisingly, received public recognition for their talents — whether by being awarded the title of Queen's Counsel, or by being elected benchers of their law society, or being made an Honorary Colonel in their army regiment, or even by receiving the Order of Canada.

THE WORK OF THE COURT

An examination of the breadth of the Federal Court's workload can quickly turn into a lesson on the extent of the impact of government on the life of a citizen. From Unemployment Insurance to Customs and Excise, the Federal Court hears a wide variety of appeals and applications for review from virtually all federal boards and tribunals. Indeed, we often forget how many different areas of legal practice are found beneath the umbrella of "**administrative law**." In its role as Canada's administrative law Court, the Federal Court hears cases dealing with human rights, labour law, tax, immigration, telecommunications, transportation and energy. And this is just a partial list. Mr. Justice MacGuigan, a distinguished member of the Court of Appeal, has aptly described the "mission" of the Court as "nothing short of civilizing the exercise of government power." And the volume of work in this area matches the breadth of the Court's work: in 1993, the Appeal Division disposed of 1,607 appeals and applications for judicial review of decisions of tribunals while the Trial Division heard 588 applications for judicial review.[32]

The Court has had the opportunity to hear many interesting cases over the years in its role of reviewing the decisions of administrative tribunals. One recent example is the Gemini merger case in which the Appeal Division held that the Competition Tribunal did not have jurisdiction to order compensation for the break up of the Gemini computer reservation system, a break up that Canadian Airlines sought in order to facilitate its association with PWA.[33] In another case, the Appeal Division held that the National Energy Board did not have the jurisdiction to impose as a condition of licences for the export of electricity that Hydro-Québec perform environmental assessments of the power generating facilities it contemplated building in northern Québec to provide the power.[34] As happens every so often, the Appeal Division was reversed on this point by the Supreme Court of Canada![35]

The review of administrative tribunals is not, of course, the only aspect of Federal Court practice. For example, hundreds of admiralty law cases are initiated in the Trial Division each year with 647 admiralty matters instituted in 1993. Concerning its role in admiralty law, a distinguished member of the admiralty bar has written:

> "In its first 20 years, the Federal Court of Canada has developed significant expertise in the maritime field, making it the forum of choice for the resolution of admiralty disputes. The court has taken the body of 'Canadian maritime law' which it inherited in 1971, has impressed it with its own stamp and has adapted and changed it to meet the requirements of new times, new technologies and new values."

The Federal Court is also the Court of practice for members of the Intellectual Property bar. Many actions in trademark, copyright and patent law are brought to the Trial Division each year: in 1993 alone, 261 trademark actions, 88 patent claims and 84 copyright matters were instituted. The subject matter of these cases is varied. In 1991, for example, the Trial Division found that the manufacturer of HUGGIES diapers was in violation of a patent held by the makers of LUVS diapers with respect to materials involved in the manufacturing of elasticized waistbands for the diapers.[36] The Federal Court is also the battle ground of breweries such as John Labatt and Molson: the most recent skirmish

ended in victory for Molson when this Court held that Molson could register the trademark "Molson's Blue" which had been in use in association with Molson Stock Ale.[37]

On top of all of this, Federal Court Judges hear cases in legal areas which one might not immediately associate with that institution. For example, a Federal Court Judge may be designated a Judge of the Court Martial Appeal Court and may hear what are essentially criminal law cases. (It is interesting to note that it is possible that a Federal Court Judge might literally decide a matter of life and death, since the *National Defence Act*[38] still allows for capital punishment under certain circumstances.) The manslaughter conviction resulting from the death of a Somali citizen while in the custody of Canadian peacekeepers was appealed to the Appeal Division.

In addition to criminal law, Federal Court Judges cannot forget their torts or contracts law. Actions against the Crown, including claims for negligence, are traditionally heard in this Court although the Superior Courts of the provinces now share the Federal Court's jurisdiction in this area. Were any litigation to proceed over the federal government's decisions not to follow through with the helicopter purchase contract or the contract for the privatization of Lester B. Pearson airport, those cases could be heard in the Federal Court.

Although not in any way a major part of the Federal Court's work, it is possible that a family law matter could end up before the Federal Court, since the Court has jurisdiction to hear matters instituted under the *Divorce Act*.[39] Divorce cases have actually been initiated, although none have proceeded to trial.

One might be excused for thinking that such a varied and interesting workload would be enough to keep any Court busy. But an unanticipated growth in the Immigration work done by the Court—particularly refugee claims—over the last six or seven years has meant that it is now the most important source of work for the Court. As Mr. Justice Heald pointed out in an address given at the Canadian Bar Association's 1991 conference on the Federal Court:

... in 1984 the total number of applications for leave to appeal to the Court of Appeal was 84. In 1989, with the coming into force of the amendments, the figure was 684, of which 651 were immigration applications. As of August 31, 1990, 1299 applications for leave had been filed, of which 1288 related to immigration issues. By October 12, 1990, 1581 immigration applications had been filed. As of September 1, well over 300 notices of appeal had been filed pursuant to leave granted by the Court.[40]

This trend continued into 1993 when the Appeal Division rendered 1,355 judgments and orders in the area of immigration law while 8,454 immigration matters were instituted in the Trial Division.

There can be no doubt that the explosive expansion in immigration law, which occurred after the Supreme Court of Canada decision in *Singh v. M.E.I.*,[41] has tested the resources of the Federal Court. Yet the Court manages its responsibilities in this area, as in all others, with the proper mix of diligence and expediency. The future promises some relief to the Appeal Division since amendments to the *Immigration Act*[42] have done away with preliminary hearings by immigration adjudicators to determine whether refugee claims have credible bases. Decisions from the credible basis hearings were reviewed by the Appeal Division and formed a substantial portion of the Court's immigration work. A further reduction in the Court's workload comes through amendments to the *Immigration Act* and the *Federal Court Act* which provide that applications for judicial review of decisions or orders made under the *Immigration Act* will be heard by the Trial Division and then only with leave of the Trial Division. No appeal may be taken to the Appeal Division from decisions on applications for leave, and appeals from decisions on applications for judicial review may only be taken where a Judge of the Trial Division certifies that a serious question of general importance is involved.

Refugee cases bring many different issues before the Court. For example, the Court recently considered whether the forced sterilization of women in China under the one child policy constituted persecution on the basis of membership in a particular social group.[43] The Court also hears cases which concern whether people with otherwise valid refugee claims should be excluded on the basis that there are serious reasons for considering that they have committed war crimes or crimes against humanity.[44] Further, the Court hears immigration matters of which one example was whether it was contrary to the *Charter*[45] to deport a permanent resident of Canada, who had lived in Canada since his youth, for conviction of a serious criminal offence.[46]

There are few areas of practice which the *Canadian Charter of Rights and Freedoms* has not touched in one way or another. As you might expect, practice before the Federal Court has also felt the impact of the *Charter*. Citizens are now able to raise constitutional challenges to the enabling legislation of administrative boards and tribunals. Federal Court Judges may now be called upon to determine if a statutorily created body has violated the *Charter*. The Federal Court has dealt with a wide range of *Charter* issues, including those of equality, life, liberty and security of the person, and the freedoms of association, expression, conscience and religion. The Federal Court has dealt with hundreds of cases with a *Charter* angle, in areas as diverse as immigration and citizenship, penitentiaries, the public service, government, benefits, taxation and a variety of other matters. For example, the Supreme Court will be hearing an appeal from a decision of this Court which held that it was not contrary to the *Charter* to restrict the availability of the spouses allowance program for the elderly to heterosexual couples.[47] As another example, the Federal Court decided that it was not contrary to the *Charter* for the government to restrict the tax deductibility of child care expenses, a decision which was affirmed by the Supreme Court.[48] Also in the area of taxation law, the Appeal Division recently held on an application for judicial review from the Tax Court that the taxing of child support payments in the hands of the custodial parent was contrary to the *Charter*.[49] Another well-known case involving the *Charter* heard in the Federal Court was whether Operation Dismantle could get an injunction against the testing of cruise missiles in Canada. The Appeal Division, in a judgment affirmed by the Supreme Court, held that Operation Dismantle's statement of claim should be struck out on the basis that it did not contain facts which, if true, would support a violation of the *Charter's* protection of life, liberty and security of the person.[50]

The Federal Court hears many cases that impact in the political arena. For example, the Appeal Division granted the Native Women's Association of Canada a declaration that the *Charter* rights of native women had been violated by the federal government's decision to exclude the Association from consultation regarding the formulation of the Charlottetown Accord.[51] During the referendum on the Charlottetown Accord, the Appeal Division held, in a case brought by citizens who moved to Quebec just prior to the referendum and could not vote in either the national or the Quebec referendum, that it was not unconstitutional for the federal government to hold a referendum in some but not all of the provinces.[52]

This work, as you can see, is varied and often complex. For us, it is also interesting and important. Our dossiers are full indeed, and with every passing year new legislation is passed and new boards and tribunals are created. As these administrative tribunals become ever more varied, and the law surrounding them ever more complex, the Federal Court will be faced with new challenges in the years to come.

CONCLUSION

The Federal Court has had a history of praise and criticism, of change and growth. What the future holds for the Court will, of course, depend greatly upon the course that future governments take. As the "Federal" Court, this institution is in the business of dealing with federal legislation and administrative bodies. The *Federal Court Act* was recently amended to change some parts of jurisdiction and the structure of the Court. One can state with certainty that this will not be the last change the Court will encounter. The Federal Court was created to respond to changes

in Canadian society, and these changes will no doubt continue. Whatever the future brings — new Judges, new jurisdiction, a new Court building, possibly — the Federal Court will continue to be an integral part of the Canadian legal community. Let us hope that it will cease to be the "Unknown Court" and will become better known as the "People's Court" so as to fulfil the dreams of its founders.

NOTES

1. Department of Justice press release, March 2, 1970, p. 1.
2. See *The Judiciary in Canada: The Third Branch of Government*, Peter H. Russell, Toronto: McGraw-Hill Ryerson Limited, 1987, p. 312; and "The Federal Court of Canada: Some Comments on Its Origin, Traditions and Evolution" by the Honourable Mr. Justice Frank Iacobucci, in 11 *Advocate's Quarterly*, p. 318.
3. Debates of the House of Commons, March 25, 1970, p. 5471.
4. *The Federal Court of Canada: A Manual of Practice*, W.R. Jackett, Ottawa: Information Canada, 1971, p. 22.
5. Ibid.
6. R.S.C. 1985, c. F-7, as am.
7. Debates of the House of Commons, March 25, 1970, p. 5470.
8. Ibid. p. 5474.
9. Russell, p. 314. See also Minutes of Proceedings of the Standing Committee on Justice and Legal Affairs, 14 May, 1970, p. 10.
10. Jackett, Introduction, p. 13.
11. Debates of the House of Commons, October 28, 1970, p. 665.
12. Editorial, *The Gazette* [Montreal], Mar. 5, 1970.
13. Editorial, *The Toronto Star*, Mar. 7, 1970.
14. Editorial, *The Globe and Mail* [Toronto], Mar. 7, 1970.
15. Editorial, *The Journal* [Ottawa], Mar. 10, 1970.
16. Minutes of Proceedings of the Standing Committee on Justice and Legal Affairs, No. 27, p. 27:25.
17. *Federal Court Act*, s. 28(1)(c).
18. Committee minutes, Professor Nichols, p. 27:25.
19. "The Federal Court Act: A Misguided Attempt at Administrative Law Reform?" D.J. Mullan, in University of Toronto L.J. 1973, vol. 23, p. 14 at 17.

20. All of these problems are canvassed in D.J. Mullan's article, *supra*, fn. 19.

21. *Federal Court Practice*, Sgayias et al., p. 1.

22. N.A. Chalmers, "The Federal Court as an Attempt to Solve Some Problems of Administrative Law in the Federal Area," McGill L.J., Vol. 18, No. 2, p. 206 at 217–218.

23. "Report of the Canadian Bar Commission on the Federal Court," A. Lorne Campbell, Q.C. (Chairman), D.M.M. Goldie, Q.C., B.A. Crane, Q.C., 1977.

24. Special Committee on the Federal Court *Report to Council on the British Columbia Proposal for Merger of the Federal Court into Provincial Superior Courts*, Legislation and Law Reform, 1990.

25. Russell, p. 316.

26. *The Role of the Federal Court in the 1990's*, J.M. Evans, delivered to the C.B.A. conference on the Federal Court held in Toronto, January 25, 1991.

27. Russell, p. 324.

28. *Report of the Canadian Bar Commission on the Federal Court*, p. 15.

29. Russell, p. 326, commenting on David Mullan.

30. Russell, p. 327.

31. The sources for the information in this section are the *Annual Reports of the Federal Court* for 1988 and 1989 and *Canadian Who's Who 1990* and *1993*.

32. All statistics in this portion of the paper are drawn from *Federal Court of Canada Statistics, December 31, 1993*.

33. *Canada (Director of Investigation and Research, Competition Act) v. Air Canada* (July 30, 1993), File No. A-302-93 [unreported] (F.C.A.).

34. *Quebec (Attorney General) v. Canada (National Energy Board)*, [1991] 3 F.C. 443 (C.A.).

35. *Quebec (Attorney General) v. Canada (National Energy Board)* (February 24, 1994), File No. 22705 [unreported] (S.C.C.).

36. *Procter & Gamble Co. v. Kimberley-Clark of Canada Ltd.* (December 13, 1991), File No. T-1493-86 [unreported] (T.D.).

37. *John Labatt Ltd. v. Molson Cos.* (June 11, 1992), File No. A-577-90 [unreported] (F.C.A.).

38. *National Defence Act* R.S., c. N-4, s.1.

39. *Divorce Act*, R.S. 1985, c. 3 (2nd Supp.).

40. "The Role of the Federal Court in the 1990's" presented by the Honourable Mr. Justice Darrel V. Heald, January 25, 1991, in Toronto, and February 1, 1991, in Vancouver, p. 17.

41. *Singh v. M.E.I.* [1985] 1 S.C.R. 177.

42. S.C. 1976–77, c. 52, as am.

43. *Cheung v. Canada (Minister of Employment and Immigration)*, [1993] 2 F.C. 314 (C.A.).

44. See, for example, *Sivakumar v. Canada (Minister of Employment and Immigration)* (November 4, 1993), File No. A-1043-91 [unreported] (C.A.).

45. *Constitution Act, 1982*, Schedule B, *Canadian Charter of Rights and Freedoms*.

46. *Chiarelli v. Canada (Minister of Employment and Immigration)*, [1990] 2 F.C. 299 (C.A.), rev'd [1992] 1 S.C.R. 711.

47. *Egan v. Canada*, [1993] 3 F.C. 401 (C.A.).

48. *Symes v. Canada*, [1991] 3 F.C. 507 (C.A.). aff'd [1993] 4 S.C.R. 695.

49. *Thibaudeau v. The Queen* (May 3, 1994), File No. A-1248-92 [unreported] (C.A.).

50. *Operation Dismantle Inc. v. Canada*, [1983] 1 F.C. 745 (C.A.), aff'd [1985] 1 S.C.R. 441.

51. *Native Women's Assn. of Canada v. Canada*, [1992] 3 F.C. 192 (C.A.).

52. *Haig v. Canada*, [1992] 3 F.C. 611 (C.A.), aff'd [1993] 2 S.C.R. 995.

Elections, Representation, and Political Parties

CLOSE-UP: WHEN VOTING WAS ELITIST AND DANGEROUS

In the nineteenth century, voter participation varied dramatically across a range of social groupings in Canada. During Canada's early years the **voting franchise** was quite restricted. **Suffrage** was denied various groups, not only women.

One of the first political questions that confronted Canadians was "Am I eligible to vote?" Indeed, most people were not. It was widely believed that voting was a privilege too important to entrust to the masses. Aboriginal people, the poor, and women were, for the most part, excluded. Women won the right to vote in 1918 (although certain groups were **enfranchised** in 1917); aboriginals had to wait until 1960. Until 1918, voting was restricted to men who owned property, paid taxes, and demonstrated loyalty to a political party. They had to own either land that yielded an income of £12 a year or urban property that brought in more than £5 a year. Tenants who paid at least £10 a year in rent were also enfranchised.

Today, all Canadian citizens age 18 or over, male and female, have the right to vote. We vote by what is called the "Australian ballot"—a secret ballot that is prepared, distributed, and counted by party appointees (scrutineers) at public expense. First used in the 1880s, the Australian ballot represented a significant change in electoral procedures.

We take the Australian ballot for granted today, but there was a time when voting in Canada was a very public exercise, for all to see and hear. Early in Canadian history voters cast their votes orally at the polling place—often at their own peril. Obviously, knowing which way a person was voting made it easy to apply pressure to change his vote. Vote buying was also quite common. In fact, elections were known to be so tumultuous that Canadian advertisements for liniments made reference to casting one's ballot as a cause of aches and pains. Growing concern over voter intimidation and fraud resulted in pressure for secret ballots, printed by public authorities and exercised in a private polling place provided and administered by the state.

Early Canadian voters needed stamina and courage as well as the will to participate in the political system. A voter might have to travel 50 or 100 km to a polling place (there was usually only one in each riding). On his approach, supporters of the candidates might try to buy his vote outright or by treating him to a drink at a nearby tavern. Alternatively, they might threaten him with a beating, or worse. Violence was common.

Before casting his vote, the voter had to show his property deeds or other proof of eligibility. Then, before a boisterous crowd, he had to state his choice out loud. The vote was entered in a poll book for all to see; those who bought votes could check the book to find out whether the voter had fulfilled his commitment to support the candidate he had been paid to support. The poll book served as a receipt for such transactions as well as an obvious record of partisan leanings.

The polls would stay open for days, sometimes weeks. On the first day of voting, candidates delivered speeches from the hustings (high platforms erected near polling places). Afterward members of the opposing factions would retire to the nearest bars and taverns, where loud demonstrations were not uncommon. It was in these drinking establishments that club-swinging gangs would harass their opponents. These were particularly violent occasions, fuelled by the combination of drink and partisan politics in close quarters. When rival gangs clashed, men were often attacked and sometimes killed.

The business of electoral fraud went unhampered in these early Canadian elections. Sometimes people who had learned to forge property deeds would be on hand in the drinking establishments to service requests for bogus documents from disqualified voters determined to participate in the elections.

It was in 1842 that the Assembly of the United Canadas passed a law against election violence, bribery, and intimidation. The secret ballot was adopted in New Brunswick in 1855, for federal elections after 1874, and in the rest of the then-existing provinces by 1877. It is now a fundamental provision of Canada's constitutional law.

INTRODUCTION: ELECTIONS AND THE RIGHT TO VOTE

Most Canadians believe that casting a ballot is not only the way we choose our leaders, but also a source of **legitimacy** for provincial and federal governments and a means by which qualified citizens can influence public policy. But does the system we have in place in Canada really fulfil our expectations of democracy?

Like most things in Canadian politics, the expected effect of elections is not always forthcoming. Andrew Heard discusses this issue in Chapter 24. Although elections sometimes have an effect on policy, their results are often nebulous. Sometimes policy takes second place to a major national issue such as Quebec's possible separation from Canada. Many voters are unable to distinguish party platforms, and tend to focus only on leaders. Some voters choose a party or a candidate on the basis of a single issue, such as the economy, the national debt, or health care. Sometimes specific policy issues appear to have no impact on voters during an election at all; instead, they are intent on expressing their negative views about "government" in general, wanting, simply, something *new* — a new government, new leadership, new policy options.

For most Canadians, voting is the only form of political participation they voluntarily experience.

Yet in today's federal elections, more than 25 percent of eligible Canadians typically do not vote at all, and the majority of those who do remain undecided about their vote well past the start of the election campaign. Although voter participation in Canada is much higher than in the United States, it appears to be much lower than in many other democracies. Canadian laws give the electorate the right to vote but do not make voting compulsory, as some states do.

Does gender affect political participation? Do men and women vote differently in elections? Are there gender differences in the way we understand issues, in our party affiliations, in our reactions to ideologies, or in our views on the fundamental roles of government? In Chapter 25, "Does Gender Make a Difference in Voting Behaviour?," Peter and Joseph Wearing analyze some of the similarities and differences in men's and women's perceptions of politics and government from a policy perspective. In Chapter 26, Manon Tremblay considers the obstacles to electoral and political participation for women in Quebec.

OUR SYSTEM OF ELECTION RULES

The success or failure of campaigns and candidates is greatly influenced by the system in place that governs elections. Canada's **electoral system** sets the rules that determine the results of our elections.

Most Canadians are not aware of these rules, cannot explain how their electoral system functions, and do not understand the **disproportional electoral results** attributable to the system in Parliament and provincial legislatures. If Canadians knew how their electoral system really worked, they might want to change it significantly.

One major feature of our electoral system, the "single-member constituency with plurality," has received very little national debate. We elect a single member per constituency, using a "first-past-the-post," "winner-take-all" system. As in a horse race, the candidate who finishes "first," with the most votes at the end of the election, gets the seat in the legislature; the votes cast for all the other competing candidates count for nothing. We choose among candidates, and the one who receives more votes than any of the others is elected; there is no requirement that the candidate win a majority of the votes.

An alternative system, that of proportional representation (PR), allocates seats in the legislature in proportion to the vote received by each party. Most PR systems have multimember constituencies (as there is no way to divide one representative). Many analysts consider PR superior to the single-member constituency system. One reason is that, unlike PR, the single-member constituency tends to overrepresent the government party and underrepresent opposition parties.

Groups underrepresented in plurality systems — for example, women and racial and religious minorities — are more likely to receive a greater legislative representation under a PR system. However, the major criticism levelled against PR is that it tends to encourage more political parties to organize and run in elections. **Minor parties** have a better chance of getting their members "elected" to the legislature under PR.

In an era characterized by concern over who gets to participate in our political and governing system and which of all the diverse groups in our population are to be represented in Parliament, an informed Canadian public is becoming increasingly interested in the possible applications of PR.

ELECTIONS AND EFFECTIVE GOVERNMENT

One key question political scientists ask is whether our electoral system is capable of producing effective government and effective opposition. Do our election rules allow all the various voices in our political system a point of access to the decision-making institutions that govern them? Manon Tremblay's contribution, in Chapter 26, gives us some solid insights into this question as it pertains to Quebec women and electoral politics.

In studying how well we are governed, we must also ask whether constituents feel that their votes draw them closer to or distance them from the governing process. Does our system make people feel that government is inaccessible or remote? A general sense of distance on the part of constituents from their representatives and their governments can threaten the legitimacy of the entire political system — especially if governments feel that they are not obligated to respond to those who voted *against* them.

THE CANDIDATES

Even though political parties play a major role in Canada's elections, candidates' personal attributes frequently influence voters' decisions. Some analysts tell us that Canadian voters prefer tall candidates over short ones, candidates with shorter names over candidates with longer names, candidates with lighter hair over ones with darker hair. Frivolous as they may be, these criteria give us an idea of the range of characteristics voters respond to.

The more important candidate characteristics that affect voter choices are race, **ethnicity**, gender, social background, political experience, party affiliation, even religion. In general, voters tend to lean toward the candidates who most resemble them in terms of these categories. People like to see someone of their own ethnic or religious background and from their own geographic region seeking a position of leadership.

In deciding whether to run for a seat in the House of Commons or in a provincial legislature, a prospective candidate has to consider the costs and risks of running as well as the probabilities of winning. Under the rules of our first-past-the-post electoral system, most candidates have little chance of getting elected. To complicate a candidate's difficulties in getting past the post first, ours is a party-based and party-structured system that can attract support for or opposition to individuals who run under a party label.

Being likely to win or lose because of one's affiliation with a particular party is, in fact, a direct effect of the electoral system. In the 1993 federal election more than two thousand candidates running for nineteen registered political parties competed for only 295 Commons seats in this complex electoral environment. In Chapter 23, Robert Campbell and Leslie Pal provide an insightful review of that election, discussing the candidates and their campaign strategies and the results that continue to shape the political future of Canada.

Because there are so many competing political parties in contemporary Canadian federal elections, many candidates are unknown to the public and run the risk of defeat from the start. Candidates and their party supporters work hard trying to maximize their chances of winning a parliamentary seat; short of that, they try at least to survive the election campaign as credible political competitors and nominees of their particular parties. Some candidates attempt to survive the electoral process by picking a particular policy or interest in the riding and promoting themselves as *the* candidate for the concerned group.

CAMPAIGNS

The goal of every election campaign is the same: to win. In Canada, unlike most European states that have PR, there are no rewards for the candidate who comes in second; the winner takes all. The party campaign organization must therefore plan a strategy to maximize the candidate's chances of winning. In their analysis in Chapter 23, Campbell and Pal discuss the complexities of party campaigns, raising questions in the process about Canadian democracy and its electoral system.

We take it for granted that election campaigns are what determines who wins. The staffing of the party campaign organization is crucial if talented people with considerable campaign experience and knowledge of complex issues are to have the best chance of being elected. The candidate's own personal organization is only part of the overall campaign organization. National party organizations and their provincial counterparts are also influential, especially in rallying loyal party supporters, getting them to the polls, and trying to make sure that high-profile party members or government ministers visit the ridings to help the party's federal or provincial candidates.

To run a successful and persuasive campaign, the constituency organization must be able to raise funds for the effort, get effective and favourable coverage from the media, produce and pay for advertising, effectively schedule the candidate's time with constituent groups and prospective supporters, convey the party's position on the issues, and get the voters to the polls on election day.

Undecided voters include not only those who are well educated and issue oriented but also many who are not particularly interested in politics or well informed about candidates or issues. In an election campaign the goal is to give such voters the kind of information and incentives that will make them come on-side.

In the early 1990s the Royal Commission on Electoral Reform and Party Financing addressed many of these questions, making recommendations and proposals for change in the way we conduct our elections. The reforms concerning the way Canadians vote and the way officials calculate who wins an election will involve harmonizing the democratic rights of voters with their Charter rights, enhancing Canadians' access to elected office, promoting greater equality and efficacy in voting results, facilitating the ability of new political parties to form and to compete in the political system, monitoring the fairness of elections, and maintaining the confidence of the public in the electoral process.

POLITICAL PARTIES

Political parties are not mentioned in our Constitution, but they have taken on an institutional character that appears to be inseparable from the workings of all of those formal institutions of government and politics that *are* mentioned. Political parties have a long tradition in Canada: Over the years, starting even before Confederation, most of the various conceivable sorts of political parties have indeed been formed within the Canadian political system.

The function and character of our major political parties today, as well as the emergence of many other parties at both the federal and provincial levels, have much to do with the historical forces operating in this country since its beginnings as an independent nation-state.

On the surface, Canada might resemble states with a stable two-party system, but the presence of various other political parties that compete at both levels of government and that sometimes win significant victories modifies our system significantly. The fact that only two political parties have ever governed Canada at the federal level contributes to the illusion of a stable two-party system, but the other parties seeking political power are in fact able, under certain circumstances, to capture numerous seats in the House, as evidenced by the Bloc Québécois's ability to form the official Opposition after the 1993 federal election.

One effect of our electoral system is that it tends to encourage the growth of regional parties and works against the ability of parties to act as institutions that can integrate the country nationally. In Chapter 28, Brian Tanguay explores the ongoing transformation of our party system and what that transformation might mean to our entire political system.

Over the years many minor parties, sometimes called **third parties**, have acted as barometers of change in the political mood of Canadians. They have forced the larger and more traditional parties to recognize new issues or trends in the thinking of Canadians, perhaps most notably of Quebeckers who argue for a sovereignist government for Quebec. Political scientists know that minor parties in Canada can act both as a safety valve for relieving the pressures felt by various political groups, sometimes preventing the eruption of major confrontations, and as a source of political stress on the governing system and on the unity of the country. Minor parties have a difficult time competing, especially at the federal level, because the rules of our electoral system discourage both the emergence and the survival of small parties. Nonetheless, minor parties have played an important role in the political life of Canada, both provincially and federally.

WHAT POLITICAL PARTIES DO

The functions of political parties also include keeping the public informed, recruiting and selecting leaders, representing and integrating group interests, and controlling the direction of the government. Party activities centre on the processes of recruiting, electing, and appointing political leaders. They provide the conditions under which hundreds of legislative seats can be filled in an organized manner. In Chapter 27, Paul Thomas reflects on the role and effectiveness of political parties and the party system with respect to representation in our democratic state. By selecting and campaigning for specific candidates, political parties bring a degree of order and predictability to our political and governing process.

Usually, the goal of party activities is to obtain the power and other advantages associated with parliamentary representation. In pursuing this goal the parties also provide various services to the Canadian public: They help to educate people on current issues and to simplify the choices voters have to make on election day. Political parties do what ordinary people cannot do on their own: build a political agenda for formal public discourse.

In addition to their role in facilitating representation, another important function of political parties is the integration of group interests. Paul Thomas gives us some important insights into this important function as well. Political parties essentially act as brokers among interest groups. They must consider the claims of each group, accepting some and modifying or rejecting others in a process of continuous bargaining and compromise.

Finally, political parties strive to win enough legislative seats to control government. But although only one political party can normally be said to form the government, it cannot be said that the government party always controls parliamentary decision making. Governments are, after all, defeated in Parliament from time to time.

THINKING IT OVER

1. You are asked to submit concise definitions of certain terms to be included in a political science dictionary. The terms are as follows:
   a. political party
   b. universal suffrage
   c. plurality result
   d. first-past-the-post system
   e. proportional representation
   f. electorate

2. What does Andrew Heard (Chapter 24) mean by "first-past-the-post"? How does the single-member constituency with plurality tend to distort the result of elections in Canada? Why is it that governments rarely get a majority of voters to support them but still enjoy majorities in the legislature? How could our electoral system be improved to enhance the representation of people who vote against the winning party? What groups are most obviously excluded from representation by our electoral system? Review the results of the 1993 federal election as presented by Campbell and Pal (Chapter 23) in the light of Heard's observations.

3. Based on your reading of the analysis by Peter and Joseph Wearing (Chapter 25), do you think women make a difference in politics and government, and if so, how? Do the authors find that men and women agree or disagree on major questions of policy? Do men and women have different political agendas? Is education level a variable in explaining the similarities and differences in the political choices men and women make?

4. According to Manon Tremblay (Chapter 26) what are some of the main factors that contribute to the underrepresentation of women in Quebec political institutions? How does she evaluate Canada's electoral process in Quebec? How significant is sexist prejudice as an obstacle to the election of women to the Quebec National Assembly? Does Tremblay identify other barriers in the electoral process to women's entry into legislatures?

5. Review the role of political parties as outlined by Paul Thomas in Chapter 27. How do political parties contribute to the representation of Canadian legislative interests? How does our electoral system affect party competition? Are political parties the most effective instruments for stimulating government action on issues of importance to Canadians?

6. Describe Canada's political party system. Why does Brian Tanguay (Chapter 28) think it is changing? Did the 1993 federal election produce a critical realignment of political parties in Parliament? What does Tanguay mean by a "regional protest party"? Is Canada becoming a multiparty system? Must Canadian political parties constantly readjust their platforms to meet changing demands in the political marketplace or can they remain loyal to their traditional ideologies?

GLOSSARY

aggregation The ability of organizations, such as governments and parties, to bring together many divergent groups under one political framework for the purpose of achieving common goals.

campaign A series of political strategies and manoeuvres undertaken by political parties and/or individual candidates seeking to capture parliamentary seats by winning the support of the electorate.

constituents People who reside in a particular electoral district (usually called a "constituency" or a "riding"). Elected politicians represent their constituents.

countersocialization A process of social and political learning whose values, norms, and expectations are fundamentally at odds with those promoted through socialization in a dominant culture. Countersocialization challenges many of the basic attitudes and values of mainstream society.

disproportional electoral results The discrepancies between how people vote and how they are represented in their legislatures. In Canada such disparities are the inevitable result of the plurality rule, which permits a candidate to win a riding not with a majority but with only a plurality of votes (i.e., more votes than any other opposing candidate receives).

electoral system A process that comprises all the rules that govern elections—how officers who supervise voting procedures are selected; how votes are tallied or recounted; what arithmetic rules and formulas are applied to determine who wins; the procedures for deciding who is eligible to vote; the rules governing campaign spending and raising money; the appropriate and legal use of the media; and how votes are translated into parliamentary seats.

enfranchised The condition of having been granted the right to vote, as when that right is extended to certain groups and categories of individuals who may formerly have been excluded by law and procedure.

ethnicity The designation used to describe social groups who are distinguished by traits such as language, national origin, custom, religion, and race.

legitimacy As it pertains to voting and elections, the rights and duties that flow from participation in the electoral process according to all its rules and procedures, and from winning the privilege to exercise power.

major parties The political parties that win the largest share of the popular vote, regularly gain seats in the legislature, and are able to form the government from time to time. They normally run candidates in every constituency, have permanent party organizations, and have political leaders poised to occupy Cabinet positions or the position of premier or prime minister.

minor parties Parties that emerge and are organized to challenge one or all of the traditional dominant political parties (or "major parties"). Minor parties consistently win a minority of the popular vote and sometimes even win seats in a legislature. Even though they may disappear over time, their presence in the political system is seldom without influence. They are sometimes called "third parties."

mobilization The ability to organize and use available resources, such as time, money, people, and the media.

ombuds services The services performed by officials acting on behalf of individual citizens to sort out problems they have encountered in their dealings with the government bureaucracy.

party system The political environment in which parties compete for popular support and for seats in Parliament, according to electoral rules for organizing and financing their platforms.

plebiscite The term used to describe any means for securing an expression of popular opinion for the purpose of political decision making.

proportional representation An electoral system based on the principle of tabulating results in a way that ultimately provides for a political party's share of the seats in the legislature being generally proportional to its share of the popular vote in an election.

simple regression A technique for measuring the relationship between or among variables, specifically, the amount of change in a dependent variable (the focus of study) that is associated with a given amount of change in an independent variable (what is found to explain the significance of a dependent variable or any changes that might condition it).

socialization The process whereby individuals learn and internalize the attitudes, values, and behaviours appropriate to persons functioning as social beings and responsive, participating members of society.

suffrage The right to vote; the franchise.

third parties *See* minor parties.

voting franchise The legal right to exercise the vote after meeting certain qualifications, such as age, residency, and citizenship.

ADDITIONAL READINGS

Archer, Keith. 1990. *Political Choices and Electoral Consequences.* Montreal: McGill-Queen's University Press.

Bakvis, Herman. 1991a. *Canadian Political Parties: Leaders, Candidates and Organization.* Toronto: Dundurn Press.

———, ed. 1991b. *Voter Turnout in Canada.* Toronto: Dundurn Press.

Brook, Tom. 1991. *Getting Elected in Canada.* Stratford, Ont.: Mercury Press.

Canada. Royal Commission on Electoral Reform and Party Financing. 1991. *Reforming Electoral Democracy.* Vol. 1. Toronto: Dundurn Press.

Carty, Kenneth, Lynda Erickson, Donald Blake, eds. 1992. *Leaders and Parties in Canadian Politics: Experiences of the Provinces.* Toronto: Harcourt Brace Jovanovich, Canada.

Christian, William, and Colin Campbell. 1995. *Political Parties, Leaders and Ideologies.* Toronto: McGraw-Hill Ryerson.

Harrison, Trevor. 1995. *Of Passionate Intensity: Right-Wing Populism and the Reform Party of Canada.* Toronto: University of Toronto Press.

Johnson, R. et al. 1992. *Letting the People Decide: The Dynamics of a Canadian Election.* Stanford, Calif.: Stanford University Press.

Johnston, Paul, and Harvey Pasis. 1990. *Representation and Electoral Systems: Canadian Perspectives.* Scarborough: Prentice-Hall Canada.

Macquarrie, Heath. 1992. *Red Tory Blues: A Political Memoir.* Toronto: University of Toronto Press.

Simpson, Jeffrey. 1995. *Discipline of Power: The Conservative Interlude and the Liberal Restoration.* Toronto: University of Toronto Press.

Small, David, ed. 1991. *Drawing the Map: Equality and Efficacy of the Vote in Canadian Electoral Boundary Reform.* Toronto: Dundurn Press.

Thorburn, H.G., ed. 1996. *Party Politics in Canada.* 7th ed. Scarborough, Ont.: Prentice-Hall Canada.

Wearing, Joseph, ed. 1991. *The Ballot and Its Message.* Toronto: Copp Clark Pitman.

A Country Divided:
The 1993 Federal Election

ROBERT M. CAMPBELL

LESLIE PAL

The 25 October, 1993, federal election was historic in so many ways that it almost defies summary. A ruling majority party, the Progressive Conservatives, was reduced to 2 seats, the worst defeat of any federal political party since 1867. The New Democratic Party went from 44 seats to 8, virtually extinguishing social democracy at the national level. Elected in place of the discredited Conservatives was a Liberal government under Jean Chrétien with 178 seats. Chrétien's triumph was diminished, however, by the success of two other parties, Reform and the Bloc Québécois. The Bloc, committed to Quebec separation, won 54 seats and became the "Loyal" Opposition. Reform won 52 seats, principally in Alberta and British Columbia, on a conservative platform that split the right-wing vote in Canada and consequently did much to allow Liberal wins in ridings across the country. Two regional parties, one committed to separatism and the other to a fundamentally changed political agenda for the country, promised one of the most bizarre Parliaments in living memory. Elections are perhaps the most "real" world of all the worlds of politics, the moment when voters exercise their ultimate sovereignty in a democratic system. In this case they expressed more than sovereignty—they took their revenge against a Conservative government that simply could not shake the legacies of nine years under Brian Mulroney. Nonetheless, the voters did not speak with a single voice. The election of Liberals, Reformers, and the Bloc suggested a Canada in 1993 closer to the brink of fundamental division than solidly behind a Liberal agenda for change.

Kim Campbell, leaving the governor general's residence on 4 November after submitting her resignation as prime minister (one of the shortest stints in Canadian history), was asked about rumours that she had a new boyfriend. Smiling, Campbell said that her "lips were sealed." Would that she had followed that rule during the election campaign before the October 25 vote. Virtually from the moment she opened her mouth as the writs were issued, through the next forty-seven days, Campbell managed to conduct the most inept national campaign in Canadian history. Jean Chrétien, Liberal leader and eventual victor, made his share of mistakes as well, but every time he stumbled Campbell obliged with an even bigger pratfall that drew all the media and public attention her way. The summer media schmooze with Campbell as she travelled at taxpayers' expense from one barbecue to another had played up her intellect, candour, her sense of humour and wit. By mid-October what had seemed like intellect looked more like smarminess, and her fabled candour came across as a mix of rudeness and indifference. Her campaign jokes fell flat. Her wit evaporated. She lost, and lost hugely.

Modern election **campaigns** focus so relentlessly on leaders that it would be tempting to blame the Tory defeat on Kim Campbell. The paradox of

SOURCE: Excerpted from *The Real Worlds of Canadian Politics*, 3rd ed. (Peterborough, ON: Broadview Press, 1994), pp. 273–76. Reprinted by permission of the publisher.

campaigning, however, is that while the leader is the focus and carries the blame or the kudos, millions of voters actually make their decision for a host of reasons, only one of which is their perception of the leader. In the 1993 campaign, which was notable for its absence of key "defining events" or substantial policy debates, voters across the country cast their ballots for any one or a combination of the following reasons: fear of economic decline, nationalism, resentment against the failed Meech Lake and Charlottetown constitutional accords, regional alienation, dissatisfaction with Tory policies because they were too right wing, dissatisfaction with Tory policies because they were not right wing enough. Infusing each of these reasons, however, and not far from the minds of most voters as they stood with pencil poised to mark their ballot, was the performance of Brian Mulroney's governments over the previous nine years. Mulroney himself had recognized what a liability he was for the party, and orchestrated his resignation and the subsequent leadership convention that elected Kim Campbell as his successor. The summer barbecue circuit and festival of international photo-ops had been part of the plan as well. The strategy had recognized that the deep dissatisfaction with the Tory party could only be neutralized with a new, attractive face. Kim Campbell was it. On the threshold of the election, the plan had seemed to work perfectly. Though the Tories were still less popular than the Liberals, Campbell herself had high popularity ratings. Had she been a better campaigner, she might have pulled it off. But to do so, she had to overcome an extraordinary antipathy in virtually every area of the country, principally in Quebec and the West, the two key partners in the national coalition Mulroney had forged in 1984 and that had carried him to two election victories.

A national election campaign is thus an amalgam of strategic actions by political parties, individual behaviours of political leaders, hard-fought campaigns in 295 ridings across the country, a media frenzy for news and sound bites, and deep structural reactions in the electorate itself as millions of Canadians acting individually somehow give rise to broad patterns and constellations of power. Anything this complex and operating at this many levels defies simple summary — we cannot say, for example, that the Canadian people "decided" any single thing, since the "people" do not vote as a mass. To complicate matters further, the millions of votes cast in a federal election are filtered through an electoral system or set of rules that skews outcomes in certain directions. Canada's is a "first-past-the-post" or plurality system, meaning that the country is divided into single-member constituencies whose representatives are elected on the basis of the single largest bloc of votes in each constituency or riding. When there are only two candidates, the winner logically will have the majority (at least 50 per cent plus one) of the votes. If the vote is split fairly evenly among more than two candidates — and for the first time, in 1993 that was truly the case in many ridings across Canada — the winner can gain the seat with much less than 50 per cent of the vote. The peculiar result of this is that more people may vote *against* than *for* the riding's "representative." This feature of Canada's electoral system played an important part in assuring the Liberal majority.

Despite the complexity of forces unleashed in an election, several characteristics of the 1993 federal election stood out. First, though Kim Campbell's campaign tried to avoid even mentioning his name, the election quickly became a **plebiscite** on Brian Mulroney's record and his style of government. Once Campbell assumed office, Brian Mulroney disappeared from the public scene (with the exception of a small but telling brouhaha over an attempt to sell his furniture at Sussex Drive to the government), but Campbell could never shake the sly Liberal and NDP insinuations that she had been part of the Mulroney team and therefore would carry forward the Mulroney agenda. Her commitment to the North American free trade deal, deficit reduction, and social program review all seemed cut from the same dreary cloth as Mulroney's policies. What did the election mean, therefore, in terms of Mulroney's success at consolidating the right in Canada? At first blush, it looked like a disaster, given the performance of Reform and the Bloc. But if one counted Reform and Tory support together as the right-wing vote, in many parts of the country the strength of the right actually increased over 1988. This was not Mulroney's doing, but it suggests that the legacy of nine years of Conservative rule, while in part repudiated was also in part affirmed. This is especially true if we consider that in substance, many of the Liberal policies do not differ from their Tory predecessors.

Second, there is the election as campaign, as theatre and human drama. This is, after all, how the media relentlessly present an election, as a "horse race," a contest, a joust, a slugfest. This framing is partly the result of lazy journalism that finds it easier to focus on personalities than issues, though the media realized their own foibles in this campaign and tried (with only minor success) to overcome them. But media or not, for a good deal of the campaign this is what the electorate sees: the tightrope-walking to avoid gaffes and commitments that can come back to haunt you once you are in power; the carefully crafted daily message that is repeated in speeches and press releases and interviews in order to capture attention and control the agenda; the underdog and rising contenders; the early sense that anything is possible, replaced in mid-campaign with the impending sense of doom, that nothing can be undone. In a way, campaigns are a mix of military manoeuvres and Greek tragedy. They simultaneously appear as strategic conflicts wherein every move has its potential countermove, every defeat has the possibility of being followed by triumph, and as an unfolding of something predetermined that nothing can alter. How did this campaign evolve, what strategies were undertaken, what mistakes made, and did any of it make any difference?

Finally, the 1993 federal election raises vital questions about the direction of Canadian democracy.

The result, as noted earlier, was not the severely divided and dysfunctional parliament that many had feared on the brink of a five-party fight, but the Liberal majority was a mirage. While it won seats in each province and the Territories, Liberal strength was heavily concentrated in eastern Canada (148 of 177 seats, or 83 per cent), and especially Ontario (98 seats). The Bloc won 54 of 75 seats in Quebec, the only province in which it ran. It went to Ottawa to defend and promote Quebec's interests, and in particular a separatist agenda — only in Canada could a separatist party become the Official Opposition. Within days of the election, the Bloc was agreeing with the cancellation of the infamous EH-101 helicopter contract but arguing that Quebec should receive compensation for the cancellation. While it spoke of being a responsible Opposition party that would speak for Canadian interests as well as Quebec's (when the two coincided, as for example, with the need to reduce the deficit), it was clear that the Bloc would pursue an unprecedented political strategy in the heart of Canada's political institutions. The Reform Party was no less bent on change, and indeed had built its early political fortunes on opposing special status for Quebec in either the Meech Lake or Charlottetown accords. It could be counted on to speak with a regional accent as well: all but one of its 52 seats were gained in the western provinces, principally Alberta and British Columbia. The presence of two diametrically opposed regionally based parties in the Commons will make it hellishly difficult for even a majority national government to respond effectively to this threat.

The 1993 election was thus a plebiscite on a political record, a war of strategic and impassioned campaigns, and a marker for Canada's historical destiny.

The First-Past-the-Post Electoral System: Does It Provide Effective Representation?

ANDREW HEARD

Canadians have lived with variants of a first-past-the-post electoral system since the first elections were held for colonial legislatures over two centuries ago, but this traditional method of selecting representatives faces a modern challenge.[1] The electoral system has been a subject of debate for some time, because of the disproportionate way it translates popular votes into seats.[2] A broader dimension is added, however, with the Charter of Rights. The Supreme Court has ruled that the right to vote, found in section 3, extends beyond the casting of a ballot to guaranteeing "effective representation."[3] Thus, a question emerges about whether the single-member plurality system can provide the effective representation required by the Charter.

A discussion of the electoral boundaries cases reveals that the courts have been uniquely concerned with the collective representation of territorial communities. There is little doubt that Canada's political culture has placed a premium upon the articulation of regional or local community interests, and the distribution of electoral populations is an important issue with practical consequences. However, such a strong focus on geographic representation obscures another fundamental dimension of representation that elections serve: that the Canadian electorate are represented by partisan legislators. The whole election and subsequent legislative process is structured along party lines. How well the electoral system translates voters' party choices into the legislative chamber is an issue of profound importance to our political system. After a review of the Supreme Court's views on effective representation arising from the decision on electoral boundaries, the analysis here will be extended to the electoral system's ability to provide Canadians with effective representation through the members of political parties that get elected to the legislatures.

The vulnerability of the single-member plurality system to a test based on effective representation could focus debate in the proper forum, the legislature, on whether another method based on **proportional representation** should be adopted. The analysis of the electoral system will be based principally upon the results of the last two general elections in each of the Maritime provinces and for the federal parliament. The Maritime provinces are chosen to show how differently the electoral system can work within fairly similar political cultures, while the national results provide an insight into the way the electoral system works in a larger, more varied setting.

THE COURTS AND EFFECTIVE REPRESENTATION

The quality of representation realized by the single-member plurality system becomes of special interest when the Charter of Rights is brought into the

SOURCE: "The First-Past-the-Post Electoral System: Does It Provide Effective Representation?" unpublished paper. Reprinted by permission of the author.

analysis. In the *Electoral Boundaries Reference*, the Supreme Court of Canada expounded on the meaning of "the right to vote" found in s.3 of the Charter in a decision that might have significant consequences for the electoral system. In that case, a concern was raised about the wide variety in constituency populations allowed under the Saskatchewan scheme of distributing seats across the province. The Court did not even consider whether the right to vote might be restricted to just the act of casting a ballot.[4] All three judges who wrote opinions simply accepted that it meant more, involving the relative worth of the effect of each citizen's casting their ballot.

Justice McLachlin wrote the majority opinion and distilled the issue down to whether the right to vote entailed either the notion of complete voter parity in "one person–one vote" or a modified view of "effective representation." In the former view, the right to vote means that each elector must have an equal opportunity to elect a representative and be served by that legislator. In this perspective, electoral districts must be of the same size to ensure the equality of all votes cast across the political system. The notion of effective representation, examined separately by McLachlin, may be described as voter parity with justifiable variations. The initial assumption in McLachlin's model is that rough equality in riding size should be the starting point.

But the majority opinion also concluded that the historical context of the Canadian franchise revealed that variations in electoral district sizes were positively pursued in order to ensure the more effective representation of voters. Deviations in constituency sizes could be justified on pragmatic grounds for sparsely populated regions; it is argued that the citizens of these ridings would be denied effective access to, and representation from, their legislators if the ridings had to be large enough to encompass the same number of voters as all other ridings.

Quite a large body of academic literature has emerged from this decision, principally because the meaning of "effective representation" was left so undeveloped by McLachlin's opinion.[5] She came closest to explaining her notion of representation in the following passage:

> Ours is a representative democracy. Each citizen is entitled to be *represented* in government. Representation comprehends the idea of having a voice in the deliberations of government as well as the idea of the right to bring one's grievances and concerns to the attention of one's government representative; as noted in *Dixon v. British Columbia (Attorney General)* ... elected representatives function in two roles — legislative and what has been termed the "ombudsman role."[6] (original emphasis)

For the most part, the judges seem to have focused on the relationship between **constituents** and whomever their legislator may be, and on the need for basic voter equality as the starting point. The reason for this concern relates to the relative access of each voter to his or her representative's **ombuds services** and to the relative contribution each voter has, through his or her representative's legislative function, in forming the government and public policies of the day.

There are some relationships between the electors and their legislator that apply no matter whom they have elected; all that counts is that the individual who won the election performs certain tasks with respect to the constituents. In the clearest example of these generic roles of representation, any legislator has an ombuds function to fill, in which he or she intervenes on behalf of the constituents to smooth out their dealings with the government. Once elected, MPs and MLAs should be the representatives of all their constituents and not just those who voted for them; this adage applies most uniformly to the ombuds function. Equality in riding size allows equal access of all citizens to the ombuds services of their legislator, but some variation is said to be needed in the largest rural constituencies to permit more effective access.

The ombuds functions of representatives mean that whoever is chosen by the electors should perform in much the same way. Some elections in specific ridings may involve debate about the incumbent's constituency service record. But these aspects should be the least important in an election, from a democratic point of view, since the choice among candidates has little value beyond which of them might be more efficient at those tasks.

There are many other, perhaps far more important, aspects of representation that cannot be so easily ascribed to any warm body sitting in a riding's legislative seat. The consequences of emphasizing "effective representation" become much more remarkable when these larger dimensions are examined.

While the personal qualities of the candidates can be at issue in modern democracies, the electors are usually faced with a choice based primarily on competing policy proposals. If an incumbent is running, the electors may hold that person to account for the policies he or she has pursued; if voters like those policies they may well vote to let that legislator continue in office. In any other circumstance, the voters look for another candidate who will advocate or implement their preferred set of policies. While these choices are filtered through the voters' perceptions of the candidates' parties and of those parties' leaders, the most fundamental level of electoral competition ultimately revolves around policy choices. In other words, it matters who is elected because different winners would try to implement different policies.

The formulation, articulation, and implementation of the winners' policies will lead them to represent various groups of their constituents differently—especially those constituents who advocate or organize support for competing policies. When it comes to opposing policy choices, legislators cannot often represent all their constituents equally; in the end, some kind of preference usually must be given to those who support the legislator's chosen policies. Indeed, our political system presupposes that MPs and MLAs will follow a particular set of policy and value choices at the expense of others.

For at least a century, Canadian politics have been defined by party politics. The concentration of power in the hands of the Cabinet has been built upon, and in turn fostered, competition between disciplined party organizations. Twentieth-century Canadian government is *party* government.[7] Elections fundamentally are contests between parties rather than candidates. This structuring and filtering of political competition into party channels is one of the most basic characteristics of our political system. The party basis of electoral competition and of virtually all the legislative work of elected officials has a profound impact upon the nature of representation that results from our electoral system. When we discuss "effective representation," therefore, we must examine the many ways in which party interests come to be represented by the results of an election. There are other important dimensions of representation, but this crucial and determining party dimension has been largely overlooked in debates over the repercussions of the *Electoral Boundaries Reference*.

Elected legislators have a web of responsibilities in a representative democracy, which mix the trustee and delegate functions. The trustee view of a representative has been most clearly associated with the views advanced by Edmund Burke, who told his electors in 1774, "Your representative owes you not his interest only, but his judgment; and he betrays, instead of serving you, if he sacrifices it to your opinion."[8] In other words, voters should choose someone for the soundness of his or her personal judgment, and that individual is guided only by his or her own wisdom in pursuing policies until the next election. In the delegate approach, a legislator is there to advocate and try to implement the views of his or her constituents, regardless of the legislator's personal views.

In practice, Canadian legislators both try to exercise their personal judgment on some issues and to advocate the views of their constituents on other occasions. The two views of representation become all the more intertwined because of the near impossibility of separating them in any given situation. Elected officials will not make personal judgments without regard for their constituents' views if they have any hope of getting re-elected.

Another dimension of representation involves the participation of representatives because they belong to a particular group within society. This is sometimes called "mirror" representation, and it has theoretical roots in Mill's argument that all interests within a society must be represented, be present, within the legislature. It is not clear from the ongoing debate that representatives who sit in the legislature as a sample of their group must act as delegates of that group, or whether they can use their own judgment as trustees.

Regardless of the theoretical model one advocates about the representative role of a legislator, however, the overriding practical determinant of a legislator's action lies in his or her party. As Dorothy Pickles wrote of Britain, "The representative's first loyalty is to the party under which label he has been elected."[9] This loyalty is owed because of the importance of disciplined political parties to elections and to the legislative process that occurs in between. In general, legislators toe the party line in order to get elected and to get something done once elected. They do indeed act as advocates and conduits into the party of local interests and sentiment, but they still remain bound by the resulting party policy. The electoral system's ability to translate votes into seats is a significant concern because of the importance of parties to Canadian elections and to the representation that is subsequently realized in the legislature.

Canadian elections are primarily contests between parties, not candidates. Canadian electoral studies have consistently shown that the decisions of Canadian voters are based primarily on which party to support rather than which individual candidate to elect. National electoral surveys covering the 1974–93 federal elections have revealed that there has been a steady increase in the number of people who cite political parties as the most important factor in their voting decision; after the 1974 election, 40 percent of respondents said that the choice of party was the central deciding factor, and by the 1993 election 57 percent felt the same way.[10] Even though Canadians hold increasingly transitory and shallow identifications with individual parties, their voting decisions are still based on parties.

Many Canadians believe that political parties are not performing nearly as well as they should, but there is still a strong belief in their central role. A national survey conducted in 1991 by Clarke and Kornberg found that while Canadians rated the performance of the federal parties as very low, 50 percent agreed with the statement "Political parties and democracy go together — no parties, no democracy"; only 26 percent disagreed.[11] As for making their choice between individuals, voters were most likely to base their voting decision on a choice of party leaders; a high of 37 percent in the 1979 election and a low of 20 percent in the 1988 election said that party leaders were the most important consideration in their voting choices.[12] But even this dimension is related to parties, as voters can "choose" the leaders only by voting for the candidates of that leader's party.

Individual candidates rank quite low in most Canadians' voting decisions. Only 20 to 27 percent of respondents have said that the choice of candidates has been the most important factor in their voting decision.[13] Not only do voters not place much stock in their specific candidates, but a study by William Irvine has concluded that representatives are not required to develop strong constituency service records in order to get elected:

> A major justification for our present electoral system . . . is that the present electoral system obliges our elected representatives to retain close links with their constituents and to tend carefully to their needs. *It does nothing of the sort.* Few are under any electoral compulsion to behave in this way.[14] (original emphasis)

In Irvine's statistical analysis, candidates' constituency service counted for one-fourth to one-seventh the weight of their party's record in voters' choices.[15]

Discussions of the electoral system and the representation which it realizes must account for the pivotal role played by political parties. Elections are primarily about voting for a party's candidate. Modern Canadian elections are *not* fundamentally concerned with voting for a specific candidate. The primacy of place for parties is not simply due to their work during a campaign in informing and simplifying voter choices. Parties are also important to elections because of their significance in government after the elections.

Political parties completely structure the legislative process. The party that wins the most seats gets to form the cabinet, and through party discipline the cabinet directs the work in the legislative chamber. As the electoral system usually rewards one party with a majority of seats, that group can effectively dominate all aspects of the legislature's work. Opposition parties must have a significant portion of the membership in order to measurably affect the conduct of affairs. An opposition caucus cannot play a meaningful role if it does not have enough members to share and participate effectively in committee work, or receive a visible share of the time allotted for questions or speeches in the chamber. The virtual disappearance from the public stage of the NDP and the Conservatives since the 1993 federal elections has been significantly affected by their inability to be heard or contribute in any other way in the House. The Conservatives and the NDP were similarly denied effective input to the political processes following the 1987 New Brunswick elections and the two most recent elections in PEI.[16] Thus, the substantial representation of political parties within the legislature is crucial to their participation in the legislative process.

The electoral system's failure to provide parties with a share of the legislature's seats in proportion to their share of the votes can effectively force many parties to work outside government institutions. Where political parties are left with only a few, or no, members of a legislature after an election, they must rely on extra-parliamentary processes to continue their participation in the policy process. Large segments of the population can be left without an effective voice in the institutions of government because their parties won only a few seats or were totally excluded from the legislature. It is difficult to imagine that any electoral system can provide "effective representation" when up to 40 percent of the population can vote for parties that win no seats, as happened in the 1987 New Brunswick elections, or just one or two seats, as was the case in the 1989 and 1993 PEI elections. The 1993 federal elections allowed the Liberals to sweep all but one seat in all of the Atlantic provinces, and all but one seat in Ontario. About one out of six voters supported the Conservatives nationally, but they were left to have their policy preferences represented by just two MPs. When such large groups of voters find their policy choices unrepresented in the legislature, they are left with highly ineffective representation.

The distortions in seat shares won by parties matter in the end only if voters are not properly represented by those candidates who did win. If there is a real convergence of policy platforms between parties, then it may not matter so much which party's candidate wins a seat. Or, if the voters did not cast their vote with any particular set of policies in mind then the policy choices made by the elected candidate will not affect the representation of those voters. Also, the whole constituency may be represented by any winning candidate if all people in that riding hold the same views on important issues. In theory, at least, it may be possible for winning candidates to advocate and represent various views on an issue at the same time. Finally, those who voted for parties' losing candidates may still have their policy interests represented by their parties' candidates who did win. However, all these conditions run essentially against either the reason for elections or their practical results. If we can say that at the end of the election it does not make much difference who got elected, then the election may not have had much meaning.

Substantive policy differences still remain at the heart of the party divisions in most Canadian elections. Different policy choices on specific issues still separate Canadian parties and drive Canadians' voting decisions.

Only a few Canadians have voted for their choice of candidate without giving great weight to that person's policy stands. In the 1988 election study, 57 percent of those citing the candidate as the most important factor in their voting choice said that the candidate's stand on specific issues was what made up their minds for that person; over 70 percent of those most influenced by the party leader made up their minds mainly on the leader's policy positions.[17] Thus, we cannot conclude that Canadians are indifferent to the policy choices their representatives will pursue once in office.

Canadian communities are seldom homogeneous in their views; there may be strong prevailing opinions in a community, but it is rare for there to be no division of opinion even on the issues that matter most to that community. Those who represent territorial communities will always have to cope with trying to represent the differing factions within their electorate.

Only in those aspects of the legislators' job that do not concern the issues which separated them from their rival candidates can they effectively represent their rivals' voters. One flirts with nonsense to imagine that an MLA or MP who was elected on the promise "I will do X" would represent with any fervour or effectiveness those who voted for rival candidates because they promised "I will NOT do X."

The impossibility of legislators' representing two sides of a policy dispute is well illustrated by the animated attack by Liberal MP Roseanne Skoke on her government's Bill to extend the Criminal Code's anti-hate protection to sexual orientation; her religious views led her to denounce homosexual activity as "unnatural" and "immoral." In contrast, NDP MP Svend Robinson has called for the censure of Skoke for her comments. Skoke can no more represent the gay-rights supporters in her riding than Robinson can represent the Christian opponents in his riding.[18] On the many controversial issues that face them, legislators must make a choice of which position they will advocate.

Furthermore, those citizens who voted for a party's losing candidates cannot always rely upon being represented by that party's winning candidates in other constituencies. Far too often, voters are left with no-one to champion their policy positions effectively in the legislature. Admittedly, there is also the broader problem that all parties face, with the distillation of party platforms down to a set of choices that do not reflect the positions of all party members. Many Canadians feel that no party reflects their interests adequately.[19] However, parties

that win any significant share of the votes must be able to represent at least those core interests that make up their official policy platform. Unrepresented interests may lead to the benign pressures that generate new parties, but they may also lead to civil disobedience and violent demonstrations to find their voice.

In the discussions of the effective representation which s.3 of the Charter is said to embody, the focus has been on the representation of territorially defined interests. The representation of communities and geographically concentrated minority groups has been the prime concern. Non-territorial matters have been briefly raised, with respect to the representation of geographically dispersed social groups; some have mooted separate, province-wide constituencies for aboriginal groups.[20] But one factor characterizes all these debates — there is an assumption that both communities and social groups can be represented collectively. This assumption in turn is reliant upon those communities and groups having single positions on issues to articulate, pursue, and implement. Through political parties, the voters within any community are faced with a choice of approaches to issues and they divide their votes, each supporting the one that suits them best. As important a place as territorial representation has in Canadian political culture, political parties play just as fundamental and continuing a role in our elections and legislatures.

Therefore, an examination of the effectiveness of the representation resulting from elections must account for the role of parties. A crucial issue to be tackled is the degree to which our electoral system provides a legislature that represents the diversity of interests among the citizenry. If an election is primarily concerned with choices by the electorate about future directions of public policy, then does the legislature reflect those choices? Because political parties frame the choices in elections and then completely structure the policy-making process in the legislature that results, the legislature should arguably be composed of party representatives in proportions similar to the number of votes received by those parties.

ELECTION RESULTS AND EFFECTIVE REPRESENTATION

The inability of the electoral system to provide a legislature that reflects the choices of the voters raises fundamental concerns about the quality of representation.

The principal weakness that one can see for individual constituencies is that legislators are elected by simply winning more votes than their competitors. As a consequence, many MPs and MLAs are elected with less than a majority of the votes in their ridings. Where there is strong competition among three or more candidates, it is possible for someone to win with quite a small portion of the votes. In four of the eight elections reviewed, a majority of winning candidates received less than a majority of votes. In three of the elections every MLA won with a majority of the votes, but, as we shall see later, this record poses its own problems. Candidates can get elected with a very small share of the vote in their ridings; 6.1 percent of the MPs elected in 1993 and 10.3 percent of the MLAs elected in New Brunswick in 1991 received less than 35 percent of the vote. In the 1993 federal election, Kim Campbell was defeated by a candidate who won 31 percent of the vote in Vancouver Centre. In the smallest plurality registered in the eight elections reviewed, Paul Forseth won the New Westminster-Burnaby riding in the same election with just 29 percent of the vote.[21]

When legislators win with less than a majority of seats, it means that the majority of their electors have voted against their policies. The lack of a majority becomes especially problematic when candidates, such as Reform or Bloc candidates in the 1993 federal election, win with a small share of the vote and yet seek to pursue policies that differ fundamentally from those favoured by the majority who supported other contestants. It also poses problems when some quality or experience of an individual candidate is at issue. For example, Billy Joe MacLean was elected by 40 percent of his voters in a 1987 by-election held after his expulsion from the Nova Scotia House of Assembly for fraud convictions; in this instance 60 percent of the voters felt someone else should represent them, but MacLean was returned on the strength of winning 165 more votes than his nearest rival.

The most important set of problems arises when the results of the individual elections in all the ridings are added together. Tremendous discrepancies can arise between a party's share of the total vote and its share of the seats. The single most important factor is the relative geographical spread of support for the various parties. A party can have a fairly large share of the total vote, but win a much smaller portion of the seats because their votes were concentrated in huge majorities in a few seats. Conversely, a party with significant and evenly spread support can do badly if it is consistently lower than its rivals. Where party support is evenly spread across the political unit, the electoral system will reward hugely the party in front and punish the other parties. In 1987 the Liberal party won every single seat in New Brunswick because its 60 percent vote share was fairly evenly spread across the province; every single Liberal candidate won with more than 50 percent of the vote in their riding. The Tories won a respectable 28.6 percent of the vote in that election but were completely shut out of the Assembly because their vote was not sufficiently concentrated to beat out any individual Liberal candidate. Much the same story was repeated in the 1989 and 1993 elections in PEI. In 1989 the Liberals won 60.7 percent of the total vote and all but 2 of the 32 seats; in 1993 the Liberals won all but 1 seat even though their share of the vote had dropped to 55.1 percent. The Conservatives won a very slim share of the seats even though they won 35.8 percent of the vote in 1989 and 39.5 percent in 1993; these poor showings were due simply to a fairly evenly spread support that was consistently less than the Liberals'.

The electoral system plays particular tricks with minor parties. The problems facing minor parties are amply illustrated by the 1993 federal elections. The Bloc's support base was concentrated in one province, Reform's in four provinces, while the Tories had fairly evenly spread national support. The Bloc were able to win 18.3 percent of the seats because their 14.0 percent vote share was all concentrated in one province; Reform received 17.6 percent of the seats because most of its 19 percent share of the national vote was concentrated in the four Western provinces; the Tories, however, won only 0.7 percent of the seats because their 16.0 percent vote share was spread right across the country. Because of these differences in geographic concentration, the Bloc became the Official Opposition even though they placed fourth in terms of the national popular vote.

The NDP has been consistently battered by the electoral system, winning a significantly smaller share of the seats than of votes in every single election they have contested federally, as well as in the provincial elections in the Maritimes. In its strongest showing in these provincial elections, the NDP won 17.7 percent of the vote in the 1993 Nova Scotia elections; however, because its support base included only a few areas of concentration, it won only 5.8 percent of the seats.[22] In the sixteen federal elections held between 1945 and 1993 the CCF/NDP won on average 43.9 percent fewer seats than they would have received under purely proportional representation.

There are several ways to measure the extent to which an electoral system has managed to translate votes into seats, which can be usefully applied to the elections studied here. The Lortie Commission on electoral reform devoted only three pages of its report to the desirability of changing to a system of proportional representation (PR). In part, the Commission defended the present system on the grounds that it was actually quite successful in comparison with countries that have some form of PR; however, it did allow that the results of a national election in Canada could be quite disproportionate when examined on a provincial or regional basis. To measure the success of the national electoral system in achieving a share of seats proportional to vote share, the Commission used a modified version of the Index of Proportionality developed by Taagepera and Shugart; the higher the value on this Index, the more closely the distribution of all parties' seats in the legislature approximates their share of the votes.[23] The 1988

federal election in Canada rated 86 on this index, while the most recent elections held in seven countries with some form of PR ranged from 91 to 99; Canada's showing was felt to be quite strong and not nearly disproportional enough to justify serious consideration of adopting another electoral system. When the Index of Proportionality is calculated for the eight elections studied here, however, the results are not nearly as comforting as the Lortie Commission would imply.

The figures in Table 24.1 indicate that the first-past-the-post system does a very poor job of translating votes into a proportionate share of seats. Six of the eight elections scored below 74 on the Index of Proportionality, with the 1993 PEI and 1987 New Brunswick elections registering extremely low tallies. Michael Cassidy has compared Canadian election results over two decades with those of 24 other countries, and, using his own measure of proportionality, ranks our federal elections 20th out of 25. If the Maritime provinces were added to this list, PEI, New Brunswick, and Nova Scotia would respectively rank 24th, 26th, and 28th out of 28.[24] There can be no doubt that the single-member plurality system serves Canadians abysmally in providing a legislature that reflects the party choices made by the electorate.

These disquieting results are further reinforced by the distortion seen in each party's share of seats. For this paper, I have calculated the distortion in seat share that each party receives in an election. The method of calculating this is somewhat different from previous methods. I have chosen a measure that is similar to that used to describe the variation in seat size that has been discussed by the courts in cases dealing with electoral boundaries. The amount of distortion in seat share is obtained by calculating the percentage variation of the actual seat share from the vote share; the vote share is the proportion of seats that a party should receive under an ideal proportional representation. Thus, if a party received 20 percent of the vote and 10 percent of the seats, the distortion is -50 percent; 10 percent is 50 percent less than the 20 percent share it should receive under strict PR. Similarly, if a party receives 30 percent of

Table 24.1

Maritime and Canadian Elections on the Index of Proportionality

Election	Index of Proportionality	Avereage Seat Share Distortion per Party
NB 87	60.7	+/– 88.5%
NB 91	67.7	+/– 65.0%
NS 88	88.4	+/– 34.0%
NS 93	73.6	+/– 55.4%
PEI 89	67.0	+/– 79.0%
PEI 93	58.2	+/– 89.4%
Canada 88	86.0	+/– 24.2%
Canada 93	68.0	+/– 47.1%
All Elections	71.5	+/– 59.5%[a]

[a] *This is a composite figure representing the average of all the individual party showings in these elections, not just the simple average of the figures listed (which would be +/–66.2%). The composite figure gives a more accurate indication of the electoral system as a whole. Only parties that received 5% or more of the vote are included.*

SOURCE: Unless otherwise noted, all data in this and subsequent tables are calculated from the official results published by the relevant Chief Electoral Officer.

the vote and 40 percent of the seats, its distortion value is +33.3 percent. This approach gives an accurate indication of the difference between the size of a party's actual caucus and the size it would have been under purely proportional representation.[25]

Table 24.1 includes the average distortion for parties running in each election. This column gives a clear idea of the great extent to which parties can expect to see their share of seats fluctuate. Only the 1988 federal election saw caucus fluctuations of less than plus or minus 25 percent per party, while the next smallest average distortion was +/– 34 percent in the 1988 Nova Scotia elections. The mean distortion of all parties in the eight elections analyzed was +/– 59.5 percent. This tremendous variation in seat share underscores the fundamental capriciousness of the single-member plurality system.

This very high level of distortion appears enormous in comparison with the variation in riding sizes that judges have appeared willing to tolerate. Judges have been somewhat circumspect on the precise fluctuations they will tolerate, but it appears that the range of +/– 10 to 25 percent covers the

preferences of the judges who have dealt with this issue. Those levels of riding variations are very much smaller than the range of fluctuations that the electoral system produces in the share of seats won by political parties. The issue is the same in both riding size and caucus size—that there should be more rough equality in voters' representation within the legislature, and that there should be concern about the effects of both types of deviation.

These distortions in seat shares are readily felt in another manner in national elections. When the voting results are broken down by province or region, one sees again consistent disparities between the share of votes and seats that each party wins. The Liberals won extremely few seats in the four Western provinces throughout the 1970s and 1980s, despite respectable vote shares. By the same token the Conservatives never won more than 3 seats in Quebec between 1972 and 1980, even though they won up to 20 percent of the provincial vote. This lack of caucus members from important parts of the country hurt both parties when they tried to form "national" governments; in 1979 and 1980, Joe

Clark and Pierre Trudeau, respectively, were forced to include extra Senators in their cabinets in order to ensure better representation for these regions. There has been an ongoing debate about whether consistent under-representation of whole regions in national parties has led to substantial changes in party policies and strategies in order to concentrate on attracting seats in the "winnable" region.[26]

How many seats each party gets can matter in other ways as well. The whole tenor of Canadian federal politics has been set by the over-representation of the Bloc Québécois in the 1993 elections. The Bloc would not be able to command such attention from their Commons seats if they were the fourth-placed party in the House, instead of enjoying all the agenda-setting, procedural opportunities of the Official Opposition.

A particular share of the votes can give wildly varying seat shares in different elections. Table 24.2

shows the seat share of three parties that won roughly the same proportion of the vote in three different elections. With about 40 percent of the vote, the seat share can vary from 3 percent to 60 percent. The single-member plurality system cannot consistently translate votes into seats. The results are completely dependent upon the number of parties running, as well as the relative size and geographic distribution of their support bases.

The distortions in seat shares are related to another singular effect of the electoral system: only a subset of the electorate actually vote for the winning candidates. If all the votes cast for winning candidates are added up and their portion of the total calculated, we find one somewhat comforting result in Table 24.3: in 6 out of 8 elections, the majority of the electorate have voted for a winning candidate. This is perhaps the one solid measure out of all those contained in this paper to indicate that an electoral majority can

Table 24.2

Varying Seat Shares with Comparable Vote Shares in Three Elections

Election	Party	Vote Share	Seat Share	Distortion
Canada 93	Liberal	41.0%	60.0%	+ 46.3%
NS 88	Liberal	39.5	40.4	+ 2.3
PEI 93	Conservative	39.5	3.1	− 92.2

Table 24.3

Percentages of Votes and Seats Won by All and Majority Party Winning Candidates

Election	% of All Votes Won by All Winning Candidates	% of All Votes Won by Majority Party's Winning Candidates	% of Seats Won by Majority Party
NB 87	60.4	60.4	100.0
NB 91	47.8	36.8	79.3
NS 88	50.2	29.1	53.8
NS 93	51.3	41.6	76.9
PEI 89	61.1	58.9	93.8
PEI 93	55.9	52.8	96.9
Canada 88	48.5	29.9	57.2
Canada 93	51.3	30.8	60.0

underlie the work of our legislatures. Even so, the figures also reveal that 40–50 percent of the electorate have voted for losing candidates. It is the quality of representation afforded these losing voters which is at issue in this discussion.

However, there is a much more disquieting message in the second column of numbers in Table 24.3. This set of figures clearly indicates that a very small minority of voters can directly determine the government in an election. While Canadian observers are well used to allowing that a majority government can be formed by a party that wins about 40 percent of the popular vote, one should understand that the number of voters who actually voted for that party's winning candidate is a much smaller fraction. In the 1988 and 1993 federal elections, as well as the 1988 Nova Scotia elections, only about 30 percent of the electorate voted for the specific candidates who won and formed a majority government. Another illustration of a small minority of voters effectively creating a majority government is found in the 1990 elections in Ontario. While the NDP was able to form a majority government in an election where they won 37.6 percent of the total provincial vote, only 24.9 percent of the electorate voted for the candidates who actually formed the government caucus. Depending upon the mix of parties and the distribution of their supporters, a majority government can be formed under our electoral system by less than a third or even a quarter of the electorate.[27]

The power of a small minority of voters to elect a majority government poses some disturbing challenges to the electoral system. One of the reasons the courts have favoured electoral districts of roughly equal size as a starting point in apportionments lies in the relative equality of each voter in contributing to the government and public policies of the day. This concern was best expressed by McLachlin in the *Dixon* decision she wrote when she was a member of the B.C. Supreme Court:

> In the legislative role, it is the majority of elected representatives who determine who forms the government and what laws are passed. In principle,

the majority of elected representatives should represent the majority of citizens entitled to vote. Otherwise, one runs the risk of rule by what is in fact a minority. Moreover, party majorities may be small and coalitions or minority governments formed. Governments may stand or fall depending on the decisions of one or two members of the legislature. If there are significant discrepancies in the numbers of people represented by the members of the legislature, the legitimacy of our system of government may be undermined.[28]

However, McLachlin's uneasiness is based on the relative contribution of whole constituencies, but the realities of elections are that legislators are elected by factions of their voters. It is the relative distribution of seats among the political parties that determines the government of the day. With the pervasive disparity between vote share and seat share, small minorities of voters can and do elect those who form the government. There is something very disturbing in the effects of our electoral system that a majority government can be formed with the votes of 25 to 30 percent of the electorate.

Another serious effect of disproportionate electoral systems may be voter disaffection, especially among those who support minor parties. Canadian federal elections have developed a very poor record of voter turnout in comparison with other liberal democracies, ranking 28th out of 32 countries for elections held in the 1980s.[29] A study by Blais and Carty has found that plurality systems have significantly lower voter turnout than systems with proportional representation: "Our evidence indicates that, everything else being equal, turnout is seven percentage points lower in a plurality system, and five percentage points lower in a majority system, as compared with PR."[30] In their view, it was primarily the symbolic effects of the election outcomes that influenced voter participation. If voters generally perceive that the election will produce a legislature that bears little resemblance to the voters' wishes, then they may be much less inclined to vote.

All these problems combine to pose a serious challenge to the value of our electoral system. With such drastic shortcomings in the outcome of elections, significant questions arise as to the quality and nature of the representation provided by first-past-the-post elections.

NOTES

1. The more formal name for this system is the single-member plurality system.

2. Some of the flavour of the debate can be found in Alan C. Cairns, "The Electoral System and the Party System in Canada, 1921–1965," *Canadian Journal of Political Science* 1 (1968), 55; Michael Cassidy, "Fairness and Stability: How a New Electoral System Would Affect Canada," *Parliamentary Government* 42 (1992), 3; William P. Irvine, *Does Canada Need a New Electoral System?* (Kingston: Institute of Intergovernmental Relations, 1979); I. Johnston and J. Paul (eds.), *Representation and Electoral Systems* (Toronto: Prentice-Hall, 1990); J.A.A. Lovink, "On Analyzing the Impact of the Electoral System on the Party System in Canada," *Canadian Journal of Political Science* 3 (1970), 497.

3. *Reference re Electoral Boundaries (Sask.)*, [1991] 2 S.C.R. 158; (1991) 81 D.L.R. 16.

4. A little more attention was given by Madame Justice McLachlin in a related decision she gave while a member of the British Columbia Supreme Court: *Dixon v. British Columbia (Attorney General)* (1989), D.L.R. 247 at 259.

5. For example, see John C. Courtney, Peter MacKinnon, and David E. Smith (eds.), *Drawing Boundaries: Legislatures, Courts and Electoral Values* (Saskatoon: Fifth House, 1992); David Johnson, "Canadian Electoral Boundaries and the Courts: Practices, Principles and Problems," *McGill Law Journal* 39 (1994), 224.

6. *Reference re Electoral Boundaries* (1991), 81 D.L.R. 16 at 35.

7. The exception to this observation lies in the Northwest Territories, whose elections and legislature are still conducted without political parties.

8. Quoted in Dorothy Pickles, *Democracy* (New York: Basic Books, 1970), p. 49.

9. *Ibid.*, p. 118.

10. 1974 data from Harold D. Clarke, Jane Jenson, Lawrence Leduc, and Jon H. Pammet, *Absent Mandate: Interpreting Change in Canadian Elections,*

2nd ed. (Toronto: Gage, 1991)), p. 115; 1993 data from Alan Frizzel, Jon H. Pammett, and Anthony Westell, *The Canadian General Elections of 1993* (Ottawa: Carleton University Press, 1994), p. 148.

11. Harold D. Clarke and Alan Kornberg, "Evaluations and Evolution: Public Attitudes toward Canada's Federal Political Parties," *Canadian Journal of Political Science* 26 (1993), 287 at 291.

12. Clarke et al., *Absent Mandate*, p. 115. Only in the 1988 elections were party leaders rated lower than candidates in the respondents' voting decision.

13. *Ibid.*, p. 115.

14. William P. Irvine, "Does the Candidate Make a Difference? The Macro Politics and Micro Politics of Getting Elected," *Canadian Journal of Political Science* 21 (1982), 675 at 781.

15. *Ibid.*, p. 772.

16. In a similar vein, legislators elected as Independents are almost completely shut out of any legislative role because they lack a party affiliation that will provide opportunities to join committees and speak in the chamber with any frequency.

17. Clarke et al., *Absent Mandate*, pp. 114–16.

18. *Globe & Mail*, Sept. 28, 1994, pp. A1–2.

19. In the 1979, 1984, and 1988 election studies, about 12 percent of respondents claimed not to identify with any political party; even more professed to hold only a weak attachment to a party. See Clarke et al., *Absent Mandate*, pp. 52–54.

20. Royal Commission on Electoral Reform and Party Financing, *Final Report*, Vol. 1 (Ottawa: Supply and Services, 1991), pp. 169–93.

21. Chief Electoral Officer of Canada, *Thirty-Fifth General Election 1993: Official Voting Results* (Ottawa: CEO, 1993), at 1521 and 1446.

22. This figure is calculated from the election results given in Joy Esberey and Larry Johnson, *Democracy and the State* (Toronto: Broadview, 1994), p. 451.

23. Royal Commission on Electoral Reform and Party Financing, *Final Report*, Vol. 1, p. 19; Rein Taagepera and Matthew S. Shugart, *Seats and Votes: The Effects and Determinants of Electoral Systems* (New Haven: Yale University Press, 1989), pp. 104–105. See also Arend Lijphart, *Electoral Systems and Party Systems: A Study of Twenty Democracies, 1945–1990* (Oxford: Oxford University Press, 1994), pp. 60–67.

24. Cassidy, "Fairness and Stability," pp. 8–9.

25. It must be noted that no PR system provides parties with a share of the seats that is absolutely identical to their vote share.

26. See the debate between Cairns and Lovink that has laid the basis for the discussion: Cairns, "The Electoral System," and Lovink, "On Analyzing the Impact of the Electoral System." For complete tables for the regional results from 1867 to 1988, see Paul G. Thomas, "Parties and Regional Representation," in Herman Bakvis (ed.), *Representation, Integration, and Political Parties* (Toronto: Dundurn Press, 1991), pp. 179–205.

27. These results are intimately linked to the relative size of constituencies as well.

28. *Dixon v. British Columbia (Attorney General)* (1989), 59 D.L.R. (4th) 247 at 266.

29. Jerome Black, "Reforming the Context of the Voting Process in Canada: Lessons from Other Democracies," in Herman Bakvis (ed.), *Voter Turnout in Canada* (Toronto: Dundurn Press, 1991), pp. 87–88.

30. André Blais and R.K. Carty, "Does Proportional Representation Foster Voter Turnout?" *European Journal of Political Research* 18 (1990), 167 at 179; Michael Cassidy included these countries in his study and found that plurality systems had on average a turnout of 11.1 percentage points below that found in PR systems with voluntary voting: Cassidy, "Fairness and Stability," p. 20.

Does Gender Make a Difference in Voting Behaviour?

PETER WEARING
JOSEPH WEARING

It is difficult to know why the question posed in the title of this chapter has received so little attention in Canadian voting studies, which have preferred to till the unfertile fields of class cleavage or to explicate the religious cleavages that are relics of a bygone era. Differences between men and women are both obvious and eternal. Moreover, issues of particular interest to women — such as abortion, equal pay for work of equal value, and daycare — are now important items on the political agenda. Recently there has been a good deal of popular speculation about whether the parties and their leaders have had differing degrees of success in appealing to female voters. Is there a "gender gap" between men's and women's support for the major parties? Do women assess politics differently from men? Are women's positions on issues different from men's? Can women harness their political power in order to extract concessions from government as other interest groups do? If the answers to these questions are "yes," then their political pressure could be very formidable indeed. But if, on the other hand, women are not yet a voting bloc, can they be organised as one?[1] If such a feminist strategy were successful, would it risk producing a counteraction from politically aware men? We cannot hope to answer all these questions within this short article, but we hope at least to provide an initial investigation of the territory.

Historically, women in western democracies — after being enfranchised earlier in this century — voted for conservative parties in larger proportions than men. The difference was not large and was probably related to other factors such as age and religion. Older people and regular church-goers also tend to be more conservative. Since women live longer than men and attend church more frequently, their conservatism may have been related as much to these other social factors as to gender. A particularly striking example is the Italian Christian Democratic party, whose electorate was 60 per cent female, while the other major Italian parties were quite predominantly male. Studies done in the 1970s, however, found that "the most important reason for this high level of female support for the CD was the greater degree of church attendance among women." When church attendance was held constant, the difference between men's and women's voting became much smaller.[2] A similar situation existed with respect to German women, who were also more "statist" — they supported whatever party formed the government.[3]

In the last decade or so, however, women in most western democracies have become less inclined to support conservative parties. U.S. women are now less likely to vote Republican than men, and British women have abandoned their age-old allegiance to

SOURCE: *The Ballot and Its Message: Voting in Canada* (Toronto: Copp Clark Pitman, 1994), pp. 342–50. Reprinted by permission of the publisher.

the Conservative party—ironically, when it was headed by a woman.

In Canada, women have supported the Liberal party more enthusiastically than men in all five elections from 1974 to 1988, although the difference was small in 1984 (see Table 25.1). There also seems to be some growing female support for the NDP. It used to do better among the male electorate than among the female,[4] but the party now gets more or less the same support from male and female voters. The NDP, like parties of the left elsewhere, is no longer at a disadvantage in appealing to women voters.

Various avenues can be explored in order to explain the differing responses given by women to

Table 25.1

Men's and Women's Party Votes, 1974–1988

	Male	Female
1974		
Liberal	48.0%	56.8%
PC	33.2	28.3
NDP	13.4	9.6
1979		
Liberal	38.2	46.0
PC	43.9	34.6
NDP	14.3	14.0
1980		
Liberal	43.0	52.1
PC	40.6	28.8
NDP	15.4	17.0
1984		
Liberal	23.3	26.7
PC	58.9	55.8
NDP	15.3	15.3
1988		
Liberal	22.4	29.0
PC	46.2	38.6
NDP	16.7	17.7

NOTE: *Columns do not total 100 due to exclusion of other parties, refused, and don't knows.*

SOURCE: Canadian National Election Studies, 1974–79–80, 1984, 1988.

the three parties. Is the phenomenon related to another socio-demographic factor, as it was in some European countries? Or do Canadian women have different policy concerns from men? Have activist women begun to mobilize their fellow female voters in accordance with a feminist agenda? We argue that the gender gap is real and cannot be explained away with other socio-demographic factors. While men and women do share many policy concerns, they diverge on several key concerns of present-day politics. It appears, however, that the policy preferences of men—and especially of men with higher education—are the ones making a distinctive contribution to the current political agenda.

Historically, the social characteristic that was most closely linked with party preference was religion. One might have expected that, as in the European examples referred to earlier, religious affiliation might be a surrogate for the gender gap. But Table 25.2 shows that the age-old link between religion and voting is finally beginning to dissipate. Moreover, *within* religious groups, differences between men and women are not great, especially in the two large Protestant and Catholic groups in 1984. In 1988, Protestant men and women divided among the three parties in more or less equal proportion, although Catholic women were more Liberal and Catholic men were more Conservative.

Another possible area of explanation lies in marital status. A study of U.S. women voters found that single women and working women were more Democratic than married women and women not in the work force. In other words, the latter group was not only more conservative, but also more closely aligned with men, who were strongly Republican.[5] Something similar happens in Canada. As Table 25.3 shows, men and women who are or who have been married are much more similar in their voting behaviour than those who have never married. It is never-married females who diverge most sharply from the rest of the population.

In some instances, education is a social factor that can explain a variation in vote among females. Some writers have suggested that, as women gain more access to higher education, their "life experience" will

Table 25.2

Party Vote by Religion and by Sex

	Protestant		Catholic		Other		None	
	Male	**Female**	**Male**	**Female**	**Male**	**Female**	**Male**	**Female**
1984	(534)	(572)	(582)	(624)	(53)	(27)	(151)	(93)
Liberal	17.2%	19.0%	31.8%	34.8%	25.5%	34.9%	11.3%	17.0%
PC	66.2	63.4	53.6	50.8	50.7	35.9	55.9	49.0
NDP	14.1	16.2	11.5	11.9	21.6	23.8	32.1	30.1
1988	(448)	(491)	(572)	(526)	(91)	(55)	(149)	(102)
Liberal	21.6%	22.9%	25.0%	36.0%	27.5%	29.1%	12.2%	25.3%
PC	43.8	46.0	49.4	34.3	35.2	32.7	49.7	27.2
NDP	17.6	17.6	13.2	14.5	19.8	18.2	26.1	31.9

NOTE: *Columns do not total 100 due to exclusion of other parties, refused, and don't knows. Numbers in parentheses indicate sample size.*

SOURCE: Canadian National Election Studies, 1984, 1988. Reprinted with permission.

come to resemble men's and so their political views will converge.[6] Data from the 1984 and 1988 elections on voting by level of education and by sex indeed show that men and women with only elementary education diverged greatly: women were more Liberal than men; men were more inclined than women to vote NDP (Table 25.4). The gap narrowed for those with high school education and virtually disappeared for those who had been to a community college. At university level, however, the gap widens — women are more likely to vote Liberal or NDP than men, while men are more Conservative. The most striking differences occurred in 1988. The margin within this group of men over women voting PC was 16 per cent. Women preferred the Liberal party by 11 per cent. The sexes split in an even more startling way when the university-educated are broken down by region. In western Canada, men and women hardly diverged. In Ontario and Quebec, they split sharply, with Quebec men more than women favouring the PCs by a 2:1 ratio. In Ontario, the sexes divided into opposing camps; the Liberals received the most votes from women, and the PCs the most from men.

Various explanations can be advanced to account for this unexpected gender gap separating the most

highly educated men and women of central Canada. Perhaps it is because these women come face-to-face with the harsh realities of discrimination as they attempt to establish careers in the male-dominated upper echelons of the business world. As such, they may consciously distinguish themselves from their male counterparts and become, in a

Table 25.3

Party Vote by Marital Status and Sex

	Never Married		Ever Married	
	Male	**Female**	**Male**	**Female**
1984	(276)	(219)	(1043)	(1097)
Liberal	30.0%	36.5%	21.5%	24.7%
PC	52.3	47.9	60.6	57.4
NDP	14.7	13.5	15.5	15.7
1988	(267)	(222)	(1008)	(996)
Liberal	20.8%	42.4%	22.9%	26.0%
PC	46.3	29.1	46.1	40.7
NDP	17.9	21.1	16.4	16.9

NOTE: *Numbers in parentheses indicate sample size.*

SOURCE: Canadian National Election Studies, 1984, 1988. Reprinted with permission.

Table 25.4

Party Vote by Level of Education and Sex

	Elementary		High School		College		University	
	Male	**Female**	**Male**	**Female**	**Male**	**Female**	**Male**	**Female**
1984	(187)	(139)	(531)	(656)	(244)	(246)	(357)	(273)
Liberal	30.5%	36.9%	22.7%	26.3%	22.0%	23.1%	21.3%	25.6%
PC	52.1	51.6	60.6	56.9	61.7	61.9	57.9	49.9
NDP	16.8	11.2	15.0	14.9	13.0	13.5	16.7	20.2
1988	(99)	(77)	(586)	(563)	(217)	(245)	(367)	(293)
Liberal	20.3%	34.7%	24.2%	25.4%	21.5%	30.5%	20.8%	33.5%
PC	50.3	42.3	40.9	37.7	43.6	39.9	55.3	38.5
NDP	11.2	7.8	20.8	19.1	16.8	17.2	11.7	17.6

NOTE: *Numbers in parentheses indicate sample size.*

SOURCE: Canadian National Election Studies, 1984, 1988. Reprinted with permission.

sense, "feminized" voters with different attitudes, policy agenda, and voting patterns.

The National Election Studies pose questions about policy and the proper role of government, where women's views can be compared with men's. Studies in other countries show that, while men and women do agree on a wide range of issues, they differ significantly in a number of areas. In the United States, women tend to be more "dovish" on foreign policy issues and men more "hawkish"; women support gun control and oppose capital punishment.[7] In Britain, women are more concerned about protecting the environment and getting rid of nuclear weapons.[8]

As in the United States and Britain, Canadian men and women hardly differ in the degree of support or opposition that they show for many issues. On abortion, for example, where given the nature of the issues, the sexes might be expected to divide, the percentages in favour and in opposition are quite similar. Nor do gender differences appear on other issues, such as whether government should be responsible for ensuring adequate housing or for providing sufficient income for older people. Women, however, are particularly more inclined to support censorship of pornographic magazines and movies, while men are most apt to favour increased contributions to NATO.[9]

In particular, we want to address the policy priorities of university-educated men and women in order to explain their divergence in voting as outlined above. An analysis of these data, however, lends little support to the hypothesis that the split among the well educated is a female-driven gender gap — rather, it would appear to be male initiated. Specifically, university-educated male voters appear to have a relatively cohesive and fairly conservative policy agenda which they, in the last two federal elections, have been able to harness consistently and to translate into voting power, whereas university-educated women would appear to have been less successful in establishing political policy priorities and in transferring these priorities to the ballot box.

The 1988 National Election Study raised a host of issues, and Table 25.5 sets out a number of these where university-educated men and women mostly differed.[10] Men, much more than women, inclined towards giving free rein to market forces and competition. They were prepared to cut back on social programs as a means of reducing the deficit and they took a hard-nosed approach to those at the bottom of the economic system.

How do these differing opinions on issues manifest themselves in opinions of government in general? In 1984, respondents in the National Election Study

Table 25.5

Replies of University-Educated Men and Women on Issues Relevant to the 1988 Election

	Statement	Percentage Agreeing with Statement		Net Difference Males/Females
		Males	Females	
FREE MARKET/COMPETITION		(327)	(246)	
i	General principle	77.9	66.0	+ 11.9
ii	Market set energy price	52.6	31.5	+ 21.1
iii	Let poor farmers go into another line of work	39.9	22.4	+ 17.5
WAYS TO REDUCE DEFICIT				
iv	Family allowance to needy	73.6	62.1	+ 11.5
v	Restrict unemployment insurance	70.8	62.0	+ 8.8
vi	Reduce welfare payments	36.9	30.9	+ 6.0
vii	Sell Petro-Canada	61.2	52.9	+ 8.3
viii	Sell CNR	58.6	46.6	ı 12.0
ix	Reduce defence budget	59.9	58.1	+ 1.8
WORKERS AND MANAGEMENT				
x	Important decisions made by management	45.2	29.3	+ 15.9
xi	Wages for unskilled about right for skill required	59.1	42.3	+ 16.8
xii	Working people earn what they deserve	57.2	26.2	+ 31.0
CIVIL LIBERTIES/MORALITY				
xiii	Catholic hospital not required to perform abortions	35.9	30.4	+ 5.5
xiv	Encourage immigration from countries like us	47.5	24.0	+ 23.5
xv	Capital punishment never justified	35.5	36.9	− 1.4
xvi	Not prevent adults from buying pornography	58.4	32.4	+ 26.0

NOTE: *Numbers in parentheses indicate sample size.*

SOURCE: Canadian National Election Study, 1988. Reprinted with permission.

were asked to state the most important tasks of government.[11] Those tasks mentioned as the first- and second-most important by all men and women and by university-educated men and women are set out in Table 25.6. Only five of these tasks reached double-digit figures. Most frequently mentioned was the task of dealing with unemployment, and on this men and women differed not at all. On the next most frequently mentioned items, women rated more highly the task of controlling inflation, while men were slightly more concerned that government be run competently. The biggest gap between the sexes occurred on the fourth and fifth most frequently

mentioned tasks of government. By a substantial margin (7.8 per cent) women gave high priority to working for world peace, while men by a margin of 9.4 per cent gave paramount importance to handling the deficit. Among the university educated the split was even wider on these two issues: 12.6 and 12.9 per cent, respectively.

Respondents were also asked to state which party was the best for each specific task. We tried to assess the consistency of voters by establishing which individuals voted for the party they identified as being "best" on their highest priority task. Thus a "consistent" voter would be someone who, for example,

Table 25.6

First- and Second-Most Important Tasks of Government: Percentage Mentioning . . .

Tasks	All		University Educated	
	Men	**Women**	**Men**	**Women**
	(1653)	(1725)	(410)	(327)
Controlling inflation	39.5	43.2	32.2	36.9
Dealing with provincial governments	8.3	7.0	8.1	9.4
Dealing with the U.S.	4.8	2.6	4.3	2.2
Handling relations with Quebec	4.5	3.3	3.6	2.6
Running the government competently	30.0	28.1	34.8	38.4
Dealing with unemployment	47.0	47.0	44.2	43.4
Providing social welfare measures	6.1	6.0	7.6	7.1
Protecting the environment	4.5	4.1	5.9	4.4
Limiting the size of government	3.9	3.0	5.7	2.8
Dealing with women's issues	1.3	4.8	1.5	4.8
Working for world peace	13.6	21.4	13.2	25.8
Handling the deficit	28.0	18.6	34.9	22.0

(N = 3380)

NOTE: *Numbers in parentheses indicate sample size.*

SOURCE: Canadian National Election Study, 1984. Reprinted with permission.

identified unemployment as the most important task of government, considered the NDP as the most appropriate party to address this, and then voted NDP. Of course, when examining National Election Study data we cannot be certain that attitudes precede behaviour in this way. However, for comparative purposes we make this assumption.

To a certain extent, these expectations of attitudinal differences were borne out. Men appear to have been much more successful than women in harnessing voting power behind their issues. Of those university-educated males who believed that handling the deficit was the most important task of government, two-thirds actually voted for the party best able, in their opinion, to do it. On the other hand, only one-third of university-educated women with world peace as their paramount issue actually voted for the party cited as doing the best job on that. On the issue that set them apart from female voters, this group of men more often voted according to what they said was important to them.

CONCLUSION

Differences in political behaviour between males and females, while not overly pronounced, consistently surface in national election studies. On most major questions of policy and government priority, women and men in aggregate tend to concur with each other. The areas in which there tends to be disharmony are usually less relevant to the electorate as a whole. One area of striking divergence occurs between highly educated men and women, although education level appears to have a greater impact on men's political attitudes and behaviour than on women's. In 1988, university-educated men tended to have a somewhat different political agenda than either their less well educated counterparts or women. This group's agenda tends to be more free-market oriented and perhaps, due to a greater cohesiveness of attitudes, they have been more successful in establishing their agenda as the government's agenda.

This is not to say that the agenda of university-educated men will always be more prominent; rather, in the past they seem to have been more successful in identifying issues of importance to them and harnessing their voting power in a more united fashion. In the future, however, as we enter an era when government will have to make decisions on disarmament and the environment, women (the larger portion of the electorate) could have significant influence on government policy because these are the very issues of particular concern to them.

NOTES

1. Two thoughtful discussions of these and related questions are Thelma McCormack, "Examining the Election Entrails: Whatever Happened to the Gender Gap?" *This Magazine* (March–April 1989), 31–35; Naomi Black, "Where Does the Gender Gap? or: The Future Influence of Women in Politics," *Canadian Woman Studies* 6 (Spring 1985): 33–35.

2. Douglas A. Wertman, "The Christian Democrats: Masters of Survival," in *Italy at the Polls, 1979: A Study of the Parliamentary Elections*, ed. Howard R. Penniman (Washington: American Enterprise Institute for Public Policy Research, 1981), 74–76.

3. David P. Conradt, *The German Polity*, 2d ed. (New York: Longman, 1982), 131–32.

4. Harold D. Clarke, Jane Jenson, Lawrence LeDuc, and Jon H. Pammett, *Political Choice in Canada*, abridged ed. (Toronto: McGraw-Hill Ryerson, 1980), 88. The National Election Studies used in this analysis were made available by the Inter-University Consortium for Political and Social Research. Neither the original investigation nor the Consortium bear any responsibility for the analysis or interpretation presented here.

5. N.W. Polsby and A. Wildavsky, *Presidential Elections: Contemporary Strategies of American Electoral Politics*, 7th ed. (New York: Free Press, 1988), 171–72.

6. Marian Sawer and Marian Simms, *A Women's Place: Women and Politics in Australia* (North Sydney: Allen & Unwin, 1984), 161–62; McCormack, "Examining the Election Entrails," 33.

7. Polsby and Wildavsky, *Presidential Elections*, 171.

8. Pippa Norris, "The Gender Gap in Britain and America," *Parliamentary Affairs* 38 (1985): 192–201.

9. National Election Study, 1984.

10. For items ii, iii, xiii, and xvi, respondents were given two alternative policy positions and they could also indicate "Neither" or "Undecided." For items iv–ix, we combined those strongly approving with those approving. The policy statements referred to in the table were as follows:

i. Competition, whether in school, work, or business, leads to better performance and a desire for excellence.

ii. The price Canadians pay for energy should be left to the market.

iii. Farmers or fishermen who cannot make a living should shift into another line of work just like any other small business has to do.

iv–ix. Below are listed some ways in which government could cut their deficits. Please indicate if you strongly approve, approve, disapprove, or strongly disapprove of each way by writing the number that best represents how you feel in the space provided to the right of each statement.

   iv. Make Family Allowance payments only to low-income families.

   vi. Reduce welfare payments.

   vii. Sell Petro-Canada to private investors.

   viii. Sell Canadian National Railways to private investors.

   ix. Reduce the defence budget.

x. When it comes to making decisions in industry, the important decisions should be left to management.

xi. Unskilled workers (such as janitors, dishwashers, and so on) usually receive wages that are about right, considering the amount of skill required.

xii. Working people in this country usually earn what they deserve.

xiii. If the only hospital in a region is run by Roman Catholics it should be required to provide abortion services, because it would be unjust to deny women in this region the same rights that women enjoy elsewhere.

xiv. Canada should try harder to encourage immigration from countries most like us, such as those in Europe.

xv. Capital punishment is never justified, no matter what the crime.

xvi. Adults should not be prevented from buying pornographic books and movies, because it is impossible to define what is pornographic.

11. The question was worded as follows: Which of these tasks is the most important in how you personally judge the parties?

Quebec Women in Politics: Obstacles to Electoral Participation

MANON TREMBLAY

The political history of women in Quebec is interesting in many respects. It should be emphasized, first of all, that although some women voted in Quebec between 1791 and 1849 in the context of a voting system based on the poll tax, they were the last Canadians to gain the right to vote and to run as candidates for office at the provincial level. By 1849, women were completely denied their right to vote (a right which had already been weakened in 1834), the explicit message being that public affairs were not part of the feminine sphere. Throughout years of suffragist battles in Quebec, the many arguments against women's right to vote included the following: "maternity prevents women from participating in public roles," "suffrage will oppose women to men," "the right to vote will degrade women," "a woman's vote will cancel that of her husband," "the man represents his family, including his wife," and so on. In sum, most of the arguments revolved around the *idéologie de conservation*, according to which women became the guardians of traditional French-Canadian culture, responsible for the preservation of the French language, the Catholic faith, and the traditions and rights inherited from France.

Women in Quebec finally gained the right to vote in 1940, from Louis-Adélard Godbout's Liberal government, but it was not until 1947 that the first female candidate appeared, running for Parliament in a by-election. The following year, two women ran in the provincial elections. In all, fourteen women were to be candidates before one of them was elected to the Salon de la race. Claire Kirkland-Casgrain, succeeding her deceased father Charles-Aimé Kirkland, was elected Liberal member of the Jacques-Cartier riding in the by-election of 1961. This delay of more than twenty years from the granting of the vote to women in Quebec is in sharp contrast with the relatively rapid ascension of the first woman to the House of Commons in 1921, two years after the women of Canada had won the right to vote and to be candidates in federal elections. In addition, it was not until Pierre E. Trudeau's second government that women from Quebec sat in the House; one of them, Jeanne Sauvé, became the first Quebec woman to be a member of a federal Cabinet.

These facts contrast curiously with the current situation relating to the political participation of women in Quebec. In fact, when Brian Mulroney's first government was elected in 1984, one female parliamentarian in two came from Quebec. In 1988, however, the figure had dropped to one in three. But, in the 1979, 1980, and 1984 federal elections, the province of Quebec had a larger number of female candidates than any other province, even Ontario, despite the latter's large number of ridings. Before the New Democratic Party took power in

SOURCE: Adapted from "Quebec Women in Politics: Obstacles to Electoral Participation," in Jane Arscott and Linda Trimble, eds., *In the Presence of Women: Representation in Canadian Governments* (Toronto: Harcourt Brace, 1997), pp. 230–42. Used by permission of the publisher.

Ontario in 1990, the Quebec National Assembly was the most feminized legislature in Canada, with female members constituting 18.4 per cent. At the municipal level, the percentage of female mayors and city councillors in Quebec increased steadily from the early 1980s until the November 1993 election. Today, 8.3 per cent of mayors and 17.7 per cent of city councillors are women.

The decline of the image of Quebec women as political outsiders and the emergence of their image as politically active occurred during the 1970s. During that period, there was an increase in the proportion of women candidates in all political parties, at both the federal and provincial levels. More females were elected to Quebec's legislature as well: whereas there had been only one female member since 1961, five women entered the National Assembly simultaneously with the first victory of the Parti Québécois in 1976. As noted above, it was during the early 1970s that the traditional absence of Quebec women in the House of Commons was reversed.

The fact that the feminist and nationalist movements developed simultaneously in Quebec seems essential to understanding the process of progressive integration of women into Quebec politics: nationalism stimulated and nourished feminism, the latter being a source of personal and social affirmation for women (Dumont 1992). In effect, the movement for Quebec's emancipation, in combining politics and culture, became a model for all social movements in Quebec, and inspired specific expectations. The writing of the *Manifeste des femmes Québécoises*, for example, may be seen as an echo of the demands of the Front de libération du Québec; in it, female activists denounce the unequal status of women and men within nationalism, a movement that presented itself as egalitarian.

In addition, the Quebec nationalist movement provided feminism with some important theoretical and conceptual tools that allowed it to formulate analyses of the situation of women in terms of oppression and liberation (Lamoureux 1986: 99–106). Furthermore, it was with the emergence, in 1966, of the Rassemblement pour l'indépendance nationale (R.I.N.) and of the Ralliement

national (R.N.)—two radically nationalist parties—that female candidacies began to increase; six out of eleven female candidates in the 1966 Quebec election came from these parties. Some years later, the Parti Québécois in its program of 1973 became the first partisan organization to commit itself to women's issues and to elect more than one woman to the National Assembly (four were elected in 1976).

OBSTACLES TO THE POLITICAL PARTICIPATION OF WOMEN IN QUEBEC

Many publications, primarily from English Canada, the United States, and Europe, identify barriers likely to restrict the political participation of women in Quebec. These obstacles can be divided into three categories: socialization and gender roles, the socio-political environment, and political parties and the electoral system. If we look at the conditions limiting the aspirations and actions of women interested in becoming involved in Quebec political life, these categories are all interrelated.

Obstacles Related to Socialization and Gender Roles

Two obstacles frequently mentioned in English Canada (Bashevkin 1983; Brodie 1985: 25–42, 77–97) and elsewhere (Darcy, Welch, and Clark 1987: 93–108; Sapiro 1982, 1983: 113–142) as inhibiting the representation of women in political institutions are socialization and gender roles. The process of socialization and the formation of gender identity, on the one hand, and obligations imposed by gender roles, on the other, are believed to combine to limit the capacities of women to develop some of the psychological and social qualifications frequently associated with political involvement (notably political ambition, the right sort of education and occupation, influential social relations, and involvement in organizations). The effect of these obstacles would be to place women outside the informal eligible pool from which political elites are recruited.

This argument explains, at least in part, some of the difficulties Quebec women have had in engaging in politics and gaining entry into the National Assembly and the House of Commons. Its validity was supported by the results of interviews, conducted in 1990–91, with 24 female and 24 male Quebec parliamentarians at the Salon bleu and in the House of Commons. The women were more likely than their male counterparts to see their political careers disturbed by parental responsibilities: not only had a majority of them delayed their entry into politics because of young children (whereas no man had), but far fewer of them had children under the age of 12 when they were elected.

Insofar as women still have the primary responsibility for young children (Gunderson and Muszynski 1990: 29; Secrétariat à la condition féminine 1993: 20), there is no reason to believe that the gender-role barrier will cease to limit the capacity of women to become involved in Quebec politics. It might do so, of course, if sufficient family support structures were set up, but this does not seem to coincide with the Quebec government's priorities regarding women's issues for the next few years.

In our research on Quebec members of Parliament, we did not include questions pertaining specifically to the process of **socialization**, and it is consequently difficult to evaluate the importance of this obstacle for women in the context of Quebec. However, the majority of the female legislators interviewed came from a politicized milieu; that is, either their mother or their father had been involved in politics, or their spouse was politically active, or a more distant relative (such as a grandfather, an uncle, or an aunt) devoted time to some kind of political activity. These results are consistent with the theory of **countersocialization**, which would suggest that women actively involved in politics have been exposed to unusual socialization experiences (for example, having a mother who was involved in political life) that have helped them go beyond the cultural norms proscribing political participation for women (Clark and Clark 1986; Fowlkes 1983, 1984; Rinehart 1985/86). Other research in Quebec has found similar results

(Gingras, Maillé, and Tardy 1989: 82; Tardy et al. 1982). It remains to be seen to what extent this theory can elucidate the experience of Quebec women in provincial and federal politics.

Obstacles Related to Socio-political Environment

Socio-political environment represents another obstacle for women interested in becoming active in politics. Take, for example, the political culture of a particular region or riding. American research has shown that certain cultural contexts favour the electability of women (Diamond 1977: 21–24; Nechemias 1987; Rule 1990; Welch and Studlar 1990). It has been demonstrated that female candidates adapt their electoral style to the dominant political culture of the constituency, conforming more to gender-role stereotypes in traditional cultures (Pierce 1989). The complete absence of this topic from Quebec research on women and politics must be remedied; it will be important to investigate the effects on the political participation of women of variables such as a constituency's level of urbanization, level of education (in general, and of women, in particular), level of feminization of the work force, and industrial structure.

A brief glance at the regions of Quebec in which women candidates have run or been elected suggests astonishing results. In fact, based on Quebec's current administrative divisions, the 589 female candidates running in provincial elections from 1948 to 1994 have clearly been concentrated on the Island of Montreal: nearly one in two candidates run in Montreal. There has, however, been a regionalization of female candidacies since the 1981 Quebec general election: from 1948 to 1976, 77.5 percent of women candidates in Quebec general elections came from the regions of Montreal, Quebec, or Laval (north of Montreal), but this figure fell to 49.6 percent in the three elections of the 1980s and the 1994 election, combined. Given that it was only in 1976 that women began to strengthen their presence in the Salon de la race, however, it is not surprising that 60.5 percent of the

Assemblywomen elected between 1962 and 1994 came from a region other than Montreal, Quebec, or Laval.

Canadian publications have shown that female candidates in provincial elections across the country are more likely to be elected in urban rather than in rural constituencies (Moncrief and Thompson 1991; see also Brodie 1977). But this does not seem to be the case in Quebec, since only a minority of female legislators represent a constituency in the Montreal, Quebec, or Laval areas, the most urbanized regions of the *Belle province*.

Obstacles Related to Political Parties and the Electoral System

Many political scientists — primarily women — in English Canada and elsewhere have suggested that political parties and the electoral system constitute a strong barrier to fair representation of women in political institutions (Bashevkin 1993; Erickson 1993; Norris et al. 1990; Rule 1987; Vallance 1988). This explanation focuses on political environment, proposing that the formal and informal rules of the political game favour men, offering them more opportunities than they give women. The effects of partisan and electoral systems combine to limit women's access to high-level decision-making positions.

It has been suggested that the choice of local candidates is often influenced by an informal model whose traits bear little resemblance to women's experience (Deber 1982; Norris and Lovenduski 1989; Studlar and McAllister 1991). One possible consequence of the prevalence of this male-biased model — called *homo politicus* — for women is to make it more difficult to be nominated for a safe seat. The Report of the Royal Commission on the Status of Women in Canada (the Bird Commission) recognized this barrier as early as 1970. More recently, Erickson (1991) has shown that women were less likely than men to be nominated by acclamation by one of the three major parties at the federal level in the 1988 general election. In the same vein, Maillé (1990: 137–38) has noted that passing the selection process successfully seems to

be a difficult step for women in Quebec. In the interviews conducted in our research, many female legislators confessed that they experienced sexism within their own political parties. Some had seen their presence as candidates diminished by sexist prejudices, whereas others found they had to clearly demonstrate their capacity to be in politics. This dimension of the political participation of women in Quebec must be studied in more detail.

Concerning the claim that parties discriminate against female candidates, it has been argued both in Canada (Bashevkin 1982; Brodie and Vickers 1981; Erickson 1993; Gotell and Brodie 1991; Vickers and Brodie 1981) and elsewhere (Appleton and Mazur 1993; Lovenduski and Randall 1993: 165–66; Rasmussen 1981, 1983; Vallance 1984) that women tend to be run as candidates in unwinnable constituencies, and that parties leave the safe ridings to men. It should be mentioned that the results of our own research, based on the 1976, 1981, 1985, and 1989 Quebec general elections, do not support this argument (Pelletier and Tremblay 1992). Taking into account three factors that would distinguish safe from unsafe constituencies — the success or failure of a party in a specific constituency for the two previous general elections, the status of adversaries (incumbents or challengers), and the margin of victory in each constituency at the last general election — we found that, from a statistical point of view, female Liberal and PQ candidates were not more likely than their male counterparts to run in uncompetitive constituencies. In the Canadian context, Studlar and Matland (1994) have obtained similar results.

There is one factor that garners little attention in research on women and politics, namely, that although we track increases in the number of women candidates and the number of constituencies in which at least one woman runs, such increases do not have as an inevitable corollary improvements in the numerical representation of women in legislatures. In fact, during the 1976, 1981, 1985, 1989, and 1994 Quebec general elections (that is to say, when larger numbers of women sought to be elected), between 22.2 percent (8 out of 36 in 1976) and 44 percent (37 out of 84 in 1994) of constituencies had at least two female prospective legislators. According to Quebec and Canadian electoral rules (notably, the first-past-the-post system and the single-member constituency), regardless of the number of female candidates in a constituency, only one can be elected and become a member of the Salon bleu or the House. In other words, having many female candidates in the same constituency does not serve to increase the presence of women in Parliament. However, it should be noted that of the 127 constituencies in which at least two women competed against each other in Quebec general elections from 1976 to 1994, only 18 of them included both a female PQ and a female PLQ candidate. The PQ and the PLQ were the two most competitive political parties during this period — that is, the two most likely to have their candidates elected and, consequently, to constitute the government. Could this be interpreted as an effort on the part of those parties to promote the election of women? This question deserves consideration in future work.

For constituencies in which only one woman ran, most often she represented a "minor" party, not one of the two major ones (the PQ or the PLQ). In the 1976 Quebec general election, 28 constituencies contained a lone female candidate; in three of them, this was a PQ candidate, in one, a Liberal, and in the remaining 24, a candidate from another political party. The figures for female candidates in subsequent general elections in Quebec are as follows: 14 PQ or Liberal candidates vs. 24 "others" in 1981; 16 PQ or PLQ vs. 35 "others" in 1985; 27 PQ or Liberal candidates vs. 18 "others" in 1989; and, most recently, 17 candidates from the PQ or PLQ and 30 representing other parties in 1994. We can only regret that the tendency evident in 1989 was not maintained in the 1994 election. As noted above, in that last election of the 1980s, female PQ and PLQ candidates were most likely to be the only females in their riding (this was the case for 36 PQ or PLQ candidates but for only 18 candidates from other parties), a situation that could potentially be effective in reducing the under-representation of women

in the National Assembly. It should, of course, be mentioned that even if a female PQ or Liberal candidate is the sole woman in her constituency, she may not, in fact, have a real chance of being elected if the past performance of her party in that riding was unspectacular. This is another issue that should be dealt with in future research.

The fact that few female PQ and PLQ candidates have recently been in a position to increase the proportion of women in Quebec's assembly may have something to do with the possibility that political parties do not trust women. It has been suggested, in fact, that women get fewer votes than their male counterparts because the electorate views them as less qualified to be MPs and as lacking the necessary experience, and, above all, because, according to traditional gender roles, being an MP is considered an inappropriate role for women. Nevertheless, in line with much foreign work (Burrell 1990; Studlar and Welch 1987; Studlar and McAllister 1991), Hunter and Denton (1984), in their study of the 1979 and 1980 Canadian general elections, failed to show that women obtained fewer votes than men.

My present research on female and male candidacies in Quebec, however, reveals a few more nuances. A statistical analysis of the number of votes obtained in federal general elections since the end of World War II (up to and including the 1993 election) by each of Quebec's 5,487 candidates (562 female and 4,925 male) shows that, on average, without controlling for political party, women win fewer votes than men: 11.5 percent compared with 22.7 percent. If we exclude third parties, however, and consider only the Liberal and Progressive Conservative parties (the only two parties to have sent a Quebec female MP to the House of Commons) between 1972 and 1993, the result changes. In terms of average votes obtained, female Conservative and Liberal candidates who ran in Quebec constituencies during this period were not significantly less successful than males: women won 35.1 percent of the vote, and men, 36.8 percent. In addition, women won with margins of victory comparable to those of men: since 1972, female deputies from

Quebec have been elected to the House of Commons with a margin of victory of 30.7 percent on average, compared with 32.6 percent for men. The differences, in terms of both margins of victory and number of votes obtained, are not significant from a statistical point of view. It should be noted that in the 1974 and 1993 elections, the margin of victory for women was significantly higher than that for men. This difference means little, however, since only three women were elected in each of these years.

In Canada, as well as elsewhere, it has been suggested that both the conditions and pace of renewal of the parliamentary elite can impede the election of women (Brodie 1985: 106–99; Darcy, Welch, and Clark 1987: 150–51 and 134–42; Studlar and Welch 1987; Studlar, McAllister, and Ascui 1988; Studlar and McAllister 1991). In fact, members of both the Canadian House of Commons and the Quebec National Assembly may seek re-election as often as they wish. Thus, Krashinsky and Milne (1983, 1985, 1986) have shown that incumbent MPs in the federal House have the advantage over challengers. This is also true in Quebec: in general elections between 1976 and 1989, 74.2 percent of incumbents seeking re-election to the Salon bleu were victorious, compared with 53.1 percent of the challengers who confronted them, while only 20.9 percent of those who aspired to be deputies opposing an incumbent were elected (see Pelletier and Tremblay 1992). So, it appears clear that electoral success varies according to the status of the adversaries. Young (1991) tempers this bleak scenario by suggesting that the high turnover in the Canadian House is a factor facilitating, rather than impeding, women's pathway to the federal Parliament (see also Erickson 1993).

From this an important question arises: either as incumbents or as challengers, are women as successful as men? First of all, since Quebec women entered the House of Commons relatively late (in 1972) and since few have been elected since that time (54 in all, some having been members more than once), a smaller number of female deputies than of their male counterparts have been in a position to seek re-election: from 1945 to 1993, 35 female versus 967 male legislators. Of this number, 62.9 percent of women (22 out of 35) have been re-elected compared with 74.4 percent of men (719 out of 967). The difference is not significant statistically. So, once membership in the House has been secured, gender does not seem to have a negative effect on the continuation of a political career. In reality, the difficulty lies in the capacity to be elected to the House a first time, a task that appears to be more arduous for women than for men in Quebec: of the 527 female challengers at Canadian general elections between 1945 and 1993, 6.1 percent (32 out of 527) were successful compared with 10.5 percent (415 out of 3,958) of male challengers. Are female first-time candidates more likely than their male counterparts to compete against an incumbent deputy?

To conclude this discussion of barriers related to political parties and the electoral system, we may ask the following question: Do women candidates face a larger number of opponents than do men? Such a proposition would in fact be in accordance with the idea that women tend to be candidates in unwinnable constituencies, where the number of adversaries would be a factor contributing to making a victory more difficult. Once again, the analysis of Quebec female and male candidacies in Canadian general elections from 1945 to 1993 offers conclusive results: 62.0 percent of males ran in constituencies with five or fewer candidates, whereas the figure for women was 29.9 percent. In other words, women were candidates in constituencies where there were, on average, 6.5 contestants, whereas men, as a rule, ran in constituencies with 5.2 contestants.

Women tend to encounter more opposition when they run, but this does not seem to reduce their chances of being elected: 74.1 percent of female candidates from Quebec constituencies with at least six adversaries were elected into the House. Moreover, one statistical test embracing both elected and defeated female candidates shows that the number of opponents does not significantly impede women's electoral success. A **simple regression**, using "votes obtained" as the dependent variable and "number of contestants" as the independent variable, indicates that when an additional candidate is added to a constituency, women lose 1.2 percent of the votes, on average, as compared with 4.1 percent for men. It should be noted that 75.1 percent of male parliamentarians from Quebec were elected in constituencies in which at most five aspirant-deputies opposed one another, compared with 25.9 percent for women. Would female candidates encourage competition? This question must be examined in future study.

Sexist prejudices, family responsibilities, and the challenge of being elected for the first time remain obstacles to more gender-balanced political institutions in Quebec. Nevertheless, many of the results described above inspire optimism about the political representation of Quebec women. It may be equally important, however, to consider the matter from another perspective: beyond a quantitative analysis of the political representation of women, a qualitative perspective would pose the question, Why is it so important for more women to sit in the House?

REFERENCES

Appleton, Andrew, and Amy G. Mazur. 1993. "Transformation or Modernization: The Rhetoric and Reality of Gender and Party Politics in France." In Joni Lovenduski and Pippa Norris (eds.), *Gender and Party Politics*, 86–112. London: Sage.

Bashevkin, Sylvia B. 1993. *Toeing the Lines: Women and Party Politics in English Canada*. Toronto: Oxford University Press.

———. 1985. "Political Participation, Ambition and Feminism: Women in the Ontario Party Elites." *American Review of Canadian Studies* 15, 4: 405–19.

———. 1983. "Social Background and Political Experience: Gender Differences Among Ontario Provincial Party Elites, 1982." *Atlantis: A Women's Studies Journal/Journal d'études sur la femme* 9, 1: 1–12.

———. 1982. "Women's Participation in the Ontario Political Parties, 1971–1981." *Journal of Canadian Studies/Revue d'études canadiennes* 17, 2: 44–54.

Brodie, Janine. 1985. *Women and Politics in Canada*. Toronto: McGraw-Hill Ryerson.

———. 1977. "The Recruitment of Canadian Women Provincial Legislators, 1950–1975." *Atlantis: A Women's Studies Journal/Journal d'études sur la femme* 2, 2 (Part I): 6–17.

Brodie, M. Janine, and Jill Vickers. 1981. "The More Things Change . . . Women in the 1979 Federal Campaign." In Howard R. Penniman (ed.), *Canada at the Polls, 1979 and 1980: A Study of the General Elections*, 325–33. Washington: American Enterprise Institute for Public Policy Research.

Burrell, Barbara. 1990. "The Presence of Women Candidates and the Role of Gender in Campaigns for the State Legislature in an Urban Setting: The Case of Massachusetts." *Women & Politics* 10, 3: 85–102.

Clark, Cal, and Janet Clark. 1986. "Models of Gender and Political Participation in the United States." *Women & Politics* 6, 1: 5–25.

Darcy, Robert, Susan Welch, and Janet Clark. 1987. *Women, Elections, and Representation*. New York: Longman.

Deber, Raisa B. 1982. "'The Fault, Dear Brutus': Women as Congressional Candidates in Pennsylvania." *Journal of Politics* 44, 2: 463–79.

Diamond, Irene. 1977. *Sex Roles in the State House*. New Haven: Yale University Press.

Dumont, Micheline. 1992. "The Origins of the Women's Movement in Quebec." In Constance Backhouse and David H. Flaherty, eds., *Challenging Times: The Women's Movement in Canada and the United States*, 72–89. Montreal and Kingston: McGill-Queen's University Press.

Erickson, Lynda. 1993. "Making Her Way In: Women, Parties and Candidacies in Canada." In Joni Lovenduski and Pippa Norris (eds.), *Gender and Party Politics*, 60–85. London: Sage.

———. 1991. "Women and Candidacies for the House of Commons." In Kathy Megyery (ed.), *Women in Canadian Politics: Toward Equity in Representation*, 101–25. Toronto: Dundurn Press. (Volume 6 in a series commissioned as part of the research program of the Royal Commission on Electoral Reform and Party Financing)

Fowlkes, Diane L. 1984. "Ambitious Political Women: Countersocialization and Political Party Context." *Women & Politics* 4, 4: 5–30.

———. 1983. "Developing a Theory of Countersocialization: Gender, Race and Politics in the Lives of Women Activists." *Micropolitics* 3, 2: 181–225.

Gingras, Anne-Marie, Chantal Maillé, and Évelyne Tardy. 1989. *Sexes et militantisme*. Montréal: CIDIHCA,

Gotell, Lise, and Janine Brodie. 1991. "Women and Parties: More than an Issue of Numbers." In Hugh G. Thorburn (ed.), *Party Politics in Canada*, 53–67. 6th ed. Scarborough, Ont.: Prentice-Hall Canada.

Gunderson, Morley, and Leon Muszynski. 1990. *Women and Labour Market Poverty*. Ottawa: Canadian Advisory Council on the Status of Women.

Hunter, Alfred A., and Margaret A. Denton. 1984. "Do Female Candidates 'Lose Votes'? The Experience of Female Candidates in the 1979 and 1980 Canadian General Elections." *Canadian Review of Sociology and Anthropology/Revue canadienne de sociologie et d'anthropologie* 21, 4: 395–406.

Krashinsky, Michael, and William J. Milne. 1986. "The Effect of Incumbency in the 1984 Federal and 1985 Ontario Elections." *Canadian Journal of Political Science/Revue canadienne de science politique* 19, 2: 337–43.

———. 1985. "Additional Evidence on the Effect of Incumbency in Canadian Elections." *Canadian Journal of Political Science/Revue canadienne de science politique* 18, 1: 155–65.

———. 1983. "Some Evidence on the Effect of Incumbency in Ontario Provincial Elections." *Canadian Journal of Political Science/Revue canadienne de science politique* 16, 3: 489–500.

Lamoureux, Diane. 1986. *Fragments et collages. Essai sur la féminisme québécois des années 70*. Montréal: Remue-ménage.

Lovenduski, Joni, and Vicky Randall. 1993. *Contemporary Feminist Politics: Women and Power in Britain*. New York: Oxford University Press.

Maillé, Chantal. 1990. *Les Québécoises et la conquête du pouvoir politique*. Montréal: Saint-Martin.

Moncrief, Gary F., and Joel A. Thompson. 1991. "Urban and Rural Ridings and Women in Provincial Politics in Canada: A Research Note on Female MLAs." *Canadian Journal of Political Science/Revue canadienne de science politique* 24, 4: 831–40.

Nechemias, Carol. 1987. "Changes in the Election of Women to U.S. State Legislative Seats." *Legislative Studies Quarterly* 12, 1: 125–42.

Norris, Pippa, R.J. Carty, Lynda Erickson, Joni Lovenduski, and Marian Simms. 1990. "Party Selectorates in Australia, Britain and Canada: Prolegomena for Research in the 1990s." *Journal of Commonwealth & Comparative Politics* 28, 2: 219–45.

Norris, Pippa, and Joni Lovenduski. 1989. "Pathways to Parliament." *Talking Politics* 1, 3: 90–94.

Pelletier, Réjean, and Manon Tremblay. 1992. "Les femmes sont-elles candidates dans des circonscriptions perdues d'avance? De l'examen d'une croyance." *Canadian Journal of Political Science/Revue canadienne de science politique* 25, 2: 249–67.

Pierce, Patrick A. 1989. "Gender Role and Political Culture: The Electoral Connection." *Women & Politics* 9, 1: 21–46.

Rasmussen, Jorgen S. 1983. "Women's Role in Contemporary British Politics: Impediments to Parliamentary Candidature." *Parliamentary Affairs* 36, 3: 300–315.

———. 1981. "Female Political Career Patterns and Leadership Disabilities in Britain: The Crucial Role of Gatekeepers in Regulating Entry to the Political Elite." *Polity* 13, 4: 600–620.

Rinehart, Sue Tolleson. 1985/86. "Toward Women's Political Resocialization: Patterns of Predisposition in the Learning of Feminist Attitudes." *Women & Politics* 5, 4: 11–26.

Rule, Wilma. 1990. "Why More Women Are State Legislators: A Research Note," *Western Political Quarterly* 43, 2: 437–48.

———. 1987. "Electoral Systems, Contextual Factors and Women's Opportunity for Election to Parliament in Twenty-Three Democracies." *Western Political Quarterly* 40, 3: 477–98.

Sapiro, Virginia. 1983. *The Political Integration of Women: Roles, Socialization, and Politics*. Urbana: University of Illinois Press.

———. 1982. "Private Costs of Public Commitments or Public Costs of Private Commitments? Family Roles versus Political Ambition." *American Journal of Political Science* 26, 2: 265–79.

Sécrétariat à la condition féminine (Québec). 1993. Un avenir à partager... *La politique en matière de condition féminine: Les engagements gouvernementaux, 1993–1996*. Québec: Sécrétariat à la condition féminine.

Studlar, Donley T., and Ian McAllister. 1991. "Political Recruitment to the Australian Legislature: Toward an Explanation of Women's Electoral Disadvantages." *Western Political Quarterly* 44, 2: 467–85.

Studlar, Donley T., Ian McAllister, and Alvaro Ascui. 1988. "Electing Women to the British Commons: Breakout from the Beleaguered Beachhead?" *Legislative Studies Quarterly* 13, 4: 515–28.

Studlar, Donley T., and Richard E. Matland. 1994. "The Growth of Women's Representation in the Canadian

House of Commons and the Election of 1984: A Reappraisal." *Canadian Journal of Political Science/ Revue canadienne de science politique* 27, 1: 53–79.

Studlar, Donley T., and Susan Welch. 1987. "Understanding the Iron Law of Andrarchy: Effects of Candidate Gender on Voting in Scotland." *Comparative Political Studies* 20, 2: 174–91.

Tardy, Évelyne, et al. 1982. *La politique: un monde d'hommes? Une étude sur les mairesses au Québec.* Montréal: Hurtubise HMH.

Vallance, Elizabeth. 1988. "Two Cheers for Equality: Women Candidates in the 1987 General Elections." *Parliamentary Affairs* 41, 1: 86–91.

———. 1984. "Women Candidates in the 1983 General Election." *Parliamentary Affairs* 37, 3: 301–309.

Vickers, Jill McCalla, and M. Janine Brodie. 1981. "Canada." In Joni Lovenduski and Jill Hills (eds.), *The Politics of the Second Electorate: Women and Public Participation*, 66–74. London: Routledge & Kegan Paul.

Welch, Susan, and Donley T. Studlar. 1990. "Multi-Member Districts and the Representation of Women: Evidence from Britain and the United States." *Journal of Politics* 52, 2: 391–412.

Young, Lisa. 1991. "Legislative Turnover and the Election of Women to the Canadian House of Commons." In Kathy Megyery (ed.), *Women in Canadian Politics: Toward Equity in Representation*, 81–99. Toronto: Dundurn Press. (Volume 6 in a series commissioned as part of the research program of the Royal Commission on Electoral Reform and Party Financing)

Representation, the Electoral System, and Political Parties

PAUL THOMAS

REPRESENTATION AND POLITICAL PARTIES

The Role of Political Parties

Political parties have long been considered essential to representative and responsible government. Party is the means by which the public puts governments in place and seeks to hold them accountable for their performance. Parties help to shape and organize the various opinions found in society by structuring them in the form of votes and other types of political activity. They give expression to regional and other diversities and integrate them into a definition of the national interest. They act as giant personnel agencies for the recruitment, election and placement of individuals in public office. The party with the greatest number of MPs elected to the House of Commons forms the government and is expected to provide policy leadership in the form of legislative, financial and other initiatives. The other parties perform the function of an institutionalized opposition, something that is considered valuable as a means for holding the political executive, in the form of the Cabinet, accountable for its actions. In theory, MPs from all parties provide parliamentary scrutiny of the bureaucracy, but in practice this function belongs more to the opposition parties,

who perform it indirectly by holding responsible ministers directly and continuously answerable in public for the performance of departments and other agencies. Opposition parties are also a valuable means for the expression of minority opinions and permit peaceful alternation in office. Finally, political parties organize most aspects of legislative life and provide the energy that drives the institution of Parliament on a daily basis.

The Effectiveness of Canadian Political Parties

Although the importance of political parties to parliamentary democracies is widely recognized, there is a growing unease about their capacity to perform successfully the various functions ascribed to them. Any discussion of the decline of political parties must necessarily take into account these various functions. Because the functions are interrelated and not always complementary, assessments of the effectiveness of the party system vary depending upon which function is under examination.

Canadian parties have been described as both too weak and too strong. They are held to be less than successful in structuring the vote, mobilizing opinion and integrating the mass public into a shared definition of the national interest. Parties

SOURCE: "Parties and Regional Representation," in Herman Bakvis, ed., *Representation, Integration, and Political Parties in Canada*, Volume 14 of the Research Studies of the Royal Commission on Electoral Reform and Party Financing (Ottawa: Privy Council Office, 1991), pp. 191–98. Reproduced with the permission of the Minister of Supply and Services Canada, 1996.

have lost ground to other institutions as sources of policy ideas over the last three to four decades. Within parties the focus has been primarily on winning elections, not on preparing to govern. There has not been the willingness to spend the energy, time and resources necessary for serious policy development. Instead, the parties have used their recently gained affluence (largely the result of the election expense law passed in 1974) to employ the new campaign technologies, not to sponsor policy development.

With respect to the recruitment of personnel, the filling of public offices and the organization of government, parties have suffered little or no loss of function. More people seek nominations than in the past, although there are concerns about the "packing" of nomination meetings and the free-wheeling spending that occurs in some nomination contests. In the eyes of many critics, parties have become almost too successful in structuring the operations of cabinet-parliamentary government. They dominate most aspects of parliamentary life. Disciplined and cohesive parties make leadership and coherence possible in terms of legislation and spending. They also enable the public more easily to assign accountability for actions since it is the prime minister and Cabinet who normally control the parliamentary process when a majority government is in place. At the same time, the pervasive influence of parties and the strict partisanship in the House of Commons limit the contribution of both Parliament and its individual members to the process of governing. Members may speak for their regions, but normally they must vote for their parties.

The Brokerage Model

How party caucuses contribute to the expression and accommodation of regional viewpoints is central to the so-called "brokerage model" of political parties. This model has been the dominant metaphor for interpretation of the party system and has been the ideal that the party leaders have sought, at least at the level of rhetoric, to approximate. The classic statement of the brokerage ideal

was made by J.A. Corry (1952, 22): "In the aptest phrase yet applied to them, parties are brokers of ideas. They are middlemen who select from all the ideas pressing for recognition as public policy those they think can be shaped to have the widest appeal and through their party organization, they try to sell a carefully sifted and edited selection of these ideas (their programme) to enough members of the electorate to produce a majority in a legislature." Following a market analogy of democracy, one version of the brokerage model sees political parties as profit-seeking entrepreneurs who try to maximize their vote to gain power, and views voters as self-interested consumers who vote for the party whose policies are most likely to benefit them individually.

A second version of the brokerage interpretation sees pragmatic, moderate, accommodationist parties as crucial in a diverse, pluralistic society where national unity is fragile. In this view, Canadian political parties have avoided imposing political debate along social class lines on a country that is already divided along regional, linguistic, religious and other cleavages. The principal function of political parties is said to be the **aggregation** and accommodation of diverse interests. To do this, the primary concern of party leaders is to keep the party united, not to articulate policy positions. It is desirable that the parties themselves are pluralistic institutions reflecting internally the main interests within society, and there must be "political room" for the élites within the parties to build coalitions through bargaining, compromise and accommodation without excessive pressures from the outside.

Both variants of the brokerage model have attracted their fair share of critics (Brodie and Jenson 1989). Party competition, according to the market analogy, is said to make the political system more responsive and to facilitate accountability, but the critics challenge it on several fronts. They reject the underlying assumption of "consumer sovereignty" in the electoral market, wherein the public has identifiable and stable policy preferences. Mass political beliefs are not fixed, but highly ambivalent and subject to manipulation by political élites. Competition for votes involves not simply responsiveness to mass preferences, but also the shaping of public opinion and the **mobilization** of political support (Edelman 1971). A second challenge to the market analogy involves the issue of whether parties offer voters any real choice. There is a disagreement among scholars over whether the two parties that have contended for power at the national level really offer voters clear policy alternatives. The majority opinion appears to be that the main parties have avoided principled stands and have not spelled out their policy plans for the benefit of the electorate. Consequently, most elections have settled little in policy terms. Despite the lack of policy differences, voters still develop loyalties to particular parties and these serve as barriers to the entry of new parties into the electoral marketplace.

The market variant of the brokerage model has been less popular than the pluralist version, which calls more direct attention to the sociological realities of Canadian society. In a society characterized by "complex cleavages," political parties are compelled to stress the function of social integration, according to brokerage proponents. There is disagreement, however, over the best way for parties to perform this function. Advocates of the "creative politics" of left–right political debate insist that the development of class-based politics would result in loyalties that transcend regional, linguistic and other conflicts. It is also argued that political parties have been brokerage institutions in terms of incorporating various interests only at the level of votes. Internally, they have been dominated by élites. It was easy for political élites to adopt a "pragmatic" political style emphasizing compromise and mutual adjustment because their issues dominated the parties. The concerns of excluded or politically marginal groups received limited or no attention.

David Smith (1985) provides another criticism of the brokerage model. Writing prior to the victory of the Mulroney Conservatives in the 1984 general election, Smith argued that recent prime ministers had followed a pan-Canadian, rather than a brokerage, approach to national leadership. Prime Ministers Diefenbaker (1958–63), Pearson (1963–68) and Trudeau (1968–79 and 1980–84) sought to transcend regional loyalties by appealing to Canadians on the basis of certain national values and policies, such as northern development, linguistic justice, patriation of the Constitution, the *Canadian Charter of Rights and Freedoms* and a national energy program. Their relative refusal to cater to regional concerns forced provincial governments to become more aggressive in defending their interests and led to demands for reforms to national institutions to make them less centralist in orientation.

The pluralist version of brokerage politics operated more successfully during earlier decades, when the underlying social cleavages and the issues of the day were more amenable to the politics of élite accommodation and consensus building. Since the 1960s, the rise of more numerous pressure groups expressing new values has fragmented the political culture. New avenues for political participation were opened, with the somewhat ironic result of increased dissatisfaction among groups who found that their demands could never be fully met. A slowdown in economic growth beginning in the mid-1970s increased controversy over the role of government and created the impression that all public policy decisions involved clear winners and losers. A decline in public confidence, trust and deference toward governmental élites occurred. In this changed social-political context, political parties have faced grave difficulties in achieving the national consensus that brokerage theory ascribes to them. The containment of conflict has become more difficult because of the nature of the issues faced by governments today. In summary, recent history suggests that Canadian political parties are best understood not as bulwarks against social and political conflicts, but as institutions that function best in the absence of such conflicts.

THE ELECTORAL AND PARTY SYSTEMS

There is a dispute among scholars about what contribution, if any, the electoral system has made to the relative weakness of political parties as unifying agencies. The debate was launched by Alan Cairns in an article calling attention to the problems caused by the simple-plurality electoral system (Cairns 1968). Cairns attributed considerable significance to the electoral system, arguing that the party system would not have developed in the way it had without "the selective impetus" provided by the electoral system. It had fostered a party system that "accentuated sectional cleavages." It had reduced the visibility of other types of social cleavages that cut across sections. It had made sections or provinces appear monolithic in their support for particular parties and it had undervalued the partisan diversity that existed within provinces. It had provided parties with an incentive to make sectional appeals during elections, and the highly regionalized character of the Cabinets and caucuses of the governing parties may have led to regional biases in national policies. Cairns observed that whether a party adopted policies favourable to provinces where it had strong parliamentary representation or whether it designed policies with an aim to achieve breakthroughs in provinces where it was weak was a matter for investigation in each case. The basic point, he argued, was that sectionalism had been given increased importance by the electoral system and the result was to call into question the political integrity of the country. If these were the disadvantages of the electoral system, it also had a mediocre record in terms of its supposed virtues. During the period from 1921 to 1965, the electoral system had produced majority governments where none would otherwise have existed on half of the occasions; and in about one-third of the elections during the period, the electoral system reduced the opposition parties to "numerical ineffectiveness."

J.A.A. Lovink (1970) argued that the propositions presented by Cairns could not be verified on the basis of the available evidence. The indictment of the electoral system, he said, was premature and probably too severe. He began by pointing out that Cairns had not clearly identified what constituted a regional policy and that in the "real world" almost all national policies had regional significance. According to Lovink, it was not clear to what extent the federal political parties had pursued regionally discriminatory policies. The regional composition of the various parliamentary parties may have led to greater sensitivity to the interests of certain provinces, but this pattern might be the result of pressures from within caucus or of decisions by autonomous leaders playing to their regional strengths or taking into account considerations outside the realm of electoral strategy. Much more research was needed, Lovink concluded, before the sectional nature of Canadian politics could be blamed on the impact of the electoral system on party policy.

The Cairns–Lovink debate over the impact of the electoral system turned more on differing emphases than on fundamental disagreements. Cairns did not argue that the electoral system conjured up regional discontent where none would otherwise exist and Lovink did not suggest that the electoral system was simply a technical factor that contributed nothing to the weakness of parties as unifying agencies. The influences of the electoral rules on parties and on the representation of regional concerns within Parliament can be both direct and indirect and, therefore, the identification of such influences is difficult. The procedures for assigning seats to provinces and for converting votes into seats for the political parties clearly affect electoral outcomes. Seats are the real currency of the parliamentary game, and votes are important as they affect the probability of winning or losing seats. The electoral system makes some votes more valuable than others to particular parties. Electoral calculations are bound to figure prominently in both campaign strategies and the formulation of party policies. Pushed to a logical extreme, the winning strategy for political parties would consist of making campaign and policy appeals to marginal voters in marginal ridings so as to maximize the efficiency of the party's votes. However, such a pure vote-maximization approach presumes better political intelligence than is available to parties. Furthermore, party decision making involves more than simple electoral calculations. Parties do not act solely on the basis of the electoral consequences; they are often motivated by more public-spirited considerations, such as national unity and fairness.

Regional Balance

The most negative consequence of the electoral system has been to create an image of a highly regionalized party system in which whole sections of the country are excluded from the governing process during the terms in office of different parties. Many observers would argue that for the ideal model to work requires that the governing party have breadth of regional support. A "working" majority in the House of Commons is not necessarily a broadly based majority. In an electoral landslide, the winning party inevitably wins seats in all parts of the country. However, such landslides are relatively rare in Canada, especially recently. In the 34 elections held since Confederation (1867–1988), the winning party has won 60 percent or more of the seats in the House of Commons on 13 occasions. Only seven times over the 33 elections since 1872 has the governing party captured a majority of the seats in all four regions of the country — the Atlantic provinces, Quebec, Ontario and the West. Canada's most recent electoral history has featured six minority governments in the 12 elections held since 1957. Only the Progressive Conservatives in 1958 and in 1984 captured more than 60 percent of the seats and managed to win a majority of the seats in all regions. Historically, Canadian governments have not enjoyed broad regional support in their parliamentary caucuses.

Regional justice will probably not be seen to be done if a government completely lacks representation from particular regions. Even if a region gives a disproportionately small number of MPs to the governing party, there will still be a concern that the region is at a disadvantage when it comes to government attention and favours. Exactly how many seats from a region are needed to induce confidence that regional fairness will prevail is not clear. Writing about the long period of almost uninterrupted Liberal rule from 1921 to 1957, Alan Cairns (Williams 1988, 107) pointed to the success of the party in straddling the two language groups while still achieving "politically adequate representation from western Canada." It may be that the designation of "politically adequate representation" can be

assigned only retrospectively. Perceptions of the adequacy of a region's representation within the national government depend on the type of issues that arise and on how a particular region fares in comparison to other parts of the country. It is plausible to argue that the main issues of partisan disagreement during the thirties, forties and fifties related to the development of the welfare state and that because such issues cut across regional boundaries, the Liberal party was able to avoid the appearance of regional bias.

Underrepresentation for a region on the government side of the House of Commons does not necessarily mean underrepresentation in the Cabinet. Prime ministers can strive, and usually do, to make their ministerial teams more regionally balanced than the parliamentary party as a whole. Provided that some MPs are returned from each province, the prime minister usually seeks to include a member from each province in Cabinet, and certain portfolios are usually assigned to MPs from the regions most directly affected. Regional representation in the Cabinet can be a considerable compensation for a region's underrepresentation in the parliamentary party as a whole. An experienced and politically skilful regional minister can protect regional interests, even without the backing of a large regional caucus. In fact, a large provincial or regional caucus can be a liability at times if it lacks political direction, cohesion and discipline. Adequate political representation, to use Cairns's phrase, may not require balanced regional caucuses.

Depending on the dynamics of party competition within a particular province, the simple-plurality electoral system tends to "over-reward" the leading party. In so doing, it sometimes assigns whole provinces to particular parties. The most notable example has been the stranglehold that the Liberal party had on the province of Quebec for most of this century. Being able to count on a large number of seats from Quebec (which once had approximately 30 percent of the total seats in the House of Commons and now has about 25 percent) meant that the Liberals began with a built-in advantage in terms of achieving a majority government.

Quebec was described as the Liberals' "solid South," a comparison to the role played by the American southern states in placing Democrats in office almost continuously earlier this century.

References

Brodie, Janine, and Jane Jenson. 1989. "Piercing the Smokescreen: Brokerage Parties and Class Politics." In *Canadian Parties in Transition*, ed. Alain G. Gagnon and A. Brian Tanguay. Scarborough: Nelson Canada.

Cairns, Alan C. 1968. "The Electoral System and the Party System in Canada." *Canadian Journal of Political Science*. (March): 55–80.

Corry, J.A. 1952. *Democratic Government and Politics.* Toronto: University of Toronto Press.

Edelman, Murray. 1971. *Politics as Symbolic Action: Mass Arousal and Quiescence.* Chicago: Markham.

Lovink, J.A.A. 1970. "On Analyzing the Impact of the Electoral System on the Party System." *Canadian Journal of Political Science* 3: 497–516.

Smith, David. 1985. "Party Government, Representation and National Integration in Canada." In *Party Government and Regional Representation in Canada*, ed. Peter Aucoin. Vol. 36 of the research studies of the Royal Commission on the Economic Union and Development Prospects for Canada. Toronto: University of Toronto Press.

Williams, Douglas E., ed. 1988. *Constitution, Government and Society in Canada: Selected Essays by Alan C. Cairns.* Toronto: McClelland and Stewart.

The Transformation of Canada's Party System in the 1990s

A. BRIAN TANGUAY

THE 1993 ELECTION: HARBINGER OF A NEW PARTY SYSTEM?

A *critical realignment*, according to Walter Dean Burnham, occurs when the blocs of voters supporting the major parties are reshuffled and the issues dominating political debate are radically altered. These electoral sea changes are often preceded by "major third-party revolts which reveal the incapacity of 'politics as usual'" (1970: 10). It is clearly too early to determine whether the 1993 federal election in Canada represented such a permanent realignment in Canadian politics; too early because future developments in the **party system** will depend to a large degree on how, or if, the constitutional question is resolved. Should Quebec ultimately separate from Canada, obviously, the party system will itself be profoundly transformed, and it would be pointless to predict the precise shape of any new arrangements after separation. Thus the question of whether the Progressive Conservatives in Canada have gone the way of the British Liberal Party, their position in the political spectrum taken by the right-wing populist Reform Party, cannot be answered by anyone without access to a crystal ball.

Despite this uncertainty, there is clearly enough evidence to demonstrate that 1993 was a pivotal year in Canadian political history. Consider the figures in Tables 28.1 and 28.2: in 1993, the Liberals' and Conservatives' combined share of the popular vote was 57 percent, the lowest figure since Confederation (the previous low was 68 percent in 1945). The Conservatives managed only 16 percent of the vote and were reduced to a pathetic rump of two in Parliament, their worst performance by far since 1867. The NDP managed to win only 7 percent of the vote (its worst showing since the CCF entered its first federal election in 1935) and nine seats. Moreover, the dramatic breakthrough of two relatively new protest parties, the independence-minded Bloc Québécois (which, in an ironic but fitting twist of fate, now forms Her Majesty's Loyal Opposition) and the Reform Party, point up the fact that "politics as usual," to use Burnham's phrase, is no longer operative in Canada.

Both the Bloc Québécois and the Reform Party can be considered the progeny of Brian Mulroney's abortive effort to forge a coalition of western populists and Québécois nationalists (which itself was an attempt to heal the wounds opened up during the years of constitutional bickering during Pierre Trudeau's tenure as Prime Minister). The first sign of cracks in this alliance appeared during the Conservatives' first term in office: westerners who had supported the Conservatives became increasingly

SOURCE: "The Transformation of Canada's Party System in the 1990s," in James P. Bickerton and Alain-G. Gagnon, eds., *Canadian Politics*, 2nd ed. (Peterborough, ON: Broadview Press, 1994), pp. 124–31. Reprinted by permission of the publisher.

Table 28.1

Federal Election Results (Percentage of Popular Vote and Number of Seats), 1980–1993

	1980 %	1980 Seats	1984 %	1984 Seats	1988 %	1988 Seats	1993 %	1993 Seats
Liberal	44	147	28	40	32	83	41	177
PC	32	103	50	211	43	169	16	2
NDP	20	32	19	30	20	43	7	9
Reform	—	—	—	—	2	—	19	52
Bloc	—	—	—	—	—	—	14	54
Other	4	—	3	1	3	—	3	—
Total	100	282	100	282	100	295	100	295

SOURCE: 1980–88: Canada, Report of the Chief Electoral Officer. 1993: *The Globe and Mail* (unofficial figures). Reprinted by permission of *The Globe and Mail*.

Table 28.2

1993 Election Results (Percentage of Popular Vote and Number of Seats) by Province

	Nfld. %	Nfld. Seats	PEI %	PEI Seats	NS %	NS Seats	NB %	NB Seats	Que. %	Que. Seats	Ont. %	Ont. Seats
Liberal	68	7	60	4	52	11	56	9	33	19	53	98
PC	26	—	32	—	23	—	28	114	1	18	—	—
Reform	1	—	1	—	13	—	8	—	—	—	20	—
Bloc	—	—	—	—	—	—	—	—	49	54	—	—
NDP	4	—	5	—	7	—	5	—	1	—	6	—
Other	1	—	2	—	5	—	3	—	3	1	3	—

	Man. %	Man. Seats	Sask. %	Sask. Seats	Alta. %	Alta. Seats	BC %	BC Seats	NWT/Yukon %	NWT/Yukon Seats	National %	National Seats
Liberal	45	12	32	5	25	4	28	6	50	2	41	177
PC	12	—	11	—	15	—	13	—	17	—	16	2
Reform	22	1	27	4	52	22	36	24	10	—	19	52
Bloc	—	—	—	—	—	—	—	—	—	—	14	54
NDP	17	1	27	5	4	—	16	2	21	1	7	9
Other	4	—	3	—	4	—	7	—	3	—	3	—

SOURCE: *The Globe and Mail* (unofficial figures). Reprinted by permission of *The Globe and Mail*.

restive as they came to the realization that the huge contingent of Tories that the region had sent to Ottawa did not translate into commensurate influence over the government's policy making. Enduring complaints, held in check by the appointment of prominent westerners to key cabinet posts, began to resurface: that the government in central Canada was either oblivious or unsympathetic to the concerns of the west, that its agenda was dominated by the interests of Ontario and Quebec (where the bulk of the votes and seats necessary for a majority just happened to be). This grousing reached a crescendo in late 1986 and early 1987, just after the Mulroney government awarded a multimillion dollar maintenance contract for the CF-18 jet to Canadair of Montreal rather than Bristol Aerospace of Winnipeg, even though the latter firm had submitted a bid that was cheaper than, and technically superior to, Canadair's. This decision infuriated most westerners, who drew the conclusion from the Conservative government's actions that the political system itself, including the two so-called "national" parties, was biased against the west. What was needed was a new party to act as the voice of western protest; the Reform Party's founding convention was held in Winnipeg in the fall of 1987.[1]

Reform Party ideology is a populist grab bag, containing proposals for direct democracy (recall mechanisms, referenda, citizen initiatives, and so on); a plan for administering radical shock therapy to the federal deficit (akin to Ross Perot's ideas in the United States); and a desire to scale down the welfare state in dramatic fashion, through such measures as the privatization of unemployment insurance and the "provincialization" of health care (whereby the provinces would be free to introduce user fees or whatever other steps they deemed necessary to control expenditures). Reformers oppose "comprehensive language legislation, whether in the nature of enforced bilingualism or unilingualism," and promise to abolish the Department of Multiculturalism (Reform Party of Canada 1991: 33, 35). Law and order is another recurrent theme in the Reform Party's pronouncements: just prior to the 1993 election campaign, Preston Manning unveiled his party's proposals to restructure the country's criminal justice system, which he and his party feel gives priority to the rights of criminals over the concerns of victims and law-abiding citizens. One proposal, nightmarish in its legal (and moral) implications, was to hold "irresponsible parents" financially responsible for the crimes of their children.

On the issue of immigration, the party proclaims that it is merely interested in creating a policy that would be "essentially economic in nature. Immigrants

should possess the human capital necessary to adjust quickly and independently to the needs of Canadian society and the job market" (Reform Party of Canada 1991: 34). As the party's critics have pointed out, this seemingly benign view betrays the unfounded assumption that many immigrants are a drag on the economy; it also dovetails with the Reform Party's frequently articulated opinion that the level of immigration in Canada is too high.[2] As Dobbin notes (1992: 201–2), of all of the party's policies (save those on Quebec, of which more below), its views on immigration have sparked the greatest controversy. The party has been dogged by frequent charges of racism, and although Manning has strived mightily to deflect this allegation, his efforts are continually and spectacularly being undermined by some of the party's loose cannons at the grassroots level. One of the more sensational incidents of this kind occurred in the middle of the 1993 election campaign, when the Reform candidate in the York Centre riding, John Beck, was expelled from the party when he acknowledged that he had described immigrants in an interview with a university newspaper as "criminals" who take away the jobs of Canadians. Despite this unsavoury side to the Reform Party's populist ideology, there is no denying that it strikes a responsive chord in a distressingly large segment of the Canadian population.

Some observers have dubbed the Reform Party "Tories in a hurry" (Dobbin 1992: 211). A preliminary analysis of the 1993 election results confirms that Manning's party acted as "Tory killers," especially in Ontario, where Reform drained away enough votes from the Conservatives to put many of the ridings in Liberal hands (Howard 1993b: A4). All of the Conservatives' efforts to outflank Reform went for nought: electing as leader a westerner with "anti-politics" credentials (as a relative newcomer to the federal political scene), genuflecting before the altar of political reform by promising vaguely to "do things differently" in Parliament, jumping on the law-and-order bandwagon, and promising to be tough on the deficit without being as brutal as the Reformers in their cutbacks. With the virtual annihilation of the Conservative Party in

1993, along with its current financial difficulties, stemming from the costly campaign (donations began to dry up in the final weeks, as everyone realized that the party was doomed), the Reform Party is well positioned to take the Tories' place on the right of Canada's political spectrum.

In many ways, the Reform Party is locked in a kind of perverse symbiosis with the other new party of regional protest, the Bloc Québécois. Each party feeds off the other, with the result that the prospects for national unity have never been bleaker. Preston Manning is fond of stating that his party represents the voice of "new federalism," as opposed to the old federalism of the Liberals and the Tories. But "new federalism" is simply a catchy slogan designed to soften the Reform Party's blunt message to the Québécois: either remain in a federal arrangement in which Quebec is strictly equal to every other individual province, or get out. Take it or leave it. Manning believes that his party's strong presence in Parliament will ensure that the "old-line" parties do not go soft on Quebec and try to bribe it to remain in Confederation with concessions of various sorts. Moreover, he claims, his party will serve to dispel any illusions BQ supporters might harbour about sovereignty-association, which Manning dismisses as "that mushy middle ground between independence and federalism."[3] This kind of aggressive posturing is music to the ears of Jacques Parizeau and Lucien Bouchard, who can point to the sympathetic response among many English Canadians to Manning's message as further evidence of the impossibility of federalism.[4]

All of this places Jean Chrétien's Liberal government in an extremely delicate position. Although the Liberals did manage to win seats in every region of the country (see Table 28.2), their nineteen seats in Quebec are mostly from Montreal ridings with heavy concentrations of anglophones and non-francophone minorities; the BQ, overwhelmingly, is the voice of francophone Quebec. This leaves the Liberals with a fairly restricted margin for manoeuvre: invocations of Pierre Trudeau and the glory days of "French power" will clearly do little to assuage Quebec nationalists, who want, at a minimum,

further devolution of powers to the province. But any hint of "pandering" to Quebec, of giving it special status surreptitiously through bilateral deals and the like, will be seized on by Manning and the Reformers as softness, and denounced as such to a receptive audience in English Canada. How skillfully Chrétien and his cabinet can pilot the government between these twin shoals will determine not only the fate of the party system in Canada, but of the country itself.

Along with the rise of two powerful regional protest parties and the possible demise of one of Canada's two **major parties**, one of the most important results of the 1993 election was the near extinction of the NDP. This outcome can be attributed to a combination of short-term and long-term factors. Among the more important short-term causes were the tensions within the federal party over campaign strategy (the issue of free trade was dropped in the middle of the campaign, when it appeared not to be eliciting much enthusiasm among the voters, and replaced by a defence of the integrity of universal health care against the deficit-slashing Reform and Tory parties); a bizarre advertising strategy which vainly sought to reprise the success of the Ontario NDP in 1990, with grainy black-and-white shots of actors ranting about a variety of injustices;[5] and, of course, the perennial issue of Audrey McLaughlin's lacklustre leadership. Focussing on the perceived failings of the leader, however, is simply a way of avoiding the more fundamental problems within the NDP; after all, it is not at all certain that Tommy Douglas himself could have rescued the party from its fate in 1993.

More important than leadership or campaign strategy in accounting for the collapse of the NDP in 1993 is the "demonstration effect" that the unpopular provincial NDP administrations in British Columbia and Ontario had on their federal counterpart.[6] Tremendous hopes were invested in the trio of NDP administrations that came to power in Ontario, Saskatchewan, and British Columbia in the early 1990s. Sadly, for long-time NDP supporters, not one of these governments has been able to implement more than a tiny fragment of traditional social democratic ideology (labour law reform in Ontario, for instance). All three governments have embraced deficit-cutting with a vengeance. In Ontario, the internecine warfare between the Rae administration and the public-sector unions over the "Social Contract"—a bold attempt to extract voluntary wage cutbacks from the government's employees in exchange for job security—has opened up a gaping rift in party ranks and threatens to end the historic relationship between organized labour and the NDP. In the wake of the 1993 election debacle, Steven Langdon, an Ontario Member of Parliament associated with the left wing of the NDP who himself had been soundly thrashed in a Windsor-area riding, called on Bob Rae to resign, stating that the outcome was a referendum on both the Social Contract and the Ontario government's general backsliding on party policy.[7]

Defenders of the Rae government have sought to explain, or at least justify, its dizzying policy gyrations—from Keynesian stimulation to New Zealand–style deficit slashing—and its administrative incompetence in the early years of its mandate (the string of minor scandals and miscues that broke with distressing regularity soon after it took office) by observing that the NDP was woefully unprepared for power in 1990. This was certainly true, and the effects of the new government's inexperience were compounded by the strained relations between the NDP and the Queen's Park bureaucracy (Tanguay 1993). Moreover, as Bob Rae is quick to point out, the economic conditions confronting the NDP government in the early 1990s were much worse than anyone could have anticipated, and they have drastically limited the administration's ability to implement traditional social democratic policies, which usually entail significant increases in state spending. While all of this may be true, to a certain extent, it is nevertheless obvious that the Rae government's performance in office has exposed the utterly threadbare nature of NDP ideology in the 1990s; it consists largely of warmed-over Keynesian nostrums more appropriate for the 1950s than the contemporary era. Despite the NDP's reluctance to overhaul its program and philosophy, it can no longer avoid

doing so in the wake of the 1993 election fiasco. This necessary renovation could be extremely fruitful, *if* the party takes bold steps to eliminate some of the sacred cows from its program and if it comes up with some kind of convincing response to the question of what it means to be a social democrat in the 1990s. The NDP can comfort itself with the knowledge that virtually every other social democratic and socialist party in the western world is now undertaking a similar process of self-examination and self-criticism, a process precipitated by a string of electoral disasters during the past decade.[8]

In some respects, the Bloc Québécois is one example of a retooled social democratic party of the 1990s, though it is far too heterogeneous an organization to be easily categorized. While most commentators (especially in English Canada) have focussed on the BQ's constitutional policies, it is worth noting that the party includes a good number of former *péquistes* and union officials (Gilles Duceppe and Francine Lalonde being two prominent labour activists). The Bloc's program is slightly left-of-centre, combining fiscal prudence—the party calls for $10 billion a year in budget cuts, in order to attack the federal deficit—with traditional social democratic measures such as tax reform and job creation (Picard 1993). With the NDP reduced to a mere nine MPs, the Bloc Québécois will be the largest left-leaning party in the new Parliament, and it may well be that the two might have to collaborate to draw up progressive alternatives to the Reform Party's brand of right-wing populism, which seeks to gut the existing welfare state.

Before concluding this rapid survey of Canada's party system in the 1990s, it should be noted that although the 1993 federal election provided ample justification for pessimism about the future of the country, one piece of good news can be gleaned from the results. This is the apparent rejection of the politics of manipulation by a large number of voters. It is perhaps a fitting result of the election that the party that devised the most vapid and manipulative campaign—the Tories—fared the worst. From its reliance on meaningless catch phrases ("the politics of inclusion"), to its overwhelming focus on leadership, to its repugnant television commercials poking fun at Jean Chrétien's facial paralysis (commercials that were masterminded by one of the gurus of media politics, Decima Research's Allan Gregg), the Conservative campaign of 1993 was a cynical exercise in the politics of style over substance.[9] Its central theme was to *trust* the new leader to do the right thing once elected, but voters seemed always to want more. From the moment Kim Campbell made the unguarded remark that an election campaign was no time to discuss a serious policy matter like the modernization of the country's social welfare programs, the Tory campaign seemed to implode. If there was one moment during the election that summed up the hollowness and superficiality of the Conservatives' approach to winning power, it was probably during the English-language television debates when, after hectoring the other leaders about their lack of a "plan" to deal with the deficit, Kim Campbell remained mute before Lucien Bouchard's repeated challenges to reveal the exact figure for that year's deficit.

This is the Canadian party system, however, and so one ought not to assume that the parties will attempt to emulate their more ideological European cousins in the future by presenting to the voters detailed plans of what they intend to do if elected. After all, Jean Chrétien and the Liberals had their own version of "trust me," and their much ballyhooed policy manifesto, the so-called "Red Book," was sufficiently vague to provide the Liberal government with more than enough room to delay or postpone their promises after the election (see Liberal Party of Canada 1993). One senses, however, a growing unwillingness on the part of many voters to tolerate the kind of back-sliding (saying one thing to win an election and doing something completely different once in office) that has been so typical of Canadian politics for the past few decades. Chrétien and his government would do well to heed the warning with which the Spicer Commission concluded its report: "The voters are watching and waiting" (Canada, Citizens' Forum on Canada's Future 1991: 137).[10]

CONCLUSION: POLITICAL PARTIES AND THE FUTURE OF DEMOCRACY IN CANADA

Canada's party system is undergoing a radical transformation, as increased voter cynicism has culminated in the rise of two regional protest parties, the Bloc Québécois and the Reform Party, and left the Progressive Conservatives and the NDP teetering on the brink of extinction. The long-standing pattern of elite accommodation within the national parties has been shattered, probably permanently, by these developments. Increasing numbers of citizens, sickened by the shenanigans of their politicians, eschew party politics altogether, and instead join one or more of the rapidly proliferating interest groups or new social movements. These latter organizations, however, can never completely displace political parties as linkage mechanisms between state and society, if only because their focus is so much more narrow and sectoral than that of the parties. If the parties are to recapture their former dynamism, and regain favour among the voting public, then they will have to undertake *meaningful* organizational change. The Lortie Commission made this observation in its report, appropriately entitled *Reforming Electoral Democracy*. Among the changes it called for were measures to encourage the selection of greater numbers of women and minorities as candidates; reform of party financing in order to eliminate or reduce the opportunities for graft and corruption; and strengthening the parties' *educational* function, in order to stress the fact that these organizations have loftier purposes than simply winning elections. Sadly, as Dobrowolsky and Jenson (1993) have argued, the Lortie Commission report was effectively shelved by the Mulroney government, and thus an ideal opportunity for reforming party politics in Canada was squandered. "Politics as usual" triumphed, in this particular instance, though this victory was short-lived, as the 1993 election demonstrated. It is safe to say that the parties will ignore the message implicit in the 1993 election results at their own peril.

NOTES

1. For more on the origins and ideology of the Reform Party, see Dobbin (1992), Sharpe and Braid (1992), and Pearson (1990).
2. Of all the party leaders participating in the English-language televised debates, Preston Manning was the only one to state openly that immigration should be scaled back, to about half its current level.
3. This was the thrust of Manning's televised speech to the Empire Club in Toronto on 1 October 1993.
4. See Bercuson and Cooper (1993), in which they denounce "accommodationists" who are trying to keep the country together through some form of special status for Quebec. This article is a distillation of the line of reasoning found in their popular book, *Deconfederation* (Bercuson and Cooper 1991).
5. A number of pundits questioned the propriety of the NDP's decision to blur the line between fiction and reality. The same technique had been utilized by the Ontario NDP in its advertising campaign during the 1990 election; a number of commercials referred to events that *sounded* as though they might have occurred, when in fact they had not. In the case of the federal NDP's advertisements in 1993, the party was attacked for using canned outrage in its commercials. It was also forced to pull one of its ads because one of the actors claimed that she had lost her job "because of free trade with Mexico"—which, of course, was not yet a reality.
6. I exclude the Saskatchewan government here because it remains, interestingly, fairly popular with its citizens. This may be because Roy Romanow never promised the voters in Saskatchewan anything but "tough love"—a fixation on the deficit and getting the province's fiscal house in order. In the case of the Harcourt and Rae governments in British Columbia and Ontario, respectively, the gap between pre-election rhetoric and post-victory behaviour has been too great for many of the NDP's traditional supporters to stomach.
7. For a highly critical account of the Rae government, see Ehring and Roberts (1993: 265–375). Written by two long-time NDP activists *before* the Social Contract was imposed on Ontario's public-sector workers, the book concludes with an appropriate epitaph for the Rae administration: "Rae's term in office has

caused NDP supporters to lose faith in a set of values that let them hope the world would be a better place if social democrats were in government" (1993: 375). On the travails of the federal party, see Bradford and Jenson (1991).
8. For comparative perspectives, see Mouzelis (1993), Paterson (1993), Piven (1991), and Therborn (1993). For the Canadian case, see Bradford and Jenson (1991), Milner (1991), Richards, Cairns, and Pratt (1991), and Rosenblum and Findlay (1991).
9. See Howard (1993a) for a withering account of Allan Gregg's role in masterminding the ill-fated Tory campaign.
10. Chrétien's quick cancellation of both the multi-billion dollar EH-101 helicopter deal and the Pearson Airport privatization plan in the early weeks of his mandate suggest that he personally has heeded the warning issued by the voters. Whether his government can live up to its promises on major economic policy issues like NAFTA and the GST, however, is another story altogether.

REFERENCES

Bercuson, David. J., and Barry Cooper. (1991). *Deconfederation*. Toronto: Key Porter Books.

———. (1993). "Why Voters are Rallying Around Reform." *The Globe and Mail*. October 14, A29.

Bradford, Neil, and Jane Jenson. (1991). "Facing Economic Restructuring and Constitutional Renewal: Social Democracy Adrift in Canada." Frances Fox Piven, ed. *Labor Parties in Postindustrial Societies*. New York: Oxford University Press, 1990–211.

Burnham, Walter Dean. (1970). *Critical Elections and the Mainsprings of American Politics*. New York: W.W. Norton & Co.

Canada. Citizens' Forum on Canada's Future [Spicer Commission]. (1991). *Report to the People and Government of Canada*. Ottawa: Supply and Services Canada.

Dobbin, Murray. (1992). *Preston Manning and the Reform Party*. Goodread Biographies. Halifax: Formac Publishing.

Dobrowolsky, Alexandra, and Jane Jenson. (1993). "Reforming the Parties: Prescriptions for Democracy." Susan D. Phillips, ed. *How Ottawa Spends,*

1993–1994: A More Democratic Canada . . . ? Ottawa: Carleton University Press, 43–81.

Ehring, George, and Wayne Roberts. (1993). *Giving Away a Miracle: Lost Dreams, Broken Promises and the Ontario NDP.* Oakville: Mosaic Press.

Howard, Ross. (1993a). "The Man Who Fell to Earth." *The Globe and Mail.* December 18, D1.

———. (1993b). "Reform Party Was Tory Killer." *The Globe and Mail.* October 29, A4.

Liberal Party of Canada. (1993). *Creating Opportunity: The Liberal Plan for Canada.* Ottawa.

Milner, Henry. (1991). "What Canadian Social Democrats Need to Know about Sweden, and Why." John Richards, Robert D. Cairns, and Larry Pratt, eds. *Social Democracy Without Illusions.* Toronto: McClelland and Stewart, 56–78.

Mouzelis, Nicos. (1993). "The Balance Sheet of the Left." *New Left Review,* no. 200 (July/August), 182–185.

Paterson, William E. (1993). "Reprogramming Democratic Socialism." *West European Politics* 16, 2–4.

Pearson, Ian. (1990). "Thou Shalt Not Ignore the West." *Saturday Night.* December, 34–43, 74–75.

Picard, André. (1993). "Rookie Field at the Starting Block." *The Globe and Mail.* October 29, A9.

Piven, Frances Fox, ed. (1991). *Labor Parties in Postindustrial Societies.* New York: Oxford University Press.

Reform Party of Canada. (1991). *Principles and Policies: The Blue Book.* Calgary.

Richards, John, Robert D. Cairns, and Larry Pratt, eds. (1991). *Social Democracy Without Illusions.* Toronto: McClelland and Stewart.

Rosenblum, Simon, and Peter Findlay, eds. (1991). *Debating Canada's Future: Views from the Left.* Toronto: James Lorimer & Company.

Sharpe, Sydney, and Don Braid. (1992). *Storming Babylon.* Toronto: Key Porter Books.

Tanguay, A. Brian. (1993). "On Winning the Battle and Losing the War: Labour Relations Reform in Ontario and the Crisis of Social Democracy." Paper presented to the annual meeting of the Canadian Political Science Association. Ottawa. June 6–8.

Therborn, Göran. (1993). "Reply to Mouzelis." *New Left Review,* no. 200 (July/August), 185–191.

Public Opinion, the Media, and Interest Groups

CLOSE-UP: THE DANGERS OF MEDIA CONCENTRATION

The idea that one man could control more than $3 billion worth of the Canadian media industry created some alarm in business and academic circles. In 1994, cable TV magnate Ted Rogers became that man when he gained control of the cable and publishing empire of Maclean Hunter Limited, Canada's fourth-largest cable company, owner of TV and radio stations, holder of major investments in newspapers, printing plants, and communications services in Canada and the United States, and publisher of more than two hundred periodicals in ten countries. Rogers Communications has extensive investments in all areas of cable broadcasting, cellular telephones, and long-distance telephone service.

Even as a boy, Ted Rogers was buying shares of media companies, such as Standard Broadcasting and CFRB, that he thought had a profitable future in the broadcast industry. Soon after he graduated from Upper Canada College, he bought up all the shares of CHFI, a tiny radio station in Toronto that offered its patrons a new frequency modulation for FM receivers.

By 1967, Rogers was investing heavily in cable TV businesses and expanding beyond the Toronto area. In the 1970s, he bought out his two biggest competitors — Canadian Cablesystems and Premier Cablevision — both larger than his own company. In 1980 he became the world's largest cable operator, with millions of subscribers in Canada and the United States. Then Rogers decided to take on the challenge of competition with Canada's most entrenched communications monopoly — Bell Canada — by joining with Canadian Pacific Ltd. of Montreal to create Unitel Communications Inc.

In Canada, there is a decided trend toward concentrated ownership of the media, increasing the risk that a few owners could control the news and promote their own political and economic interests, much as political parties influenced the content of some of Canada's earliest newspapers.

Regulation of the broadcast media arose out of necessity. Today, the Canadian Radio-television and Telecommunications Commission (CRTC), one of eleven regulatory agencies organized under Communications Canada, licenses radio and television stations and monitors the phenomenon of media concentration. A corporation interested in establishing a television station in Canada cannot simply purchase the necessary equipment, hire staff, and begin broadcasting. The CRTC must license it to operate on a particular frequency.

All of this may seem unnecessary; at first glance, concentration of ownership of the media does not appear to be a problem. After all, although there are only a few major networks in Canada, these networks do not usually own their affiliates. As well, most Canadian communities seem to have ample choice among the media they use. The electronic media offer diverse viewpoints and do not appear to be adversely affected by the trend toward greater concentration of ownership.

The situation becomes more complicated, however, when ownership is concentrated across several different media. The same corporation can own television stations, radio stations, and newspapers in the same region or across the country. Before Rogers acquired Maclean Hunter, his was already Canada's largest cable company, with fourteen cable systems serving nearly two million subscribers. His company also owned nine AM and eleven FM radio stations in Ontario, British Columbia, Alberta, and Manitoba. In addition, it controlled Toronto's CFMT TV, a multicultural television station, and YTV, a youth-oriented cable channel, as well as holding major shares in Viewer's Choice Canada, a user pay cable service. Rogers also held 32 percent of Unitel and 80 percent of Cantel Mobile Communications, a Canada-wide cellular phone and paging service.

Some people fear such concentration of media ownership in the hands of a single, private owner, and they consequently expect government to regulate media ownership, as well as other aspects of media operation. In Canada, the broadcast media have always operated under more stringent regulations than the print media, initially because of the complex technical aspects of broadcasting that have special needs to be regulated. Critics of deregulation or nonregulation argue that the information provided by a single, privately owned corporation may be controlled by corporate owner, whether it is owned by Canadians or foreigners.

After all, the media largely determine what information is received by the public and have a corresponding obligation to objectivity, fairness, and relevance. Increasing concentration of ownership of the mass media has raised concerns about the reduced competition among information sources and the enhanced possibilities for control and domination.

Besides Rogers, three of the wealthiest men in the world, also Canadians, control vast corporate empires that include the mass media in Canada. K.C. Irving, worth nearly $7 billion (US), owns most of the media outlets in New Brunswick. Kenneth Thomson, worth an estimated $6 billion (US) and described as a "newspaper magnate," owns nearly 60 percent of Canada's English-language newspapers. Conrad Black, another billionaire, controls a chain of daily and weekly newspapers as part of his vast corporate empire. One of his companies, Hollinger Inc., acquired a 23 percent stake in Southam Inc., another of Canada's largest media corporations.

Two federal royal commissions have documented the concern of Canadians about increased concentration of media ownership throughout the country. In 1970, the Davey Report drew attention to the extent of corporate concentration in the Canadian media and left it to us to decide how much we should tolerate. In 1981, the Kent Commission concluded that the concentration of ownership in the hands of fewer and fewer large corporations is "entirely unacceptable for a democratic society."

But are the fears about who owns the media well founded? Does it really matter if Ted Rogers and a few other Canadians like him own a substantial portion of Canada's media capabilities in a communications world that offers great choice? In the final analysis, does the concentration of ownership increase the political power of these corporations and ultimately affect the governability of the country? Perhaps—but it is all a matter of interpretation: For Rogers, the takeover of Maclean Hunter represents a corporate step toward creating a nationwide electronic superhighway capable of delivering a vast array of new services to Canadian homeowners—a development that might remain unrealized in the absence of a high degree of concentration of ownership. Will the costs outweigh the benefits?

INTRODUCTION: INFLUENCING THE POLITICAL AGENDA

In this section, we turn our attention to the ways in which public opinion, the media, and interest groups affect the political agenda in Canada. We know that public opinion is complicated because there is not just one Canadian "public," but many individuals, and because opinions vary not only over time but in intensity and sophistication across groups as well. Indeed, across the country, Canadians differ widely in their interest in and knowledge about politics and government. A clear example of the lack of uniformity in public opinion among Canadians was evident during the 1995 Quebec referendum debate, when, as is often the case, the political opinions of Quebeckers on such issues as the meaning of being Canadian, federalism, provincial powers and jurisdictions, and government spending in the economy differed dramatically from those of Canadians in the rest of the country.

We also know that the media play a pivotal role in determining how and what opinions are expressed and heard in our society. Increasingly, the media influence the political agenda as well as the government agenda. When deciding what to cover, the media focus on certain aspects of public life to the exclusion of others. Because the media's choices often constitute the only information the public receives, what they do not focus on might just as well not exist. Studies have shown that the media are most influential in shaping the public agenda when the events and issues concerned are either outside the public's direct experience or are new to society. By highlighting some issues and ignoring others, the media influence the standards by which Canadians judge their governments, their public officials, and their candidates for public office.

Finally, we will learn that interest groups have come to wield increasing political power in Canadian society. Differing widely in size and composition, they pursue varying objectives and serve as organizational links between their members and elected and appointed government officials. Interest groups can be extremely effective in making Cabinet members, other parliamentarians, and government bureaucrats aware of people's needs and concerns: This capacity is both what justifies their existence and what causes people to question their role in the political system. Many people join interest groups to promote their own economic well-being or to effect social and political change, in the belief that the collective action of pressure groups is more effective than belonging to a political party.

POLITICAL OPINIONS

No Canadian government or political leader can afford to ignore political public opinion. Stated formally, a political public opinion is a collective evaluation of political issues, policies, institutions, and individuals. Political opinion has become the ultimate standard against which we judge the conduct of Canadian governments and political leaders, the relevance of their institutions, and the effectiveness of public employees.

Political opinion can be defined as the opinions held by ordinary people that governments and political leaders take into account in making decisions of political consequence. One frame of reference that guides Canadian political opinion is cultural beliefs (underlying, for example, people's support for a publicly funded health care system), which can determine a range of acceptable or unacceptable policy alternatives. Opinion can also stem from **ideology**, as in the case of strong and consistent attachments to liberal or conservative policies. People can also develop political opinions as a result of their group orientations, notably those influenced by religion, income, occupation, region, race, or gender. Partisanship is perhaps one of the principal sources of political opinions; members of the Liberal, Bloc Québécois, Reform, New Democratic, and Progressive Conservative parties differ in their voting behaviour and views on policy issues.

Political opinions vary in intensity, **salience**, stability, and direction. Not every issue evokes intense feelings, and not all issues are equally salient or stable. Opinion also varies in terms of direction, that is, in favour of or against a particular issue. There may be various levels of support for an issue but no clear or precise direction of opinion.

Political opinion can vary considerably in terms of its stability. On many issues—difficult ones in particular—public support is far from stable, but rather fluctuates with the changing expectations and demands of the people. On less complex and confusing matters, public opinion tends to be more reliable; for example, public support for government funding of education and health care has remained relatively stable, even in the face of severe budgetary constraints.

Public officials find it necessary to know about the intensity, saliency, stability, and direction of the public's political preferences. If a majority, or even an active minority, of the public seem indifferent to a particular issue, or if opinions on the matter are unstable and shifting, officials may disregard them in whatever action they choose to take, or they may choose not to act at all. In contrast, salient issues that arouse intense feelings and popular passions, such as abortion and gun control, are more likely to stimulate government action.

Rais Khan and James McNiven's piece on how political opinions are formed and on the factors that influence them (Chapter 32) will help us understand some of the fundamental forces at play in our thinking about politics. What Canadians *think* about politics is important because it determines, in part, how they *act* politically. The diverse but generally moderate character of Canadian political opinions, and the modest intensity with which most Canadians advance their views, set the tone for the whole political process. To understand how people think about politics is to understand an essential element of how a country's political process functions.

THE MEDIA

The **mass media** are the various forms of communication that reach a large audience without any personal contact between the senders and the receivers of the messages; they include newspapers, magazines, books, television, radio, movies, videos, computers, and audio recordings. There are also minor mass media, such as posters and various forms of public signage. These are all potential agents of political socialization that introduce individuals to an extraordinarily diverse array of political personalities who are usually "known" to the public only indirectly — historical political figures, political party leaders, and other politicians and government leaders.

The media provide Canadians with almost instant coverage of political and social events. They are the disseminators of the complex political and social ideas — that is, the ideologies — that shape our society. The media offer political viewpoints and analysis, and reflect our attitudes, beliefs, and expectations. In Chapter 29, "Ideology and the Media," David Cheal and Graham Knight explore the concept of **dominant ideologies** and examine how the media reflect them, becoming the looking glass through which we perceive the world around us.

Studies of the media's effects generally agree that the media help set the country's political agenda by influencing what is uppermost in the minds of policy-makers and the Canadian people. The media may not always have a powerful influence on the attitudes of Canadians, but they certainly help determine where we direct our attention. Indeed, as Richard Jenkins suggests in Chapter 30, "Public Opinion, the Media, and the Political Agenda," the media are not usually successful in telling people *what* to think, but they are highly successful in telling people what to think *about*.

Although the agenda-setting power of the news media does not affect the attitudes of Canadians directly, it has an important indirect influence. Richard Jenkins's article focusses on the extent to which the media set the political agenda with respect to two sorts of issues — "symbolic" issues, such as national unity, and "non-symbolic" issues, such as unemployment. But he also makes the important connection between the role of the media and the formation of public political opinion. In this regard, the political agenda is very much a product of the direction and intensity of public opinion, which is often influenced by media reporting.

Since the ascendancy of the mass media and, in particular, the advent of television, there has been a dramatic change in the leadership role of the prime minister and the premiers in parliamentary government. More than any other figure in the Cabinet, the prime minister relies on and is the focus of the media: The two are mutually dependent, typically locked in a kind of love–hate relationship. In Chapter 31, "The Prime Minister's Media Arsenal," David Taras explores that relationship, demonstrating how a prime minister can use the media to survive in a job that is fraught with potential pitfalls.

Public support can have a powerful effect on a prime minister's or a premier's ability to lead a Cabinet and achieve policy goals. This ability resides in large part in a prime minister's claim to national leadership, and the legitimacy of that claim is roughly proportional to public support for the government and its performance.

INTEREST GROUPS

An interest group (often called a **pressure group** or lobby group) is defined as an assembly of people who share common attitudes and **interests** and who try to influence the political system by shaping public and parliamentary opinion, opposing or supporting candidates in elections, and trying to influence governments on the direction and implementation of public policy. Unlike political parties, pressure groups are not interested in getting their own members elected to Parliament. Instead, they seek to influence government indirectly.

As Paul Pross informs us in Chapter 34, almost all Canadians either belong to one or more interest groups or are represented by such groups without being formal members. In this way, interest groups are unlike political parties. They represent the opinions and demands of people and use their strength to win benefits from the government. Interest groups are highly significant forces in the formulation of public policy in Canada.

In Chapter 33, Sandra Burt traces the development of organized women's groups in Canada from the nineteenth century, when the women's social movement began to take shape, to the present. It should be noted that women are not just a special interest group: They are also the majority of the Canadian population.

More and more, Canada is becoming a political system of special interests. Organized interest groups have been increasingly successful in **lobbying** legislators and administrators and articulating the needs of their members, and have earned special benefits from successive governments. The power of interest groups in Canada's parliamentary system results from a number of factors, some of which are inherent in the groups themselves and some of which derive from the structure of our government. And, as Pross tells us, the ability of interest groups to adapt to change gives them an advantage over political parties and over the very governments from which they seek to gain benefits.

Our governing system has many points of access for the strategic intervention of interest groups in the decision-making process. Lobbying targets legislators before a bill becomes a law, but if, in spite of all efforts, the legislation passes, the interest group can lobby Cabinet or the department responsible for implementing the law in the hope of influencing how the legislation is applied.

THINKING IT OVER

1. Based on the brief analysis by David Cheal and Graham Knight (Chapter 29), what are some of the values and beliefs that Canadians subscribe to as part of their ideological framework? Research the subject in some of the textbooks used in the related disciplines of sociology and social psychology: You may find that the observations and generalizations they make about ideologies will enhance your understanding of political ideology as outlined by Cheal and Knight. Do the media themselves subscribe to a particular ideology? Do the media enforce or challenge the dominant ideologies in Canadian society?

2. Put together a "needs list," or "wish list," for your community. What ideological stance adopted by a government would be the most likely to enable your community or country to achieve the goals on your list? How would you describe the ideological positions you take on community issues? What is the difference between a general public opinion on a matter of social interest and a political opinion?

3. Richard Jenkins (Chapter 30) tries to explain the link between the role of the media, public opinion, and the political agenda. Is he

successful? How influential are the media in defining the public interest? Identify the various media you are most frequently exposed to and try to evaluate how much political information they provide you. How do the media transmit political information in our society?

4. David Taras (Chapter 31) also has some ideas on how the media can set the political agenda. What are some of the ways in which governments manipulate the media? What opportunities are available to a prime minister to use the powers of the media to his or her advantage?

5. Khan and McNiven (Chapter 32) connect political culture with opinion formation. What are the agents of political opinion that they identify as highly influential in our political culture? How do these factors contribute to the formation of our opinions on politics and government in Canada?

6. Using the arguments presented by Sandra Burt (Chapter 33) and Paul Pross (Chapter 34), identify the reasons why interest groups are often more likely than political parties to influence the political process and gain the attention of governments. In recent years, a number of pressure groups claiming to represent the "public interest" have emerged. Identify and discuss the activities of some of these groups, focussing in particular on women's groups. How effective do you believe women's groups have been and are likely to be in getting their interests on the government agenda? Would a Canadian Feminist party be more effective?

GLOSSARY

agenda building The choices made by a government, the media, or political groups to determine which public policy questions should be debated and evaluated by Parliament.

dominant ideology The principal set of ideas, particularly political ideas, advanced and supported by those in positions of power and influence in a society at a particular time.

gatekeepers A term used in reference to the mass media, in their function of determining what information the public will be exposed to. In mass-media organizations, it is the editors, producers, and owners of media outlets who decide what stories will be printed or broadcast and analyzed in the public domain.

hegemony The ideological domination of one class by another. The term is also used to refer to the dominant influence of one state over another or over a group of states.

ideology A system of ideas that collectively describe, explain, and justify existing social arrangements, or propose alternatives to them, and that identify appropriate lines of action for people to follow.

interest accommodation The ability of a political organization to meet the range of demands placed upon it by its members or by coalitions of groups seeking to co-ordinate their strategies across many levels of society.

interests The desires, values, or objectives held in common by individuals and groups.

investigative journalism The in-depth research by journalists into a particular social or political problem in order to discover information that may not be immediately evident, and the public disclosure of such findings.

leak Information released strategically to the media by government, a political group, or a political party in an attempt to control public reaction to and interpretation of certain information and events.

lobbying Activity geared to influencing government decision-makers through both direct and indirect contact with them. The term refers to the public places in which such activity originally took place.

mass media The instruments of public communication that transmit political and social knowledge to all members of society; they include computers, radio, television, books, newspapers, movies, documentaries, public billboards.

mobilization The organization and use of available resources, such as time, money, people, and the media.

news values The various criteria by which news media try to define and represent issues or events and thereby attract an audience. Examples include immediacy, personalization, novelty, reportorial neutrality, impartiality, and relevance, and often entail conflict, confrontation, deviance, or disorder.

opinion poll A survey of public thinking conducted by pollsters to obtain a precise measure of opinions.

pack journalism The tendency of reporters to shape their stories by following the lead of other journalists.

political action All purposeful and goal-oriented behaviour by individuals and groups that leads to social and political change.

political culture The patterns of beliefs, symbols, and conduct associated with a political community, its constitutional system, and the government of the day.

pressure groups Organized interests that try to achieve at least some of their goals by influencing the process of making public policy by means of pressure tactics and strategies. Also called *interest groups* and *lobby groups*.

public opinion The vast array of beliefs and attitudes that people hold about any social matter or issue. Political scientists and governments are interested in *political* opinions — those that reflect opinions about government and the political system.

salience The perceived importance of an issue.

spin An interpretation of an event or of election results that is deliberately and intensely biased in favour of or against a particular political figure or candidate, party, or political policy or strategy.

ADDITIONAL READINGS

Associations Canada 1991: An Encyclopedic Directory. 1991. Mississauga, Ont.: Canadian Almanac & Directory Publishing Co.

Babe, Robert. 1990. *Telecommunications in Canada: Technology, Industry, and Government.* Toronto: University of Toronto Press.

Coleman, William, and Grace Skogstad. 1990. *Policy Communities and Public Policy in Canada.* Mississauga, Ont.: Copp Clark Pitman.

Cooper, Barry. 1994. *Sins of Omission: Shaping the News at CBC TV.* Toronto: University of Toronto Press.

Desbarats, Peter. 1996. *Guide to Canadian News Media,* 2nd ed. Toronto: Harcourt Brace.

Dobbin, Murray. 1993. *Preston Manning and the Reform Party.* Toronto: James Lorimer & Company.

Funderburk, Charles, and Robert Thobaben. 1994. *Political Ideologies: Left, Center, Right.* New York: HarperCollins College Publishers.

Hoy, Claire. 1990. *Margin of Error.* Toronto: Key Porter Books.

Lachapelle, Guy. 1992. *Polls and the Media in Canadian Elections: Taking the Pulse.* Toronto: Dundurn Press.

Singer, Benjamin. 1992. *Communications in Canadian Society.* Scarborough, Ont.: Nelson Canada.

Taras, David. 1990. *The Newsmakers: The Media's Influence on Canadian Politics.* Scarborough, Ont.: Nelson Canada.

Vipond, Mary. 1990. *The Mass Media in Canada.* Toronto: James Lorimer & Company.

Ideology and the Media

DAVID CHEAL

GRAHAM KNIGHT

IDEOLOGY

An **ideology** is any system of ideas that describes and explains the experiences of certain people, and either justifies their situation or proposes alternatives to it. It identifies appropriate lines of action for them to follow and suggests strategies by which they can achieve their goals. Political parties that seek radical change often have well-developed ideologies that describe how they plan to gain political power and how they intend to use it. The Parti Québécois is a good current example. Its ideology claims that the Canadian federal state is broken and cannot be mended, and so it is best for the different parts of Canada to go their separate ways.

Another example of an ideology is the conservative, fundamentalist Christian world view that underlies belief in Satanism. It describes social change in terms of a moral struggle between good and evil. It explains current problems as attributable to the increased power of evil, because religion is in crisis and the churches have lost their traditional control, especially over children. The ideology proposes solutions to this situation, by identifying the need to counteract the subversive influence of Satanists. And it suggests concrete strategies for finding out who the Satanists among us are and for preventing their work.

By comparison with its far greater influence in the United States, conservative Christian fundamentalism is not a very important ideology in most parts of Canada today. Seymour Martin Lipset (1990) notes that ideologies in America are often intensely moralistic. They are the bases for recurring movements to eliminate evil. The tendency to see the "other" as an agent of Satan has deep roots in American history. It has been expressed in a variety of confrontations with "evil empires," a term applied to the former Soviet Union in the context of the anticommunist zeal of the post–Second World War period. By contrast, Canadians have generally been more willing to tolerate a measure of human imperfection and to accept that opponents are not necessarily completely evil. Box 29.1 illustrates the point.

Ruling Ideas

Despite their ideological differences in certain areas, Canadians and Americans have similar interests in the ideology of the free market economy. This is one of the most powerful ideologies in the world today. For example, it provides the theoretical underpinning for policies to increase trade between countries through treaties such as the North American Free Trade Agreement (NAFTA).

SOURCE: Excerpted from David Cheal, "Culture and the Postmodern," pp. 7.11–7.12 and 7.5–7.6, and Graham Knight, "The Mass Media," pp. 8.8–8.11, in Robert J. Brym, ed., *New Society: Sociology for the 21st Century* (Toronto: Harcourt Brace, 1995). Reprinted by permission of the publisher.

The ideology of the free market describes social change in terms of a struggle for survival among individuals, companies, and countries as they compete with one another for scarce resources. It explains current problems as the result of interference by governments, because they tend to drive up the cost of doing business and so make industries in certain places uncompetitive. The market ideology proposes solutions to this situation by reducing government intervention in the management of trade and by cutting expensive government programs. Finally, the market ideology suggests concrete strategies, such as negotiated agreements between governments of different countries stipulating that each is to stop subsidizing certain industries domestically and is to reduce duties on imported goods. Although the ideology of the free market economy has been very influential in recent years, it is by no means new. It has been around for well over two centuries, although the extent of its influence has fluctuated over the years.

In 1848, a German writer living in England gave a speech in Brussels that went almost unnoticed. In it, he outlined the sociology of the market ideology. He argued that this system of ideas was created and communicated by people who stood to gain the most from it. He thought that industrial workers would benefit very little because their wages would fall, but that the owners of industry would make bigger profits as a result of their lower manufacturing costs. Therefore, he argued, workers and owners could not relate identically to the free market ideology. The speaker insisted that, although the people who argued for free trade claimed it to be in the general interest of everybody, in reality it served the particular interests of those capitalists who had invested their money in manufacturing. The speaker was Karl Marx (1976).

Marxist sociologists view ideologies such as that of the free market as forms of **hegemony**. What they mean by this is that the most influential ideas, the "ruling ideas," are the ones that benefit the wealthiest economic class. The class of wealthy owners, or the ruling class, is generally successful in making its ideas appear to be the only plausible or

---

Box 29.1 Core Values in Canadian Culture

Between November 1, 1990, and July 1, 1991, some 400 000 Canadians participated in an unprecedented process of national consultation. That process was known as the Citizens' Forum on Canada's Future. Citizens who spoke to the Forum focussed on what it meant to them to be Canadians. They expressed their sense of a distinct Canadian identity that sets Canadians apart from Americans and from people in other countries. The final report from the Forum presented the following list of core values that emerged strongly from participants in all regions of Canada:

- ◆ Belief in equality and fairness in a democratic society
- ◆ Belief in consultation and dialogue
- ◆ Importance of accommodation and tolerance
- ◆ Support for diversity
- ◆ Compassion and generosity
- ◆ Attachment to Canada's natural beauty
- ◆ Commitment to freedom, peace, and non-violent change in world affairs

SOURCE: Based on Citizens' Forum on Canada's Future, *Citizens' Forum on Canada's Future: Report to the People and Government of Canada* (Ottawa: Minister of Supply and Services, 1991).

---

feasible ideas. People who are not as well off therefore accept their lesser economic fortune because they believe what they have is the best deal they can get, or because they believe it is the outcome of a system that is basically just.

MASS MEDIA

One of the main ways in which certain ideas come to dominate popular thinking is through their diffusion by the media. The mass media are means of communicating messages to very large numbers of people. They depend on a variety of technologies for recording and copying symbols, and for sending them across great distances. Books, newspapers, and magazines, as well as movies and radio and television programs, are distributed to large numbers of individuals, who are thereby exposed to identical messages from the same source. As a result, the mass media have contributed greatly to increased cultural diffusion in this century.

Cultural diffusion is the spreading of ideas from their original source to other places, which may be very remote. For example, movies made in the United States have exported the subculture of American truckers to long-distance truck drivers in Norway. One consequence is that some of the latter now prefer to communicate via CB radio in English rather than Norwegian.

The long-term effects of cultural diffusion can be enormous. The fall of the Berlin Wall and the collapse of communism in Eastern Europe were attributable in part to the fact that the Communist regimes could not prevent their populations from being exposed to information about Western lifestyles and consumer goods. Local shortages of desirable goods, such as jeans, which are part of the international culture of youth, contributed to the alienation of teenagers in Eastern Europe in particular.

REPRESENTATION AND IDEOLOGY: THE MEANING OF THE MESSAGE

The media communicate on different levels — the pleasurable as well as the meaningful, the entertaining as well as the informative. Such communication entails the process of representation, that is, the use of language, visual images, and other symbolic tools to create messages people can understand and find satisfying or enjoyable. Representation, however, is a selective process. It involves countless decisions — only some of which are conscious — about what is to be included and what is to be left out, what is to be emphasized and what is to be downplayed, and about the sequence in which the elements are to be connected into a coherent message. Any representation — a news report, an advertisement, a TV show — is ideological to the extent that it contains any particular inflection or bias. Every representation is only one of several ways of seeing and talking about something.

News and Ideology

Outside our immediate experience, the news media are one of our principal sources of information about social reality. Conservative and critical writers have disagreed considerably about the nature of selectivity in the news, and its ideological effects. Conservatives argue that the news media have a "left-liberal" bias that runs counter to the views and interests of the mainstream of society. They believe that this bias operates in two ways: (1) the media give disproportionate attention to the views of more marginal and/or radical interest groups and constituencies, such as unions and environmentalists, at the expense of the majority, and (2) the media concentrate on negative events, issues, and news angles, ignoring the positive aspects of social life (see Box 29.2).

The conservative perspective is evident in the work of the National Media Archive (NMA), which analyzes news coverage of major issues and events, comparing different media in terms of extent of coverage, angle of the coverage, and types of sources used. In its analysis of immigration coverage, for example, the NMA found that both CBC and CTV "rather than reporting the successes . . . focussed on the negative experiences of refugees and immigrants in Canada" (National Media Archive, 1993: 3). CBC reporters, in particular, have been identified as guilty of unbalanced coverage: "CBC journalists were more than twice as likely to express negative as positive views on privatization, free trade, the management position in labour disputes, and private delivery of health-care services" (National Media Archive, 1989: 7). Although NMA research does not systematically examine the origins of these biases, its analyses imply that they stem primarily from the individual biases of reporters, editors, and other news staff.

In contrast to the conservative perspective, those who employ a critical perspective believe that the news media function chiefly to reproduce dominant ideology. This is not seen as a conscious conspiracy,

Box 29.2 The Conservative Critique: Is News Too Negative?

Anybody scanning the news would be hard pressed to avoid concluding that the Canadian economy is dog-paddling into a sludge of slow growth and perpetual joblessness. *Maclean's* magazine set the national tone with a cover headline six centimetres high that said: "1,550,000 UNEMPLOYED: Will they find work in the '90s?"

The same headline, of course, could have been written ten years ago. In fact, it often was. In early 1983, the total number of unemployed in Canada reached 1 512 000, generating a stream of stories about how the unemployment rate will remain high for years to come. Where on earth, everybody asked then as they do now, will the jobs come from?

Other themes from a decade ago: The unemployment rate didn't really capture the true level of unemployment because it didn't include all the discouraged workers who simply gave up looking. Youth unemployment remained disturbingly high and job prospects looked impossible. Most jobs, moreover, were part-time rather than full-time.

That was 1983, when unemployment peaked at 12.8 percent and the headline was: Will they find work in the 1980s? In the following years, of course, the number of jobs created soared, contrary to the worst expectations. They *did* find work.

As the graph shows, the number of jobs—employed people—rose to more than 12.5 million from 10.5 million in 1983. Two million jobs created during the period drove the unemployment rate down to 7.5 percent.

Despite all the turmoil of the past two years, including the rise in the unemployment rate to a high of 11.6 percent, the number of people employed has remained well above 12 million. In recent months, it has been climbing, reaching 12 431 000 in June, about 200 000 more jobs than existed in June last year.

The Canadian economy also continues today to produce a healthy amount of goods and services relative to 1983. In constant 1986 dollars, average output per person is currently about $20 000—$2000 higher than in 1983.

Another measure of employment in the economy is the number of people working as a proportion of total population. More people work in Canada today as a percentage of the population (about 58 percent) than worked during the same period of the slump of the early 1980s, when the employment rate fell to below 56 percent.

The decline in the proportion of people working during the past three years has many causes that do not justify the current national depression over the state of the economy or the level of unemployment.

Employment Rebound

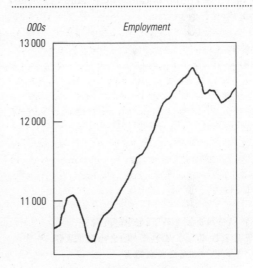

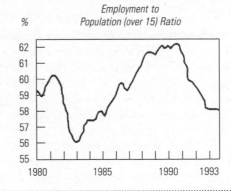

DATA: Statistics Canada

(continued)

Immigration alone accounts for a significant change in the numbers. Between 1988 and 1993, more than one million immigrants arrived in Canada.

Exactly how many of these people have been looking for jobs and have been showing up among the unemployed is not known. But there's no doubt that if you add a million people to the population just as the economy is going through a recession and recovery, the employment statistics are inevitably going to be thrown a curve.

Our understanding of the labour market and the non-working population is also seriously deficient. Statistics Canada has only recently started to investigate the 7.5 million Canadians not in the labour force. Who are they? Why are they not working? A recent Statistics Canada study, the first of its kind, found that more than half are over the age of 70, and another 1.5 million people over the age of 50 describe themselves as retired. Others cite disabilities, child-care responsibilities, or a simple lack of interest in working.

Canada's unemployment rate is nothing to be complacent about. Three or four decades ago, 4 percent unemployment was considered high. There is obviously a problem somewhere. But it should not be, as it is today, a cause of national anguish. Jobs can and will be created.

SOURCE: Terence Corcoran, "12,431,000 Employed—And Climbing!" *The Globe and Mail*, July 30, 1993, p. B2. Reprinted by permission of *The Globe and Mail*.

---

but as the unconscious effect of the values and practices that journalists employ when they define and gather news. Let us consider the critical perspective in greater detail.

DEFINING THE NEWS

What is news? In the first place, it is a representation of reality that is unavoidably selective. We must therefore ask what are the criteria, or **news values**, that the media use to select what goes into the newspaper or the newscast.

As the word itself implies, news is about what is new or immediate. Although the media are often unable to capture events as they actually happen, the accent is on reporting them as quickly as possible after they have occurred. *Immediacy* has always been a major element in the competition between different media, and the history of media technology is dominated by the goal of making communication faster. Whenever possible, news is written in the present tense, to convey the sense that events are occurring as they are being reported, and to compensate for the fact that the media often get to the scene of an event only after it has already taken place.

The emphasis on immediacy, however, goes beyond the present and into the future. To generate interest and curiosity on the part of the audience, news stories attempt to create a sense of uncertainty about what will happen next. The effect of this approach is that news tends to be concerned with the consequences of events and issues at the expense of their causes and development (Knight, 1982b). Causes belong to the past, and news generally lacks a strong sense of historical perspective and context.

When news does deal with causes and explanations, it often reduces them to the level of individual motives and individual psychology. This is an effect of *personalization*. To communicate with an anonymous audience, news has to make events that are often remote from everyday experience more concrete and more familiar in order to enable the reader or viewer to identify with them. The consequent emphasis on personalities has been intensified by the growth of TV news, where the need to be visual makes it even more difficult to deal in abstractions (such as unemployment) and even easier to deal with people (such as the unemployed). The personalizing effect of TV news was especially apparent in coverage of the Gulf War, which seemed at times to be reduced to a conflict between just two men, George Bush and Saddam Hussein.

In political news coverage, the media spotlight typically shines primarily on leading political figures such as prime ministers and opposition leaders, and it does so at the expense of a fuller understanding of the political processes and structures within which these people operate. The emphasis on personalities is even more narrowly focussed during elections, when the media are almost completely preoccupied with the actions and statements of the major party leaders and with the "horserace" between them for first place at the polls (Wilson, 1980; Knight and Taylor, 1986). The effect of this emphasis on personalities is that the media tend to overlook the more substantive aspects of political policy (Taras, 1990).

Despite their importance, immediacy and personalization are nevertheless secondary news values. The cardinal or primary value is that news concerns events and issues that are *out of the ordinary*, and entail *conflict, confrontation, deviance*, or *disorder* (Hall et al., 1978; Knight, 1982a). The implication of this, as conservative critics also point out, is that news is normally about the negative. For critical theorists, however, the negative emphasis of news does not undermine mainstream values and beliefs, but in fact reinforces dominant ideology in at least two ways.

First, by dwelling on the negative, news invokes and reproduces dominant definitions of what is socially normal and desirable. It identifies events and actors that deviate from these definitions, and represents them as a threat to what is socially desirable (Knight, 1982a). News media do not work in a vacuum, inventing the reality they represent out of thin air. Rather, they take up the dominant values, assumptions, and understandings of the society in which they are themselves embedded. The raw materials of news are already given in the preoccupations and concerns of the wider social context. These preoccupations and concerns, however, are themselves the result of an ongoing selection process that values the experiences and viewpoints of dominant groups over those of others. The events and issues that make it into the news are already defined in negative terms — as dangerous, sickening, bizarre, threatening, and so on — by the dominant culture.

By assuming that the dominant culture generally reflects the interests, values, and understandings of society as a whole, the news media tend to reproduce a tacit consensus about what is right and wrong, normal and deviant, desirable and undesirable. One effect of this is to exclude or downplay oppositional and alternative perspectives by associating them with deviant or marginal behaviour. In his study of press coverage of the peace movement in Canada during the 1980s, for example, Hackett (1991) shows how the orientation to "bad" news helped stigmatize peace activists by focussing on the visibly more disruptive aspects of their actions, such as street demonstrations, at the expense of their arguments about the need for arms control and disarmament.

Second, news coverage of deviance and conflict tends to focus on the actions of the appropriate social-control authorities — the government, the police, the experts — to restore social order and limit disruptive effects. Newsworthy events and issues come to the attention of the media because the media rely on organized ways of knowing about the activities of official control agencies and organizations, including news releases, phone tip-offs from inside contacts, and routine monitoring of the radio communications of the police and other emergency services. Because they exercise official authority, these agencies are seen as the major source of credible and reliable information about what has happened, how it has happened, who is involved, and what the immediate consequences seem to be.

Crime news, for example, consists largely of information derived from the police about incidents of law-breaking. This information deals primarily with police activities and procedures such as investigation, interrogation of witnesses and suspects, and the charging of the accused (Ericson et al., 1989). The ideological effect is that the media view crime from the perspective of the police and police procedures. Consequently, deviance and disorder are represented in the news as discrete, isolated events, rather than as broader social processes that are part of the structure and functioning of society. They are, moreover, portrayed after the fact, in terms of the process of social control and restoration of order by the authorities. In this way, the threat of bad news is offset by reassurance that things are being put right: news of crime is news of police activities to solve crime and catch offenders.

REFERENCES

Ericson, R., et al. (1989). *Negotiating Control: A Study of News Sources.* Toronto: University of Toronto Press.

Hackett, R. (1991). *News and Dissent: The Press and the Politics of Peace in Canada.* Norwood, NJ: Ablex.

Hall, S., et al. (1978). *Policing the Crisis: Mugging, the State and Law and Order.* London: Macmillan.

Knight, G. (1982a). "News and Ideology." *Canadian Journal of Communication, 8*(4), 15–41.

Knight, G. (1982b). "Strike Talk: A Case Study of News." *Canadian Journal of Communication, 8*(3), 61–79.

Knight, G., and I. Taylor. (1986). "News and Political Consensus: CBC Television and the 1983 British Election." *Canadian Review of Sociology and Anthropology, 23*, 230–46.

Lipset, S.M. (1990). *Continental Divide.* New York: Routledge.

Marx, K. (1976). Speech on the question of free trade, delivered to the Democratic Association of Brussels at its public meeting of January 9, 1848. In K. Marx and F. Engels, *Karl Marx and Friedrich Engels: Collected Works.* Vol. 6 (pp. 450–65). New York: International Publishers.

National Media Archive. (1989). "Priming Canadian Media Audiences." *On Balance, II*(6), 1–8. Vancouver: Fraser Institute.

National Media Archive. (1993). "Immigration I: The Human Interest Story." *On Balance, 6*(3), 1–8. Vancouver: Fraser Institute.

Taras, D. (1990). *The Newsmakers: The Media's Influence on Canadian Politics.* Scarborough, Ont.: Nelson.

Wilson, J. (1980). "Media Coverage of a Canadian Election Campaign: Horserace Journalism and the Meta-Campaign." *Journal of Canadian Studies, 15*(4), 56–68.

Public Opinion, the Media, and the Political Agenda

RICHARD JENKINS

Since 1980, Canada has undergone significant social, economic, and political changes. A period of economic growth in the 1980s was bracketed by two recessions, both of which were characterized by high unemployment and economic restructuring. The Constitution was patriated in 1982 without the approval of the Quebec government, and the failures of the Meech Lake and Charlottetown Accords would follow within a decade. Canada entered a free trade agreement with the United States, the deficit continued to grow, and the aboriginal peoples demanded to have their voices heard.

In the context of these events and changes, how do members of the public come to their evaluations of the political agenda? The *political agenda* refers to a set of issues ordered in terms of their importance for the community and in particular for government action. This paper examines the agenda-setting hypothesis — that is, that political manipulation or media coverage sets the political agenda — and alternatively the possibility that public concern is driven chiefly by changes in real conditions and not by political or media manipulation. The second hypothesis is that the process by which an issue becomes *salient* for the public is dependent upon the degree to which the issue is grounded in day-to-day experience. One would expect there to be a different process involved for symbolic as opposed to non-symbolic issues.

These hypotheses will be considered by analyzing how the salience of unemployment and national unity changed in relation to the unemployment rate and other real-world events, and the amount of media coverage of these issues between 1980 and 1992. These two issues were chosen because political events and economic changes made them potentially salient at times during the period of study. They also represent different issue areas, which enables a preliminary analysis of the second hypothesis, that agenda-setting is more likely to occur when the issue is of a symbolic nature.

IDENTIFYING PUBLIC OPINION ABOUT THE POLITICAL AGENDA

Public opinion about the political agenda is basically a measure of the salience of issues in a political system, where salience includes both a realization of the problem and an attachment of priority or importance to that issue.[1] The public does not prefer one issue over another, but rather one issue is more salient or more of a priority. The most important problem question is the general approach for quantifying this type of public opinion.

One of the central debates in the study of public opinion revolves around the question of whether public opinion is meaningful or short-lived and

SOURCE: "Public Opinion, the Media, and the Political Agenda," unpublished paper. An earlier version of this paper was presented at the Annual Meeting of the Canadian Political Science Association, Calgary, 1994. Reprinted by permission of the author.

whether it is subject to manipulation and persuasion.[2] The literature on agenda-setting gives the media a considerable role in the salience of issues for the public through coverage of issues and the ability to put a **spin** on the content of the news.

One important consideration that may help us understand how issues become salient for the public is the role of predispositions in orienting the public to react in certain ways to events and news coverage. In the spirit of Converse, MacKuen makes the argument that the public is "open" to influence about what issues are important because "Citizen political priorities are apparently not firmly embedded in a broader conceptual framework."[3] One needs to consider whether the public may have ways of reacting to issues that affect what becomes a high priority on the political agenda.

In developing views about what issues are important, the public has several potential sources of information. The first is personal information derived from one's own life situation. For example, one may be or may know someone who is unemployed. If personal experience is relevant to a person's view of the political agenda, then the question becomes, Why does an issue go from a private to a public concern?

The second is that the state of national or regional conditions is a key determinant of the agenda. In this sense, individuals act as citizens making judgements and evaluating consequences in the formation of their view of the agenda. For these types of judgements, one would expect the media to play a role as a supplier of information, often by means of **investigative journalism**.

Some have taken an extreme position that everything people know is derived either second or third hand from the media.[4] For example, Page, Shapiro, and Dempsey claim that "nearly everyone is exposed either directly or indirectly to what the media broadcast."[5] In contrast, Samuel Popkin, in making the argument that the media and daily-life information interact, recognizes the importance of personal experience.[6] The agenda-setting hypothesis has a particular way of understanding the type of information that the media supply and the public uses.

THE AGENDA-SETTING ROLE OF THE MEDIA

"Agenda-setting" refers to the ability of the media to tell people what to think about, while not being able to tell them what to think.[7] For example, the media are able to tell the public that they should be concerned with the abortion issue but are unable to persuade them to share their view as to which side of the issue is the correct one. The media have this effect because the public uses the amount of coverage as a cue that the issue is important; it is in this sense that the media are thought of as **gatekeepers**. As a result, the political agenda is imposed on the public and some evidence has suggested that this affects how the public evaluates candidates and parties.[8]

A considerable amount of evidence has been gathered that supports the agenda-setting hypothesis. Iyengar and Kinder use an experimental approach to show direct links between the amount of coverage and the amount of concern with issues.[9] Others rely on comparing the amount of media content (number of stories) with the level of public concern with an issue.

This latter strategy has been challenged because it ignores the effect of "real-world" conditions and individual characteristics on the salience of issues. In defence, McCombs and Shaw argue that one cannot support the conclusion that the media/opinion association is artificial unless one "assumes that voters have alternative ways of observing day-to-day changes in the political arena."[10]

In fact, when researchers have considered "real-world" conditions in their models, they have sometimes found important exceptions to the agenda-setting theory. Several U.S. studies have shown that the variation over time in unemployment salience is a function of real-world conditions, not of the coverage provided by the media, despite the importance of the media in other issue areas.[11]

Given the finding that agenda-setting does not occur for some issues, such as unemployment, there is some support for Neuman's observation that the effectiveness of agenda-setting is constrained by the type of issue involved.[12] The public responds to different issues in different ways.

Neuman develops a four-category classification system: crisis, symbolic crisis, problems, and non-problems. A crisis issue is defined by being a real-world condition that is limited in time, such as the dramatic rise in oil prices in the 1970s. A symbolic crisis is the result of an enduring social problem being transformed into a crisis for a limited period of time. Problems and non-problems are less clear, but generally refer to the existence or non-existence of a real-world change in conditions. For Neuman, unemployment is a problem and crime is a non-problem.

In studying the dynamics of public opinion about the agenda, it is important to recognize that there may be more than one process at work. The reasons why some issues are salient for the public may not explain the salience of other issues. Rather than pursuing Neuman's rather complex categorization, it may be more useful to consider the difference between symbolic and non-symbolic issues. The difference between the issues may sometimes be unclear, but is based on the extent to which the issue involves an actual change in societal conditions, whether or not the issue is based in the everyday experiences of the public, and the nature of the discourse used by the media and political elites to communicate the importance of the issue.

The assumption is that the media will have a larger effect with regard to symbolic issues because the public must rely on cues from the media about the importance of these issues. Other issues, such as inflation, are so intrusive into everyday life that the public does not need the media to find out about them. The issues of national unity and unemployment allow for an investigation into the possibly different processes involved in the salience of one kind of issue compared with another.

A key factor in how members of the public respond to the unemployment issue is the more general way in which they understand economic changes. Based on the assumption that the public follows the state of economic conditions (both national and personal), many people have sought to identify the political consequences of economic conditions. The evidence so far is inconclusive and the findings depend largely upon the mode and level of analysis. Nevertheless, attitudes about economic issues appear to reflect perceived changes in the economic environment.

Evaluations of how the economy is performing and evaluations of how the federal government is managing the economy move in the same direction as economic conditions. Johnston (1986) argued, based on his analysis of responses before 1984 to a question he asked, "what is the most important problem," that the public tends to feel an issue is "important" when the measure of that problem crosses a particular threshold; hence, when unemployment and inflation are high, they need to be addressed.[13] Depending on the ability of the government to enhance the performance of the economy, the salience of these issues in the mind of the public will diminish or intensify in response to changing economic conditions.

The national unity issue has consumed a considerable amount of political energy in the past twenty years, without a successful resolution. While Canadians have preferences for how they would like to see the issue resolved, the issue is not grounded in the daily life experiences of most people. During the course of everyday life, few things arise that bear directly on the national question. While the distribution of powers between the federal and provincial governments may have implications for the lives of Canadians, it is unlikely that most people recognize them, because federal and provincial powers do not have a real-life manifestation, as unemployment does.

The two issues will be considered independently, starting with a look at how the change in salience of these issues relates to actual conditions and ending with an examination of the agenda-setting hypothesis.

THE DYNAMICS OF THE SALIENCE OF UNEMPLOYMENT FOR THE PUBLIC

Issues become salient and then become dormant in a manner that appears to be consistent with the general economic and social circumstances of the time.

The 1980s began with large percentages of people citing inflation and national unity as the most important problems facing Canada [according to the Johnston study], but after 1982, inflation was of only minor importance. National unity did, however, resurface and capture the attention of the public in the early 1990s. About 10 percent of Canadians regarded government and taxation as the most important category until the end of the 1980s, when there was a significant climb in its salience. This climb was probably driven by the public's reaction to the Goods and Services Tax (GST). International concerns were significant only when the Free Trade Agreement (FTA) became a salient political issue, despite international problems such as the Gulf War. Another thing worth mentioning is the lack of concern with energy and interest rates for most of the decade.

The salience of unemployment for the public tends to follow the prevailing economic climate. For the first two years of the 1980s, unemployment was considered the most important problem by about 10 percent of the population. During the recession of the early 1980s concern with unemployment rose quickly, to 48 percent in the spring of 1983 and over 50 percent for two quarters in 1984. Despite the economic recovery that began in 1984, the issue did not return to its pre-recession level of public concern until the last quarter of 1988, which is consistent with the way that the unemployment rate dropped during the recovery. At the beginning of the second recessionary period, concern about employment rose, but it is important to note that it never reached the high rate that it had during the earlier recession.

Unemployment and Inflation as Salient Concerns

Traditionally, economic policy was couched in terms of the trade-off between unemployment and inflation as macroeconomic policy goals. Consequently, when considering how public concern

changes in relation to unemployment, we need to consider the effect of the inflation rate as well as the unemployment rate.

Richard Johnston analyzed the relationship between public opinion on unemployment and inflation and the actual rates of unemployment and inflation between 1980 and 1984. Extending the analysis through to 1992, there are only minor changes: The data continue to support Johnston's conclusion that Canadians are "more sensitive, in the short run, to unemployment than to inflation, but with an underlying permanent bias against inflation."[14]

A one-percentage-point change in the unemployment rate produces a change of more than 5 percentage points in the proportion of people who rate unemployment as our most important problem, and a rise of one percentage point in the inflation rate is associated with about a one-point rise in public concern about inflation.

As the unemployment rate returned to its pre-recession level in about 1986, several issues emerged and gained significant public attention. After the 1984 election, the Conservative government, following a recommendation by the Macdonald Royal Commission, negotiated the Free Trade Agreement with the United States. Public concern with the FTA is included in the "International Concerns" coding category in Johnston's study, which registers its first significant rise in the fall of 1986. From the fall of 1987, when the Liberal-controlled Senate blocked the agreement, to the winter of 1989, more than 20 percent of the public was concerned with this issue.[15] While the FTA is important in and of itself, it is also important to remember that one of the central themes of the discourse on the FTA was its potential effect on jobs. Consequently, some of the drop in unemployment concern may reflect a shift away from current conditions to future considerations driven by the FTA.

The second issue to gain public attention was the introduction of the Goods and Services Tax (GST). There is no doubt that the GST was universally hated by the public from its inception. In early 1989, there was a significant climb in the proportion citing a government/taxes concern, which can be attributed to the GST. In the summer of 1990, 30 percent of the public was concerned with this issue, and concern remained high into 1991. Although the GST, unlike the FTA, has no direct effect on unemployment, it clearly affected all Canadians in a monetary way that everyone could identify. It is not surprising that concern with unemployment was not rising as swiftly as it had in the early 1980s, given that many people were experiencing the hardship of the GST at the same time.

Finally, in the late 1980s and early 1990s, unlike in the early 1980s, unemployment and national unity were salient at the same time. While national unity is the subject of analysis in the latter half of this paper, it is important to reinforce the fact that issues are salient in the context of competing priorities.

The Role of the Media in the Process of Issue Salience

One possible explanation for the public's awareness of the unemployment rate and for the difference in public concern about unemployment between the early and late 1980s is the news coverage of the issue by the media. In considering the role of the media, one must deal with three questions. How did the newspapers cover the issue? Did the coverage change in relation to changes in the rate of unemployment? And, can the agenda-setting hypothesis explain the change in concern with unemployment between 1980 and 1992?

There is an identifiable pattern to the newspaper coverage of the unemployment issue between 1980 and 1992. For most of the period, there were fewer than 40 stories per quarter, but between the first quarter of 1982 and the first quarter of 1985, there was a dramatic rise in that number. Leading up to 1981 the average number of articles per quarter was 22, but over the course of the next two years the average rose to 144. The bulge continued through the recession of the early 1980s, when unemployment rose above 10 percent. Interestingly, however, when the unemployment rate rose above 10 percent again in 1990, the number of articles increased only slightly.

One would expect that coverage of unemployment would reflect changes in the unemployment situation. Behr and Iyengar's study of the United States between 1974 and 1980 shows that national economic conditions do affect the amount of unemployment coverage.

> A shift of .25 percent *in either direction* in the level of unemployment brings forth four additional stories on that subject, while a change of slightly over .5 percent warrants a lead story.[16]

In Canada newspaper coverage between 1980 and 1992 resembled but diverged significantly from the actual unemployment rate. Much of the divergence can be explained by the overwhelming coverage of the issue during the first recession, followed by more modest coverage during the second recession.

Given this pattern it is arguable that the media could have been engaged in agenda-setting by leading the public to attach more or less significance to the issue than would be merited based on the unemployment rate itself. The 1980–92 period is a useful example because it took into account two recessions and a mid-term period of growth, so one would expect that there was room for agenda-setting to occur. The number of newspaper stories did not, however, lead the public to be more concerned with unemployment. No agenda-setting effects were evident.

It should be remembered, however, that Canadians have been sensitized to the issue of unemployment because of past media exposure and no longer rely on the amount of coverage as a signal of issue importance.[17] So while agenda-setting is not evident after 1980, this finding may be explained by the public's consciousness of the issue and the general politicization of the economy. This would suggest that the public has predispositions and a framework for understanding some of the information that they receive.

The salience of unemployment changed dramatically throughout the period of study and these changes in public opinion reflect changes in the actual unemployment rate. Because there was no effect of the media on the public's perception of the importance of unemployment, it is clear that the media did not have agenda-setting effects. The media may or may not have influenced public opinion by providing information about the state of the economy to the public, but the amount of coverage was irrelevant. While we did not test directly for the relationship between opinion change and elite direction, the strong link between opinion and the rate would suggest only minor effects. This would confirm the observation made by Nadeau and Blais that "It would seem that incumbent governments in Canada have been unable to escape the blame for, or direct attention from, rising unemployment."[18]

THE NATIONAL UNITY ISSUE

Before examining how public opinion about the importance of national unity changed between 1980 and 1992, it is important to clarify what it means to be concerned with national unity. A concern with national unity reflects a concern with the character of the nation and in particular the relationship between English and French Canada and is therefore not limited to a fear that Quebec will separate.

The importance of national unity for the public changes significantly from 1980 to 1992. While a significant percentage considered it a matter of importance in 1980 and into 1981, between summer of 1982 and the winter of 1989, national unity never scored higher than 7 percent. During the early 1990s, it was a salient concern for a sizable minority of the public. Thus in the two periods of sustained government activity in the realm of the Constitution, national unity was more salient for the public than at other times. Despite these changes, national unity never reached the high levels of salience found with unemployment. At the peak of concern only 30 percent of the public felt that national unity was the most important problem.

Relationship Between Public Opinion Change and the Real World

Although there is no direct way to quantify the "real-world" manifestation of the national unity issue in the manner that the unemployment rate quantifies unemployment, one can make observations about the relationship between public concern and the context of the issue. Government activity preceded public concern about national unity, and without government activity only a minuscule proportion of the public was concerned about the issue. Consider, for example, the period around Meech Lake. The level of concern about national unity did not rise significantly until months after the agreement was signed.

At any given time between the summer of 1981 and the winter of 1989, less than 10 percent of the public was concerned about national unity. Political elites explained the need for a constitutional agreement by referring to the fact that Quebec had not signed the Constitution in 1982, but public opinion in the country as a whole showed a general lack of concern with national unity during the period preceding the 1987 accord.

While the constitutional debate in Canada has implications for all of Canada, Quebec has been the key protagonist in the debate because it did not assent to the constitutional amendments of 1982. As a result, it is important to determine the extent to which the Quebec public differed from the rest of Canadians in feeling that national unity was the most important problem.

The province of Quebec does differ from the rest of Canada with respect to the salience of national unity, but it does so in a particular way. In general, being from Quebec tends to increase the chance of feeling that national unity is the most important problem when the activities of governments are focused on addressing the national question. During other periods, however, Quebecers, like other Canadians, are more concerned with other issues.

The Role of the Media

In order to understand the role of the media in affecting the importance of the national unity issue as a public concern, it is necessary to answer two questions. How does the media cover the national unity issue and is the salience of the national unity issue related to this coverage?

The newspapers devoted a substantial amount of their coverage to constitutional issues, specifically focused on the periods of constitutional negotiations. Coverage of the issue takes dramatic swings in response to events, often as a result of **pack journalism**.

Public opinion followed the pattern of newspaper coverage very closely. Concern rose with events and the increase in coverage. For every 100 stories, the level of concern with national unity increases by 1 percent.

For our purposes, finding that there is a strong association between media coverage and public opinion is consistent with the literature on agenda-setting. This is significant in the light of the finding that there is a lack of agenda-setting with regard to the unemployment issue. It may be the case, however, that real-world conditions, which are difficult to measure, are a significant influence on opinion about the importance of national unity. Nevertheless, the importance of the media–opinion association cannot be dismissed, because even if real-world conditions are a major causal factor, the media are covering them in such a way as to mirror the changes.

Constitutional negotiations are primarily the object of elite discourse and preoccupation. The media played a role in informing the public about the problem, and public opinion responded. The public, however, did not respond to the issue to the same extent that they did to the unemployment issue. Hence, the national unity issue can appropriately be described as an enduring problem that is unlikely to be resolved in the short term, and "a combination of events and the responses of government, the public and the media leads to a public

definition of the issue as a problem of crisis proportions." [19] While the Quebec public was more likely to feel the issue was important and responded more quickly to the presence of the issue on the agenda, this follows from its more direct interest in the outcome of the constitutional negotiations.

CONCLUSIONS

Several observations can be drawn from the study of unemployment and national unity as public concerns. Of primary importance is that the public's definition of the political agenda is not simply derived from the media or political elites, although some issues and some people are susceptible to these influences.

The environment plays a substantial role in the importance of some issues for the public. The unemployment issue demonstrated this most clearly; the unemployment rate was a good predictor of the level of concern with unemployment.

National unity was only a concern during periods when changes were proposed to the constitutional order. While it seems reasonable to expect that public concern would rise during periods of constitutional change merely because of the possible implications of that change for Canada, it is arguable that the issue was constructed as a problem to which the public responded. Thus the elites set the agenda and set the environment in which public opinion developed.

The evidence for agenda-setting is contradictory. Media coverage was not associated with the public's concern about unemployment. If the media played a role in the salience of this issue, it was limited to supplying information about the state of the national economy and in particular the change in the unemployment rate to which the public reacted; more or less coverage in and of itself did not provide the public with new information.

Media coverage was, however, a good predictor of the public's concern with national unity. The public reacted to the issue, at least to some degree, because of the existence of it in the media and the activities of political elites and not because of fundamental concern with national unity or the Constitution. National unity never reached the high level of salience that is found with other issues, however, which suggests that the public is less responsive to direct cues from political elites or indirect ones from the media.

Throughout the period of study both issues revealed that there is a tendency for the public to come to a collective view of the most important problem. The way that the salience of issues changed across time as reflected in the responses to the "most important problem" question cannot be explained simply by the changed circumstances of individuals. For example, in 1983 almost half of the population felt that unemployment was the most important issue, but this does not reflect the number of people affected by the increase in the unemployment rate.

The findings from the unemployment and national unity case studies support the hypothesis that the characteristics of the issue are important for understanding the role of the media and the general process by which issues become salient.

NOTES

Public opinion data used in this paper were originally collected by Decima Research. The data were made available by Queen's University, Kingston, Ontario. Neither the original source or collectors of the data nor Queen's University bear any responsibility for the analyses or interpretations presented here. Special thanks to Professors George Perlin and Monroe Eagles.

1. John Geer, "Do Open-Ended Questions Measure 'Salient' Issues?" *Public Opinion Quarterly* (1991) 55: 361.

2. See Philip Converse, "The Nature of Beliefs in Mass Publics," in David Apter, ed., *Ideology and Discontent* (New York: Free Press, 1964), and John Zaller, *The Nature and Origins of Mass Opinion* (New York: Cambridge University Press, 1992) for general discussions of the debate about the meaningfulness of public opinion.

3. Michael MacKuen, "Exposure to Information, Belief Integration, and Individual Responsiveness to Agenda Change," *American Political Science Review* (1984) 78: 382.

4. Kurt Lang and Gladys Lang, "The Mass Media and Voting," in Bernard Berelson and Morris Janowitz, eds., *Reader in Public Opinion and Communication*, 2nd ed. (New York: Free Press, 1966), p. 466.

5. Benjamin Page, Robert Shapiro, and Glen Dempsey, "What Moves Public Opinion?" *American Political Science Review* (1987) 81: 25.

6. Samuel Popkin, *The Reasoning Voter* (Chicago: University of Chicago Press, 1991), p. 27.

7. Maxwell E. McCombs and Donald L. Shaw, "The Agenda-Setting Function of the Mass Media," *Public Opinion Quarterly* (1972) 36: 177.

8. See Shanto Iyengar, *Is Anyone Responsible?* (Chicago: University of Chicago Press, 1991); Arthur Miller, Lutz Erbring, and Edie Goldenberg, "Typeset Politics," *American Political Science Review* (1979) 73: 67–84.

9. Shanto Iyengar and Donald Kinder, *News That Matters* (Chicago: University of Chicago Press, 1987).

10. McCombs and Shaw, "The Agenda-Setting Function," p. 185.

11. Roy Behr and Shanto Iyengar, "Television News, Real-World Cues, and Changes in the Public Agenda," *Public Opinion Quarterly* (1985) 49: 50, and Michael MacKuen, "Social Communication and the Mass Policy Agenda," in M. MacKuen and C. Coombs, eds., *More than News: Media Power in Public Affairs* (Beverly Hills: Sage, 1981), p. 91.

12. W. Russell Neuman, "The Threshold of Public Attention," *Public Opinion Quarterly* (1990) 54: 169.

13. Richard Johnston, *Public Opinion and Public Policy in Canada* (Toronto: University of Toronto Press, 1986), p. 138.

14. Johnston, *Public Opinion*, p. 124.

15. There were no other equally visible issues during this rise, and given the generally low percentage of people concerned about international issues as revealed by the data, we can be confident that the FTA is the driving issue in public concern.

16. Behr and Iyengar, "Television News," pp. 45–46.

17. MacKuen, "Social Communication," p. 97.

18. Richard Nadeau and André Blais, "Explaining Election Outcomes in Canada: Economy and Politics," *Canadian Journal of Political Science* (1993) 26: 787.

19. Neuman, "The Threshold of Public Attention," p. 169.

The Prime Minister's Media Arsenal

DAVID TARAS

As **agenda building** is critical to the prime minister's survival, the Prime Minister's Office has developed formidable resources in dealing with the media. The prime minister has a director of communications, a press secretary, speech writers, and a battery of other staff to help formulate an overall media strategy and deal with reporters' daily news requirements. Cabinet documents now contain communications strategies that describe, often in considerable detail, how policies are to be sold. The Prime Minister's Office constantly monitors media coverage, wages image-building campaigns, and attempts to orchestrate issues, events, and situations so that the most favourable public relations juice is squeezed out. The art of media management rests on the ability to direct reporters to stories and points of view that the government wants reported, while hindering the coverage of events or perspectives that would detract from the government's message or prove to be embarrassing.

One weapon that is sometimes used is access to the prime minister. Under Trudeau, access was limited and held out as a reward to favoured reporters; Mulroney has also used this approach. The basic understanding is that access will be given in exchange for favourable coverage. Journalists who receive an exclusive tip or lead or are allowed to interview the prime minister have an advantage over other reporters and gain enhanced stature and credibility

within their own news organizations. The news organization itself can benefit by co-operating with the prime minister. One network reporter remembers being upbraided by a member of Brian Mulroney's staff and told that "If you don't shape up (names a TV program) won't get an interview with the prime minister."[1]

Leaking a story to a favoured reporter has a number of advantages. A **leak** about an impending policy announcement, for instance, gives the government two opportunities instead of one to promote its policy. The first opportunity comes with the reporting of the leak. The second is the coverage that occurs when the policy is announced. As the first reports about a policy are often the ones that have the most impact on public opinion, the government has a great deal at stake in ensuring that these reports are favourable. Leaking information to reporters is also a means of testing public opinion. If news reports about a proposed initiative or appointment produce a hostile reaction from the public, then the government can deny the reports' validity and retreat without losing face. The launching of "trial balloons" is undoubtedly the favoured aerial sport of Canadian politicians.

Leaking information to favoured journalists can also backfire, as it can arouse the resentment of other reporters. One CBC reporter interviewed for this study still retains a measure of resentment

SOURCE: *The Newsmakers: The Media's Influence on Canadian Politics* (Toronto: Nelson, 1990), pp. 125–31. Reprinted by permission of the publisher.

against Joe Clark because "he played friends."[2] Politicians also have to play the game with subtlety. Reporters are suspicious about being co-opted and resent attempts to manipulate them. Michael Grossman and Martha Kumar have described how White House officials would allay these fears among reporters by "letting them through the line."[3] Reporters would be permitted to "discover" a new development through questioning instead of just being handed the information.

Journalists who are seen as hostile risk being frozen out by the prime minister, as well as by ministers and key government and party officials. Being put in "deep freeze" can impair a reporter's ability to do daily reporting because reporters often need basic background information and facts confirmed before they file their stories. George Radwanski has observed that "nothing hurts a journalist more than being denied access, because we lose favour with our bosses."[4] He believed that journalists were constantly afraid of this kind of retaliation. "They watch for it to a degree you wouldn't believe," he said.[5] The danger is not only that other reporters will get the story at the expense of those frozen out but that even their own organizations may view them as abrasive and, hence, as a liability. In some cases, reporters will be frozen out for short periods, as a warning. TV journalist Mike Duffy recalls being on Mulroney's freeze list for over three months. Questions put to Mulroney were simply ignored. Then suddenly, for no apparent reason, Mulroney started talking to him again.[6] Sometimes the snub is so direct and brutal that there is no mistaking the degree of hostility involved. Claire Hoy recounts how in a scrum following a cabinet session that had been held in St. John's, Newfoundland, Canadian Press reporter Tim Naumetz asked Mulroney a question about a particular policy. According to Hoy, "Mulroney just glared at him, turned around, and walked away, ending the scrum on the spot."[7]

According to one knowledgeable Ottawa journalist, the severest form of retaliation is the "burn." In his memory it had only been used once. A reporter is deliberately fed false information and then burned when the story proves to have no basis in fact. The reporter is made to look foolish and his or her bosses are left wondering about the person's ability to carry out their job.

For some reporters the message is clear: conflict must be tempered by co-operation. Criticisms leveled at the government cannot be so harsh that they lead to a severing of communications. Their self-interest is to ensure that the bridges over which they must travel to do their work remain intact.

One well-worn tactic is to release information late on Friday afternoons. Correspondents facing deadlines have little choice but to go with the information that the government has supplied, for opposition MPs and interest group spokespeople who might have critical comments are likely to have left for the weekend. The end result is that the government has "at least a twenty-four hour free ride before the critics get their turn."[8] The item is also likely to receive greater media play because news organizations are often starved for news to report on weekends. The problem is particularly acute for newspapers that have large Saturday or Sunday editions to fill. One CBC producer who worked in Ottawa admitted that he always got edgy as Friday afternoons approached. By then everyone in the Press Gallery "was tired and didn't want to scramble."[9]

A related tactic is to make policy announcements close to the times when correspondents have to file their stories. Without the time required to analyse the substance or significance of the new policy or search out the opposition point of view, reporters often have little choice but to give verbatim accounts of the government's position and reasoning. Having been boxed in, they go with what they have — the government line.

Another well-known method of manipulating the media is for politicians to provide reporters with "prepackaged" news. News is manufactured for the media; a story line is presented in briefings, photo opportunities are available so that reporters have good visuals, and press releases explain the background and significance of the event or policy that is being promoted. As reporters have to produce news stories almost every day, whether or not there is real news, some reporters depend on the government to serve up a steady diet of stories. Indeed, politicians have come to expect, if not depend on, a certain degree of laziness and inertia among journalists: journalists who will take the path of least resistance and report the "news" they have been given. According to Michel Gratton, a former press secretary to Brian Mulroney, journalists "are considerably more docile when well-nourished with material." [10] A former Reagan press aide has described how the policy of "manipulation" was orchestrated in the Reagan White House: "You give them the line of the day, you give them press briefings, you give them facts, access to people who will speak on the record. . . . And you do that long enough, they're going to stop bringing their stories, and stop being investigative reporters of any kind, even modestly so." [11] Some reporters, of course, dismiss government press releases and pre-packaged news as "gainsburgers" and will vigorously pursue all aspects of a story.

Many reporters have come to view Question Period as an attempt to create pre-packaged news. Reporters are often forewarned about the questions that the opposition parties intend to ask so that they know when the sharp confrontations — the sparks that make for good visuals — are likely to occur and over which issues. The prime minister and cabinet ministers come well armed with answers that have been scripted and rehearsed in advance. The "House book" prepared for the prime minister and cabinet ministers contains dozens of answers to anticipated questions. Playing to the media's need for drama and sensationalism, snappy rejoinders, humorous one-liners, and bitter accusations have replaced any obligation to address the questions being asked. Question Period has become a kind of theatre where each side plays out the ritual of political combat for an audience of cameras and reporters. As Brian Mulroney once put it, "It's all theatre; once I understood that, I was all set." [12] Although journalists often see Question Period in terms of winners and losers, the reality is that Question Period doesn't necessarily produce a long-term winner or a positive image for any of the participants. The public is routinely exposed to shouting matches, insults, and the emotions of blind partisanship, and this can undermine attempts to build positive images.

Scrums, with reporters milling tightly around the person being questioned and jostling against each other for position, are also an opportunity for the prime minister or a party leader to convey a tightly scripted message. The line of the day has been well thought through, and key phrases are repeated so that reporters will include them in TV and radio clips or as quotes in articles. If the questioning becomes too intense or uncomfortable, the politician can cite pressing engagements and beat a hasty retreat. Colin Seymour-Ure warns, however, that scrums can prove dangerous: "An unstructured exchange increases the risks for the person giving out information: he is more likely to be caught off guard, or to make a mistake, or to be misunderstood — even at the simple level of the answer to one question being taken to refer to another. There may be difficulty in ending the exchanges, too, if the prime minister is almost literally boxed in." [13]

Diversions are another commonly used tactic. Governments often attempt to blunt the harmful effects of a negative story by scheduling a "good news" event for the same day. The hope is that more attention will be given to the news that shows the government in a flattering light than on the news that is damaging. For instance, the Mulroney government announced its new day care initiative on the same day as the release of the Parker Inquiry report into the activities of former cabinet minister Sinclair Stevens. That Mulroney announced a cabinet shuffle on the same day as Pierre Trudeau was scheduled to testify before a parliamentary committee on the Meech Lake Constitutional Accord, testimony that was scathing in its criticism, was unlikely to have been only a coincidence.

Above all, prime ministers attempt to set the ground rules for reporting. Interviews are only granted under conditions that are likely to produce favourable coverage. Prime ministers may insist that television interviews be done live, for example, so that the interviews will be aired fully and not extensively edited. One former press secretary to Joe Clark described how he arranged for a TV interview to run for the length of air time so that the producers were forced "to go with what had been said" rather than cutting and stitching the interview together to make it more sensational.[14] One of the cardinal rules of American media advisor Roger Ailes is to avoid having politicians appear on programs that are heavily edited. Ailes' experience is that "The network will use their most controversial 18 seconds. Those seconds could be remarks out of context or could be the one moment they lose their cool." [15] David Gergen, who worked in both the Nixon and Reagan White Houses, recalls the approach that Nixon used to avoid editing. Nixon would "go out and deliver one hundred words, and he'd walk out. Because he knew that they had to use about one hundred words. They had to use what he wanted to say. And if you gave them five hundred words, they would select part of it and determine what the point of his statement was.[16] Patrick Gossage, a press secretary to Prime Minister Trudeau, described the "old PMO trick" of stipulating that the text of an interview be published in its entirety as the condition for granting the interview. This ensured that "the PM's views get out clean." [17]

Another device is to do an "end-run" around the Ottawa Press Gallery by making key announcements outside Ottawa. The logic, according to Graham Parley of *The Ottawa Citizen*, is that "Moving out of Ottawa you get more uncritical coverage. Local reporters are not as informed on some of the issues and as familiar with the nuances." [18] While prime ministers cannot avoid being followed around the country by a caravan of Press Gallery reporters, some benefits can be garnered through favourable local coverage. The pace and pageantry of prime ministerial travel, rather than his pronouncements on issues, will sometimes dominate local reporting.

A new wrinkle in attempts to bypass the Ottawa media was developed during Brian Mulroney's first term in office. The Conservative party set up its own broadcast facilities and began to market interviews with ministers and MPs to TV stations across the country. A number of smaller stations, starved for access to leading newsmakers, regarded this as a bonanza; and being able to do a big Ottawa story seemed to outweigh any concerns they might have had about Liberal or NDP MPs not being given the same opportunity to appear. Among Ottawa reporters the Conservative operation became known as "the tiny Tory network" and was treated derisively as a marriage of party propaganda and bogus journalism.

A more subtle method of influencing media coverage is by creating a climate of expectations among reporters, expectations that become the standard against which the prime minister's or the government's performance will be judged. An attempt is made to condition reporters over weeks or months into accepting certain assumptions. Geoffrey Stevens has described how prime ministers can create a sense of crisis, for instance, that will make them appear to be the saviours of a particular situation.[19] Stevens remembers that during the battle over the Constitution in 1981, government representatives repeatedly stressed that a deadlock had been reached and that a resolution was virtually impossible. When an agreement was finally concluded, the media, having been conditioned to expect that the talks would prove fruitless, proclaimed it as a historic breakthrough even though Quebec had not given the deal its approval and the provinces had the power to sidestep the Charter of Rights and Freedoms. Nonetheless, the prime minister appeared to have triumphed over seemingly insurmountable odds. Similarly, the Mulroney government launched a major public relations campaign prior to bringing down its 1989 budget. The clear message was that the government was going to take action on the deficit and that the budget would contain "radical" cuts to government spending.[20] When the budget was finally brought down, reporters, who expected drastic spending cuts, tended to describe the reductions that were announced as moderate and relatively insignificant. Media coverage probably helped dampen public outcries.

Public relations experts suggest that there are a number of basic rules to successful political salesmanship. The message must be simple (message composition), it must be newsworthy (message salience), and it must be credible; it must ring true (message credibility).[21] Simplicity, newsworthiness, and credibility are the cornerstones of image-making. Without this basic formula, it is argued, threats, stunts, leaks, pre-packaging the news, and creating expectations will all, in the long run, fall short. George Reedy, a former press secretary to Lyndon Johnson, contends that at the end of the day the only thing that really matters about media relations is whether it is believable. As he put it, "When the press is satisfied that it is getting straight answers, even if it does not like the answers, everything has been accomplished that can be accomplished by the press office." [22] Attempts to manipulate situations artificially, or to pump up images that are not congruent with reality, are ultimately doomed to failure. Others would argue, however, that on the mean streets of Canadian politics, image, especially television image, has become reality.

NOTES

1. Confidential interview.
2. Confidential interview.
3. Michael Grossman and Martha Kumar, *Portraying the President* (Baltimore: Johns Hopkins University Press, 1981), p. 174.
4. Interview with George Radwanski, Toronto, 23 May 1986.
5. Ibid.
6. *TV Guide*, 18 June 1988, p. 9.
7. Claire Hoy, *Friends in High Places* (Toronto: Key Porter Books, 1987), p. 310.
8. Interview with Jeff Dvorkin, Toronto, 21 May 1986.
9. Ibid.
10. Michel Gratton, *"So What Are the Boys Saying?"* (Toronto: McGraw-Hill Ryerson, 1987), p. 110.
11. Mark Hertsgaard, *On Bended Knee: The Press and the Reagan Presidency* (New York: Farrar, Straus & Giroux, 1988) p. 52.
12. Graham Fraser and Ross Howard, "Commons Floor a TV Studio Where MPs Play to Camera," *The Globe and Mail*, 4 April 1988, p. A1.
13. Colin Seymour-Ure, "Prime Ministers, Political News and Political Places," *Canadian Public Administration* (Summer 1989), p. 313.
14. Interview with Jock Osler, Calgary, 10 July 1986.
15. Fred Barnes, "Pulling the Strings," *The New Republic*, 22 February 1988, p. 12.
16. Hedrick Smith, *The Power Game* (New York: Random House, 1988) p. 406.
17. Patrick Gossage, *Close to the Charisma* (Toronto: McClelland and Stewart, 1986), p. 112.
18. Interview with Graham Parley, Ottawa, 9 July 1987.
19. Interview with Geoffrey Stevens, Toronto, 22 May 1986.
20. Claire Hoy, *Margin of Error* (Toronto: Key Porter Books, 1989), p. 90.
21. W. Lance Bennett, *News: The Politics of Illusion* (White Plains, N.Y.: Longman, 1988), pp. 73–74.
22. Grossman and Kumar, p. 88.

Opinions and Interests

RAIS A. KHAN
JAMES D. McNIVEN

Political culture is to a political system what a stage set is to a play: it establishes boundaries for the production. If the set is a room in a house, the actors must stage a play which takes place in a room. It would be inappropriate for them to stage the same play using sets which represent the middle of a desert or the side of a mountain.

Likewise the political culture of a society constrains political actors. They must behave within accepted norms, otherwise they risk confusing the people who could eventually reject them. The interaction of opinions and interests, which the political culture of a community moulds, generates politics. This analysis will explore why and how individuals and groups within the community form and express opinions and interests, and the extent to which the system facilitates this activity.

Decision makers in a political system must maintain an awareness of what the public feels and/or wants in relation to specific issues. This is all the more important in a democratic system where outputs of the system must relate to the wishes of the people. However, it is not always possible to determine what the public *does* want. For instance, Canadians generally believe that murder is not justifiable. But under certain circumstances, they are willing to condone the taking of a human life: for example, in self-defence, as a punitive measure (capital punishment), or in defence of one's

country. Thus, it is not the sanctity of life that is important to the decision makers, but rather the specific conditions under which the Canadian public feels that exceptions are warranted.

Opinions and interests are articulated in a variety of ways. These can be categorized into two main types — informal and formal — as shown in Table 32.1. *Informal articulation* takes place through the eliciting of public opinion, spontaneous and unorganized activity, personal relationships with decision makers, and uninvolved third-party advocacy of a cause. Most of the people holding an opinion are seldom directly involved in articulating it: this explains the classification of "public opinion" as *passive* in Table 32.1. *Formal articulation*, on the other hand, is achieved through permanently or semi-permanently organized and politically *active* groups.

A fine line divides passive and active articulation. Generally the distinction is made when a person or group simply thinks about an issue as opposed to acting in the context of an opinion. Thinking and acting are the twin dimensions of political participation. Aristotle, for instance, saw participation as a function of belonging — of sharing attitudes and values. Medieval scholars considered participation as the pursuit of private interests. Rousseau in the eighteenth century viewed participation as continuous involvement in public affairs.

SOURCE: *An Introduction to Political Science* (Toronto: Nelson, 1991), pp. 98–106. Reprinted by permission of the publisher.

There is a wide disparity in the extent and level of political participation between modern systems. The stereotype of Russian participation is the passive sharing of attitudes and values: everything has political implication. The American stereotype is one of active involvement in the pursuit of private or group interests: politics is a necessary evil. Neither stereotype is accurate, but they do point out how political systems differ in their view of participation in everyday politics.

PASSIVE ARTICULATION

Passive articulation refers to unexpressed attitudes and opinions about issues and personalities which must be sought out. This is more commonly referred to as *public opinion* and is quite distinct from active articulation, in which individuals or groups publicly express opinions and interests in an organized manner.

A distinction should be made between political culture and public opinion. Political culture consists of basic attitudes about the political system and its environment as a whole. In contrast, *public opinion is the viewpoint individuals hold about specific issues and personalities in politics.* A combination of political socialization and life experiences conditions public opinion. The values of the political culture determine the limits, context, and content of public opinion.

Public opinion is difficult to fathom because it is dispersed in erratic patterns amongst the population. This encourages the development of organizations called "interest groups" and "political parties," which facilitate and channel the active expression of opinion and serve as a medium of contact between decision makers and the public at large.

These voluntary organizations attract only those people who are interested in the organization's objectives and policies. The vast majority of the public is unorganized and unaffiliated. As societies become more complex and direct contact between decision makers and the public becomes sparing, regular and systematic methods of finding out the opinions and desires of the public become necessary.

Table 32.1

Articulation of Opinions and Interests

	Passive	Active
INFORMAL	Public opinion	Anomic representation
		Personal representation
		Proxy representation
FORMAL		Interest groups
		Nonassociational
		Associational
		Institutional

Enterprises are established to develop and conduct surveys of public opinion. These surveys, or **opinion polls**, have become increasingly scientific and reliable and have gained widespread acceptance in academic, commercial, and political circles. A discussion of public opinion, at least in democratic systems, must therefore include a discussion of polls.

Public opinion is also important in non-democratic systems. Authoritarian governments establish an elaborate network of political institutions to do more than just control the public: they are intended to serve as lines of communication, for it is important that leaders know the mood of the public. An authoritarian government which is not attuned to the public mood could lose public support in a crisis and thereby imperil its existence.

Factors Influencing Public Opinion

People reach similar opinions through very different routes and each opinion is intelligible if not logical. Often a respondent's inability to recall all the experiences that moulded his or her basic outlook, or to describe accurately how he or she became aware of the issue and acquired knowledge about it, frustrates the attempt to unravel the contributing influences on individual opinion. There are so many factors influencing a person's opinion on any given matter that while the probable influences are identifiable, their interaction with each other can only be guessed. They include considerations such as gender, race, occupation, ethnicity, income, language, and regional loyalty. We discuss below some of the primary influences on public opinion.

FAMILY

Family influence is widely recognized in the study of opinion formation. For example, polls indicate that the majority of voters support the same political parties as their parents. At the same time, it is not uncommon for members of a family to differ, a natural reflection of their varied experiences as individuals. Changes in economic and social status also affect political attitudes. There is nothing to prevent members of a family from belonging to the same political party while, at the same time, holding differing views on specific issues or personalities. The way in which family disputes are handled, or even discussed, encourages differences of opinion in some families. Family structures in some countries are more dramatic than in others, so the nature of their influence varies from country to country.

RELIGION

The impact of religion on public opinion in societies where most people profess the same faith is obvious. But in a diverse society such as Canada the multiplicity of religions and the values they seek to preserve complicates this relationship. Certain religious groups encourage their members to act politically as a bloc: in some cases this is done out of a general sense of group solidarity, and in others out of a sense of special group interest in a particular issue. The abortion issue, for instance, has triggered considerable religious solidarity.

The North American tradition of religious group involvement in social and political issues is rather ambiguous. Some religious groups actively attempt to influence opinion on economic and social problems through involvement in the political process; others are opposed to this involvement. Some groups have a liberal, others a conservative influence. Surveys show that only the Jews are consistently liberal on social and political questions; Protestants and Catholics tend to be more conservatively oriented.[1] The influence of religion often conflicts with

individualistic values in a pluralistic society: regular churchgoers are less tolerant than others of nonconformist behaviour. The only major religious group to deviate from this is, again, the Jewish.

The concept of an operational, if not a legal, separation of church and state shapes the relationship between religion and politics in North America. Citizens can express their religious beliefs in political terms where relevant, but religious organizations should stay away from direct involvement in political activity. Conversely, the state must not interfere in religious affairs. This separation often breaks down when religious leaders publicly oppose government involvement in social issues closely related to religious morality. In contemporary North America and Europe, for instance, controversy over the permissibility of abortion and its funding through public medical care plans has brought churches into open conflict with governments.

The Catholic Church in Quebec before 1960 sponsored a large number of "subsidiary" bodies to assist in the task of promoting social welfare and economic development. However, the growth of a more interventionist government deprived the church of these social instruments, forcing it to reevaluate its role in society. A similar but more rapid divestiture of such functions in nineteenth-century France led to generations of conflict between church and state. The involvement of the Catholic Church in Polish politics since the upheavals of 1980–81 shows that the influence of religion on political opinion continues to prevail even in some communist states.

Religious groups in other parts of the world are overtly active and in some countries they constitute an integral part of the political establishment: the Catholic Church publicly favours the Christian Democrats in Italy; religious leaders have controlled and run the Iranian government since Ayatollah Khomeini overthrew the Shah in 1979. Such close ties between religion and politics do not always meet with the approval of all religious leaders in the countries concerned, but the involvement of religion in politics is real in most parts of the world.

EDUCATION

The relationship between religion and political opinion is well documented, but such is not the case with education and public opinion. The educational system fosters certain impressions of the world which reinforce basic cultural values. An educational system which stresses independent work and thought will produce independent and tolerant people. Higher education encourages more tolerant attitudes than primary or secondary education, but is still accessible to only a minority of the population.

Survey data indicate that the higher one's education, the higher is the level of political knowledge, opinion formation, and activity. Higher education enhances individual willingness and ability to think about political issues and to hold and express opinions about them. Advanced education also fosters a high degree of confidence in the political process and in the efficacy of one's participation in it.

Researchers are divided in their views on the consistency and stability of public opinion in relation to educational levels. While many people give inconsistent, spur-of-the-moment responses to public opinion survey questions, researchers are uncertain whether people with a low level of education are less coherent and consistent in their opinions than those who are better educated.

PEER GROUPS

Everyone has friends and most people join groups of one sort or another. Generally these groups have no political orientation, but they do encourage common behaviour patterns and values among their members. Street gangs, Rotary Clubs, sports teams, and the "guys at the pub" are groups that encourage certain norms of behaviour and attitude. Acceptance and approval of an individual into a group is a measure of the individual's adoption of group norms.

The implications of group norms for politics are quite clear. The influence of one's associates and friends creates, reinforces, or diminishes many essentially non-political attitudes. But the values and attitudes learned as part of a group often become the basis for reaction to overtly political questions.

ECONOMIC FACTORS

The influence of economic factors on public opinion arouses controversy among political researchers. Both sides in the argument agree that people possess unequal economic resources. Beyond that, one school of thought believes that those who possess an abundance of economic resources are the elite, whose opinions are different from those of the less privileged. At its most deterministic level the elitist school blends into Marxism. Another school feels that elite opinions are different from others but, depending upon the nature of the issue, opinions are shared regardless of economic circumstances. This is the pluralist school, which appeals more to conservatives and liberals. Survey data suggest a complex interaction between economic factors and public opinion, which further complicates the debate over elite formation and cohesion.

MASS MEDIA

The **mass media** exercise considerable influence over the intensity and direction of public opinion and deserve special attention. Content of the mass media in North America is generally non-political. Even prestigious newspapers devote less space to strictly political matters than to sports or social notes, to say nothing of advertising. The same is basically true of the electronics media. Much of the programming on television and radio is directed at the mass audience, which is essentially non-political in nature, reflecting the average individual's inclination toward programmes of entertainment rather than more serious matters of politics.

The lack of political content in the media does not, however, diminish their potential influence in shaping opinions. Television, for instance, brings the tragedies of the Middle East and Central America into people's living rooms and has undoubtedly deglamourized warfare. Dramatic events such as election campaigns, political assassinations, and airplane hijackings illustrate the impact that television can have.

Studies indicate that people have more confidence in television than in the printed word, because on TV they can "see it for themselves." But the knowledge that television is just as biased as newspapers or magazines has undermined its credibility in recent years. (One only sees the edited clips which dramatize a story.)

The ties between the electronic media and the government vary between countries. The profit motive dominates where the media are largely privately owned. The emphasis is on reaching large audiences so as to attract sponsors who underwrite programmes and subsidize the usually unprofitable public service broadcasts. Newspapers, too, are not immune from catering to popular interest: they commission opinion polls to find out what kind of news the public wishes to read.

In countries where the electronic media are largely government controlled the need to cater to advertisers is not as pressing so long as sufficient public funds are available to finance programming. Most government networks around the world try to reduce, and ultimately to eliminate, advertising. They are under persistent pressure to increase "national" content in programming which, in turn, requires more public funds. For instance, the Canadian Radio-television and Telecommunications Commission (CRTC) frequently revises its rules on "Canadian" content in broadcasting, putting pressure on the Canadian Broadcasting Corporation (CBC) as well as private networks to reduce imported programmes from the United States and Britain.

The spread of cable and pay television facilitated an even wider dispersal of American programmes. As an incentive toward increasing Canadian content, tax laws were revised in the early 1980s to discourage Canadian advertising on U.S. border stations. The aim of the revision was to provide Canadian networks with more advertising revenue so that they would invest in producing Canadian programmes. The tax measures did not promote a substantial increase in Canadian content, but they did cause economic tensions between the two countries through the 1980s.

The use of electronic media is a sensitive subject. In France, for instance, the government network generally allows, even during election campaigns, only limited access to radio and television for the opposition political parties. Direct ownership or control over the media is not the only way in which the government can influence what is presented to the public. Government officials may simply not provide information about, or explanation of, events to the media, or they may present facts in such a way as to create a favourable impression of the government's actions, thus "managing" the news. The United States was treated to a variation of this phenomenon during the Nixon administration, when some rather obvious efforts were made to use federal regulatory agencies to discipline the television networks for their critical reporting of government policies.

A fine line exists between legitimate government attempts to present its interpretation of an event and a conscious attempt at news "management" to manipulate opinion. Efforts to monopolize or control the media in a democratic system are a threat to the system itself. Democracies can operate properly only if the channels of communication are open.

The media in authoritarian systems are used as instruments of propaganda and socialization. Consequently, alternative sources of information and ideas are limited to clandestine channels: the "grapevine," foreign radio and television broadcasts, illegal newspapers such as the *Samizdat* in Russia, and illegally imported books. Listening to foreign radio stations such as the Voice of America or the BBC was illegal in many Eastern European countries after World War II. Many still transmit static to "jam" Western stations.

The issue of news management has arisen in another form in recent years as a result of the Third World allegations that the Western news agencies, such as Reuters and the Associated Press, do not accurately portray events in their countries to North American and European audiences. The Western media greeted their call for a new "world information order," with its overtones of government control over news releases, as an attempt by non-democratic countries to stifle unpleasant or disagreeable news items.

One could dismiss the concern of the Third World countries as "sour grapes," but there is more to it than the egos of military juntas and dictators.

The news media are instruments of change. They focus on specific events and thus create communities. But these are not events which customary values, traditional beliefs, and moral standards mould. Instead, the news focuses on what is "new." It is a method of endless self-criticism and self-renewal for societies. In this way, the media foster more open and less controlled societies. These pressures run counter to the nation-building efforts of the Third World leaders who feel that they have to build on traditional moral values (as in Iran and Pakistan), to control criticism so as to keep down tribal tensions (as in Africa), or control economic aspirations (as in Latin America). Even the non-political media, in these contexts, become a threat.

Commercial culture does not manufacture ideology; it relays and reproduces and processes and packages and focuses ideology that is constantly arising from social elites and from active social groups and movements.[2]

If American sitcoms and football cause concern among the Canadian political elite, think of the political implication of punk rock, "Dallas," and even "Sesame Street" to elites in Cairo, Bangkok, and Accra!

NOTES

1. See John H. Redekop, *Religious Pressure Groups in the Canadian Political System*, Research Paper series no. 8470 (Waterloo: Wilfrid Laurier University, n.d.).
2. Todd Gitlin, "Prime-Time Ideology: The Hegemonic Process in Television Entertainment," *Social Problems* 26, no. 3 (February 1979), pp. 251–66. Copyright 1979 by the Society for the Study of Social Problems.

Organized Women's Groups and the State

SANDRA BURT

Since the late 1800s, women's groups in Canada have sought policy changes from governments. Their activity has been continuous, although varying significantly over time in both intensity and focus. The first clustering of **political action** occurred in the early 1900s when social feminists, who wanted to transfer the values prevalent in the private world of the family to the public world of politics and labour, worked to obtain franchise rights for women. Beginning in the 1960s, liberal, radical, and socialist feminists (Code, 1988: 43–46) have sought changes ranging from equality rights to a reshaping of the values informing all facets of social, economic, and political life. And more recently anti-feminists have lobbied for a return to traditional family forms and life styles.

The literature on these groups and their interactions with the Canadian state has grown dramatically in the past ten years (Black, 1988; Burt, 1986, 1988a, 1988b; Findlay, 1987). Yet although the amount of information on women's groups has increased, an understanding of the relationships that have developed between these groups and policymakers has not developed at the same rate. Analyses of the overall policy patterns have concentrated on feminist theory in the general context of policy-making frameworks, and conclusions have focussed on the end result of feminist lobbying rather than on the processes that lead to these results.

It is now clear that, over time, Canadian policymakers have become increasingly sympathetic to the feminist claim that women should have equal access with men to the competitive spheres of politics and work. But they have consistently resisted demands for a fundamental restructuring of relations among both women and men to reflect the feminist values of participation, nurturing, caring, and peace. To a somewhat lesser degree, they have resisted as well attempts by feminists to redefine gender roles within the family. This pattern is similar to that found in other Western, industrialized countries, and in the case of Canada at least reflects the growing emphasis on individual rights developing since the end of the Second World War, and accelerated by the adoption in 1982 of a Charter of Rights and Freedoms. The most dramatic manifestation of the federal government's commitment to the equal rights claim of feminists came in 1981 when the Ad Hoc Committee on the Constitution convinced both levels of government to give notwithstanding status to section 28 in the Charter of Rights and Freedoms (Burt, 1988a).

But within the boundaries of this equal rights thinking, the process of **interest accommodation** is not well understood. Paul Pross (1986) discusses the qualities needed by groups that seek a consultative role in the policy-making process, and some

SOURCE: "Organized Women's Groups and the State," in William D. Coleman and Grace Skogstad, eds., *Policy Communities and Public Policy in Canada: A Structural Approach* (Toronto: Copp Clark Pitman, 1990), pp. 191–200. Reprinted by permission of the publisher.

studies (Adamson et al., 1988) have examined the level of institutionalization of women's groups. On the basis of these studies it can be concluded that the strongest groups, such as the National Action Committee on the Status of Women (NAC), the Business and Professional Women (B&PW), or the Canadian Congress on Learning Opportunities for Women (CCLOW) have, on most issues, undergone organizational development that equips them to move from policy advocacy to policy participation. The nature of their policy participation, the pattern of women's group–government interaction *within* the general boundaries of the prevailing policy climate, is best furthered by a sectoral level of analysis.

With sectoral-level analysis "much greater attention must be paid to specific bureaucratic arrangements and to the relationships that the officials involved maintain with key societal actors" (Atkinson and Coleman, 1989: 50). The relationships among groups as well as between groups and governments within a policy sector are important. Women's groups have rapidly proliferated and diversified since 1970. And although these groups have moved away from the state direction exercised in the 1960s, they are still fragmented, diverse in their goals, and organizationally weak, partly as a consequence of their continued reliance on government funding. At the same time, the federal government has put in place a set of agencies and status of women officers to accommodate the claims of women's groups. These government agencies are fragmented as well. The argument advanced here is that the network linking women's groups with the state has evolved from state direction in the 1960s to pressure pluralism in the 1980s. This transition (see Figure 33.1) is explored in the context of two issue areas: maternity leave in the 1960s and child care in the 1980s.

WOMEN'S GROUPS AND THEIR POLICY COMMUNITY

Prior to 1970, only a small number of groups were concerned with women's roles and status in Canada.

Some, like the National Council of Women, which was formed in 1893, were still committed to social feminist principles (Black, 1981). Other groups, such as the B&PW, formed in the 1900s in the context of women's growing labour force participation, sought equal opportunities for women in the work world. Links between the early groups and public officials were weak, and often limited to yearly formal presentations to Cabinet. Although the groups lobbied successfully for changes in women's status — notably improved family property and labour laws — they lacked organizational skills, were only weakly coordinated, and were few in number.

In the 1970s, the number and range of women's groups increased dramatically. There are now thousands of women's groups across Canada which focus on a wide variety of issues affecting both women's and men's roles, such as abortion, maternity leave, employment equity, and equal opportunity. The largest increase in numbers occurred after 1970, for a variety of reasons. First, throughout the 1900s, but most dramatically in the past two decades, women's labour force participation has increased. The wages paid to women have been lower than those paid to men, leading to demands for equal treatment and equal opportunity in the work place. A second catalyst to **mobilization** was the United States example of action, with Betty Friedan leading women into the liberation movement. Third, in 1970, the federal government published the report of the Royal Commission on the Status of Women. This report directed the government's and the public's attention to the status of women in Canada, and recommended federal government support for women's groups working to improve women's status. In 1973, in the context of preparations for International Women's Year, the federal government acted on this recommendation and created the Women's Program in the Secretary of State to provide both core and project funding for women's groups.

The goals of women's groups today are much more diverse than those of the groups in existence before 1970. From a survey conducted in 1984,[1] it is possible to identify three major categories of feminist

Figure 33.1

The Changing Community on Status of Women Issues at the Federal Level

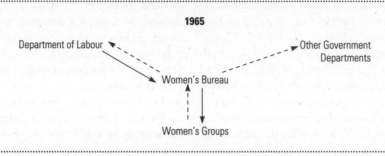

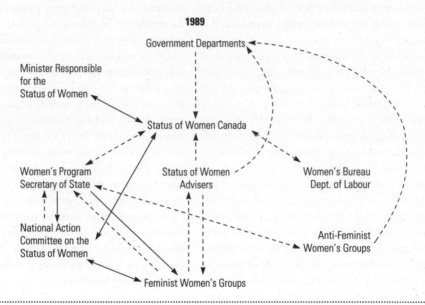

groups. The largest category consists of service providers—groups that make counselling, referral, educational, or shelter services available to women. Equal rights groups are almost as numerous. They seek to break down the barriers to equal opportunities in employment and politics. Finally, there are still some groups committed to social feminist goals. Since the 1984 study, a fourth category of groups, those seeking to maintain the traditional division of responsibilities between women and men, has gained significance as well.

About one-half of these groups are small in size (with less than 50 members) and operate with annual budgets of less than $50,000. A national umbrella group, NAC, has attempted to serve as a coordinator of women's claims since its origins in 1972. With a membership of over 500 groups, NAC tries to accommodate most of its members by serving as a lobbyist on issues with policy relevance to women. Issue priorities are set each year at the annual general meeting, and positions on these priority issues are then presented to the federal cabinet at an annual lobby session. In addition, informal links with public officials, especially those in Status of Women Canada, together with the publication of position/research papers, help to publicize their positions (Morris, 1983).

NAC has had some difficulty exercising its leadership. Since it brings together a wide variety of women's groups, some of which hold conflicting positions, NAC's strength as a national lobby group is sometimes weakened by internal dissension. In 1980, for example, NAC lost its position as the leading lobby group in the struggle for women's equality rights in the Charter of Rights and Freedoms. Today, some member groups oppose NAC's pro-choice position on the abortion issue. In addition to problems arising within NAC, the group has recently faced a loss of legitimacy with the federal government as the major representative of women's views in Canada. For the first time, in 1989, the minister responsible for the status of women refused to meet with NAC in a closed session to receive its annual cabinet submission.[2]

Overall, since 1970, women's groups have improved their organizational skills, and developed lines of communication with both levels of government. Although the groups are fragmented, many of those committed to feminist goals work with NAC on issues upon which there are common positions, and their commitment to the principle of cooperation also leads to some collaboration. For example, in the 1984 survey 17 per cent of the groups interviewed reported spending at least one-quarter of their time networking with other women's groups. But the links among feminist groups are still weak, and the emergence of new anti-feminist positions suggests that the women's organizational community is becoming increasingly pluralist.

In the 1970s, a further factor contributing to pluralism in the policy community is that a separate set of policy advisers was established by the federal government. These Status of Women advisers sometimes have been important in affecting the impact of the women's lobby on policy formation. There is even evidence that they have performed an advocacy function within government when interest groups

have been silent on an issue. And there have been variations over time in their autonomy or ability to insulate themselves from societal influence while drawing on their own internal resources and expertise in defining policy objectives. There have been variations as well in their ability to operate independently of their host agency or other parts of the federal bureaucracy.

The federal government made its first administrative arrangements for the development of policy for women in the 1950s. At that time, its main interest was the employment status of Canadian women. In the booming postwar economy, the focus was on increasing the labour force, and governments started to look to women for help. By 1951, already 24 per cent of women were working for pay outside the home, an increase from only 16 per cent at the turn of the century. Gradually women were being accepted as long-term and low-wage labour, and the proposals of the 1945 reconstruction committee following the Second World War included the recommendation that a women's bureau be established in the Department of Labour. The minister of labour, Milton Gregg, a Liberal member from New Brunswick who throughout his career was concerned with the removal of discriminatory practices from the employment field, announced in 1953 in the House of Commons the creation of a women's bureau. It was charged with the following functions:

- providing research on women workers;
- through speeches, and so on, making information on women workers available to the public;
- developing channels between the Department of Labour and other public and private agencies;
- advising the Department of Labour on its programmes affecting women workers.[3]

The Bureau was formed in 1954, and from the outset it served as a vehicle for bringing the positions taken by groups to the attention of policymakers. But the Bureau was not autonomous within the Department of Labour, with its weak administrative position being demonstrated in many ways.

Marion Royce, the first Director, complained in 1955 that, although she was a member of an inter-departmental committee to examine the problems of older workers, she was not invited regularly to meetings.[4] In 1965, she was overruled in her effort to have the Women's Bureau housed in the Research and Development Section of the Department of Labour, rather than the less supportive Labour Standards Section. The Bureau was moved to Standards, where it remained until 1985. It is a tribute to Royce's skills that the Bureau survived the transition.[5] Royce was forced to work with a small staff (never more than five people) and a starting budget of $24,000. She concentrated on the publication of information about women's changing labour status, together with liaison work with women's groups. Under her directorship, the Bureau began a listing of national women's organizations. When Royce retired in 1966, she was replaced by Jessica Findlay, a woman with no involvement in women's groups or awareness of status of women concerns. During her brief directorship, the staff of the Bureau shrank to three full-time people, including the director, and a budget of $45,000. Findlay resigned after one year, and her resignation sparked a debate in the House of Commons which focussed on the Director's lack of authority and funds to carry out her functions. Findlay was replaced by Sylva Gelber, and under her directorship the Bureau became a much stronger working unit within the Department of Labour. The functions shifted from information-gathering to coordination of policies affecting women in the federal government. To this end, an interdepartmental committee was established "consisting of representatives of the main government departments concerned with women's affairs in general and with working women in particular."[6]

However, the Bureau's greatest successes remained within the realm of information-gathering and -dissemination. Under Gelber's leadership, the Bureau upgraded the yearly publication begun by Royce of facts and figures about women in the labour force, and undertook studies of the needs of these women. But her efforts to promote interdepartmental cooperation failed. This setback is obvious from her letter to the assistant deputy minister of Labour on the subject of the wording in the 1969 publication, *Labour Highlights*: "The inclusion of the Interdepartmental Committee on Women's Affairs as a highlight of the work of the Bureau is not only a source of annoyance but a source of real embarrassment. You will recall that we discussed the failure of the Interdepartmental Committee as long ago as last spring."[7] Gelber was most successful in pointing out the pattern of women's labour force participation, using this knowledge as her ammunition in the fight to gain equality rights. Under her leadership the Bureau developed a reputation within the Department of Labour for conscientious research and expertise.

But the Bureau's new-found autonomy was short-lived. In 1970, the Royal Commission on the Status of Women submitted its report. The Commission recommended that the federal government improve the process for implementing policy changes to enhance the status of women. The government struck an Interdepartmental Committee to consider implementation of the report. The committee, chaired by Freda Paltiel, a senior bureaucrat from Health and Welfare with an interest in status of women issues, proposed that many of the Bureau's functions be redistributed to new agencies. When these new agencies were created, the Bureau suffered a loss of power and personnel. It now focusses on the publication of information related to women in the labour force; activities associated with the International Labour Organization; and the administration of a small grants programme (started in 1985 with a budget of $25,000) designed to assist individuals or groups with projects to improve the situation of women in the workplace. In 1985, the Bureau was moved from Labour Standards to Policy within the Department of Labour. The staff was increased to 13 person years in 1987, and the budget reached $1,002,000 (Canada, House of Commons, 1987: 128).

Between 1970 and 1975 the federal government decided to accept the recommendations of the interdepartmental committee studying the Royal Commission's report, and put in place a collection of status of women agencies. This decision reflected cabinet's commitment to the principle of equal opportunity. In later recollections about the process, Florence Bird, the Commission Chair, reflected that the creation of multiple agencies was a mistake. The Commission had pressed for several, hoping to get one. Of these new agencies, the most powerful was Status of Women Canada, a central agency that was situated first within the Privy Council Office, and was designed to assist the minister responsible for the status of women. In addition, Status of Women was involved in "monitoring the activities of government departments, and coordinating new initiatives to improve the status of women."[8] This responsibility included the former Bureau function of serving as a link between women's groups and the government.

From the outset Status of Women encountered difficulties. Unlike the Women's Bureau, which by the 1970s had developed a strong working relationship with its host department, Status of Women Canada was an independent agency, without close links with any departments. Officials charged with the task of considering status of women concerns who were placed within some departments (for example, Health and Welfare, the Public Service Commission, and the Justice Department) had only nominal power to recommend policies, and real power only to promote research and offer advice.

The relationship between the Women's Bureau in Labour and women's groups was further weakened by the development of a granting programme within the Women's Program of the Secretary of State. The Women's Program provides both core and project funding for groups which serve to "promote increased understanding of, and action on, women's issues among women and the general public in the form of advocacy and information exchange" (Canada, Secretary of State, 1982: 1). The first budget of the Women's Program was only $223,000, but by 1987 over 650 groups received funding from a total budget of $12.4 million. Of this amount, 61 per cent was targeted for special projects, and 39 per cent for operational grants. National groups received 37 per cent, and regional, provincial, or local groups the rest (Canada, Secretary of State, 1987: 10). According to the funding guidelines, operational funding, the most sought-after commodity, is available to groups that promote action and provide information to the public on women's issues. The granting guidelines have been interpreted by some groups as an attempt by the federal government to exert control over programmes which lie within the boundaries of provincial responsibility. Social service groups in particular (rape crisis centres, transition homes, and educational counselling groups) have been granted both types of funding. The government controls the groups' agenda by setting a priority list for funding. For example, in 1983–84, funding priorities were violence against women, communication, and women in the economy. In addition, the government directs money to be spent in specific activity areas, requires its approval for budget transfers, and according to some groups, discourages service providers from taking public stands on issues related to women (Saskatchewan Action Committee, 1983).

The Women's Program acts as "the main federal programme of financial assistance, advice and information to women's and other voluntary organizations" (Secretary of State, 1987: 2). Until 1989, directors of the programme understood these guidelines to mean that only those groups which work to improve the status of women in Canada (that is, improve the potential for equal opportunity) are eligible for funding. They have worked within what they have interpreted as the federal government's commitment to equality. However, that interpretation may be changing. In 1989 a group seeking a return to pre-feminist definitions of women's roles, Realistic Equal Active for Life (REAL women), received funding, in accordance with the recommendations in the 1987 report of the Standing Committee on the Secretary of State, "Fairness in Funding."

Throughout their existence, the status of women agencies within the federal government have struggled to develop autonomy. Some of them have been assisted by central policy directives. The cabinet has been particularly anxious to improve the position of

Status of Women Canada. In 1975, in the context of International Women's Year, the minister responsible for the status of women (Marc Lalonde) undertook a review of the government's record in advancing women's claims to work as equal partners with men in the economy. His report led cabinet to declare in 1976 that "each department or agency should establish or designate a mechanism to ensure the integration of status of women concerns into all phases of department activity." It recommended as well that each departmental mechanism maintain continuing contacts with the Office of the Coordinator, Status of Women.[9] At the same time, Status of Women Canada was granted independent status as a central agency, reporting directly to the minister responsible for the status of women. Somewhat later in 1987, the Neilsen Task Force studying government organization recommended that the minister responsible for the status of women be a member of the Priorities and Planning Committee in cabinet, and that each minister mandate an existing assistant deputy minister to ensure that all departmental proposals contain a thorough study of their impact on women.

The record of Status of Women has been mixed. Successive coordinators have worked to establish good working relationships with women's groups, and the agency houses the past publications and policy recommendations made by these groups. Status of Women grew to 43 person years by 1986, with a budget of $2,804,000. But the agency has not been able to coordinate the activity of other departments on status of women questions. Status of Women advisers meet only occasionally, and rarely to discuss policy concerns of mutual interest. The Neilsen Task Force concluded that the main success of Status of Women Canada lay in pulling "the provinces together for national awareness of issues relating to women and for consensus building." It further concluded that the agency's coordination function was hampered by the fact that, with the exception of Labour Canada, no federal department systematically reviews its policies to determine their impact on women (Canada, House of Commons, 1987: 109, 111).

In summary, the agencies within the government for dealing with status of women issues have never enjoyed positions of autonomy within the bureaucracy. But some organizations, especially the Women's Bureau in the Department of Labour in the late 1960s and Status of Women Canada after 1975, have been more capable of generating their own "professional ethos" (Atkinson and Coleman, 1989: 52) than those embedded in existing department bureaucracies. And the overlap of mechanisms across bureaucratic divisions, without effective coordination among them, creates the potential for conflicting interpretations of status of women needs. The policy networks linking women's groups to these status of women agencies have undergone significant changes as both the groups and governments have become more fragmented.

NOTES

Much of the information reported in this paper was obtained from interviews conducted with activists within women's groups, status of women officials in the federal government, and elected officials responsible for the policies discussed. These interviews were conducted between 1984 and 1989, and were supported by Grant 410-86-0170 from the Social Sciences and Humanities Research Council of Canada.

1. This study was conducted by the author in 1984. The 686 women's groups listed in the 1982 publication of the Women's Program, Secretary of State, were sent questionnaires. The response rate was 24 per cent.
2. See Paul Koring, "Antibudget Campaign by Women's Group Off to Confused Start," Toronto *Globe and Mail*, May 16, 1989, A13.
3. National Archives of Canada, RG 27, vol. 1903, file 38-2-2, part 1, "Seminar on the Work of the Women's Bureau, Department of Labour," May 5, 1960.
4. Canada, Department of Labour, Women's Bureau Library, memorandum from M. Royce, Director, Women's Bureau to H.L. Douse, January 18, 1955.
5. National Archives of Canada, RG 27, vol. 3209, file 1-4-12, "Interim Report of the Task Force on Manpower," December 30, 1965.

6. National Archives of Canada, RG 27, vol. 4160, file 722-4-3, memo to J. Despres from S.M. Gelber, October 23, 1968.
7. National Archives of Canada, RG 27, vol. 38-6-2-8, letter to J.P. Despres from S. Gelber, Dec. 29, 1969.
8. National Archives of Canada, RG 106, vol. 29, "Report of the Ad Hoc Committee on Mechanisms to Integrate the Status of Women," Appendix A, p. 2.
9. National Archives, RG 106, vol. 29, "Briefing for Deputy Ministers on Status of Women Policy," p. 3.

REFERENCES

Adamson, N., Linda Briskin, and Margaret McPhail (1988). *Feminist Organizing for Change: The Contemporary Women's Movement in Canada.* Toronto: Oxford University Press.

Atkinson, M.M., and W.D. Coleman (1989). "Strong States and Weak States: Sectoral Policy Networks in Advanced Capitalist Economies." *British Journal of Political Science,* 19: 47–67.

Black, Naomi (1981). "Introduction." In Elsie Gregory MacGill, *My Mother the Judge.* Toronto: Peter Martin Associates: xi–xxiv.

———. (1988). "The Canadian Women's Movement: The Second Wave." In Sandra Burt, Lorraine Code, and Lindsey Dorney, eds., *Changing Patterns: Women in Canada.* Toronto: McClelland and Stewart.

Burt, S. (1986). "Women's Issues and the Women's Movement in Canada." In Alan Cairns and Cynthia Williams, eds., *The Politics of Gender, Ethnicity, and Language in Canada.* Toronto: University of Toronto Press.

———. (1988a). "The Charter of Rights and the Ad Hoc Lobby: The Limits of Success." *Atlantis,* 14: 74–81.

———. (1988b). "Legislators, Women, and Public Policy." In Sandra Burt et al., eds., *Changing Patterns.* Toronto: McClelland and Stewart.

Canada. House of Commons, Task Force on Program Review (Neilsen Task Force) (1987). *Report.* Ottawa. Ministry of Supply and Services.

Canada. Royal Commission on the Status of Women (1970). *Report.* Ottawa: Information Canada.

Canada. Secretary of State (1982). *Funding Guidelines.* May.

———. (1987). "Notes for the presentation of the Undersecretary of State Before the Standing Committee on the Secretary of State." February 3.

Code, Lorraine (1988). "Feminist Theory." In Sandra Burt et al., eds., *Changing Patterns.* Toronto: McClelland and Stewart.

Findlay, S. (1987). "Facing the State: The Politics of the Women's Movement Reconsidered." In H.J. Maroney and M. Luxton, eds., *Feminism and Political Economy.* Toronto: Methuen.

Morris, C. (1983). "Pressuring the Canadian State for Women's Rights: The Role of the National Action Committee on the Status of Women." *Alternate Routes,* 6: 87–108.

Pross, A. Paul (1986). *Group Politics and Public Policy.* Toronto: Oxford University Press.

Saskatchewan Action Committee, Saskatchewan Status of Women (1983). "The Pink Papers: Government Funding and Government Control in the Women's Movement." Unpublished document available from Canadian Women's Movement Archives. Toronto.

Pressure Groups

A. PAUL PROSS

The most difficult of all governmental tasks is that of communicating with the public. Despite the millions of words expended in public debate every day, modern governments have great difficulty finding out what the public wants and needs, and what it feels about the work that the state is already doing. Equally, although its payroll is laden with press officers, writers, and others skilled in the arts of communication, government has immense problems in explaining itself to the public, in reporting back to it, and in persuading and leading it.

Pressure groups are one of three communication systems used by most modern states to overcome these problems. The other two are the internal apparatus of the government itself, such as the press officers and writers mentioned above, and the party system. Political parties are best equipped to transmit the demands and views of individuals and of groups of individuals concerned about specific localities. This is because political parties tend to be built around an electoral system created to fill a legislature that is territorial or *spatial* in orientation; i.e., each member represents the people who live in a specific area, or constituency.

Pressure groups have become prominent because they are effective where parties fail. They can identify and articulate the views and needs of individuals who may live far apart but who share common interests. In modern society, with its interdependent economy, its multinational corporations, and its very large and specialized government bureaucracies, this sectoral approach of pressure groups is an essential complement to the spatial orientation of political parties. Even so, as we shall see later, the rapid growth and rising influence of pressure groups gives concern to many observers, some of whom feel that democratic government is threatened thereby.

Pressure groups are organizations whose members act together to influence public policy in order to promote their common interests.[1] Unlike political parties, they are not interested in directly wielding the power of the state, through sometimes a group representing a particularly large socio-economic block (the Acadians are a good example) will decide to transform itself into a political party. In general, pressure groups are interested in exerting influence and in persuading governments to accommodate the special interests of their members.

To achieve this, pressure groups have to be more than mere assemblages of people. Their members have to be organized, brought together in structured relationships with one another, and dragooned into identifying and expressing their common interests. Pressure groups are consequently distinct, clearly identifiable elements in the body politic. While their chief role, as far as the political system is concerned, is to provide a network for

SOURCE: "Pressure Groups: Talking Chameleons," in Michael Wittington and Glen Williams, eds., *Canadian Politics in the 1990s* (Toronto: Nelson, 1990), pp. 285–90. Reprinted by permission of the publisher.

policy communication, in the following paragraphs we shall see that they have several other functions as well.

THE FUNCTIONS OF PRESSURE GROUPS

Whenever we try to set down precisely what it is that pressure groups do, we have to remember that, like most institutions, they are different things to different people. Leaving aside for the moment those who feel that pressure groups are a curse and an abomination, let us look briefly at the ways in which government officials and group members relate to them.

Most of us are unaware of the number of pressure groups we belong to. Because we join many associations in order to share our interests and concerns with others, we tend not to think of them as pressure groups. Each September, as Canadian universities resume classes, thousands of students pay dues to their campus student associations. Most of that money supports local campus activity that has nothing to do with politics, but some of it is channelled to provincial and national federations of student associations, which in turn devote considerable time and money to **lobbying** governments concerning matters such as tax breaks for students, university funding, tuition fees, student loans, and national and international issues that have pricked the conscience of the university community. Acquiring a university degree is a serious business, and if government is to be deeply involved in education we should expect student associations to act as pressure groups.

We do not expect our leisure associations to camp as regularly on the doorsteps of government, yet they are among the most active pressure groups to be found in Canada. For instance, many a rural politician has trembled as provincial legislatures have debated hunting and fishing legislation; game laws have often been the most hotly contended items on legislative agendas, and provincial associations of hunters and anglers have been slow to forget the transgressions of politicians who have opposed their

ideas. Similarly, associations of camping enthusiasts, naturalists, bird watchers, and wilderness buffs have a surprising degree of influence with government agencies, such as Parks Canada, that cater to their interests. In fact, the wilderness orientation of Canada's national parks system is in large part a reflection of the strength of this lobby.

These examples illustrate a basic point: very few pressure groups exist simply to influence government. Their members have joined in order to obtain some special benefit that each organization alone can offer. Yet, because government intrudes so much into our daily lives, these associations become a very convenient vehicle for communicating with government. While most associations inevitably develop some capacity in this role, the members often only very grudgingly allow this to happen — lobbying governments is an expensive business. But as the need to express their views becomes more urgent, they hire consultants, undertake studies, appoint "government liaison officers," meet with officials and politicians, and generally join the babble of tongues that surrounds the policy process.

From the group members' point of view, then, the lobbying activities of their associations are first and foremost intended to *communicate*. People in government also see pressure groups in this light, though not always happily. Communication may take many forms, some of them violent, many of them distinctly noticeable to the general public — and therefore usually embarrassing. However, the great majority of them are unobtrusive, involving the careful negotiation of technical and regulatory details of policy. Although often unwelcome — after all, no official or politician likes to be told that a pet project or policy is faulty — pressure groups are frequently the most reliable and the best-informed link between government agencies and the portions of the public that they particularly serve. Indeed, so important is this function that governments have often gone out of their way to encourage the creation of special-interest groups. In the Atlantic provinces the federal and provincial governments did exactly this in the late 1970s when they encouraged independent fishermen to form bodies able to participate in developing policies for managing Canada's newly expanded fishery. "If I had to write the manual for dealing with government," federal Fisheries Minister Romeo LeBlanc told one group, "I would put two main rules of the road: carry a flag—that is, have an organization—and sound your horn. Let people know you are there." By the early 1980s, the Eastern Fishermen's Federation, the chief product of the exercise, was a recognized actor in the fisheries policy community.[2] Similarly, core funding from the federal government was an important factor in developing the modern Canadian Indian movement.[3]

Nor does communication flow in only one direction. Most lobbying organizations present governments with a convenient means of reaching a special audience. Annual meetings can be addressed by ministers and senior officials intent partly on flattering and winning over a special clientele or constituency, but also on conveying various messages: a hint at policy change, an explanation of action, warnings, encouragement, and so on. Eyes watering from cigar and cigarette smoke, perspiring under the television lights, wondering whether they can be heard above the clatter of coffee cups and the hum of comment, guest speakers drone through their after-dinner jokes, their compliments, and their pious reminders, knowing that alert minds in the audience will soon have interpreted the speech's central message and passed it on to the less discerning. Similarly, organization newsletters, regional meetings, and informal get-togethers offer government spokespersons networks for the rapid transmission of information.

If communication is the primary function of pressure groups, *legitimation* is not much less important.[4] That is, pressure groups play a very significant part in persuading both policy makers and the general public that changes in public policy are worthwhile, generally desired, and in the public interest. Because pressure groups frequently speak for a significant proportion of the public that will be affected by a change in policy, governments find it reassuring to have their proposals endorsed by the relevant groups. As Romeo LeBlanc told fishermen

in the speech previously quoted, "Push the officials . . . they like it." Cabinet ministers know how helpful it is to have a pressure group leader tell a legislative committee, as one did in 1975, that "we provided extensive comments . . . with respect to the first draft. When we saw the new bill most of the corrections, changes or criticisms we had found with the first draft had been corrected, modified or vastly improved."[5] In a similar way, group leaders sell their members on the desirability of policy changes.

On the other hand, officials are aware that a disaffected group can use its many connections with the media, the opposition parties, and perhaps other governments to attack policy and so undermine its legitimacy. The mining industry did this between 1967 and 1972 when it disagreed with the federal government over tax reform. Using a combination of general appeals to the government and behind-the-scenes lobbying with provincial governments, the mineral industries eventually forced the federal government to revise its proposals. One of the reasons for their success lay in their ability to persuade the public and the provinces that the new laws would discourage investment in the mining industry and so hurt the economy. In other words, they undermined the legitimacy of the proposed changes.[6] Similar interest group reactions to Finance Minister Allan MacEachen's 1981 budget had the same effect, ultimately leading to a number of changes and an attempt on the part of the finance minister, and his successor, to reform the budget-making process so that interests would have an opportunity to discuss possible tax changes before they become government policy. Fear of the embarrassment caused by such incidents, to say nothing of the disruptive effect on policy, gives government agencies a powerful incentive to consult with pressure groups that has become more pressing as our policy process has become increasingly diffuse.

Administrative and regulatory activities are much less prominent functions than communication and legitimation, but they occur often enough to deserve mention. Provincial administration of social services is often supplemented by the work of groups such as the Children's Aid Society or church-affiliated organizations. In the years when Canada was receiving large numbers of immigrants, voluntary associations provided many facilities that helped newcomers move to, and settle at, their destinations.[7] Today, as tight budgets constrain governments' ability to pay for services we once took for granted, we have begun to revive the practice of encouraging voluntary associations to provide supplementary services, particularly in support of food banks and in home care for the elderly. Often the groups involved in these activities are not thought of as pressure groups, but because they often do contribute to the development of policy in their areas of interest, we are justified in thinking of them in this way.

Groups perform administrative functions for several reasons. Often, as we have suggested, governments cannot afford to offer the services that they provide through a combination of volunteer and paid help. Sometimes governments are not willing, for policy reasons, to provide special services, though they are willing to help voluntary associations provide them. The community is so divided over many issues related to birth control, for example, that some governments prefer to support birth control counselling indirectly through general grants to organizations such as Planned Parenthood rather than to advocate directly one position or another. Finally, many groups administer programs that could as easily be carried out by government officials, simply because they have traditionally offered such services. Periodically, as in the case of the Children's Aid Societies in Ontario, these roles come under review and sometimes they are taken over by government.[8]

Regulatory functions are delegated to groups for quite different reasons. Lawyers, doctors, chartered accountants, and other professional groups have been given considerable authority to govern themselves through their associations, largely because governments are reluctant to thrust themselves into the complicated and often treacherous debates that surround professional accreditation and ethics. As well, though, some professional groups have a great deal of influence, and quite probably that has been

exerted to keep government at arm's length. Even so, we see governments increasingly cutting back on this autonomy — for instance, forcing the medical profession, by and large, to accept publicly approved fee schedules or, as in Quebec, by imposing a high degree of regulation on all professional groups.[9]

In summary, we have argued that as far as the political system is concerned, pressure groups serve four functions: they communicate, legitimate, administer, and regulate, though to their members these are often the least important roles that they play. We have suggested that the communications function is the most important.

NOTES

1. This definition was first presented in "Pressure Groups: Adaptive Instruments of Political Communication," in *Pressure Group Behaviour in Canadian Politics*, ed. A. Paul Pross (Toronto: McGraw-Hill Ryerson, 1975), pp. 1–26, and has been elaborated in my *Group Politics and Public Policy* (Toronto: Oxford University Press, 1986).
2. *Lunenberg Progress-Enterprise*, 5 April 1978, p. 16.
3. J. Hugh Faulkner, "Pressuring the Executive," *Canadian Public Administration* 25, no. 2 (1982): 240–44, 248.
4. See David Kwavnick, *Organized Labour and Pressure Politics* (Montreal: McGill-Queen's University Press, 1972) for a useful discussion of this aspect of pressure group life.
5. W.L. Canniff, Technical Director, Canadian Chemical Producers' Association, House of Commons, Standing Committee on Fisheries and Forestry, *Minutes of Proceedings and Evidence*, 17 April 1975, p. 18:4 (Re: "An act to protect human health and the environment from substances that contaminate the environment.")
6. See Arthur Drache, "Improving the Budget Process," *Policy Options* 3, no. 5 (1982): 15–19, and Douglas Hartle, *The Revenue Budget Process of the Government of Canada* (Toronto: Canadian Tax Foundation, 1982).
7. Freda Hawkins, *Canada and Immigration: Public Policy and Public Concern* (Montreal: McGill-Queen's University Press, 1972), p. 301.
8. The role of Children's Aid Societies in Ontario has

been vigorously debated in the past. See particularly *The Globe and Mail*, 16 December 1977, and the debate over the provincial government's intervention in the operation of the Kenora District Office of the Children's Aid Society, in the provincial legislature. See also National Council of Welfare, *In the Best Interests of the Child: A Report by the National Council of Welfare on the Child Welfare System in Canada* (Ottawa: The Council, 1979).

9. See René Dussault and Louis Borgeat, "La reforme des professions au Québec," *Canadian Public Administration* 17, no. 3 (1974): 407.

Governing the Provinces in a Federal System

CLOSE-UP: SEPARATE JURISDICTIONS — FEDERALISM AND THE DEADBEAT DADS

Federalism both connects and separates us in many ways. To the outside world, Canada appears united in a parliamentary system of government, the prominent federal government superimposing its presence on a multiplicity of provinces, territories, and thousands of municipalities and other governing bodies. But as Canadians know, governments separate us by jurisdiction, area, region, vast distances of political geography, and public policy.

On a daily basis, Canadians experience the intermingling of government jurisdictions and of services from all the levels of government. The provinces and municipalities have substantial discretionary powers in many of the policy areas that affect the lives of Canadians most directly — among them, for example, public education, health and safety, family law, transportation, and curbs and gutters.

You can drive to work on the Trans-Canada Highway, which is mostly federally financed, get stopped for a traffic violation by a federal officer, and lose points on your provincial driver's licence. Or, as you walk through the town or city in which you live on the way to your provincially funded college or university, you might pass by a Canada Post letter carrier delivering mail and a municipal police officer patrolling the neighbourhood. The jurisdictions of the three levels of government are interconnected everywhere in one way or another.

The complexities of federalism can open the door to a range of problems — including providing individuals with opportunities to avoid the spirit and the letter of the law. The system naturally produces a patchwork of different policies to be pursued in different provinces and different regions. Such a configuration tends to prevent, among other things, the emergence of a fully unified legal system, thus creating opportunities for certain classes of individuals, under certain circumstances, to evade the law.

At the social level, for example, federalism can foster an unequal division of parenting responsibilities. For instance, provincial laws require mothers to provide by far the major portion of the nurturing and financial support their children need. At the same time, the federal system gives fathers the opportunity to avoid paying the maintenance and child-care costs required by law by making them free to move from one provincial jurisdiction to another.

Fathers who elude their legal responsibility to maintain and support their families are commonly referred to as "deadbeat dads" (although some mothers are guilty of similar omissions). Many deadbeat dads remain in the province in which the families for which they are responsible live, but others move out of the legal jurisdictions of their families entirely. They may work in another province or leave the country altogether in the hope that their family-maintenance responsibilities will somehow disappear, or at least diminish substantially.

Deadbeat dads' frequent and deliberate failure to make their family support payments can have dire consequences for the financial and emotional health of their families. (Across the country, more than 50 percent of the families who should receive support payments do not get them regularly.) All provinces have cracked down not only on fathers who stay in the provinces where their families live, but also on those who choose to leave. Provincial governments pursue these negligent parents partly to prevent families from ending up on provincial welfare roles and creating a burden on the provincial social-assistance system.

The issue of deadbeat dads is one of the many political controversies in Canada that have hinged on the question of federal versus provincial/municipal jurisdiction. Provincial and municipal governments face the problem of limiting the ability of spouses, especially men, to escape the payments they are ordered to make by the courts on the breakup of a marriage. They are currently implementing new ways to prevent people from moving to another province to avoid making payments. Intergovernmental agreements under which spouses who default on payments in one province can be pursued in another are slowly being implemented.

Some provinces want the power to set a formula on which to base their orders for child support. In Quebec and Ontario, for example, provincial governments can require automatic deductions from the paycheques of spouses who have a history of defaulting on payments. In 1996 Nova Scotia passed a hard-line law enabling bureaucrats to take strong action. The government can now seize the property, bank accounts, salaries, and even the driver's licences of deadbeat dads. (The latter option is particularly useful in the case of defaulting parents who make their living on the black market.)

The federal government has been reluctant to alter the tax system to permit the implementation of a system of support payment that is more equitable for the spouse who is raising a family alone. Because divorce law falls under federal jurisdiction, the provinces are usually unable to set levels of support payments. Most provinces want Ottawa to change tax laws that discriminate against custodial parents to permit provincial governments to establish automatic systems of future support payments. In cases where the defaulting parent is not receiving a salary, the provincial government agency would have the power to confiscate and sell goods and furniture, and to seize payments by the federal government, such as unemployment insurance, as well as by the province, such as worker's compensation.

Provinces have always differed to some extent in their approach to public policy on family and other matters. As a result, loopholes have been created that allow individuals to get around provincial laws by moving to other provinces without fear of prosecution. This situation clearly demonstrates that federalism involves the different levels of government in ways that can and do have direct and significant effects on the lives of individual Canadian citizens.

INTRODUCTION: FEDERALISM — A CONTENTIOUS IDEA

Since Confederation, the most contentious feature of Canada's governing system has been the relationship between the federal and provincial levels of government. As Michael Howlett and Martin Robin note in Chapter 35, "Provincial Governments and Province Building," the provinces were once colonies of imperial England and France, and the colonists' ideas of what was desirable government with respect to local matters had a profound impact on the range of powers provinces were granted under Confederation. The colonists' notions about national government also influenced the nature of what would become, by the latter part of the nineteenth century, the federal government of Canada.

Canadian federalism evolved as a system of government in which two levels, national and provincial, were constitutionally assigned governing authority over the same territory and the people who lived and worked there. But as federalism evolved, the responsibilities of the different levels of government were sorted out through a political and legal, but not a procedural, process. To understand why federalism in Canada is always up for negotiation, we need to start with an appreciation of the historical setting that contributed to the original expectations of the early Canadian federalists.

In the 1860s the Fathers of Confederation were determined to create a strong central government that would permit the original provinces to make and administer public policies at the regional and local levels. But the people who wrote our Constitution in the 1860s foresaw a federation in which the central government would gradually, if not immediately, come to exercise control over everything the provinces did, notwithstanding the cultural distinctiveness of Quebec and the suspicions of some of the Quebec delegates. In fact, as Keith Brownsey and Michael Howlett note in Chapter 36, legend has it that Canada's first prime minister, John A. Macdonald, believed provincial governments might eventually disappear. After all was said and done, strong centralizing powers were delegated to, and reserved for, the federal government; other powers were assigned to the provinces, and some were left for both levels to share.

THE FORCES OF DECENTRALIZATION

The British North America Act (Constitution Act, 1867) provided the initial outline of jurisdictions for the provinces and the national government. Few observers at the time would have predicted that the political dynamics among the provinces and the federal government would alter the original distribution of powers very much. In Chapter 37, James J. Guy takes us through the evolution of Canadian federalism from Confederation to the present.

As the provinces gained more ground against the federal government, they developed a confrontational attitude comparable to that of the opposition parties in the House of Commons. Another major cause of decentralization lies in the changing priorities of Canadian society since the nineteenth century. When the Constitution Act, 1867, was adopted, provincial powers in the areas of education, health, municipalities, and welfare were not regarded by Canadians as paramount government services. Today, Canadians no longer consider the role provincial governments play in their lives as secondary to that of the federal government.

In effect, federalism has not always enhanced the centralizing powers or the jurisdictions of the federal government. Rather, federalism has constrained the federal government and continues to limit its ability to govern decisively, without the consent and cooperation of the provinces. Simultaneously, it has enabled each province to create its own distinctive patterns of economic and social development, as discussed in Chapter 38, "The Provinces and Regional-Economic Conflicts," by Rand Dyck.

In the 1990s, the tyranny of the global market combined with the massive public indebtedness of the Canadian economy has forced the federal government to consider shifting many of its original responsibilities to the provinces. As part of Ottawa's strategy to reduce government spending and indebtedness, the size of government has been shrunk, and federal transfer payments and cost-sharing programs have been cut. Although Canada's federal system is still constitutionally centralized, the present reality is that the federal government cannot govern Canada on its own.

The evolution of Canadian federalism has been influenced most by the socio-political culture of Quebec and by that province's strong demands for sovereign empowerment. Quebec's has been the strongest and most constant movement for provincial autonomy in Canada ever since the British officially recognized the special status of the "French fact" in the Quebec Act, 1774, thereby effectively acknowledging it as the basis for the creation of a sovereign and independent society.

PROVINCIAL EQUALITY AND FEDERALISM

Quebec has relentlessly challenged the framework and procedures of Canadian federalism by maintaining a nationalistic political and governmental culture distinct from that of any other province in Canada. The enduring nationalism in Quebec has kept Canadian federalism sensitive to the issue of provincial autonomy and made the federal government reluctant to use its constitutional powers to keep the provinces subordinate.

Quebec has argued for **asymmetrical federalism** and has pursued a special status among provinces to buttress its role as the legitimate protector and promoter of francophone interests. This most fundamental divergence between Quebec, the federal government, and the other provinces will need to be settled if Canada is to resolve its problems of government.

However, Canadian federalism has created many obstacles for achieving national unity. As Rand Dyck points out in Chapter 38, federal–provincial economic relations have been a source of continuing conflict and controversy. Moreover, federal governments have not been very attentive to their capacity to produce enormous debt, to the point of national crisis. Quebec sovereignists have used Canada's enormous debt burden as evidence of the failure of the federal system, and as a good reason to leave it.

Is the Canadian federal system essentially cooperative, or is it competitive? Can federalism be interpreted both as a rivalry between the provinces and Ottawa, and as a partnership and fraternity among all governments? A bewildering system of more than six thousand governments could not operate without a substantial measure of co-operation, but there is also a great deal of tension built into the system, and it will probably never disappear.

THINKING IT OVER

1. What do Michael Howlett and Martin Robin (Chapter 35) mean by province building? The status of provincial governments has fluctuated throughout Canadian history. How would you describe that status today, and in what direction is it likely to evolve? Do Canadian provinces have too much power? Do Canadians need a strong central government in the contemporary global economy?

2. Keith Brownsey and Michael Howlett (Chapter 36) discuss the phenomenon of the "provincial state" in Canada. Are Canada's provinces "states" in the same sense as independent states in the international system? What does this say about the nature of Canadian federalism?

3. James J. Guy (Chapter 37) traces the development of Canadian federalism. Did the Fathers of Confederation intend Canada to develop into its present federal configuration? Explain. Trace the evolution of Canadian federalism. Can we say that Canadian federalism works in theory but not in practice, or is the reverse true?

4. Based on what you have learned from all the presentations in this section, explain what makes Quebec such a special province. What are some the most distinctive characteristics of Quebec, compared with the other provinces?

5. What does Rand Dyck (Chapter 38) mean by "regional-economic conflicts"? Give some examples. How have regional economic conflicts affected the character of Canadian federalism? Does the increasingly decentralized nature of governance in Canada, coupled with rising debt, erode the federal government's capacity to deal with regional economic disparities? Rand Dyck describes the federal system in terms of winners and losers. Are there any winners left in our federal system?

6. How safe is the future of our federal system in view of the Quebec question? Can Canada change its federal structures without unravelling in the process? Should Canada make fundamental changes to what has evolved to be its federal system? Or are the present structures in the federal system adaptive enough?

GLOSSARY

asymmetrical federalism A departure from the intended symmetrical arrangement of provinces within a centralized or decentralized intergovernmental system, wherein some provinces would exercise more powers than others.

autonomous state The autonomy of a state is partly a matter of power (whether the state has the capacity to enforce its own laws) and partly a matter of recognized authority (whether it is regarded by other states as the legitimate governing entity).

disallowance The constitutional power of the federal government to annul a provincial law within a year of its passage.

equalization A concept in Canada's federal system that assumes that the "have" provinces will provide enough transferable wealth to the "have not" provinces to ensure that all provinces are able to dispense equal benefits and opportunities to Canadians from coast to coast to coast. Equalization payments were entrenched in the Constitution in 1982.

federalism The constitutional division and sharing of government responsibilities and jurisdictions between the national and provincial political systems.

federal–provincial dialectic The differential and argumentative character of federal–provincial relations that sometimes results in conflict, and other times in co-operation.

First Ministers' Conferences A feature of Canadian federalism dating back to 1887 that brings together premiers or Cabinet ministers of provincial governments, the prime minister, and members of the federal Cabinet in summit meetings devoted to discussing and negotiating solutions to problems and issues facing the country.

intergovernmental relations The workings of the federal system of government, by which is meant the entire set of interactions among the federal, provincial, and municipal levels of government.

reservation A constitutional provision allowing federally appointed lieutenant-governors to reserve royal assent on a provincial bill, placing the final decision before the federal Cabinet.

subnational politics All political and governing behaviour that is conducted at a level below that of the national or federal government and that is specified or implied by the distribution of powers outlined in a constitution.

welfare state A state in which the government assumes responsibility for the welfare of people within its jurisdiction, especially with respect to the redistribution of income to reduce social inequality and the administration of public policy programs that service the social and economic needs of communities.

ADDITIONAL READINGS

Banting, Keith, Douglas Brown, and Thomas Courchene, eds. 1994. *The Future of Fiscal Federalism.* Kingston: School of Policy Studies, Queen's University.

Brownsey, Keith, and Michael Howlett, eds. 1992. *The Provincial State: Politics in Canada's Provinces and Territories.* Toronto: Copp Clark Pitman.

Cairns, Alan C. 1992. *Charter versus Federalism: The Dilemmas of Constitutional Reform.* Montreal and Kingston: McGill-Queen's University Press.

Coates, Ken, and William Morrison. 1992. *The Forgotten North: A History of Canada's Provincial Norths.* Toronto: James Lorimer & Company.

Dyck, Rand. 1996. *Provincial Politics in Canada.* 3rd ed. Scarborough, Ont.: Prentice-Hall Canada.

Forbes, E.R., and D.A. Muise. 1993. *The Atlantic Provinces in Confederation.* Toronto: University of Toronto Press.

Gagnon, Alain, and M.B. Montcalm. 1990. *Quebec: Beyond the Quiet Revolution.* Scarborough, Ont.: Nelson Canada.

Goudzwaard, Bob, and Harry de Lange. 1995. *Beyond Poverty and Affluence.* Toronto: University of Toronto Press.

Randall, Stephen, and Roger Gibbins. 1994. *Federalism and the World Order.* Calgary: Calgary University Press.

Russell, Peter, et al. 1990. *Federalism and the Charter: Leading Constitutional Decisions.* Ottawa: Carleton University Press.

Simeon, Richard, and Ian Robinson. 1990. *State, Society and the Development of Canadian Federalism.* Toronto: University of Toronto Press.

Stevenson, Garth. 1993. *Ex Uno Plures: Federal–Provincial Relations in Canada,*

1867–1896. Montreal: McGill-Queen's University Press.

Tomlin, Stephen. 1995. *Ottawa and the Outer Provinces*. Toronto: James Lorimer & Company.

Vipond, Robert. 1991. *Liberty and Community: Canadian Federalism and the Failure of the Constitution*. Albany: State University of New York Press.

Young, Robert. 1991. *Confederation in Crisis*. Toronto: James Lorimer & Company.

Provincial Governments and
Province Building

MICHAEL HOWLETT
MARTIN ROBIN

Many people are not aware of all the powers and responsibilities of Canada's provincial governments. Protecting the environment, running universities, maintaining hospital insurance, and caring for the poor and elderly are all largely provincial responsibilities. If a **welfare state** is one in which governments have programs devoted to health, social security, and universal education, then in Canada we have ten welfare states, since all of these components are under provincial jurisdiction. The provinces together spend more money than the federal government, employ more people, and collectively are approaching a debt load comparable to that of Ottawa.

The study of political life in Canada, then, is not complete without a look at important subnational levels of government. This is also true of many other countries. Like national governments, subnational governments are the subjects of hypotheses, investigation, and theory testing in political science.

Recent surveys and public opinion polls have indicated that many Canadians are unaware of the role and activities of provincial governments. This is an interesting phenomenon that reflects the varied nature of Canadian federalism and the substantial range of opinions expressed about the proper role and responsibilities of subnational government during Canada's history.

Most of the provinces have colonial histories that predate the creation of the federal political system in 1867. Only Manitoba, Saskatchewan, and Alberta — created in 1870 and 1905 out of land purchased from the Hudson's Bay Company in 1869 — have non-Native histories shorter than that of the federal government. The other provinces have much longer histories, extending back to the days of the French, British, Russian, and Spanish colonization of North America in the sixteenth and seventeenth centuries.

Throughout that time, what are now provinces were separate colonies. By the mid-nineteenth century most had obtained self-governing status under British rule. This entailed the creation of colonial legislative bodies and administrations with control over their lands and resources. Confederation was negotiated by representatives of three of those provinces — Nova Scotia, New Brunswick, and the United Province of Canada (made up of Quebec and Ontario) — with the aim of creating a common market throughout the northern half of North America. However, virtually from the inception of unity talks in 1864, politicians have debated the proper roles of the provincial and national governments.

Canada's first prime minister and one of the original negotiators of the Confederation arrangement, Sir John A. Macdonald, argued that provincial governments were no more than glorified municipal governments whose role in the new confederation would be minor and would decline over time. Provincial leaders did not share this view and

SOURCE: "Provincial Politics," in Michael Howlett and David Laycock, eds., *The Puzzles of Power: An Introduction to Political Science* (Toronto: Copp Clark Longman, 1994), pp. 451–58. Reprinted by permission of the publisher.

engaged the federal government in public struggles over provincial rights and powers.

The most bitter struggles were waged by Ontario over the Manitoba boundary question and by British Columbia over the question of Chinese immigration. Other major struggles involved the Manitoba and federal governments over north–south railway construction and the Nova Scotia and federal governments over freight rates and railway tariffs. These struggles were resolved in the courts, with the provinces winning a series of crucial cases before the highest court of appeal in the British Empire, the Judicial Committee of the Privy Council. Between roughly 1890 and 1949, provincial governments also forced the federal government to stop vetoing provincial laws through the federal powers of **reservation** and **disallowance**. Provincial governments simply continued to pass the same pieces of legislation until the federal government eventually abandoned its exercise of formal constitutional powers.[1]

By the turn of the century, these provincial actions had forced the federal government to recognize the continuing powers and responsibilities of the provinces. This ushered in a new era of federal–provincial diplomacy in which the two orders of government attempted to resolve their differences through negotiation. By 1896, Sir Wilfrid Laurier had taken many leading provincial politicians into his federal cabinet in Canada's first attempt at constitutional reconciliation. Although this effort only temporarily halted such wrangling, which soon began again in earnest over the division of tax revenues in the country,[2] it resulted in a great deal more attention being paid to the provinces in studies of Canada's political system.

Thus, in 1914, when two of Canada's first political scientists set out to explain the country to the outside world, they named their multivolume work *Canada and Its Provinces*. Adam Shortt and Arthur Doughty organized their texts around the politics, economics, cultures, and societies of the country's then nine provinces and two territories.[3]

The status of the provinces waned during the First World War, when the federal government's war effort led it to assume many provincial powers. While those powers were returned to the provinces in the 1920s, the provinces suffered during the Great Depression of the 1930s, when large demands were placed upon them for welfare and unemployment relief when they could ill afford them.[4] During the Second World War the federal government again took over direction of the economy and usurped many provincial powers over natural resources, labour, and taxation under the terms of its emergency powers.[5] By the end of the war, the federal government completely dominated the provinces.

During this lengthy period, academic efforts tended to mirror political practice, and the provinces were virtually ignored in studies of Canadian politics. Major works by Dawson and Corry, for example, concentrated exclusively on the "colony-to-nation" theme — Canada slowly earning its own place in the international system — and failed to devote any attention to the provinces' role in Canadian government.[6]

In the 1950s and 1960s, academic attention swung once again to provincial politics, with increased provincial exercise of their constitutional rights and responsibilities and a widespread questioning of federal dominance of national affairs. Intrigued by the election of North America's first socialist government, in Saskatchewan in 1944, American foundations funded studies of provincial governments in Western Canada in the 1950s[7] and then in several other provinces in the early 1960s.[8] The development of the independence movement in Quebec[9] and the continual problems plaguing Newfoundland's economy sparked studies of those provinces.[10] Development issues emerging in the territories resulted in the first studies of the Canadian North.[11]

Provincial governments continued to expand in size and scope throughout the 1960s and 1970s. They asserted their jurisdiction in areas such as pensions, resources, and transportation and developed a broad array of regulatory agencies and Crown corporations to pursue their ends.[12] By the 1970s many Canadian scholars had recognized that understanding the general dynamics of Canadian government required a careful examination of the provinces. The modern era of studies of provincial governments and societies had begun.

These studies emphasized chronicling the development of specific provinces, comparing developments from one jurisdiction to another, and developing theoretical models to explain the differences and similarities among provinces. Several case studies helped fill the gaps in coverage of the provinces occasioned by the earlier piecemeal approach.[13] The first serious effort at comparative treatment of the provinces was produced,[14] as was the first theoretical treatment of provincial life, Simeon and Elkins' "political culture" approach.[15]

Simeon and Elkins utilized a framework developed in American studies of comparative politics, which emphasized the impact of national differences in values, attitudes, traditions, and beliefs on the nature and type of national political institutions. Different regime types were identified as correlating with characteristic "political cultures" in different countries. Simeon and Elkins applied the same techniques to analysis of subnational governments and societies. Utilizing survey research tools similar to those employed in national studies, they found that different provincial populations had distinct attitudes towards both government and modes of political participation. However, they themselves questioned the usefulness of such findings, given historical and contemporary similarities in provincial political regimes. They often had difficulty explaining the origins of the differences they had found. Other critics called the entire approach into question, noting that it was apparent that most provincial governments adopted similar policies and engaged in similar activities despite some differences in the attitudes held by their populations.

An alternative theoretical perspective emerged from the interest in Canadian political economy, which was occasioned by concerns about American penetration of the Canadian economy in the early 1970s. In the course of re-examining Canada's role in the continental and international economies, the provinces were analysed from a resource–hinterland perspective.[16] This perspective argued that the provinces and provincial governments were significant players in a system of continental resource exploitation in which Canadian wheat, timber, minerals, and energy were exported to the United States in exchange for manufactured goods.

Such trade, it was argued, resulted in the systematic underdevelopment of the eastern and western regions of the country, which remained resource hinterlands to wealthier metropolitan areas in the United States and Central Canada.[17] However, as critics of this approach noted, many areas of Quebec and Ontario were as dependent on resource exploitation as the eastern or western provinces. More significantly, critics noted that trade in resources, especially energy resources like oil, gas, and hydro-electricity, could result in large amounts of money remaining in the producing provinces. Like the political culture approach that preceded it, the political economy approach was substantially modified in the face of such criticism.

In the 1980s many insights of the political culture and political economy perspectives were synthesized into a third general approach to Canadian provincial politics. This focussed not only on the nature of provincial societies and economies but also on the capacity of provincial states to alter and affect the pattern of provincial development. Building on early work that had noted the key role played by provincial political institutions in the life of the nation,[18] this approach called for a fundamental reinterpretation of the dominant perspective on Canadian federalism. It proposed complementing a focus on the federal government's role in "nation building" with one on the provinces' role in a concurrent historical process of "province building." This province-building approach stimulated examination of the effect of political institutions on social and economic development, reversing a theoretical perspective focussing on societal actors and events that was characteristic of earlier perspectives on provincial government and politics.[19]

Although criticized for its exaggerated claims and lack of precision,[20] the province-building perspective's impact should not be underestimated. It has greatly influenced contemporary research of two general types — case studies and comparative subnational politics. In the 1980s and 1990s there has been a plethora of new case studies of provincial governments, tending to focus on a common set of political, economic, social, and cultural characteristics. These studies are concerned with the development of provincial states and societies in the context of their governments' modernization efforts. Research focusses on social services, public sector growth, economic development, and alterations in provincial social structures and political systems.[21] Rather than simply describing the historical development of provincial states and societies as did many earlier case studies, these studies attempt to examine the nature of provincial and territorial states and societies and the interactions and interrelationships existing between them.

Many present-day studies are more explicitly comparative than in the past, often involving systematic evaluation of provinces' experiences to determine the causes and consequences of state action. Such studies have examined, among other things, causes of public expenditure growth, determinants of provincial party systems, methods of provincial budgetary control, and conscious provincial emulation of each others' policy initiatives.[22]

Studies of provincial government and politics have come a long way since 1970. The major problem encountered with the fluctuating status of the provinces in Canadian affairs has been largely overcome, and the provinces accorded their due status as important state institutions. Different theoretical approaches have been tried, and the political significance of distinctive provincial societies and economic structures underlined, while the need to carefully evaluate state–society linkages at the provincial level has also been made apparent. Case studies continue to examine specific aspects of social and political relationships, and provincial comparisons reveal similarities and differences in provincial experiences with government and politics. Perhaps this is setting the stage for comparisons of Canadian **subnational politics** with those of other countries and for integrating such findings with general theories of national politics and political life. The

large range of case and comparative studies now being undertaken will help ensure that the dynamics and impact of Canadian provincial politics will no longer be received with surprise by anyone.

NOTES

1. On the history of these disputes see E.R. Forbes, *The Maritime Rights Movement, 1919–1927* (Montreal: McGill-Queen's University Press, 1985); G.V. LaForest, *Disallowance and Reservation of Provincial Legislation* (Ottawa: Department of Justice, 1955); and J.C. Morrison, *Oliver Mowat and the Development of Provincial Rights in Ontario: A Study in Dominion-Provincial Relations* (Toronto: Department of Public Records and Archives, 1961).

2. J.A. Maxwell, *Federal Subsidies to the Provincial Governments in Canada* (Cambridge: Harvard University Press, 1937).

3. Adam Shortt and Arthur G. Doughty, *Canada and Its Provinces: A History of the Canadian People and Their Institutions, by One Hundred Associates*, 23 vols. (Toronto: Glasgow, Brook, 1914–17).

4. William Archibald Mackintosh, *The Economic Background of Dominion-Provincial Relations: A Study Prepared for the Royal Commission on Dominion-Provincial Relations* (Ottawa: King's Printer, 1939).

5. P.A. Crepeau and C.B. Macpherson, eds., *The Future of Canadian Federalism* (Toronto: University of Toronto Press, 1965).

6. J.A. Corry, *Democratic Government and Politics* (Toronto: University of Toronto Press, 1951), and Robert MacGregor Dawson, *The Government of Canada* (Toronto: University of Toronto Press, 1947).

7. See S.M. Lipset, *Agrarian Socialism* (Berkeley: University of California Press, 1950), and C.B. Macpherson, *Democracy in Alberta* (Toronto: University of Toronto Press, 1962).

8. Among the works included in this series were Murray S. Donnelly, *The Government of Manitoba* (Toronto: University of Toronto Press, 1963); Frank MacKinnon, *The Government of Prince Edward Island* (Toronto: University of Toronto Press, 1951); F.F. Schindeler, *Responsible Government in Ontario* (Toronto: University of Toronto Press, 1969); and Hugh Thorburn, *Politics in New Brunswick* (Toronto: University of Toronto Press, 1961).

9. See, for example, K. McRoberts and D. Postgate, *Quebec: Social Change and Political Crisis* (Toronto: McClelland and Stewart, 1980), and Herbert Quinn, *The Union Nationale: Quebec Nationalism from Duplessis to Quebec's Quiet Revolution* (Toronto: University of Toronto Press, 1979).

10. For example, S.J.R. Noel, *Politics in Newfoundland* (Toronto: University of Toronto Press, 1971).

11. K.J. Rea, *The Political Economy of the Canadian North* (Toronto: University of Toronto Press, 1968).

12. See M. Chandler and W. Chandler, *Public Policy and Provincial Politics* (Toronto: McGraw-Hill, 1979); M. Chandler and W. Chandler, "Public Administration in the Provinces," *Canadian Public Administration* 25, 4 (1982): 580–602; and Margot Priest and Aron Wohl, "The Growth of Federal and Provincial Regulation of Economic Activity, 1867–1978," in *Government Regulation: Scope, Growth, Process*, ed. W.T. Stanbury (Montreal: Institute for Research on Public Policy, 1980).

13. Martin Robin, ed., *Canadian Provincial Politics: The Party Systems of the Ten Provinces* (Scarborough: Prentice Hall, 1972), and Martin Robin, ed., *Canadian Provincial Politics* (Scarborough: Prentice Hall, 1978).

14. See David J. Bellamy, Jon H. Pammett, and Donald C. Rowat, eds., *Provincial Political Systems: Comparative Essays* (Toronto: Methuen, 1976).

15. See David Elkins and Richard Simeon, eds., *Small Worlds: Provinces and Parties in Canadian Political Life* (Toronto: Methuen, 1980).

16. See T.W. Acheson, "The National Policy and the Industrialization of the Maritimes, 1880–1910," *Acadiensis* 1 (1972); David Alexander, *Atlantic Canada and Confederation* (Toronto: University of Toronto Press, 1983); H.V. Nelles, *The Politics of Development* (Toronto: Macmillan, 1974); and J. Richards and L. Pratt, *Prairie Capitalism: Power and Influence in the New West* (Toronto: McClelland and Stewart, 1977).

17. See, for example, R.J. Brym and R.J. Sacouman, eds., *Underdevelopment and Social Movements in Atlantic Canada* (Toronto: New Hogtown Press, 1979), and Michael Clow, "Politics and Uneven Capitalist Development: The Maritime Challenge to the Study of Canadian Political Economy," *Studies in Political Economy* 14 (1984).

18. E.R. Black and A.C. Cairns, "A Different Perspective on Canadian Federalism," *Canadian Public Administration* 9, 1 (1966): 27–44.

19. See Harold Chorney and Phillip Hansen, "Neo-Conservatism, Social Democracy, and 'Province-Building': The Experience of Manitoba," *Canadian Review of Sociology and Anthropology* 22, 1 (1985): 1–29, and Larry Pratt, "The State and Province-Building: Alberta's Development Strategy," in *The Canadian State: Political Economy and Political Power*, ed. L. Panitch (Toronto: University of Toronto Press, 1977).

20. R.A. Young, Phillipe Faucher, and André Blais, "The Concept of Province Building: A Critique," *Canadian Journal of Political Science* 17 (1984): 783–818.

21. See, for example, James Bickerton, *Nova Scotia, Ottawa, and the Politics of Regional Development* (Toronto: University of Toronto Press, 1990), and Keith Brownsey and Michael Howlett, eds., *The Provincial State: Politics in Canada's Provinces and Territories* (Toronto: Copp Clark Pitman, 1992).

22. For example, L.R. Jones and Jerry L. McCaffery, *Government Response to Financial Constraints: Budgetary Control in Canada* (New York: Greenwood Press, 1989).

The Provincial State in Canada

KEITH BROWNSEY
MICHAEL HOWLETT

There is a legend in Canadian politics that John A. Macdonald believed the provinces would wither away. He argued that the British North America Act gave the important powers to the federal government and that the provinces would soon become no more than municipal governments providing a few insignificant services to individuals within their boundaries. But John A. Macdonald was wrong. The provinces have become much more than municipal governments. Not only have the powers assigned to them in the original Confederation agreement become increasingly important, the very fact that they are separate political entities has given them the institutional and political legitimacy to seek further powers and support from both the national government and from their own constituents.[1]

One of the most neglected areas in the study of Canadian history and politics is the development of the "provincial state." There has been a lot of talk in the last few years about "the state." Much has been written about the **autonomous state**, the state in capitalist society, the Canadian state, and about the world state system. The literature is extensive; it encompasses a wide ideological range from Weber/Hintze concepts of the rational and autonomous state to instrumental Marxist notions of the state as captive of the bourgeoisie. An important question it does not address, however, is whether Canada's provinces and territories are

"states" in the same sense as the better-known nation states of the world system.

States, as Rueschemeyer and Evans claim, are sets of organizations that have the ability to make binding decisions for people and organizations located within a territory. Moreover, they are able to implement these decisions by force if necessary.[2] They are a mix of social tensions, class struggles, and external influences that define their territory and frame their policy communities.[3] In this sense Canada's provinces and territories qualify as "states." They are constitutionally empowered to make binding decisions on their citizens and they are shaped and defined both by the very constitutional arrangements that give them their authority and by their internal class structures and external economic relations.[4]

The provinces and territories share a number of ideological and institutional features which have created a system of political interaction and discourse in Canada that helps to hold the country together. But this is only one part of the **federal-provincial dialectic**. Faced with specific problems—from the preservation of a distinct society to the protection of the family farm—the provinces have responded in ways that constitute variations on the common Canadian theme.

Out of these qualities of provincial life have developed two historical patterns. First, there has been a continuous connection between the construction of

SOURCE: "Introduction: The Provincial State in Canada," in Keith Brownsey and Michael Howlett, eds., *The Provincial State: Politics in Canada's Provinces and Territories* (Toronto: Copp Clark Pitman, 1992), pp. 1–8. Reprinted by permission of the publisher.

regional and national centres and the process of building economic and cultural institutions. Institution building in the provinces and territories has been essential to what various authors have described as province building. The strength of provincial governments has been judged according to their capacity to construct such institutions as a provincial bureaucracy, provide a diversified economic structure, and maintain social harmony. Second, there has also been competition between different groups within the provinces over access to and control of these local centres of power. It is this competition for control of provincial and territorial institutions that has led to confrontation between the different elements of society over the proper role and purpose of provincial and territorial government. Different interests within provincial and territorial societies have led to differing ideological visions of the purpose and content of provincial and territorial government. Yet there is another dimension to these traditional ideological battles in Canada. Provincial and territorial political life has turned not only on issues of government intervention in the marketplace and the legitimacy of the welfare state, but also on such tensions as those between strong provinces and strong central governments, between centralization and decentralization.[5]

Associated with the institutions of Canadian provincial and territorial life has been the development of unique patterns of change. These patterns are characterized by a predisposition of provincial governments aligned with the federal government to be transmitters of economic, political, and social innovations such as extensions of the franchise or medicare. Second, there has been a tendency of provincial and territorial parties to establish their bases of support in a broader social stratum than the parties at the federal level and hence to be more closely allied with movements of protest and reform. Finally, there is an accompanying predisposition for provincial and territorial governments and groups to develop institutions away and apart from the central or national government.

While Canadian provinces share characteristics of subnational units in other federal states, they have also tended to develop specific institutional profiles of their own. The most common problem for the provinces has been and remains the maintenance of a general standard of economic and socio-cultural development which is more or less the same level as that prevailing in the most prosperous areas. As a number of social scientists have pointed out in a variety of contexts, however, small internal markets such as those found in the provinces and territories are not — with a few exceptions — large enough to obtain sufficient economies of scale necessary for any kind of autonomous development.

The economies of the provinces and territories are neither large enough nor diversified enough to produce all that the province needs or to consume all that it produces. The result is that provinces have tended to specialize for external markets. This specialization was based on geographic location, resources, social structure, and cultural traditions but has also been led in certain directions by provincial states. Quebec, for example, has, with the help of the federal government, attempted to specialize in aerospace, pharmaceuticals, and other technology-intensive goods and services in order to offset a reliance on declining industries such as low-wage manufacturing and resource exploitation. Because of particular resource endowments, other provinces have tended to specialize in particular goods such as grain, fish products, oil and natural gas, automobiles, and forest products. This specialization has been further reinforced by "the pressures of a liberal international economy."[6] Yet unlike a number of small European states, the provinces and territories have not been able to make the necessary economic adjustments to the new globalized economy without political, economic, and social dislocations such as those experienced in the Atlantic provinces in the 1970s, British Columbia in the mid-1980s, and the Prairies and Ontario and Quebec in the 1990s. The politics of Canada's provinces and territories have been shaped by the various responses of their governments to rapidly changing economic circumstances.

Different provinces and territories have developed different strategies for coping with these problems.

Alberta, for example, has tried to develop a petro-chemical industry through generous incentive programs and loan guarantees, while Quebec has attempted to forge a new alliance between business, government, and labour in order to lessen the harsher aspects of a changing economy. Ontario, on the other hand, has done little since the restraint program of the mid-1970s to cope with a new global economic context. Instead of policies and programs designed to promote economic flexibility and political stability, Ontario governments of various political ideologies have relied simply on crisis management with little thought or money given to long-range solutions. Whatever the response to changing economic conditions, specialization has created a dependency on and sensitivity to changes in international markets. As Saskatchewan's grain farmers have understood for generations, a province or territory cannot directly influence the demand for its products.

These problems are present not only in the economic life of the provinces and territories but also in the areas of cultural, technological, and political life. In the area of technology, one of the major problems is how various scientific discoveries with economic promise can be exploited when the necessary investment in facilities and personnel is not forthcoming in Canada from either private or public sources. The small scientific communities in the provinces and territories face a problem of maintaining their autonomy and distinctiveness from either transnational corporations or the larger and better-funded scientific communities in the United States, Western Europe, and Asia. In the area of education, the provinces and territories are under enormous international pressure to bring their educational systems into line with those in Japan and the European Community as well as other nations.[7] As trade barriers continue to crumble in Canada — not only in external markets but internally as well — provincial societies are finding it increasingly necessary to standardize their educational systems with those in their competitors' jurisdictions. In order to compete in the globalized economy, a trained and flexible work force, as Robert Reich argues, is increasingly necessary.[8] But

this standardization may endanger the distinctive identities of the provincial and territorial societies. Instead of accepting the more universal reforms of their economic competitors, provinces and territories may emphasize their own traditions, history, and internal problems. In terms of culture, each province and territory is faced with the problem of how to absorb the flood of cultural "goods and services" from the United States and elsewhere and still maintain its own identity.

Nevertheless, the types of specialization open to Canada's provinces and territories, and the nature of their economic circumstances, may change over time. One of the problems they may encounter is a reliance on a single, international market. Any downward shift in the demand for the product(s) they produce leads to both economic and social problems that are destructive of provincial and territorial society. The classic Canadian example of Saskatchewan's dependence on the production of grain and oil seeds illustrates this point. Since 1900 Saskatchewan has adapted to a particular type of international market and pattern of trade. With powerful ministers in Ottawa, the province had been able to focus the national government's attention on its needs in the international and domestic setting. But once grain prices begin to decline — as they first did in the 1920s and again in the 1980s — there was little that either the provincial or federal government could do for Saskatchewan's farmers. The province did not and does not have enough flexibility to change in the face of changing international conditions. The problem of economic inflexibility now conforms all of Canada's provinces and territories.

While the ten provinces and two territories have sought different solutions to the problem of modernization in a small, open economy, they are remarkably similar in their methods. Governments of both the left and the right have intervened in their provincial and territorial economies to preserve and foster economic growth. They have not been passive bystanders willing to act simply as rule makers and umpires. Provincial and territorial governments have aggressively promoted economic and social development. Even the most avowedly free-market governments have acted to stimulate economic development in their jurisdiction. For example, as Howlett and Brownsey argue, the government of British Columbia in the 1980s, while cutting back various social programs and making substantial cuts in the civil service, spent billions of dollars on a world's fair and the development of the province's northeast coal fields. The provincial state is seen as an integral part of economic and social development in the provinces and territories. Such are the necessities of provincial and territorial government in Canada. Although there is a growing literature on the politics of individual provinces, there have been surprisingly few overviews of provincial and territorial politics in Canada. As well, these collections have focussed on the themes of political culture and electoral analysis or have been descriptive histories. None has attempted an overview of provincial politics in Canada within the broadly defined intellectual tradition of political economy.

NOTES

1. Alan C. Cairns, "The Governments and Societies of Canadian Federalism," *Canadian Journal of Political Science* 10 (December 1977): 695–734.

2. Dietrich Rueschemeyer and Peter B. Evans, "The State and Economic Transformation: Toward an Analysis of the Conditions Underlying Effective Intervention," in *Bringing the State Back In*, ed. Peter B. Evans, Dietrich Rueschemeyer, and Theda Skocpol (New York: Cambridge University Press, 1985), 46–47.

3. Otto Hintze, "The Formation of States and Constitutional Development: A Study in History and Politics," in *The Historical Essays of Otto Hintze*, ed. and trans. Felix Gilbert (New York: Oxford University Press, 1975), 159–61.

4. Alan C. Cairns, "The Governments and Societies of Canadian Federalism," 695–725.

5. Christopher Dunn, "Do Canadian Provinces Have Too Much Power?" (Paper delivered at the annual meeting of the Canadian Political Science Association, Victoria, May 1990).

6. Peter J. Katzenstein, *Small States in World Markets: Industrial Policy in Europe* (Ithaca, NY: Cornell University Press, 1985), 10.

7. Jeffery Simpson, "The counter-revolution Canada needs to get in step with the world," *Globe and Mail*, 2 January 1992, A14.

8. See Robert B. Reich, *The Work of Nations* (New York: Alfred A. Knopf, 1991), especially Parts Two and Three.

The Provinces and Federalism

JAMES J. GUY

The Fathers of Confederation did not foresee a federal system like the one we have now. The federal government has maintained the enormous range of governing powers they wanted it to have. But, over the years, the politics of Canadian **federalism** has produced one of the most decentralized federal systems in the international community.

One of the paradoxes of our political system is that the great expansion of government powers has conferred important jurisdictions on the provincial governments. In fact, all levels of government have expanded the services they administer to an extent never imagined by the original nineteenth-century architects of federalism.

The federal and provincial governments have grown hand in hand. Canadians have come to believe strongly that their provincial government is the cradle of local control and grass-roots governing. In many ways, Canada's federal system is a logical outcome of the contradictory impulses of Canadians who want to find national solutions for building a large nation-state yet who fiercely want to retain local and regional control over their lives.

The role of the provinces in how we govern ourselves is fundamentally that they can meet regional and local demands. Federalism also assumes that, when provinces get rich, they contribute to national wealth. At the same time, provincial governments provide opportunities for experimentation on a small scale as a counterweight to extensive national standards that can be imposed on the provinces by the federal government. In 1994, the federal government began to dismantle the Department of Indian Affairs and Northern Development, beginning with the province of Manitoba so as to monitor the effects that the change might have on aboriginals living in the other provinces.

Provincial governments can usually act more swiftly than the federal government in response to local problems. Provinces and their municipal government structures keep government closer to the people and provide more opportunities for residents to participate in how they are governed. Canada's federal system creates multiple points of public access to federal and provincial government bodies to satisfy the political demands of the people.

But, while federalism as it has evolved here created many opportunities to expand the role of our governments, it has also created many road blocks to achieving national unity. The relations between the provinces and the federal government have been a source of continuing conflict and controversy in the Canadian political system and raise a number of questions of fundamental importance.

Who benefits from and who loses in our federal system is an important question to ask if we want to know how effective our governments are. Do the advantages of federalism outweigh the price of

SOURCE: *How We Are Governed: The Basics of Canadian Politics and Government* (Toronto: Harcourt Brace, 1995), pp. 349–57. Reprinted by permission of the publisher.

fragmented government and a sovereigntist and independent Quebec? Because of the enormous debts our governments have racked up serving our needs, must Canada reconstruct its federal system? Are there better ways of governing ourselves, using different rules and structures? Should we consider these or proceed to reform the existing parliamentary system?

Canadian-style federalism has placed its stamp on a broad range of informal activities in Canadian society. The nature of representation in the Canadian House of Commons reflects the consequences of federalism from the provincial perspective. Each province, no matter how small, has a certain number of MPs and senators who represent ridings within the province (see Table 37.1).

MPs also constitute an informal political delegation to the federal government from their province. Similarly, senators are appointed, but they make up a provincial constituency in Parliament and can influence the dynamics of government in Ottawa as well as their provinces.

Our court system reflects our federal system. Provincial and municipal courts exist side by side with federal courts. However, because provincial courts handle the vast majority of cases, the provincial court system is much larger and busier than the federal system. The federal courts appear distant, and beyond the range of most Canadians. Contact with a federal court in Canada is thus a much rarer occurrence than contact with a provincial court.

Interest groups respond to Canada's federal system as well. Many of them are federations of provincial associations and groups. It is at the provincial level that interest groups build their membership, raise their money to organize and advertise, and create strategies for lobbying the federal government. This is true of the Canadian Medical Association and the Canadian Bar Association, which take their membership from the provincial and territorial organizations.

The contours of Canadian party politics are also driven by **intergovernmental relations**. Political parties reflect federal politics because political parties are organized along federal lines. To a party

Table 37.1

Legislative Representation in Parliament

Province/ Territory	House of Commons Seats	Senate Seats
Newfoundland	7	6
Nova Scotia	11	10
P.E.I.	4	4
New Brunswick	10	10
Quebec	75	24
Ontario	99	24
Manitoba	14	6
Saskatchewan	14	6
Alberta	26	6
British Columbia	32	6
Yukon	1	1
Northwest Territories	2	1
Total	295	104

out of power nationally, the existence of provincial party organizations takes on special importance. By building the strength of a political party from the provincial level and demonstrating its governing ability there, a political party can consolidate its position and prepare for the next federal election. Sometimes a strong premier or former premier will emerge as a contender for national party leadership.

Since the adoption of the Constitution Act, 1867, the single most persistent source of political and governing conflict in Canada has been relations between the federal and the provincial governments. The basic political fact about Canada's federal system is that it has created separate, self-sustaining centres of governing power across the country.

The Constitution Act, 1867, gave the federal government enormous governing powers and control over all areas that are both national and provincial in interest and scope. These areas include navigation, fisheries, the fiscal and monetary system, public debt, aboriginal territories, and defence (see Table 37.2). The provincial governments were given important powers as well — over resources, education, health

Table 37.2
What the Federal Government Can Do

- Amend the Canadian constitution
- Control public debt and property
- Regulate trade and commerce
- Administer unemployment insurance
- Raise monies by any means of taxation
- Borrow money on public credit
- Operate the postal service
- Take the census and gather statistics
- Raise an Army, Navy, Air Force, and Militia
- Fix salaries for all public officials
- Establish and maintain all beacons, buoys, light-houses, and Sable Island
- Control navigation and shipping
- Declare quarantines and maintain marine hospitals
- Manage seacoastal and inland fisheries
- Operate ferries
- Coin money, incorporate banks, and set national fiscal and monetary policy
- Set national weights and measures
- Set interest rates
- Establish policy on bankruptcy and insolvency
- Register patents and discoveries
- Register copyrights
- Administer for aboriginal peoples and lands reserved for them
- Grant citizenship
- Legalize marriage and divorce
- Establish and codify criminal law
- Establish, maintain, and manage penitentiaries
- Administer agriculture and immigration
- Administer old-age pensions

Table 37.3
What Provincial Governments Can Do

- Propose amendments to the constitution except as regards the lieutenant-governor
- Determine direct taxation within the province
- Borrow money on the credit of the province
- Establish the payment and appointment tenure of public servants and public officials
- Management and sale of public lands and forests
- Establish, maintain, and manage hospitals, asylums, charities, and eleemosynary institutions in and for the province, other than marine hospitals
- Municipal institutions within the province
- Grant shop, saloon, tavern, auctioneer, and other licences issued for the raising of provincial and municipal revenues
- Fund and administer local public works
- The incorporation of companies with provincial business interests
- The solemnization of marriage in the province
- Property and civil rights in the province
- The administration of justice in the province, including the maintenance and organization of provincial courts, both of civil and of criminal jurisdiction, including procedure in civil matters in these courts
- The imposition of punishment by fine, penalty, or imprisonment in enforcing any law of the province relating to any of the aforesaid subjects
- Generally all matters of a merely local or private nature in the province
- Administer education
- Administer agriculture and immigration

services, business, industry, transportation, and municipal governing institutions (see Table 37.3).

Over the years, Canada's federal system has greatly decentralized our politics and government. The federal system decentralizes not only our politics but also our policies. The history of the federal system is one of tension between the provinces and the federal government about jurisdictions of public policy—who controls it and what it should be. Most of our public-policy issues in Canada are based on federalism.

AN EVOLVING FEDERALISM

Since 1867, the Canadian federal system has changed significantly. But, from the start, a sizable part of the transactions among Canadian governments involved money (Cody 1977). The federal government began extending grants to the provinces early in the country's political history. This involved using the enormous economic resources, derived from the extensive taxing powers of the federal government, to transfer money to the provinces or to absorb their debts. For example, in 1867, the federal government absorbed pre-Confederation provincial debts and agreed to pay the provinces certain subsidies and annual grants to fund provincial programs and services.

Early in this century, the federal government gave conditional grants to the provinces, the "condition" being that the money was to be spent on federally approved projects and to meet national standards. However, it soon became evident that these grants would not eliminate the fundamental weakness of Canada's federal system — namely, that the provinces' capacity to produce wealth is not uniform. Moreover, the provinces were quick to resent the paternalistic manner in which these grants were provided.

Conditional grants were supposed to give the provinces some freedom in deciding how to spend the money while helping many provinces to relieve their tax burdens and raise the living standards of their residents. But the amount of money available for conditional grants did not grow as fast as the provinces had hoped. Furthermore, the federal government attached numerous strings to these grants in terms of how the money could be spent (Moore, Perry, and Beach 1966).

The Fathers of Confederation initiated a quasi-federal system because, in 1867, Ottawa assumed major administrative responsibilities for the bulk of public services. The constitution had deliberately centralized how we govern Canada, such that the federal government dominated, exercising national governing authority. At that time, federalism seemed to be all about the division of powers. It was the belief of many of the Fathers of Confederation that the provinces might even wither away.

Less than 30 years after Confederation, Canadian federalism has already evolved beyond its quasi-federal origins. In the period between 1896 and 1914, the provinces demanded more power and consultation from the federal government. Emergency federalism characterized the war period, when Parliament delegated sweeping authority to Ottawa to levy personal and corporate income taxes, to apply wage and price controls, and to prohibit strikes in wartime. The federal government was now expected to play a central role in the economic and social life of the country. This quality of federalism would return just prior to the Depression and last until the end of the Second World War.

In Canada, federal powers have always grown in wartime. During both world wars, Ottawa made heavy use of the federal powers granted by the constitution. In fact, federal powers actually expanded under the state of emergency.

But, during the 1920s, provincial autonomy grew as a result of revenues drawn from licensing automobiles, and taxing gasoline and liquor. During the Great Depression, many of the provinces were not able to deal with the trauma of economic and social decline. By the 1930s, it was necessary to restructure the fiscal relations between the provinces and the federal government because tensions were mounting over how to undertake economic recovery and how to deal with the high levels of unemployment.

In 1937, the Royal Commission on Dominion–Provincial Relations (the Rowell-Sirois Commission) was established. For the next three years, this commission studied the problems of Canadian federalism. Its recommendations included, among others, that the federal government should collect personal and corporate income tax, assume the accumulated debt of the provinces, and support the unemployed through a social security program. The commission also recommended that certain grants provided by the federal government be used to assist the poorer provinces and standardize government services across the country.

The advent of the Second World War enabled the federal government, under certain emergency powers, to assume some of the responsibilities recommended in the Rowell-Sirois Commission's report. The war solidified the central role of the federal government in fiscal and monetary matters. Wartime prosperity produced strong economic growth almost everywhere in the country and eased the financial squeeze on the provinces. The federal government consolidated its powerful centralist position, steering the national economy and taking responsibility for our economic well-being.

What has been called "Father knows best" federalism resulted from the enormous post-war taxing powers of the federal government and its ability to penetrate the jurisdictions of the provinces by funding certain shared-cost programs. The federal government entered into a series of taxation agreements with the provinces, preparing the way for fiscal co-operation in the federal system.

Co-operative federalism began in the 1960s as provincial governments experienced unprecedented demands for expanded services in health, education, welfare, and resource development. Today, all provinces spend more than half their budgets on these areas. Since the 1960s, personal income taxes have been collected by Ottawa, and the provincial portion is transferred back to the province, except in Quebec, where the government collects its own personal income tax. For this reason, Quebeckers must complete two income tax forms. As well, the rise of nationalism in Quebec spawned the concurrent spread of provincial autonomy in the other provinces.

Since the 1940s, shared-cost programs in the form of conditional grants and block grants have continued to be a source of provincial revenues. Examples are the block grants to provinces for post-secondary education (established in 1952), the conditional grant for hospital insurance (1957), the conditional grant for the Canada Assistance Plan (1966), and the conditional grant for medical insurance (1968).

Provinces also gain substantial revenues through equalization payments. **Equalization** is an instrument used to reduce disparities between the rich and poor partners in the Canadian federal family. The idea of equalization payments came out of the Rowell-Sirois Commission, but it was not implemented in Canada's federal system until 1957.

Equalization payments are unconditional grants to the so-called have-not provinces — there are seven — in order to bring them up to the national average in terms of tax yield per capita. The equalization formula tries to ensure that the seven have-not provinces enjoy roughly the same services as Ontario, British Columbia, and Alberta.

The formula used to determine whether a province qualifies takes the base average of per-capita revenues of the provinces of Quebec, Ontario, Manitoba, Saskatchewan, and British Columbia. If any province has a total per-capita revenue below this base average, the federal government prepares a payment based on the per-capita shortfall multiplied by the province's population. So payments vary from province to province. At the high end of the scale, in 1994 Newfoundland received $1655 per capita, and Saskatchewan, at the low end, received $521 per capita.

During the late 1960s and early 1970s, another federal style emerged in Canada, usually referred to as "executive federalism." Executive federalism changed the conduct of federal–provincial relations, transforming them from negotiations among provincial and federal bureaucrats who met behind closed doors to formal meetings among premiers and the prime minister at **First Ministers' Conferences** to resolve problems of federalism in front of television cameras. This convention format, in which eleven political executives work out "deals" on intergovernmental affairs, was largely the framework used in the Constitutional Conferences that produced what came to be known as the Meech Lake and the Charlottetown accords.

First Ministers' Conferences have addressed many of the issues at the root of federal–provincial differences over the years. One persistent issue has been regionalism. Because Canadians are so regional in outlook, it is difficult for the federal and provincial governments to find coast-to-coast agreement on every issue. Because the regions are host to such different economic and political cultures, it has been natural for disagreements to occur. Other contentious issues have involved transfer payments, cable and pay TV, energy prices, off-shore resources, and the state of the economy.

Executive federalism has been criticized for creating public political forums that give First Ministers the opportunity to appeal to their voters rather than to negotiate in the national interest. Premiers have also used the conference format to oppose the federal government as a group, often appearing to be an extraparliamentary opposition.

But, by the early 1980s, the public began to view the federal system as bloated and out of control. Successive governments promised to reduce the deficit and debt, and the size and cost of the federal government. They began to criticize the contemporary version of federalism, charging that it concentrated too much authority at the federal level of government. The federal government was indeed the senior partner in intergovernmental relations, but it was being asked to pay for too many services provided under provincial jurisdiction. The share of provincial costs footed by the federal government began to fall, and Ottawa became very reluctant to take on any new funding programs.

Eventually the provinces were expected to pick up the costs themselves for the new programs they wanted to offer and to cut funding to existing programs to pay for them. Federal attempts at downsizing government aroused intense opposition at the provincial level. If the Progressive Conservative governments of the 1980s did not achieve a wholesale reorganization of the federal system, they did prompt a re-evaluation of the role of the federal government in that system.

By the time Prime Minister Mulroney left office in 1993, the federal government was no longer a benefactor, bestowing generosity on worthy provinces. The debt and deficit pressures on the provinces had mounted enormously, such that many provinces began to speak of their treasuries as being in crisis. The sober reality of federal budget deficits erased the hopes among provincial governments that the rest of the country could come to their assistance. For the first time in decades, provinces had to consider raising taxes as well as initiating major cuts in health, education, and welfare services.

QUEBEC AND FEDERALISM

The reality of Quebec's distinctiveness has deep historical roots, as does the legal recognition of its cultural identity within the federal system (Young 1991). Long before Confederation, in 1838, Lord Durham described "Lower Canada" (Quebec) as "two nations warring in the bosom of a single

state." Concern with Quebec as a distinct society has been a powerful force throughout Canada's federal history.

When Confederation was being debated, the pattern for key protections of the French language and aspects of Quebec's distinctiveness had already been set. Almost immediately, the unique political culture of Quebec began to alter the federal landscape of Canada. The British North America Act recognized the status of French as an official language in the Parliament of Canada and the Assembly of Quebec. Latent within the legalistic language of the constitution was the basis for Canadian bilingualism, and for the status of French as an official language equal to English in federal, Quebec, and New Brunswick law.

From the beginning, Quebec challenged one of the main underpinnings of the Canadian federation — the equality of the provinces. As the argument has been made through the years, treating any province differently under the constitution leads to "special status." However, Confederation did confer special status on a number of provinces, including Quebec.

In 1871, under its terms of union, British Columbia agreed to join Canada if a transcontinental railway was built to link it to the East within ten years. And Newfoundland, under its terms of union in 1949, protected denominational schools and colleges. The equality of the provinces may have been a wish of the Fathers of Confederation, but the terms of the union laid the foundations for something quite different.

But what was to have a significant effect on the dynamics of Canadian federalism was the emergence and strengthening of Quebec nationalism. Although Confederation tied French-speaking Quebeckers to the rest of British North America, it also provided them with a separate province in which they were the majority and could eventually use provincial governing institutions to protect their distinctive culture. For many Quebeckers, Confederation did not mean assimilation into the larger English community of provinces and federal institutions; rather, it meant the opportunity to remain distinctive and free to develop a political culture that might one day launch itself on a separate course.

In the era of Premier Jean Lesage, the so-called Quiet Revolution of the 1960s, this sentiment was expressed in the idea that Quebec was not "une province comme les autres" (a province like the others). Lesage altered the spirit of Canadian federalism with the phrase "maîtres chez nous" (masters in our own house), a doctrine that would eventually challenge the federal assumption that all provinces are equal entities within Canada.

In the 1970s, the victory of the Parti Québécois showed the strength of Quebec nationalism in the province and reflected the challenges that Canada's federal system would come to face (Posgate and McRoberts 1976). Quebec's claim to be a distinct society within Canada led the Quebec government to propose "sovereignty association." Under this policy, the province would be a separate state but remain associated with Canada with respect to currency and defence.

A referendum on the issue was held in 1979 to see if the Quebec voters wanted their government to negotiate sovereignty association. The "Non" vote won, and by 1985 a federalist government, headed by Liberal leader Robert Bourassa, was returned to power.

In 1987, the question of Quebec as a distinct society in the Canadian federation came to a head. Quebec had not signed the Canada Act, 1982, the act patriating and amending the constitution, because the constitution did not recognize Quebec as a "distinct society within Canada."

But, in 1987, the federal government and the provinces agreed upon amendments to the constitution, recognizing Quebec's distinctiveness. The Meech Lake Accord would have made it more difficult for the federal government to encroach on areas of exclusive jurisdiction. The accord's recognition of Quebec's distinctiveness would have increased the decentralization of Canadian federalism as it involves all provinces.

In the failed Charlottetown Accord, the recognition of Quebec's distinctiveness was included as one of only eight "fundamental characteristics" in the Canada Clause. But in a subsection that followed the list of fundamental characteristics, the accord confirmed Quebec's distinctiveness: "The role of the legislature and Government of Quebec to preserve and promote the distinct society of Quebec is affirmed."

Within Canada's federal structure, the distinctiveness of Quebec extends beyond its major language and cultural uniqueness. Its distinctiveness is a considerably broader canvas. This was recognized even in the 1960s, when the Royal Commission on Bilingualism and Biculturalism referred in its preliminary report to Quebec's political and economic institutions and its "autonomous network of social institutions."

The flexibility of Canada's federal system has permitted Quebec to do a number of important things its way. Quebec has, in the past, chosen to take a different route from the rest of Canada in several areas of public policy and public administration. Quebec is the only province that has its own public pension plan, which came into effect in 1965, a few months before the Canada Pension Plan. Both plans emerged from a period of lively public debate and intergovernmental negotiations. A number of elements in the original Canada Pension Plan were strengthened in response to the Quebec government's proposal for its own plan.

The Quebec government has also developed what most agree is a unique approach to encouraging economic development, particularly to strengthen the province's economic infrastructure. At the forefront has been the Caisse de dépôt et placement, created in 1965 to manage the funds of various Quebec insurance plans. The Caisse also invests in government bonds — both inside and outside Quebec — and in Quebec businesses. It provides assistance to Quebeckers seeking to acquire control over Quebec corporations. The Caisse is the largest of any Canadian corporation to invest on the stock exchange.

Quebec's special character in Canada's federal system is also exemplified by its participation in international affairs (Munton and Kirton 1992, 156–74). As the homeland and mainstay of the majority of French-speaking people in North America, Quebec has assumed responsibilities peculiar to it alone by its active participation in the international community. Bolstered by the 1867 constitution, which gave the provinces formidable powers in economic and cultural areas, Quebec has taken initiatives in external affairs with many of the francophone nation-states in Europe, Africa, and the Caribbean. The efforts by Quebec to conduct its own external relations as a province of Canada by participating in international conferences, and by developing independent agreements in the educational and cultural fields with France and La Francophonie, are examples of Quebec's ability to act as a special entity in Canada's federal system.

REFERENCES

Cody, Howard. 1977. "The Evolution of Federal-Provincial Relations in Canada: Some Reflections." *American Review of Canadian Studies* 7, no. 1 (Spring): 55–83.

Moore, M., J.H. Perry, and D.I. Beach. 1966. *The Financing of Canadian Federalism: The First Hundred Years.* Toronto: Canadian Tax Foundation.

Munton, Don, and John Kirton. 1992. *Canadian Foreign Policy: Selected Cases.* Scarborough, Ont.: Prentice-Hall Canada.

Posgate, Dale, and Kenneth McRoberts. 1976. *Quebec: Social Change and Political Crisis.* Toronto: McClelland & Stewart.

Young, Robert. 1991. *Confederation in Crisis.* Toronto: James Lorimer.

The Provinces and Regional-Economic Conflicts

RAND DYCK

More often than not, demands from one region conflict with those from another. The most pervasive expression of such regional-economic conflict has undoubtedly been between the Prairie and Ontario regions. Since Ontario's regional interests are often persuasive with the federal government, the analysis is usually put in terms of the central core versus the periphery of the country.[1]

The problem began in 1870 with the creation of the province of Manitoba. While the eastern provinces and British Columbia had jurisdiction over their own natural resources, Ottawa decided to retain such control in the case of Manitoba, and when Saskatchewan and Alberta were created in 1905, these provinces were placed in the same subordinate position. The logic of prime ministers Macdonald in 1870 and Wilfrid Laurier in 1905 was that the federal government (i.e., central Canada) should control such resources in the national interest, allowing Ottawa to guide the development of the West. The Prairie provinces fought vehemently against this discrimination, and were finally successful in gaining control of their natural resources in 1930.

In the second place, the West complained for generations that Canadian tariff policy was designed in the interest of Ontario (and to a lesser extent Quebec) at the expense of the Prairies. As early as the 1879 National Policy, Macdonald saw the tariff as a means of protecting the industrial heartland of central Canada. Adding a tariff (an import tax) to the price of imported manufactured goods would raise their price above that of goods manufactured in Canada, even if Canadian production costs were slightly higher, and allow domestic goods to be sold more cheaply than imports. In practice, it was largely foreign firms that established themselves in central Canada behind this tariff wall, but the tariff at least had the beneficial effect of creating jobs in Canada rather than in Britain or the United States. Ontario thus gained employment in producing tractors for western Canada, for example, but western Canadians felt that this was contrary to their interests because in the absence of such a tariff they would have been able to buy a cheaper tractor from abroad. Furthermore, when Canada resorted to tariff protection of its manufacturing industry, other countries were likely to respond by restricting their imports of Canadian grain. The West demanded lower tariffs at every opportunity, and especially in the 1920s sent its own farmer representatives to the House of Commons to fight on this front. Tariffs among all countries have gradually come down since 1945, but the issue took on a new life in the 1980s with the western demand for a free trade agreement between Canada and the United States. Thus the controversial Canada–U.S. Free Trade Agreement, which took effect in 1989,

SOURCE: *Canadian Politics: Critical Approaches* (Toronto: Nelson, 1993), pp. 34–41. Reprinted by permission of the publisher.

can be seen as a response to 110 years of western discontent with the tariff aspect of the National Policy.[2]

Another aspect of Macdonald's National Policy that displeased the West was transportation, especially railways. Here the western case was not quite as convincing, because in choosing to live so far from the central core of the country, westerners should have expected to pay additional transportation costs. Some acknowledged this, although others demanded that railway freight rates be subsidized by Ottawa. Indeed, the Crow's Nest Pass Act (or Crow Rate) of 1897 was an attempt to do just that, and provided a very low rate for transporting prairie grain to eastern ports. About eighty years later, the Trudeau government's decision to increase these rates greatly upset many westerners. But a more legitimate complaint concerned peculiar inequities within the freight rate structure, including higher rates for finished goods than for raw materials (which discouraged manufacturing in the West), discrimination against short hauls, and deviations from the principle of distance determining price.

The West was probably on more solid ground in protesting against national banking policy. In contrast to community-based unit banks as in the United States, Canada deliberately developed a centralized branch banking system. This policy was in part an attempt to construct a sound, stable banking community that would avoid frequent local collapses, but the lack of competition it involved was also favoured by the established banking interests themselves, and provides evidence of corporate pressure on government policy. The result was a handful of large national banks, usually with headquarters in Montreal or Toronto, and with local branches spread across the country. From a hinterland perspective, money deposited in the local branch of a national bank would not remain in the community to be lent out for local purposes, but was sent to headquarters in central Canada to be used in the economic development of Ontario or Quebec. Moreover, decisions to lend money were largely centralized at the head office so that western

entrepreneurs would have to travel east in order to borrow substantial sums. This was another reason for the farmers' revolt of the 1920s, and displeasure with the Canadian banking system had much to do with the rise of Social Credit in Alberta in the 1930s. For many decades Ottawa refused to make any changes to this policy, but in the 1970s, when the West became stronger in spite of it, the federal government finally responded. On the one hand, Ottawa eased restrictions on chartering regional banks, and several new western banks were established. On the other hand, the existing national banks saw the merit in decentralizing decision-making within their own operations, so that larger decisions could be made on location. Unfortunately, several of these new western financial institutions faltered in the 1980s, largely because of a downturn in the western economy.

By that time, the original conflict over natural resources had re-emerged, especially with respect to petroleum pricing. National energy policy in the 1950s and 1960s had actually favoured the West, for Alberta was guaranteed a market for its oil and natural gas as far east as Ontario. But the West quickly forgot that fact after the Organization of Petroleum Exporting Countries (OPEC) cartel agreed on an artificial rise in the international price of oil in 1973. At this point, federal policy began to favour the consumer/manufacturing interest of central Canada at the expense of the producer interest of the West. The height of the regional-economic conflict occurred in 1980 with the Trudeau government's National Energy Program (NEP), which imposed new federal taxes, retained a larger share of petroleum revenues for Ottawa, kept the national price below the world level, encouraged frontier development, and promoted Canadianization of the industry, all objectives inimical to most westerners. Eventually a partial compromise between central and western interests was reached in 1981, and the Mulroney government later scrapped the NEP entirely. Nevertheless, the NEP had a profound effect on the western Canadian psyche, especially when combined with the region's simultaneous opposition to the federal bilingualism policy.

These four policy areas — tariffs, transportation, banking, and resources — represent the most serious regional-economic conflicts in Canadian history, but they can be put in a broader context. The metropolitan–hinterland thesis suggests that Western Canada was created as a colony of central Canada and was intended to be held in a subordinate and dependent relationship.[3]

Many of the western economic conflicts with central Canada were echoed by the Atlantic provinces. This was especially true of post-Confederation tariff policy, which also appeared to do the Maritimes more harm than good. Nova Scotia and New Brunswick entered Confederation in 1867 as proud and prosperous colonies, and while changes in marine technology (from wooden sailing ships to steel steamships) were probably the principal factor responsible, their economies quickly declined. Whatever the reason, Maritimers preferred to blame federal economic policy for much of their difficulty. The Atlantic provinces shared the West's concerns about federal freight rates, although they received subsidization in this area, too, and they opposed federal resource policy in the 1980s, prompting them to fight for provincial ownership of offshore petroleum. They differed from the West to some extent on the Canada–U.S. Free Trade Agreement, fearing that it would eliminate many of their subsidy programs. They also complained of an insufficiently aggressive federal government when it came to protecting Atlantic fish stocks from foreign overfishing. Another common complaint of the Atlantic and western regions is that the federal government does most of its purchasing or procuring in central Canada. While the economic complaints of the two outlying regions have thus generally coincided, they have occasionally been at odds, such as in the relative decline of Maritime representation in federal political institutions as the West's population expanded.

Smaller-scale regional-economic disputes are also a routine occurrence in Canadian politics. Attempts to support the steel plant in Sydney, Nova Scotia, arouse opposition in Sault Ste. Marie, Ontario; awarding the CF-18 maintenance contract to Canadair of Montreal infuriates supporters of Bristol Aerospace of Winnipeg (and further reinforces western alienation);[4] extending drug patent protection for multinational pharmaceutical firms in Quebec offends Canadian generic drug producers in Ontario; promoting frontier petroleum exploration (including federal assistance to Newfoundland's Hibernia project) upsets conventional oil and gas producers in Alberta; assisting foreign automobile plants in Ontario raises the ire of Quebec; and the attempt to fight inflation in Toronto with high interest rates angers those in almost every other part of the country who wish to see such rates lowered. (One of the few regional conflicts that Ontario lost was its bid to have Toronto included with Montreal and Vancouver in the designation of international banking centres.) The list of regional economic conflicts is almost endless, and most readers can probably add their own examples. Even subsidizing western grain farmers or Atlantic fishermen, which could be seen to be of indirect benefit to central Canada, is increasingly opposed by those in Ontario who feel that they are paying most of the cost. Besides these regional-economic conflicts that engaged the attention of Ottawa, interprovincial conflicts may also develop. The most serious of these was probably the fight between Quebec and Newfoundland over the Churchill Falls hydroelectric project in Labrador.

REGIONAL-ECONOMIC DISPARITIES

Conflict between regions of equal economic status would be one thing, but these are exacerbated in Canada because of regional-economic inequalities or disparities. As mentioned, some have-not regions blame federal economic policies for their fate, but even if this charge has some truth to it, no observer can overlook the facts that Canada's primary resources are not evenly distributed and that the regions are of different sizes, have different populations, and are variable distances from key export markets.

Among the available measures of regional-economic disparity are provincial gross domestic product (the total value of all goods and services produced), per capital personal income, provincial unemployment rates, and provincial sales taxes. These measures are provided in Table 38.1.

The table generally indicates three categories of provinces: three rich ones, Ontario, Alberta, and British Columbia; three poor ones in the Atlantic provinces; and four intermediate provinces, Quebec, Nova Scotia, Manitoba, and Saskatchewan. Quebec has a larger economy than any province other than Ontario, of course, but this figure is not so impressive when expressed on a per capita basis. Per capita income statistics show that the average Ontarian received almost twice as much money as the average Newfoundlander, with the other provinces arrayed in between. It is also true as a general rule that the provinces with the highest unemployment rates have the highest provincial taxes, while Alberta's petroleum revenue allows it to get by without a provincial retail sales tax at all. Needless to say, provinces and regions select whichever figures put them in the worst possible light when they demand that Ottawa do something to reduce such disparities.[5]

In addition to developing national social programs and to assisting various industries in a uniform national policy, successive governments have focused on two principal means to deal with the specific question of regional-economic disparities. One is to give federal funding to have-not provincial governments, and the other is to provide grants to individual firms in designated have-not regions of the country.

In 1957 Ottawa finally responded to repeated demands and began to make equalization payments. These annual cash grants to the have-not provinces are designed to allow them to raise their services to an acceptable national level, but can be spent for any purpose. In other words, they are unconditional grants, with no strings attached. The formula according to which provincial eligibility is calculated is extremely complex, now taking into account over thirty sources of provincial income, and designed to equalize the per capita yield of such provincial revenues across the country. Ever since 1957, all four Atlantic provinces have qualified on an annual basis, as have Quebec and Manitoba. Saskatchewan has usually qualified, Alberta and

Table 38.1

Provincial Gross Domestic Product, Per Capita Personal Income, Unemployment Rate, and Retail Sales Tax

	Gross Domestic Product 1990 (millions)	Per Capita Income 1990	Unemployment Rate Aug. 1991	Sales Tax 1991
Ontario	$281 210	$24 017	9.9%	8%
Alberta	71 203	21 076	7.9	0
B.C.	81 085	21 099	10.0	6
Quebec	157 210	19 613	12.0	9
Manitoba	23 990	18 332	9.7	7
Saskatchewan	20 494	17 109	7.5	7
N.S.	16 916	17 158	12.8	10
N.B.	13 187	16 097	12.8	11
P.E.I.	2 001	15 300	16.1	10
Newfoundland	8 732	14 996	19.2	12

SOURCE: Statistics Canada, *Provincial Economic Accounts, Preliminary Estimates, 1990*, Cat. no. 13-213P (May 1991); *National Income and Expenditure Accounts, Annual Estimates, 1978–1989*, Cat. no. 13-201 (December 1990); and *The Labour Force, September 1991*, Cat. no. 71-001 (August 1991). Reproduced with the permission of the Minister of Supply and Services Canada, 1992.

British Columbia did so for a few years, but Ontario has never received a cent from this source. (The formula had to be changed in 1981 in order to exclude Ontario, at its own request.) The equalization formula has been renegotiated every five years since 1957 at federal–provincial conferences, but in recent times Ottawa has unilaterally altered the formula in order to curtail its obligations in this sphere. Nevertheless, the sums involved are astronomical, as Table 38.2 reveals.

Equalization payments were entrenched in the Constitution in 1982, so that while the federal government may change the formula at any time it cannot withdraw from its responsibility in this regard:

> Parliament and the government of Canada are committed to the principle of making equalization payments to ensure that provincial governments have sufficient revenues to provide reasonably comparable levels of public services at reasonably comparable levels of taxation.

Many find it puzzling that Quebec should qualify as a "have-not" province, and indeed, that when its revenue shortfall is multiplied by its large population, it should receive approximately as much in equalization payments as all the other have-not provinces combined. The explanation seems to rest with the following facts: Quebec has less natural

Table 38.2

Equalization Payments, 1991–1992

Quebec	$3 765 400 000
Manitoba	956 800 000
Newfoundland	943 000 000
Nova Scotia	919 900 000
New Brunswick	855 400 000
Saskatchewan	570 400 000
P.E.I.	192 000 000
Total	$8 202 800 000

SOURCE: Provided to the author by the Department of Finance and published by permission.

resource wealth than is commonly assumed, its industry was historically small-scale, business profits were often taken out of the province and sent to corporate headquarters elsewhere, its steel industry was slow to get started, it did not enjoy the proximity to the U.S. automobile industry that favoured Ontario, and until 1960 its labour force was not well trained and the Roman Catholic Church in the province discouraged entrepreneurial activity among its deferential flock. Whatever the reasons, Quebec does well by these federal payments, to which people in all provinces contribute via their federal taxes.

Many attempts have been made to identify the overall "winners" and "losers" of Confederation, that is, which provinces have a net gain or loss when all their federal taxes and benefits have been totalled. This debate has been particularly centred in Quebec, but the results of federalist and sovereigntist studies have often been contradictory. On a per capita basis, at least, there is no question that the Atlantic provinces are the largest beneficiaries.[6]

The second means of trying to reduce regional-economic disparities is to establish federal regional development and job-creation programs.[7] Among the early versions of such policy were the Prairie Farm Rehabilitation Administration of 1935; the Maritime Farm Rehabilitation Act of 1948; the Agricultural Rehabilitation and Development Act of 1961, renamed the Agricultural and Rural Development Act in 1966; the Atlantic Development Board of 1962–63; the Area Development Agency of 1963; and the Fund for Rural Economic Development of 1966. These payments and programs culminated in the establishment of the Department of Regional Economic Expansion (DREE) in 1969, which has undergone many changes of organization and emphasis since, and was later renamed the Department of Regional Industrial Expansion (DRIE). The basic thrust of this program was to designate those parts of the country that were in need of economic assistance (essentially the whole country except Ontario's Golden Horseshoe, that is, Toronto and westward around the head of Lake Ontario), and then to provide grants to firms that would locate or expand existing operations in such areas. An element of federal–provincial cooperation was usually involved, primarily through Economic and Regional Development Agreements. Some grants also went to provinces or municipalities in order to provide the basic infrastructure that might attract industry, such as highways, water and sewage systems, and industrial parks. In 1987 another reorganization occurred that created several separate regional-economic development agencies, principally the Atlantic Canada Opportunities Agencies (ACOA), FEDNOR for northern Ontario, and the Western Diversification Initiative for the West. Southern Ontario does not qualify for such programs, and Quebec was left to operate on an ad hoc political basis. What remained of DRIE became the Department of Industry, Science and Technology.

This is not the place to analyze the overall results of these attempts to reduce regional-economic disparities in Canada. The many rearrangements of economic development programs, however, are an indication of their recognized deficiencies. Many cases could be documented of corporations that received money without being in need of it, or of taking the money and not living up to their commitments to create jobs. On the other hand, some positive results have also occurred. In any case, whatever the policies and programs in place, federal politicians face a never-ending stream of appeals from have-not communities, have-not provinces, and companies in difficulty (as well as have-provinces and companies not in difficulty) to use the federal power of the purse to make their life a little easier.

NOTES

1. For recent discussions of the western point of view, see David Kilgour, *Uneasy Patriots: Western Canadians in Confederation* (Edmonton: Lone Pine Publishers, 1988), and *Inside Outer Canada* (Lone Pine, 1990), as well as Don Braid and Sydney Sharpe, *Breakup: Why the West Feels Left Out of Canada* (Toronto: Key Porter Books, 1990), and Roger Gibbins, Keith Archer, and Stan Drabek, eds., *Canadian Political Life: An Alberta Perspective* (Dubuque, Iowa: Kendall Hunt, 1990).

2. By this time many large central Canadian corporations also saw advantages for themselves in such a policy.

3. For an excellent summary of this position, see Donald Smiley, *The Federal Condition in Canada* (Toronto: McGraw-Hill Ryerson, 1987), p. 159.

4. Robert Campbell and Leslie Pal, *The Real Worlds of Canadian Politics* (Peterborough: Broadview Press, 1989).

5. See Donald J. Savoie, *The Canadian Economy: A Regional Perspective* (Toronto: Carswell, 1986).

6. See, for example, a study by the Fraser Institute, *Government Spending Facts* (Vancouver, 1990). For a contrary opinion, see Phil Hartling, *Federal Expenditures as a Tool for Regional Development* (Halifax: Council of Maritime Premiers, 1990).

7. See Anthony Careless, *Initiative and Response: The Adaptation of Canadian Federalism to Regional Economic Development* (Montreal: McGill-Queen's University Press, 1977); Economic Council of Canada, *Living Together: A Study of Regional Disparities* (Ottawa, 1977); and Donald J. Savoie, *Federal–Provincial Collaboration: The Canada–New Brunswick General Development Agreement* (Montreal: McGill-Queen's University Press, 1981).

Governing Our Cities

CLOSE-UP: FROM FEDERAL TO MUNICIPAL RESPONSIBILITY— THE CASE OF HOMELESSNESS

Homeless people have become fixtures on the streets of many Canadian cities. They are constant reminders that when it comes to being responsible for the poor, federalism passes its social responsibilities down the levels of government until they hit the streets of our cities. What follows is a case study of one of the thousands of homeless people in our country today.

His real name was Terry MacD, but he liked to be called Buddy. In 1991 his home was an exhaust vent in the back of a restaurant in Halifax. He was raised in a hardworking Cape Breton family, but by the time he was 16 he was an alcoholic runaway. He had a job at the Sydney steel plant, but his bizarre and unpredictable behaviour led to his firing. After quarrelling with his sisters, who had housed him and put up with his angry rantings for so many years, he got on a bus to Halifax one day, eventually finding his way to the vent in the downtown area.

By age 23 Buddy was addicted to heroin and crack. By 41, he had compiled an arrest record that included breaking and entering "just to keep warm," property damage, drug trafficking and possession, shoplifting, and disturbing the peace. From the age of 32, Buddy had been hearing voices, talking to himself, shouting at strangers, and racing out into traffic "just to scare the shit out of the yuppies." By 1993 Buddy had become resigned to his life on the streets.

The police found Buddy's body under a car near the place he slept almost every night—the victim of a bad drug deal in the early hours of a cool September morning in 1994. Not very many people noticed he was gone.

Most Canadians live in cities and most have adequate shelter wherever they live. But every year an increasing number of Canadians must live in cities and towns without adequate shelter.

Homelessness in contemporary urban Canada has become a symbol not only of poverty but also of social and political failure. It is not an isolated phenomenon: It happens in most Canadian communities, even in small towns and in every city across the country.

Many Canadian municipalities are unable to provide accurate figures as to the number of homeless on any given night. The lowest estimate for all of Canada is about 10 000, although it is guesstimated that in Toronto alone there are about 20 000. Surveys conducted by the Canadian Council on Social Development (CCSD) have come up with figures as high as 250 000 for Canada.

Despite genuine attempts to accurately count the homeless, most tallies are nothing more than estimates, most of them low. The fact that they are low tends to reflect the relative importance governments attach to the problem and obscures its actual magnitude. However, two things do seem clear: the scale of the problem is greater than the public and the government know, and the problem is on the increase.

In cities such as Toronto, Montreal, and Winnipeg, so many people are homeless because in recent years larger cities have tended to experience higher levels of unemployment in recessionary times, and a lower rate of job creation during recoveries. Moreover, government funding for special programs designed to help people avoid homelessness has dried up under fiscal constraints. Individuals with nothing to live on but the sale of their labour have consequently found themselves dependent on overcrowded emergency hostels for shelter.

Many of the jobs that were plentiful in an industrialized economy have disappeared in the current information-based global economy. During the days when the classic image of the "hobo" characterized the homeless, and when the homeless comprised single men almost exclusively, men survived by moving from city to city to sell their labour in urban labour markets. "Skid row" areas developed in many urban communities, as the transient workers who provided inexpensive labour tended to cluster in the industrial parts of the city, in areas that were not considered residential. Because the work was sporadic, shelters developed as a temporary emergency service, usually provided by Christian missions or by the owners of cheap rooming houses and hotels. The result was a system that provided a readied labour force at close hand to industries at relatively little cost. As the Canadian economy transformed during the 1980s, the demand for casual and sporadic labour to serve industries declined significantly, and the jobs that remained were filled by overqualified workers.

Between the late 1960s and the early 1980s, Canada's social welfare system seemed prepared to take on the challenge of the homeless. But economic recession, coupled with the **downsizing of governments** at all levels, has greatly reduced the capacity of policy-makers even to address homelessness as an issue. The idea that the provision of shelter is a government responsibility, undertaken out of a community sense of charity and a commitment prescribed by social policy, is not widely accepted by legislators in Canada today. And to compound the plight of the municipalities, health care "reform"— usually amounting to the closing of community hospitals and the shrinking of health-care and mental-health service institutions — has, among other consequences, swollen the ranks of the homeless in all Canadian cities.

Today, about half of Canada's homeless are families. Women and children constitute the fastest-growing segment of those who become homeless. Many of them simply cannot afford to pay rent and buy food on the income they receive from their low-wage jobs or from public assistance.

What can be done about the homeless? Are Canadians willing to spend more public money to help them, even if it means raising taxes? Are Canadians inclined to blame the homeless for the situation in which they find themselves? Most Canadians today can identify the homeless in their own communities; it is harder to ignore them than it is to ignore city slums, the working poor, and other social problems.

Provincial legislatures are likely to react to the problem of the homeless by embarking on new programs geared to helping people get off the streets. But any lasting solution must take into account some of the deeper causes of homelessness. Funding for community-based mental-health and drug-treatment programs and for day-care services must accompany efforts at training homeless people to find work.

INTRODUCTION: GOVERNING URBAN CANADA

While cities offer some of the best features of Canadian life, they also harbour some of the gravest problems and reflect our greatest economic, social, and political challenges. It is hard to define "city" in a way that will please everyone.

In Chapter 39, C. Richard Tindal and Susan Nobes Tindal analyze the foundations of local government, explaining that municipal governments were the first to be established in Canada; some, including those of Montreal, Quebec City, and Trois-Rivières, were founded in the seventeenth century. In the mid-1600s, each of these outpost towns contained fewer than 1000 people; by 1765, Quebec and Montreal had grown into towns of more than 5000 inhabitants. At this time New France was about 25 percent **urban**—a much higher percentage than that in the growing populations of the thirteen American colonies, where less than 10 percent of the population lived in urban centres.

By contemporary standards, these first urban settlements were strong and cohesive. Small as they were, they represented our primary municipal institutions, and the decisions their town councils made enabled our municipalities to become the dynamic crossroads for trade, communication, and ideas, and the centres of learning and political organization, that they are today.

Canadian urbanization moved westward rapidly. In 1851, Halifax, Saint John, and Kingston were the fourth-, fifth-, and sixth-largest cities; within a century all three were surpassed by western cities. The newer cities—Edmonton and Calgary—were the fastest growing in Canada by the mid-1980s; by the 1990s, they were surpassed only by Vancouver and Victoria. Today, these cities are known worldwide as important centres of the arts, business, education, politics, science, and technology. Today, Canada is one of the most highly urbanized societies in the world. Most governments in Canada are municipal governments, and most Canadians live in cities.

THE BASIC STRUCTURES OF MUNICIPAL GOVERNMENT

All of Canada's provinces contain municipalities that are administered by some form of local government. Because municipalities are the responsibility of provincial governments, local government organizations vary from province to province. All provinces have strict rules and regulations for organizing local governments as cities and towns. Some

also divide their territory into counties and regional municipalities; some further subdivide their counties into townships.

Every level of municipality has its own governing council. At the lower level of city, town, and township, the council is usually elected by direct popular vote. All municipalities have the power to collect property taxes. They also receive grants from the provincial government, which, in turn, receives grants from the federal government.

MUNICIPAL REFORM

By the 1990s, most Canadian towns and cities were faced with problems associated in part with a shrinking employment base. When employers move out of a municipality or go out of business, more people are put out of work, and there is a smaller tax base. Less tax revenue means less money to pay for curb and gutter repair and to meet most other municipal obligations, including fighting crime and assisting those who make up the urban underclass. These problems feed on themselves, leading to more social and economic pathology, increased crime and poverty, an even smaller employment base, and other related problems.

Many of the critical issues that face Canadians today, such as the safety of our drinking water and what to do with our garbage, are examples of local issues. As governments devolve their responsibilities within Canada's federal structure, it is the municipal governments that must come up with solutions to these problems. Consequently, the work of municipalities is almost always unfinished and will be as long as social and economic problems confront people on a day-to-day basis. Increasingly Canadian communities are considering **municipal reform**.

There are and will continue to be many plans to consolidate and streamline governments, and generally to make them more efficient. In Chapter 40 Beryl Davis reminds us of the need to continually rethink what municipal governments do, how they finance their work, and the relationships they have with other governments.

With about six thousand separate and often overlapping governmental units within Canada, the trend toward municipal reform and consolidation is understandable. The restructuring of local governments has been a focus of reform for many years. One of the first provinces to consolidate its municipal districts was Alberta, under the government of William Aberhart during the depression years of the 1930s. In the 1960s the government of British Columbia initiated a program of local government reform with a policy for the creation of regional districts throughout the province. Perhaps the most renowned case of municipal reorganization in Canada was the creation of the municipality of Toronto in 1953.

The **consolidation** (sometimes called "amalgamation") of two or more municipal governments into a single one has had great appeal in recent years among municipal reformers, because of the efficiencies in service delivery it is thought to entail, as well as the savings of public dollars from reduced administrative and public-personnel costs. Typically, provincial governments designate the procedures for consolidating and amalgamating municipalities. For example, in August 1995 in Cape Breton, Nova Scotia, eight municipal governments (including the City of Sydney, a county, and towns such as North Sydney, Sydney Mines, Glace Bay, Louisbourg, New Waterford, and Dominion) were consolidated into a single regional "supercity." This provincial initiative was made in anticipation of saving millions of dollars on the salaries of seven mayors, a warden, and other administrative officers, as well as from the consolidation of fire protection, police, and other municipal services, such as curb and gutter, and street and road, maintenance and repair.

Not everyone thinks consolidation is a good idea. In Chapter 42, "Governing Canada's City-Regions," Andrew Sancton defines and analyzes the concept of regional government, looking at the example of Montreal, Toronto, and Vancouver. He questions the wisdom of implementing widespread institutional change as an approach to resolving the difficulties of living in our urban communities.

Municipal reform goes well beyond reducing and reorganizing governments. Local governments acting alone cannot introduce any real reforms. The buck-passing from one level of government to the next ends up squeezing local governments and local taxpayers. Real reform would involve major shifts in the responsibilities and jurisdictions of governments in Canada, affecting everything from the environment to taxation. Municipal planners across Canada are concerned that the devolution of federal and provincial government responsibilities, including the requirement that municipalities have policies on air quality, contaminated properties, and the quality and quantity of surface and groundwater, will overburden municipal resources.

MONEY AND MUNICIPALITIES

All of this comes down to money and how to raise it under a constitution that does not give much status to municipalities and grants all of the taxing powers to the federal and provincial governments. Thus, local tax reform is one entanglement that involves the whole Canadian tax system, and requires a definition of which level of government is responsible — practically and financially — for what. In Chapter 41, David Siegel puts all of this in the context of municipal finances and funding. His contribution helps us understand the restrictive financial parameters under which most municipalities must operate.

The financial underpinning of all Canadian municipalities is a tax based on property. This rather limited and regressive way of raising money for the many services local governments provide has been the fiscal culprit responsible for keeping cities and towns in the condition of what some have called "puppets on a shoestring."

Historically, the idea has been that the owners of property are the consumers of **municipal services** such as garbage collection and disposal, sewers, roads, and firefighting. Municipalities assess a value of a piece of property and set their taxes as a percentage of that value, usually referred to as the "mill rate." This tax system has been in use in most of North America for two centuries. Local governments have relied heavily on **property taxes** for their self-generated revenue. Other taxes contribute relatively little to the treasuries of municipal governments.

Heavy reliance on property taxes creates a number of inequities for local governments. Communities with high property values can afford to do more than poorer communities. Because of the wide range of property values from one place to the next, cities and towns in the same province are often unable to provide the same standard of municipal services.

There is no doubt that the most burdensome restrictions on the ability of municipalities to deliver services, and ultimately on how well Canadians are governed at the municipal level, are those related to finance and revenues. With the rising costs of operating municipal governments, the ability of provincial treasuries to assist their municipalities is critical. What provinces provide has a great impact on the level and quality of the services people will receive in their cities and towns. But in the end, the provincial governments can channel enough money to their municipalities only if the federal government maintains or increases **transfer payments** to the provinces.

The federal government is no longer in the position of operating as a wealthy benefactor, bestowing funds generously on provincial and local governments. Yet the spending pressures on local governments are enormous. The public demands better municipal services, better schools, and better roads. The sober realities of federal and provincial deficits and debts erases the hope of increased transfers to local governments.

In a world of competing governments, it is what municipalities have to offer that is of interest to foreign and domestic investors, entrepreneurs, and governments. The construction of **infrastructure** undertaken by municipalities — public works in the form of streets, bridges, sewers, signage, street lighting, utilities, and industrial, commercial, and technological incubation parks — means large-scale public expenditures. Infrastructure is an important incentive drawing talented, skilled people and capital- and labour-intensive business to municipalities.

In theory, responsibility for governance in Canada is dispersed throughout the federal system and includes decisions made by provinces and municipal governments. But in practice there has been a major shift in the direct location of the responsibilities of governing. Cities, towns, and regional governments will have to do much more for themselves, without being able to seek additional funds from the federal and provincial governments. Because of the unequal distribution of economic power in Canada, the powers, responsibilities, and effectiveness of local governments will vary considerably from province to province. This may lead to inequities between and among communities within and between provinces.

One of the benefits of localizing government is that it brings governments closer to the people, giving them an opportunity for greater control over the political process, and for a more direct impact on policy. However, it also means increased taxes, on top of an already burdensome federal and provincial tax system.

Which level of government do Canadians think gives them most for their tax dollars? The answer has changed over time. During the 1960s, most people had more confidence in how the federal government spent money than in how local and provincial governments did. Since the 1980s, however, the public's confidence in the federal government has waned, and people today are just as likely to think that their provincial and municipal governments are giving them the most for their money.

THINKING IT OVER

1. Discuss the origins of Canadian municipalities, focussing on the influence of these early communities on municipal government today. Based on your reading of the article by C. Richard Tindal and Susan Nobes Tindal (Chapter 39), describe the role of provincial governments (and, in the case of Yukon and the Northwest Territories, of the federal government) in creating our municipalities. Do the authors identify parallels in the development of municipalities between the various regions? Was the development of municipal governments in Newfoundland different from that in the rest of Canada? In what way? How is your municipality governed? Describe the type of governing structure.

2. Do Canadians need to "re-invent" municipal government? Why is it so necessary to reform these original governing structures? Beryl Davis (Chapter 40) asks us to rethink local government. How does she think municipal governments will restructure themselves? Trace the growth of your city or town since it was first incorporated. Take a walking or automobile tour of your community. In what ways is it developing? What can government do to improve living conditions in your community?

3. David Siegel (Chapter 41) discusses municipalities in the context of our federal system. What does he say about the status of local governments at the time of Confederation? What services did they provide, and why could they not be described as "puppets" on the provincial "shoestring"? How has the situation changed since that time? According to Siegel, what are some of the problems connected with relying on property taxes as the primary revenue source for municipalities? In what other ways can municipalities raise revenues? List ten different taxes that Canadians pay and the level of government to which each is paid. Which of these taxes benefit municipalities most?

4. What does Andrew Sancton (Chapter 42) have to say about the governance of our large municipal areas, such as Greater Montreal and Greater Vancouver? Why does he think that large city-regions need a regional governing institution? What relationship would this level of government have with the provinces and the federal government?

5. Some people suggest that the reason we have so many local governments and governing bodies is that Canadians want to keep decision-making control firmly in hand at the local level. What are the advantages and disadvantages of having multiple municipal governments? Do we have too many municipal governments? What kinds of reforms should we consider? Should we consolidate our municipal governments for greater efficiency in terms of cost and program delivery?

6. Using information introduced by Tindal and Tindal in Chapter 39 and by Siegel in Chapter 41, discuss the proposition that the evolution of municipal governments in Canada has been greatly influenced by their lack of constitutional status. Can municipal structures do a good job of governing as long as they represent an inferior level of jurisdiction, subordinate to federal and provincial jurisdictions?

GLOSSARY

charter The governing instrument and certificate of municipal incorporation for towns and cities in Canada. Originally these were regarded as a contract between colonial authorities (the Crown) and the local municipality, subject to amendment without the consent of both parties. After Confederation, charters were granted by provincial legislatures as ordinary legislative acts, subject to ordinary legislative amendment.

city Each province creates its own special provisions and specific determinations about what might constitute a city, which is generally defined as a place where a concentration of people reside and interact, where a market for consumption and production is created, and where an organized system of municipal government exists.

consolidation The union of two or more government units to form a single unit.

constitutional status All that comprises constitutional law in written and unwritten provisions, such as the division of powers between levels of government, designated rights and freedoms, amendments, judicial interpretations, and conventions.

Courts of Quarter Sessions Courts of criminal jurisdiction that had the power to try misdemeanors and that exercised certain functions of an administrative nature.

downsizing of governments Refers generally to the reduction in the size of governments at all levels in Canada and elsewhere, which has been one of the consequences of massive government debts and deficits, and of the "New Public Management" approach to government, which focusses on a more entrepreneurial style in the administration and management of the public service.

infrastructure Refers generally to the basic structures and services needed to operate a community, such as streets, sidewalks, roads, power grids, garbage removal technologies, information technologies and delivery systems, and basic government services and related private-sector services.

intergovernmental relations Refers generally to the interactions of government at all levels, federal–provincial, provincial–municipal, municipal–federal.

local autonomy The recognition of the authority or power to make laws at the municipal level.

metropolitan Describes an approach to local and regional government under which the number of overlapping levels of municipal governing bodies is reduced and a regional authority is established, with wide responsibilities for policy-making and administration.

municipal planning Strategies designed by municipal councils to develop their communities, often relating to population growth or decline, commercial and business development, changes in the use of information technologies, and municipal reforms.

municipal reform The drive to change the structures, functions, and constitutional status of municipal government.

municipal services General municipal services usually include fire protection, planning and maintenance, refuse collection and disposal, municipal libraries, police, water supply, parks and recreation, public welfare, pollution control, hospitals, public housing, transportation, and public education.

progressive tax A tax that requires wealthier individuals and corporations to pay a higher percentage of their income than poorer individuals and corporations.

property assessment The various formulas and means of tabulation that provincial governments and municipalities use to place a value on a property and or on buildings located on properties, in order to set taxes as a percentage of that value.

property tax A tax on property set by municipal governments based on an assessed market value as of a certain date. Property taxation funds the annual operations of governments.

regional government An approach to governing that involves the joining of cities, towns, and other municipalities to form a new municipality with a regional level of government that is responsible for services that affect the entire region, such as water supply, sewage disposal, roads, and police and fire protection. One of the most important functions of a regional government is to plan economic and demographic growth, land use, and services for the whole region.

regressive tax A tax system under which those with high incomes pay a lower percentage of their income in taxes than do those with low incomes.

statutory law Laws that are laid down in statutes or statutory instruments and express the will of Parliament or provincial legislatures, as distinct from common law, which is the sum of the principles contained in and developed through the decisions of judges.

transfer payments Annual transfers of money based on complex formulas and calculations made by the federal government and allocated to the provinces to preserve and enhance national standards of government services across the country.

urban Describes large municipal centres that receive similar services within any given province and in which populations of significant density cluster, attracting service and manufacturing industries, technological corporations, stores, banks, and other features of a modern city. The term also connotes the spread of influences, including certain cultural patterns, associated with living in cities.

urbanization The growth of cities by means of rural transformation, natural population increase, or populations' migrating to and settling in a concentrated area.

ADDITIONAL READINGS

Andrews, Vian, ed. 1991. *The Encyclopedia of Canadian Municipal Governments*. Burnaby, BC: Venture Page Design.

Bourne, Larry, and David Ley, eds. 1993. *The Changing Social Geography of Canadian Cities*. Montreal: McGill-Queen's University Press.

Bunting, Trudi, and Pierre Filion, eds. 1992. *Canadian Cities in Transition*. Don Mills, Ont.: Oxford University Press.

Driedger, Leo. 1991. *The Urban Factor: Sociology of Canadian Cities*. Don Mills, Ont.: Oxford University Press.

Fowler, Edmund. 1992. *Building Cities That Work*. Montreal: McGill-Queen's University Press.

Hampton, William. 1991. *Local Government and Urban Politics*. Essex, UK: Longman Group Ltd.

Harrigan, John. 1993. *Political Change in the Metropolis*. New York: HarperCollins College Publishers.

Loreto, Richard, and David Price, eds. 1991. *Urban Policy Issues: Canadian Perspectives*. Toronto: McClelland & Stewart.

Maclaren, Virginia. 1992. *Sustainable Urban Development in Canada: From Concept to Practice*. Toronto: ICURR Press.

Tindal, C.R., and S. Nobes Tindal. 1990. *Local Government in Canada*. Toronto: McGraw-Hill Ryerson.

The Foundations of Local Government

C. RICHARD TINDAL
SUSAN NOBES TINDAL

How did our municipal governments evolve, and why in the particular form which we find in Canada? One answer — which is correct as far as it goes — is that they were shaped by decisions made by the provincial governments to which they owe their very existence (and by the federal government in the case of municipalities in the Yukon and Northwest Territories).

This explanation is based on the constitutional, legal arrangements provided by the British North America Act (now the Constitution Act). While both the national and provincial levels of government were given separately defined spheres of operation within which each would act relatively autonomously, municipal governments were accorded no such status. Instead, municipal governments were only mentioned in the British North America Act as one of the responsibilities allocated to the provinces. It follows, therefore, that from a strict legal perspective, municipal governments only exist to the extent that the provincial governments have seen fit to provide for them. The types of municipality and their boundaries, responsibilities, and finances must be authorized through provincial legislation.

The basic features of Canadian local government evolved before Confederation, and the new provincial governments established in 1867 inherited existing municipal institutions and/or operating philosophies of how local governments ought to operate. It is necessary, therefore, to look beyond the legal explanation, important though it is.

The earliest municipal governments in Canada evolved in response to the settlement of the country. As the population increased, and particularly as it became concentrated in the limited urban centres of the early years, it was necessary to administer a growing variety of programs and regulations. With pockets of population scattered in a vast area, and with very rudimentary forms of transportation and communications, the responsibilities could not be handled directly by a centralized colonial government.

While some form of local administration was inevitable for quite practical reasons, therefore, the particular form which did evolve was strongly influenced by the political values and traditions of the settlers of this country and the beliefs which they held or developed about municipal government. In this connection, the extent to which this country was settled through immigration was a significant factor, especially because of the belief in local self-government held by many of the United Empire Loyalists who entered this country in the years during and after the American War of Independence.

CENTRAL CANADA

Local government made its first, although somewhat brief, appearance in Canada under the French

SOURCE: Excerpted from *Local Government in Canada* (Whitby, ON: McGraw-Hill Ryerson, 1995), pp. 15–40. Reprinted by permission of the publisher.

regime in the settlements of Montreal, Quebec, and Trois Rivières. As early as 1647 a mayor, councillors, and *syndics d'habitations* (who made representations on behalf of local residents to the provincial authorities) were elected in Quebec. This practice was strongly discouraged by the very authoritarian and centralized home government in France, which felt that it was a dangerous innovation, and in 1663 the mayor and aldermen of Quebec resigned. The whole issue of local self-government was allowed to lapse until 1760 and the advent of British rule.

After the British conquest all government was vested in the military and subsequently in a Governor and an appointed council. In 1763 a proclamation was issued which promised to introduce English law and the English system of freehold land grants in Quebec, in order to encourage English settlement. In the following year the Governor-General did establish the ancient English system of local justices of the peace meeting in the Courts of Quarter Sessions for the three districts around Montreal, Quebec, and Trois-Rivières for the trial of unimportant matters.

Despite the rule by British Governors and the promise of the benefits of English law, little occurred to interrupt the traditional running of the affairs of Quebec. There was little interference with the Roman Catholic Church, the Court of Common Pleas continued to administer French civil law, and land was still granted through the feudal French system, "en fief et seigneurie." The Quebec Act, which was passed in 1774, formally recognized this situation and also extended the Quebec boundaries west to the Great Lakes and Mississippi River and north to Labrador.

The American Revolution broke out soon after and precipitated a flow of United Empire Loyalists to Nova Scotia and the western part of Quebec. The peak years of this immigration were 1782–1783, when about 10 000 arrived in the Saint John area of the Bay of Fundy, 25 000 arrived in Nova Scotia (doubling its previous population), and 20 000 arrived in the unsettled areas around Lake Ontario, particularly around Kingston, Toronto, and Niagara.[1]

These immigrants came chiefly from New York and the New England colonies, where they had enjoyed a certain measure of local self-government. They brought with them the tradition of municipal government through the town meeting. Under this system, selectmen (councillors) were elected at the annual town meeting by the inhabitants residing within one-half mile of the meeting house. These selectmen were to oversee the affairs of the town between meetings. In theory their appointment and actions were to be approved by the Governor but in practice they operated independently of the central authorities.

UPPER CANADA (ONTARIO)

Needless to say, these Loyalists were unhappy under French civil law, especially the system of land grants under the seigneurial system, and the limited local autonomy. There soon were numerous petitions from the Loyalists around Lake Ontario for some form of local courts and administration, English civil law, and separation from that area of Quebec which was east of Montreal. Because of population growth pressures, but much against their better judgment, the British acquiesced and in 1787 passed an ordinance which divided the western settlements, previously a part of the District of Montreal, into four new districts with various appointed officials, including justices of the peace, who constituted the **Courts of Quarter Sessions**. The Quarter Sessions assumed judicial, legislative, and administrative responsibilities, including maintaining the peace, regulating domestic animals running at large, the conduct of licensed taverns, the appointment of minor officials, and the superintending of highways.[2] As new problems arose, the Quarter Sessions, which were the only official agency dealing with local matters, were simply given more powers to deal with them.

However, this new system proved to be unworkable under the French feudal laws and institutions which had been established with the Quebec Act, and pressure continued for a separate province with English civil law and an English system of land tenure. This continuing pressure finally culminated in the Constitutional Act of 1791 (also referred to as the Canada Act).

The main provisions of the act were:

1. The creation, from the province of Quebec, of the provinces of Upper and Lower Canada, with the Ottawa River roughly as the dividing line.
2. The provision of a government for each province consisting of a British Lieutenant-Governor, an appointed executive council, an appointed legislative council, and an elected legislative assembly.
3. The use of English law and land tenure in Upper Canada.
4. The allotment of land as clergy reserves for the support of the Protestant clergy.

Lord Dorchester, then Governor-General, was reluctant to approve the Constitutional Act because he felt that the Loyalists would be safer under French than British law since, in his view, too free an indulgence in British political institutions had led to the American Revolution. Therefore the Act contained certain precautions against the rise of democratic institutions such as the establishment of an hereditary political aristocracy (through the appointed councils) and the establishment of an episcopal state church (clergy reserves).

Both Lord Dorchester and also J.G. Simcoe, the first Lieutenant-Governor of Upper Canada, strongly discouraged any form of local government. To this end surveys were to be of royal seigniories and not townships, and they were to be numbered and not named as was customary, to discourage any strong attachment to a particular place. However, the Loyalists had already set up town meetings and designated their settlements townships named after King George and his family, even before the Constitutional Act was passed.

In 1792 Simcoe divided Upper Canada into counties for militia purposes and for the election of representatives to the newly created assembly. He was very keen to develop an aristocracy in an effort to reproduce the highly classed society found in England. From this privileged class he planned to appoint his executive council to oversee the actions of the assembly. He therefore promoted half-pay army officers as candidates in the first provincial election, most of whom were rejected by the voters in favour of men of lower classes. Instead of heeding this indication of popular thought and giving up his plans, Simcoe redoubled his efforts to eradicate all democratic tendencies and in time an aristocracy known as the Family Compact became organized around the executive branch of the provincial government. This group had developed both family and economic ties throughout the province.[3] Its members felt it was their duty to "guard the body politic from the corrupting influences of republicanism" and fought all efforts at establishing any kind of responsible government at any level.[4]

On the other hand, the Loyalists, who constituted most of the population of the province, felt that they had proven their loyalty to the Crown by fleeing the rebellious colonies and therefore deserved to have local self-rule. Perhaps it is not surprising then that the first bill introduced in the first session of the legislative assembly of Upper Canada was "to authorize town meetings for the purpose of appointing divers parish officers." Although not passed in that session, it was passed in 1793 as the Parish and Town Officers Act. The Act permitted annual town meetings[5] to appoint a town clerk, assessors, a tax collector, road overseers and fence viewers, a poundkeeper, and town wardens. The town wardens were to represent the inhabitants in the Quarter Sessions of the District in which the town(ship) was located. The only legislative authority the town meeting had was to fix the height of fences and to regulate animals running at large. An assessment act was also passed in 1793 to provide for raising money to pay for the costs of court and jail houses, paying officers' fees, and building roads.

By the turn of the century, urban concerns of sanitation, streets, education, welfare, and local police were becoming sufficiently pressing that the powers of the justices of the peace had to be extended.

A severe fire in Kingston in 1812 persuaded central authorities that some action was needed and in 1816 an act to regulate the police[6] was passed for Kingston. This act gave the magistrates the power to make and publish rules and regulations for the safety and convenience of the inhabitants and to finance local improvements through a special tax. By the end of the year, Kingston had fourteen rules which covered such areas as streets, slaughterhouses, weights and measures, and animals running at large.

Another potentially important event in 1816 was the passage of the first public school act. This act enabled local residents to meet together to elect three trustees who were to hire a teacher and authorize school textbooks. This was the first example of the true local self-government, whereby local people could elect representatives to administer a local need. Unfortunately, this was not a successful attempt at local government because of the lack of funds and experienced trustees.

The end of the War of 1812 in North America and the Napoleonic Wars in Europe saw the beginning of a new wave of immigration from the British Isles. Between 1815 and 1850 approximately 800 000 came to British North America, the great bulk of whom settled in Upper Canada. This population growth magnified the already existing urban problems and petitioning continued for some form of municipal government. In 1828 Belleville applied to be incorporated as a town. The Legislative Council rejected this application, saying that:

> Since men do not like to be forced, they are pretty certain to elect only such persons as will not make effective rules or adequately enforce them; hence in the interest of efficient administration, such innovations much be discouraged.[7]

Despite this setback for Belleville, in 1832 the Legislature capitulated and created a distinct corporate body in the President and Board of Police of the town of Brockville. This body was, in essence, the first form of elected municipal council and it assumed responsibility for all of the local government functions previously undertaken by the

Quarter Sessions, with the justices of the peace retaining only their judicial functions within Brockville. This movement to representative local government proved to be popular. In 1834 York was created the self-governing city of Toronto and by 1838 there were eight police towns and two cities.

One should not overstate the significance of this development, however.[8] Only the members of the boards of police were incorporated, not the town inhabitants. The qualifications to be a member of the board required that a town inhabitant be a freeholder or a householder paying a certain amount of rent per annum for his dwelling. A governing elite was formed whose obligation was to govern the town. The qualification to be a voter in the election required that the town inhabitant be a male householder, a subject of the King, and possessing a freehold estate. "These qualifications for board membership and voting demonstrate the calculated restrictions that were put upon participation in town politics."[9] Moreover, the terms of incorporation for these boards suggest that the Upper Canada legislature was very cautious in conferring corporate capacities on towns.

> The boards of police had more duties and obligations than rights and liberties. Or, stated another way, these bodies politic were constituted so as to make them accept the delegated powers of the State; and, by empowering a qualified elite to govern through taxation, these communities also relieved the State of the costs of governance.[10]

While the urban areas of Upper Canada were gaining more local self-government, the rural areas were still functioning under the Parish and Town Officers Act with the magistrates of the Quarter Sessions in almost total control of local affairs. Reform newspapers of the time charged that many magistrates were unfit, intemperate, and ready to stir up the mob against reformers.[11] The magistrates decided which local works were to be carried out, often ignoring areas in which they had no personal interest, and how much tax revenue was to be raised. In 1835 the assembly came under the control of a reform group which produced a report stating that magistrates were half-pay officers and strangers who often became members of the Family Compact.[12] Similar conditions existed in the other provinces, with the unrest culminating in the Rebellion of 1837 in Upper and Lower Canada.

After the Rebellion, the Earl of Durham was appointed to investigate the insurrection particularly and the general state of government in all of the provinces. Durham produced a comprehensive report dealing with the conditions in British North America, and of particular importance for our purposes are his recommendations dealing with local government. He wrote that "municipal institutions of local self-government . . . are the foundations of Anglo-Saxon freedom and civilization."[13] Further he stated: "The latter want of municipal institutions giving the people any control over their local affairs, may indeed be considered as one of the main causes of the failure of representative government and of the bad administration of the country."[14] Durham recommended that the two Canadas be reunited and that local matters should be looked after by municipal bodies of a much smaller size than the province.

Governor-General Sydenham, who replaced Durham in 1840, recognized the importance of the recommendations in Durham's report and he wrote to the Colonial Secretary:[15]

> Since I have been in these Provinces I have become more and more satisfied that the capital cause of the misgovernment of them is to be found in the absence of Local Government, and the consequent exercise by the assembly of powers wholly inappropriate to its functions.

Sydenham also sent the Colonial Secretary a draft bill for union of the Canadas which incorporated Durham's recommendations. Unfortunately at this time Durham had fallen into personal unpopularity and the Colonial Office considered the Family Compact and the Chateau Clique as the loyal heart of the country.[16] The principle of responsible government and the clauses on local government were dropped from the Union Act introduced

and passed by the English Parliament. One cannot overstate the importance of this omission. Had the Union Act contained clauses providing for a system of municipal government, then such a separate and distinct provision might well have been reproduced in the British North America Act, which brought Canada into existence. Instead, while a number of specific municipalities were incorporated before Confederation, municipal government received no formal recognition or legal status in the constitution of Canada.

In any event, Lord Sydenham persisted in spite of his initial setback. In 1841 he persuaded the new Canadian legislature to pass an act which established an elected district council to take over the administrative authority formerly exercised by the Courts of Quarter Sessions in rural areas. There were no drastic changes in the general way that local government was carried on; the annual town meeting still elected various officers and passed town laws. But it also elected one or two district councillors from each township. The head of the district council, the warden, was appointed by the Governor-General although subsequently the councils were given the right to choose their own warden. The councils were given responsibility for roads, municipal officers, taxing, justice, education, and welfare. Their expenses could be met by tolls or taxes on real or personal property or both. The Governor-General could disallow any by-laws and could dissolve any or all of the district councils.

The District Councils Act is perhaps even more important than any succeeding act because it was the first real break with the system of local government by Courts of Quarter Sessions and preceded by almost 50 years the abandonment of this system in England.[17] While it was too radical for conservative elements in the legislature and not radical enough for the reformers, it did provide for a transition period in the rural areas between no local self-government and full local self-government. The central authorities retained much power because it was genuinely felt that local people would not be able to manage their own affairs.

Despite initial fears, the first district councillors were apparently fairly capable people who were able to stimulate the development of their townships because of their knowledge of local needs. By far the most important functions were the construction and repair of roads and bridges and the laying out and creating of school districts. The councils were hampered, however, by problems with assessment, provincial control, and scarce finances — problems which persist to this day. It has been written of the revenues available to district councils that:

> These were paltry sums for the needs of large districts, and it is quite certain that the very light direct taxation on which Canadians long prided themselves was a rather important factor in the backward condition of the country for so many years.[18]

[In a rather fascinating parallel, one could argue that the backward and dangerously deteriorated condition of the infrastructure of many municipalities today is at least partly a result of the modest levels of property tax demanded by local citizens.]

In 1843 the Baldwin or Municipal Act was introduced, although because of a rupture with the Governor-General it was not passed until 1849. A primary function of the act was the consolidation of all municipal legislation under one measure. It built upon the District Councils Act while extending certain powers. The Baldwin Act differed *in two major respects*:

1. the country rather than the district became the upper tier of municipal government, and
2. for the first time townships were recognized as a rural unit of municipal government.

As well, the act established villages, towns, and cities as urban municipal units. **Cities** and separated towns were not a part of the county for municipal government purposes. This municipal system established in 1849 has endured to the present in many areas of Ontario. Moreover, even the reformed structures introduced in recent decades (the controversial

regional governments) are essentially modified county systems.

LOWER CANADA (QUEBEC)

It will be recalled that under the French regime the province of Quebec enjoyed little or no autonomy, and the first attempts at local government were strongly discouraged. This was undoubtedly because of the extent of local control by central authorities and the lack of a French tradition of local self-rule. The British conquest and takeover in the 1760s made little impact on this situation, although by 1764 the Quebec grand jury petitioned for regulations regarding markets, schools, and poor houses. In 1777 an ordinance was passed to "empower the Commissioners of the Peace to regulate the Police of the Towns of Quebec and Montreal for a limited time." [19] But this must have proven inadequate since both Quebec and Montreal petitioned for incorporation because of the bad conditions existing in the towns. In 1799 districts were established under justices of the peace to supervise roads and bridges and by 1807 a market was established in Montreal under the magistrates.

In Lower Canada, as in Upper Canada, government by the magistrates grew to be very unpopular. A citizen meeting in Montreal in 1828 expressed the need for an improved local administration

> ... to cope with police and financial problems of the prosperous town, the long neglected harbour, the insanitary conditions of surrounding swamps, and the lack of a general and effectually prosecuted plan of improvements.[20]

It was not until 1832 that Quebec and Montreal were granted charters which enabled the citizens to elect a mayor and two aldermen per ward. According to Isin,[21] the long delay since the 1785 incorporation of Saint John as the first incorporated city in British North America reflected the caution and hesitancy of colonial and British authorities about the use of this legal device. Indeed, the incorporations were limited to a four-year term. When the provisions expired in 1836, they were not renewed until after 1840 because of the political turmoil caused by the 1837 Rebellion.

Although Lower Canada was subject to almost the same urban pressures as Upper Canada, the first 80 years of British rule saw little progress in the establishment of local government. Lord Durham made the following observation on Lower Canada in 1839:

> In fact, beyond the walls of Quebec all regular administration of the country appeared to cease; and there literally was hardly a single public officer in the civil government except in Montreal and Three Rivers, to whom any order could be directed.[22]

Thus the need for some system of municipal government was apparent and in 1840, under the guidance of Lord Sydenham, an ordinance was passed which provided for a system of local government that in many respects resembled the district councils established soon after in Upper Canada. Lower Canada was divided into districts which were to be governed by an elected council and an appointed warden. Another ordinance passed at the same time provided for the election of a clerk, assessors, tax collector, surveyors, overseers of roads and the poor, fence viewers, drain inspectors, and poundkeepers. Townships and parishes with sufficient population were constituted corporate bodies and elected two councillors each to the district councils. Although the district councils were given the power of taxation, much of the real power remained with the Governor.

Both of the 1840 ordinances proved to be unpopular in Lower Canada. The execution and deportation of rebels of the 1837 Rebellion caused resentment and mistrust and the people were especially wary of Lord Sydenham and his motives. The Union Act itself was unpopular and local government was seen as another means of oppression. But perhaps the most unpalatable measure was the power of taxation, which, except for customs duties, had previously been unknown in Lower Canada. Therefore, it is not surprising that in 1845 an act

was passed which repealed both ordinances and constituted each township or parish a body corporate with an elected council with most of the duties of the district councils.

In 1847 a county system roughly based on the district councils was established. This system lasted until 1855, when the Lower Canada Municipal and Road Act was passed which became the foundation of Quebec municipal institutions. This act established parishes, townships, towns, and villages, while retaining the county level as an upper-tier unit. The heads of the local councils sat on the county council and chose their own warden. Each level could appoint the officers it felt were necessary and could levy taxes. Cities continued to be provided for by special **charters** rather than being incorporated under the provisions of the general act. This system remained in effect with minor changes until the turn of the century.

ATLANTIC PROVINCES

The development of municipal institutions in the Atlantic provinces initially paralleled that in Ontario. In the early 1700s the area known as Acadia was ceded by France to Britain. The area soon became known as Nova Scotia and gradually people from New England spread north and settled in the new province. These settlers brought with them a tradition of local government through the town meeting, although officially local government was to be carried on by the Courts of Quarter Sessions and a grand jury.

After the American Revolution, a wave of Loyalists migrated to the area, this time less from New England than from New York, New Jersey, Pennsylvania, and the South. The Southern Loyalists brought with them a different tradition of local government, based on the classed society of the American South in which the Courts of Quarter Sessions discharged local government functions and the Governor appointed local officials. Because of anti-American feelings caused by the Revolution, the New England Loyalists were unsuccessful in promoting local self-rule. Despite dissatisfaction with corrupt practices of certain magistrates, the system of the Courts of Quarter Sessions was to prevail for over 100 years.

At this point, developments in the Atlantic provinces proceeded on a different course from those in Ontario. Far from fighting for local municipal institutions, many Loyalists actively discouraged their development. Many reasons have been suggested for this attitude. They include the feeling that the town meeting had contributed to the revolutionary tendencies of the Americans, a fear of increased taxation, a concern that local officials would lose patronage, and public apathy.

NOVA SCOTIA

Early local government in Nova Scotia was provided by Courts of Quarter Sessions established by the British authorities around 1750. A wave of immigration from New England at the beginning of the 1760s brought settlers accustomed to the town meeting form of local government. The colonial authorities were unwilling to consider such a democratic approach, especially after the American War of Independence. It wasn't until 1841 that the first municipal incorporation occurred, with the granting of a charter to Halifax.

After the introduction of responsible government in 1848 the authorities showed more willingness to allow local government. Legislation permitting the incorporation of counties was enacted in 1855, and the following year the incorporation of townships was authorized. Ironically, now that the right to local government was finally granted, Nova Scotians did not exercise it. According to Higgins, the early enthusiasm waned with the realization that incorporation would bring with it higher taxation.[23] However, the provincial government was determined to shift some of the financial burden for local services onto local residents.

The result was the 1879 County Incorporation Act.

That Act was conceived in secrecy at the provincial level and it was the direct offspring of the financial difficulties of the provincial government. The then Attorney General, J.S.D. Thompson, who later became Prime Minister of Canada, frankly stated that the main object of the Act was "to compel Counties to tax themselves directly to keep up their roads and bridges."[24]

Under the Act, the rural areas of the province were incorporated as counties or districts, single-tier municipalities governed by a warden and an elected council. Urban areas were dealt with in the Towns Incorporation Act of 1888. It stipulated geographic and population requirements which would enable a town to apply for a charter of incorporation. (Eight such towns had already been incorporated by charter prior to the passage of the statute.) These provisions for separate rural and urban municipalities have remained the basis for the Nova Scotia system to this day.

PRINCE EDWARD ISLAND

In 1769 Prince Edward Island separated from Nova Scotia. Two years earlier the island had been divided into counties, parishes, and townships for judicial purposes and for the election of representatives to the provincial legislature, but these areas were never used as municipal units. Indeed, there wasn't any obvious need for municipal government, or even for a decentralization of the colonial administration, given the small size and tiny population of Prince Edward Island.

The first municipal government appeared in 1855 with the incorporation of Charlottetown as a city. In 1870 an act was passed which enabled the resident householders of a town or village to petition the provincial authorities to allow the election of three or more wardens who could appoint local officers and pass by-laws with regard to finance and police matters. Summerside was incorporated as a town in 1875 but, presumably because of the very small population of most settlements, only six more towns had been incorporated by the time the procedure fell into disuse, in 1919. It was abolished in 1950. That same year, the Village Services Act was passed, but the villages established under this statute were not municipalities. They were governed not by elected councillors but by commissioners appointed by the provincial government. These villages are now known as communities, of which there are currently 80. The main difference between towns and communities is that the town councils adopt their own budgets whereas communities must get their budgets approved at an annual meeting of residents.[25] Half of the province's area, and 40 per cent of its population, is still not municipally organized, with the province continuing to provide many of the usual local government services.

NEW BRUNSWICK

Fifteen years after Prince Edward Island separated from Nova Scotia, New Brunswick followed suit — the break being precipitated by an influx of United Empire Loyalists. The following year, 1785, Saint John was incorporated as a city, preceding by almost fifty years the creation of cities in the rest of Canada. Elsewhere in the colony, however, local government was carried on by the Courts of Quarter Sessions and a grand jury. The local citizenry, according to Higgins, seems to have been largely indifferent to the idea of local self-government.[26] This attitude has been partly attributed to the smaller population of Loyalists who came from New England and had thus experienced local government. Whalen, however, rejects this viewpoint, contending that only about 7 per cent of the Loyalists came from the Southern Colonies with their system of Quarter Sessions and that, in any event, even the Loyalists from New England made little demand for more democracy at the local level.[27] Certainly the substantial French population of the province, with their tradition of centralism, did not push for local government.

Interestingly, much of the impetus for the incorporation of municipalities came from the central authorities, who were concerned about "reducing the time consumed on endless debates and squabbles over parish and county issues in the legislature" and anxious to shift a growing expenditure

burden.[28] Finally, in 1851 an act was passed for the incorporation of counties, but its provisions were permissive and only six counties were established over the next three decades. However, the Municipalities Act of 1877 made county incorporation mandatory, thus bringing the entire population and area of the province under municipal government. The county system was two-tiered like that in Ontario, but differed in that councillors from the rural areas were directly elected to county council while all urban areas, except Fredericton, were represented at the county level, usually by ex-officio members.

During this period a number of urban communities sought corporate status. Fredericton had received its charter in 1848, over 60 years after the first urban incorporation in Saint John. By 1896 nine towns had been established by separate charter. In that year the Town Incorporation Act was passed, providing for a uniform system for the creation of towns with an elected council consisting of a mayor and aldermen.

The basic municipal system of New Brunswick was established in this 1896 statute and the 1877 Counties Act. Cities each have their own separate charters of incorporation and a 1920 act provided for the incorporation of villages. However, a major reorganization of local government in New Brunswick begun in 1967 resulted in the abolition of county governments and a number of other major changes.

NEWFOUNDLAND

The development of municipal institutions in Newfoundland has been a slow and arduous process, attributed to several factors.[29] The settlements which developed in the early years were numerous but geographically isolated from each other, generally quite limited in population, and financially unable to support any form of local government. Moreover, since Newfoundlanders gained the right to own property only in 1824, they jealously guarded this right against the taxation which would inevitably come with local government.

Newfoundland, because of its geographic isolation, was not influenced by the development of municipal government elsewhere; nor did its early settlers have prior experience with such a system. In any event, there was little apparent need for municipal government in much of the province. Transportation needs were partly served by water, and the central government provided services such as roads that were provided at the local level in other provinces.

After some unsuccessful attempts, St. John's was created a town in 1888, but once again the impetus was not the demand for local democracy but the desire of the colonial authorities to shift some of their expenditure burden. As Higgins explains, municipal status for St. John's was imposed partly to facilitate costly improvements to the sewerage and street systems and partly to be a mechanism whereby the privately owned and heavily indebted St. John's Water Company would become the financial responsibility of the City—a Water Company in which the Premier of Newfoundland and other prominent government supporters and business people were shareholders![30]

No other municipalities were formed for fifty years. Acts were passed in 1933 and again in 1937 providing for the incorporation of municipalities. However, no community requested incorporation and the central authorities did not use their authority to impose such incorporations. Instead, a new approach was attempted which offered subsidies and provided a special act giving a municipality any taxation form it desired if it would incorporate. By 1948 twenty municipalities had been incorporated by special charter and only five of these imposed the real property tax.[31]

After Newfoundland joined Confederation in 1949, the provincial legislature passed a general local government act which bestowed municipal status by proclamation for areas with a population of at least one thousand, and also provided for rural districts. Since that time the number of municipalities has grown steadily, as have such quasi-municipalities as local improvement districts and local government communities. Newfoundland made prolonged efforts to bring about restructuring in the St. John's area as well as its ambitious municipal consolidation program.

WESTERN PROVINCES

The provinces of Manitoba, Saskatchewan, and Alberta were part of the original Hudson's Bay Company land grant and later of the Northwest Territories. For most of their early history these provinces were governed by the Company, which had complete judicial, legislative, and administrative authority. In 1869 the Company's rights in Rupert's Land and the Northwest Territories were acquired by the newly created Dominion of Canada. It was not until late in the nineteenth century that a substantial amount of settlement occurred in the Prairie provinces. When population growth pressures finally necessitated the provision of local services and subsequently a local government system, it was only logical for these provinces to look to their nearest eastern neighbour, Ontario, for a model upon which to base their systems. Because of the different physical characteristics of the West, the Ontario model was somewhat modified to suit local needs.

MANITOBA

In 1870 Manitoba was created a province separate from the Northwest Territories. The first provincial legislature provided for a system of local government by a grand jury and Courts of Sessions which were to administer a County Assessment Act and a Parish Assessment Act. As well, the judges of the Sessions selected local officers such as treasurers, assessors, highway surveyors, poundkeepers, and constables from lists presented by the grand jury.

The first municipality was established in 1873 with the incorporation of Winnipeg as a city—although not without a struggle. Apparently the Hudson's Bay Company and four other property owners, who together owned well over half of the assessable property in Winnipeg, had opposed the incorporation and the resultant taxation of that property.[32] In that same year, general municipal legislation was also passed which provided for the establishment of local municipalities upon petition of the freeholders within a district. Only six areas became incorporated during the decade that this act was in force.

This permissive approach was dropped in 1883 when the Manitoba Government decided to introduce a municipal system for the whole province modelled on the two-tier county system of Ontario. The new act established twenty-six counties with councils composed of the heads of both rural and urban local (lower-tier) municipal councils. The county council elected a warden from among its own members. This Ontario county system proved to be ineffective, however, because of the large areas covered, the often sparse and scattered population, and the local objections to a two-tier system. It was abandoned after only three years, and the province was divided into smaller rural municipalities.

In 1902 a general act established cities, towns, villages, and rural municipalities as the basic units of local government, although Winnipeg was given its own special charter. This system has continued to the present, except for major changes in the structure of government for the Winnipeg area.

SASKATCHEWAN

Like Manitoba, Saskatchewan had been part of the lands granted to the Hudson's Bay Company. It was taken over by the Canadian Government in 1870 and administered essentially as a colony until it gained provincial status in 1905. The territorial council first provided for municipal government in 1883 by enacting a municipal ordinance which was patterned on the previously cited Manitoba legislation of that year, which, in turn, had been modelled on the 1849 Municipal Act of Ontario. The ordinance provided for either rural municipalities or towns, depending on area and population and on whether local citizens petitioned for municipal status. Regina received town status that very year and four rural municipalities were organized in 1884, but little initiative was evident thereafter. By 1897 only one additional town had been created and two rural municipalities had dropped their municipal status. One major problem was the vast area and small, scattered population which made it

difficult to generate the financial base needed to support municipal government.

However, since some form of local organization was necessary to provide roads and protection against prairie and forest fires, an ordinance was passed allowing the creation of "statute labour and fire districts" in areas not organized as rural municipalities. By 1896 these local improvement districts, as they were now called, were made mandatory, and the following year legislation was passed which allowed for elected committees to administer the districts. In 1903 the districts were reorganized into large units made up of four of the former districts, each with one elected councillor on a municipal district council. Meanwhile, a revision and consolidation of municipal ordinances in 1894 provided for the incorporation of cities, towns, and rural municipalities.

Throughout this period the federal government was strongly encouraging Western settlement, and large numbers of settlers arrived from Europe and from Eastern Canada, the latter bringing previous experience with municipal government. The impetus which these developments gave to the creation of municipal institutions is evident from the fact that when Saskatchewan became a province in 1905 there were already 4 cities, 43 towns, 97 villages, 2 rural municipalities, and 359 of the local improvement districts.[33]

The new province appointed a Commission to carry on with a study previously started by the assembly of the Northwest Territories, which was to consider all aspects of municipal government. In 1908 Saskatchewan adopted the Commission's recommendation that a system of municipal units be established with a separate act covering each type of unit. Accordingly, the City Act, Town Act, and Village Act were passed in 1908 and the Rural Municipalities Act in the following year. One result was a very rapid increase in rural municipalities — to 200 by 1912. However, many rural residents opposed municipal organization, mainly because of a fear of increased taxes,[34] and the provincial government had to force remaining local improvement districts to become rural municipalities. This municipal structure has remained basically unchanged through to the present.

ALBERTA

Since Alberta was also part of the federally administered Northwest Territories from 1870 until 1905, its municipal background resembles that of Saskatchewan. The first municipal government was introduced in Calgary, which was incorporated as a town in 1884 under the previously described municipal ordinance of 1883. In what has by now become a familiar pattern, incorporation efforts were initially thwarted by large landowners, among them the CPR, opposed to the prospect of property taxes.[35] Two more urban municipalities were created over the next decade (Lethbridge and Edmonton in 1891 and 1892, respectively), but because of the very sparse, scattered rural population, there were no petitions for the creation of rural municipalities under the ordinance. As in the area which later became Saskatchewan, the main form of local government was the statute labour and fire district or local improvement district.

Toward the end of the century, however, the large influx of settlers began to stimulate the creation of local governments. When Alberta became a province in 1905 its population was about 170 000 (compared to 18 000 in 1881) and it had two cities, fifteen towns, and thirty villages. By 1912 a new municipal system was established with cities, towns, villages, and local improvement districts. The latter could be erected into rural municipalities upon reaching a specified population, but here again few incorporations were requested because of local fears about tax increases.

The organization of municipal government in rural Alberta has undergone considerable change over the years.[36] Beginning in 1942 the provincial government began to reduce the number of local improvement districts (by now called municipal districts) through amalgamation. A much more radical change was introduced in 1950 with the creation of single-tier county governments in the rural areas handling virtually all local government functions

including education. The main structural changes since have involved annexations around Calgary and Edmonton.

BRITISH COLUMBIA

The area of what is now British Columbia was also under the jurisdiction of the Hudson's Bay Company during its early years of settlement. In 1849 the British assumed responsibility for Vancouver Island. By this time there was a general movement of population to the west side of the continent because of the discovery of gold in California (in 1848). A significant influx of population to the mainland of British Columbia occurred with the discovery of gold on the Fraser River in 1858, and that year the British also assumed control of the mainland from the Hudson's Bay Company. The mainland and Vancouver Island were administered as two separate colonies until 1866.

The physical characteristics of British Columbia played a significant role in the development of municipal institutions in the province. Because of the mountainous terrain, early settlements were scattered and isolated. New Westminster, the capital of the mainland colony, became a municipality in 1860, and two years later Victoria, the capital of the Vancouver Island colony, was incorporated as a town. Shortly after gaining provincial status in 1871, British Columbia enacted the Consolidated Municipal Act providing for local petitions for municipal incorporation, but by the end of 1874 there were still only five municipalities in the province.

In 1892 the Municipal Clauses Act was passed, governing all new municipalities formed and providing for a system similar to that in Ontario, but without a county level. Municipalities were either cities with a mayor and council or rural districts with a reeve and council. By 1900 there were some 52 of these municipalities. In 1920 a Village Municipalities Act was passed allowing for smaller urban areas to incorporate with limited powers.

It is noteworthy that most of the larger towns established in the period from the 1870s to the

1920s were incorporated under their own "charters," statutes that were drafted locally by the applicant citizens and dealt with by the legislature as private bills. These arrangements contributed to the strong tradition of local autonomy that continues to characterize municipal government in British Columbia.

Even with these incorporations, however, the vast majority of the area of the province remained unorganized territory. The British Columbia Government was directly responsible for the provision of all necessary services.[37] Under this centralized administration, a government agent received local revenues and supervised public expenditures, and often was stipendiary magistrate, gold commissioner, mining recorder, water commissioner, issuer of marriage licences, assessor, tax collector, and policeman. A municipal response to the governing of the vast rural areas was introduced beginning in 1965 with the creation of regional districts. These have proven to be among the most flexible of the various structural reforms introduced in the various provinces in recent decades.

NORTHERN TERRITORIES

The area of the Yukon and Northwest Territories was controlled by the Hudson's Bay Company until acquired by the federal government in 1870.[38] Its territory was reduced that year by the establishment of Manitoba as a separate province, and further reductions occurred in 1905, when Alberta and Saskatchewan became provinces, and in 1912, when the northern boundaries of Ontario, Quebec, and Manitoba were extended north to their present positions. The discovery of gold in the Klondike in 1896 sparked a rapid increase in the population of the Yukon and in 1898 it was established as a separate territory.

Dawson City was incorporated as the first municipality in 1901, but its charter was revoked in 1904 and the provision of local services reverted to the territorial administration for a number of years. Also in 1901, a provision was made for the establishment of unincorporated towns upon petition. These units were not full municipal governments,

however, since residents could only elect one official and only a very limited range of services could be provided. In any event, the one unincorporated town created was disbanded when its population subsequently declined.

This often temporary nature of northern settlements has added to the problems caused by the extremely small, scattered population. Therefore, while both the Yukon and Northwest Territories have municipal ordinances authorizing the establishment of municipal governments, relatively few units were created until the past couple of decades. As late as 1964 there were only three incorporated municipalities — the towns of Yellowknife and Hay Bay and the village of Fort Smith.

Prior to 1960, virtually all real government within the Northern Territories came from Ottawa. With the relocation of the Territorial Council from Ottawa to Yellowknife in 1967, however, new municipal structures were introduced which allowed for more decision making at the local level.[39] The category of city was introduced in 1969, with Yellowknife becoming the first city.

There has been increasing emphasis on the passing of authority down from the Territorial Government to local governments, along with an attempt to strengthen the political role of the municipalities. One government study claimed that "[In] the NWT the importance of the local level of government is of particular magnitude because of the cultural diversity and the vast distances between communities." [40]

While only a very small portion of the vast area of the Northern Territories is organized municipally, the organized portion contains three-quarters of the population. The few cities, towns, and villages, which contain the bulk of the population, are basically modelled upon the structure of municipal government found in Southern Ontario. In addition to these tax-based municipalities, there are some 40 non-tax-based municipalities (mostly hamlets) with more limited powers. Of particular interest is a relatively new form of municipal unit called the charter community, whose specific features depend on what is spelled out in the charter establishing it.

This flexibility is especially useful in areas where band councils have provided the traditional leadership in the community. Natives have tended to view municipalities as "foreign" structures. The charter community approach allows the creation of a new governing arrangement which can incorporate elements of the band council structure and that of municipalities.

In addition to these municipal structures, a very large number of local boards and special purpose committees are found in the Northern Territories.[41] Many of these bodies were established to obtain feedback from the local communities, to compensate for the fact that there were few elected members of the territorial council (now the Legislative Assembly) and few elected municipal councils. Even though municipal councils are now more widespread, these special purpose bodies have proven difficult to eradicate — a problem also experienced in Southern Canada.

Further changes and boundary adjustments are inevitable as a result of reviews which will be carried out in response to the several aboriginal land claim settlements which are changing jurisdictions in the north. Particularly dramatic is the Nunavut land claim of the Eastern Arctic, which will lead to territorial division before the end of this century. The Nunavut Political Accord signed in October 1992 sets out guidelines establishing a new region to be carved out of the Northwest Territories by 1999, essentially cutting it in half.[42]

NOTES

1. K.G. Crawford, *Canadian Municipal Government*, Toronto, University of Toronto Press, 1954, p. 21.
2. *Ibid.*, p. 23.
3. In Lower Canada the Family Compact had a counterpart known as the Chateau Clique, with whom it also had family and economic ties. An elite group surrounding the Lieutenant-Governor, such as the Family Compact and Chateau Clique, was found in most of the provinces.
4. Adam Shortt, *Municipal Government in Ontario, An Historical Sketch*, University of Toronto studies, History and Economics, Vol. II, No. 2, p. 8.
5. In Ontario, town meetings were actually township meetings.
6. Use of police in this sense meant regulation, discipline, and control of a community.
7. Shortt, *op. cit.*, p. 19.
8. See Engin F. Isin, *Cities without Citizens*, Montreal, Black Rose Books, 1992, pp. 112–114, on which this discussion is based.
9. *Ibid.*, p. 113.
10. *Ibid.*, p. 114.
11. Fred Landon, *Western Ontario and the American Frontier*, Toronto, McClelland and Stewart Limited, 1967, p. 223.
12. John M. McEvoy, *The Ontario Township*, University of Toronto studies, Politics, 1st series, No. 1, 1889, p. 22.
13. Gerald M. Craig (ed.), *Lord Durham's Report*, Toronto, McClelland and Stewart Limited, 1963, p. 60.
14. *Ibid.*, p. 67.
15. Landon, *op. cit.*, p. 223.
16. Thomas H. Raddall, *The Path of Destiny*, Toronto, Doubleday and Company, Inc., 1957, p. 31.
17. Crawford, *op. cit.*, p. 31.
18. Adam Shortt and Arthur G. Doughty (gen. eds.), *Canada and Its Provinces, A History of the Canadian People and Their Institutions*, Toronto, Glasgow, Brook and Company, 1914, Vol. XVIII, p. 437.
19. *Ibid.*, Vol. XV, p. 301.
20. *Ibid.*, p. 304.
21. Isin, *op. cit.*, p. 142.
22. Shortt and Doughty, *op. cit.*, p. 290.
23. Donald J.H. Higgins, *Local and Urban Politics in Canada*, Toronto, Gage, 1986, pp. 39–40.
24. A. William Cox, Q.C., in a 1989 paper "Development of Municipal-Provincial Relations," quoted in *Task Force on Local Government*, Report to the Government of Nova Scotia, April 1992, Briefing Book, p. 13.
25. Allan O'Brien, *Municipal Consolidation in Canada and Its Alternatives*, Toronto, Intergovernmental Committee on Urban and Regional Research, May 1993, p. 27.
26. *Ibid.*, p. 40.
27. H.J. Whalen, *The Development of Local Governments in New Brunswick*, Fredericton, 1963, Chapter Two.
28. *Ibid.*, p. 20.
29. Higgins, *op. cit.*, pp. 33–34.
30. *Ibid.*, pp. 34–35.
31. Crawford, *op. cit.*, p. 41.

32. Higgins, *op. cit.*, pp. 50–51.

33. Horace L. Brittain, *Local Government in Canada,* Toronto, Ryerson Press, 1951, p. 179.

34. Higgins, *op. cit.*, p. 53.

35. *Ibid.*, p. 54.

36. See Eric J. Hanson, *Local Government in Alberta,* Toronto, McClelland and Stewart Limited, 1956, and Jack Masson, *Alberta's Local Governments and Their Politics,* Edmonton, University of Alberta Press, 1985, Chapter Four.

37. Shortt and Doughty, *op. cit.*, Vol. XXII, p. 355.

38. The description in this section is partly based on Higgins, *op. cit.*, pp. 59–60.

39. This discussion is based on Government of the Northwest Territories in conjunction with the Association of Municipal Clerks and Treasurers of Ontario, *Municipal Administration Program,* 1984, Unit 1, Lesson Two.

40. *Constitutional Development in the Northwest Territories, Report of the Special Representative* (Drury Report), Ottawa, 1980, quoted in *ibid.*, p. 33.

41. See Report of the Project to Review the Operations and Structure of Northern Government, *Strength at Two Levels,* November 1991.

42. *Canada Year Book 1994,* Ottawa, Statistics Canada, p. 288.

Rethinking Local Government

BERYL DAVIS

As the third level of government in Canada, local government is frequently overlooked in the study of government institutions. The third level of Canadian government is generally perceived in terms of providing services and raising revenue, while the other two levels are involved with what are thought to be more significant issues of national and international dimensions.

Local government, because it is local, is of vital importance to the health of Canada's democracy. Local government in Canada has developed to embody the principles of participatory democracy, but it also reflects the politics of the federal system by which this country is governed. Popular participation is encouraged and is possible at the local level while the opportunity for such participation is limited at the federal and provincial levels. The complex administrative structures that exist at both senior levels leave little room for democracy in operations that are remote and inaccessible.[1]

As Canadians have become better educated, their desire to participate and to have a role in the community has increased. On the local level, this remains possible. Because local governments are the most accessible and closest to the people, they impact on our everyday lives in ways other levels of government do not. Local government enables Canadians to settle their own problems and to establish services that will meet their particular needs. Local problems are usually more easily and effectively solved by local authorities, although a growing number of problems are beyond the fiscal capacity of many municipalities.

In the Canadian federal system, the basic unit of local government is the "municipality." A municipality may be defined as a political body formed by the residents of a particular region and having powers of a local nature that it can exercise autonomously.[2] The very existence of a municipality assumes three fundamental characteristics: first, a specific geographical region; second, a region that is governed by its residents through elected representatives; and third, a degree of governing autonomy, along with financial resources that allow the municipality to exercise its powers without external supervision.

While there are three distinct levels of government in Canada — federal, provincial and municipal — only two are protected by the Constitution. Local government has no **constitutional status** of its own and functions as a mere delegate of the senior levels of government, primarily the provincial government. As a result, municipal governments differ from province to province; there are ten municipal systems that are quite different from one another. In Prince Edward Island, for example, with its small geographical size and population of about 100,000, municipalities barely exist because it is possible to govern the whole province from the provincial capital of Charlottetown. In Ontario,

SOURCE: Written for this volume. Used by permission of the author.

however, which is larger in size and population than many independent countries, municipal governments are highly developed. In addition, there is great variety among municipal institutions and no single uniform structure prevails. Municipalities may be either urban or rural. Rural municipalities may be counties, parishes, townships, rural and district governing bodies; while urban municipalities are cities, towns and villages. There are also innumerable special purpose bodies attached to the more developed municipalities that perform specific functions, usually to enhance efficient delivery of services.

Canadians elect far more representatives to local government offices than the number who serve on the other two levels. In 1991, for example, Nova Scotians elected some 600 representatives to serve on 66 municipal councils and 66 school boards across the province. By comparison, Nova Scotia elects only 52 members to its provincial legislature and 11 Members of Parliament to the federal House of Commons.

WHERE WE HAVE BEEN . . .

Municipal government evolved slowly in Canada, and its development in the various provinces has not been uniform.[3] This diversity was due to early settlement patterns and the cultural and political values immigrants brought to this land. The struggle for local government involved conflict between local citizens and provincial/colonial authorities. Often those in more **urbanized** areas struggled for its establishment while rural residents struggled against it.

Three cultural and political influences — British, French and American — played an important role in shaping municipal government in early Canada. Immigrants from Great Britain and the southern United States were accustomed to the English system of the Courts of Quarter Sessions but they had no experience with local self-government. The French colonists were used to the rule of a highly bureaucratized and authoritarian system of central government that strongly discouraged any attempt to foster local self-government. It was the New

England Loyalists who brought with them their heritage of local self-government and practices of democratic expression that eventually won them the right to establish local government in Central Canada. The Ontario model in turn strongly influenced municipal development in the other provinces. This basic framework for local government has endured to the present day, with certain modifications introduced by the turn-of-the-century proponents of the Municipal Reform Movement.

As Canada has grown from an agrarian to an industrial to an informational/technological society, the demands on Canadian municipalities have increased enormously. Municipal government has been dramatically affected by urbanization, technological advances and the resulting pressure for specialized services. Urban municipalities especially have had difficulty in coping with changes that have taken place. There are numerous explanations for this, but all seem to turn on one fundamental issue — that municipal government, unlike the other two orders of government in Canada, does not have constitutional status. As a result it is difficult, if not impossible, for municipalities to function as autonomous units of government within the federal system.

Early local government did not develop as units of mature democracy. Government at the local level was not established as a result of popular pressure for local self-governing legislatures but rather it was imposed upon local communities by provincial fiat. Initially, Canadian municipalities started with robust tax bases, having access to property taxes, sales taxes, estate taxes and income taxes, and they were adequately empowered to fulfill their responsibilities. This position changed tremendously, however, during the course of the twentieth century, as municipal autonomy was steadily eroded by structural weaknesses, fiscal inadequacy and increased dependency on other levels of government. Indeed, there are those who question whether the form of local government we have in Canada today, acting as an administrative extension of the province and functioning in many ways like the corporate model, is either "local" or "government."

WHERE WE ARE NOW

Although attempts have been made to change the inherently subordinate role of municipalities within the Canadian federation, the constitutional status of Canadian municipalities remains essentially the same today as it did in 1867. As a result, three major areas of concern have continued to be problematic: intergovernmental relations, fiscal responsibilities and urban policy.

Intergovernmental Relations

Intergovernmental relations in the federal context usually refers to relations between the federal and provincial governments. The relations between the province and the municipalities, like relations between the federal and provincial governments, involve two levels of government, but there are significant differences. Dupre has summarized these differences under three headings: law, hierarchy and structure.[4] First, in legal terms, the federal–provincial relationship is based on constitutional law; the provincial–municipal relationship is based on **statutory law**.

Second, in hierarchical terms, the federal–provincial relationship is one of equal to equal; the provincial–municipal relationship is one of superior to subordinate. At First Ministers' Conferences, a hierarchy of federal and provincial relationships meet to discuss overall policy but there is no equivalent of this at the provincial–municipal level.

Third, in structural terms, the federal–provincial relationship is a relatively simple one in contrast to the complexity of provincial–municipal relations. The former involves the national government with a set of ten provincial governments, each of which has jurisdiction over its territory; the latter, however, involves the provincial governments and a diverse array of municipal governments, which may take the form of regional governments (i.e., counties or metropolitan municipalities), general-purpose local governments (i.e., cities, towns or villages); and highly specialized governments (i.e., school boards, health units or planning commissions).

As a result of the subordinate nature of the municipalities to provincial governments, relations between the two tend to be administrative. The administrative nature of provincial–municipal relations tends to fractionalize these relations among the various provincial departments: municipalities become bogged down in administrative detail that could have been avoided if power had been delegated to the municipal authority.

In reality, the provincial–municipal constitutional relationship exists within a political framework in that political factors limit the ways provinces can exert their influence on their municipalities. These political factors have tended to reinforce institutional decentralization by limiting provincial influence and by shaping the growth of government functions into a highly fractionalized pattern. Dupre succinctly describes the nature of the relationship between the provinces and their municipalities as one of "hyper-fractionalized quasi-subordination."[5]

Federal–municipal relations, in contrast, are largely subject to the control of the provinces, which are constantly vigilant against constitutional impropriety on the part of the federal government. The period of greatest federal involvement in local affairs was during the 1970s, when Ottawa responded to the increased problems of local governments which were experiencing the effects of urbanization. The federal government attempted to improve intergovernmental relations by creating the Ministry of State for Urban Affairs (MSUA), a federal ministry which functioned from 1971 to 1979 but was beset with problems from its inception due to the fact that its mandate was for research and coordination. Also, it lacked any real authority with which to control the legislative or spending proposals of other agencies. MSUA's powers of persuasion did not prove very successful. Its demise in 1979 may have demonstrated the difficulty of direct federal–municipal involvement through such a ministry in the present constitutional arrangement. MSUA's attempts to promote coordination among all three levels of government resulted in the establishment of national tri-level conferences. The municipalities hoped to raise their stature in the Canadian political arena, but found themselves relegated to the position of interest groups. The provinces were particularly hostile to these meetings, and the tri-level effort may have ultimately reinforced the inferiority complex of municipalities.

Revenues and Responsibilities

As Lord Durham anticipated over a century before, the provinces did not provide their municipalities with adequate tax sources to allow them to fulfill their responsibilities. Because of the limited tax base allowed by provincial governments, municipalities have become increasingly dependent on grants from the two senior levels of government. Since the Second World War, the role of local government has changed substantially as a result of urbanization, technological advances and rising incomes. In many instances, municipalities have been forced to give up to the provinces their dominant position in financing local services. In 1993, for example, the municipalities in Ontario collected $15 billion in local taxes.[6] Still, municipalities have not been able to respond to the ever-increasing demands for their services. Thus, the federal and provincial governments, with access to greater tax sources, have assumed the responsibility for many municipal services either directly, by actually providing these services, or indirectly, by providing conditional grants. As a percentage of total local expenditure, conditional transfers to municipalities grew from 4 percent in 1913 and 6.2 percent in 1930 to 17.1 percent in 1953 and 40.4 percent by 1982.[7] Unconditional grants are also provided by the provinces but to a much lesser degree; in 1980 only 9.8 percent of total transfers to municipalities were in the form of unconditional grants.[8] Federal transfers amounted to only 1.5 percent of total grants to local governments in 1980.[9]

Transfers from the federal and provincial governments, whether conditional or unconditional, are not an adequate method of attempting to solve the financial problems of municipalities. They have had damaging consequences that have weakened municipal accountability and have undermined local fiscal responsibility. Municipalities tend not to exercise restraint in spending funds that have not been raised by taxes and for which they are not directly accountable. They also look more often to the federal and provincial authorities to solve problems of a local nature. Municipal dependency on transfers makes long-term planning next to impossible because grants can be reduced or eliminated from one year to the next and confirmation of grant funding is often received late in the stages of **municipal planning**, causing uncertainty and resentment.

Conditional grants are damaging to municipal autonomy in that the local government no longer controls the area for which a grant is provided; instead, federal or provincial authorities impose their own standards and conditions on the municipality, which is unable to formulate its own policies for local matters. Municipalities therefore tend to be reactive rather than proactive in initiating and developing policy and planning, because they begin to anticipate intervention from the other levels of government. Provincial governments prefer the use of the conditional grant system; it provides a means by which they can delegate difficult services to municipalities and still retain control. Unconditional grants are preferable for municipalities in that they allow for more local control in spending.

Municipal governments view their lack of an adequate fiscal base as having a number of detrimental effects. An inadequate fiscal base has limited their role in areas where the provinces have assumed greater responsibility but where local input is important; it has reduced local autonomy in providing local services due to the dependency on conditional transfers; and it has produced weak local governments, unable to handle local issues because of the fiscal discrepancy between expenditure requirements and revenue-raising capacity.[10] Because the provinces are responsible for their municipalities, they assume a supervisory role of activities at the local level in order to reduce the possibility that the local units will not function properly or encounter financial difficulties. If financial difficulties do occur at the local level, as was the case during the depression years when many municipalities declared bankruptcy, it would be expected that the provincial government would assist the affected local units. With its broader economic and political base the provincial government is better able to provide advice and direction, particularly to smaller municipalities. There should be a balance, however, in provincial–municipal relations whereby the province may protect its legitimate interests without unduly interfering with the responsibilities of the municipal government.

Urban Policy

As Canada's municipalities have evolved from "outpost to service centre to specialized place"[11] so too their needs have grown enormously. Since 1867 Canada has changed from an agrarian society with smaller, more isolated municipal units to a transformed information-technology society in the 1990s. The constitutional arrangements for the municipalities of 1867 do not reflect the urban life of Canada today. Urban indicators clearly show that the concentration of Canada's population in only a few urban centres has proceeded at an unprecedented rate since the 1960s. By the year 2000 it is likely that well over one-third of this country's projected population of about 30 million will live in three major cities: Montreal, Toronto and Vancouver.

Following the Second World War the Canadian governments became increasingly sensitive to the fact of urbanization and its impact on major cities. Feldman and Graham have identified four perceived results of the urbanization process on which government concern became focused. The first was the problem of urban growth itself, stemming from the relocation of Canadians and newly arrived immigrants and problems of planning and servicing growing areas. Second, there was concern for slow-growth or no-growth areas which had to be dealt with to provide them with government and services that built on tradition and met the needs of a changing world. A third area of concern was the federal government's interest and direct involvement in the provision of basic municipal infrastructure

and housing in spite of possible jurisdictional problems. The federal government established the Central Mortgage and Housing Corporation (CMHC) in 1946 to provide direct funding of mortgages for low-cost housing and to assist in the construction of basic municipal services through a program of capital funding. Fourth, the provincial governments were concerned that, like their American counterparts, the major cities in Canada would become "hollow shells."[12]

In light of these concerns, programs of urban reform were initiated in most provinces. The creation of Metropolitan Toronto in 1954 launched the modern era of local government reform, followed by the Montreal Urban Community (1970) and Winnipeg Unicity (1972).

Canadian **metropolitan** centres have responsibilities and requirements that are much different from those of smaller urban or rural municipalities. The greater territorial dimensions associated with larger urban centres bring into question two particular issues. First, if local government is in essence the government of local communities as consistent with the principles of democracy, then in the case of large metropolitan governments, is it the metropolis or the neighbourhood which becomes the unit of local government? Second, it is questionable that provincial governments will be willing to continue to create local governments of agglomerations (25,000 or more people) or metropolitan areas (100,000 or more people) which would represent the potential strength of or significantly challenge provincial authority.

WHERE WE ARE GOING

If municipalities are to be expected to function effectively within the Canadian federation, certain changes must be considered. Canadian municipalities are not fulfilling either of their basic representative or administrative roles largely as result of their subordinate constitutional status. Municipal units can only be as strong and effective as their provincial governments are prepared to make them.

First, then, in order to increase administrative capacity, changes must be considered in the securing of adequate financial resources for local governments. The Constitution restricts the provinces to only direct forms of taxation [Section 92 (2)], sale of licences and permits [Section 92 (9)], and the levying of fines and penalties [Section 92 (15)]. These limitations also apply to the municipalities, which are further restricted to only those services granted them by the province.

In its "Puppets on a Shoestring" report, the Canadian Federation of Mayors and Municipalities (CFMM) proposed three ways in which the financial plight of local governments could be alleviated. First, to reduce the need for municipal financial support, the provinces could take over responsibility for some of the service functions that municipalities perform. Changes have taken place in Nova Scotia, for example, in the areas of education, health and social services. If this trend continues, municipalities may become functionally insignificant as governments. Second, additional funding from the federal and provincial governments could be transferred to the municipalities. This approach would only be effective if the municipalities were guaranteed set levels of federal and provincial tax revenues on an unconditional basis or with no strings attached. A third approach would involve having the municipalities increase their own levels of taxation using revenue sources now available to them.[13]

CONCLUSION

The development of municipal government in Canada has been largely influenced by its status within the Canadian constitution. The provinces are ever vigilant to guard against constitutional impropriety on the part of the federal government in its relations with the municipalities. For the municipalities, intergovernmental relations have involved a relationship of superior to subordinate which makes their relationship with senior levels difficult, as the natural attitude of the inferior is to be on the defensive. Increasingly, municipalities have been unable to balance revenues with responsibilities due to the inadequate financial sources delegated to them by the provinces. The larger urban municipalities are confronted with special problems, different from those of other municipalities, particularly in land-use planning and development.

Municipalities are being urged to become more technologically advanced, innovative and competitive in the expanding global economy. In order to do this, certain financial and structural problems need to be addressed, but changes in these areas of concern will not be easily achieved by the "creatures of the province."

In the 1990s, the availability of financial resources to municipalities has decreased, nevertheless public demands for more specialized services have increased. Fiscal problems at the local level persist — municipalities are unable to raise sufficient funds on their own to meet rising expenditures. The federal decision to reduce transfer payments to the provinces has resulted in the provinces passing on those cuts to the municipalities. Faced with the fiscal dilemma of simply accepting the cuts or raising taxes, some local governments have done both, and as a result, have endured the political cost of upsetting the electorate.

Structural problems persist as well. Across the country there are hundreds of small municipalities that struggle for survival with limited resources to provide basic services. Some provinces have responded to this problem by consolidating smaller municipalities into regional and metropolitan governments in order to capture economies of scale and improve land-use development. Structural reform at the provincial level, such as strengthening the department of municipal affairs, would serve to expedite dealings between municipalities and provincial departments. The fragmentation in the present system leads to duplication, indecision and financial waste.

With all its past and present challenges, local government has nevertheless proved to be quite resilient for well over a century in this country. Given its longstanding record of endurance, it is likely that local government will continue to provide services and raise revenues well into the twenty-first century.

NOTES

1. Jacques L'Heureux, "Municipalities and the Division of Powers," in R. Simeon, ed., *Intergovernmental Relations*, Vol. 63, prepared for the Royal Commission on the Economic Union and Development Prospects for Canada (Ottawa: Minister of Supply and Services, 1985), p. 180.
2. *Ibid.*, p. 179.
3. Donald Higgins, *Urban Canada* (Toronto: Macmillan, 1977), p. 3; also see James J. Guy, *How We Are Governed* (Toronto: Harcourt, Brace, 1995), pp. 371–404.
4. J.S. Dupre, *Intergovernmental Finance in Ontario: A Provincial–Local Perspective* (Toronto: Queen's Printer, 1968), pp. 1–2.
5. *Ibid.*, p. 5.
6. Durham Report, 1839, p. 113.
7. Donald McFetridge, "Canadian R&D Incentives: Their Adequacy and Impact" (Toronto: Canadian Tax Foundation, 1983), pp. 97, 197.
8. H.M. Kitchen and M.L. McMillan, "Local Government and Canadian Federalism," in Simeon, ed., *Intergovernmental Relations*, p. 223.
9. *Ibid.*, p. 223.
10. Kitchen and McMillan, "Local Government and Canadian Federalism," p. 231.
11. James and Richard Simmons, *Urban Canada* (Toronto: Copp Clark, 1969), p. 46.
12. L. Feldman and K. Graham, "Local Government Reform in Canada," in Arthur B. Gunlicks, ed., *Local Government Reform and Reorganization* (Port Washington, N.Y.: Kennikat Press, 1981), pp. 152–53.
13. Canadian Federation of Mayors and Municipalities, *Puppets on a Shoestring: The Effects on Municipal Government of Canada's System of Public Finance* (Ottawa: CFMM, April, 1976).

The Financial Context for Urban Policy

DAVID SIEGEL

LOCAL GOVERNMENT IN THE FEDERAL SYSTEM

In the early years of Confederation, federal and local governments were the most important orders of government (in terms of level of expenditure). Local governments provided education, roads, and such social assistance as was provided at that time. Provincial governments provided very few services.

The depression of the 1930s and evolving technology changed this situation. During the depression, many municipalities suffered serious financial difficulties and had to be shored up by provincial governments, which in turn were heavily supported by the federal government.

Technology also spawned some significant changes. The improved quality of the motorcar and truck and the growth of the suburbs increased the importance of inter-city highways and commuter trains. These methods of transportation were clearly in the sphere of provincial governments. The high cost of modern education caused an increasing share of this burden to be borne by provincial governments. The overall effect of this on government expenditures was that provincial government expenditure eclipsed local expenditure during the 1930s and local governments have remained in third place ever since (Bird, 1970: 15, 239, 268).

This change in the financial status of local governments had ramifications in other areas. In general, provincial control of municipal activities has become tighter over the years. A quantum leap was made in the 1930s when provinces, which had to bale out bankrupt or virtually bankrupt municipalities, strengthened provincial control over debt issuance and other financial aspects of municipal operation. There are some who would say that provincial control has tightened considerably over the years, although this is an arguable position.

Figure 41.1 illustrates the trend in the relative importance — in financial terms — of the three spheres of government in the Canadian federal system for the period from 1946 to 1985. It focuses on two measures of revenue — own-source revenue and revenue including transfers from other governments.

Own-source revenue consists of taxes, charges, and fees a government imposes by its own authority. *Revenue including transfers* includes all revenue received by the government — both own-source revenue and transfer payments from other governments. There is an important distinction between the two. Local governments are free to make their own decisions about raising (and spending) own-source revenue, within some fairly broad constraints established by general provincial policies on tax assessment and other matters.

SOURCE: Excerpted from "The Financial Context for Urban Policy," in Richard Loreto and Trevor Price, eds., *Urban Policy Issues: Canadian Perspectives* (Toronto: McClelland & Stewart, 1990), pp. 13–30. Reprinted by permission of the author. This article was originally written in 1988. An updated version will be available in the second edition of *Urban Policy Issues.*

Figure 41.1

Revenue by Order of Government as a Percentage of Total Government Revenue, 1946–1985 (National Accounts Basis)

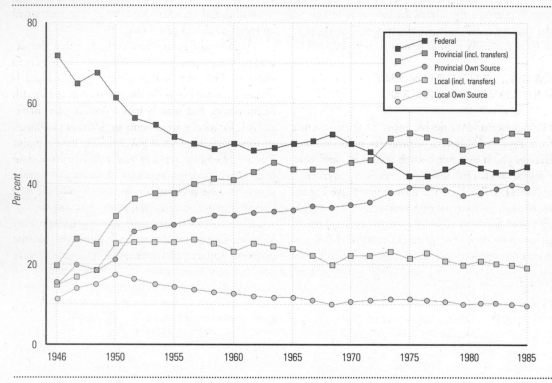

SOURCE: Adapted from Canadian Tax Foundation, *The National Finances, 1984–85* (Toronto: Canadian Tax Foundation, 1985), p. 33. Reproduced with the permission of the Canadian Tax Foundation.

Transfer payments are more problematic because these funds usually come with fairly stringent conditions attached. Also, local governments are forced to rely on the benevolence of other orders of government to provide these funds and there is no assurance about the levels of funding from year to year.

The major trends in the 1946–85 period are the declining role of the federal government and the increasing role of provincial governments. The beginning point of the graph — 1946 — is immediately after the Second World War, which was a time of strong federal dominance. The period since then has witnessed the increasing importance of such social services as health care, education, and social assistance, all of which are predominantly provincial responsibilities. Also, in the immediate post-war period, the federal government returned certain revenue sources it had used during the war (most notably, the income tax) to the provinces.

The position of local government during this period has been relatively stable. Local own-source revenue as a percentage of total government revenue declined slowly and steadily over the first part of the period but has not changed much since 1974. Revenue including transfers has been subject to greater short-term fluctuations, but has held fairly steady when viewed in the long term.

The changing financial positions of the three orders of government in the post-war period can be summed up rather quickly. The provincial governments' position has strengthened considerably at the expense of the federal government. The position of local governments has remained relatively stable.

LOCAL GOVERNMENT REVENUE SOURCES

Local governments derive most of their revenue from four main sources — property taxes and user charges (both are own-source revenues), and conditional and unconditional transfer payments. Figure 41.2 illustrates the changing relative importance of these four revenue sources over the period 1967–84 for the total local government domain[1] in all ten provinces. The general thrust of this figure is that the property tax is a declining, but still very

important, source of revenue for local governments. Conditional transfers have been a significant and stable source of revenue. Both user charges and unconditional transfers have been relatively small and stable sources of revenue.

These total figures obscure the fact that the situation varies considerably from one province to another. The wide variance between provinces is caused to some extent by the variance in the wealth of provinces, but mostly it is reflective of a different role for local governments in different provinces. In some provinces, local governments have a major role in providing services and this is mirrored in their need for large amounts of revenue; in other provinces, the provincial role is so significant that there is less scope to local government activity.

While the revenue per capita varies quite widely between provinces, the relative importance of the different sources of revenue really does not vary

Figure 41.2

Revenue by Source as a Percentage of Total Local Government Revenue, 1967–1984

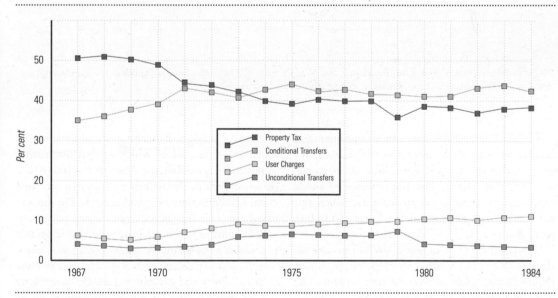

NOTE: Miscellaneous revenue is not included.

SOURCE: Statistics Canada, *Local Government Finance* (Cat. no. 68-204), various years. Reproduced by authority of the Minister of Industry, 1996.

much. The property tax and conditional transfer payments are almost invariably the major sources of revenue. The only two exceptions are Prince Edward Island and New Brunswick, where the property tax is basically a provincial tax. Newfoundland and New Brunswick are the only provinces in which unconditional transfers are very important and these are the two provinces with the smallest local government sectors — measured on a revenue per capita basis.

The specific methods employed in raising local government revenue have an impact on **local autonomy**, on the welfare of citizens, and on the manner in which the burden of supporting local government is divided among citizens. Particular issues associated with each revenue source will be discussed below.

Property Tax

The property tax is a major source of revenue for local governments and it has also been a controversial form of taxation in recent years. This section will first review the mechanics of calculating the tax and determining the tax base, and then proceed to a discussion of some of the controversial aspects of the property tax.

(A) THE ASSESSMENT SYSTEM The assignment of specific dollar values to properties — **property assessment** — is the basis of the property tax system. This function was at one time a municipal responsibility. It has been almost universally moved to provincial governments in recent years. All provinces have a system of assessing property based either on market value or on some vaguer idea of the fair value of the land in its current use. Where provinces have used fair market value based on periodic re-assessments to establish assessed values, the system has worked fairly well. However, where provinces have allowed their systems to get out-of-date, serious problems have occurred.

The lack of a sound periodic re-assessment system causes the property tax to be less buoyant than other taxes. Income taxes are buoyant because

they increase automatically as personal incomes increase. The same process *can* occur with the property tax, but only if there is systematic market value re-assessment. There are probably some benefits in depriving local governments of this automatic "inflation dividend" (Bird and Slack, 1983: 15), but weaknesses in assessment also allow problems of equity to develop in the system.

There would be no serious equity problems if all property was systematically under-assessed in the same manner. The lower *values* would require higher tax *rates*, but would not change the distribution of the tax among properties. However, poor assessment practices lead to situations in which some properties are unintentionally assessed at values closer to market than others; this causes some properties to bear more than their fair share of the property tax.

The prevailing wisdom is that buildings constructed in recent years are assessed at a value higher than those built in earlier years and that multiple-unit buildings are assessed at a higher level than single-family homes. It must be emphasized that these are not conscious decisions. The problem comes about because an assessor must examine a building completed yesterday and estimate what it would have been worth at some date in the 1960s or whenever the last complete re-assessment was performed. This makes the job of assessors so difficult that it should not be surprising that their results are often disputed.

Those owning the buildings with higher assessments argue on grounds of equity that all property should be assessed in the same manner, i.e., fair market value. Those owning older buildings argue that each owner knew what the assessed value was when the property was purchased and that, on grounds of equity, that value should not be changed.

Both sides seem to have a valid point and this discussion has generated heated debate in provinces such as Ontario, which has been slow to move to market value assessment. It usually pits the older established areas of the community, which will suffer large tax increases, against the newer areas, which will see tax reductions. There can also be significant shifts in the relative tax borne by residential, commercial, and industrial taxpayers. It is important to understand that this controversy is not just a matter of abstract theories. The method of assessment has real distributional consequences for residents and property owners in a municipality.

Another consequence of this situation is that it hampers provinces that would like to provide some form of equalization to municipalities. The principle of equalization means that the province would provide larger transfer payments to municipalities with weaker tax bases in order to equalize the ability of all municipalities to provide a basic level of services without imposing excessive taxes. The problem is that when the province cannot have confidence in the property tax assessment system, then there is no sound basis for determining which municipalities are in the greatest need.

(B) CALCULATION OF THE TAX The property tax is calculated by multiplying the assessed value of a piece of property by a *mill rate*. The mill rate is expressed as a certain number of mills (one-tenth of a cent) per dollar of assessed valuation. Alternatively, some people view the mill rate as dollars per thousand dollars of assessed value. Mathematically, either view produces the same result.

Generally, this tax is imposed on the value of land and buildings. Some provinces have imposed taxes on inventory, machinery, and other personal property, but these seem to be falling into disuse (Finnis, 1979: 5). Farm land is usually assessed on the basis of its value as farm land, not on its fair market value, which could be much higher if it is located close to an urban area. This is to prevent farmers from being forced into selling their land for urban development because of a heavy property tax burden. Some kinds of property, such as pipelines, railways, and utility distribution systems, are taxed on a different basis altogether (Canadian Tax Foundation, 1986: 150–71).

In every province, the effective tax rate borne by commercial and industrial property is greater than that borne by residential property.[2] The general rationale for this is that businesses can bear a greater

tax burden than individuals. The specifics of how this differential is achieved vary among provinces, but there are three general ways in which this is accomplished. First, commercial and industrial property is sometimes assessed at a rate closer to its true market value than is residential property (Boadway and Kitchen, 1984: 222–23). Second, in most provinces, commercial and industrial property attracts a higher mill rate than residential property (Canadian Tax Foundation, 1986: 165). Third, some provinces apply an additional business tax assessment that increases the assessed value of the property by some stated percentage (Finnis, 1979: 82). For example, businesses could pay a *property tax* based on 100 per cent of the assessed value of the property and a *business tax* based on 75 per cent of that same value.

(C) THE BENEFITS OF THE PROPERTY TAX The property tax has traditionally been a very attractive tax for local governments. It is easy to administer because it attaches to the land and buildings and so is virtually impossible for taxpayers to evade. The method of computation is quite straightforward as compared to the income tax, for example.

One traditional theoretical justification for the property tax flows from a distinction between services to property and services to people. The argument is that the property tax should bear the cost of all services to property, i.e., "hard" services such as sewers, water, and roads. The rationale for this is that provision of these services increases the value of property so the cost of providing them ought to fall on the property benefited.

The difficulty with this argument is that all services are ultimately services for people. Making the distinction between services for people and services to property is not always an easy task. Education would seem to be a classic "service to people," but it is clear that proximity to a school will increase the value of a particular property.

Another argument for the property tax stems from the adage that "an old tax is a good tax." This has two complementary interpretations. One is that taxpayers have become accustomed to an "old tax" and so will offer less political resistance to it than to a new source of taxation. The second, economic interpretation of this statement is that old taxes have become built into price and market structures over time. New taxes can have unpredictable consequences on prices and markets. In short, a number of factors make the property tax attractive, but there have been some problems with its use in the last few years.

(D) EXEMPTIONS FROM TAXATION Not all property is subject to taxation. The specific exemptions vary by province, but they generally relate to property owned and used by governments and to educational, charitable, and religious institutions. Property of the federal government is exempt from all provincial and municipal taxation because, under the terms of the Constitution Act, no other government can impose a tax on the federal government. In all provinces, except Prince Edward Island, provincial property is also exempt under terms of provincial legislation. Property owned by charitable and religious institutions and used for charitable or religious purposes has traditionally been provided an exemption because these organizations are usually considered deserving of government support.

The value of exempt property can be quite significant. A 1973 Ontario study indicated that exempt property amounted to 17 per cent of the overall property tax base. It was estimated that if this amount had been included in the tax base, the property tax bill of the average household could have been reduced by $100 per year (Boadway and Kitchen, 1984: 226).

Federal and provincial governments usually make a voluntary payment to local governments referred to as a "grant or payment in lieu of taxes." Municipalities frequently complain that this payment is not equal to the full amount of taxes that would have been imposed on the property. Charitable and religious organizations do not provide such payments.

However, exempt property does not just reduce a municipality's tax take, it can also create inefficient land-use patterns. Organizations benefiting from exemptions feel little pressure to economize on the use of even very expensive land. Municipalities have argued that the tax exemption for some organizations ought to be terminated and replaced by cash grants. If this happened, these exempt organizations would probably find ways of using less (or less expensive) land to reduce their property tax burden. In turn, municipalities would benefit from the release of new land for development purposes.

For practical political reasons, this is unlikely to occur. In many jurisdictions, providing overt subsidies to religious organizations would be such a contentious activity that politicians would rather that these subsidies remain hidden, as they currently are.

(E) LEVEL OF THE PROPERTY TAX A great many taxpayers complain about the amount of the property tax and its presumed escalation in recent years. However, perceptions are not always reality. Many people are keenly aware of the annual increase in the property tax, but forget that some of that increase is accounted for by inflation and some of it could be offset by increases in their incomes. Kitchen and McMillan (1985: 225) have found that property tax as a percentage of disposable income did increase from 1947 to 1971, but that it has leveled off or even been reduced since then.

The high levels of dissatisfaction voiced about the property tax likely stem from the fact that it is a highly visible tax that must be paid in a lump sum, unlike federal and provincial taxes, which are either hidden totally (manufacturer's excise tax) or deducted at source before taxpayers are aware they have the money (income tax). You might try an experiment with those you know who own property. Ask them if they know how much property tax they pay to the nearest ten dollars. They will likely know exactly. Then, ask them if they know how much federal income tax they pay to the nearest thousand dollars. Not many people know that, because it is deducted at source.

(F) INCIDENCE OF THE PROPERTY TAX: REGRESSIVE, PROPORTIONAL, OR PROGRESSIVE? The incidence of the property tax has been another cause of controversy. "Incidence" refers to the technical question of who actually bears the burden of a particular tax. Incidence can be very difficult to determine because the people who ultimately bear the tax are not necessarily those who pay it in the first place. For example, manufacturers must pay the federal sales tax when a good is completely manufactured, but the amount of that tax is usually added to the price of the product so that the ultimate consumer really bears the cost of the federal sales tax. In economic parlance, the manufacturer pays the tax but shifts it to the consumer.

A **regressive** tax is a tax that falls proportionally more heavily on low-income taxpayers.[3] Conversely, a **progressive** tax falls proportionally more heavily on high-income taxpayers. For example, on the surface the income tax is a progressive tax because higher incomes are taxed at higher rates than lower incomes. A proportional tax is borne equally by taxpayers in all income groups. It is usually argued that progressive forms of taxation are more desirable than regressive ones because progressive taxes involve a redistribution from the rich to the poor.

Traditionally, the property tax has been considered to be regressive because, regardless how low a person's income is, he or she must still purchase some minimum amount of shelter. The person would pay the property tax either directly to the municipality (if he or she owns the property) or indirectly when the landlord adds in the property tax to arrive at the monthly rent. In economic terms, this scenario assumes that the landlord is able to shift the tax to the renter. The argument continues that as a person's income increases, he or she spends a lower percentage of income on shelter, which is taxable, and more on such luxuries as yachts or jewelry, which do not attract an annual tax. Thus the argument goes that the property tax ought to be minimized because it is regressive.

This argument was accepted for many years and played a significant role in local politicians' rhetoric when they wanted additional money from the provincial or federal governments. However, the so-called new view of the property tax challenges this assumption (Bird, 1976b). The basis of the traditional view of the incidence of the property tax is that landlords are able to shift the tax by increasing rents so that tenants in effect pay the tax. The "new view" of the property tax makes the assumption that landlords are unable to shift the tax to renters because of certain market conditions, so that the tax reduces landlords' incomes. If it is assumed that landlords have higher incomes than tenants, then the tax is effectively borne by a higher-income group and so will more likely be progressive. Finally, in those provinces with geared-to-income property tax rebate systems (Canadian Tax Foundation, 1986: 154–69), any initial regressivity in the imposition of the property tax is reduced considerably by the rebate.

There have been a number of empirical studies of this question in the last few years (Bird and Slack, 1978: 53–64). The basic problem in arriving at a conclusion about the regressivity of the property tax is that no definitive answer is available about the question of shifting. A recent, comprehensive study by Meng and Gillespie (1986) suggests that if one assumes the traditional view is correct, the property tax is generally regressive over all income levels and in all regions of the country. However, if one accepts the new view, then the findings are mixed but seem to indicate that the tax is either proportional or progressive.

Boadway and Kitchen (1984: 234) summarize this debate in the following careful and tentative manner.

What conclusions can be drawn from the evidence of the regressivity of the residential property tax? Unfortunately, there is no simple or obvious answer to this question, especially in view of the numerous conceptual and statistical problems haunting all quantitative incidence exercises. Perhaps the safest and best comment that can be made as a result of these studies is that the new view indicates that the property tax is not as regressive as the traditional view claims nor is it likely to be as progressive as some of the advocates of the new view have suggested. Empirically and theoretically, the incidence question is in an embryonic state. Further research and analysis are required before any definitive and conclusive position can be taken.

The public policy implications of this question are enormous. One of the strongest arguments local politicians have made against the property tax is that it is regressive and that society ought not rely too heavily on a regressive form of taxation. However, if the property tax is actually progressive or proportional, then it becomes a very attractive form of taxation because of its ease of administration.

(G) SHARING THE PROPERTY TAX BASE Another problem with the property tax is that a number of different units of local government must share the same tax base. In a few provinces this includes the provincial government, but more generally it would include a metropolitan or regional government, a lower-tier municipal government, several school boards, and possibly some other special-purpose bodies. Each of these bodies can have the right to impose a property tax without consulting any of the other organizations.

This problem is particularly acute for the lower-tier municipalities because they must usually collect the full tax on behalf of the other units. This creates confusion in the minds of the general public and forces lower-tier municipal governments to shoulder much of the blame for tax increases that are actually the shared responsibility of several governments.

User Charges

User charges are fees imposed on users of services where the fee imposed bears some relation to the benefit enjoyed. The most obvious examples are transit fares, water rates, and fees to use recreational facilities. These have traditionally been a rather limited source of local government revenue, but councils seem to be turning to them more frequently in recent years as a response to financial restraint (Ridler, 1984).

The two arguments most frequently advanced in favour of user charges are that they are equitable and that they further economic efficiency (Bird, 1976a: 101–04). The equity argument holds that where specific groups benefit from a service, they ought to pay for the service. User charges further

economic efficiency because they act as signalling devices to local councils to identify which services are in greatest demand. Where services are provided free, the demand is likely to be unlimited; the imposition of some price helps determine how interested people really are in a particular service.

However, there are certain negative aspects of user charges as well. User charges for such municipal services as recreational facilities can be a political minefield. In some municipalities, sports groups such as hockey and softball leagues are very well organized. They are in a good position to bring strong pressure to bear on councillors who want to increase user charges. Even picking on unorganized groups can be dysfunctional. Who wants to be responsible for beginning to charge six-year-olds to use the municipal swimming pool?

Probably one of the greatest concerns about user charges is their distributional effect. Some services are provided by government precisely because society does not like the distribution that would occur if they were provided by the private sector. For example, if families were forced to purchase education for their children, some would not be able to afford it. Most would agree that this circumstance is undesirable. There are clearly cases where the application of user charges is quite appropriate, but the distributional consequences of these charges should not be overlooked.

In sum, user charges can be desirable from both equity and efficiency viewpoints and as a source of new funds, but they do have serious distributional consequences. Politicians have learned that they must proceed carefully in this area because of the strength of some organized groups.

Transfer Payments

Transfer payments are made to local governments by federal or provincial governments, but they are not made for the provision of any current good or service; the government providing the transfer payment is under no legal obligation to do so. Boadway (1980: 41–52) suggests that there are three main rationales for the provision of transfer payments — fiscal gap, interjurisdictional spill-over, and fiscal equity.

A significant *fiscal gap* or *fiscal imbalance* has emerged between local government expenditure and local government own-source revenue in recent years. The main source of local government own-source revenue — the property tax — has not been a particularly buoyant source of revenue in the last few years. At the same time, local governments have been forced to cope with expenditures generated by increasing urbanization and demands for improved services. These two trends have generated the fiscal gap that provincial governments have been called on to fill.

Following sound economic theory (and concern for local autonomy), a fiscal gap should be bridged by the provision of an unconditional transfer because it allows the municipality to decide which services should be funded. However, some provinces have used the fiscal gap as a rationale for the provision of conditional transfers as well.

Interjurisdictional spill-overs or *externalities* occur when expenditures made by one locality benefit other jurisdictions. Some examples are the cost of educating a young person who then moves to another area and the cost of pollution control, which benefits downstream municipalities. Municipal councillors are understandably reluctant to spend money on programs that benefit other jurisdictions. However, the provincial government is aware that these expenditures are necessary for the good of the entire province. Therefore, it provides a conditional transfer to offset this spill-over and so encourage municipalities to spend more on this service.

The third rationale for intergovernmental transfers — concern for *fiscal equity* — arises because of differences in the abilities of local governments to raise funds. Municipalities with large, stable industrial and commercial tax bases can raise sizable amounts of revenue through the property tax without imposing unduly high mill rates on residential property owners. Municipalities with weaker tax bases or higher costs are forced to impose much higher mill rates to provide the same level of service

as the wealthier municipalities. Federal and provincial governments usually step in to reduce this problem by providing transfers to the municipalities with the weaker tax bases. Theoretically, transfers provided for this purpose should be unconditional, but some conditional transfers are calculated in a manner that takes this concern for fiscal equity into account.

One of the major problems with provincial transfers from the standpoint of municipalities is that the province has absolute control over the level of these payments. Thus, they can change significantly from year to year. Municipalities fear that provinces will use a reduction in transfers to save money because this does not have a direct impact on services provided by the province.

Conditional Transfers

Conditional transfers are payments made to local governments by either the provincial or federal government to be used for a specified purpose. In most cases, these are shared-cost programs, meaning that the federal or provincial government agrees to fund a certain percentage of the cost of a program undertaken by local governments. Conditional transfers can also be calculated on the basis of a flat amount for each municipality or an amount per capita or per household. These transfers are conditional because stipulations attached to the money require that it be spent in a specified manner.

The usual rationales for conditional transfers relate to externalities and the establishment of minimum provincial standards. Because municipalities are relatively small units of government, they frequently provide services used by residents in other municipalities. For example, on any average day you might drive on roads provided by several different municipalities without even thinking about it. Equity would suggest that municipalities should be compensated for this; conditional transfers provide that compensation.

For certain services, there is a feeling that all citizens of a province should receive the same level of service or at least a certain minimum standard regardless of where the person lives. For example, Canadians feel strongly about the value of education and usually believe that a child should not be subjected to an inferior level of education just because he or she grows up in a poorer area of the province. Conditional transfers frequently come with minimum standards to ensure that this does not happen.

The largest portion of conditional transfers comes from provincial governments for programs in the areas of education, health, and transportation and communications. The federal government, through several of its departments and agencies, also supplies some funding to municipalities for transportation, communications, and environment control services.

Local governments are always pleased to receive funds, but conditional transfer payments are sometimes a mixed blessing. One of the most frequent complaints is that conditional transfers tend to skew the priorities of the recipient government. For example, where a transfer payment provides that the province will share 50 per cent of the cost of a program, the argument is usually made that the program is really spending only "fifty-cent dollars," i.e., each fifty cents of *municipal* expenditure results in one dollar of *total* expenditure on the program. This makes programs that receive conditional transfers more attractive than those that do not. But in turn, such transfers can result in municipal governments bending their priorities to attract these payments.

When this occurs, municipalities are conscious that they are vulnerable to shifts in provincial priorities. The provincial government could be very interested in a program for a number of years and encourage municipalities to develop extensive delivery systems on which local citizens become dependent. Later, provincial priorities could change, resulting in a reduction or total withdrawal of provincial funding for this service. However, the municipality cannot shift gears so easily because it has an extensive delivery system in place and a clientele that has come to rely on the service. Thus, the municipality must continue to provide the service, but without provincial assistance.

This points to another problem with conditional transfers. They can tend to muddle accountability. Stripped of all the administrative niceties, a transfer payment is basically one level of government spending money raised by another level of government. If the service is not provided properly, whose fault is it? Did the government making the transfer provide too little funding or impose inappropriate conditions? Or did the recipient government use the funds unwisely? It is difficult for a citizen to know which government should be held accountable for problems in this situation.

There can also be significant administrative costs associated with conditional transfers. Municipalities must maintain records to prove that they have spent the funds in accordance with the sometimes very detailed conditions of the program. Then, the provincial government must establish a group of auditors and program specialists to check up on municipalities to ensure that they are complying with the conditions of the transfer.

Conditional transfers have some beneficial consequences, but they also pose certain difficulties. Unconditional transfers avoid some of these problems.

Unconditional Transfers

Unconditional transfers can be used by the recipient government for any purpose. They are provided to municipalities only by provincial governments. The method of calculation varies widely by province but there is frequently some flat amount for each municipality and additional amounts based on either a percentage of total property taxes levied or on a per capita or per household basis (Canadian Tax Foundation, 1986: 210–20).

There is also frequently an equalization factor in the calculation of the transfer, which deals with the fiscal equity problem. A typical arrangement would provide extra payments to municipalities whose property value per capita fell below the provincial average. Some provinces also provide supplemental transfers to northern municipalities in recognition of the high cost of providing services in remote locations. While most provinces pay lip service to this concern for equalization, some unconditional transfers work better than others at actually accomplishing this equalization (Eden and Auld, 1987).

New Revenue Sources

Municipalities have seen themselves in a financial bind in recent years. Their own-source revenue, mostly property tax, has not been buoyant. Most municipalities have become more dependent on transfers from other governments, but these can fluctuate beyond the control of local governments. The fiscal gap has been an increasing concern.

The usual manner of dealing with this problem has not been an auspicious one from the standpoint of local government. There has been a general trend for provincial governments to take over certain functions that were previously local government responsibilities. This type of movement was seen in the 1960s and 1970s when most provinces took over responsibility for administration of justice and correctional facilities. Following the advice of the New Brunswick Royal Commission on Finance and Municipal Taxation (1963), more commonly called the Byrne Commission, New Brunswick undertook one of the most extreme programs in 1967 when it abolished many rural municipalities and took over complete control of education, health, social assistance, and some other functions (Krueger, 1970; Higgins, 1986: 183–85; Tindal, 1977: 18–20).

This reduces the fiscal problems of local governments but could make local governments hollow shells with only minimal responsibilities. A better arrangement from the standpoint of local autonomy would be to find new sources of revenue or to re-arrange existing sources to minimize both the fiscal gap and the local dependence on provincial transfers, without reducing the role of local government in service delivery.

A very innovative and extensive reform occurred in Quebec in 1979 (Lapointe, 1980). A long-standing grievance of municipal governments is that they must share the property tax with other local bodies, most notably school boards. Quebec changed this by funding school boards almost entirely through provincial transfers and allowing municipal governments to have virtually full control of the property tax. At the same time, provincial transfers to municipalities were reduced drastically. This change left municipalities with the same amount of funding they had previously but increased their autonomy by eliminating conditional transfers and providing an enriched source of taxation.

Several provinces have incorporated a tax-sharing provision into their unconditional transfer. This arrangement provides that a certain percentage of the provincial income tax is allocated to municipalities. For example, in British Columbia, municipalities receive 1 per cent of the individual income tax, 1 per cent of corporate taxable income, and 6 per cent of a large number of other taxes such as fuel and sales taxes (Canadian Tax Foundation, 1986: 219). Provincial treasurers have been slow to adopt this idea because it means that some portion of the provincial budget is earmarked and so beyond their control.

Tax-sharing is beneficial to municipalities because it allows them to estimate their future revenues (at least, as well as they can estimate future provincial revenue), and it gives them a piece of what has usually been a buoyant source of revenue. However, this arrangement means that when provincial revenue declines, municipalities share in the pain just as they shared in the gain.

Other revenue sources have been explored but the small size of municipalities eliminates some potential taxes because they can be avoided too easily. For example, a municipal sales tax would simply encourage people to shop in neighbouring municipalities with a lower tax rate or no tax whatsoever. A tax on hotel accommodation and amusements seems attractive at first because most of it would be paid by non-residents of the community. The problem is that it could cause tourists to avoid the community. Likewise, a municipal income tax could cause people to shun living in a community and also raises assessment and collection problems.

The General Trend

The trend of local government revenue has varied between provinces, but the general idea is clear. The property tax has not been a buoyant source of revenue. The reason for this is unclear and should be the subject of further research. Municipalities argue that the tax base itself is not buoyant and so their only option is to increase the tax rate on this allegedly regressive form of taxation. This might have some validity, but probably only in provinces that do not engage in periodic re-assessment. Another interpretation might be that municipal politicians simply find it easier to cry poverty and get funds from other governments than to raise taxes themselves.

The other trend has been a greater reliance on conditional transfers from provincial governments. Concern about the stability of this source of revenue has spurred a search for new revenue sources, which so far has proven fruitless. The problem is not that municipalities are facing a grave financial crisis; conditional transfers have ensured that they are not. The problem is that the increasing importance of conditional transfers will tend to erode local autonomy.

NOTES

1. In this chapter, "municipal government" refers to the multifunctional unit usually thought of as "the city"; the phrase "local government" includes both municipal government and such special-purpose bodies as boards of education.
2. The effective tax rate is defined as the tax payable divided by the market value of the property. This could vary considerably from the stated mill rate because of differences between the assessed and market values of property.
3. In the case of the property tax, an argument could be made that the more relevant measure is the relationship between the amount of the tax and the taxpayer's *accumulated wealth*. Many would say that a retired person with low current income (but significant accumulated wealth) would be better able to pay the property tax than a young family with higher current income but little accumulated wealth.

REFERENCES

Bird, Richard M. (1970). *The Growth of Government Spending in Canada.* Toronto: Canadian Tax Foundation.

———. (1976a). *Charging for Public Services: A New Look at an Old Idea.* Toronto: Canadian Tax Foundation.

———. (1976b). "The Incidence of the Property Tax: Old Wine in New Bottles?" *Canadian Public Policy*, 2 (Supplement): 323–34.

———. (1979). *Financing Canadian Government. A Quantitative Overview.* Toronto: Canadian Tax Foundation.

Bird, Richard, and N. Enid Slack (1978). *Residential Property Tax Relief in Ontario.* Toronto: University of Toronto Press.

———. (1983). *Urban Public Finance in Canada.* Toronto: Butterworths.

Boadway, Robin W. (1980). *Intergovernmental Transfers in Canada.* Toronto: Canadian Tax Foundation.

Boadway, Robin W., and Harry M. Kitchen (1984). *Canadian Tax Policy*, 2nd ed. Toronto: Canadian Tax Foundation.

Bossons, John, Michael Denny, and Enid Slack (1981). *Municipal Fiscal Reform in Ontario: Property Taxes and Provincial Grants.* Toronto: Ontario Economic Council.

Canadian Tax Foundation (1986). *Provincial and Municipal Finances—1985.* Toronto: Canadian Tax Foundation.

Eden, Lorraine, and D.A.L. Auld (1987). "Provincial-Local Fiscal Equalization" (Department of Economics, Brock University, discussion paper 1987-2).

Finnis, Frederic H. (1979). *Property Assessment in Canada*, 3rd ed. Toronto: Canadian Tax Foundation.

Higgins, Donald J.H. (1986). *Local and Urban Politics in Canada.* Toronto: Gage Educational Publishing Company.

Kitchen, Harry M. (1984). *Local Government Finance in Canada.* Toronto: Canadian Tax Foundation.

Kitchen, Harry M., and Melville L. McMillan (1985). "Local Government and Canadian Federalism," in Richard Simeon (ed.), *Intergovernmental Relations.* Toronto: University of Toronto Press.

Krueger, Ralph R. (1970). "The Provincial-Municipal Government Revolution in New Brunswick," *Canadian Public Administration*, 13 (Spring): 51–99.

Lapointe, Jean-Louis (1980). "La reforme de la fiscalité

municipale au Québec," *Canadian Public Administration*, 23 (Summer): 269–80.

Meng, Ronald, and W. Irwin Gillespie (1986). "The Regressivity of Property Taxes in Canada: Another Look," *Canadian Tax Journal*, 34 (November-December): 1417–30.

New Brunswick Royal Commission on Finance and Municipal Taxation (1963). *Report*. Fredericton.

Ridler, Neil B. (1984). "Fiscal Constraints and the Growth of User Fees Among Canadian Municipalities," *Canadian Public Administration*, 27 (Fall): 429–36.

Saskatchewan Local Government Finance Commission (1985). *Alternative Local Sources of Revenue and Utilization of the Property Tax Base*.

Tindal, C.R. (1977). *Structural Changes in Local Government*. Toronto: The Institute of Public Administration of Canada.

CHAPTER

42

....

Governing Canada's City-Regions

ANDREW SANCTON

What are the institutional requirements for the effective governance of Canada's city-regions? The greatest need, especially for the purposes of economic development policy, is to have one regional institution capable of taking into account the interests of the region as a whole. Establishing such an institution requires neither the consolidation of existing municipalities nor the creation of rigidly structured, two- or three-tiered municipal federations. Rather than new governments, city-regions need flexible and efficient institutions that can respond rapidly to changing economic circumstances.

I follow Statistics Canada in defining a "city-region" as "a very large urban area [population 100,000 or more], together with adjacent urban and rural areas which have a high degree of economic and social integration with that urban area." There are 25 CMAs in Canada.

During the 1960s and early 1970s Canadian city-regions were subjected to great changes in their systems of municipal government. These changes were supposed to improve the quality of our urban life by facilitating the planning of outward expansion, capturing economies of scale and reducing inequities in service levels and tax burdens. To the extent that the new structures forced people in the wealthy enclave municipalities to start paying a fair share of costs, they have at least been successful in reducing inequities. But the other alleged gains

from structural changes have been elusive at best. Three central lessons have emerged.

MULTIPLE TWO-TIER SYSTEMS SERVE NO USEFUL PURPOSE Montreal and Toronto both have two-tier systems of municipal government that work somewhat like mini-federations. A top-tier government is responsible for certain municipal services (e.g., regional planning) for which individual municipalities (the lower tier) are considered too small to provide on their own. But in neither case is there any one top-tier government that includes more than 80% of the city-region's total population. By this definition, there is no territorially comprehensive local government in either region.

Greater Montreal has one relatively strong top-tier government (the Montreal Urban Community, or MUC) and a number of weak ones (the *municipalités régionales de comté*, or MRCs). The Greater Toronto Area (GTA) has one metropolitan government and four strong **regional governments**. There is no possible justification for such a state of affairs. Both Montreal and Toronto must live with all the disadvantages of two-tier systems (inefficiencies caused by duplication, overlap, conflict) while still having no one local government capable of effectively dealing with issues affecting the city-region as a whole.

It is relatively easy to point out the problem but much more difficult to suggest remedies. The Task

....

SOURCE: "Governing Canada's City Regions," *Policy Options* 15, 4 (May 1994): 12–15. Reprinted by permission of the Institute for Research on Public Policy.

....

Force on Greater Montreal has made a valiant effort but has come perilously close to recommending a *three*-tier system of local government. By limiting the functions of the proposed new agency for the whole city-region and by downgrading the MUC to an inter-municipal service-provision agency, the task force has attempted to avoid the three-tier label. But if or how it will ever be made to work in practice remains to be seen.

In the case of Toronto, the provincial office of the GTA has so far carefully avoided issues related to municipal structures. But sooner or later these will have to be faced. There are three alternatives. The first is to maintain the *status quo*, but with a possible strengthening of the Greater Toronto Coordinating Committee. Such an approach would be similar to that adopted by the Task Force on Greater Montreal. The problem here, as in Montreal, is the subtle introduction of a third level of local government at a time when the popular view is that institutions of government need to be streamlined, not made more complicated.

A second alternative is to consolidate all municipalities within each of the five two-tier systems. A new top-tier planning and infrastructure authority could then be created for the whole GTA. This plan seems logical in principle but provokes a number of potentially difficult questions. Would inner-city residential areas in Toronto survive in a municipal system dominated by commuters from North York, Scarborough and Etobicoke? Would there be anything local about municipal governments stretching from Steeles Avenue to Lake Simcoe (York), from Lake Ontario to Lake Simcoe (Durham), from Mississauga to Caledon (Peel) or from Burlington to Acton (Halton)? Is there any evidence that such huge authorities would be more effective and efficient, especially given the wide variations in the kinds of residents they would be expected to serve?

The third alternative is to abolish the five existing top-tier governments and replace them with a single new one. The new two-tier system would then contain 30 lower-tier municipalities. The main problem with this solution is figuring out what to do with services currently provided by the existing

top-tier units — services that might not be appropriate for a new authority covering the entire GTA. The most obvious problems are policing and social services. All the same, as long as municipal police forces in Ontario remain under the control of police services boards rather than municipal governments, there is no need to change their territorial jurisdictions. Police services boards can continue to be made up in exactly the same way as they are now.

The future of municipal social services in Ontario has been in question for many years. It seems entirely possible to pass the income-security function (general welfare assistance) to the province, to have the new GTA authority responsible for social-service planning and to place some operational functions (old-age homes, seniors' services, and child care) with the lower-tier municipalities or with new special-purpose bodies.

New top-tier authorities for Greater Montreal or for the GTA would not simply be the MUC or Metro Toronto writ large. Their territories would be larger but their political structures and their staffs would be less elaborate and more flexible. Greater Vancouver can provide the model (see below).

MUNICIPAL CONSOLIDATION IS NOT THE ANSWER
At a time when Canadians are searching for cheaper, more efficient government as a means of improving their overall economic situation, it is not surprising that some are advocating fewer governments. Since the one federal, ten provincial and two (soon to be three) territorial governments are unlikely to be consolidated, people's attention inevitably turns to the hundreds of municipal governments in Canada. In the past 25 years, proposals in various parts of the country to consolidate two or more contiguous municipalities have provoked bitter local controversies. Two of the best-known examples of consolidation are Winnipeg and London, Ontario. Edmonton and Halifax have also gained territory, but schemes under which they would completely absorb neighbouring suburban municipalities were never implemented. In all these cases, the final outcome was decided by the province.

British Columbia is the one Canadian jurisdiction in which changes to municipal boundaries are always decided by local residents through referenda; however, there have been no recent examples in which significant changes have been approved. In Quebec, there have been two recent cases of consolidation (in Lévis and Sorel) to which the relevant local councils consented. A proposal to amalgamate Gatineau, Hull and Aylmer was defeated in a local referendum conducted in 1990.

Municipal consolidations that are approved by the affected local residents need hardly be questioned. In particular circumstances there might also be powerful cases for consolidations — for example, if a municipality is not financially viable or if there are glaring inequities among contiguous municipalities. But the most common justification for consolidation is that it will reduce costs, thereby making the municipal system as a whole more efficient. The problem with such a justification is that there is no empirical evidence to support it.

Data from a *Financial Times of Canada* survey suggest that one-tier systems (i.e., with a single municipal structure) are more efficient than two-tier systems but, since there were no examples of "non-comprehensive" single-tier systems (that is, systems that cover less than 70% of the population of the relevant city-region), we cannot arrive at any conclusions concerning the virtues of consolidations within a single-tier system. Likewise, there is no evidence to suggest that there would be efficiency gains from consolidating all the lower-tier municipalities *within* a two-tier system. The fact that the Task Force on Greater Montreal, when confronted with 136 municipalities within its territorial frame of reference, recommended against any immediate municipal consolidations is highly significant.

CITY-REGIONS NEED A REGIONAL INSTITUTION

Can a large city-region contain a number of municipalities, establish a regional local-government institution and avoid the pitfalls of two-tier municipal government? This is the biggest structural question facing urban government today.

Strict adherents to the public-choice approach might still reject the need for any form of metropolitan or regional government. They argue that the best way to prevent the self-serving behaviour of politicians and bureaucrats is to subject governments as much as possible to the discipline of the marketplace. One way to do this is to insist that components of government compete with the private sector; hence the pressure for privatization and contracting out. Another way, especially relevant at the municipal level, is to force governments to compete with one another. Once one considers the notion that competition among governments, like competition among retailers, might be good, then many of the arguments about the virtues of a single comprehensive government for a city-region are turned on their head.

However, the views of public-choice advocates are now not likely to be completely accepted even by those most interested in making government more entrepreneurial. For example, after a very brief survey of "regional government" issues in the U.S., David Osborne and Ted Gaebler (in their book, *Reinventing Government*) vaguely conclude that "most areas are under pressure to find some way to get their hands around the new problems of the metropolitan region."

It is not at all clear exactly what Osborne and Gaebler have in mind but it seems quite likely that the flexible, adaptable structures of the Greater Vancouver Regional District, established to take over the functions of special purpose bodies such as sewage and water supply and to provide a framework for increased municipal cooperation, would meet their criteria for "reinvented" government. It seems unlikely that they would be much interested in Ontario's longstanding debates about direct election to the top tier or in solving coordination problems between the two tiers for certain functions by declaring one level or the other as sole authority.

The GVRD is far from perfect. To be an effective decision-making institution for the entire city-region, its original land-use planning authority needs to be fully restored and perhaps even expanded. The fact that it has little or no involvement in public transit seems quite unjustified. There are perhaps ways in which its control over sewers and water-supply systems can be better integrated with the needs of the municipalities. But the GVRD does cover almost the entire city-region and its territory can easily be expanded. It is already involved in hospital planning and clearly has great potential as a locus for multi-functional planning for the whole area.

City-regions with single-tier comprehensive systems — Edmonton, Calgary, Winnipeg, London — need not be much concerned about bringing together all the area's municipal leaders to pursue common objectives. The city council serves the purpose well enough. From time to time, however, they will have to consider whether their respective areas need to be expanded still further, or perhaps (as was the case in Winnipeg) contracted.

Most Canadian city-regions are not governed by single-tier comprehensive municipal systems. They require an institution similar to the GVRD: one that is comprehensive in territory and flexible in function. Such institutions do not require large bureaucracies. In fact, they will probably work best if they have no operational responsibilities at all. Their aim should be to provide a forum where regional issues can be discussed, to act as a catalyst for the creation of inter-municipal agreements and special-purpose bodies, and to enact planning documents with sufficient legal status to coerce municipalities into adhering to broad strategic objectives

for the use of land. Inevitably, one of the central concerns of such an institution would be to facilitate local adaptation to changing economic conditions. At a minimum, the regional institution would collect economic data and provide information. In some circumstances the need could be much more substantial: it could be called upon to prepare a comprehensive plan for economic renewal, in cooperation with other levels of government.

Much more so than Americans, Canadians have been quick to adopt institutional change as a solution for urban problems. The Municipality of Metropolitan Toronto and Unicity in Winnipeg, the 1972 reform that brought Winnipeg's 12 lower-tier municipalities and the Corporation of Greater Winnipeg under a one-tier structure, have been institutional innovations that have quite properly attracted attention throughout the industrialized world. The basic idea was to establish a new government for an entire city-region. But the days of creating new governments are over. As a way of solving urban problems, such a response is too costly, too inflexible, and too disruptive of democratic local decision making. The current challenge in Canada is to create institutional frameworks for entire city-regions in which decisions can be made and services arranged. The framework would not itself be a distinct level of government. Its purpose would be to enhance the capacity of provincial and municipal leaders to serve the needs of the people who elected them.

PART

▼
10

....

Governing the Canadian Economy

CLOSE-UP: WHAT'S A TRILLION ANYWAY?
....

What would happen if the Canadian government defaulted on the **national debt**? What would happen if the provinces defaulted on their debts? How would Canada be able to govern itself? How would the world react to this kind of financial crisis in a so-called developed economy?

We often hear about the burden of the **public debt**. Some argue that the government is eventually going to go bankrupt, but could that really happen? As we approach the end of this century, Canada's national or public debt is pointed directly at the awesome figure of $1 trillion.

Most Canadian families go into debt. Indeed, a typical family in Canada goes into debt to purchase almost any big-ticket item, such as a house or a car. Businesses go into debt, too, in order to expand their inventory or their production capacity or to purchase other businesses. Even the most successful and highly profitable corporations in Canada carry a debt at all times. Owing money is a Canadian way of life — in the household, in the corporate world, and in the government.

When households take on too much debt they often have difficulty making their payments. And when a household misses a few months of payments on a credit account at a local department store, its credit dries up and no more purchases are permitted until the debt is reduced to manageable proportions in relation to the family income. However, a bad mark on a household's credit rating will make it more difficult to borrow money in the future. If a household misses its payments on a mortgage, something more serious may occur — the mortgage could be foreclosed and the family could lose its home.

Businesses often get into trouble because they are unable to make payments on their loans. They may run into a cash-flow problem and may have to renegotiate the interest payments they owe on large debts. When a business is unable to come up with the money it owes to make interest payments, its credit line is normally eliminated. In a worst-case scenario, the business will default on its debt, and its creditors will force it into bankruptcy.

But what happens when the government defaults on the public debt? Such an event is not an impossibility. Growing **deficits** mean that governments must pay higher interest costs to cover them. Canada or any number of its seriously indebted provinces could find themselves in the position of being unable to make payments on the public debt to keep up with interest payments, let alone reduce the size of the principal. Canada and its provinces owe hundreds of billions of dollars to American, Canadian, and European banks and bondholders. Most of its politicians and many economists and political scientists believe that continuing large deficits will threaten the long-term health of the economy, because our debts could become unmanageable.

....

One of the first consequences of defaulting on the debt would be an abrupt drop in the government's credit rating. Foreigners would no longer purchase Canadian public bonds. The federal government would no longer be able to keep borrowing to finance its deficit every year and to continue spending more than it receives in revenues. Federal government spending would have to drop dramatically overnight. Many social and defence programs would have to be cut.

Another grave consequence would be the Canadian public's loss of faith in the ability of the federal government to establish sound monetary and fiscal policy. The market value of government debt in Canada would fall because debt holders would have no confidence as to when the government could pay the interest it owes on the debt. The debt holders—numbering in the millions of Canadians—would consequently see their own wealth diminished. As a result, they would invest less and consume less, leading to a serious recession, if not another depression.

If the Canadian government defaulted on its public debt, the economies of other nation-states would be seriously affected as well. Some of the debt is held by American, British, French, German, and Japanese investors, including individuals, corporations, and governments. Defaults by Canadian governments would shake the confidence of investors in all financial markets, perhaps leading to defaults by other governments.

Are there any monetary, fiscal, or other measures that our governments can take to avoid such a scenario? Fortunately, there are. The main guarantee is the taxing and other revenue powers of governments. They can raise taxes and customs and excise duties to pay the interest on the public debt. As long as Canadians are willing to pay taxes, the ultimate consequence of national financial collapse can be avoided.

Other measures involve the painful restructuring of the Canadian economy. In the early 1990s all Canadian governments set out to improve their competitive positions within the emerging North American integrated economy. But just at the time that governments were adjusting their economic policies to adapt to the new international realities, Canada was slumped in a **recession**. In response to the tough monetary and fiscal restraints governments were imposing in an effort to squeeze down their deficits and accumulated debts during these years of economic malaise, most business enterprises were forced to restructure their own operations and approaches.

Despite the determination of Canadian manufacturers, wholesalers, and retailers to change the ways in which they do business, in reality they had little choice but to compete within an emerging North American continental economy. Proponents of the Canada–U.S. Free Trade Agreement (FTA) argued that free trade with the United States was the only way Canada could become a competitive exporter of its goods and services in the twenty-first century.

Notwithstanding certain complications on the road to achieving **bilateral co-operation**, the FTA gave Canada preferential access to the lucrative U.S. market, a market more than ten times larger than its own, and the multilateral North American Free Trade Agreement (NAFTA) has provided similar access for both Canada and the United States to the burgeoning economy of Mexico. But trade co-operation and integrated markets do not necessarily lead to reductions of deficits and debts. They can, however, generate enough economic growth to produce a more positive tax return for the governments involved. The opportunities are there if Canadian firms and governments can make the adjustments necessary to take advantage of them. With an abundant supply of natural resources and an advanced manufacturing and technological sector, Canada's economy is in a position to experience significant growth.

INTRODUCTION: THE ECONOMIC ROLE OF GOVERNMENTS

Canada's first parliamentary governments, in the nineteenth and early twentieth centuries, gave little consideration to the ups and downs of the economy. For them, the economy was like the weather, something dependent on natural forces that people liked to talk about but certainly did not expect their governments to try to control.

Federal and provincial governments in Canada were not considered responsible for the successful operation of the economy or for the improvement of economic life. It would not have occurred to government officials in the first years after Confederation to tell farmers, bankers, business leaders, employers, or employees how to run their affairs. The economic concerns of governments did not go beyond protecting the country so that corporate and individual enterprises could pursue their affairs, developing territory for western expansion, and enacting some protections to mitigate the effects of competition from the United States and abroad. As the twentieth century unfolded, Canada's governments gradually played a greater role in the economy.

Today, Canada's federal and provincial governments influence the country's economic health through a variety of public policies and international associations. The economic policy activities of the federal government include **monetary** and **fiscal policies**, government spending policies, the size of government, the performance of government, and treaties of economic consequence with other nation-states around the world. The short presentation by Laurence Hewick and Christopher Sarlo in Chapter 43 provides a good thumbnail sketch of the role of government in the Canadian economy and succinctly explains the nature and effects of fiscal and monetary policies.

Canadians commonly hold the prime minister, the provincial premiers, and their Cabinets responsible for the economy's performance. In reality, this perception of the economy and of the ability of governments to direct it is oversimplified. But it serves to make the point that our economies *are* powerfully influenced by politics (thus the expression "political economy"). Indeed, politics — as exemplified by the public's resistance to cutbacks in government services — is what prevents Cabinets from reducing their deficits to zero in one year. Such an action would create great pain for most Canadians — pain that could instantly translate into political revenge against the governments that caused it.

Taken together, government disbursements (spending on goods and services plus transfers to provinces) totalled about 40 percent of Canada's gross domestic product (GDP) by the early 1990s. Severe restrictions on all government spending have transpired since 1994, but some analysts still consider governments to have a powerful role to play in the Canadian economy.

One special aspect of Canada's make-up has a significant effect on the country's economic stability and future: the position of Quebec with respect to the rest of Canada. The Quebec referendum of 1995 settled very little with regard to the goal of hard-line sovereignists to negotiate some kind of **sovereignty association** with Canada. But it did settle one important question for individuals and institutions investing in Canada: that uncertainty about Quebec will persist over the long term.

As Christopher Dunn suggests in his article on NAFTA in Chapter 46, the future of Quebec is central to Canada's economic stability and to its competitiveness in the **global economy**. His analysis focusses especially on Canada's free-trade associations in the Western Hemisphere.

Notwithstanding the persistent influence of Quebec on Canada's fate, it is the basic laws of economics that determine how Canadians build their economic future. The Canadian economy, based on a mixture of capitalism and government intervention and regulation, as well as the public's perception of the government's credibility, is influenced by both the decisions of Cabinets and the decisions of millions of economic players.

Ordinary consumers influence the economy through their everyday decisions about spending and saving. Businesses influence economic vitality through their decisions about hiring workers, purchasing raw materials, and setting production levels. Banks and financial institutions make lending decisions that enable businesses to expand and consumers to make purchases on credit. In addition, the decisions made outside Canada — those of foreign investors and foreign companies seeking to export their products to Canada — also contribute to the overall health of the economy.

THE POWER OF POLICY

Fiscal policy refers to the body of government strategies relating to spending, taxing, and borrowing in terms of their effect on economic growth and stability. This policy instrument is used to promote economic growth by raising or lowering taxes and increasing or decreasing federal spending.

Canadians believe that it is the legitimate goal of fiscal policy to ensure that the burden of taxes falls somewhat more heavily on wealthier people than on poorer ones. Fiscal policy has reflected the idea that national income should also be redistributed from wealthier regions to regions that are relatively poorer. Since the 1950s this consensus on fiscal policy has enabled governments to promote "regional equality" in their budgets.

Monetary policy controls the amount of money in circulation, interest rates, and the functioning of credit markets and the banking system. When interest rates are low, easier credit makes it more feasible for new businesses to start and for existing ones to expand. In the resulting business climate, jobs are created and consumer spending rises, which leads to growth in the economy, usually through private-sector investment.

The Bank of Canada administers Canada's monetary policy. Its most direct effect on the economy comes from its responsibility for setting the overnight financing rate. While the Bank's day-to-day decisions are focussed on bringing about a particular level for that rate, these decisions are taken with a view to influencing overall monetary conditions in a direction consistent with the broad anti-inflationary thrust of federal government policy. During times of unusual volatility in financial markets, and with uncertainty in the exchange-rate markets, the Bank of Canada tries to encourage greater steadiness in the financial marketplace, strongly influencing the demand and supply of money in the Canadian economy.

DEFICITS AND DEBTS

In Canada, particularly since the 1970s, the persistent deficits of federal and provincial governments have had a predominant influence on the economy. The concept of the deficit is quite simple. Over a one-year fiscal period, if governments spend more than they collect in taxes and other revenues, they incur a deficit, which becomes reconciled in the public accounts as a part of the national debt.

Long-term deficits create many economic problems. First, when deficits persist, so too does government borrowing, which puts the federal and provincial governments in competition with private corporations and consumers for borrowing money (businesses use the money to expand and modernize, and consumers borrow to spend). This competition crowds the borrowing markets and reduces the capital available for public- and private-sector borrowing, requiring the Bank of Canada to drive up interest rates. In this way, federal and provincial borrowing becomes a negative influence on the economy, as Bryne Purchase and Ronald Hirshhorn point out in Chapter 44, entitled "Courting a Financial Crisis."

Second, deficit spending in previous years causes a financial burden in the current and future years. Since the start of the 1990s, about 40 cents of every dollar of federal and provincial expenditures has been going to pay interest and other carrying charges on funds borrowed in the past. This means that substantial government budget dollars must be spent on repaying interest, instead of being used to achieve pressing national and regional goals.

The rapid growth of Canada's national debt has made reducing federal and provincial budget deficits a hot political topic. Governments can reduce budget deficits by increasing revenues — which usually (but not always) means raising taxes, reducing the size of the public service, and cutting spending.

The most harmful economic impact of persistent budget deficits and growing debts, however, is the need to increase federal and provincial taxes. Taxes are regarded by most Canadians as a significant burden on their spending powers, which sometimes encourages them to try to avoid paying taxes by buying goods and services from individuals and companies that do not charge the required range of taxes.

THE UNDERGROUND ECONOMY

The reliance of governments on individual Canadians for most of their revenues has tremendous political ramifications. People feel the impact of taxes daily, often reacting with an angered attempt to avoid them. Rolf Mirus and Roger Smith's commentary in Chapter 45 sets the drama of Canada's underground economy alongside its legal one. No longer can governments ignore the underground network of productive exchanges that dodge the tax system.

A significant number of Canadians seek relief by participating in the underground economy, sometimes called the "unreported economy" or the "subterranean economy." The underground economy consists of individuals and groups who work for cash payment and thus avoid paying taxes. It also consists of those who engage in illegal activities, such as prostitution, gambling, and drug trafficking. As tax rates increase in the legal economy, individuals and groups find greater incentive to work "off the books." The broader concept of tax resistance is also discussed in Chapter 44, by Purchase and Hirshhorn, who analyze the general malaise of national indebtedness in Canada.

The question, of course, is how big the underground economy is. If it is small (less than 2 percent), it does not pose a very serious problem. Estimates of its size range from 5 percent to over

15 percent of the gross national income annually. This means that the underground economy in Canada represents anywhere from $30 billion to more than $90 billion a year. At 5 percent, the underground economy is at least the size of the federal government's deficit. At 15 percent and above, the underground economy could greatly reduce Canada's national debt if that added part of the gross national product was taxed. The loss of tax revenues is thus a significant factor with respect to Canada's competitiveness in the global economy.

THE EFFECTS OF FREE TRADE

The most significant influence on the restructuring of Canada's economy in the twentieth century was free trade between Canada and the United States, ratified in January 1988. The powerful forces of free trade in the context of a continental North American economy would reverberate throughout the Canadian economy, affecting everything from corporate competitiveness, fiscal and monetary policy, policies of **economic nationalism**, labour–management relations, and the tax system to the widespread use of information technologies.

Canada approved NAFTA at the end of 1993, following in the footsteps of the FTA, the historic free trade agreement between Canada and the United States that took effect in January 1989. In Chapter 46, Christopher Dunn gives us a short but clear presentation of the consequences of free trade for Canada and explains the scope of the treaty. The goal of NAFTA was to eliminate high tariffs (taxes on imported goods) on furniture, textiles, appliances, petrochemicals, plastics, metals, paper, and fish products. The Canada–U.S. Free Trade Agreement guaranteed that the two countries would have access to each other's petroleum, gas, coal, and electricity at prices paid by nationals under comparable commercial circumstances. NAFTA basically extended this agreement to include Mexico.

NAFTA enforces a highly competitive economic regime on all three signatories. For example, Mexico will now import more information technology and grain from Canada, as well as more financial services, but the Canadian footwear, steel, and clothing industries will face much stiffer competition from Mexico. Over time, the so-called playing field will level out, and the comparative advantage of economic production and distribution will produce more of a continental, North American economy.

NAFTA has also had an effect on how Canadians govern themselves, requiring governments in Canada under specific clauses of the treaty to harmonize their functions with public sectors in Mexico and the United States. It was inevitable that the quality and universal character of Canada's social net would be adversely affected by the broad harmonization of public policy needed to comply with the provisions of this free trade agreement. The treaty encourages a **fiscally conservative** philosophy among all participating governments, constraining them from expanding government expenditures for the **subsidization** of jobs, business productivity, and benefits to labour. Canadian governments have adopted a new vocabulary, which includes terms such as "disentitlement," "contracting out," "privatization," and "divestment" (or "offloading") of social services—all part of a new approach to governing Canada in the name of efficiency and competitive advantage.

THINKING IT OVER

1. Using the article by Laurence Hewick and Christopher A. Sarlo (Chapter 43) for suggestions, prepare a list of economic roles for government in the Canada of the 1990s. Discuss what the authors mean by the "key areas of government influence" in today's economy. Do the authors believe that Canada's economy is governable? Do you? Explain why or why not?

2. According to Bryne Purchase and Ronald Hirshhorn (Chapter 44), Canada is in some sort of financial crisis. What do the authors mean by this? Given the gloomy scenario they describe, should governments tax Canadians any more to defuse the "financial time bomb"? Can Canada survive the economic difficulties it faces?

3. Many Canadians agree that our tax system contributes to the underground economy. How big is this economy, according to Rolf Mirus and Roger S. Smith (Chapter 45)? What "corrective actions" are necessary to get all qualified taxpayers to pay taxes in a legal economy? Is having too many taxes the only reason why an underground economy exists?

4. Are you as optimistic about the effects of NAFTA on the Canadian economy as Christopher Dunn (Chapter 46)? Is it still possible for the Canadian government to make its own fiscal and monetary policies and fully participate in NAFTA? Is Canada more prosperous under NAFTA than it would have been outside of it?

5. Can Canada survive as a credible political economy without Quebec? How should the Canadian economy react to a separate Quebec? From an economic perspective, is it imperative for Canadians to consider sovereignty association? What are some of the anticipated reactions from the international community of a Canadian federal system without Quebec? Would an independent Quebec's membership in NAFTA make the Quebec economy less dependent on the rest of Canada for its economic growth? After reading the section on "Canadian National Integrity" in the article by Christopher Dunn (Chapter 46), do you think Canada's position in NAFTA would be compromised by an independent Quebec being included in the same treaty?

GLOSSARY

big government Refers generally to the size and scope of contemporary governments, their extensive involvement in the social and economic system, and the large number of people who work directly or indirectly for government departments and agencies.

bilateral co-operation An understanding between two states to foster friendly relations in matters of trade and related economic matters, as well as in other aspects of international relations. It can involve diplomatic, educational, and scientific exchanges.

consumer protection laws Laws administered by federal and provincial consumer affairs departments to protect consumers from the potential harmful effects of foods and manufactured products and from consumer fraud, among other things.

deficit The financial condition that results when government expenditures exceed revenues.

economic nationalism A public-policy approach that endeavours to shield the domestic economy from foreign competition.

fiscally conservative Describes the philosophy that governments should balance their operating budgets, eliminate deficits, and reduce public debt to minimal or controllable levels.

fiscal policy Government decisions about taxing, borrowing, and spending that affect the economic life of Canadians.

global economy All of the international economic interactions relating to trade, borrowing, debt, production, and distribution of goods and services for world markets.

globalization The growing tendency of corporations to conduct business on a global basis in order to meet the demands of a global marketplace and to produce and distribute goods and services throughout the world, without much regard to the special interests of the country in which the corporate headquarters are located.

International Monetary Fund A specialized agency of the United Nations established in 1944 to promote international monetary co-operation and exchange stability, help member states overcome balance-of-payments problems, and establish a worldwide payments system among different currencies.

macroeconomic indicators Predictors of the behaviour of large-scale economic phenomena, particularly inflation, unemployment, and national or provincial economic growth.

monetary policy Federal economic policies that involve the control of, and changes in, the supply of money in the Canadian economy.

national debt or **public debt** The total accumulated amount of money that the national and subnational governments owe to lenders, such as domestic and foreign banks, individual investors, insurance companies, and the variety of financial institutions that purchase government securities. It is the total indebtedness of all levels of government as a result of past borrowings and shortfalls in government revenues.

public debt *See* national debt.

recession A period during which real output falls for six months or more.

sovereignty association A concept advanced from time to time by the Parti Québécois since it won the Quebec provincial election of 1976, calling for a form of semi-independence wherein a formal economic association with Canada would be retained, including free trade and a common system of currency.

stabilizing the economy Efforts by the government to control the level of national income and related conditions of inflation, unemployment, and the balance of payments, using taxation and expenditure as tools.

subsidization Direct or indirect economic and financial assistance offered by government to private individuals or corporations to increase their competitive positions in the economy.

tax reform All measures taken by a government to change the tax system, including reducing tax rates, closing loopholes, punishing tax evaders, generally making the tax system fairer, and changing or eliminating a variety of deductions, tax credits, and tax shelters.

underground economy Economic activity by those who do not pay taxes on the money they earn and whose productivity and spending are not directly measured by government statisticians; also called the "illegal economy," the "unreported economy," or the "subterranean economy."

ADDITIONAL READINGS

Bothwell, Robert. 1995. *Canada and the United States: The Politics of Partnership*. Toronto: University of Toronto Press.

Chodos, Robert, et al. 1993. *Canada and the Global Economy*. Toronto: James Lorimer & Company.

Doern, Bruce, and Brian Tomlin. 1991. *Faith and Fear: The Free Trade Story.* Toronto: Stoddart.

Gillespie, W. Irwin. 1991. *Tax, Borrow and Spend: Financing Federal Spending in Canada, 1867–1990.* Ottawa: Carleton University Press.

Grinspun, Ricardo, and Maxwell Cameron, eds. 1993. *The Political Economy of North American Free Trade.* Montreal: McGill-Queen's University Press.

Hart, Michael. 1992. *Trade . . . Why Bother?* Ottawa, Ont.: Renouf.

Howlett, Michael, and M. Ramesh. 1992. *The Political Economy of Canada.* Toronto: McClelland & Stewart.

Johnson, David. 1993. *Public Choice: An Introduction to the New Political Economy.* Toronto: McClelland & Stewart.

McBride, Stephen. 1992. *Not Working: State, Unemployment and Neo-Conservatism in Canada.* Toronto: University of Toronto Press.

Quarter, Jack. 1992. *The Social Economy.* Toronto: James Lorimer & Company.

Russell, Steven, et al. 1992. *Governing in an Information Society.* Ottawa, Ont.: Renouf.

Savoie, Donald. 1992. *Regional Economic Development.* Toronto: University of Toronto Press.

Starling, Grover. 1993. *Managing the Public Sector.* New York: Nelson.

Stubbs, Richard, and Geoffrey Underhill. 1994. *Political Economy and the Changing Global Order.* Toronto: McClelland & Stewart.

Williams, Glen. 1993. *Not for Export: Toward a Political Economy of Canada's Arrested Industrialization.* Toronto: McClelland & Stewart.

Business and Government

LAURENCE HEWICK
CHRISTOPHER A. SARLO

THE ROLE OF GOVERNMENT

Canada is a federal democracy. It is a federation of ten provinces and two territories. Each province has jurisdiction over important matters (health care, education, welfare, housing, energy, and natural resources) within its provincial boundaries. Provincial governments have the authority to pass laws and make policies regarding these and other areas of provincial responsibility. For example, minimum wage laws, rent controls, welfare rates, and urban pollution standards are matters of provincial concern.

The federal government has the constitutional authority to make laws and policies on issues affecting the whole of Canada. Such areas as international trade, monetary and fiscal policy, regional policies, income tax, goods and services tax (GST), old age pensions, and national defence are matters of federal government responsibility.

It is a fact that government's role in the economy and in our everyday lives has increased sharply. Since World War II, total government spending as a proportion of GDP has more than doubled and is currently (1993) at about 50 percent. Major increases occurred during the 1960s and early 1970s when many new social programs were established and existing ones expanded.

Governments (at all levels) are supposed to promote the general good. They have the exclusive legal authority to impose any taxes necessary to pay for the programs and policies they establish. There is a vigorous debate about both the moral legitimacy of government's involvement in the economy and the effectiveness of using governments to solve economic problems. Nevertheless, **big government** is a fact of life and is an imposing part of the business environment. While the government sector is a substantial source of uncertainty, it is imperative that for-profit enterprises be as knowledgeable as possible about the state's role in their industry. Because of government's profound effect on business, the cost of ignoring it is too high.

KEY AREAS OF GOVERNMENT INFLUENCE

Governments affect businesses in a number of ways. They pass laws that lay out the permissible limits of behaviour by all individuals, groups, and organizations. They set up regulatory bodies that establish guidelines or rules for particular sectors and monitor compliance. They develop policies that are designed to solve specific problems. And finally, by virtue of its enormous size, government and its borrowing needs dominate Canadian financial markets. Let us examine some specific areas of government influence.

SOURCE: *Introduction to Canadian Business and Management* (Toronto: Captus Press, 1994), pp. 10–12. Reprinted by permission of Captus Press, McGraw-Hill Ryerson, and the authors.

LAWS AND REGULATIONS Some of the laws and regulations that have a direct effect on business enterprises are labour laws, including minimum wages, hours of work, rules regarding unionization, statutory holidays and overtime, mandatory retirement, and human rights guidelines; health and safety regulations in such areas as food (wholesale, retail, restaurants), drugs, children's clothing and toys, vehicles and licensing, building construction, factory air and noise pollution, and the transport of hazardous materials; regulations limiting competition, especially in the transportation and telecommunication industries; and other laws including contract law, corporate law, tax laws, and **consumer protection laws**.

POLICIES Monetary policy deals with the control of the money supply and interest rates with the goal of promoting price stability and a strong, healthy economy. In Canada, monetary policy is run by the Bank of Canada. The Bank has considerable independence to conduct its money policies as it sees fit.

A popular theory of monetary policy suggests that the authorities should administer an "easy money" policy (i.e., increase the supply of money, lower interest rates) during recessions and a "tight money" policy (decrease money, raise interest rates) during boom periods. Although this approach, if successful, would have the beneficial effect of reducing the severity of business cycles, it is much easier said than done. Uncertainty regarding both the natural path of the economy and the lagged impact of monetary shocks makes it very difficult to fine-tune the economy using monetary policy.

One increasingly credible approach suggests that the private sector and the economy as a whole would be better served by a monetary policy that kept money growth and interest rates as stable as possible. This would more effectively promote price stability (zero or low inflation) and establish an environment (low, stable interest rates) more favourable to business investment.

Fiscal policy deals with government's spending and taxing and their effect on the economy. Again, the popular theory (Keynesian) is that government should spend more (or tax less) during recessions and spend less (or tax more) during boom periods. As mentioned earlier, fiscal stabilization policy has not been very successful. Over the past twenty or so years, what seems to have happened is that governments have run deficits during recessions and bigger deficits during boom times, when more tax revenue was coming in. This has led to the problem of the permanent deficit, one that afflicts all levels of government and one that they seem unable to solve.

Government assistance to private, for-profit enterprises is a very controversial issue. Some business people see it as little more than welfare for inept entrepreneurs. The other view is that, on occasion, a timely government grant, loan, or tax holiday can keep a venture alive and healthy. Supporters of this view argue that letting weaker firms close or delaying some new ventures may be costly, in terms of production and especially employment.

Skeptics deny that governments ever really create any jobs. The assistance they provide to one (usually weaker) firm will be at the expense of production and jobs elsewhere in the economy. Their preference is for government to provide fairly low level assistance (mainly information), substantially reduce regulations and "red tape," and then let private firms fight it out in the marketplace.

While the debate goes on about government assistance, it is a fact that tens of millions of dollars flow from the federal and provincial governments to private enterprises every year. These monies are in the form of direct cash grants for the purpose of starting up, stimulating, or bailing out private firms. Additional amounts in the form of loans, tax holidays, free information, and favourable tax provisions provide assistance to some businesses. While a manager may disagree in principle with the idea of government assistance, it may be quite rational to take advantage of programs that have obvious financial benefits.

BUDGET DEFICITS AND THE POLITICAL ENVIRONMENT

Very recently, governments at both the federal and provincial levels have begun to talk tough about their deficit problems. It seems that there is no longer a "no problem" attitude regarding our mounting public debt. There appears to be an appreciation that future generations will have to pay off every dollar of that huge debt and that this is an unfair burden to place on them. In addition, there is the more immediate concern that, at some point, lenders (especially foreign lenders) will require a much higher risk premium to buy our government bonds. This means that the cost of debt service will rise sharply, which in turn will push governments to take more drastic action.

A glance at the 1992 budget (Table 43.1) shows the broad breakdown in revenue and expenditure. As of the summer of 1993, the federal government deficit was approximately $30 billion and the total debt was about $490 billion. At the provincial level, there was some variation, but most provinces had substantial deficits. Overall, the total combined government debt in Canada is about $650 billion or roughly $25 000 for every person. Currently, almost one-third of every tax dollar goes to pay interest on the federal government debt. All these numbers are growing! This deficit/debt problem is exerting an unfavourable influence on the business environment. In practical terms, the large debt service costs severely constrain other kinds of government spending. Unless the government is willing to raise taxes still further, increases in interest costs must be matched by reductions elsewhere in the budget.

Table 43.1
Federal Budget 1992

Revenue	$132.2B	%	Expenses	$159.6B	%
Personal income tax		47.7	Social costs		26.6
UI premiums		14.6	Debt costs		25.2
GST		14.2	Provincial costs		15.2
Sales & excise tax		8.9	Government operation		11.2
Other		7.6	Subsidies		8.5
Corporation tax		7.2	Defence		7.7
			Other		5.6
Total		100.0			100.0

Courting a Financial Crisis

BRYNE PURCHASE
RONALD HIRSHHORN

INTRODUCTION

The cost of carrying the public debt now represents 18 percent of all government spending and 9.4 percent of the gross domestic product in Canada. In fact, it might be argued that this huge debt service cost is driving the current discontent with government. In the past, governments serviced the debt by more borrowing. That option is now being slowly closed off, and governments must cut back on their core activities — redistributing income, **stabilizing the economy**, and providing public services — or raise taxes. As we shall see, governments have already raised taxes substantially. The response to government action so far has been a heightened demand for a more fundamental public examination of the efficacy and effectiveness of government itself. This chapter examines how this situation has developed by providing a brief overview of the growth of government and the federal-provincial structure of intergovernmental finance in Canada.

A GROWING GOVERNMENT SHARE

The period from the end of World War II until the early 1970s was a time of unprecedented and almost continuous growth in prosperity for Canadians,

with relatively low inflation and low unemployment interrupted only briefly by comparatively shallow recessions. The Canadian version of an industrial, urban, affluent, capitalist, welfare state was effectively invented between 1941 and 1975. The major social program initiatives undertaken are chronicled in Table 44.1. Rapid growth of new government programs and expenditures coincided with an equally strong growth in government revenues; the economy, driven by strong productivity growth and low unemployment, generated a fiscal dividend. Interest on the public debt hovered around 3 to 4 percent of gross domestic product.

Even though impressive, these charts understate the growth of "government" activity since they do not reflect all the costs associated with regulatory interventions. They include only those costs of administration, monitoring, and enforcement borne by government. But most of the costs of regulation are borne in the private sector. As well, there is no account here of governments' conscious use of the tax system ("tax expenditures") to manipulate the behaviour of individuals, families, or corporations.

Developing Fiscal Federalism

The welfare state in Canada was a joint federal-provincial initiative. Aside from funding its own

SOURCE: Excerpted from *Searching for Good Governance: Government and Competitiveness Project Final Report* (Kingston, ON: School of Policy Studies, Queen's University, 1994), pp. 25–29, 32–39. Reprinted by permission of the School of Policy Studies.

Table 44.1

Building the Welfare State — The Invention of the Sharing Society

A Chronology of Important Social Programs

1942	Unemployment Insurance Plan (employer-employee contributions with federal subsidization)
1944	Family Allowances Act (federal payments for children under 16)
1947	Hospital Insurance Plan (province of Saskatchewan)
1948	Program of federal grants for provincial health services
1949	Hospital Insurance Plan (province of British Columbia)
1951	Old Age Security Act (federal payments without means test to persons aged 70 and older)
....	Old Age Assistance Act (federal-provincial sharing of income-tested pension for persons aged 65 to 69)
1952	Blind Persons Act (arrangement similar to those above)
1954	Disabled Persons Act (arrangement similar to those above)
1956	Federal Hospital Insurance and Diagnostic Services Act (joint federal-provincial hospital insurance plan)
1962	Medical Care Insurance (province of Saskatchewan)
1963	Pension Benefits Act (government of Ontario)
1964	Medical Care Insurance (province of British Columbia)
1965	Old Age Security Act (amended to provide non-means tested pensions to all persons over 65)
....	Canada Pension Plan and analogous Quebec Pension Plan (wage-related pensions based on employer-employee contributions)
1966	Medical Care Act (joint federal-provincial system of medical insurance)
....	Canada Assistance Plan (expansion of federal grants to provinces for social services)
1967	Guaranteed Income Supplement (income-tested addition to old age security payments)
1971	Unemployment Insurance Act (substantial expansion and extension of original UI system)
1974	Family Allowances (substantial increases in payments)
1975	Old Age Security (allowances for spouses aged 60 to 64)
1977	Established Programs Financing Act (EPF) (regularized federal-provincial shared cost programs funding to postsecondary education and health insurance)
....	Extended Health Care Act (provision of additional health services)
1979	Child Tax Credit (federal)

programs, the federal government also supplied an important element of financing to programs delivered at the provincial-local level.

Federal revenues grew very quickly relative to federal spending in the period 1958 to 1974. Revenues had grown even more strongly immediately after World War II, but at that time excess federal revenues were applied to paying down the war debt. After 1957, the federal government similarly might have further reduced the federal debt or reduced taxes. Instead, excess federal revenues were increasingly transferred to other governments, and fiscal federalism, which had gained ground during the depression and the war, was given a significant boost.

Finding ways to transfer excess revenues to the provinces to support their increased program spending is constitutionally complicated because health, postsecondary education, and welfare are provincial responsibilities. As well, the federal government is, in principle, accountable to its electorate for federal revenues no matter who actually spends them. Nevertheless, the funds were transferred to the provinces with few strings attached, notwithstanding much ado about national standards (Leslie 1993). This process was sometimes a federal initiative; at other times it was motivated by provincial requests.

Would the welfare state in Canada have developed as rapidly and to the same extent had the federal government not used its fiscal capacity to support provincial programs? There is no doubt that many of the programs would still have been implemented, but there is equally no question that they would not have been as rich. Some provinces simply did not have the fiscal capacity for this type of spending. Interprovincial tax competition also would have limited the redistributive capacity of any one provincial government. Deals would have had to emerge between provinces — a possibility but not a high probability. In short, decentralization of government taxing powers very likely would have generated less revenue and therefore less total government expenditure.

Canadian productivity performance in the early years also was favourable, particularly compared to the United States. Other countries were growing more rapidly, but their productivity levels initially were lower. However, over the period from 1979 to 1990 total factor productivity did not increase at all in Canada.

Of course, poor economic performance was reflected in lower government revenues, higher expenditures, and higher deficits. It also has been the backdrop for a sea-change in the fortunes of competing ideas on how the economy functions and on the role of governments in it. The postwar growth of government had been explained or justified largely in terms of the evident failings of private markets. But with the economy faltering despite continued expansion of government, the built-in failings of public organizations and public decision processes have received new attention. Some blamed government for the deteriorating economic performance of the country.

DETERIORATING ECONOMIC PERFORMANCE

As measured by virtually all **macroeconomic indicators**, the performance of the Canadian economy deteriorated sharply in the 1970s. Except for inflation, it grew worse in the 1980s, and has fallen further in the 1990s. Each successive recession has been deeper and more prolonged and has ratcheted long-term unemployment upward. The government share of the economy has grown during the period, in large part because of increased support payments and subsidies to persons and business and, of course, interest on the public debt.

After World War II, the income per capita of the Western European countries and Japan was well behind that of the United States and Canada. Since 1945 the other industrialized countries have been catching up with the front-running United States, largely through more rapid growth in productivity (Dudley and Montmarquette 1993; Baumol 1986; Denny and Wilson 1993).

A Financial Time-Bomb

Whether or not there is a strong causal link between government activity and the slowdown in productivity, few would argue that there were in the 1980s obvious problems in the making for governments in Canada. The relatively poor performance of Canadian governments compared with the governments of other major industrial countries in respect of controlling the growth of debt is immediately obvious. A comparison of Canada with other G7 countries shows that Canada's current tax burden is very high, particularly relative to the United States and Japan. But then, so is Canada's public spending level. Tax costs have their corresponding benefits.

However, debt levels, by implication a future tax burden, are a major concern; only Italy's debt level is higher than Canada's. Part of the reason for the poor performance was a lack of early tax effort as deficits first arose — in fact, taxes were in many ways reduced. But that is no longer the case. Since the mid-1980s taxes have been increased sharply. Canada's total tax effort is now only just behind France, Germany, and Italy; yet debt continues to mount. As a result, debt and deficits are the most obvious and immediate constraints confronting all Canadian governments. To make matters worse, the economy is still operating well below capacity, and unemployment hovers around 10 percent. These conditions are unlikely to be eliminated quickly, even with a comparatively robust medium-term economic recovery.

CRIPPLING DEBT INTEREST

After 1974, the fiscal system in Canada "went tilt." The federal government began annually to borrow the resources necessary to pay the interest on the public debt. The government effectively "capitalized" the interest, charging it to the future. Occasionally, the government also borrowed to finance current public spending and public-debt interest. As long as the real interest rate was less than the real growth rate of the economy, public debt as a share of GDP did not rise (Hartle 1994).

In the 1980s, however, the economic environment turned hostile to this fiscal strategy. The real interest rate and real growth rate reversed, and interest rates were consistently higher than growth rates. The debt burden ballooned (see also Dungan and Wilson 1994).

In the fall of 1984, a new federal government inherited a major fiscal problem. The 1984–85 deficit was $38.5 billion or 8.7 percent of GDP. The government had a mandate for deficit reduction. Eight budgets later, in 1991–92, the budgetary deficit was $34.6 billion or 5.1 percent of GDP. In 1984–85, the national debt had been $206 billion; in 1991–92, it was $423 billion, more than double. Compound interest on the debt had added $237 billion to costs. Roughly speaking, the government had simply borrowed the funds necessary to pay the debt service charges. It was able to run cumulative budgetary operating surpluses — that is, excluding public-debt interest — of $20 billion as an offset to the growth of debt.

Of a total federal expenditure of $161.9 billion in 1992–93, the largest item was $39.4 billion in public debt interest charges. Some $27.1 billion was transferred to other governments, of which $11.2 billion was for health and postsecondary education, $7.3 billion for the Canada Assistance Plan, and $7.4 billion for equalization payments to the poorer provinces, which excludes Ontario, Alberta, and British Columbia. The federal government's own largest social spending programs are Unemployment Insurance ($19 billion) and Old Age Security (also $19 billion). The latter includes the Guaranteed Income Supplement and Spouses' Allowance.

THE ROLE OF FISCAL FEDERALISM

The growth of debt has been, at least until recently, heavily concentrated at the federal level. The federal government simply continued to borrow the money it was still transferring to the provinces after its own "surplus" tax revenues had disappeared. The transfer process was not, of course, a smooth one. The past 15 years have been devoted to reforming, then capping, federal transfers to other governments as well as attempting to restore the income elasticity of the federal tax base. In both cases, the federal government necessarily squared off against the provinces in a squabble first about cost sharing, then for resource rents, and then for tax room.

Federal financing for health care and post-secondary education has been moved from 50-50 cost sharing to a block-funding basis under Established Programs Financing (EPF), made up of cash plus tax points. One purpose of the move to block grants was to improve the incentive structure for provincial governments, which, under the previous system, had been making unilateral decisions for which they paid only 50 percent of the costs. Since then, the overall block grants have been subjected to various further restraints that imply that the cash portion will be gradually phased out. The Canada Assistance Plan (CAP) has also been subjected to ad hoc restraints, although ostensibly it is still a 50-50 cost-sharing arrangement.

However, even after the new federal government in 1984 made deficit reduction a goal, federal cash transfers to the provinces grew by 4.5 percent per year while all federal program spending grew by 3.6 percent per year in the period 1984–85 to 1989–90.

> It was only in 1990, when it became clear that the tolerance for tax increases had been reached if not exceeded and that significant further spending cuts would require cuts to transfers, that the first Expenditure Control Program was introduced, freezing EPF transfers and reducing the growth rate of CAP in the non-equalization receiving provinces. (Gorbet 1994, p. 76)

Concentration of the debt at the federal level has an important effect on incentives. Only the provinces can redesign their own programs, even those partially financed by the federal government. And, as long as the emerging deficit problem was concentrated largely at the federal level it could be treated by the provinces as a federal problem. Moreover, at this level it could more easily be rationalized as national stabilization policy. At least until the late 1980s, most continued to believe the federal government had the capacity and the responsibility to stabilize the macroeconomy through fiscal actions. However, had the provinces, and through them the local governments, shared the federal deficit problem more fully and sooner, then provincial and local program reforms would have taken place earlier. The structure of federal-provincial financing blunted the incentive to reform spending programs in the provinces.

One justification for continuing the same levels of federal-provincial transfers despite the growing federal deficit is the presumed greater federal ability to absorb cyclical revenue fluctuations through borrowing. This fits with the basic notions of countercyclical fiscal policy and the greater capacity of the federal government to carry it out. Specifically, this may also have been the logic behind leaving CAP as a cost-shared program since its client base is cyclical. However, the federal deficit, as indicated, is largely structural, not cyclical. A degree of financial stability for spending programs was maintained only by borrowing the funds necessary to pay the interest on the growing national debt — a strategy that has begun to destabilize the financial centre.

Now, of course, the financial situation of most provinces has also deteriorated. In consequence, some provincial credit ratings have suffered sharp reductions. Ontario, for example, went from a triple-A rating in 1990 to a double-A in late 1993.

INCREASING TAXES AND TAX RESISTANCE

To some degree, governments have been overtaken by the relentless arithmetic of compound interest. Their primary response has been to raise taxes heavily while putting off major program expenditure reforms. Compared with other industrialized countries, Canada's tax effort is, and has been, substantial.

Total tax revenues for all governments in Canada increased from 31.3 percent in 1983 to 37.0 percent in 1992, some 5.7 percentage points. This compares to a 0.9 percentage point increase in the United States and a decline of 4 percentage points in the United Kingdom.

The corporate tax burden in Canada, not measuring program benefits, is very similar to that in the United States, and Canadian governments work rigorously and consciously to keep it at a similar level. In part, this reflects the considerable mobility of capital in North America (Thirsk 1993). The Canadian and U.S. economies are particularly highly integrated by trade and investment flows. These flows are concentrated in a few industries and a few companies, most of which are multinational. Accordingly, corporate investment location decisions are inevitably and principally focused on competing provincial and state jurisdictions within North America.

Social security taxes (that is, payroll taxes for unemployment insurance, workers' compensation, Canada and Quebec pension plans, and health care) are lower in Canada than in the United States (Damus 1992). Often this is cited as a Canadian investment location advantage, although most economists believe that the burden of such taxes is eventually shifted to workers. Nonetheless, these taxes have been rising, and there are concerns that they will continue to rise sharply. Their levels depend on program costs. And very often, these costs are raised by perverse incentive structures inherent in program design.

While corporate income taxes were kept competitive with those in other jurisdictions, taxes on individuals have been increased sharply. As a result of tax increases between 1984 and 1992, federal personal income tax revenues increased by $6.2 billion, commodity tax revenues by $10.8 billion, and UI and CPP/QPP contributions by individuals by $3.6 billion. During the period, the total net impact of federal tax and transfer changes on individuals was $20.6 billion (Grady 1993).

As a result, Canadian governments now rely even more heavily than do governments in the United States on income, sales, and excise taxes. These increases in personal taxes have affected the economy in three very important ways: they have exacerbated cross-border shopping, fuelled the underground economy, and contributed to wage inflation. In respect of the latter, the Economic Council of Canada (Damus 1992) estimated that during the period 1980 to 1990, Canada's manufacturing costs increased from 2 percent to 40 percent above U.S. costs. About 60 percent of this deterioration in cost competitiveness was attributable to faster growth of labour compensation in Canada. Wilton and Prescott (1993) examined the impact of taxes and regulated prices on increases in base-wage settlements. Their work revealed that roughly one-quarter of the deterioration in Canada's manufacturing labour costs could be attributed to increased sales taxes, increased payroll taxes, and faster increases in the prices of government-regulated industries compared to non-regulated prices.

In short, initially at least, the growing financial problems of government were addressed by raising taxes, particularly on those least able to escape those taxes. Resistance to these higher taxes has escalated and contributed to the growth of the underground economy, higher wage costs, and even, for a time, increased cross-border shopping. It is now fair to suggest that taxes have reached their outer limits, and reform of expenditure programs must now be on the agenda.

CONCLUSION

The data amply demonstrate that after the mid-1970s Canadian governments were dealing with a structural, not a cyclical, deterioration in the performance of the Canadian economy. How much of the deterioration can be attributed to government is not clear. It is clear, however, that government programming was not immediately and fundamentally altered to meet this new condition, and large structural deficits have emerged.

The delayed response may have been partly due to the incentive structures inherent in cost-shared, federal-provincial financial agreements as well as to the commitment of the federal government to shield the provinces, particularly the weaker ones, from what might have been considered normal cyclical setbacks in the economy. However, the design of provincial programs cannot be changed from the federal level. As long as the debt was viewed as a federal problem, the provinces were unlikely to act. Ownership of the debt affects the incentive of individual governments to take the unpopular decisions necessary to lower deficits. This is not, however, to place blame or to excuse the federal government from failure to make significantly greater progress in reforming its own direct transfer programs.

Perhaps the failure of governance in this case was simply the attempt to offset structural rather than cyclical change or, alternatively, the inability, politically, to acknowledge the difference. The constitutional turmoil of the Canadian federation no doubt played a role and will continue to do so. It is a seemingly ever-present factor. In any case, as long as a strong response could be forestalled on the expenditure side, it was. Even a federal government publicly committed to deficit reduction failed repeatedly to meet its own targets. There was, however, no immediate consequence of that failure, aside from a loss of credibility. More generally, there was no overall mechanism to trigger action on the debt — at least on the expenditure side. On the other hand, by the end of the 1980s, all governments were aggressively raising taxes, so much so that the legitimacy of government as a reliable, cost-effective provider of basic public services was beginning to be undermined.

Even fairly optimistic forecasts of economic activity to the end of the decade show that very large and sustained primary budget surpluses will be necessary to reduce the deficit — that is, revenues must exceed expenditures on programs, excluding the payment of public debt interest (Dungan and

Wilson 1994). Such an accomplishment would be unusual by the standards of the past 20 years, or even of the past six years. Rather than continuing to borrow the interest on the debt, governments have now to pay for it out of increased current revenues or reduced program spending. Accordingly, high taxes and service cutbacks will continue.

Provincial deficits and financial pressures are now such that all provinces are engaged in serious program reform. More federal downloading is probably not necessary to stimulate provincial action, but this is not a prediction. In fact, a strong federal deficit reduction option is to allow the gradual exit now implicit in the cash payments under the Established Programs Financing program to continue or even to accelerate. It is obvious that health care, education, unemployment insurance, and pensions must be part of any large-scale expenditure review. From the point of view of this study, the question is whether or not governments will use the fiscal crisis as an opportunity to add a greater degree of accountability to the design of these and other government organizations and programs.

REFERENCES

Baumol, W.J. (1986). "Productivity Growth, Convergence and Welfare." *American Economic Review*, 76 (December): 1072–85.

Damus, S. (1992). *Canada's Public Sector—A Graphic Overview*. Economic Council of Canada. Ottawa: Supply and Services Canada.

Denny, M., and T. Wilson (1993). "Productivity and Growth: Canada's Competitive Roots." In *Productivity Growth and Canada's International Competitiveness*, ed. T. Courchene and D. Purvis. Kingston: John Deutsch Institute, Queen's University.

Dudley, L., and C. Montmarquette (1993). "Fit or Fat? Government and Productivity Growth." Government and Competitiveness Project Discussion Paper 93-06. Kingston: School of Policy Studies, Queen's University.

Dungan, D.P., and T.A. Wilson (1994). "Public Debt and the Economy." Government and Competitiveness Project Discussion Paper 94-02. Kingston: School of Policy Studies, Queen's University.

Gorbet, F. (1994). "Fiscal Federalism: Is the System in Crisis?" In *The Future of Fiscal Federalism*, ed. K.G. Banting, D.M. Brown, and T.J. Courchene. Kingston: School of Policy Studies, Queen's University.

Grady, P. (1993). "The Burden of Federal Tax Increases," *Canadian Business Economics*, Inaugural Issue: 16–24.

Hartle, D.G. (1994). "On the Efficiency of Government Policy." In *Policy Making and Competitiveness*, ed. B. Purchase. Kingston: School of Policy Studies, Queen's University.

Leslie, P.M. (1993). "The Fiscal Crisis of Canadian Federalism." In *A Partnership in Trouble: Renegotiating Fiscal Federalism*, ed. P.M. Leslie, K. Norrie, and I.K. Ip. Policy Study 18. Toronto: C.D. Howe Institute.

Thirsk, W. (1993). "Fiscal Sovereignty and Tax Competition." Government and Competitiveness Project Discussion Paper 93-08. Kingston: School of Policy Studies, Queen's University.

Wilton, D., and D. Prescott (1993). "The Effects of Tax Increases on Wage and Labour Costs." Government and Competitiveness Project Discussion Paper 93-29. Kingston: School of Policy Studies, Queen's University.

Canada's Underground Economy

ROLF MIRUS
ROGER S. SMITH

Over the last decade and a half, there seems to have been a significant increase in the size of Canada's **underground economy**. Today, economists, statisticians and academics debate the extent of the problem, the reasons for its increase, and what should be done about it.

In 1981, we published a paper in *Canadian Public Policy* that used methodologies developed by Peter Gutmann and Edgar Feige in the United States and Vito Tanzi of the **International Monetary Fund** to estimate the size of the Canadian underground economy in 1976. Working with a definition of the underground economy as "the extent to which GDP fails to record legal production activities other than do-it-yourself work," we estimated it at between 5 and 22 per cent of total economic activity, with 10 to 12 per cent as our best guess.

During the 1980s little additional work was done to refine these or other Canadian estimates. With the exception of a 1986 study by Statistics Canada that allowed for an underground economy of 2.9–3.5 per cent of GDP and a survey-based academic study, the topic was largely neglected until this year, when Statistics Canada published its view that the underground economy could not exceed 2 or 3 per cent of GDP. This contrasts with our best guess of around 15 per cent of GDP for the underground economy in 1990.

The large difference between our estimates and those of Statistics Canada is, in part, based on what is being measured. We define the underground economy as economic activity that would be taxable were it reported to tax authorities. Thus, the underground economy includes income of employees who are working for employers off the books, unreported rental and investment income, unreported tips and childcare earnings, skimming by owners of businesses, barter activities, and unreported proceeds from home-grown products and home-produced items. It also includes income from activities that are not reported in order to avoid regulation and licensing such as illegal gambling, drug dealing, smuggling and some construction activities. On the other hand, it excludes activities that are largely of a self-service nature, such as gardening, home repairs and cooking. The 1994 Statistics Canada study, in contrast, pertains to the concept of unrecorded GDP, thus excluding income from illegal activities and other unreported income that is included in our definition. Therefore, unrecorded GDP may be much lower than unreported income.

In light of the growing concern during the 1980s over the effectiveness and fairness of our tax system, we wished to determine how applicable our estimates for 1976 were to the situation today and have used available data to extend our estimates to 1990.

SOURCE: "Canada's Underground Economy," *Canadian Business Review* 21, 2 (Summer 1994): 26–29. Reprinted by permission of *Canadian Business Review*, The Conference Board of Canada.

Table 45.1

Estimates of Canada's Underground Economy
(As a Percentage of Total Economic Activity)

Method	Previous Estimates	Current Estimates
Gutmann	14.0 (1976)	21.6 (1990)
Feige	21.9 (1976)	19.3 (1984) *
Tanzi	4.8–7.2 (1976)	14.6 (1990)

* Available data do not permit us to extend estimates using the Feige method beyond 1984.

The results of our updating are the basis for the following discussion, in which we address three questions: What factors may have contributed to continued growth in underground activity after 1976? What are some problems that accompany a large underground sector? What measures might reduce the size of the underground sector?

FACTORS CONTRIBUTING TO UNDERGROUND GROWTH, 1976–1990

A number of factors may have caused Canada's underground economy to grow as a share of the total economy from 1976 to 1990. They include the following.

TAXES The burden of direct and indirect taxes has grown rapidly in Canada, with tax revenues as a share of GDP increasing at a much faster rate in Canada than in other OECD countries (including the United States but excepting Italy). Personal income taxes as a share of personal income net of transfers rose from 15.2 per cent in 1976 to 19.7 per cent in 1990. Direct and indirect taxes rose as a share of GDP from 38 per cent to 43 per cent from 1976 to 1990.

UNEMPLOYMENT The average unemployment rate was much lower for the 10 years before 1976 than for the 10 years following (5.2 per cent versus 9.3 per

cent). The unemployed can increase their casual or informal activity and may have an incentive to do so while they collect unemployment insurance. UI and informal economic activity can become a way of life.

SELF-EMPLOYMENT The self-employed in the incorporated and unincorporated sectors grew from 11.1 per cent in 1976 to 14.5 per cent in 1991. The number of self-employed in Canada grew by 71 per cent during this period, while the number of other workers grew by 25 per cent. The self-employed and small-business sector is where much underground economic activity occurs.

DEMOGRAPHICS Younger taxpayers are more likely to be non-compliant, and there is evidence that, once on this track, returning to compliance is not very likely. The ageing of the population may well lead to an increasing rate of non-compliance. It also means that while tax increases may push individuals underground, lowering rates may not bring them above ground.

IMMIGRATION The number of immigrants entering this country doubled from 1981 to 1992, and business immigration quadrupled, rising from 5 per cent of total immigration in 1981 to 11 per cent in 1992. There is evidence that underground economic activity is present to a higher degree among recent immigrant communities, both because of their small-business affinity and because of informal business relationships.

INVESTMENT INCOME The 1987 study by the International Monetary Fund on the discrepancy in the world current account found that "reported portfolio investment income is the fastest growing, and now the largest, of all individual current account discrepancies." Interest and dividends paid by companies worldwide are reported fairly accurately, as the companies file financial statements and claim deductions; on the other hand, these incomes may not be reported when received in other countries, and the necessary information may not be shared among national tax authorities to permit

---

Box 45.1 The "Monetary Aggregates" Methodology

ADVANTAGES
◆ The underground economy is believed to be largely cash (and cheque) based.
◆ Data on currency in the hands of the non-bank public and the various types of deposits at banks and other financial institutions are readily available and believed to be accurate.

DISADVANTAGES
◆ For estimates to be made, a base year must be chosen against which the development of currency holdings or monetary transactions is measured. Different base years give different results.
◆ For some monetary methods, purely financial transactions have to be eliminated. This proves difficult and requires judgement.
◆ For some monetary methods, unrealistically high estimates are obtained, not because currency holdings have grown but because financial innovation has led to diminished deposit holdings.
◆ The nature of money is national; therefore, regional estimates are not possible.

---

tracking of the payments. For the world as a whole, the excess of debits over credits rose from U.S. $33 billion in 1984 to U.S. $90 billion in 1991. The large growth in capital flows since 1976 would be expected to have a major impact on the dividend and interest flows on equity and bond investments. This is likely to be an area of substantial underreporting, although we have little data for Canada.

GOODS AND SERVICES TAX In January 1991 the federal government introduced the Goods and Services Tax (GST). This highly visible tax has proved to be an added incentive to underreport economic activity, particularly in service industries, where much of the value-added occurs in the final provision of the service. A study by Peter Spiro for the Ontario government found a dramatic growth in cash holdings after the Goods and Services Tax was introduced in 1991 and discovered no other apparent explanation for the increase.

CONCERNS ACCOMPANYING UNDERGROUND ACTIVITY

Where the underground economy accounts for a large share of total economic activity, the result is higher tax rates on reported income, lower government revenues and greater deficits. Estimates from the Canadian Tax Foundation place the loss of federal, provincial and local government tax revenues at $28.6 billion if the underground economy equals 15 per cent of GDP. Tax rates must, on average, be over 10 per cent higher to compensate for this.

Tax systems will not be, and cannot be, perceived as fair where underground activity is sizeable. Support for the public sector will erode, and public services that are crucial to business and to individuals will be undersupplied. A shift to indirect taxes and away from direct taxes may occur (as in New Zealand), and redistributive goals that might best be achieved through direct taxes may be sacrificed.

When underground activity is large, official economic indicators provide inappropriate guidance to policy makers. The equivalent of one million jobs at $50,000 per job is supported by underground activity equal to $50 billion. Official unemployment statistics may therefore be misleading and corrective actions inappropriate. Likewise, measures of GDP growth that exclude underground activity may result in skewed figures. Inflation measures will be faulty, as one response to increasing prices in the regular economy is increased activity in the underground sector. Productivity measures may be faulty for similar reasons. Less comprehensive estimates of private saving also occur. For instance, the net worth of a carpenter and electrician who swap services for home renovations may increase significantly without any addition to their reported incomes.

The "international" underground economy may alter the effectiveness of monetary policy. Large amounts of currency may be used in black markets outside the home country, although this is less likely for Canada than for some other countries. The opening of Eastern Europe, for instance, increased the demand for U.S. dollars, and measures of the U.S. money stock became misleading. Because of the leakage of currency to foreign markets, the "domestic" money supply in the United States increased less rapidly in the early 1990s than was suggested by the normal indicators. As a result, the U.S. economy did not receive the boost it needed, which may have had an impact on George Bush's chances for re-election.

If unreported income is a large share of total income, tax systems relying on self-assessment and a reasonable level of honesty are no longer viable. Italy recently imposed a tax on the presumptive income of small businesses because of the unreliability of income reporting by these businesses. Such a system may be unfair, but in the long run it may be fairer than a system that taxes some while others simply do not report income. Recently, the widely reported evasion of alcohol and tobacco taxes in this country has raised public consciousness of tax evasion, as has lesser smuggling related to cross-border shopping. The GST also contributed to a worsening of attitudes towards government; common sense and existing research support a direct relation between such negative attitudes and the level of tax evasion.

Finally, it is important to acknowledge that there may, paradoxically, be a benefit associated with underground activity. Government regulations (such as minimum wages) as well as taxation are avoided, making the sector more flexible and better able to respond to rapidly changing market conditions than may be true for the regular economy. This may help to keep real unemployment lower than would otherwise be the case. Lower prices for goods and services may also have some positive distributional effects when they help those with low incomes. This form of competition is, of course, unfair to those who operate above ground, and there are severe consequences for public policy — to say nothing of attitudes towards government — when the only way to stay competitive is to go underground!

POSSIBLE CORRECTIVE ACTIONS

What actions might be taken by tax authorities to reduce underground economic activity? No single action will markedly reduce the size of the underground economy, but a series of actions can be helpful.

TAX REFORM There is a strong case for broader tax bases and lower tax rates. The **tax reforms** of the 1980s, in Canada and elsewhere, moved towards broader bases, lower rates and diversified tax systems to reduce the incentives to underreport incomes. None the less, we continue to have significant deductions in calculating taxable income, as well as the exemption of food and other items in the application of federal and provincial sales taxes. There are reasons for these provisions, but they also result in higher tax rates, perceptions of unfairness and complexity, and a greater incentive to evade or avoid taxes.

LINKAGE OF TAX TO BENEFIT Whenever possible, we must link taxes closely with benefits experienced by taxpayers. Compliance is much more readily achieved when the direct benefit of the tax is apparent to the taxpayer. This is an argument for applying user fees to a greater extent in the delivery of health and education programs and in the financing of public pensions and unemployment insurance programs. Such measures make it possible to lower tax rates; however, as long as taxes play a redistributional role, the ability to tie them to benefits is limited.

EASIER COMPLIANCE Compliance, particularly for the small-business sector, needs to be kept as simple as possible. This is a major issue for the GST and is related in part to a base for the tax that excludes some items and includes others. This issue is even more serious in those provinces that have maintained a retail sales tax with a base that differs from that of the GST. The federal and provincial governments must persist in their efforts to harmonize income and sales taxes, to simplify tax bases and tax rates, and generally to simplify tax rules. Both levels of government will have to sacrifice some autonomy if they want to see an improvement in taxpayer attitudes.

TOUGHER ENFORCEMENT There is an argument for tougher enforcement, but careful thought is needed in this area. Tougher enforcement that encourages either more non-taxable activity, such as do-it-yourself, or non-filing as means of avoiding audit may be counterproductive. Audit targets must be carefully selected and personnel well trained. Some studies abroad have found little agreement among taxpayers and tax inspectors concerning who is and who is not cheating. Many of those who claim to know they are cheating are not found to be, and many who truly believe they are being honest are found to be cheating. This contributes to perceptions of unfairness. One measure that might help enforcement is found in Germany,

where both the purchaser and the seller of the underground good or service may be prosecuted for breaking the law.

INTERNATIONAL CO-OPERATION We need greater international co-operation in tax enforcement. While Canadians derive growing amounts of investment income from foreign holdings, Revenue Canada cannot keep track of the investments held by Canadians in the United States or other countries. We cannot expect individuals or businesses to respect the tax system if they perceive that large amounts of investment income escape taxation.

A CALL FOR ACTION

A problem that was already large by 1976 has grown considerably in absolute size and relative to total economic activity over the past decade and a half. The government, conscious of the problem, can take some steps to alleviate it. Reform of the GST provides an opportunity to simplify the tax system and make it fairer. Business should work with government to keep the tax bases broader and rates lower by minimizing special provisions. User fees should be levied to a greater extent to finance public services that have contributed to high tax rates — rates not related to benefits received. Penalties must be punitive where evasion is clear-cut, and a well-trained cadre of tax auditors will play an important role. Good government and a healthy economy and society require that the underground economy be kept in check.

The Value of NAFTA to the Canadian Economy

CHRISTOPHER DUNN

The North American deal is thoroughly in keeping with progressive trade practices around the world and will assure Canadian prosperity for many years to come. The North American Free Trade Agreement has many of the same arguments in its favour as did the Canada–U.S. Free Trade Agreement. However, we shall not repeat them here, but instead concentrate on those particular benefits that flow from NAFTA. They relate to international trade patterns, economic benefits, international development, and Canadian national integrity

INTERNATIONAL TRADE CONSIDERATIONS

International considerations weigh heavily on Canadian trade policy-makers. These include several important areas, most notably the demonstration effect of NAFTA, the hub-and-spoke analysis, the role of other trade blocs, and the globalization phenomenon in general.

Demonstration Effect

It is sometimes maintained by opponents that NAFTA amounts to a regional trade bloc that will have the effect of discouraging global trade liberalization. This is not true. If anything, the agreement has an important demonstration effect: it shows the partners' support and encouragement for larger forms of economic integration. Such integration could be endangered if NAFTA diverted trade from the larger environment; if it harmed current efforts at multilateralism; or if it raised existing barriers to trade. However, the access clause is a guard against trade diversion, offering an inclusive rather than exclusive approach to trade, possibly hemispheric in nature; the GATT encourages comprehensive bilateral free trade, and the World Trade Organization that Uruguay Round negotiators established is based on the bilateral panel model of the FTA; and the negotiators, with the notable exception of the Auto Pact, resisted the temptation to misuse the rules of origin to shore up powerful economic interests.[1]

Hub and Spoke

Forestalling a hub-and-spoke trading pattern in the Western Hemisphere is another pressing consideration for Canada. One possibility is that the U.S. could become the predominant trade power — or hub — with Canada and other countries establishing separate — or spoke — arrangements with the U.S. on terms that are uneven and of benefit predominantly to the Americans. Now, with both the United States and Canada on an even footing vis-à-vis

SOURCE: *Canadian Political Debates: Opposing Views on Issues that Divide Canadians* (Toronto: Oxford University Press, 1995), pp. 306–20. Copyright © 1995 by Christopher Dunn. Reprinted by permission of Oxford University Press Canada.

Mexico and with the access clause written in such a way as to preclude renegotiating the agreement every time a new partner wants to enter, Canadian interests are served.

Once having negotiated the FTA, it was largely common sense for Canadian policy-makers to ensure that Mexico did not get any better access to the U.S. market than Canada did, and, for that matter, that Canada would have equal access to Mexico as that accorded to the United States. A spoke arrangement was a distinct possibility, because when talks on a U.S.–Mexico deal began in the summer of 1990, Canada was not automatically considered a possible partner; in fact, Mexico was opposed to Canadian participation. Even after trilateral talks began in February of 1991, the U.S. chief trade negotiator warned that Canada could be dropped from the talks if its participation threatened to delay the negotiations.[2] Trade Minister John Crosbie noted the worry for Canada: "It might well be that if Canada were not involved in the enlarged free-trade area, important job-creating investment could well decide to go elsewhere."[3] One trade writer summed up the stakes this way:

> Mexico has 81 million people, the United States has 250 million and Canada 26 million. If the United States and Mexico strike a bilateral deal without Canada, companies looking at long-term investment opportunities might decide to put their money where the bulk of the population is, and that does not mean Canada.[4]

Globalization

Although it has a number of characteristics associated with it, the **globalization** phenomenon (as first enunciated by Theodore Levitt) simply means the emergence of global markets for standardized consumer products.[5] Multinational (or "transnational") companies downplay the importance of national policies and national preferences in their decisions about production, distribution, marketing, and standards, and think of the world as a single market. The multinationals are becoming the major actors

in a hierarchical global industrial structure; the 600 or so transnational corporations have substantial shares of world trade and many national markets, and dominate over three subordinate tiers, namely medium-size multinationals, threshold multinationals, and purely domestic companies, each of which has access to progressively smaller national markets.[6]

Other characteristics associated with the term "globalization" include:

- world-wide disaggregation of production;
- specialization by subsidiaries;
- niche products;
- footloose approach to sourcing;
- growing importance of knowledge-based service industries.

Hart's generic description of globalization is that "economic rivalry is rapidly replacing political ideology as the defining factor in international affairs."[7]

Globalization does not necessarily logically dictate any one specific form of economic integration. However, most analysts agree that the increasing intensity of international competition that globalization entails necessitates a Canadian stance supportive of international rules, as opposed to international economic power. Canada as a middle-level power has always had to seek influence in international forums, both political and economic. Predictability is the major benefit of such arrangements. NAFTA is a positive development from Canada's perspective because it offers a secure framework for trade relations that will remain intact with the addition of new members and be the model for new international trade agreements.

Regional Trade Groupings

One of the distinguishing characteristics of the postwar period has been the substantial growth of regional trade groupings in Europe, Latin America, and the Far East. Although various observers describe the three major blocs in different ways, North

America cannot afford to remain indifferent to the increased levels of world trade they account for.

Compared to Western Europe (the countries of the European Community and of the European Free Trade Association) and the Asia-Pacific region (Japan plus the countries of the Association of Southeast Asian Nations, as well as the newly industrializing countries of South Korea, Hong Kong, and Taiwan), North America is not flourishing. GATT statistics collected over the last two decades reveal the relative extent of slippage:

> North America [the U.S. and Canada] has experienced the largest relative decline in the share of world exports—five percentage points from 1970 to 1986. Its exports as a percentage of world trade have declined in every major region; bilateral Canada–U.S. trade has declined as a proportion of world trade; and the region has developed a trade balance of equal but opposite magnitude to that of the Asia-Pacific region—a deficit equal to six percent of total world exports.[8]

Western Europe's relative share also declined, but this was compensated for by the increase in intra-regional trade; and the Asia-Pacific region saw the most dramatic export growth.[9]

NAFTA is an eminently sensible strategic move for a trade group that has also seen its inter-bloc trade patterns change for the worse. Over the same period of the 1970s and 1980s, both North American exports and imports relative to the European Community declined markedly and there began a growing trade imbalance with the Pacific Rim countries.[10] North American integration may be the only workable medium-term alternative available in the face of such entrenched imbalances with other blocs. An import substitution strategy was tried by Mexico and abandoned with its entry into the GATT in 1986; economic nationalism has ceased to be a working concept in Canada; and the United States is deeply suspicious of the possibilities inherent in the multilateral route, at least for the present. As well, NAFTA offers the best demonstration model to effect multilateral reforms.

OTHER ECONOMIC BENEFITS

International trade considerations make a convincing case for NAFTA. However, when other economic benefits are also considered, the need for such an agreement seems overwhelming. The major economic benefits in question are the asymmetry in gains from the accord, sectoral advances, and the possibility of lower-cost inputs into the manufacturing sector.

Asymmetrical Gains

Both Canada and the United States have gained asymmetrically through NAFTA. As the government's White Paper notes, "NAFTA does not greatly change the access for the United States or Mexico to the Canadian market, but it does fundamentally change Canadian and U.S. access to the Mexican market."[11] There was not a level playing field in regard to access to the Mexican market. Much of the latter had been characterized by a number of trade blockages, the remnants of the country's hostility to international trade before 1986. There were Mexican import licences, government procurement preferences, restrictions on investment, and blockages to involvement in the services sector, all of which made doing business in Mexico a distinct problem. Now, practically the whole Mexican economy is open to Canadians and Americans—on a preferential basis.

There are important sectoral advances to consider as well. Mexico is a modernizing economy, and its population and economy are likely to want the kinds of goods that Canada produces on a competitive basis. Current trade between Canada and Mexico is relatively modest. However, the government's White Paper suggests that important advances in trade with Mexico could be made in several areas. Box 46.1 indicates the former Conservative government's estimation of the best areas for trade growth with Mexico.

Manufacturing Inputs

Another advantage of NAFTA is the availability of cheaper inputs into the manufacturing process.

Box 46.1 The Federal Case for Trade with Mexico (1992)

- *Agri-Food Products:* Mexico will not be self-sufficient in livestock or in meat in the proximate future; it will also need improved technology for fish harvesting and processing.
- *Transport Equipment:* Mexico is the fastest growing market for auto parts in North America, and sales of vehicles should grow even more with the lifting of the Mexican Auto Decree. As well, the tremendous transportation infrastructure program the Mexicans have undertaken to cope with growing urban populations offers inroads for the Canadian steel rail, locomotive, and rolling stock industries.
- *Petroleum Equipment and Services:* PEMEX, the state petroleum monopoly, will be spending several billions of dollars in modernization of equipment and services, and Canadian energy specialists are allowed to compete for it under NAFTA.
- *Mining Equipment and Services:* Canada is a world leader in mining technology, and Mexico badly needs to elevate its mine safety and environment standards.
- *Telecommunications:* There is a growing market for suppliers of electronic components, telecommunications equipment, and computer software in Mexico.
- *Environment Equipment and Service:* Public opinion is forcing Mexico to make its environmental regulation meaningful, and Canadian water treatment specialists and others are poised to make inroads.
- *Industrial Technology:* Canadian industrial technology is already competitive in Mexico; and the bulk of growth in this area is expected to come from imports.
- *Consumer Products:* Seventy per cent of Mexico's 85 million inhabitants are under thirty, and increasingly urbanized, offering prime targets for a variety of Canadian goods.
- *Financial Services:* Mexico has privatized and opened much of its banking, insurance, and securities sector to foreign competition, and Canada already has a strong presence in the area.

SOURCE: Adapted from Government of Canada, *The North American Free Trade Agreement: An Overview and Description* (August, 1992), pp. vii–ix.

About a quarter of Canadian imports are used in the manufacture of Canadian exports. If Canada did not belong to NAFTA, and thus missed out on the availability of low-cost manufacturing inputs from Mexico while the Americans enjoyed them, Canadian manufacturers would likely be much less competitive than their American counterparts. Exports would slide and Canadian jobs would be in jeopardy. The effects, moreover, would be cumulative. The more the Americans exported to the Mexicans, the greater would be their opportunity to increase economies of scale, and the greater would be the threat to Canada.[12]

On the employment side of the coin, it is wrong to imply, as some critics do, that an agreement like NAFTA is a direct contribution to Canada's employment problems, that relatively low Mexican wages threaten Canadian manufacturing, jobs, and wage levels. Some important facts have to be considered by Canadian critics of the agreement:

- Competitiveness is determined by more than labour costs. Also important are other factors of production and related considerations, including the cost of capital, capital productivity, knowledge and skill level of the labour force, transportation and communication networks, and product quality. Labour costs account for only 17 per cent of the average cost of production for Canadian manufacturers.[13]
- If wages were a determining factor in industrial location, their effect would have been felt

already. The average rate of duty on Mexican imports into Canada is under 3 per cent, and about 80 per cent of Mexican goods enter Canada duty-free already.[14]

♦ The productivity of Canadian labour is six to seven times higher than that of Mexican labour.[15]

If low wages were such an important factor in the modern capitalist economy, countries such as Mexico would already have been industrial powers. Canada has little to fear from the Mexican challenge on the wage front.

INTERNATIONAL DEVELOPMENT

One international argument for NAFTA is that the best way to promote Third World development is to encourage the spread of inclusive regional trade networks. Another is that the human rights, labour, and environmental records of new partners in NAFTA will improve as the force of public opinion comes to bear on the countries that lag behind the progress of the leaders.

The implications of NAFTA for Third World development are important indeed. It is instructive to consider that the impetus for NAFTA came in the first instance from a developing nation, Mexico. The interest in freer trade reaches far beyond the borders of Mexico, however. Chile, presently involved in a free trade agreement with Mexico, has expressed great interest in joining NAFTA. Its enthusiasm is closely matched by other nations. The most interested are the nations of the Mercosur free trade group (Argentina, Brazil, Uruguay, and Paraguay); Central American countries that have trade agreements with Mexico; and certain Caribbean nations that fear the loss of U.S. access after NAFTA.[16] These countries are more interested in trade as a development tool than they are in aid. They remember that free trade is the general promise the United States gave the thirty-one countries in the Western Hemisphere with which it signed framework agreements under the now stalled

Enterprise of the Americas Initiative (in return for liberalized investment regimes).

So even within the hemisphere there is a powerful demonstration effect at work. But the growing popularity of the NAFTA model is more than a bandwagon phenomenon. It stems from a disenchantment across the continent with interventionism and protectionism, the former economic model of preference. Lipsey summarizes the new outlook in Latin America:

> The less developed countries obtain many advantages by getting into close economic relations with developed nations. Free trade in goods and services probably does not pose any great threat. Inward-looking, import-replacement methods of growth are generally discredited. Free investment flows offer a technology transfer that creates faster economic growth than can be achieved by creating one's own technology behind closed trade and investment barriers. Most importantly, a regime of liberalized trade and investment flows formalized in a free trade area treaty is an important check on future populist regimes which will promise short-term gains, through such income redistribution policies as lowering profits and raising wages, that will bring long-term losses. . . . the evidence from Latin America and Africa is that the easiest way to eliminate growth prospects is for a government to be interventionist with state-owned production and major redistribution schemes.[17]

The environmental and social progress that most North Americans would like to see flourish in the hemisphere is given an important impetus by NAFTA. Some critical environmentalists have overlooked the general tone of the main agreement as well as the several specific provisions that are sensitive to environmental issues. All three countries have committed themselves to promoting sustainable development in implementing the agreement. NAFTA accepts each country's right to adopt standards and sanitary and phytosanitary measures that exceed international standards, and certain international agreements (on endangered species, ozone-depleting substances, and hazardous wastes) may even take precedence over NAFTA provisions (provided they do not constitute disguised trade restrictions). Rather than depressing environmental standards, NAFTA may elevate the standards of member countries, especially in the case of Mexico. Canadians or Americans, for example, could block imports from Mexico that failed their domestic standards. Environmental issues will be investigated by a trilateral dispute panel, but the panel will be advised by environmental experts.

The side deal on the environment does not meet every perceived need identified by the green movement — which would in itself be a doubtful and unrealistic aim, to be sure — but it is a significant beginning. William Watson sees it as having a strong potential. The fact that the Environmental Secretariat has a relatively large staff, a wide mandate, and a supportive Advisory Committee invites activism. As well, "the obligation to consider requests from private parties and to publish most of what it produces — unless the Council disapproves, which it will do at risk of public criticism — can only reinforce a penchant for activism."[18] Gilbert Winham states that the tri-national environmental commission will keep environmental issues on the agenda and provide additional focus for environmental interest groups to lobby governments. "The creation of lobby-able international structures is not an insignificant achievement for non-governmental organizations."[19] President Clinton's threat to withdraw from NAFTA in the event of Canada or Mexico withdrawing from the environmental side deal implies a certain precedence of environmental agreements over trade agreements.[20]

The whole issue of labour and human rights is a very serious one in developing countries, and trade agreements should pay them some attention. Unlike environmental matters, however, labour issues were largely outside the main agreement, appearing only in its preamble and also in a Memorandum of Understanding on Cooperative Labour Activities signed between Canada and Mexico in May, 1992.

The latter commits both governments to an exchange of information and technical assistance in the areas of labour market statistics, occupational health and safety, job training, and labour relations. This reflected a mainstream view that, in D'Aquino's words, "the best way to upgrade Mexico's labour standards is to encourage it to create better paying jobs and prosperity through freer trade and an open market."[21]

The labour side deal extends co-operation in labour matters. This deal is not as potentially activist as the environmental one, but it offers analogous opportunities for the experts on the secretariats to contribute to public policy. In addition, if informal consultation does not lead to enforcement of the domestic labour laws challenged by another NAFTA partner, an "Evaluation Committee of Experts" can be struck. The committee can issue public reports on such important issues as minimum wages, worker health and safety, equal pay between the sexes, and protection for migrant workers. Over time, the combination of international attention and the improved standard of living from enhanced trade will result in better labour laws, as has been the case in most countries. As for collective bargaining itself, this, plainly, is too important politically to be loosened from the bounds of national sovereignty.

Human rights are an analogous situation. In Mexico, as in some other areas of Latin America, human rights and civil liberties are dealt with in an extremely arbitrary fashion. As with labour issues, the question of rights is outside the bounds of the agreement *per se*; but the agreement will affect rights nevertheless. A Canadian government fact sheet on NAFTA gives the accepted wisdom on the question: "the strengthened, more prosperous economy that will result from the NAFTA will increase the Mexican standard of living, promote a higher level of education, and encourage individuals to take an active role in creating a more pluralistic society." This corresponds with the record of human rights in the more developed countries of the West.

CANADIAN NATIONAL INTEGRITY

National unity and integrity are unavoidable considerations that enter into almost every major public policy decision in Canada, and NAFTA is no exception. Careful consideration leads one to endorse the current course of economic integration in North America. In specific terms, NAFTA, like the FTA, responds to the aspirations of Quebec and perhaps weakens the argument for separatism. As well, the increasingly multicultural nature of Canada virtually dictates a more outward-looking trade perspective for Canada.

Quebec is a unique province that has often insisted on the right to undertake public policies designed by Quebecers for Quebecers. The insistence on provincial autonomy has on occasion grated on the sensibilities of those in other provinces, who are distinctly more centralist in their federal orientations. With both free trade agreements, however, Canada experiences the happy coincidence of a major policy initiative that has not turned political representatives of the two charter groups against each other. In a country where the French–English duality is the most serious cleavage threatening national unity, this turn of events should be considered a master stroke of statesmanship.

Much of the activity of Quebec in the economic policy area has been spurred by a collective sense of urgency. In fact, it can be argued that this sense of urgency has allowed Quebec to serve as an early warning system for the impending economic realities that ultimately all Canadians had to face. Realizing that international competitiveness depended on a combination of access to markets and a knowledge-based economy, Quebec insisted on forward-looking policies: [22]

- the inauguration of Quebec trade offices abroad (the earliest in 1940);
- Quiet Revolution initiatives such as the nationalization of Hydro-Québec, the building of development funds through the Caisses de dépôts et placements du Québec, and public education breakthroughs;

- reacting to the lack of opportunities and capital for young Québécois educated during and encouraged by the Quiet Revolution by establishing the Quebec Stock Savings Plan;
- the formation of a social consensus, during and after the serious recession of the early eighties, that stressed the primacy of ensuring Quebec's international competitiveness.

NAFTA is a logical culmination of these developments. The shared vision of Quebecers is that of "a strong regional economy in a world-wide global market," and the opposite vision of a protectionist Canadian national market is simply a non-starter.[23] One of the surest ways to discourage Quebec membership on the Canadian ship of state is to deny it the economic tools it has deemed necessary for its cultural survival.

Alternatively, free trade also acts as a glue for national unity because, once implemented, it discourages Quebec's exit from the Canadian national framework. Quebec, if it made a unilateral declaration of independence or opted for sovereignty-association, would most likely find itself outside the free trade framework looking in because it had not been a signatory to the original agreement(s). Its membership would not automatically be assured. As noted above, this would deprive Quebec of one of its most cherished positions in trade matters.

The hope of renegotiating its way back in after a political separation from Canada is such a risky affair that Quebec may not want to chance it. Rugman and D'Cruz are pessimistic that a sovereign Quebec could get as good a deal as it now has.

> The U.S. negotiators would be hostile to Quebec's subsidies to business, and Quebec would need to make major concessions in order to secure access to the U.S. market. Quebec has abundant energy and other resources, but there are few alternatives to the U.S. market, so for these exports Quebec's bargaining position is not as strong as that of a united Canada.[24]

The likelihood of trade concessions by a truncated Canada to help prop up the Quebec economy should not be automatically assumed, to say the very least. All in all, therefore, the free trade format has a unifying effect on Canadian federalism.

In addition, NAFTA is in tune with the world views of Canadians who are not of the original charter groups. Rightly or wrongly, Canadian immigration for the past few decades has emphasized possession of capital and entrepreneurial skill as determining characteristics in granting landed immigrant status. Authorities have interpreted the national interest as promoting a pro-business image for Canada. Potential new immigrants to Canada will be likely to be attracted to a country that is part of a broad regional framework where their investments can be accorded national treatment with those of other partner nations.

Economic integration initiatives like NAFTA offer positive benefits to Canada and to other trade partners. They promote efficiencies of scale, eliminate expensive and time-consuming *ad hoc* trade restrictions between nations, and discourage government interventionism. NAFTA in particular is in tune with the twin imperatives of globalization and global development. It embodies the historical logic of earlier movements toward Canada–U.S. economic alliances. It is not perfect; but to retreat from it now would be to return to a past imperfect.

NOTES

1. "NAFTA and the world," *Globe and Mail*, editorial, March 2, 1993.

2. "FTA may be reopened," *Globe and Mail*, February 7, 1991.

3. "3-way trade talks set," *Globe and Mail*, February 6, 1991.

4. Madelaine Drohan, "Coming to terms," *Globe and Mail*, February 12, 1991.

5. Theodore Levitt, "The Globalization of Markets," *Harvard Business Review* (May-June, 1983), pp. 92–102, as cited in Edward A. Carmichael, Katie Macmillan, and Robert C. York, *Ottawa's Next Agenda: Policy Review and Outlook, 1989* (Toronto: C.D. Howe Institute, 1989), pp. 82–83.

6. Bryan B. Purchase, *The Innovative Society: Competitiveness in the 1990s. Policy Review and Outlook, 1991* (Toronto: C.D. Howe Institute, 1991), p. 50.

7. Michael Hart, "A Brave New World: Trade Policy and Globalization," *Policy Options*, 13, 10 (January-February, 1993), p. 4.

8. As cited and interpreted in Carmichael *et al.*, *Ottawa's Next Agenda*, p. 89.

9. *Ibid.*, pp. 88–89.

10. Dorval Brunelle and Christian Deblock, "Economic Blocs and the Challenge of the North American Free Trade Agreement," in Steven J. Randall, ed., *North America Without Borders? Integrating Canada, the United States, and Mexico* (Calgary: University of Calgary Press, 1992), p. 123. Here the authors mean Canada, the U.S., and Mexico when referring to North America.

11. Government of Canada, *The North American Free Trade Agreement: An Overview and Description* (August, 1992), p. v.

12. Leo-Paul Dana, "Why we must join NAFTA," *Policy Options*, 13, 2 (March, 1992), pp. 7–8.

13. Government of Canada, *North American Free Trade Agreement: The NAFTA Manual*, August, 1992.

14. *Ibid.* See also Thomas D'Aquino, "Why We Need NAFTA," *Policy Options* (January-February, 1993), p. 23.

15. D'Aquino, "Why We Need NAFTA," p. 23. David Ricardo (1814) noted the importance of differences in relative labour productivity in establishing comparative advantage.

16. Peter Cook, "Continental Divide," *Globe and Mail* Report on NAFTA, September 24, 1992, p. C3.

17. Richard Lipsey, "The Case for Trilateralism," in Steven Globerman, ed., *Continental Accord: North American Economic Integration* (Vancouver: Fraser Institute, 1991), pp. 98–99. Reprinted by permission of the publisher.

18. William G. Watson, "Environmental and Labour Standards in the NAFTA," *Commentary*, no. 57 (Toronto: C.D. Howe Institute, The NAFTA Papers, February, 1994), p. 17.

19. Gilbert R. Winham, "Enforcement of Environmental Measures: Negotiating the NAFTA Environmental Side Agreement," paper presented at a conference on "Enforcement of International Environmental Agreements," La Jolla, California, September 30–October 2, 1993, p. 19.

20. *Ibid.*, pp. 19–20.

21. D'Aquino, "Why We Need NAFTA," p. 23.

22. Rita Dionne-Marsolais, "The FTA: A Building Block for Quebec," *American Review of Canadian Studies* (Summer/Autumn, 1991), pp. 245–52.

23. *Ibid.*, p. 250.

24. Alan M. Rugman and Joseph R. D'Cruz, "Quebec Separatism and Canadian Competitiveness," *American Review of Canadian Studies* (Summer/Autumn, 1991), p. 257.

INDEX

READER REPLY CARD

We are interested in your reaction to *Expanding Our Political Horizons: Readings in Canadian Politics and Government,* by James John Guy. You can help us to improve this book in future editions by completing this questionnaire.

1. What was your reason for using this book?

   ☐ university course   ☐ college course   ☐ continuing education course
   ☐ professional   ☐ personal   ☐ other _____
       development   interest   _____

2. If you are a student, please identify your school and the course in which you used this book.

3. Which chapters or parts of this book did you use? Which did you omit?

4. What did you like best about this book?

5. What did you like least about this book?

6. Please identify any topics you think should be added to future editions.

7. Please add any comments or suggestions.

8. May we contact you for further information?

   Name: _____

   Address: _____

   _____

   Phone: _____

(fold here and tape shut)

- -

MAIL ➤ POSTE

Canada Post Corporation / Société canadienne des postes

Postage paid   **Port payé**
If mailed in Canada   si posté au Canada

Business   **Réponse**
Reply   **d'affaires**

0116870399   01

0116870399-M8Z4X6-BR01

Heather McWhinney
Director of Product Development, College Division
HARCOURT BRACE & COMPANY, CANADA
55 HORNER AVENUE
TORONTO, ONTARIO
M8Z 9Z9